LONG-TERM CARE IN AN AGING SOCIETY

Graham D. Rowles, PhD, is founding director of the Graduate Center for Gerontology and chair of the Department of Gerontology, University of Kentucky. He is a Professor of Gerontology with joint appointments in Nursing, Behavioral Science, Geography, and Health Behavior. An environmental gerontologist, his research focuses on the lived experience of aging. A central theme of this work is exploration, employing qualitative methodologies of the changing relationship between older adults and their environments with advancing age, and the implications of this relationship for health, well-being, and environmental design. He has conducted in-depth ethnographic research with elderly populations in urban (inner city), rural (Appalachian), and nursing facility environments. Recent research includes leadership of the Kentucky Elder Readiness Initiative (KERI), a statewide project to explore the implications for communities of the aging of the baby boom cohort. His publications include *Prisoners of Space?* and six coedited volumes, in addition to 80 book chapters and articles. He is a Fellow of the Gerontological Society of America and the Association for Gerontology in Higher Education and currently serves on the editorial boards of the *Journal of Applied Gerontology* and *Journal of Housing for the Elderly*. Dr. Rowles is past national president of Sigma Phi Omega, past president of the Southern Gerontological Society, past president of the Association for Gerontology in Higher Education, and is currently chair of the Commonwealth of Kentucky Institute on Aging.

Pamela B. Teaster, PhD, is the associate director for research at the Center for Gerontology and a professor in the Department of Human Development at Virginia Polytechnic Institute and State University. She established the Kentucky Justice Center for Elders and Vulnerable Adults and the Kentucky Guardianship Association and was its first president. She is the secretary general of the International Network for the Prevention of Elder Abuse. She served as director and chairperson of the Graduate Center for Gerontology/Department of Gerontology as well as the director of doctoral studies and associate dean for research for College of Public Health at the University of Kentucky. She serves on the editorial board of the *Journal of Elder Abuse and Neglect* and *Frontiers*. Dr. Teaster is a Fellow of the Gerontological Society of America and the Association for Gerontology in Higher Education, a recipient of the Rosalie Wolf Award for Research on Elder Abuse, the Outstanding Affiliate Member Award (Kentucky Guardianship Association), and the Distinguished Educator Award (Kentucky Association for Gerontology). She has served as both board member and president of the National Committee for the Prevention of Elder Abuse. She has received funding from The Retirement Research Foundation, Administration on Aging, National Institute on Aging, Kentucky Cabinet for Families and Children, National Institute of Justice, Centers for Disease Control, National Institute of Occupational Safety and Health, Health Resources and Services Administration, and the Office of Victims of Crime. Her areas of scholarship include the mistreatment of elders and vulnerable adults, public and private guardianship, end-of-life issues and decision making, ethical treatment of vulnerable adults, human rights issues for vulnerable adults, public policy and public affairs, public health ethics, and quality of life. She is the coauthor of two books and over 100 peer-reviewed articles, reports, and book chapters.

LONG-TERM CARE IN AN AGING SOCIETY

THEORY AND PRACTICE

GRAHAM D. ROWLES, PHD
PAMELA B. TEASTER, PHD
Editors

Springer Publishing Company, LLC
11 West 42nd Street
New York, NY 10036
www.springerpub.com

Acquisitions Editor: Sheri W. Sussman
Production Editor: Michael O'Connor
Composition: MPS Ltd, India

ISBN: 978-0-8261-9456-5
e-book ISBN: 978-0-8261-9457-2

Instructors' Materials: Qualified instructors may request supplements by e-mailing textbook@springerpub.com:
Instructors' Manual: 978-0-8261-3219-2
Instructors' PowerPoints: 978-0-8261-3218-5

15 16 17 18 19 / 5 4 3 2 1

Library of Congress Cataloging-in-Publication Data

Long-term care in an aging society (Rowles)
Long-term care in an aging society : theory and practice / Graham D. Rowles, Pamela B. Teaster, editors.
p. ; cm.
Includes bibliographical references and index.
ISBN 978-0-8261-9456-5—ISBN 978-0-8261-9457-2 (eBook)
I. Rowles, Graham D., editor. II. Teaster, Pamela B. (Pamela Booth), editor. III. Title.
[DNLM: 1. Long-Term Care—United States. 2. Aged—United States. WT 31]
RT120.L64
610.73'6—dc23

2015013818

Printed in the United States of America by McNaughton & Gunn.

Contents

Contributors

Keith A. Anderson, PhD, MSW—Associate Professor, School of Social Work, University of Montana, Missoula, Montana

Robert A. Applebaum, PhD—Director, Ohio Long-Term Care Research Project, Scripps Gerontology Center; Professor, Department of Sociology and Gerontology, Miami University, Oxford, Ohio

Julie A. Brown, PhD—Assistant Professor of Gerontology, Department of Social and Public Health, Ohio University, Athens, Ohio

Nicholas G. Castle, PhD, MHA—Professor, Department of Health Policy and Management, University of Pittsburgh, Pittsburgh, Pennsylvania

Caroline Cicero, PhD—Lecturer, Davis School of Gerontology, University of Southern California, Los Angeles, California

Holly Dabelko-Schoeny, PhD, MSW—Associate Professor, College of Social Work, The Ohio State University, Columbus, Ohio

Pankaja Desai, PhD, MPH, MSW—Assistant Director, Evaluation and Tracking Program, University of Illinois at Chicago, Center for Clinical and Translational Science, Chicago, Illinois

Jessica Dornin, MSL—Recruitment and Academic Affairs Administrator, Department of Health Policy and Management, University of Pittsburgh, Pittsburgh, Pennsylvania

Jamie Ferguson-Rome, MHA—Instructor and Project Director/Research Analyst, Health Policy and Management, Department of Health Policy and Management, University of Pittsburgh, Pittsburgh, Pennsylvania

Richard H. Fortinsky, PhD—Professor and Health Net, Inc. Chair in Geriatrics and Gerontology, Center on Aging and Department of Medicine, University of Connecticut School of Medicine, Farmington, Connecticut

Joseph E. Gaugler, PhD—Professor, Center on Aging, School of Nursing, University of Minnesota, Minneapolis, Minnesota

Stephen M. Golant, PhD—Professor, Department of Geography, University of Florida, Gainesville, Florida

Carole Haber, PhD—Professor of History and Dean of the School of Liberal Arts, Tulane University, New Orleans, Louisiana

Karen B. Hirschman, PhD, MSW—Research Associate Professor University of Pennsylvania School of Nursing, Philadelphia, Pennsylvania

Martha B. Holstein, PhD—Associate for Research at the Park Ridge Center for the Study of Health, Faith, and Ethics, Long-Term Care Policy Consulting, Health and Medicine Policy Research Group, Chicago, Illinois

Amy F. Hosier, PhD—Associate Professor in Family Sciences, Department of Family Sciences, University of Kentucky, Lexington, Kentucky

Susan L. Hughes, PhD—Principal Investigator of the University of Illinois at Chicago Midwest Roybal Center for Health Maintenance, Institute for Health Research and Policy, University of Illinois at Chicago, Chicago, Illinois

Susan Lysaght Hurley, PhD, GNP-BC, ACHPN— Director of Research/ Hospice and Palliative Care Nurse Practitioner, Care Dimensions, Danvers, Massachusetts

Joan Hyde, PhD—Senior Fellow, Gerontology Institute, McCormack Graduate School of Policy and Global Studies, University of Massachusetts, Boston, Massachusetts

Melanie N. G. Jackson, MS, LAMFT—Doctoral Candidate, Department of Family Social Science, University of Minnesota, St. Paul, Minnesota

Marshall B. Kapp, JD, MPH—Director, Center for Innovative Collaboration in Medicine and Law, and Professor of Medicine and Law, Florida State University, Tallahassee, Florida

Amber S. McIlwain, ABD, MS—Assistant Professor, School of Health Administration, Texas State University, San Marcos, Texas

Linda S. Noelker, PhD, MA—Senior Vice President for Planning and Organizational Resources, Director of the Katz Policy Institute, Benjamin Rose Institute on Aging, Cleveland, Ohio; Adjunct Professor of Sociology, Case Western Reserve University, Cleveland, Ohio

Jee Hoon Park, MSW—Doctoral Student in Social Work, The Ohio State University, Columbus, Ohio

Jon Pynoos, PhD—Director of the National Resource Center on Supportive Housing and Home Modification; UPS Foundation Professor of Gerontology, Policy and Planning, Andrus Gerontology Center, University of Southern California, Los Angeles, California

Emily J. Robbins, PhD—PhD Instructor, Department of Sociology and Gerontology, Miami University, Oxford, Ohio

Graham D. Rowles, PhD—Founding Director of the Graduate Center for Gerontology and Chair of the Department of Gerontology, University of Kentucky, Lexington, Kentucky

Debra J. Sheets, PhD, MSN, RN, FAAN—Associate Professor, School of Nursing, University of Victoria, British Columbia, Canada

Noreen A. Shugrue, JD, MBA, MA—Research Associate, Center on Aging, University of Connecticut School of Medicine, Farmington, Connecticut

Pamela B. Teaster, PhD—Associate Director, Center for Gerontology; Professor in the Department of Human Development, Virginia Polytechnic Institute and State University, Blacksburg, Virginia

Amy M. Westcott, MD, CMD, FAAHPM—Associate Professor of Medicine, Penn State College of Medicine, Hershey, Pennsylvania

Carol J. Whitlatch, PhD—Assistant Director for Research, Benjamin Rose Institute on Aging, Cleveland, Ohio; Adjunct Associate Professor, Department of Sociology, Case Western Reserve University, Cleveland, Ohio

Faika Zanjani, PhD—Associate Professor, School of Public Health, Department of Behavioral and Community Health, University of Maryland, College Park, Maryland

Preface

PAMELA B. TEASTER
GRAHAM D. ROWLES

Difficulties are what makes it honorable and interesting to be alive.

—Florida Scott-Maxwell, *The Measure of My Days*

To begin, we state the obvious: Our society is an aging one. Though many of its members will remain healthy and able to care for themselves for the majority of their lives, many others will cycle in and out of various types of long-term care arrangements. Although not all persons requiring long-term care will be old, all are indisputably aging. Because the topic of long-term care is critical for younger and more mature scholars and practitioners alike, we solicited a cadre of exceptionally insightful and prominent scholars to contribute to a comprehensive volume addressing long-term care within an aging society.

Our book, which begins and ends with a focus on the individual intersecting with others on micro to macro levels and is framed against a backdrop of changing landscapes and understandings, contains chapters with theoretical grounding and empirical research that meld with current practice in order to provide readers with a cutting-edge and comprehensive understanding of long-term care. We asked our contributors to consider five key themes and, where appropriate, to weave these themes within their chapters in order to embrace diverse aspects of the ever-changing landscape of long-term care. Specifically, we asked that they consider complex relationships among independence, dependence, and interdependence. Second, we asked that they recognize the fluidity of the long-term care continuum and the reality of constant change as a feature of each person's long-term care experience. Third, we requested that they be particularly sensitive to the critical role of decision making in long-term care, considering both the individual recipient's trajectory of care and decisions affecting the evolution of the long-term care system. Fourth, in drafting their chapters, we requested that our contributors pay special attention to the myriad ethical issues that pervade all levels of long-term care and that are especially important given the vulnerability of recipients of long-term care as well as the pressures that confront many caregivers. Finally, we emphasized that our contributors should not lose sight of the lived experience of long-term care and stressed that ultimately, the purpose of the entire enterprise is to ensure the best possible quality of life for people at a time when they are likely to be most vulnerable.

Organized to progress along the long-term continuum from community-based care through supportive housing to institutional care, we include new approaches and perspectives. We suggest that the development of age-friendly communities and adaptive residential design are components of long-term care that delay entry of individuals into the formal care system. Emphasis is placed on the interface of technology and long-term care, not only a direction of immense promise but also the source of critical questions with respect to the desires of care recipients and the level of social and interpersonal contact that is maintained within our model of long-term care. Throughout the book, we seek to stress the importance of recognizing cultural diversity and the dangers of assuming that any one type of intervention appropriately fills every person's need. A critical issue to which our contributors devote attention is the complex relationship between voluntary and paid services. In a society in which family members are likely to be interacting from a distance and competing professional obligations place increased stress on traditional caregivers, this issue is of vital concern. Finally, emphasis throughout the contemporary long-term care continuum on person-centered care is featured prominently.

Long-Term Care in an Aging Society is organized in five parts: Part I: The Context of Long-Term Care, Part II: Community-Based Long-Term Care, Part III: Transitional Long-Term Care, Part IV: Facility-Based Long-Term Care, and Part V: Contemporary Issues in Long-Term Care. In Part I: The Context of Long-Term Care, we (Rowles and Teaster, Chapter 1) present case studies as exemplars of three very different long-term care situations: a fairly typical family-supported trajectory of community-based care, the care of a person with Down syndrome, and the story of an increasingly common scenario of caregiving from a distance. The three vignettes provide a context for defining long-term care, explanation of the demographic processes that have resulted in the current situation of demand for long-term care, and description of the general characteristics of persons requiring long-term care and those who care for them. Major themes that recur throughout the volume are then considered, including the role of family, friends, and acquaintances in providing informal care and the emergence over the past 50 years of an elaborate system of formal long-term care. We introduce new residential alternatives that have emerged to address the situation when aging in place in a familiar residence is no longer a viable alternative. The chapter concludes with consideration of the societal context of contemporary long-term care and a brief introductory discussion of new directions: moving beyond merely quality of care to quality of life, the role of age-friendly neighborhoods as part of an expanded view of long-term care, the growing importance of environmental design interventions and new technologies, and the culture change movement exemplified by emphasis on person-centered care.

In Chapter 2, Carol Haber provides a historical backdrop chronicling the development of long-term care in the American colonies and the United States from the 17th to the 21st century. Haber explains how economic, demographic, political, and cultural changes have influenced attitudes and practices shaping long-term care and highlights the impact of historical ideas and institutions on care provision. She discusses such topics as how the English philosophy of care shaped early colonial policy, why almshouses were established and their impact on support of the poor and aged, the role and impact of religious beliefs on 19th-century institutional care, foundations of old-age homes in 19th-century America, beliefs about older adults in the first half of the 20th century, the effect of Social Security on institutional care, and the influence of legislative and judicial rulings in the second half of the 20th century on long-term care.

Part II: Community-Based Long-Term Care, begins with Whitlatch and Noelker's interpretation of the role of the family in long-term care. The authors discuss the family-caregiving experience for older relatives caring for elderly and chronically ill elders. The prevalence of family care is described, as well as its estimated cost and value. Factors that affect the provision and consequences of caregiving, relevant theoretical paradigms, interventions to ameliorate negative effects and strengthen positive aspects of care provision, and public policies developed to meet the needs of and challenges faced by an increasing number of family caregivers provide the focus for the remainder of the chapter.

In many ways a companion to Chapter 3, Jackson and Gaugler focus on aspects of informal care in the community (Chapter 4). Their primary concern is with family caregiving of a relative with dementia. They consider various types of family involvement and the role(s) of family members in alternative types of residential long-term care-including assisted living and nursing facilities. The chapter also includes interpretation of philosophies guiding the culture change movement in nursing home environments and implications of this transition for family involvement. They round out the chapter by describing interventions for family involvement in residential settings and their limitations.

Chapter 5 (Hughes and Desai) adds another piece to the mosaic that is community-based long-term care in its exploration of the development of home care in the Unites States. This chapter includes a description of payment and regulatory policies influencing the present complex array of home care services. Elucidating the varied sectors of the home care industry, they discuss challenges for maximizing the positive impact of 21st-century home care. In particular, they explain the population, services, funding sources, and quality assurance mechanisms used for private home care and high-tech home care. They conclude with consideration of the potential of the Patient Protection and Affordable Care Act to improve coordination of care and care outcomes for persons with chronic conditions served by home care programs.

The place of geriatric rehabilitation in the continuum of long-term care is considered in Chapter 6. Sheets focuses on rehabilitation in postacute care settings: long-term acute-care hospitals, inpatient rehabilitation facilities, skilled nursing facilities, and home health agencies. Her chapter presents two conceptual models for disability, shows how each informs an understanding of rehabilitation, and illustrates how members of a rehabilitation team establish rehabilitation goals and coordinate care. In addition, the chapter includes consideration of inpatient and outpatient rehabilitation settings for postacute care, rehabilitation interventions and modalities, and explains how Medicare funds rehabilitation services.

In the final chapter of Part II, Dabelko-Schoeny, Anderson, and Park (Chapter 7) introduce the growing phenomenon of adult day services (ADS). These contributors present the history and development of ADS, demographic characteristics of the ADS population, its organizational and operational structure, services offered, and how ADS are funded. Also considered is the influence of research on the impact and effectiveness of ADS for participants, family members, and society as well as future directions and contributions of ADS in meeting the growing need and desire for home- and community-based services.

In Part III: Transitional Long-Term Care, our focus is on the ambiguous and often highly stressful portion of the long-term care continuum during which the primary goal for many older and disabled adults is remaining in the community for as long as possible or utilizing a growing array of transitional environments that provide options short of highly "medicalized" institutional long-term care settings. Chapters are included on the environmental design and the use of technologies that may prevent or delay movement along the continuum toward a higher level of dependency, on the role of age-specific housing, and on rapidly proliferating assisted living alternatives.

Employing a transactional ecological perspective, Brown, Rowles, and McIlwain (Chapter 8) expand traditional conceptualizations of long-term care by emphasizing the importance of nurturing age-friendly community environments that provide supportive settings that can delay the need for forms of long-term care intervention that are more costly for the individual. The authors describe the importance of the built environment, and the role of age-sensitive environmental design and a growing array of assistive technologies used in contemporary long-term care. Embedded within the chapter are discussions of the principles of universal design and smart-home technologies and the potential for emergent and future assistive technologies to transform the long-term care landscape. The chapter concludes with observations on practical and ethical dilemmas associated with environmental design interventions and assistive technologies and the potential social and emotional costs in becoming reliant on technological interventions.

Complementing Chapter 8, Cicero and Pynoos (Chapter 9) review the housing situation of the aging population as a component of the long-term care continuum. They focus on where, how, and why older adults strive to age in place; how home modification programs allow people with functional decline to adapt to their environment; and investigate innovative models that allow for long-term care to be delivered in the home, through shared housing and shared community experiences. They also discuss public program and service options that contribute to the long-term care continuum by providing alternatives to assisted living and skilled nursing facilities. A discussion of zoning, neighborhood design, and housing design for an aging-friendly built environment reinforces the need for broader consideration of environmental aspects of long-term care.

Golant and Hyde (Chapter 10) examine assisted living, a relatively new addition to the long-term care continuum. They define assisted living and sources of knowledge about this alternative, chronicle the historical development of assisted living, and describe the range of assisted living residences in the United States that have resulted from this history. A typology of contemporary assisted living models is provided together with an explanation of the ways in which assisted living differs from other housing-care options. Golant and Hyde explain the demographics, health status, and impairment profiles of residents, and detail the occupancy costs of assisted living. Their discussion also incorporates an examination of the regulatory environment of assisted living; commentary on the challenges of achieving both a good quality of life and a good quality of care; explanation of the role of Medicaid in making assisted living affordable; and consideration of the future prospects of assisted living as a long-term care alternative.

Part IV: Facility-Based Long-Term Care takes us into the world of institutionally based long-term care and the end of life. Despite the proliferation of alternatives and efforts to enable older and disabled adults to remain in community settings for as long as possible, a significant proportion of older Americans spend time, often at the end of their lives, in a nursing facility. Dornin, Ferguson-Rome, and Castle (Chapter 11) provide a brief history of the development and growth of nursing homes as a feature of the long-term care system. They review the contemporary operation of nursing homes and describe the characteristics of residents. Their discussion includes consideration of the culture change movement, particularly resident-centered care, as well as new options that are creating homelike environments for residents, such as the Greenhouse Movement and the Eden Alternative. The authors conclude by considering future challenges and opportunities for the nursing home industry and a variety of trends in Medicare and Medicaid reimbursement.

In Chapter 12, on hospice and palliative care, Westcott, Hurley, and Hirschman consider ways in which end-of-life care is provided by hospice and palliative care options. Their chapter is concerned with how we can best integrate high-quality end-of-life care into existing long-term care services and supports. The discussion is framed in relation to an account of the history and development of hospice and palliative care. After describing the various contemporary settings that deliver hospice and palliative care, the authors discuss benefits and challenges in ensuring the sensitive and effective delivery of hospice and palliative care.

Having described many of the components of the complex array of elements that comprise the long-term care continuum, in Part V: Contemporary Issues in Long-Term Care, the final section of this book, concern shifts to a set of contemporary topics pertaining to the entire system of long-term care or representing special situations that do not fit neatly into the continuum. Many subpopulations who receive long-term care have special needs. One such subpopulation is persons with mental illness. As Zanjani and Hosier explain (Chapter 13), in late life, mental illness can contribute to increased morbidity, disability, and even mortality. Persons with mental illness are to be found in virtually every long-term care environment. These authors point out the importance of addressing mental health of older adults, consider areas within the existing system that need improvement in order to enhance mental health management, and explore future areas of inquiry and intervention, including fostering a better understanding of managing severe mental illness and psychiatric comorbidities in late life in both community and long-term care facility settings.

In Chapter 14, Holstein explores another critical cross-cutting issue of relevance to all stages of the long-term care continuum—the ethics of care and being cared for on a long-term basis. This theme is apparent in many of the chapters, but here it is highlighted in Holstein's discussion of what it means to be a practitioner, a resident, or both in long-term care settings; how such notions influence conceptions of autonomy; and how a different way of understanding autonomy, as well as the ethical principles of beneficence, nonmaleficence, and justice, broaden the scope of justifiable action in long-term care. Holstein stresses how injustices fester and are reinforced in long-term care policy and critiques the standard paradigm for analyzing ethical problems in long-term care. She elucidates general ethical concepts, applies ethical concepts to long-term care situations, and provides examples of ethical conundrums faced by long-term care facilities.

The litany of ethical dilemmas in long-term care is paralleled by an array of legal principles and issues considered in Chapter 15 in which Kapp considers long-term care and the law. Kapp outlines the most salient aspects of interaction between the legal system and various participants involved in the provision and receipt of long-term care. He helps us appreciate the roles of the law and lawyers in shaping the long-term care environment. He also evaluates the practical impact of the legal system on the professional and personal lives of the various participants in the long-term care system. The chapter concludes with discussion of the process of working within legal parameters to improve both quality of care and quality of life for long-term care consumers. The issue becomes one of reconciling effective legal risk management with ethically and clinically appropriate long-term care.

Perhaps the most daunting challenge facing long-term care in the 21st century is the issue of financing. With a huge anticipated increase in demand along the entire continuum, a projected shortage of caregivers, and low levels of remuneration for many workers in the long-term care sector of the economy, and the inability of many families to pay for the services they need, there is cause for anxiety. Although funding of the entire long-term care system is problematic, on a human level fiscal problems become manifest in the inability of individuals to afford the costs of long-term care. Applebaum and Robbins (Chapter 16) provide important insight into these issues. They discuss financial aspects of the provision of long-term services and supports to individuals who experience disability, how services are provided, and the costs and mechanisms of funding for such services. As they note, of particular concern are the implications for consumers who are without coverage for ongoing long-term services and supports. Ultimately, the fate of long-term care and those who rely on the many options discussed in this book to receive decent care and maintain a good quality of life depends on the value that society places on providing long-term care and the way in which this becomes translated into policy. In the final chapter (Chapter 17), Fortinsky and Shugrue share insights into the politics and processes of public policy. They present a framework for understanding long-term care policy development by describing the political process by which long-term care policy decisions are made and the interrelationships among major types of long-term care policies, types and levels of decision makers in the long-term care arena, and interest groups that influence the formation of policy. Major historical milestones and current policy directions and dilemmas in policy making are outlined. The authors conclude with a description of major consensus trends in long-term care policy making: the impact of public policy decisions on persons needing long-term care, types of public policies affecting long-term care, the influence of various levels of governmental and nongovernmental policy makers, and the plethora of interest group political constituencies influencing long-term care policy decisions.

As additional aids for qualified instructors, both an Instructors' Manual and a complete PowerPoint presentation are available by request to textbook@springerpub.com.

Acknowledging the outstanding credentials of our contributors, we emphasize that we, the editors, compiled this text because of an abiding and long-standing personal and professional interest in long-term care and our awareness of the need for a comprehensive textbook that considers the state of long-term care and incorporates a full integration of theory and practice. We hope and anticipate that this text will provide a useful resource for anyone with an interest in long-term care—a topic of relevance to every person reading these words.

As we move further into the 21st century, the issue of long-term care will become an increasingly important part of our national discourse as the baby boom population ages and requires an expanding proportion of long-term care economic and human resources. There is no doubt that the current system of long-term care is inadequate to meet future needs. Change is imperative. It is our hope that this change will be guided by full awareness of the current status of long-term care and informed discussion regarding optimal ways in which to proceed. In the pages that follow, our intent is to introduce readers to information and ideas that will enable a clear understanding of the changing face of contemporary long-term care and facilitate future, critical, and informed contributions to this highly important debate.

Acknowledgments

Since its initial conceptualization several years ago, this volume has been through many phases in its progress toward the reader's desk. To our outstanding assemblage of authors we extend our deep appreciation for their tolerance and for sticking with us through a long and sometimes arduous process in developing this text, a process that involved a series of unforeseen challenges.

Thanks are due to the many people who, behind the scenes, have supported these authors in researching, writing, rewriting, and reviewing the chapters that comprise this text. Too often, research associates and others who make major contributions to scholarly works remain in the background.

We gratefully acknowledge and thank Connie Evashwick, who wrote a textbook with Delmar/Cengage that provided the framework for our volume and introduced many of the themes and ideas that we expanded and altered to fit the direction that the book took during its several years of gestation.

Special thanks are due to Sheri W. Sussman, Executive Editor at Springer Publishing Company, who quickly saw the potential of this book and, through a process of gentle nudging, and sometimes firm and decisive direction, facilitated completion of the project and brought the book to publication. An experienced master of author management, her indefatigable helpful suggestions while running interference nurtured the venture at every turn.

Coordinating and assembling the manuscripts of numerous contributors, compiling author information, securing publication releases, preparing the final version of a manuscript for the publisher, and handling much of the administrative work involved in producing a substantial book is a sometimes difficult and unrewarding task. We thank Amber McIlwain, Doctoral Student in Gerontology at the University of Kentucky, for her meticulous help with chapter drafts, assembling contact information and corresponding with contributors during early phases of the project. Sujee Kim, Doctoral Student in Adult Development and Aging at Virginia Tech, provided swift and tireless assistance in getting the final version of the book to the publisher and assisted with research for some chapters. Thank you, Sujee.

Perhaps most important is the need to thank the many people who endeavor to improve long-term care: Many of you are among those who will read these words. You provide care, you direct care, you advocate for care, and many of you are the recipients of care. You are on the front lines of innovation and your investment is essential for sustaining the quality of care. Your influence is apparent along the entire long-term care continuum. As our contributors frequently acknowledge in their chapters, it is you who ensure that care and caring remain at the heart of long-term care.

Finally, as editors, we offer thanks to the people close to us who nurture us. Pam wishes to thank her loving family members, Gerald, Evan, and Hadley, and to acknowledge their patience with all the late nights, early mornings, and stalled or foregone weekend plans that made completion of this book possible. Graham thanks Ruth for similar forbearance. In supporting our work, you provide the ultimate expression of long-term caring.

The Context of Long-Term Care

1

The Long-Term Care Continuum in an Aging Society

GRAHAM D. ROWLES
PAMELA B. TEASTER

CHAPTER OVERVIEW

This chapter provides an introduction to contemporary long-term care. We consider concepts of care and caring and provide expanded definitions of long-term care and the long-term care continuum. Demographic processes that have resulted in rapidly increasing demand for long-term care are described and the characteristics of populations in need of such care are outlined. The chapter then considers informal sources of long-term care, primarily the family, and describes the formal system of long-term care services support that has developed in the United States to enable individuals to age in place. Acknowledging that eventually community-based care may no longer be an option, the chapter introduces an array of residential options that provide progressively higher levels of social and medical support. We then explore recent trends in long-term care, including the culture change movement and the emergence of alternatives oriented toward more person-centered long-term care in both community and institutional settings. The chapter concludes with observations on some of the persistent issues confronting long-term care, including debates regarding the appropriateness of community living versus age-segregated care environments, dilemmas in financing long-term care and generating an adequately trained workforce, and the moral and ethical challenges we face, both as individuals and as a society, in providing the highest possible level of caring and practical support to those in need.

LEARNING OBJECTIVES

After completing this chapter, you should have an understanding of:

- The demographic context of contemporary long-term care
- The diversity and characteristics of populations needing long-term care

- Characteristics of persons providing long-term care
- Changing components of long-term care
- The long-term care continuum
- The political economy of long-term care
- Widening perspectives on long-term care

KEY TERMS

Activities of daily living (ADLs)
Age-friendly neighborhoods
Aging in place
Care and caring
Chronic illness
Compression of morbidity
Culture change movement
Demographic transition
Design interventions
Disability
Epidemiologic transition
Formal care
Functional status
Geographical dispersion
Impairment
Informal care
Instrumental activities of daily living (IADLs)
Lifestyle
Long-term care
Long-term care continuum
Long-term care system
New technologies
Nursing home
Person-centered care
Self-care interventions
Survivorship curves
Third age

INTRODUCTION

FAMILY STORIES

Grandma Brewster

It was easy to remember how old "Grandma Brewster" was because she was born in 1900. When she died in 1995, Margaret had lived a full life. After her husband's death in 1973, she remained in the large two-story New England colonial-style Connecticut home on the five-acre lot where she and Albert had raised their twins, Samuel and Susan. Sam lived with his family (including four of Elizabeth's grandchildren) in a ranch home, about half a mile away. Susan, her husband, and two of their three daughters lived on a dairy farm a little over a mile from Margaret. For several years, Margaret was able to remain in her home. She took up painting and devoted increasing amounts of time to her needlework. The matriarch of the family, she continued to host Thanksgiving dinner where close to 20 members of the extended family would dine beneath the Norman

Rockwell "Freedom from Hunger" framed print that adorned the dining-room wall. Over the years, members of the family played an expanding role in preparing food and coordinating the celebration. Sam and Susan were frequent visitors, with Sam assuming progressively greater responsibility for home repair, garden maintenance, and providing assistance with her finances. Nonslip strips were placed on the wooden steps outside the kitchen door, and Sam installed a handrail to reduce the possibility of a fall when the steps were wet. A telephone with a large dial, modified ring-tone, and volume control was installed to compensate for Margaret's declining hearing and vision. As climbing the stairs became more problematic, Sam moved her bed downstairs into the room adjacent to the dining room. Over the years, the locus of family events—with the notable exception of Thanksgiving (where family members pitched in more and more to help with preparation of the meal)—gradually shifted to Sam's and Susan's homes.

And then, one day, Margaret fell. She was hospitalized with a back injury. Returning directly to her home was not an option. And so, when she left the hospital, Margaret moved into Sam's house for a period of recuperation. She stayed for several months. Because of a lack of space (three of Sam's children were still living at home), staying with Sam was not a viable long-term option. As time passed, Margaret became increasingly anxious to go "home." Sam, Susan, and the remainder of the family were concerned for her safety should she do this. Following extended discussions involving Margaret and different factions of the family, some of it quite tense, they all agreed that the best option for Margaret would be to move to a smaller residence. Consequently, Margaret gave up her home of 47 years and relocated to a four-room apartment in town. She lived in a modern apartment block that had begun to develop into a naturally occurring retirement community (NORC), as a progressively increasing proportion of residents were older adults. Margaret accommodated well. She kept her car and so was still able to attend her church and her painting classes and visit family and friends. The smaller residence was much easier to maintain and keep to the level of pristine cleanliness she had always valued. Although she was on the third floor, an elevator that opened close to her door made it easy to get around. She became close friends with new neighbors, including Mary Corson, a widow only 1 year younger, who lived in the next apartment and Audrey Septian who lived at the other end of the corridor. The three ladies would spend much time together. Margaret remained fully engaged with her family as Sam, Susan, or one of her grandchildren would always pick her up so that she could attend gatherings that might extend into the evening. Margaret had decided that she would no longer drive at night.

This arrangement worked well for more than 4 years; but when her friend Mary died and Audrey moved into a nursing facility, Margaret's increasing isolation and growing frailty necessitated a move to a setting where she might receive regular onsite care. After some searching around and family discussion of various options, Sam, Margaret, and the rest of the family settled on Cavendish Place, a continuing care community that provided dining facilities, assistance with activities of daily living (ADLs), and a continuum of health care support options that would become increasingly available to Margaret as her level of impairment increased. Once again, Margaret quickly settled into her new home, this time a room with an adjacent bathroom. She surrounded herself with photographs of Albert, her children and grandchildren, a few family heirlooms she had the space to accommodate, and her craft projects. Over the next few years, she was still picked up for family events, but as her health declined, this strategy became progressively less feasible. She became increasingly reluctant to leave the familiarity and comfort of her room although she still hosted family members, including her grandchildren and great-grandchildren, who loved to hear her stories and receive the candy she always kept next to her chair. She remained cognitively competent although she tired easily and dozed more often. Eventually, she needed to be on oxygen for part of each day. On May 4, 1995, Margaret, "Grandma Brewster" died in her sleep.

Anders Swenson

Anders Swenson is now 36 years old. He was born in Tennessee at a time when the median life expectancy of individuals born with Down syndrome was less than 25 years (Yang, Rasmussen, & Friedman, 2002). By 1997, this figure had increased to 49 years, and today the life expectancy of persons with Down syndrome is approximately 60 years.

When he was a child, Anders experienced many of the comorbidities associated with Down syndrome. He had a heart condition that required surgery and was subject to frequent respiratory infections. In the small town where he lived, resources for the care and support of persons with Down syndrome and their families were limited. Both of his parents, Gunnar and Joanna, were well educated. They quickly schooled themselves on Down syndrome and soon became conversant with the condition. They became fully engaged in the local community of parents with Down syndrome children, eventually assuming a leadership role. Anders received the best possible care, with both of his parents fully invested in his future and a family context in which both Gunnar and Joanna were fully aware of and committed to their unexpected long-term responsibility for his well-being. Both accepted that their lives would be reshaped as a result of their lifelong commitment to the long-term support of their son. Though they fully embraced their parental role, both worried about how he would fare when they were much older or no longer alive (Dillenburger & McKerr, 2010). As Anders grew into adulthood, his potential was maximized at every step. Following a move to Montana, Gunnar and Joanna made sure that he continued to receive the best possible education. Also, they prepared for his future. Gunnar worked with him to the point that he was able to develop a degree of independence and become part of a father and son craft business.

In 2014, Gunnar died after a lengthy battle with a chronic form of leukemia. While Joanna remains alive, Anders can count on her continuing committed and knowledgeable support. What about the thousands of other persons with disabilities being cared for by aging parents? Who will provide the appropriate level of informed long-term care when they are gone?

Mark A. Lincoln

Mark A. Lincoln was born in 1922, the youngest boy born to an Arkansas farm family of nine. He was raised as a member of the Church of the Brethren: the women wore long dresses and covered their hair with white bonnets; the men wore plain, dark clothes and broad-brimmed hats. Their faith, a cornerstone of their work and life, demanded strict adherence to its tenets. Their religion forbade education beyond the 8th grade, but Mark was so capable that he repeated the grade twice, helping the teacher of the one-room school during his "second year." When Mark was 16, he left the farm to work in a sign business owned by his oldest brother. At age 18, he was called to fight in World War II. His goal was to be a fighter pilot, but World War II had already been won on a number of fronts, and so he ended up working on radios in the Philippines. Taking advantage of the GI Bill, he completed a degree in theater but soon realized that he could well starve before he was "discovered." He acquired a secondary school teaching certificate, returned to live with his older brother, and became a high school teacher of English and theater. There he met Ellen, an English teacher at the same high school. They married and moved to a small comfortable home. Ellen became pregnant within two years of the marriage, and the couple had one child.

Shortly after the birth of their daughter, Kaylee, Mark began a career in banking that lasted the rest of his working life. Ellen continued teaching high school English for over 30 years. The three led a modest but warm and loving life together. After graduation from the local high school, Kaylee attended a nearby state university, earned a master's degree in theater, and married an English teacher who worked at the same high school where her parents had first met. Immediately after the marriage, work opportunities led to Kaylee and her new husband moving 6 hours away. For 7 years, Kaylee taught high school English and theater while her husband also taught high school but later returned to school and completed a law degree. Upon graduation from law school, a career opportunity for Kaylee's husband enabled the couple to move 4 hours closer to her parents. Kaylee then went back to school, earned a doctorate, and was hired by the university she had attended. About a year later, Mark (now 76) and Ellen (now 74) had their first grandchild, a curly-haired boy.

All her life, Ellen had been plagued by respiratory problems, having inherited them from her father. After many years of treatments, including steroids, prednisone, and inhalants, she died at the age of 77. In the spring prior to her mother's death, Kaylee had accepted a new faculty position about a 6-hour drive from her parents' home. She was concerned about leaving her father alone so soon after her mother's death, although she knew he was surrounded by many friends (mostly around Mark's age). For the first few years after Ellen's death, Mark cooked for himself, volunteered at the church and local hospital, and visited back and forth with his daughter and her family.

About 2 years after Ellen's death, Mark fell for the first time and had to be hospitalized: during his stay he was diagnosed with dementia and peripheral neuropathy. Although he was discharged home, his fall was the first of many such incidents that followed. He also was involved in a number of minor car accidents. Over a 5-year period, Mark grew thin and pale. He became increasingly confused, and more and more often when she visited, Kaylee found remnants of old food and milk in his refrigerator but little else to eat in the house. She called her father daily and tried to visit as often as her work schedule and her own family responsibilities would allow. Her ability to provide daily support was severely limited by distance at a time when her work responsibilities were increasing and time available to take care of her father had decreased. And then Mark was diagnosed with four heart blockages requiring surgery. During the surgery, Kaylee was in constant contact with the surgeon. Shortly after the surgery, accompanied by Mark's now 4-year-old grandson, Kaylee moved in with Mark where she spent several weeks helping her father convalesce and trying to fulfill her distant work commitments. Subsequently, when he could travel, Kaylee drove her father back to her house where he would stay for a few weeks. Kaylee's husband helped when he could, but the location of his work meant that he was away for extended periods.

Though Mark regained strength and acuity and eventually returned home, it was not long before his confusion returned, he began to eat less and less, and he experienced several more falls and minor car accidents. He loved his daughter and her family and appreciated the dilemma posed by their living so far away, but he remained firm in his conviction to remain in the town where he had lived his entire adult life. Nine months later, after another car accident and a precipitous fall that again landed him in the hospital, Mark reluctantly agreed to sell the family home and move into an assisted living facility. He arranged the sale of most of the personal property accumulated over his lifetime with Ellen. Kaylee, her husband, and his grandson traveled to help him move out of the family home and into the facility. Mark fared well at Oakwood Hills for about a year and a half. Over time, he began to mix up his medications (Kaylee arranged for him to be assisted), became increasingly confused and depressed (he began to accuse Kaylee of trying to put him in a "home"), and was sometimes hostile to staff (Kaylee intervened with the facility administration and with Mark's physician). His balance gradually worsened, but he refused to use a cane or a walker, even though Kaylee and others provided him with many varieties.

Kaylee had long wished for another child. After over 6 years of waiting, she traveled to China to adopt a little girl of 2½ years. Her husband and son remained in the United States because not only Mark but also Kaylee's mother-in-law was failing and was too frail to be left with no close family member nearby. While walking to the telephone in his room to hear the first words of his new granddaughter and speak to his daughter, both in China, Mark fell again, this time slamming his head hard against a table and crashing to the floor. He had broken his neck. Despite the efforts of the medical team, his son-in-law, and Kaylee's efforts to guide his care from a distance, Mark died 10 days after she returned to the United States.

DEFINING LONG-TERM CARE

The three stories introducing this chapter are modeled on actual situations; they are among the myriad possible scenarios of long-term care considered within this book. Dilemmas of aging in place versus relocation, emergent issues resulting from success in extending the longevity of persons born with disabilities, and difficulties in providing care from a distance are examples of an array of issues in providing long-term care in an aging society—a society in which the need for such care is increasing in the face of stable or declining human and capital resources. But what then, exactly, is long-term care?

The most often used definition is that of Kane and Kane (1987, p. 4), who defined long-term care as "a set of health, personal care and social services delivered over a sustained period of time to persons who have lost or never acquired some degree of functional capacity." In this book we broaden this perspective. Fundamental to such elaboration is clear expression of what we mean by care and caring. The words *care* and *caring* can be viewed in many ways, but perhaps most important is to distinguish between the practice of care and the emotion behind caring—we care for our fellow humans and attempt to be caring individuals. We navigate the process, programs, or mechanisms through which this sentiment is manifest: the provision of care services and programs and the practical acts of serving the needs of those who have "lost or never acquired some degree of functional capacity." Care or caring about the fate of others without administrative structures, services, and programs to provide this care in a practical way is noble but ineffective. On the other hand, provision of a full array of services and programs without an underlying and fully internalized ethic of care and caring results in a system that may be effective in providing practical support but lacking in meaning for all involved (Douglas, 2010; Tronto, 1993). The trick, of course, is to develop approaches to care and systems of care that are fully integrated expressions of a caring society that acknowledges the richness of human experience and is based on the desire to enable all people to function at their highest level of human potential. The ever-growing system of long-term care options in the United States has sometimes provided care without caring because it has strayed away from the ultimate purpose of not just providing services or support to improve function but also achieving the loftier goal of facilitating the highest possible quality of life for those being served.

A diversity of definitions of care and caring and the distinction between sentiment and service is woven throughout the chapters in this book. Rather than limiting each author within the rubric of standardized definitions, we encouraged the contributors to write from their own individual perspectives on long-term care. In this introductory chapter we provide four general definitions of long-term care, but we encouraged the authors of each chapter to expand on these definitions in the most appropriate manner for expressing different aspects of the long-term care enterprise.

As we have noted, much has been written on notions of **care and caring** (Bassett, 2002; Parr, 2003; Weaver, 2013). As Kittay, Jennings, and Wasunna (2005) so eloquently articulated, "People do not spring up from the soil like mushrooms. People produce people. People need to be cared for and nurtured throughout their lives by other people, at some times more urgently and more completely than at other times" (p. 443). The need for an ethos of care and caring has been often expressed in fields such as nursing (Bassett, 2002; Dewar & Nolan, 2013).

Our definition of **long-term care**, the concrete manifestation of care and caring, blends the perspectives of Kane and Kane (1987) and Mosby's Medical Dictionary (2009): *health, personal care and social support delivered on a recurring or continuing basis to persons who have lost or never acquired some degree of functional capacity*. This definition embraces all forms of long-term support, ranging from the informal care provided by family and friends to the full array of formal services provided by both public and private service delivery programs, organizations, and institutions. In recent decades, the diversity of options has increased; there are now a plethora of alternatives for providing different types of long-term support.

The proliferation of long-term care alternatives is not a random occurrence. It represents the progressive creation of new options as the landscape of needs has evolved (see Chapter 2). What has emerged as a **long-term care system** is a linked set of supports, services, and integrating mechanisms that guide and track the provision of both informal and formal physical and mental health and social services to persons in need of long-term care (adapted from Evashwick, 2005). This system is imperfect and dynamic. For example, a generation ago, Cavendish Place was not an option for Margaret; there was no need to confront the issue of Ander's care in his 60s, as he would not be alive at that age, and Mark Lincoln's daughter would likely have been living nearby, thus obviating the need for long-distance caregiving. It is also important to acknowledge the cultural diversity of long-term care systems. Nursing facilities, assisted living, special housing options, adult day care, and the full array of alternatives discussed in this book are distinct features of contemporary American society. They do not exist as options within societies that sustain alternative cultural models of long-term care; for example, the sustained and sometimes exclusive primacy of the family in the provision of long-term care.

As the current system of long-term care in the United States developed over the past century, it increasingly became framed within a **continuum of care**, one that continues to evolve in the present century. Recognition that the long-term care needs of individuals are constantly changing necessitates a system that allows for the flow of individuals within the system, often although not invariably, in the direction of increasing dependency. Margaret Brewster and Mark Lincoln both reflect this pattern. Their stories provide unique trajectories of movement along a continuum in which a variety of pathways are available. Formally defined, we can consider the continuum of care as an integrated form of long-term care provision that provides a comprehensive and linked set of supports and services focused on meeting the health, personal care, and social services needs of individuals as their capabilities and circumstances change (adapted from Evashwick, 2005). In adopting this definition, we emphasize the importance of avoiding the negative connotation of an invariant progression from independence to dependency and, instead, frame the continuum in the context of exchanges occurring throughout the life course. As part of the human condition, human beings are interdependent from birth to death (Silverstein, Conroy, Wang, Giarusso, & Bengtson, 2002). The physical dependency of infancy is reciprocated by the gift of a new life. The social contract of adulthood necessitates the manifestation of this reciprocity through care of both the young and old as part of the accumulation of social capital. In old age, we draw on this capital as we exchange the receipt of physical care in payment for the legacy we have created and that we will leave.

Throughout this volume, notions of care and caring, the design of long-term care services, and consideration of ways in which these are linked within a long-term care system are framed within a continuum of linked options that, ideally, are constantly transitioning toward maximizing quality of life.

THE DEMOGRAPHIC CONTEXT OF CONTEMPORARY LONG-TERM CARE

PATTERNS OF CHANGE

As societies move through the process of industrialization and development, they experience a **demographic transition** that results in increased longevity, a growing elderly population, and the survival of sub–population groups that formerly might not have survived through infancy (Figure 1.1). In the first phase of the transition, essentially agrarian societies are characterized by high birthrates and high but fluctuating death rates as a result of wars, famines, and epidemics. During this phase, the population remains small and young, with few individuals surviving to old age. With development and industrialization, improvements in sanitation, fewer epidemics, enhanced health care and better living conditions, infant mortality levels drop. But a cultural lag in recognizing that fewer births are needed to ensure the survival of a viable population means that the overall population begins to rise. This growth continues although at a gradually slowing pace as birthrates drop and death rates remain low. Eventually, a situation is reached where death rates are low and birthrates are also low (although sometimes fluctuating as a result of periodic "baby booms"). The overall population stabilizes at a high level. In some developed countries, it appears that the overall population may even be moving to a point below replacement level (where the number of births is lower than is needed to maintain the population size).

As societies move through the demographic transition, patterns of illness and death gradually change as a result of an **epidemiologic transition**. Researchers generally consider this transition as involving three phases. First, corresponding to the earliest phases of the demographic transition, is a stage of pestilence and famine characterized by high death rates from periods of chronic malnutrition, plague, and epidemics of infectious diseases such as smallpox and cholera. During a second stage, there is a gradual decline in deaths from epidemics and famine and a transition to infectious diseases such as tuberculosis, pneumonia,

FIGURE 1.1 The demographic transition.

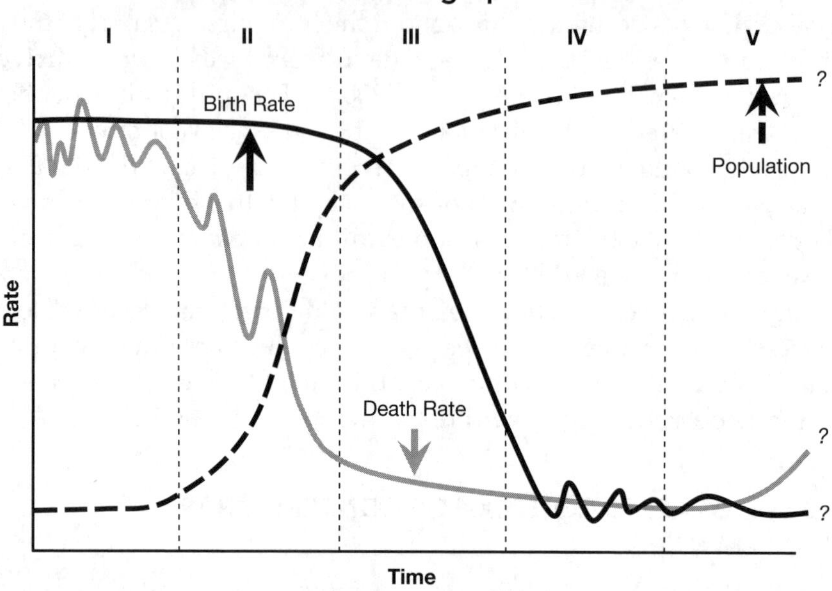

	Fertility	Mortality	Population Change
Stage I	High	High and Fluctuating	Small and Fluctuating
Stage II	High	Falling	Accelerating Increase in Size
Stage III	Falling	Low	Slowing Increase in Size
Stage IV	Low and Fluctuating	Low	Large and Fluctuating in Size
Stage V	Low ?	Low ?	Large and Stable (potential decline?)

and influenza as dominant causes of death. With improvements in medical care, these diseases become far less prevalent among younger people but become the scourges of old age. In the final phase of the epidemiologic transition, there is a shift from infectious diseases as the primary cause of death and disability to **chronic illness** as the major cause of morbidity and mortality. Today, the dominant chronic illnesses are coronary heart disease, hypertension, diabetes, arthritis, and cancers (Centers for Disease Control and Prevention, 2015).

One outcome of these processes is increasing survivorship rates as, over time, growing numbers of individuals are able to enjoy a ripe old age, albeit often experiencing the limitations of chronic disease. This process is illustrated in Figure 1.2, which portrays the progressive "rectangularization" of **survivorship curves** for the United States as higher percentages of individuals experience old age.

FIGURE 1.2 Survivorship curves: past and projected.

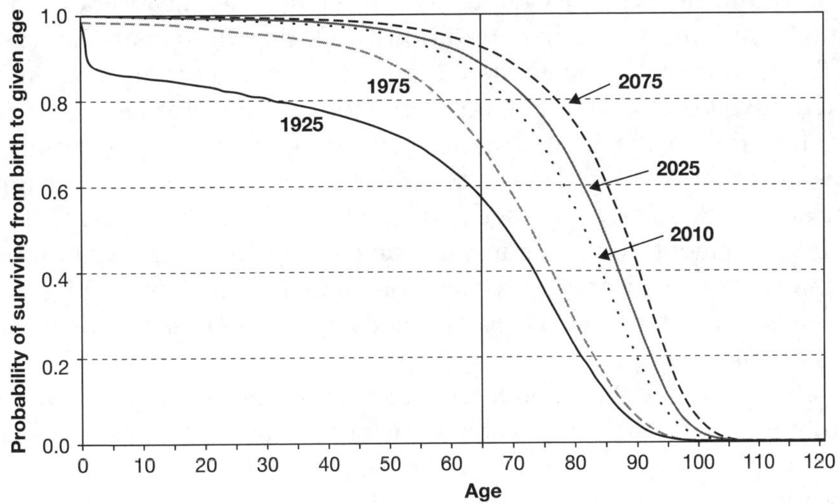

Overall, these trends have given rise to the increased importance of long-term care as a component of life in contemporary societies. This has been reinforced by a number of associated trends. First has been the **geographical dispersion** of the family resulting in transformation of the ways that long-term care is provided from an almost exclusive focus on geographically proximate family providing unpaid direct day-to-day care to increasing reliance on mechanisms of care from a distance (e.g., the daily calls that Mark Lincoln received from his daughter Kaylee and the manner in which she ran interference with his physicians and caregivers). Such geographical separation has provided added impetus to the development of paid formal services, including home care, home-delivered meals, visiting nurse services, and adult day services.

A second trend has been the **compression of morbidity**, a notion that has generated some controversy. The basic argument here is that with improved medicine and healthier lifestyles, the period of time that individuals are experiencing life-limiting effects of chronic illness gradually declines. It is suggested that this shortens the period of living with disability and hence the need for long-term care. This argument is reinforced by the emergence of a new phase of life in developed societies, often termed the **third age**, a period of active postretirement living during which individuals remain healthy and are able to engage in new pursuits and activities (e.g., the arts, second careers, volunteering) that were not available or possible to previous generations (Laslett, 1989; Weiss & Bass, 2002). This view is supported by evidence that each cohort of older adults tends to be healthier than the one that preceded it (Manton, Gu, & Lamb, 2006). On the other hand, there are those who suggest that increased longevity merely extends the length of time that individuals experience the most negative effects of chronic illness and extends the period of disability and need for long-term care.

A third trend that has accelerated in recent years has been the provision of long-term care in an array of new settings. During colonial times, the primary locale of long-term care was the family; those without family were generally cared for by almshouses (see Chapter 2). Since that time, the locations in which long-term care is provided have multiplied. During the Great Depression of the 1930s, the nursing home appeared as part of the long-term care landscape. This alternative flourished, to the point that today, there are close to 1.5 million nursing facilities in the United States. The **long-term care continuum** now includes an array of special housing options, including federally supported housing alternatives that developed from the 1960s through the early 1980s, self-contained retirement communities, assisted living facilities, continuing care communities, and comprehensive campus-like facilities providing support for all levels of needed care. These alternatives are discussed in detail in later chapters of this book.

Although there is debate about the effects of recent demographic and health status trends, there is little doubt about the increasing need for an array of long-term care options. This book is about this need and the many ways in which it is being addressed.

LONG-TERM CARE POPULATIONS

A wide range of individuals require long-term care. First are those who experience *chronic* health conditions, variously defined by the U.S. National Center for Health Statistics as lasting for at least 3 months and by other agencies and researchers as at least 12 months. Such conditions include arthritis and other rheumatic conditions, hypertension, heart disease, lower respiratory disease, cancer, diabetes, depression, and cerebrovascular disease. Data from 2005 show that 44% of all Americans had at least one chronic condition, and 13% had three or more (Paez, Zhao, & Hwang, 2009). The number of persons with chronic conditions is anticipated to grow to 157 million in 2020 with 81 million having multiple conditions (Wu & Green, 2000; Figure 1.3). The percentage of individuals with multiple chronic conditions is also increasing, as revealed in Figure 1.4, which documents increases in the percentage of people ages 45 to 64 and 65 and over with two or more of nine selected chronic conditions: hypertension, heart disease, diabetes, cancer, stroke, chronic bronchitis, emphysema, current asthma, and kidney disease (Fried, Bernstein, & Bush, 2012). As noted earlier, the prevalence of most chronic conditions increases with age as these conditions tend to worsen with age. This often necessitates higher levels of long-term care as impairment increases.

A second long-term care population consists of individuals living with **impairment** resulting from a permanent, usually untreatable defect caused by disease, injury (an amputated leg), cognitive limitation (Down syndrome—Anders would be in this category), or a congenital malformation (blindness since birth). Chronic illness and impairment result in **disability**, a reduction in a person's ability to perform self-care and complete regular functions of daily living without assistance. Traditionally, disabilities are assessed through measures of **functional status**. These measures include tools that assess physical, cognitive, emotional, and social dimensions of functional ability. For example,

FIGURE 1.3 Projected increase in numbers of persons with chronic conditions (in millions).

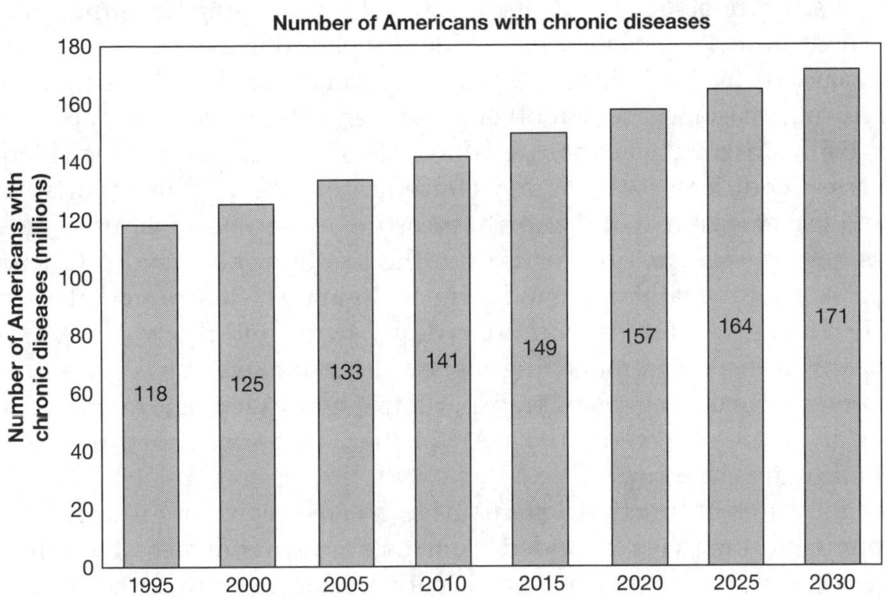

Source: Wu and Green (2000, October).

FIGURE 1.4 Percentage of adults aged 45 to 64 and 65 and over with two or more of nine selected chronic conditions, 1999–2000 and 2009–2010.

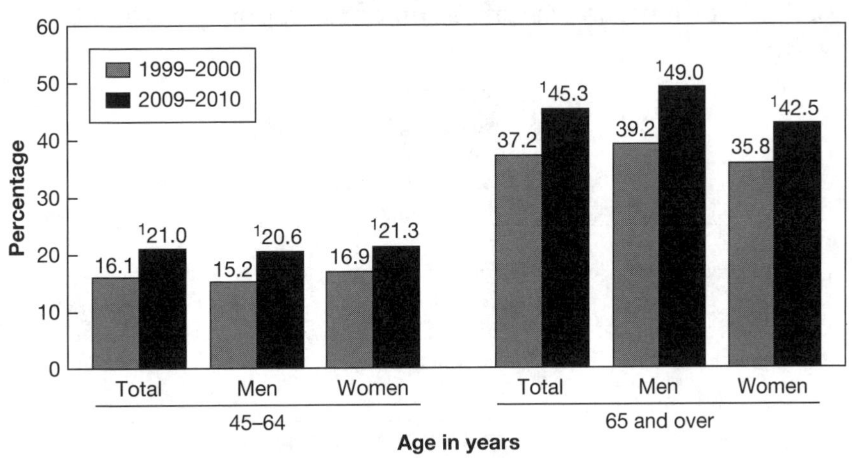

[1]Significantly different from 1999–2000, $p < 0.05$.
Note: Access data table at: http://www.cdc.gov/nchs/data/databriefs/db100_tables.pdf#1
Source: CDC/NCHS, National Health Interview Survey.

the most widely employed measure of physical function is assessment of **activities of daily living (ADLs)**, a measure initially developed during the 1960s that assesses self-care abilities with respect to eating, dressing, toileting, transferring, and continence. The measure is often employed using a four-point assessment scale: (1) totally independent, (2) requiring mechanical assistance only, (3) requiring assistance from another person, and (4) unable to perform activity (Katz, Ford, Moskowitz, Jackson, & Jaffe, 1963). This measure has been modified in a variety of different ways since its introduction, although most variants continue to use at least five of the initial measures. A second often-used measure moves beyond self-care and focuses on the ability of a person to function in ways conducive to maintaining independent living. The **instrumental activities of daily living (IADLs)**, first introduced by Lawton and Brody (1969), assesses abilities with respect to managing money, using the telephone, grocery shopping, personal shopping, using transportation, housekeeping, completing daily chores, and managing medications. Again, there are a variety of different manifestations of this measure.

As measures of functional status have become more sophisticated and all encompassing, they have expanded to embrace measures of mental health, social engagement, and environmental participation. Classic among these more recent models is the now widely employed International Classification of Functioning, Disability and Health (ICF) disablement model of the World Health Organization (WHO, 2001; Figure 1.5). Approved for use by the World Health Assembly in 2001, this measure is based on underlying principles of *universality* (applicable to all people irrespective of health condition and in all physical, social, and cultural contexts), *parity and etiological neutrality* (avoiding either explicit or implicit differentiation among health conditions (physical or mental) by making the

FIGURE 1.5 International classification of functioning, disability and health.

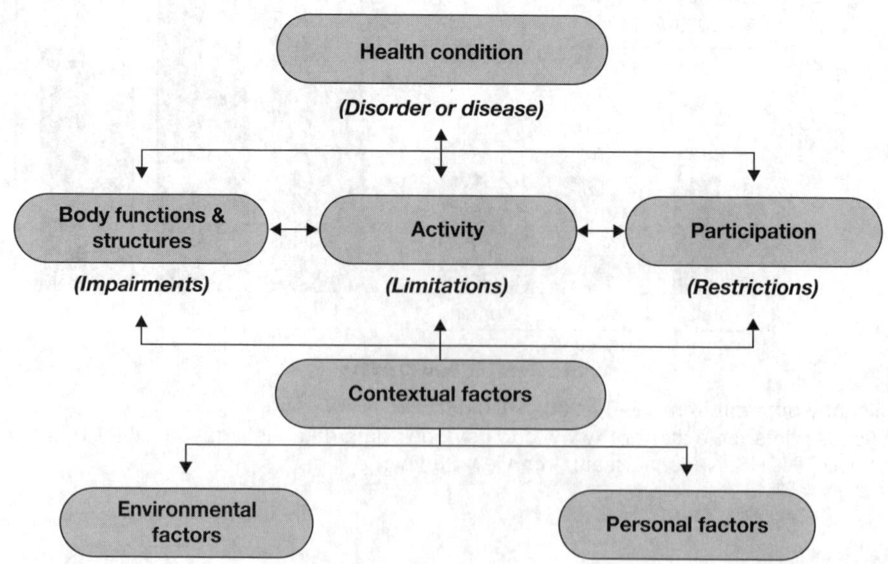

important shift from health status to functioning), *neutrality* (employing nonevaluative language wherever possible to include both positive and negative aspects of status), and *environmental influence* (recognizing the important role of physical environment factors, such as climate, terrain, and building design, as well as social factors such as attitudes, institutions, and laws, in determining functioning and disability). Since its introduction, there have been many different applications and adaptations of the ICF for use with specific populations and in specific situations. However, the model now provides a widely accepted framework for defining the situation of populations that tend to be in need of long-term care.

Regardless of the measures employed to assess levels of functional ability or disability, the population in need of long-term care is both diverse and growing. Indeed, the U.S. Department of Health and Human Services estimates that 70% of people turning age 65 can expect to use some form of long-term care during their lives (http://longtermcare.gov/the-basics/who-needs-care/, retrieved on January 4, 2015). The older a person grows, the more likely he or she is to need long-term care, especially women because they outlive men by about five years and consume more long-term care services. Also, persons with disability, including 69% of people aged 90 or older, are likely to consume significant long-term care resources. Persons with chronic illness and high blood pressure, many of whom are older adults, make heavy use of long-term care resources. Persons living alone (the proportion of older women living alone has risen to almost 50%) are more likely to need long-term care. Finally, the population in need of long-term care is influenced by heredity and by lifestyle factors (e.g., diet and exercise habits).

Although the aging of the population and other demographic processes are important determinants of an expanding demand for long-term care, rising demand is only a part of the problem. Equally important is consideration of the increasing demand for people, often family members, to provide long-term care in the face of multiple and competing demands. The other side of long-term care is the people whose lives are shaped and often transformed by the need to provide long-term care, both **informal care** (generally unpaid) received from family members, friends, and acquaintances and **formal care** (generally paid) provided by programs, services, and agencies.

INFORMAL CARE: FAMILIES, FRIENDS, AND ACQUAINTANCES

As former first lady Rosalynn Carter once expressed it, "There are only four kinds of people in the world—those who have been caregivers, those who currently are caregivers, those who will be caregivers and those who need caregivers" (Carter & Golant, 1994, p. 3). It is difficult to estimate the number of informal caregivers because definitions vary widely as to who a caregiver is and what informal care constitutes. Does bringing in the mail from a roadside mailbox for an elderly neighbor constitute care? How does such support equate with providing 24-hour assistance with ADLs and medical care for an aging parent? According to the National Center on Caregiving, 65.7 million caregivers (29% of the U.S. Adult population) provide care to someone who is ill, disabled, or aged (Family Caregiver Alliance, 2012). Of these, 43.5 million adult caregivers care for someone 50 years of age or older and 14.9 million care for someone who has Alzheimer's disease or another dementia. AARP reported that in 2009, about 42.1 million family caregivers in the United States provided care to an adult with limitations in daily activities at any given point in time, and about 61.6 million provided care at some time during the year. The estimated economic value of their unpaid contributions was approximately $450 billion in 2009, up from an estimated $375 billion in 2007. More detailed descriptions of the characteristics of these caregivers, the challenges they face, and the rewards they receive from caregiving are provided in Chapters 3 and 4. Here, we emphasize that informal care from families and friends is likely to remain the primary source of long-term care support for the foreseeable future. The majority of caregivers are women (66%), 34% of whom care for two or more people (Family Caregiver Alliance, 2012). The average age of caregivers is 48 years, an age that is rising steadily. Many caregivers are themselves growing older, with an average age of those caring for persons 65 and older being 63 years. Along with the rising age of caregivers, the average number of hours per week devoted to caregiving increases with age.

Providing care to a person in need is not without cost. There has been an ever-expanding literature on caregiver burden and the economic and social costs of providing long-term care. These costs include lost wages, reduced potential for professional advancement, impaired health, social isolation, clinical depression, and other manifestations of emotional distress (Adelman, Tmanova, Delgado, Dion, & Lachs, 2014). In the past decade there has been growing awareness that despite the stresses and strains, there are benefits to becoming a caregiver: an enhanced sense of purpose, feelings of competence in the role of caregiver, being glad to give back to the receiver, personal growth, and a sense of meaningfulness in life (Raschick & Ingersoll-Dayton, 2004; Savundranayagam, 2014). It is also increasingly recognized that the view of caregiving as a burden is culturally based: in some cultures, the provision of care is viewed as a normative aspect of life. Indeed, in their work with five reservation-dwelling tribes in the American Southwest, Hennessey and Johns (1996) discovered that caregivers were more concerned about their work and other commitments interfering with their caregiving rather than caregiving interfering with their work and other aspects of their lives.

FORMAL CARE: THE RISE OF SERVICE SYSTEMS, THE AGING NETWORK, AND CORPORATE CARE

Although the bulk of long-term care is provided by family members, the long-term care landscape has been supplemented by the development of formal (paid) long-term care. As the difficulties and stresses of family caregiving gradually increase with the deteriorating condition of the care recipient, the tendency for informal care to be supplemented by formal care resources also increases. Assistance from family members with shopping, housekeeping, mowing the lawn, changing lightbulbs, and fixing the faucet gradually becomes supplemented by participation in Meals-on-Wheels programs, three visits a week from a home care worker to provide help with bathing, or support from an array of community-based services.

Development of systems of formal long-term care was very much a feature of 20th-century Western culture. Stimulated by the Social Security Act of 1935, which provided federal resources to facilitate the financial support of older adults and those in need, the situation in the United States paralleled the emergence in many developed nations of support systems for increasing populations of aging and disabled individuals. A major reinforcement was the passage of the Older Americans Act in 1965 and the creation of Medicare and Medicaid, programs providing funding for medical care. Amendments to the Older Americans Act in 1973 created a system of long-term care service delivery by forming Area Agencies on Aging and what has come to be known as the "Aging Network." This involved the creation of 56 State Units on Aging and a nationwide system of 629 Area Agencies on Aging, 244 tribal organizations, and two native Hawaiian organizations. Under the aegis of these administrative units, the array of services and resources supporting long-term care has proliferated throughout the nation to include adult day care, adult protective services, family caregiver support, help for grandparents raising grandchildren, guardianship, health promotion, home care, legal services, nutrition, ombudsman programs, personal care attendants, and transportation. Many of these services are delivered in individual communities through local senior centers. An elaborate infrastructure and network of social services is now available to persons requiring long-term care support at home.

RELOCATION AND THE EMERGENCE OF RESIDENTIAL ALTERNATIVES

Many current programs and services reflect a priority that evolved during the 1980s on **aging in place**—enabling people to remain at home in a familiar setting (Rowles, 1993; Tilson, 1990; see Chapters 8, 9, and 10). Indeed, a priority on aging in place has evolved into a societal policy mantra even though there has been a dawning realization that this may not be the optimal situation for some older adults or persons with disabilities.

There comes a point when the combined efforts of families and community-based services are no longer sufficient (Robison, Shugrue, Porter, Fortinsky, & Curry, 2012). Often a tipping point occurs when the long-term care recipient becomes incontinent, his or her level of cognitive impairment is such that the care recipient becomes a danger to himself or herself, or the primary caregiver can no longer cope (Ryan & Scullion, 2000). At this point, and sometimes in anticipation of this point, it becomes necessary to consider alternative settings for the provision of care. In parallel with community-based options, a smorgasbord of residential and health care specialized environments has developed.

Gradually, over time, the **nursing home** emerged as an institutional alternative to family care, with the number of facilities in the United States rising from about 1,200 with 25,000 beds in 1939 to 15,465 nursing facilities with 1,646,302 beds in 2011 (Kaiser Foundation, 2015). Further impetus to this option was provided by the previously mentioned Older Americans Act and the introduction of Medicare and Medicaid. The result was expansion of the nursing home industry accompanied by increasing corporatization of this long-term care option.

In parallel with this trend, and partially in response to the abysmal circumstances of many older adults (in 1959 poverty among persons 65 and older was 35%), came a growing interest in *residential options for older adults*. Over the past few decades, alternatives between the extremes of living with family members and nursing home residence proliferated (Exhibit 1.1).

EXHIBIT 1.1 Examples of the Growing Array of Residential Settings of Long-Term Care

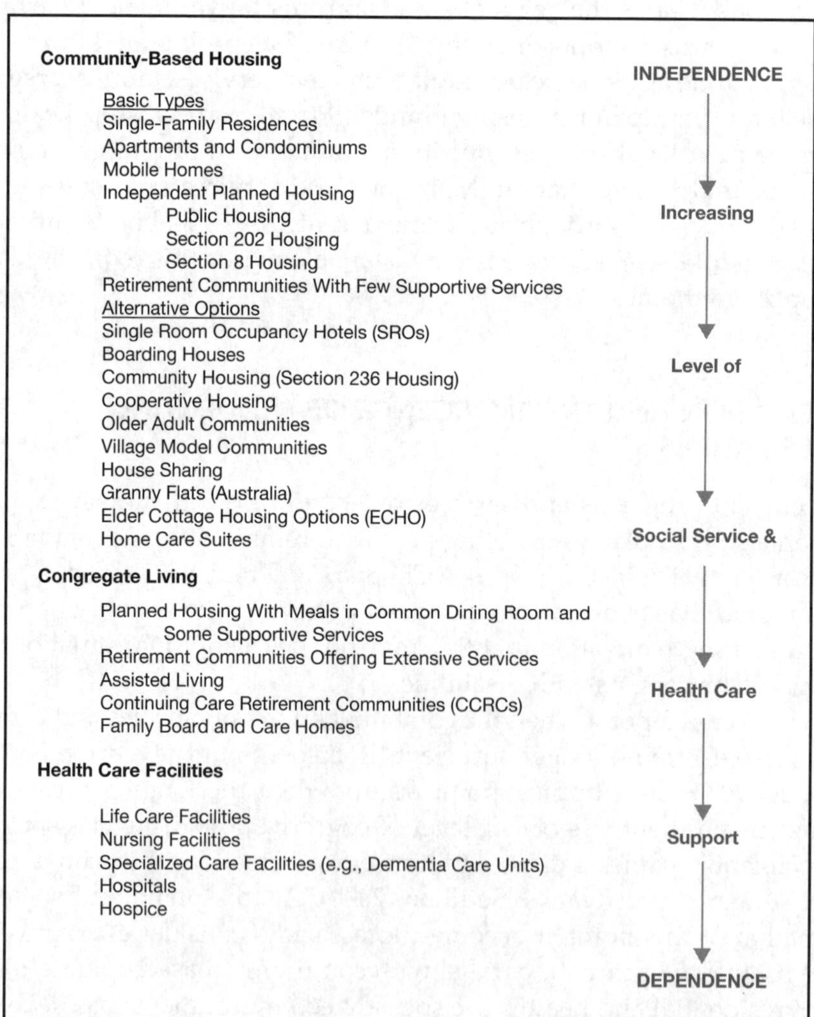

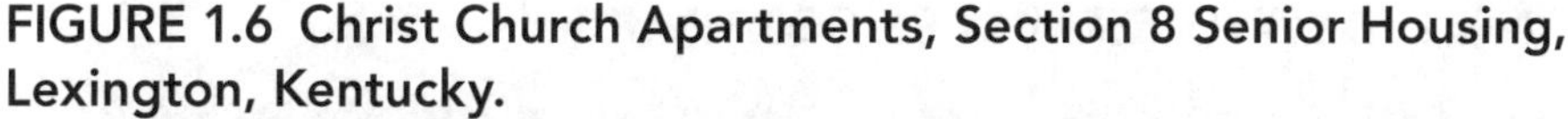

FIGURE 1.6 Christ Church Apartments, Section 8 Senior Housing, Lexington, Kentucky.

Source: G. D. Rowles.

These options can be arrayed along a continuum addressing a progressively increasing need for service and health care assistance. From the 1950s through the 1970s, federally supported housing options were developed, including public housing, Department of Housing and Urban Development (HUD)-supported Section 8, Section 236, and Section 202 housing (often constructed by faith communities and nonprofit organizations that received low-interest loans (Figure 1.6). The focus was on providing affordable housing to older adults and persons with disabilities (see Chapter 9). Change in federal policy during the 1980s led to significant curtailment of funding for new construction of such housing. As the original residents aged in place in these settings and grew increasingly frail, a need arose for supportive services.

The need to provide more services to aging populations in federally subsidized housing was complemented by the emergence of a new alternative funded by the private sector—assisted living (Golant & Hyde, 2008; Wilson, 2007; see also, Chapter 10). The idea of assisted living is based on maximizing independence but providing supportive services within a model of care in which residents have not only private and public space and maximum autonomy in controlling their daily lives and care but also ready access to both routine and specialized services. Unfortunately, although creative options abound, alternatives such as assisted living still remain prohibitively expensive for many people and are not available in many communities (Golant, 1992).

REVISITING THE LONG-TERM CARE CONTINUUM

The long-term care needs of persons who are aging or living with disability or in other situations requiring assistance over an extended period are constantly evolving as their capabilities and circumstances change. Long-term care involves far more than a set of services or institutional settings and should be considered in the context of the life course. When we are born we become part of a convoy of individuals who nurture us (Antonucci & Akiyama, 1987; Antonucci, Berditt, & Akiyama, 2009). Initially, this convoy comprises our parents, siblings, and other relatives as well as our pediatrician, the people who support us in our faith community, and the friends we accumulate as we progress through childhood. The convoy tends to expand as we continue our education or pursue a career and as our lives become intertwined with an ever-broadening population of colleagues and associates. People also fall away from the convoy as our grandparents and eventually our parents die, as we change careers, as we relocate, and as we grow older. Interwoven throughout this book are ways the convoy changes, the processes involved in this change, and the ways in which our progress is supported at different times by different human resources and environmental contexts. Progress along the continuum is rarely completely unidirectional. Rehabilitation, introduction of a new medication that counters impairment, or a psychological intervention may reverse the course.

In developed societies, the aspiration is for a continuum of care that is maximally flexible, accommodates to changing circumstances, and provides for an optimum quality of life over an individual's life course. Ideally, there should be no gaps—no circumstances in which an individual in need falls between the cracks of the long-term care system. In reality, the system is fragmented, constantly in transition, and, for many caregivers, remains extremely difficult to negotiate. Typically, each individual's progress along the continuum involves phases of moving into and out of different types of both informal and formal long-term care.

THE SOCIAL CONTEXT OF CONTEMPORARY LONG-TERM CARE

Quality of life is far more than quality of care. This distinction has become increasingly apparent during recent decades as the long-term care system has evolved in the United States. Emphasis on quality of care became an important focus during the second half of the last century, in part as a result of society's response to a number of scandals that affected segments of the formal long-term care continuum. For example, during the mid-1970s there was a major concern with corruption and fraud in the operation of nursing homes and well-publicized reports documented major deficiencies in the quality of care (Mendelson, 1974; United States Senate, 1974). Public outcry led to a tightening of regulations and renewed effort to improve the quality of institutional long-term care.

Although these changes resulted in some improvement in basic physical care and a reduction in levels of corruption and fraud in the burgeoning nursing home industry, a 1986 Institute of Medicine study found that nursing home residents still received "shockingly deficient" care. In the following year, Congress enacted the Omnibus Budget Reconciliation Act (OBRA '87), also known as the Nursing Home Reform Act. Passage of this law heralded a gradual process of transition in nursing facility care, representing expansion from a primary concern with physical care to increasing emphasis on quality of life. Significant components of this legislation included requirements for comprehensive assessment of the condition of every person admitted and development of a written plan of care; annual assessment of ADLs for all residents; preadmission screening and annual resident reviews to detect mental illness or mental retardation; and mandated services (physician, nursing, rehabilitative, pharmaceutical, dietician, dental, and medically related social services). Increased emphasis was placed on resident rights. When admitted to a nursing home, residents were to be informed both in writing and verbally of their legal rights, which include the right to choose their own physician, be free from chemical and physical restraints, enjoy privacy and confidentiality of personal and medical records and protection of personal funds, voice grievances without fear of reprisal with prompt attention to resolution of those grievances, organize and participate in resident groups (with family members able to meet in family groups), and have access to federal or state surveys of the facility and to a local or state long-term care ombudsman. The OBRA '87 legislation also provided for improved staffing and training by mandating at least one registered nurse (RN) on duty 8 hours a day, 7 days a week, and a licensed nurse on duty 24 hours a day, 7 days a week. Facilities with more than 120 beds were to employ at least one full-time social worker, and nurses' aides were to undergo at least 75 hours of approved training and pass a competency evaluation. The legislation also introduced federal requirements for regular surveys and certification of facilities. Moreover, states were to conduct unannounced standard surveys of nursing homes at least once a year, which included an audit of a sample of resident assessments and interviews with residents to determine the quality of care they were receiving. Finally, the legislation introduced procedures for enforcement and sanctioning of noncompliant facilities.

This detailed example of a piece of long-term care–related legislation provides one historical illustration of the way in which the system of long-term care in the United States has evolved as the need for and scale of supportive intervention has grown. The emergent alternative of assisted living is seeing a similar transition from an initially unregulated option to an increasingly regulated component of the long-term care continuum. At this point, most states have developed their own definition of assisted living with distinct regulations with regard to the licensing and monitoring of such facilities. The result is a patchwork of guidelines shaping the form of this component of long-term care.

WIDENING HORIZONS

Recognition that an integrated and person-centered long-term care system must focus on maximizing quality of life for both care recipients and care providers at all points along the long-term care continuum has been an important stimulus to evolutional change. **Person-centered care** is respectful of and responsive to each person's needs, preferences, and values, and ensures that care recipients' own values guide all decisions affecting their lives. This has involved both a rethinking of the underlying philosophy of care and a broader definition of what we mean by long-term care. As Kane (2001, p. 295) wrote: "Bluntly put, LTC [long-term care] policies and practices in the United States are flawed, particularly for those LTC consumers who are old." In an indictment of the contemporary system at the turn of the century she noted that there was undue emphasis on nursing home and institutional care over community-based and home care alternatives. She noted particularly skimpy geographical availability of home care alternatives and services in many localities and rued the focus on quality of care rather than quality of life. In part, Kane argued, this stemmed from overemphasis on safety and health. At the core of her argument was advocacy for the need for a complete reorientation of the way in which long-term care is conceptualized:

> One little-tested assumption is that safety—defined vaguely or not at all—is the be all and end all of LTC. Embedded in most of our rules and regulations is the idea that LTC should aspire to the best possible quality of life as is consistent with health and safety. But ordinary people may prefer the best health and safety outcomes possible that are consistent with a meaningful quality of life.
>
> (Kane, 2001, p. 296)

During the early years of the 21st century, it appears that this voice is being increasingly heeded, as the cultures of most components of the long-term care continuum are evolving in new consumer-focused directions (e.g., person-centered care, supported decision making).

One direction is growing appreciation of the role that **age-friendly neighborhoods** and livable communities can play in creating environments supportive of individual's ability to defer the need for long-term care. In 2007 the World Health Organization conducted focus group research in 33 cities in 22 countries around the world (including New York City and Portland, Oregon) to identify characteristics of communities that maximized their livability and the ability of people to actively participate in community activities regardless of age and level of functional ability. The result was *Global Age-Friendly Cities: A Guide* (WHO, 2007a) and development of a checklist identifying eight essential features of an age-friendly city that provided foci for maximizing the engagement of all residents (WHO, 2007b; Figure 1.7). In the United States, this initiative was picked up by AARP, which developed its own criteria for livable communities and established a growing network that currently embraces 41 cities, towns, and counties serving more than 28 million people (www.aarp.org/livable-communities/, accessed January 25, 2015). Both organizations developed a program whereby communities could work toward achieving recognition as an age-friendly community by developing programs of intervention and enrichment to enhance the livability of their community. Implications of the age-friendly community movement for long-term care are many because

FIGURE 1.7 Age-friendly city topic areas.

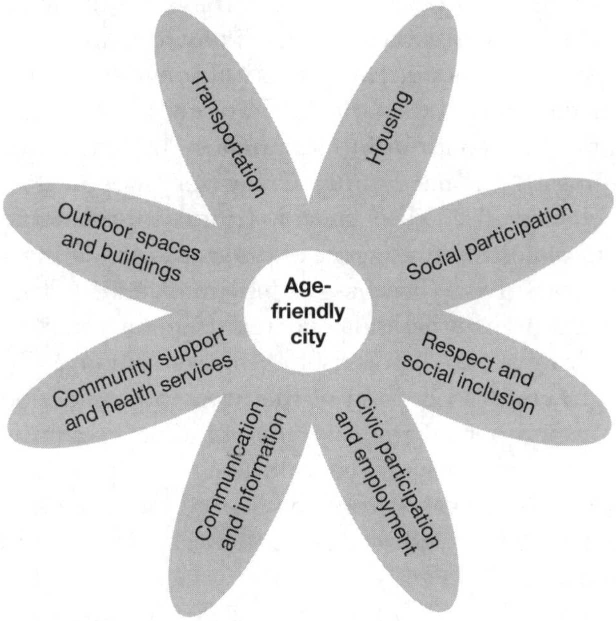

Source: Reprinted from World Health Organization (2007a).

residence in a supportive well-designed, well-serviced, and highly negotiable community is likely to enable vulnerable individuals to continue effective functioning in their community for longer than might otherwise be the case (Zur & Rudman, 2013). It will help to expand the long-term care continuum by delaying individuals' need to harness family and community resources.

Comparable interventions on the scale of the immediate residence are also increasingly viewed as options for delaying entry into the formal long-term care system. **Design interventions** and **new technologies** are enabling persons in need of long-term care to remain at home far longer than in the past. Such technologies include home modification (Kim, Ahn, Steinhoff, & Lee, 2014), smart homes (Chan, Campo, Esteve, & Fourniols, 2009), universal design (Steinfeld & Maisel, 2012), and surveillance technologies that enable caregivers to monitor older adults and persons with disabilities from a distance while enabling them to age in place in a familiar residence (Sixsmith et al., 2007; see Chapter 8).

Beyond environmental change, there has been growing emphasis on **lifestyle** and **self-care interventions** that are conducive to maintaining independence and that serve to reduce the need for long-term care support at the beginning of the long-term care continuum and limit the need for assistance as a person's capabilities decline (Clarke & Bennett, 2013; Jerant, von Friederichs-Fitzwater, & Moore, 2005; Kennedy et al., 2007). Close health monitoring with routine medical checkups and preventive screening, exercise programs, programs to reinforce good nutrition and hydration, and the development of local community self-help networks are important options for delaying the need for more costly forms of long-term care. Indeed, the recent development of consumer-driven collaborative models for aging in place, including the "village" model, represent an ever-widening array of alternatives that are likely to reduce the need for formal long-term care programs as people in need of long-term care take increasing responsibility for their future (Scharlach, Graham, & Lehning, 2012).

Moving along the continuum, stimulated by the Administration for Community Living's National Family Caregiver Support Program (NFCSP), which was established in 2000 to provide grants to states and territories, we have seen in many states the emergence of programs providing social and financial assistance for caregivers (Feinberg & Newman, 2004). These have included respite services, support groups, and psychoeducational interventions (Feinberg, 2014; Noelker & Browdie, 2012; Sorensen, Pinquart, Habil, & Duberstein, 2002). There is also a growing recognition of the need to provide long-term support for the increasing number of grandparents who are assuming full long-term responsibility for raising their grandchildren (Hayslip & Kaminski, 2005). A major source of respite for caregivers has been the proliferation of both social and medical care models of adult day service (Fields, Anderson, & Dabelko-Schoeny, 2014; see also, Chapter 7).

Underlying most of these innovations is a fundamental reorientation of thinking about long-term care. Increasingly, long-term care is guided by an emphasis on culture change, a movement that embraces a person-centered or person-directed approach in which (insofar as is possible) individuals are fully informed and engaged in decision making about their care. This philosophy involves acknowledging the personhood of each human being, knowing each care recipient in his or her biographical context, maximizing autonomy and choice, and nurturing relationships (Ekman et al., 2011; White, Newton-Curtis, & Lyons, 2008). At the home- and community-based services end of the continuum, implementation of this philosophy of care has encountered cultural and structural barriers, such as fragmentation of service delivery, restrictive regulation, and financing-related limitations, which provide an ongoing challenge (Hagenow, 2003; Ruggiano & Edvardsson, 2013).

Nowhere is the emphasis on humanizing and reframing care from a lived experience, humanistic perspective and the notion of person-centered care more important than at the institutional care end of the long-term care continuum, which is, for many, still the setting that provides the final terminus of life. We have begun to move beyond the tragedy of "double burial," where relocation to a nursing facility symbolized a kind of societal death preceding a person's corporeal demise. Efforts to delay nursing facility entry for as long as possible (for both social and financial reasons) are in some ways less pressing because the **culture change movement** is transforming the focus of institutional care from a custodial and palliative final phase of life to a less onerous phase of active life before death (Rahman & Schnelle, 2008). In addition to resident-centered care, this transformation involves the creation of a homelike atmosphere, the development of close relationships between residents and staff, empowerment of staff, collaborative decision making, and implementation of feedback strategies facilitating continuous quality improvement (Koren, 2010).

Development of the Eden Alternative by William Thomas during the 1990s provides an exemplar of this approach (Thomas, 1994). Thomas argued that the three plagues of loneliness, helplessness, and boredom account for the bulk of suffering among older adults. He advocated for the development of elder-centered communities that would replace the traditional nursing facility by creating a human habitat where life revolves around close and continuing contact with plants, animals, and children. His view was that such relationships provided young and old alike with a pathway to a life worth living (Exhibit 1.2). For Thomas, an elder-centered long-term care community should create opportunities to give as well as receive (providing an antidote to helplessness). Such a community should imbue daily life with variety and spontaneity by creating an environment in which unexpected and unpredictable interactions and happenings could take place (providing an antidote to boredom). Meaningless social activity was to be replaced by meaningful activities that would counteract the corrosion of the human spirit that typified most nursing homes. Finally, echoing Kane's (2001) sentiment, he envisaged a setting where medical treatment would be the servant of genuine human caring, rather than its master. Operationalizing these ideas entailed de-emphasizing top-down bureaucratic authority by placing maximum possible decision-making authority into the hands of residents or those closest to them. Thomas envisaged an environment in which the creation of community was a never-ending process nurtured by wise and engaged leadership in which human growth was never separated from human life.

Elements of Thomas's ideas have been operationalized in a number of facilities and in many countries (Brownie, 2011; Otsuka, Hamahata, Komatsu, Suishu, & Osuka, 2010) and have evolved into a contemporary greenhouse model of institutional long-term care that has completely transformed both the design and organization of the traditional nursing home (Jenkens, Sult, Lessell, Hammer, & Ortigara, 2011; Rabig, Thomas, Kane, Cutler, & McAlilly, 2006). Greenhouse

EXHIBIT 1.2 The Ten Principles of the Eden Alternative

1. Loneliness, helplessness, and boredom are the plagues of the human spirit
2. Close and continuing contact with children, animals, and plants builds a human habitat
3. Loving companionship is the antidote to loneliness
4. Giving and receiving care are the antidotes to helplessness
5. Variety and spontaneity are the antidotes to boredom
6. Meaning is essential to human life
7. Medical treatment is a partner in care, not its master
8. Wisdom grows with honoring and respecting elders
9. Growth is not separate from life
10. Wise leadership is the lifeblood of thriving

Source: Brownie (2011).

facilities consist of small self-contained houses for 10 or fewer residents. They employ an array of smart home technologies. A central focus is on the development of relationships that maximize the identification of and respect for resident choices. In contrast to the traditional nursing facility, the household operates on no fixed schedule. Residents may have meals, receive personal care, sleep, rest, and engage in activities whenever they choose. The vision is that residents who are so inclined will participate with staff in household activities such as planning and preparing meals, gardening, caring for the household pets, cleaning and doing laundry. Residents and caregiving staff are expected to engage in direct personal relationships and eat together, talk together, make decisions together, and play together. An additional feature of a Green House facility is its open relationship with the community in which it is located. Visitors, including individuals from the surrounding community, are encouraged to engage informally with residents and staff. The transformation is even manifest in a new language designed to completely erase traditional administrative culture and hierarchical senior/junior staff and staff/resident relationships. Exemplifying the new order, residents are "elders," the nursing assistant is now the "shahbaz" (plural "shahbazim"), the administrator is the "guide," and volunteers from the community beyond the facility are known as "sages." Even traditional activities are renamed. For example, a dining experience is referred to as a "convivium" (The Green House Project, 2014).

Emergent long-term care options take us further and further away from the time when long-term care alternatives were care at home or assignment to an almshouse. As the long-term care continuum continues to evolve with an ever-widening array of opportunities within a more comprehensive and differentiated long-term care system, it is important to remain mindful of significant challenges throughout the entire continuum. It is useful to conclude this opening chapter by noting some of these fundamental concerns.

CHALLENGES OF LONG-TERM CARE

Contemporary long-term care in the United States faces many challenges beyond the sheer numbers of people who may need assistance during the next few decades. Fundamental philosophical questions continue to focus ongoing debate. For more than 60 years since Mumford (1956) raised the issue in his seminal commentary on age-based residential segregation, there has been debate about the optimal living arrangements for older, frail, or disabled people. Should they be treated separately in segregated environments where their presumed needs can be most effectively addressed (Golant, 1985), or should they remain a part of the community and fully integrated within the stream of community life as is consistent with the 1999 *Olmstead v. L. C.* decision of the Supreme Court and the provisions of the 1990 Americans with Disabilities Act? What are the preferences of persons receiving care? Might they prefer to be among their peers? To what extent should we allow burgeoning long-term care technologies that facilitate monitoring and support from a distance to replace the intimacy of direct human contact? How will we go about funding long-term care programs and services in the face of rapidly increasing demand when the current long-term system is challenged to handle even the current level of need?

As we write this chapter, there are more than 20,000 people in Kentucky (where we both worked together for over a decade) who are eligible for services but are not receiving them because these services are not available. To what extent is the growing corporatization of long-term care compatible with the current emphasis on culture change and the humanization of care? With the dominant medical model of care under attack, how long will it remain viable? Does the pathway to the future mandate new models of care? In view of changing perceptions of the nature of care and increasing recognition of the potential for meaning in late life, can current models of care be maintained? Where will the long-term care workforce come from? Will it be able to cope with the projected increase in demand? How will the people providing long-term care be trained and by whom? Where will we find the resources to appropriately reimburse this labor force?

At the most fundamental level, these complex issues are all encapsulated within the question of both individual and societal moral responsibility toward those in our midst who are most vulnerable. On an individual level, at some time in our life, each of us is likely to be challenged to provide or secure support for a relative or friend in need of care. On a societal level, the question becomes one of communal moral responsibility and the values to which we choose to adhere. As Hubert Humphrey eloquently phrased this in 1977 "the moral test of government is how that government treats those who are in the dawn of life, the children; those who are in the twilight of life, the elderly; and those who are in the shadows of life—the sick, the needy and the handicapped." The challenge is to come up with the very best system of long-term care, a system that provides appropriate support to those in need along the entire continuum of life. This is a tall order. One way to begin is to develop a deeper understanding of the complexities of contemporary long-term care in all its dimensions. This book is designed as a contribution to this effort. We begin, in Chapter 2, by learning from history and by considering how things came to be as they are today.

DISCUSSION QUESTIONS

1. How has the provision of long-term care changed over the past three decades, and how would you explain these changes?
2. Identify and discuss at least three major long-term care issues illustrated by the chapter-framing cases of Grandma Brewster, Anders Swenson, and Mark A. Lincoln.
3. Who needs long-term care and how is this population changing?
4. How is long-term care a continuum? What types of long-term care arrangements are part of the continuum? Is thinking in terms of a continuum the best way to frame discussions of long-term care? What are some alternatives?
5. At the outset of reading this book, and given your present level of understanding, explain your preferences should you need long-term care.

REFERENCES

Adelman, R. D., Tmanova, L. L., Delgado, D., Dion, S., & Lachs, M. S. (2014). Caregiver burden: A clinical review. *Journal of the American Medical Association*, *311*(10), 1052–1059.

Antonucci, T., & Akiyama, H. (1987). Social networks in adult life and a preliminary examination of the convoy model. *Journal of Gerontology*, *42*, 519–527.

Antonucci, T., Berditt, K., & Akiyama, H. (2009). Convoys of social relations: An interdisciplinary approach. In V. Bengtson, M. Silverstein, & P. Norella (Eds.), *Handbook of theories of aging* (pp. 247–260). New York, NY: Springer Publishing Company.

Bassett, C. (2002). Nurses' perceptions of care and caring. *International Journal of Nursing Practice*, *8*(1), 8–15.

Brownie, S. (2011). Culture change in aged care: The Eden Alternative. *Australian Journal of Advanced Nursing*, *29*(1), 63–68.

Carter, R. & Golant, S. K. (1994). *Helping yourself help others: A book for caregivers*. New York, NY: Three Rivers Press.

Centers for Disease Control and Prevention. (2015). Retrieved from www.cdc.gov/chronicdisease/overview

Chan, M., Campo, E., Esteve, D., & Fourniols, J. (2009). Smart homes: Current features and future perspectives. *Maturitas*, *64*, 90–97.

Clarke, L. H., & Bennett, E. V. (2013). Constructing the moral body: Self-care among older adults with multiple chronic conditions. *Health*, *17*(3), 211–228.

Dewar, B., & Nolan, M. (2013). Caring about caring: Developing a model to implement compassionate relationship centred care in an older people care setting. *International Journal of Nursing Studies*, *50*, 1247–1258.

Dillenburger, K., & McKerr, L. (2010). How long are we able to go on? Issues faced by older family caregivers of adults with disabilities. *British Journal of Learning Disabilities*, *39*, 29–38.

Douglas, K. (2010). When caring stops, staffing doesn't really matter. *Nursing Economics*, *28*(6), 415–419.

Ekman, I., Swedberg, K., Taft, C., Lindseth, A., Norberg, A., Brink, E., … Sunnerhagen, K. S. (2011). Person-centered care—Ready for prime time. *European Journal of Cardiovascular Nursing*, *10*, 248–251.

Evashwick, C. J. (ed.). (2005). *The continuum of long-term care* (3rd ed., pp. 3–13). Clifton Park, NJ: Delmar Learning.

Family Caregiver Alliance, National Center for Caregiving. (2012). Selected Caregiver Statistics. Retrieved from https://www.caregiver.org/selected-caregiver-statistics

Feinberg, L. F. (2014). Recognizing and supporting family caregivers: The time has come. *Public Policy and Aging Report*, *24*, 65–69.

Feinberg, L. F., & Newman, S. L. (2004). A study of 10 states since passage of the National Family Caregiver Support Program: Policies, perceptions and program development. *The Gerontologist*, *44*(6), 760–769.

Fields, N. L., Anderson, K. A., & Dabelko-Schoeny, H. (2014). The effectiveness of adult day services for older adults: A review of the literature from 2000 to 2011. *Journal of Applied Gerontology*, *33*(2), 130–163.

Fried, V. M., Bernstein, A. B., & Bush, M. A. (2012, July). *Multiple chronic conditions among adults aged 45 and over: Trends over the past ten years* (NCHS Data Brief No. 100). Hyattsville, MD: National Center for Health Statistics.

Golant, S. M. (1985). In defense of age-segregated housing. *Aging*, *348*, 22–26.

Golant, S. M. (1992). *Housing America's elderly: Many possibilities, few choices*. Thousand Oaks, CA: Sage.

Golant, S. M., & Hyde, J. (2008). *The assisted living residence*. Baltimore, MD: Johns Hopkins University Press.

Hagenow, N. R. (2003). Why not person-centered care? The challenges of implementation. *Nursing Administration Quarterly, 27*(3), 203–207.

Hayslip, B., & Kaminski, P. L. (2005). Grandparents raising their grandchildren: A review of the literature and suggestions for practice. *The Gerontologist, 45*(2), 262–269.

Hennessey, C. H., & Johns, R. (1996). American Indian family caregivers' perceptions of burden and needed support services. *Journal of Applied Gerontology, 15*(3), 275–293.

Jenkens, R., Sult, T., Lessell, N., Hammer, D., & Ortigara, A. (2011). Financial implications of THE GREEN HOUSE® model. *Seniors Housing & Care Journal, 19*(1), 3–22.

Jerant, A. F., von Friederichs-Fitzwater, M. M., & Moore, M. (2005). Patients' perceived barriers to active self-management of chronic conditions. *Patient Education and Counseling, 57*, 300–307.

Kane, R. A. (2001). Long-term care and a good quality of life: Bringing them closer together. *The Gerontologist, 41*(3), 293–304.

Kane, R. A., & Kane, R. L. (1987). *Long-term care: Principles, programs and policies*. New York, NY: Springer Publishing Company.

Katz, S., Ford, A., Moskowitz, R., Jackson, B., & Jaffe, M. (1963). Studies of illness in the aged. *Journal of the American Medical Association, 185*, 914–919.

Kennedy, A., Reeves, D., Bower, P., Lee, V., Middleton, E., Richardson, G., ... Rogers, A. (2007). The effectiveness and cost effectiveness of a national lay-led self-care support programme for patients with long-term conditions: A pragmatic randomized controlled trial. *Journal of Epidemiology and Community Health, 61*(3), 254–261.

Kim, H., Ahn, Y. H., Steinhoff, A., & Lee, K. H. (2014). Home modification by older adults and their informal caregivers. *Archives of Gerontology and Geriatrics, 59*, 648–656.

Kittay, E. F., Jennings, B., & Wasunna, A. A. (2005). Dependency, difference and the global ethic of long-term care. *Journal of Political Philosophy, 13*(4), 443–469.

Koren, M. J. (2010). Person-centered care for nursing home residents: The culture-change movement. *Health Affairs, 29*(2), 312–317.

Laslett, P. (1989). *A fresh map of life: The emergence of the third age*. Cambridge, MA: Harvard University Press.

Lawton, M. P., & Brody, E. M. (1969). Assessment of older people: Self-maintaining and instrumental activities of daily living. *The Gerontologist, 9*, 179–186.

Manton, K. G., Gu, X., & Lamb, V. L. (2006). Change in chronic disability from 1982 to 2004/2005 as measured by long-term changes in function and health in the U.S. population. *Proceedings of the National Academy of Sciences, 103*(48), 18374–18379.

Mendelson, M. A. (1974). *Tender loving greed*. New York, NY: Alfred A. Knopf.

Mosby's medical dictionary. (2009). (8th ed.). St. Louis, MO: Mosby Elsevier.

Mumford, L. (1956). For older people—Not segregation but integration. *Architectural Record, 119*, 191–194.

Noelker, L., & Browdie, R. (2012). Caring for the caregivers: Developing models that work. *Generations, 36*(1), 103–106.

Olmstead v. L. C., 527 U.S. 581 (1999).

Otsuka, S., Hamahata, A., Komatsu, M., Suishu, C., & Osuka, K. (2010). Prospects for introducing the Eden Alternative to Japan. *Journal of Gerontological Nursing, 36*(3), 47–55.

Paez, K. A., Zhao, L., & Hwang, W. (2009). Rising out of pocket spending for chronic conditions: A ten-year trend. *Health Affairs, 28*(1), 15–25.

Parr, H. (2003). Medical geography: Care and caring. *Progress in Human Geography, 27*(2), 212–221.

Rabig, J., Thomas, W., Kane, R. A., Cutler, L. J., & McAlilly, S. (2006). Radical redesign of nursing homes: Applying the greenhouse concept in Tupelo, Mississippi. *The Gerontologist, 46*(4), 533–539.

Rahman, A. N., & Schnelle, J. F. (2008). The nursing home culture-change movement: Recent past, present, and future directions for research. *The Gerontologist, 48*(2), 142–148.

Raschick, M., & Ingersoll-Dayton, B. (2004). The costs and rewards of caregiving among aging spouses and adult children. *Family Relations, 53*(3), 317–325.

Robison, J., Shugrue, N., Porter, M., Fortinsky, R. H., & Curry L. A. (2012). Transition from home care to nursing home: Unmet needs in a home-and community-based program for older adults. *Journal of Aging and Social Policy*, *24*(3), 251–270.

Rowles, G. D. (1993). Evolving images of place in aging and "aging in place." *Generations*, *17*(2), 65–70.

Ruggiano, N., & Edvardsson, D. (2013). Person-centeredness in home- and community-based long-term care: Current challenges and new directions. *Social Work in Health Care*, *52*, 846–861.

Ryan, A. A., & Scullion, H. F. (2000). Nursing home placement: An exploration of the experiences of family carers. *Journal of Advanced Nursing*, *32*(5), 1187–1195.

Savundranayagam, M. Y. (2014). Receiving while giving: The differential roles of receiving help and satisfaction with help on caregiver rewards among spouses and adult children. *International Journal of Geriatric Psychiatry*, *29*, 41–48.

Scharlach, A., Graham, C., & Lehning, A. (2012). The "village" model: A consumer-driven approach for aging in place. *The Gerontologist*, *52*(3), 418–427.

Silverstein, M., Conroy, S. J., Wang, H., Giarusso, R., & Bengtson, V. L. (2002). Reciprocity in parent-child relations over the adult life course. *Journal of Gerontology: Social Sciences*, *57B*(1), S3–S13.

Sixsmith, A., Hine, N., Neild, I., Clarke, N., Brown, S., & Garner, P. (2007). Monitoring the wellbeing of older people. *Topics in Geriatric Rehabilitation*, *23*(1), 9–23.

Sorensen, S., Pinquart, M., Habil, D., & Duberstein, P. (2002). How effective are interventions with caregivers? An updated meta-analysis. *The Gerontologist*, *42*(3), 356–372.

Steinfeld, E., & Maisel, J. (2012). *Universal design: Designing inclusive environments*. Hoboken, NJ: John Wiley & Sons.

The Green House Project. (2014). Retrieved from http://www.thegreenhouseproject.org

Thomas, W. (1994). *The Eden Alternative: Nature, hope and nursing homes*. Sherburne, NY: Eden Alternative Foundation.

Tilson, D. (ed.). (1990). *Aging in place: Supporting the frail elderly in residential environments*. Glenview, IL: Scott, Foresman and Company.

Tronto, J. C. (1993). *Moral boundaries: A political argument for an ethic of care*. New York, NY: Psychology Press.

United States Senate, Subcommittee on Long-term Care. (1974). *Nursing home care in the United States: A failure in public policy*. Washington, DC: U.S. Government Printing Office.

Weaver, R. (2013). "Don't you have to care about people?" The challenges of caring. *Medical Education*, *47*, 434–435.

Weiss, R. S., & Bass, S. A. (2002). *Challenges of the third age: Meaning and purpose in later life*. New York, NY: Oxford University Press.

White, D. L., Newton-Curtis, L., & Lyons, K. S. (2008). Development and initial testing of a measure of person-directed care. *The Gerontologist*, *48*(1), Special Issue, 114–123.

Wilson, K. B. (2007). Historical evolution of assisted living in the United States, 1979 to the present. *The Gerontologist*, *47*(Special Issue), 8–22.

World Health Organization. (2001). *International classification of functioning, disability and health*. Geneva, Switzerland: World Health Organization.

World Health Organization. (2007a). *Global age-friendly cities: A guide*. Geneva, Switzerland: WHO Press.

World Health Organization. (2007b). *Checklist of essential features of age-friendly cities*. Geneva, Switzerland: WHO Press.

Wu, S.-Y., & Green, A. (2000, October). *Projection of chronic illness prevalence and cost inflation*. Santa Monica, CA: RAND Health.

Yang, Q., Rasmussen, S. A., & Friedman, J. M. (2002). Mortality associated with Down's syndrome in the USA from 1983 to1997: A population-based study. *The Lancet*, *359*(311), 1019–1025.

Zur, B., & Rudman, D. L. (2013). WHO age-friendly cities: Enacting societal transformation through enabling occupation. *Journal of Occupational Science*, *20*(4), 370–381.

2

History of Long-Term Care

CAROLE HABER

CHAPTER OVERVIEW

This chapter focuses on the development of long-term care in the American colonies and the United States from the 17th through the 20th centuries. It demonstrates the effects economic, demographic, political, and cultural changes have had on both the attitudes and practices shaping long-term care, as well as the lasting impact of historical ideas and institutions.

LEARNING OBJECTIVES

After reading this chapter, you should understand:

- The English philosophy of care that shaped early colonial policy
- Why almshouses were established and their impact on support of the poor and aged
- The role and impact religious beliefs of the 19th century had on institutional care
- The foundation of old-age homes in 19th-century America
- Beliefs about older adults in the first half of the 20th century
- The effect of Social Security on institutional care
- How legislative and judicial rulings in the second half of the 20th century affected long-term care

KEY TERMS

Almshouse
Americans with Disabilities Act (ADA)
English Poor Law
Federal Nursing Home Reform Act (OBRA '87)
Hill–Burton Act
Homer folks
Kerr–Mills Act
"Less eligibility"
Medicaid
Medicare
Old-age homes
Olmstead decision
Omnibus Budget Reconciliation Act of 1987 (OBRA '87)
Outdoor relief
Overseers of the poor
Poorhouse
Social security

EXHIBIT 2.1 Long-Term Care Timeline

1601	English poor law
1612	First hospital erected in Jamestown
1664	First almshouse built in Boston
18th century	Development of almshouses throughout the colonial era and early republic
Late 18th and	Cities attempt to eliminate outdoor relief early 19th centuries
Early 19th	The Second Great Awakening changes attitudes about
century	institutional reform
1810–1840	Cities and states build mental hospitals, orphanages, prisons
1817	First old-age home established in Philadelphia
1900–1935	Progressive attitudes reevaluate the almshouse
1935	Social Security Act established
1950	Key Social Security Amendments allow payments to public institutions
1960	Kerr–Mills Act—Medical assistance to the aged
1963	Fitchville Fire illustrates need for federal support
1965	Passage of Medicare and Medicaid
1987	Federal Nursing Home Reform Act (OBRA '87)
1999	*Olmstead* Decision

INTRODUCTION

In recent years, issues surrounding long-term care have become both a national concern and, for many, a difficult family and personal issue. Yet such matters—although certainly magnified by the number and proportion of elderly individuals in the population—are neither new nor the creation of a very recent past. In the United States, since its colonial beginnings, government authorities, welfare advocates, medical experts, family members, and the old and infirm themselves have all struggled to define and create suitable long-term care solutions. Not surprisingly, over the course of 400 years, although the problems of meeting the needs of these groups have remained, the possible options available for addressing their demands have significantly evolved. Individuals who required extensive care in the colonial era faced a very different landscape from that of their modern counterparts. Some ended their days in newly established almshouses, whereas others depended on the benevolence of their communities or assured their continued care through legal agreements with family members. No nursing home existed to provide extended care; no national government program offered financial assistance, allocated medical aid, or set institutional regulations. By the mid-20th century, the changing institutional, medical, and political conditions that defined the long-term care of the old and infirm resulted in a range of options that spoke to modern realities and attitudes. At the same time, these alternatives harkened back to the beliefs of the past and the long shadow cast by the first long-term care institutions.

COLONIAL AND EARLY 19TH-CENTURY PRACTICES

Among the first White settlers in British North America, few who dared to cross the ocean were of great age or incapacity. In the first few decades of passage, only the young seemed foolish or desperate enough to undertake the voyage. At times, nearly half of those who embarked on the journey were unable to withstand the storms and privations of the trip; the Atlantic Ocean became their final resting place. As was well known in England, the New World was hardly a hospitable place for the old or disabled. In the first century of settlement, therefore, colonial governments provided little institutional care. In Jamestown, the first hospital, built in 1612 to accommodate 80 "sicke and lame patients," burned down in 1622. Another century would pass until the establishment of a standalone hospital (Duffy, 1976).

In time, of course, the earliest surviving settlers did grow old and others were incapacitated by accident, disease, or childbirth. In fact, within a century of settlement, the British colonies boasted of some of its inhabitants' advanced age. In the 1700s, even with the high fertility rates, 5% of the population was above 60 (Wells, 1975). Among a society in which the median age of the population was around 16, such individuals often attracted the notice of commentators. Their gray hair and stooped backs were signs not only of their remarkable longevity, but also of the community's need to offer support when necessary (Haber, 1983).

For these individuals, as well as those who were incapacitated or mentally challenged, both tradition and law dictated that they be cared for in their own homes or in the residences of others. Following the principles established by the **English Poor Law** in 1601, colonial governments decreed that families were required to provide for the needs of their relatives; kin were to take in the orphaned or infirm; and the old were to be sheltered alongside their offspring. If individuals required additional support, they often received "**outdoor relief**" in the form of a cord of wood, food, or clothing.

Although relatives generally opened their doors to the needy, not everyone found coresidence to be ideal. The colonial law that specified that kin had the financial and moral responsibility to care for their relatives did not dictate how that obligation was to be met. If they chose to place the individual with others, government officials generally approved such an arrangement. In 1715, for example, Mary Thomas of Boston explained to the selectmen that she had contracted care for her mother in Dorchester. Although she did not specify why she had chosen this course, the town leaders seemed satisfied that her aging mother would not be deserted or neglected (Record Commissioners of the City of Boston, 1884).

Even in colonial society, some failed to fulfill their responsibilities entirely. In response, both ministers and magistrates railed against families who had turned their backs on their kin. Samuel Willard, for example, chastised the young who "desert their helpless parents, as thinking it now time to look to themselves, and let them shift as they can" (Willard, 1726, p. 608). Other ministers went directly to the families to remind them of their duties. In 1713, Cotton Mather, the esteemed Puritan minister, noted, "there is an aged woman in my neighborhood, poor, lame, and sick, and in miserable circumstances. I must not only releeve [*sic*] her myself but also summon together her several relatives, that they agree to have her well-provided for" (Mather, 1912, p. 208). Local officials were also quick to take action, ready to penalize those who failed to meet their obligations. In the late 17th century, for example, the selectmen of Boston notified James Barber that if he did not provide care for his father, "you may expect wee [*sic*] *shall; prosecute* the law upon you" (Record Commissioners of the City of Boston, 1692, p. 62).

The colonial tradition of providing long-term care for the needy did not rest on sermon and statute alone. Rather, the agrarian nature of society established the economic basis for long-term care. Following the practices of England, upon settlement in the New World, land was distributed to male head of households. Retaining title to the property until their deaths, aging individuals were able to rely on the valuable property to guarantee the continued residence and support of at least one family member. Sons knew that if they deserted the household, they would also be leaving behind their inheritance. Even later generations of colonists, who began to deed some of the property to their heirs before their demise, made sure they retained the status of household head with at least one child in the household (Greven, 1970).

In the early 18th century, Joseph Abbot of Andover, Massachusetts, exemplified this pattern. One of six sons, he was selected to inherit the family estate upon his father's death. As a result, Joseph remained a bachelor in his family home, responsible for the care of his aging parent. In 1731, at age 73, his father died. A year later, Joseph, now 45, married and began the family that would, in time, presumably support him in his old age (Greven, 1970).

For elderly widows, colonial landholding practices also tended to ensure care, although not necessarily the power that traditionally rested with the male head of household. According to legal statute, widows were entitled to one third of the estate. In addition, wills generally listed the wife's portion of the estate. The documents often explicitly stated the room she would inhabit as well as the livestock and property that could be used for her needs. The widow would receive "the bedstead we lie on, the bedding thereto belonging" or "two cows, by name Reddy and Cherry, and one yearling heifer" (Demos, 1978, p. 238). Well into the late 18th century, these patterns persisted. In 1789, Adam Deemus of Pennsylvania decreed in his will that after his death, his wife would have "the privilege to live in the house we now live in until another is built and a room prepared for herself if she chuses [*sic*], the bed and beding [*sic*] she now lays on, saddled bridle with the horse called Tom; like ten milch cows, three sheep" (Chelfant, 1955, p. 35).

However, even in colonial America and the early republic, not all infirm and aged individuals could find such support. In small towns and communities, well-established residents without a kinship network became the responsibility of the selectmen. Often, government officials would find a suitable family to shelter them, providing funds for the boarders' support. In other cases, they would arrange for a family to reside in the home of the debilitated individual. Although such practices did not guarantee the quality of care, they assured that the person would not be abandoned.

Others faced a more uncertain fate. Those without any ties to the community would be "warned out" and unceremoniously escorted to the town's limits. In 1707, for example, Nicholas Warner was repeatedly ordered to leave the city of Boston. Despite the fact that he was over 80 and infirm, he merited little sympathy or support from the town's leaders (Record Commissioners of the City of Boston, 1884, p. 57). Colonies even passed laws that barred individuals such as Warner from ever entering their borders. Just before the revolution, Pennsylvania ratified an Act requiring a bond from anyone who chose to bring an elderly person into the community. If the individual then became a burden on the town, the money could be used to transport the individual back to the community of origin (Assembly of the Province of Pennsylvania, 1775, p. 160). Over the course of 100 years, town after town and colony followed by colony enacted laws to dissuade any person who might require relief or long-term care from entering the community.

In making such laws and allocating relief only to their local residents, communities and colonies gave little special attention to the age or infirmity of the individual. As was evident in Boston's "warning out" of Nicholas Warner, the ties to the city, rather than his advanced years, physical condition, or mental state, dictated his treatment. In providing for long-term care, custom and statute grouped together the orphaned, the insane, the incapacitated, as well as the old. Categorized as the "worthy poor," they were judged not to be responsible for their impoverished state.

As such, and if they had long-standing ties to the community, they were seen as proper recipients of the community's assistance (Rothman, 1971).

With the growing cities of the colonies and early republic, localized solutions to the needs of these groups increasingly became insufficient. The numerous colonial wars of the 18th century brought large numbers of impoverished refugees into the cities; the high mortality rate of colonial society meant that being an orphan or a widow was a common state of affairs. Without families or established communities, individuals had needs that could not be met by reliance on kinship support.

In response, and following practices established in England, colonial cities began to create the earliest institutional solution to long-term care—the municipal **almshouse**. First founded in Boston in 1664, the almshouse became a well-known and easily recognized institution in scores of cities throughout the 18th century. Within its walls could be found the most problematic of the needy: the orphan without a family, the insane individual whose care had become too difficult for his or her kin, the widow who had outlived her relatives, and the diseased whose sickness was incapacitating.

Initially, when almshouses were established, they were both small and rather unregulated institutions. Generally, they served a minute population. The **Overseers of the Poor** continued to provide outdoor relief to most needy individuals, limiting institutional care to only the most debilitated. In 1700, for example, New York City opened its first, very small almshouse, but continued the practice of outdoor relief. Between 1724 and 1729, the Mayor's Court granted relief to 51 cases. For 18 persons they allocated outdoor relief, providing assistance to individuals within their own homes. They placed 19 individuals in the residences of others. Many of the individuals in the first two categories faced temporary illness or could survive with minimum support. The 14 they placed in the institution, however, had far greater demands. In the roster of the almshouse, they were described as extremely handicapped, blind, insane, or, in the words of the court documents, "ancient" (Rothman, 1971).

Other major cities soon followed Boston's and New York's example. Charleston founded its poorhouse in 1712; Philadelphia's first public institution opened its doors in 1732. As in the case of the earliest institutions, these homes sheltered small numbers of residents. The municipal overseers assumed that only a few—the most debilitated individuals—would require long-term institutional care.

In the growing colonial cities of the 18th century, however, as migrants and immigrants flooded into urban areas, the small almshouses quickly became outdated. Their lack of discrete space meant that rooms became crowded with all types of indigent individuals. The young mixed with the old; the insane shared space with the diseased. As a result, throughout the colonies and then into the early republic, officials in the largest urban areas began to replace the small and unregulated buildings with far more imposing institutions.

In time, the existence of these new almshouses not only provided for greater numbers, but also had a direct impact on the colonial approach to long-term care. Convinced that many individuals had come to rely needlessly on charity, officials in numerous cities attempted to eliminate all outdoor relief. They declared that anyone who needed assistance had to reside in the publicly supported buildings (Rothman, 1971). In 1769, for example, Barnet and Sarah Campbell of Great Barrington, Massachusetts, petitioned the Overseers of the Poor for outdoor relief. Old and ailing, they assumed that their advanced age and roots in the community would qualify them as worthy of such assistance. The city's authorities, however, responded that if they wanted care, they would have to enter the **poorhouse** (Quadagno, 1986).

By the early 19th century, welfare authorities across the new nation adopted this policy. Josiah Quincy of Massachusetts, a leading expert on charity allocation, demanded an end to all outdoor relief. In his influential *Report on Poor Relief,* he wrote, "the diminution of the evil is best, and most surely to be effected by making Alms Houses, Houses of Industry, not abodes of idleness, and denying for the most part all supply from public provision, except on condition of admission into the public institution" (Quincy, 1821, n.p.). Similarly, John Yates of New York asserted that even the worthy and disabled should be placed in institutions if they wished public support (Trent, 1994). Such statements did not mean that either men felt "the ancient" unworthy of assistance. Quincy, for example, stated, "of all classes of the poor that of virtuous old age has the most unexceptionable claims upon society" (Quincy, 1821, n.p.). Nonetheless, he asserted that they, too, should only receive care if they were willing to leave their homes for long-term care in the almshouse.

In requiring all who petitioned for assistance to enter the poorhouse and despite their sympathy for the needy old, welfare advocates, such as Quincy, did not then believe that the institution should be designed as a hospitable environment. Subscribing to the principle of **"less eligibility,"** they declared that the almshouse's environment could not meet or exceed conditions found beyond the institution's walls. If it did, they feared, unworthy individuals would wish to seek shelter rather than providing for themselves. As a result, the modern concern for the quality of the resident's life was turned on its head: conditions within the institutions were purposefully intended to be inhospitable. The squalid environment was created to dissuade individuals from applying for entrance or remaining within the institution (Foucault, 1972; Rothman, 1971). Given this philosophy, conditions were often abhorrent: the insane were chained; the orphan went unschooled. Infected prostitutes interacted with alcoholic men while the old languished on their beds. In southern asylums, the races were segregated, or Black inmates were placed in distinct, and far less funded, institutions (Case Study 2.1). Well into the 19th and even the early 20th century, institutions that sheltered African Americans received one third of the budget of White institutions and were generally devoid of plumbing, electricity, or mattresses. In the north, such institutions became filled with impoverished immigrants (Haber & Gratton, 1986).

In demanding that paupers relocate into the repugnant asylum if they wished assistance, welfare advocates were cognizant that even such substandard relief was more expensive than outdoor relief in the form of an occasional cord of wood or parcel of food. To limit expenses, they demanded that long-term inmates contribute to their own sustenance. All ambulatory individuals in the

Case Study 2.1: Long-Term Care in a Southern City: The Segregated Almshouses of Charleston, South Carolina

In 1712, Charleston opened the American colonies' second public almshouse. Its founding reflected the booming nature of the 18th-century city as a center for trade, a bustling port, and a magnet for immigrants and migrants. By the early 19th century, the Charleston almshouse had become a shelter to a growing number of impoverished and ailing individuals, nearly one in five of whom was of advanced age.

Although the southern poorhouse bore many similarities to northern asylums, it exhibited one striking regional difference. In 1811, city leaders dictated that Blacks could enter the institution only if they were insane, largely because all "lunatics" were to be housed in separate quarters in the basement. The authorities made it quite clear that they would not tolerate large numbers of African Americans sheltered alongside needy Whites. In 1837, Major Henry L. Pinckney declared that that the almshouse was "specifically intended for destitute whites." Moreover, despite the fact that free Blacks comprised the neediest of the city's citizens, the Commissioners for the Poor rarely extended outdoor aid to individuals of color.

By 1856, however, the city leaders began to revise the policy of excluding Blacks from the welfare system. The "aged and infirm free colored poor of the City and State," asserted the Commissioners of the Poor, "are fit and rightful objects of public relief." Rather than agree to house Blacks and Whites together, however, Charleston city officials established a new almshouse—eventually called the Charleston Home—for needy Whites and turned the old, dilapidated institution over to impoverished freed Black men and women.

Before the Civil War only a few destitute Blacks seemed to be housed in this institution; after the conflict, the notion of having two very different asylums for the long-term care of the poor became firmly established. As large numbers of impoverished, recently freed slaves sought assistance, the city opened a new long-term care institution, the Ashley River Asylum, solely for Black inmates. By 1899, it housed 91 paupers, far more than the 73 in the White institution.

But it was not only the numbers that differentiated the two shelters. The amount of resources and the resulting quality of care contrasted sharply between the institutions. Throughout the late 19th and early 20th centuries, the city routinely allocated two to three times the amount for the White asylum than for the Black. In 1928, for example, the city distributed $263 for each White inmate and only $115 for the Black resident. Thus, although the White home boasted a library, flowers, an icebox, and ample food and heat, the Black asylum had no water,

(*continued*)

Case Study 2.1: Long-Term Care in a Southern City: The Segregated Almshouses of Charleston, South Carolina (*continued*)

mattresses, sewage system, or lights. Perhaps not surprising, mortality rates also differed sharply between the two homes. At the Black Ashley River Asylum, annual death rates ranged around 40%, whereas at the Charleston Home, yearly mortality rates rarely rose to 10%.

With the implementation of Social Security, the century-long system of segregated institutions came to an end. As the federal legislation mandated that residents of the city's public asylums could not receive aid, in 1949, both the Charleston Home and Ashley River Asylum finally closed their doors. Instead, their residents now turned to support from National Old Age Assistance and private nursing homes (Charleston City Year Book for 1887, 1914, 1925, 1938, 1949; City of Charleston, 1967; Haber & Gratton, 1986).

Case Study Discussion Question:

1. To what extent do you feel it is appropriate to make special accommodation in long-term care facilities through separation on the basis of age, sex, marital status, mental status, religion, or culture?

almshouse were assigned tasks such as growing food and producing goods for sale. Although they did not require work from the bedridden, they demanded that once their health improved, these recovering individuals would serve as nurses for those in worse health than they were. In the early 19th century, for example, the Philadelphia almshouse divided the women's wards into four categories (Rosenberg, 1987):

Aged and helpless women in bad health
Aged and helpless women who could sew and knit
Aged and helpless women who are good sewers
Spinners

Despite this classification, the almshouse overseers knew very well that only a minority of inmates was able to work. Those who entered the poorhouse were not only indigent, but also extremely infirm and incapacitated. In response, many of the almshouses opened hospital wings attached to the asylum. Here, the chronically ill often passed their final days or were moved back and forth from the medical annex to the main residence depending on the availability of beds. Increasingly, the medical function of the institution came to dominate its character. By 1826, in the Philadelphia almshouse, for example, 13 of the 18 women's wards were defined as medical care wards; only three of the 19 male wards had inmates who were actually able to work. By 1849, the Philadelphia almshouse listed 756 male paupers of whom 449 were patients and 67 served as nurses (Rosenberg, 1987). Overshadowed by disease and dependence, the entire facility increasingly turned into a medical, long-term care institution.

Yet such medical attention did not mean that the almshouse provided even the old and disabled with consideration or care. In 1797, for example, the Pennsylvania Hospital received one inmate of the almshouse who, as the Overseers of the Poor noted, had received a broken jaw "occasioned by a stroke from Dr. C." Despite the degree of their infirmities, residents were seen as inmates—they were to respond properly to their betters or suffer the consequences. They could not question—or even talk to—the physicians who attended to the institution without first being addressed by the doctors and given permission to speak. They were, after all, spending their final days dependent on the city's benevolence (Rosenberg, 1987).

Basic to the philosophy behind such long-term care was the expectation that the institutionalized individuals had little hope of being cured. Long-term care in the almshouse provided food and shelter rather than hope or reform. Those who resided in its wards were categorized as society's most dissolute, destined to spend their final days relying on public support. The Overseers of the Poor did not believe that it was wise or necessary to devote considerable resources to their care.

RELIGIOUS REFORM AND LONG-TERM CARE

In the 19th century, religious and social beliefs led to a questioning of these assumptions. Followers of the Second Great Awakening challenged the biblical notion that "the poor will always be with us." Within the walls of the almshouse, they identified groups whom they believed could be transformed or saved. They saw little reason to mix, indiscriminately, the orphan who might have a redeemable future with the old or debilitated. They declared that even the insane or mentally challenged might be saved and the criminal reformed, whereas the orphan or able-bodied could be taught to live a productive existence (Grob, 1973).

Thus, over the course of the 19th century, welfare advocates established specialized institutions for those who had once spent their days among the wards of the almshouse. Almost simultaneously they founded orphan asylums, mental hospitals, chronic care hospital, prisons, and homes for the blind and deaf. In each of these institutions, their organizers believed that residents would find a beneficial environment that would lead to almost miraculous cures or reformation. Once removed from the chaos of the modern world, the inmate was to become a far more perfect individual who could then be returned to the outside community (Grob, 1973).

THE NEW ASYLUMS AND THE IMPACT ON THE OLD

In the mid-19th century, for example, reformers established private mental asylums that touted cure rates of nearly 100%. Although such figures greatly exaggerated the therapeutic nature of such care by counting each returning patient as a new case, their enthusiastic superintendents argued that they were able to eliminate insanity in America. Focusing on the newly afflicted, they promised that if they were given a patient soon after the onset of the disease, they could restore sanity by teaching order and discipline. These were not to be places where the chronic languished for years, but rather institutions of hope and restoration (Rosenkrantz & Vinovskis, 1978).

In stressing the appropriateness of such institutions for those only recently suffering the onset of insanity, the superintendents made it clear that they had little room for the old or chronically ill. Despite original intentions, by the late 19th century, such institutions became filled with the chronically ill and elderly, thereby turning the asylums into long-term care institutions. Initially, the men in charge, as well as theorists on insanity, argued forcibly against admitting elderly people. In the mid-19th century, for example, the Superintendent of the Massachusetts State Hospital strongly cautioned against any type of long-term care for the insane of advanced age. "As there is no reasonable hope for cure," wrote Dr. George Choate in 1860, "I have generally advised friends to retain them at home" (Trustees of the State Lunatic Hospital at Taunton, 1860, p. 34).

The renowned British psychiatrist T.S. Clouston supported this admonition. The old, he informed his students, should not be admitted to a mental asylum as, he wrote, the "difficulty of managing such cases satisfactorily … is extreme. They are very restive, always meddling with something or somebody, very obstinate, entirely forgetful and purposeless." Such elderly patients, he noted, required the best individualized care in order that they not get hurt or hurt others. And yet, he concluded, "all this needs to be done … under the depressing feeling that it is of no use in the long run towards the cure of the patient" (Clouston, 1884, pp. 401–402).

Not surprisingly, in the 19th century the proportion of older adults found in mental institutions was far below their expected proportion. In 1854, in a study of Massachusetts, the old had the highest reported rate of insanity of any age group. Although over 18% of the state's reported insane were of advanced age, fewer than 10% of the inmates in the asylum were above 60 (Rosenkrantz & Vinovskis, 1978). Similarly, in New York, in 1871, although 80% of all insane persons of ages 30 to 40 were placed in asylums, only 38% of the old who were identified as insane were permitted to enter such supposedly curative institutions (Board of State Commissioners of Public Charities of the State of New York, 1873).

In rejecting older people from obtaining such care, the superintendents argued that the almshouse was more suitable for their mental illness. Assuming that everyone of advanced age was simply "senile," they asserted they could do little for their disease. "We never intentionally send an insane person to the almshouse," explained Dr. Charles T. Gaynor, "except in the case of an old person who is pretty senile and can be treated as well [there] as at any other hospital" (Goldhamer & Marshall, 1953, p. 79). Although actual cure rates of insane elderly people who did enter the asylum mirrored their younger counterparts, superintendents continued to refuse the majority of older adults' entrance, asserting that their institutions were not intended for long-term care (Boston Commissioners, 1904).

A similar rejection of older adults occurred in hospitals throughout the nation. Originally established as institutions that housed their patients for extended periods of time, hospitals often set aside a ward for the long-term custodial care of old and incapacitated people. In 1869, when Roman Catholic Carney Hospital of Boston opened its doors, it reserved one of its five floors for "old people who may not be sick but come here for a home." By the 1890s, however, the hospital clearly changed its function and its willingness to provide a long-term residence for elderly individuals. In the 1890s, it made it clear that it did not want, nor would support, "chronic, lingering inmates" (Vogel, 1974, p. 138).

OLD-AGE HOMES

Not surprisingly, given such admonitions, and without the young, able-bodied, or insane who were now housed in other institutions, almshouses increasingly turned into long-term care institutions for elders. Although charity advocates and benevolent organizations deemed such a fate to be acceptable for the scores of immigrants who crowded the poorhouse, they judged the institution to be an unwarranted end for the minority of native-born persons who, without family or resources, had nowhere else to turn. Perhaps ironically, the same welfare experts who argued for the end of outdoor relief and the establishment of the detestable poorhouse also led organizations that created private, long-term care residences for specific groups among older inhabitants. In their views, individuals of their own religion or background did not deserve to die with the stigma of having been an almshouse pauper. Rather, they argued that specialized **old-age homes** should be established to provide long-term care for the upstanding, and especially, native-born elderly people.

THE GROWTH OF OLD-AGE HOMES

This initiative began early in the 19th century in Philadelphia. In 1817, horrified when they discovered two native-born Christian widows among the immigrants in an almshouse ward, a group of middle-class women established the first old- age home in the United States—the Indigent Widows' and Single Women's Society. In the view of the founders of the asylum, the ideal residents of their old-age home were women "whose earlier lives had been passed in more refined walks of life and whom experience, therefore, had not inured to the struggles of penury." Such individuals, the founders asserted, were "too respectable to be classed with the poor that come under the notice of most charitable societies, and unwilling to be inmates of an Almshouse." The new old-age home was to provide a suitable alternative (Haber, 1983).

However, the founders did not simply assume that those who applied to them deserved to be rescued from the almshouse. To ensure that, as the Society wrote, "unworthy objects would be excluded," every applicant had to provide evidence of a "character and habits beyond reproach," as well as recommendations from "acceptable persons" (Indigent Widows' and Single Women's Society, 1824).

In addition, in 1823, the Society established a sizable $150 entrance fee. This money, the benevolent women argued, would be a sign that the individual's needy state was not due to a lifetime of impoverishment. Those who lacked the funds, but had led an exemplary life, they reasoned, could appeal to their church or their friends for the necessary support (Haber, 1983).

Nonetheless, in its earliest years, the old-age home, like the almshouse, required its able-bodied inmates (as they were called) to contribute to the home through their labor. Women in the Philadelphia asylum often spent their days making shirts or participating in other domestic duties of the house. Not until the mid-1830s did the requirement to labor disappear from the old-age home's bylaws. In other asylums, inmates produced the food they ate or were required to spin and weave (Haber, 1983).

The early founders also imposed rules to "preserve perfect harmony in the family" (Indigent Widows' and Single Women's Society, 1819). Establishing a resident matron who served as the central authority figure, they decreed that any woman disagreeing with her policies would be expelled from the institution and face ending her days in the almshouse. During the first 17 years of its establishment, the Philadelphia asylum determined that 20 out of 140 inmates were not suitable members of the community and expelled them from the establishment. By 1887, to ensure that the resident met their expectations, the society established a 1-year probationary period before the individual assumed permanent resident status (Haber, 1983).

Chief among these rules was the notion that the individual would separate herself from the world and prepare spiritually for her future destiny. Proudly, the founders noted, "What is more important, many exemplary Christians devote their best efforts to instruct [the inmates] and to induce them to prepare for the awful change from their sojourn in this life to a weary rest from their labours [*sic*], and where sorrow can never intrude" (Haber, 1983, p. 95). Repeatedly, they relayed stories in their annual reports of women who had lost their beliefs as they faced increasing hardships. Forced to end their days in the almshouse, they certainly would have died without any spiritual guidance. In their asylum, however, and under the tutelage of Christian women and ministers, they died knowing that they would meet their heavenly reward.

The initiative that began in Philadelphia quickly spread to other major cities. Like the earliest asylum, Boston's first old-age home, established in 1849, was created to rescue worthy elderly women who had "a natural repugnance … to be herded with paupers of every character, condition, and clime" (Rogers, 1850, p. 3). The almshouse, Henry B. Rogers, asserted, had been taken over by "foreigners." As a result, the new asylum was to be for those who were "bone of our bone and flesh of our flesh" (Rogers, 1850, p. 3).

By the end of the 19th century, scores of homes existed across the country in both large cities and smaller towns. They housed not only Christian White widows, but men, married couples, immigrants of varied ethnicities, as well as Black men and women. In Philadelphia alone, by the end of the century, the city roster noted the existence of 24 homes. Numerous churches created asylums for their congregants, whereas labor organizations erected homes for working men of specific occupations. Separate asylums were founded for African Americans, retired actors, as well as aged soldiers and sailors (Haber, 1983). Especially for groups whose lifetime employment denied them the ability to start a family or establish a household, the old-age home offered an alternative to almshouse residency.

Although the residents within these homes often differed by religion, occupation, race, or gender, the founders shared specific beliefs about their residents. Not only were the old-age homes intended to save the inmates from ending their days in the almshouse, but they were also fashioned to reflect contemporary views of senescence. Sharing the medical view of the era that the last years of life were a time of disease and dependence, the homes segregated the old people based on chronological age and offered supposedly age-specific activities: a rare trip to the park, a young people's visit, and a Christmas concert. In their annual reports, the matrons of the homes repeatedly celebrated the fact that they had libraries stocked with appropriate books and flowers that lifted the spirit of those who faced a declining number of days.

THE MYTH OF ALMSHOUSE RESIDENCY

In portraying their homes as a superior alternative to the dreaded almshouse, the founders and managers of such homes clearly played into the widespread fear that without such institutions elderly people would inevitably end their days in the almshouse. For the great majority of aged individuals, such a concern was unfounded. Throughout the 19th century, the proportion of the elderly population in an asylum—whether in an almshouse or in an old-age home—remained rather stable. No more than 2% of the older population at any time sought such shelter. For many in the working and middle classes, industrialization actually increased their wealth and family support rather than led to impoverishment and desertion (Haber & Gratton, 1993).

Despite this reality, the popular culture of the early 20th century presented a very different picture. In movies, such as D.W. Griffith's *What Should We Do With Our Old?* and in two popular songs, each titled, "Over the Hill to the Poorhouse," even hardworking and thrifty elderly individuals were portrayed as having no choice but to end their days in the almshouse. In Griffith's film, the aged man's fate seemed inevitable. Thrown out of work by a younger laborer and arrested when he tried to steal food, he watched helplessly as his emaciated wife succumbed to starvation and old age. The subtitle explained that such a condition was hardly his fault; he had simply been "wounded in the battle of life." Without the support of family or work, he now had little choice, but to go "over the hill to the almshouse" (Braham & Catlin, 1874; Carleton, 1871; Griffith, 1911).

The stereotype of the inevitability of the almshouse was reinforced by statistical studies published by welfare advocates. In city after city, these experts noted, the municipal almshouse had become dominated by the old. In San Francisco, for example, in 1870, the average age of the inmates was 37; by 1894, it had escalated to near 60 (Smith, 1895). Nationally, the numbers seemed to reflect the same trend; whereas in 1880, only 33% of the almshouse population was above 65; by 1923, the proportion had reached 67% (Hoffman, 1909).

Investigations by government commissions also contributed to the myth that an increasing proportion of elders was now institutionalized. In 1934, in their call for federal pensions, the Committee on Economic Security argued that, with industrialization, the almshouse was becoming the final home for ever-increasing numbers of aged individuals. Using a graph composed ominously of black-silhouetted stooped men, they charted the seemingly exploding growth of "Paupers 65 & Over in Almshouses." In 1860, as the table revealed, there were 18,903 aged paupers or 25.6% of the institutionalized population. By 1923, the number had ballooned to 41,980, or 53.9% of the residents. "The predominance of the aged in the almshouse," the Committee then conclusively asserted, "is a sign of their increasing dependency" (Committee on Economic Security, 1934, n. p.).

In reality, the growing proportion of aged paupers simply reflected the removal of other groups to institutions dedicated to their specific needs, such as orphanages, mental asylums, or hospitals. Nonetheless, in often citing the ballooning absolute numbers of the old residents *within* the almshouse, social advocates stressed what appeared to be an indisputable fact: not only the very poor, but also the native born and upstanding were likely to face impoverishment in old age and the danger of institutionalization. "The risks of being left without means of meeting [the needs] of old age," wrote Lucille Eaves in her influential study, *Aged Clients of Boston's Social Agencies*, "are not confined to workers with low earning capacity, but are shared by persons in all ranks of society" (Eaves, 1925, p. 3). Bent down by age and impoverishment, they then had little choice but to die amid the almshouse's squalor.

Even attempts to make the almshouse appear more like a benevolent institution did little to allay such fears or lessen the horror of ending one's life in the institution. In 1903, for example, the New York City almshouse changed its name to the Home for the Aged and Infirm; in 1913, the city of Charleston followed suit, now calling their almshouse "The Charleston Home" (Charleston City Year Book, 1914). Other superintendents focused on the amenities in the home, such as food, heat, or indoor plumbing. Regardless of these actions, the stigma of the almshouse remained. "The poorhouse," as social analyst Henry C. Evans wrote, "is a word of hate and loathing, for it includes the composite horrors of poverty, disgrace, loneliness, humiliation, abandonment, and degradation" (Evans, 1900, cited by Epstein, 1929, p. 128).

This belief in the inevitability of the almshouse and the terror it evoked among older people had a significant impact on welfare philosophy. Even charity advocates whose predecessors had stressed the importance of the poorhouse as a deterrent now began to argue against its existence. If the almshouse could not be avoided, it now seemed to make little sense to punish the unfortunates who had nowhere else to turn or to follow the philosophy of "less eligibility." Those needing institutional care had obviously done nothing to deserve this fate. Rather than a preventive option, therefore, the institution had become little more than a reflection of the nation's lack of concern for its elderly citizens. "The placing of these unfortunate poor in the almshouse," declared Earnest

C. Marshall in 1898, in his *Annual Report of the Institutions Commissioners to the City of Boston*, "is not the kind, humane or just way of treating them. ... It should no longer be known that Massachusetts brings shame to old age, the blush to wrinkled faces, by classing them under the shameful name of paupers" (Marshall, 1898, n.p.).

THE ATTACK ON THE ALMSHOUSE

Given increasing animosity toward the almshouse, the attack on the very existence of the institution became widespread. Over the course of the first three decades of the 20th century, welfare advocates were joined by religious, fraternal, and government officials in their rejection of the asylum's central role in providing long-term care for elderly individuals. By the time of the Great Depression, few could seem to remember why the institution had even come into existence. Rather, opponents of the institution agreed there were myriad reasons for its elimination.

First, they argued, not only was the almshouse a barbaric way to treat the old, but it was not even cost-efficient. In fact, the large and ever-increasing budgets necessary to run the asylums seemed to negate their very purpose. When the almshouse was first established, the Overseers of the Poor knew all too well that supporting a pauper in the institution cost far more than an occasional cord of wood, a small allocation of money, or basket of food. They believed, however, that the loathsome nature of the institution would deter individuals from seeking any relief at all. Convinced now that older people could not avoid the institution, and that the numbers of the needy older population were exponentially increasing, charity experts now asserted that the costs of such institutionalized long-term care were neither prudent nor manageable. "It is well known," wrote the Illinois State Federation of Labor in 1923, "that the cost of maintaining an aged person in a public institution is far in excess of the amount it proposed to pay an individual in the form of a pension" (Illinois State Federation of Labor, cited by Quadagno, 1986, pp. 170–171). According to the Massachusetts Commission on Pensions, support of an individual outside the institution would at best be a dollar a day or $365; the cost of a couple would be no more than $500. Both these sums, the Commission declared, would be far less than the expense within an institution (Massachusetts Commission on Pension, 1925).

Moreover, opponents of the asylum noted, regardless of these high costs, the institution rarely provided suitable care. Even as early as 1903, a study of Boston's Long Island almshouse concluded that, although considerable sums were spent, the inmates often lacked sufficient food, heating, or clothing. By 1923, the Department of Labor echoed this finding. Calculating that the average cost per inmate in 2,183 almshouses was $440, the study found that given the great fixed costs of the asylums, they had few resources left to devote to the care or sustenance of their inmates (United States Bureau of the Census, 1923). It mattered little whether the institution was called an almshouse or had changed its name to an "old folks" home; the residents' basic needs were not being met. The elderly people in the almshouse spent their final days surrounded by disease and impoverishment.

Finally, advocates for the old asserted that reliance on the almshouse for support of older adults not only threatened their dignity, it also had a negative impact on their family members. For too long, the relatives of older people had been faced with an untenable choice. Either they watched their aged parents go "over the hill to the poorhouse," or they sacrificed their own needs and those of their children to rescue their aged family members from dying in an almshouse. "Consider the dilemma," wrote Mabel Nassau in 1915 in her landmark study, *Old Age Poverty in Greenwich Village*, "of the middle generation trying to decide whether to support the aged parents and thus have less to eat for themselves and their children ... or to put the old people in an institution" (Nassau, cited by Lubove, 1968, p. 153). A decade later, Reverend George B. O'Conor, director of Boston's Charities, agreed. His parishioners, he declared, would rather "starve to death" than allow family members to enter the poorhouse (O'Conor, *The Boston Globe*, January 9, 1923, cited by Haber & Gratton, 1993, p. 136).

PENSIONS, SOCIAL SECURITY, AND LONG-TERM CARE

As numerous segments of society joined together to condemn the existence of the almshouse, they were also unanimous in their support of the solution to long-term care: pensions based on advanced age would eliminate the need for institutional aid. Previously, such funds had been allocated by the government for veterans and their families, as well as provided by select industries for long-time workers (Skocpol, 1992). By the first decades of the 20th century, the movement for national pensions became viewed not only as a way of rewarding the aged worker or disabled veteran, but also as a means to escape almshouse residency.

For fraternal and labor organizations, the symbol of the almshouse loomed large; they repeatedly evoked its seeming inevitability in their campaigns to increase membership. Only through dues-supported pensions, they argued, could even the most hardworking avoid such an ignominious fate. A 1925 illustration from *The Eagle*, the magazine of the Fraternal Order of Eagles, clearly portrayed this message. Despite the middle-class appearance of the elderly couple's home, complete with "bless our home" framed needlepoint, a sign outside the window on the factory door reading "young men only need to apply" sealed their destiny. Held in the elderly man's hand was the inescapable future: the certificate declared that it was the couple's "Passport to the Poorhouse" (*The Eagle*, January 1925, cited by Haber & Gratton, 1993, p. 58).

By the 1920s, the call for pensions was also supported by government officials and candidates for political office. In unison, they claimed that the benefits of a pension system would not only restore the dignity of old age, but also would forever eliminate the almshouse as the means of providing the old with long-term care. In his campaign for governor of New York, Franklin Roosevelt, for example, evoked the symbol of the poorhouse in his call for government pensions. The great majority of aged inmates, Roosevelt declared, were institutionalized not as a "result of lack of thrift or energy," but "as a mere by-product of modern life. … The worn-out worker, after a life of ceaseless effort and useful productivity must look forward for his declining years to a poorhouse." Roosevelt and others knew that the attack on the almshouse was a salient campaign issue; those who opposed such measures risked their political futures (Roosevelt, Box 16, 1928).

In the enactment of **Social Security**, therefore, legislators took direct aim at the poorhouse. Through the measure, they not only provided assistance to the needy older adult and insurance for the long-time worker, but also attempted to eliminate the poorhouse as a welfare institution. In its initial formulation, Social Security strictly barred pensions for any resident of a public asylum. According to the legislation, individuals needed to be "sixty-five years of age or older and … not an inmate of a public institution" ("Title 1 – Grants to the States, Section 3, Payments to the States," Social Security Act, 1935). In including this clause, the creators of the bill were well aware of its impact. "We were" as the Deputy Secretary of Public Assistance of Pennsylvania explained, "rather enthusiastic to empty the poorhouses" (Thomas, 1969, p. 97). Only at a risk to their political future could legislators object to a measure that would eradicate the greatest fear of growing old.

Even after the passage of Social Security, deep-seeded fear of the almshouse served to support arguments that the Act was both necessary and constitutional. In 1937, the Supreme Court upheld the measure, declaring that the fear of the almshouse was a very real threat. Writing for the majority, Justice Cardozo proclaimed that "the hope behind this statute is to save men and women from the rigors of the poorhouse as well as from the haunting fear that such a lot awaits them when journey's end is near" (*Helvering v. Davis*, 1937). With pensions, guaranteed support was to provide funds to replace the need for institutional care.

Had the promises of the welfare advocates been accurate, the history of long-term care would have ended with Social Security's goal of eradicating the almshouse. Individuals would have lived out their days in the comfort of their own homes or in the residences of their children supported by small, but guaranteed monthly annuities. Following the passage of the measure, in fact, scores of smaller almshouses disappeared from the country's landscape. Public officials quickly moved the residents to private facilities, or, in some cases, simply restructured the institution. In Kansas, for example, although the supervisors of the public county homes remained the same, the asylums were transferred to private control. No longer an almshouse in name, and now able to receive its residents' pensions, the institution continued to provide for the long-term needs of the elderly people (Fischer, 1943). In other states and cities, as the almshouse population was transferred to private asylums or individuals were given support in their own homes, the institution lost its reason for being.

But not all the old who needed long-term care were able to live independently. Even before Social Security was enacted, some welfare advocates asserted that pensions would not eliminate the need for long-term care. In the 1930s, welfare advocate **Homer Folks** argued against the notion that the old ended their days in the almshouse simply because they were poor. Only about 15% of the residents, he stated, fit this description. Although this group would be able to live independently on a pension, "the others," he declared at a hearing of the New York Commission on Old Age Security, "are physically infirm and sick, and have various kinds of ailments and conditions that require personal attention of the kind that you could not get in an individual home." In response, he asserted, the government should include in the Social Security legislation a provision for the institutional support of the infirm elderly (Folks, cited by Thomas, 1969, p. 40).

Immediately following the passage of the bill, the economist and future senator Paul H. Douglas made a similar argument. Writing in 1936, he asserted that:

> the dislike for institutional care has, however, commonly been carried too far, so that there is a movement to prevent the pensions from being paid to those who are in any private institution for the aged or who may be receiving treatment in a state hospital, etc. The truth of the matter is of course that while a large proportion of the aged ought not to be in an institution, there is nevertheless a large group who need the skilled and specialized care which only an institution can present. A great many of the old people are ill or crippled and need specialized nursing and medical care. This can commonly be furnished more effectively in a home for the aged or an infirmary than in the private home or lodgings of the aged person.
>
> (Douglas, 1936, pp. 244–245)

Both Folks and Douglas, of course, had been correct. A significant proportion of the almshouse population continued to require long-time care. In Charleston, for example, though the authorities did remove the great majority of aged inmates from the almshouse, most of these individuals could not live on their own. Rather, they were transferred to local, private sanitariums where their health needs could purportedly be addressed (Charleston City Year Book, 1938). Other individuals found themselves in boarding and rooming houses now labeled as "homes for the aged."

As government investigations revealed, in the move to create "private" asylums in which residents could receive pensions, many of these homes fell far below any acceptable standard. Fires in which the old lost their lives or homes in which they were victims of abuse and substandard care became front-page news. Studies found that some states had skirted the regulations entirely by simply changing the names of the institutions. In Kansas, for example, a 1943 federal investigation concluded that the state's private asylums were, in reality, public institutions (Fischer, 1943). Moreover, as almshouse doors closed, mental asylums were flooded with elderly people for whom the state would now bear the expense. Once excluded from such institutions due to assumptions that they could not be cured, the institutions now became warehouses for the elderly residents who had been classified as chronically "senile." Inspections revealed that, for large numbers of older adults, the shame of the almshouse had often just been transferred into state-supported mental asylums (Grob, 1973; Rosenkrantz & Vinovskis, 1978).

A decade after passage of the legislation, weaknesses in the initial formulation of Social Security had become widely acknowledged. In 1948, the authors of the "Report of the Advisory Council on Social Security" argued that the government needed to reassess the restriction against supporting the old in public institutions. Finding that 50,000 aged individuals were living in commercial nursing homes, the report concluded that large numbers of these received "very unsatisfactory care." The study also noted that another 300,000 recipients of pensions were bedridden and in need of assistance in eating and dressing. "Of these living in their own homes or with others," the report asserted, "many need prolonged treatment in medical institutions." Authors of the study did not want to return to the system of almshouses. They felt that by extending support to public medical institutions that were regulated by the state, superior care would be provided. "We believe that," the report concluded, "as a condition of eligibility for federal funds, a State aiding needy aged persons in public and private medical institutions and commercial nursing homes should be required to have an authority or authorities that would establish and maintain adequate minimum standards for institutional facilities and for the care of aged persons living in these facilities." The Council argued that to meet such standards, institutions would have to "maintain and operate facilities for the diagnosis, treatment, or care of persons suffering from illness, injury, or deformity, and be devoted primarily to furnishing medical or nursing service." They concluded, however, "the additional annual cost to the Federal Government under this recommendation would range from a low of $20,000,000 to a high of $32,000,000" (Advisory Council on Social Security, 1948, p. 116).

In the 1950 Social Security amendments, Congress accepted many of the recommendations of the Advisory Council. For the first time, payments were allocated for individuals living in public medical institutions as long as they met State regulations. As Wilbur J. Cohen and Robert J. Myers explained in the October 1950, *Social Security Bulletin*:

> the Federal Government will match expenditures for assistance to aged and blind persons in certain types of public medical institutions. Under the old law no expenditures made to persons in public institutions were matchable. Further, if the State plan includes provision for payments to persons in any private or public institution, the State must establish or designate some State agency that will be responsible for establishing and maintaining standards for such institutions. This requirement will raise the standards of those institutions that have been understaffed and underfinanced, that have been firetraps, and in which people have been badly treated.
>
> (Cohen & Myers, 1950, p. 5)

EXPANSION OF THE NURSING HOME INDUSTRY

This measure obviously had a tremendous impact on federal support of long-term care. In contrast to the 1940s, individuals living in public medical facilities could now receive a pension. Studies in the 1950s revealed that generally more than half of the residents of nursing homes were recipients of public assistance (Committee on Nursing Homes Regulation, 1986). Moreover, additional legislation propelled the growth of these institutions. In 1946, Congress passed the **Hill–Burton Act**, which supported hospital construction throughout the nation. Within two decades, 4,678 institutions had been constructed, especially in the south and in cities with fewer than 100,000 people (Committee on Nursing Homes Regulation, 1986; Stevens, 1989).

Although the original measure was intended to create state/federal partnerships to build modern hospitals, in 1954, amendments to the law promoted the erection of long-term care facilities. According to the new legislation, the federal government would provide matching funds to states that built nursing homes that conformed to mandated regulations. Moreover, in 1959, a newly devised program of the Department of Housing and Urban Development encouraged the construction or rehabilitation of nursing homes through the allocation of federal mortgage insurance, allowing private lenders to make low-interest loans (Committee on Nursing Homes Regulation, 1986).

Not surprisingly, these measures led to an explosion in the number of nursing home beds. Yet, the rule that these institutions had to conform to federal or state standards was, at best, ill defined, and most homes remained unregulated. Additional Social Security legislation in 1953 required, "If a State plan for old-age assistance, aid to the blind, or aid to the permanently and totally disabled provides for payments to individuals in private or public institutions, the State must have a State authority to establish and maintain standards for such institutions" (ElderWeb, "States Create Nursing Homes Licensing"). Nonetheless, in 1958, an investigation of the Public Health Service concluded that a large proportion of homes remained poorly staffed and largely unregulated. This finding was reiterated by the Senate Subcommittee on Problems of the Aged and Aging, originally convened in 1959. "Because of the shortage of nursing home beds," the Subcommittee concluded, "many states have not fully enforced the existing regulations, failure to do so reflecting the policy of the states to give ample time to the nursing home owners and operators to bring the facilities up to standards. Many states report that strict enforcement of the regulations would close the majority of homes." In 1960, 44% of the 308,000 beds in skill-nursing facilities did not meet the standards set by Hill–Burton (Committee on Nursing Homes Regulation, 1986).

Aware of the need to provide additional medical support for old people, in 1960, Congress passed the Medical Assistance to the Aged program as a provision of the **Kerr–Mills Act**. The federal government now allocated funds for older adults who, although not poor enough to receive old-age assistance, still could not cover the cost of the medical care. This measure provided support for those in skilled nursing homes. As the Act dictated that the states, rather than the federal government, determined the level of eligibility, the impact was limited. In the first year, 60% of those elderly people receiving such support were in New York, California, and Massachusetts (Moore & Smith, 2005–2006).

The Special Committee on Aging, established by Congress in 1961 and chaired by Senator Frank Moss, underscored the lack of regulation and substandard care in many nursing institutions. Years later, in his book, *Too Old, Too Sick, Too Bad,* Moss called nursing homes "The greatest fear of the elderly." For most old people, he stated that the asylums—much like the poorhouses of the past—embodied the horrors of growing old: the "fear of losing liberty, identity, and human dignity," the "fear of death," and the "fear of poor care and abuse."(Moss & Halamandaris, 1977, pp. 12–14).

Reflecting the Special Committee on Aging's finding, in 1963, 3 years after the enactment of Medical Assistance to the Aged, a Senate subcommittee judged the program to be "an ineffective and piecemeal approach to the health problems of the nation's 18 million older citizens." "It is still," concluded the report of the subcommittee, "not a national program and there is no reason to expect that it will become one in the foreseeable future" (Hunter, 1963, p. 16). The 1965 hearings of the Senate Subcommittee on Long Term Care echoed these findings. Appropriate residential care was beyond the financial reach of most elderly Americans. Enforcing regulations to raise the standards in these asylums would simply lead to the closing of many of these residences and expand the already desperate necessity for affordable nursing home beds for the old (Moss & Halamandaris, 1977).

Thus, in response to the obvious crisis in the medical care of elders, in 1965, the government enacted **Medicare** as a health insurance plan for individuals covered by Social Security. The program focused largely on doctors visits and hospital care. The Act, however, did cover 100 days of nursing home stay following a 3-day or more hospital stay and if the nursing home residency was for rehabilitation. In addition, for the very poor, Kerr–Mills was transformed into **Medicaid** in order to provide funds for the medical care of those who were covered by Social Security Assistance. Because of these measures, in the years between 1960 and 1975, the number of nursing homes grew from 9,582 to 23,000, whereas the number of patients ballooned from 290,000 to over 1,000,000. With expenditures that skyrocketed from $500,000,000 to $10,500,000,000, institutional care of the elderly has grown into a major industry (Moss & Halamandaris, 1977).

The growth in the industry, however, was not met by a parallel increase in the quality of care. Investigations, both before and after the passage of federal legislation, underscored the substandard nature of many nursing homes. In the 1950s, newspapers reported that nearly 150 elderly people lost their lives in nursing home fires; by the 1970s, this number had nearly doubled. On February 17, 1957, alone, 72 people died in the flames of one nursing home fire Warrenton, Missouri; on November 23, 1963, another 63 were victims of a nursing home fire in Fitchville, Ohio (Case Study 2.2). In 1971, in one nursing home

EXHIBIT 2.2 The Fitchville Fire

On November 23, 1963, the nation's attention was captivated by the recent assassination of John F. Kennedy. In Ohio, however, another event shared front-page news. In Fitchville, in the early morning, a fire consumed the Golden Age Nursing Home. Once built as a toy factory, the 60-year-old building now served as the shelter to 84 elderly residents, ages 68 to 93. When the fire broke out, according to one observer, the home "went up like a tinderbox." In the chaos, it became clear that no exit strategy existed: some residents ran for the doors, others refused to leave their beds. Telephone lines that might have allowed calls for help were immediately destroyed. When a truck driver seeing the flames finally contacted the Norwalk Fire Department, the department refused to respond as the home was beyond its jurisdiction. According to newspaper reports, no fire hydrants were on site; water had to be carried from 5 miles away.

When the smoke finally cleared, only the front door of the home was left standing. Sixty-three residents lost their lives, some to smoke, others to fire. Even when the bodies were recovered, 15 could not be immediately identified because of their condition. In other cases, relatives were asked not to view the remains. Twenty-one individuals who were never claimed by family members were buried in a common grave. Another 21 residents escaped from the institution, along with all three of the night attendants.

Arriving in Fitchville within a day of the fire, Governor James A. Rhodes demanded an investigation. The president of the company that owned the nursing home, Robert Pollock, had immediately asserted that the home was not at fault; it had been recently certified by health officials as an "efficient, clean, safe nursing home." Eventually, the cause of the fire was determined to be three-fold: "1) the probable extensive shorting along over fused and improperly wired electrical circuits under an overload; 2) the simultaneous ignition of fires at a number of different points, and delay in turning in the alarm to the fire department having jurisdiction; and 3) lack of prompt evacuation based on an orderly plan since the first five minutes of any building fire are critical." The report concluded that the fire was caused not "from design but carelessness" (Anderson & Quarnatelli, 1964, p. 9).

As a result of the disaster, officials called for homes to have mandatory sprinklers, automatic fire detection systems, and electrical wiring codes. The governor charged the Ohio legislature to determine what control a state should have over such institutions. In Washington, editorial writer Drew Pearson linked the fire to the poverty-stricken nature of the residents, whose inability to provide for their own medical needs led them to seek shelter in the substandard home. Calling on Wilbur Mills, head of the Ways and Means Committee, to release the long-stalled Medicare Bill from his committee, Pearson asserted that the Fitchville fire proved the need to provide medical care for impoverished individuals who had nowhere else to turn (Anderson & Quarnatelli, 1964; "63 Elderly Patients," 1963; "Fire Inquiry," 1963; "Ohio to Study," 1963; Pearson, 1963).

in Maryland, food poisoning killed 36 residents (ElderWeb, "1950–1980: Nursing Home Fires"). Such events made clear that even with the passage of Medicare, nursing homes not only needed to address accessibility, but also to improve conditions within the institutions. In 1987, according to the Federal Nursing Home Reform Act from the **Omnibus Budget Reconciliation Act of 1987 (OBRA '87)**, institutions receiving Medicare or Medicaid had to guarantee that residents could maintain the "highest practicable, mental, and psycho-social well-being." Not only were the supervisors of homes to be concerned about the nature of care; they had to expand their focus to assure that individuals had a high quality of life. Staff had to be trained, restraints had to be limited, family members were to have a voice in their care of their relatives (Turnham, n.d., n.p.).

Moreover, with the passage of the **Americans with Disabilities Act (ADA)** in 1990, Congress mandated, a "public entity administer ... programs ... in the most integrated setting appropriate to the needs of qualified individuals with disabilities" (U.S. Department of Justice, Civil Rights Division "Statement of the Department of Justice on Enforcement of the Integration Mandate of Title II of the Americans with Disabilities Act and *Olmstead v. L. C.*," n.p.). Originally, the measure largely addressed "services, programs, or activities." Businesses, schools, and other public organizations had to provide "a reasonable modification" to "avoid discrimination based on disability." Nine years later, however, the measure was interpreted to address the institutionalization of persons with disabilities as well. In 1999, the Supreme Court found in the ***Olmstead* Decision** that, under the ADA, it was unconstitutional to institutionalize those who could live in the community with reasonable modifications. Such persons, they declared, were suffering from "unjustified institutional isolation." In their ruling, the justices noted "confinement in an institution severely diminishes everyday life activities of individuals, including family relations, social contacts, work options, economics independence, educational advancement, and cultural enrichment" (*Olmstead v. L. C.*, 1999, p. 3). This decision, as well as the regulations contained in OBRA '87 clearly reflected the new emphasis in long-term care.

Over the course of America's history, methods for dealing with the long-term needs of the older adult population have been transformed from reliance on the almshouse or outdoor relief into a variety of public and private institutions and initiatives. Although initially long-term facilities had been structured to allocate basic—and often substandard—food and shelter, they have come to focus on providing appropriate assistance and to ensure the residents' quality of life. This transformation did not come easily or quickly. Rather, over time, the changes reflected evolving attitudes toward those who needed institutional care as well as significant legislative and judicial decisions.

Yet, despite the transformation that has occurred, current policies and attitudes toward long-term care still reflect their historical roots. Although in the 20th century, policy makers consciously attempted to separate long-term care from any association with the almshouse, the institution and the terror it evoked have continued to cast a long shadow. Since its founding, the poorhouse had become a symbol of all that was wrong with growing old in America. Not only did it seem to punish even hardworking elderly people for their assumed inescapable decline into poverty, but also it was eventually judged to be costly and inefficient. Although other institutions, such as orphanages, old-age homes, and mental hospitals, were developed in the 19th century as preferable alternatives, the old still feared ending their days amid the squalor of the poorhouse. As a result, in creating Social Security, lawmakers purposefully targeted the long-standing institution. Hoping that pensions alone would provide for the needs of the old, they barred the residents of all public institutions from receiving these funds. Without such resources, they concluded, the long-despised almshouse would finally disappear from the landscape.

Although legislators were largely successful in this aim, numerous federal and state investigations revealed that they had overestimated the ability of pensions alone to provide for elderly individuals. Institutional care was still a necessity for older people who were not just poor, but in need of residential medical assistance. The "private" homes that had sprung up to fill the void rarely provided appropriate care. Even when new laws allowed pensions to go to the recipients of public asylums and supported the construction of institutions, a crisis in nursing home care remained. In the decades following the passage of Social Security and Medicare, the difficulties of trying to balance the cost and regulation of long-term facilities with the nation's ever-growing need for such institutions became all too apparent. Attempts to close unregulated homes critically reduced the number of available beds, enforcing standards that ensured proper care often raised the cost beyond what most elderly people could afford. These issues continue to shape the public debate over the best means of providing for the medical and residential support of older adults. The concerns are not new; they have roots deep in the historical evolution of long-term care.

DISCUSSION QUESTIONS

1. Why were the few provisions for long-term care made in the first century of colonial America?
2. Why and how did this change in the 18th century? What types of long-term care for the needy were established?
3. Why did leading 19th-century welfare advocates reject the notion of outdoor relief?
4. Why were elderly individuals excluded from many institutions in the first half of the 19th century?
5. What factors explain the rise in the old-age homes in the United States?
6. How do you explain the changing attitudes about the almshouses that occurred in the first half of the 20th century?
7. Why did welfare authorities assume that a growing proportion of elderly persons were likely to end their lives in the almshouses in the first half of the 20th century?
8. Why were individuals in public institutions first excluded from receiving Social Security? Why did this change?

9. Contrast the belief in "less eligibility" with the concern for "quality of life." How did these two differing philosophies shape the nature of long-term care?
10. To what extent have conflicts among state, family, and personal responsibility remained a dominant motif throughout the history of long-term care?

ADDITIONAL RESOURCES

Achenbaum, W. A. (1978). *Old age in the new land*. Baltimore, MD: Johns Hopkins Press.
Cole, T. (1992). *The journey of life*. New York, NY: Cambridge University Press.
Fischer, D. H. (1977). *Growing old in America*. New York, NY: Oxford University Press.
Gratton, B. (1986). *Urban elders*. Philadelphia, PA: Temple University Press.
Haber, C. (1983). *Beyond sixty five*. New York, NY: Cambridge University Press.
Haber, C., & Gratton, B. (1993). *Old age and the search for security*. Bloomington, IN: University of Indiana Press.
Katz, S. (1996). *Disciplining old age*. Charlottesville, VA: University Press of Virginia.
Premo, T. (1990). *Winter friends*. Urbana, IL: University of Illinois Press.
Schaie, K.W., & Achenbaum, W.A. (Eds.). (1993). *Societal impact on aging*. New York, NY: Springer Publishing Company.
Van Tassel, D., & Stearns, P. (Eds.). (1986). *Old age in a bureaucratic society*. Westport, CT: Greenwood Press.

REFERENCES

Advisory Council on Social Security. (1948). *Report of the advisory council on social security: Part 3 public assistance*. Retrieved from http://www.ssa.gov/history/reports/48advisegen.html
Anderson, W., & Quarnatelli, E. L. (1964). *A description of organizational activities in the Fitchville Ohio Nursing Home Fire*. Retrieved from http://udspace.udel.edu/bitstream/handle/19716/1317/RN8.pdf?sequence=1.
Assembly of the Province of Pennsylvania. (1775). *Acts of the assembly of the province of Pennsylvania*. Pennsylvania: Assembly of the Province.
Board of State Commissioners of Public Charities of the State of New York. (1873). *Sixth annual report*. Boston, MA: State Commissioners.
Boston Commissioners. (1904). *Majority and minority reports of an investigation of the Boston alms house and hospital*. Boston, MA: Municipal Printing Office.
Braham, D., & Catlin, G. (1874). Over the hill to the poor house. In D. Scott & B. Wishy (Eds.), *America's families* (pp. 283–284). New York, NY: Harper & Row, 1975.
Carleton, W. (1871). *Over the hill to the poor house*. Retrieved from http://www.poorhousestory.com/over_the_hill.htm
Charleston City Year Book for 1887. (1888). Charleston, South Carolina: City of Charleston.
Charleston City Year Book for 1914. (1915). Charleston, South Carolina: City of Charleston.
Charleston City Year Book for 1925. (1926). Charleston, South Carolina: City of Charleston.
Charleston City Year Book for 1938. (1939). Charleston, South Carolina: City of Charleston.
Charleston City Year Book for 1949. (1950). Charleston, South Carolina: City of Charleston.
Chelfant, E. (1955). *A goodly heritage*. Pittsburgh, PA: University of Pittsburgh Press.
City of Charleston. (1867). *Poor house journal*. Charleston, SC: Charleston City Archives.
Clouston, T. (1884). *Clinical lectures on mental disease*. Philadelphia, PA: Henry C. Lea's Sons.
Cohen, W., & Myers, R. (1950). *The Social Security bulletin*. Retrieved from http://www.socialsecurity.gov/history/1950amend.html

Committee on Economic Security. (1934). *The need for economic security in the United States.* Retrieved from http://www.ssa.gov/history/reports/ces/cesvol9theneed.html

Committee on Nursing Homes Regulation. (1986). *Improving the quality of care in nursing homes*. Washington, DC: Institute of Medicine.

Demos, J. (1978). Old age in early New England. In M. Gordon (Ed.), *The American family in social-historical perspective* (pp. 220–256). New York, NY: St. Martin's Press.

Douglas, P. (1936). *Social security in the United States*. New York, NY: Whittlesey House.

Duffy, J. (1976). *The healers*. New York, NY: McGraw Hill.

Eaves, L. (1925). *Aged clients of Boston's agencies*. Boston, MA: Women's Education and Industrial Union.

ElderWeb. (n.d.). 1950–1980: Nursing home fires. In *History of long term care*. Retrieved from http://www.elderweb.com/node/2856

ElderWeb. (n.d.). States create nursing home licensing. In *History of long term care*. Retrieved from http://www.elderweb.com/node/9683

Epstein, A. (1929). *The problem of old age pensions in industry*. Harrisburg, PA: Pennsylvania Old Age Commission.

Fire inquiry is on at nursing home. (1963, *November 25*). *The New York Times*, p. 11.

Fischer, V. (1943). Kansas county homes after the Social Security Act. *Social Service Review, 17*(4), 442–465.

Foucault, M. (1972). *The archeology of knowledge*. New York, NY: Pantheon Books.

Goldhamer, H., & Marshall, A. (1953). *Psychosis and civilization*. Glencoe, IL: The Free Press.

Greven, P. (1970). *Four generations*. Ithaca, NY: Cornell University Press.

Griffith, W. D. (1911). *What should we do with our old?* Biograph Company. Retrieved from http://www.youtube.com/watch?v=zjaVhjD4IG4

Grob, G. (1973). *Mental institutions in America*. New York, NY: The Free Press.

Haber, C. (1983). *Beyond sixty five*. New York, NY: Cambridge University Press.

Haber C., & Gratton, B. (1986). Old age, public welfare and race. *Journal of Social History, 21*, 263–279.

Haber, C., & Gratton, B. (1993). *Old age and the search for security*. Bloomington, IN: University of Indiana Press.

Helvering v. Davis , 301 U.S. 619. (1937).

Hoffman, F. (1909). State pensions and annuities in old age. *Journal of the American Statistical Association, 11*, 363–408.

Hunter, M. (1963, October 29). Medical plan for aging scored. *The New York Times*, p. 16.

Indigent Widows' and Single Women's Society. (1819). An act to incorporate. In the *2nd annual report from the managers of the Indigent Widows' and Single Women's Society*. Philadelphia, PA: Author.

Indigent Widows' and Single Women's Society. (1824). *Seventh annual report*. Philadelphia, PA: Author.

Lubove, R. (1968). *The struggle for social security, 1900–1935*. Cambridge, MA: Harvard University Press.

Marshall, E. (1898). *Annual report of the institutions commissioners to the city of Boston*. Boston, MA: City Publishers.

Massachusetts Commission on Pensions. (1925). *Report of the commission on old-age pensions.* Boston, MA: Commonwealth of Massachusetts.

Mather, C. (1912). *Diary of Cotton Mather*. Boston, MA: Massachusetts Historical Society.

Moore, J., & Smith, D. (2005–2006). Legislating Medicaid. *Heath Care Financing Review, 27*(2), 45–52.

Moss, F. E., & Halamandaris, V. J. (1977). *Too old, too sick, too bad*. Germantown, MD: Aspen Systems.

Ohio to study aged care. (1963, November 28). *The New York Times*, p. 37.

Olmstead v. L. C., 527 U.S. 581 (1999). Retrieved from http://www.law.cornell.edu/supct/html98-536.ZS.html

Pearson, D. (1963, December 10). Golden years end tragically. *The Washington Post*, p. 11.

Quadagno, J. (1986). The transformation of old age security. In D. Van Tassell & P. Stearns (Eds.), *Old age in a bureaucratic society* (pp. 129–155). Westport, CT: Greenwood Press.

Quincy, J. (1821). *The Quincy report on poor relief.* Boston, MA: The Massachusetts General Court Committee on Pauper Laws.

Record Commissioners of the City of Boston. (1692). *Report of the record commissioners of the city of Boston containing miscellaneous papers*. Boston, MA: City Printers.

Record Commissioners of the City of Boston. (1884). *Report of the record commissioners of the city of Boston containing the records of the Boston selectmen 1701-1715*. Boston, MA: City Printers.

Rogers, H. B. (1850). *Remarks before the Association for Aged Indigent Females at the opening of their home*. Boston, MA: Association for Aged Indigent Females.

Roosevelt, F. (1928). Campaign speeches, October–November 1928. *Papers of Franklin Delano Roosevelt: Legislation: Old age pensions*. New York State Archives, Box 16.

Rosenberg, C. (1987). *The care of strangers*. New York, NY: Basic Books.

Rosenkrantz, B., & Vinovskis, M. (1978). The invisible lunatics. In S. Spicker, K. Woodward, & D. Van Tassell (Eds.), *Aging and the elderly* (pp. 95–126). Atlantic Highlands, NJ: Humanities Press.

Rothman, D. (1971). *The discovery of the asylum*. Boston, MA: Little, Brown.

63 Elderly patients are killed as fire razes Ohio rest home. (1963, November 24). *The New York Times*, p. 1.

Skocpol, T. (1992). *Protecting soldiers and mothers*. Cambridge, MA: Harvard University Press.

Smith, M. R. (1895). Almshouse women. *Journal of the American Statistical Association*, *4*(31), 419–462.

Stevens, R. (1989). *In sickness and wealth*. New York, NY: Basic Books.

Thomas, W., Jr. (1969). *Nursing homes and public policy*. Ithaca, NY: Cornell University Press.

Trent, J. (1994). *Inventing the feeble mind*. Berkeley, CA: University of California Press.

Trustees of the State Lunatic Hospital at Taunton. (1860). *Seventh annual report*. Boston, MA: State Hospital.

Turnham, H. (n.d). *Federal Nursing Home Reform Act*. Retrieved from http://www.allhealth.org/briefingmaterials/OBRA87Summary-984.pdf

United States Bureau of the Census. (1923). *Paupers in the almshouse*. Washington, DC: U.S. Government Printing Office.

U.S. Department of Justice, Civil Rights Division, Statement of the Department of Justice on Enforcement of the Integration Mandate of Title II of the Americans with Disabilities Act and *Olmstead v. L. C.* Retrieved from http://www.ada.gov/olmstead/q&a_olmstead.htm.

Vogel, M. (1974). *Boston's hospitals, 1870–1930*. PhD dissertation, University of Chicago, Chicago, Illinois.

Wells, R. (1975). *The population of the British colonies in North American before 1776*. Princeton, NJ: Princeton University Press.

Willard, S. (1726). A *compleat body of divinity in two hundred and fifty expository lectures*. Boston: B. Eliot and D. Henchman. Sermon 180.

Community-Based Long-Term Care

3

The Role of Family in Community-Based Long-Term Care

CAROL J. WHITLATCH
LINDA S. NOELKER

CHAPTER OVERVIEW

This chapter provides a broad discussion of the experience of family caregivers who provide in-home care to older relatives with chronic health conditions. The prevalence of family care is first described along with information about its estimated cost and value. Next, we move to a discussion of factors that have an impact on the provision and consequences of caregiving. We describe interventions designed to ameliorate the negative effects and strengthen the positive aspects of care provision. The chapter ends with a description of public policies that have been developed to meet the needs and challenges faced by the growing number of family caregivers.

LEARNING OBJECTIVES

After completing this chapter, you should have an understanding of:

- The breadth, depth, and type of care provided by family and friends to older persons with chronic illnesses living in the community
- The demographic characteristics of the informal providers of community-based long-term care
- Theoretical paradigms that describe the connection between informal and formal helpers
- Interventions designed to ameliorate the stress experienced by family and friends who assist older adults in the community
- Public policies that address the needs and well-being of informal providers of community-based care to older adults

KEY TERMS

Elder abuse
Evidence-based intervention
Family caregivers
Formal care
Hierarchical compensatory model
Informal care
National Family Caregiver Support Program (NFCSP)
Primary caregiver
Respite services
Substitution model
Supplementation model
Task-specific model

INTRODUCTION

Older adults with chronic health conditions who need assistance with daily activities typically turn first to family members and friends. These family or **informal care** providers are the preferred source of care for older adults and provide ongoing assistance with a broad range of tasks such as personal care, household help, and activities of daily living. Family caregivers help with tasks ranging from housework, gardening, home maintenance, finances, cooking, and shopping to more personal tasks such as eating, bathing, toileting, and dressing. Regardless of the type and duration of care provision, family members and friends are the preferred source of care for the millions of older adults with chronic conditions living in the community.

DEFINITION OF INFORMAL CARE

For the purposes of this chapter, informal care is the assistance provided by a broadly defined and inclusive network of family and friends. This network is typically unpaid and includes care by spouses and unmarried partners; biological and nonbiological children, grandchildren, nieces, nephews, and other family kin; neighbors; church members; and close friends. Most persons with chronic disabilities could not remain living outside of institutional settings without help from these "informal" caregivers. Persons providing informal care, often termed **family caregivers**, are a broad group of individuals who vary greatly in their backgrounds, the care tasks with which they help, and their relationship and commitment to the person they are assisting.

PREVALENCE

It is challenging to determine the exact prevalence of family caregivers at any one point in time because of the wide variation in how the terms *family caregiver, caregiving*, and *care recipient* are defined. Many family members who are providing assistance do not self-identify as a "caregiver." Rather, these family members see themselves as fulfilling a duty or giving back to the older relative who needs the extra assistance. According to the National Alliance for Caregiving (NAC, 2009), approximately 28 million households in the United States in 2008 had one or more family members who had provided care to an older relative. Approximately 43.5 million adults in the United States served as unpaid caregivers to persons aged 50 and older (NAC, 2009). Other estimates put this number closer to over 50 million unpaid caregivers (National Family Caregivers Association, 2000). The federal Administration on Aging estimated that at any one time, 22.4 million persons are providing family care (Administration on Aging, 2003).

Additional challenges to estimating the prevalence of family care will result from recent changes to diagnostic procedures that identify memory-impairing conditions such as Alzheimer's disease. Continued improvements in diagnostic accuracy and specificity will lead families to receive diagnoses earlier in the disease progression. In turn, the prevalence of dementia will increase as will the number of family members involved in providing care in the home and who self-identify as a "caregiver." For example, research findings on the trajectory of mild cognitive impairment (MCI) as a prodromal or preclinical phase of Alzheimer's disease suggest that persons who previously would not be defined as caregivers would now be categorized as providing assistance to an older relative with Alzheimer's disease (Wilson, Leurgans, Boyle, & Bennett, 2011). Of the households reporting that a family member is involved in providing care, 22% (about 5 million) indicate they are helping someone with dementia symptoms (National Alliance for Caregiving, 1997). It is estimated that 60% to 70% of persons with Alzheimer's disease live at home, and 80% receive assistance from a family member (Alzheimer's Association, 2010a, 2013).

Demographic changes will also influence the prevalence rates of informal caregiving. These changes include: (a) an increasing proportion and number of older adults who require assistance because of increased longevity; (b) a shrinking pool of potential family members available to provide care as a result of lower fertility rates, reflecting the growing number of employed women and postponed child bearing; and (c) geographically dispersed family members (Noelker & Whitlatch, 2005; for more information on demographic changes, see Chapter 1). It is important to note that estimating the number of family caregivers based on the number of older adults who receive help from family will yield inaccurate estimates of caregiving's prevalence. The reason is that many older adults rely on more than one family caregiver. Thus, even though we know that 83% of chronically disabled adults under age 65 and 73% of those over age 65 received help exclusively from family members (Noelker & Whitlatch, 2005; Stone, 1995), we cannot use these figures to estimate the number of family caregivers.

TYPES OF CARE PROVIDED

The type of care provided to older adults depends greatly on the nature and severity of the chronic illness and related functional impairments for which the older adult requires assistance. Approximately 80% of older adults report at least one chronic condition, whereas about 50% report having two or more chronic conditions (Centers for Disease Control and Prevention, 2011). The types of disabilities associated with limitations in activity for older adults living in the community include arthritis and other musculoskeletal conditions (31%), heart and circulatory problems (28%), vision and hearing loss (11%), fractures and joint injuries (8%), diabetes (8%), and emotional and mental disorders (2%). The percentage of community-dwelling older adults who require help with activities of daily living increases with age. Specifically, 10.9% of persons aged 65 to 74, 21.8% of persons aged 75 to 84, and 48.8% of adults 85 years of age and older require assistance with personal activities of daily living (PADLs; bathing, dressing, toileting, feeding, grooming) and instrumental activities of daily living (IADLs; grocery shopping, meal preparation, transportation, finances, legal assistance, mobility, arranging appointments; Stone, 2000).

Additional factors that have an impact on the type, duration, and intensity of assistance provided by family caregivers include characteristics of both the caregiver and the older adult who requires care (Noelker & Whitlatch, 2005). Adults with memory loss (e.g., MCI, Alzheimer's disease, degenerative dementia) have different care needs compared to physically impaired but cognitively intact adults. Caregivers of adults with physical impairments (e.g., stroke, traumatic brain injury, multiple sclerosis) provide a great deal of hands-on assistance with self-care activities such as bathing, eating, dressing, and walking. In addition to assisting with self-care activities, caregivers of adults with memory loss spend a great deal of time and energy assisting with their relative's problem behaviors (e.g., agitation, memory deficits, wandering, and other behaviors such as inappropriate sexual or physically disruptive behaviors; Noelker & Whitlatch, 2005).

Care tasks can also vary depending on the older adult's symptoms and disease progression. Persons in the early stages of dementia or memory loss exhibit more deficits in memory and personality than in self-care tasks. As the disease progresses, cognitive functioning further deteriorates, leading to deficits in self-care activities. With most dementing illnesses, physical difficulties occur later in the disease. Conversely, with conditions such as traumatic brain injury or stroke, adults can be bedfast from the start, with only minor deficits in cognitive functioning. For persons with nondementing illnesses, the progression and outcome of their condition is less certain, and they can experience periods of remission or stability punctuated by acute episodes (Noelker & Whitlatch, 2005). Finally, as hospitals and home-health care agencies increasingly discharge patients who require more complex and technical medical interventions, family caregivers will be expected to provide more medically based care (Levine, 2008). Examples of more medically based care include wound care, feeding tubes, and intravenous therapy.

Family members who do not live near their older relatives provide assistance as well, although this assistance is typically less "hands on." Tasks more common to long-distance caregivers include instrumental assistance such as arranging and/or paying for services (e.g., house cleaning and lawn care), providing financial assistance, in-person visits that provide relief to the local caregivers, and telephone support. Anecdotal evidence from our own work with family caregivers suggests that support is also increasingly provided through electronic resources such as e-mail, text, instant messaging, and social network exchanges that are supportive and encouraging.

COST ESTIMATES AND THE VALUE OF FAMILY CARE

The economic value of providing family care to older adults in the community has been estimated to total $450 billion in 2009, an increase from $375 billion in 2007 (Feinberg, Reinhard, Houser, & Choula, 2011). The assistance provided by family caregivers who are women has an annual estimated value ranging from $148 to $188 billion (Arno, 2002). For persons with Alzheimer's disease, family caregivers provided 17 billion hours of unpaid care, a contribution to the nation valued at over $202 billion (Alzheimer's Association, 2011). In addition to the health care cost savings to society associated with the provision of family care, there are also financial costs to caregivers due to lost wages. It has been estimated that direct health care costs and costs associated with lost wages totaled between $80 and $100 billion for older adults with Alzheimer's disease and the family members who assist them (Hoyert & Rosenberg, 1999; National Institute on Aging, 1998). It is likely that the economic value of family care will continue to increase as will the financial costs incurred by family caregivers.

Given the vast amount of care provided by families and the significant cost savings for publicly funded long-term care programs, it is not surprising that increased attention is being paid to developing policies and programs to support family caregivers in their role. If family members and other informal helpers were to discontinue their care activities, either because they were unwilling or unable to fill this role, the burden would shift to the formal long-term care sector. This increased demand would have a significant impact on the existing long-term care system, which, in its current form, would be unable to support the increased care needs of older and other impaired adults (Noelker & Whitlatch, 2005). In recognition of the changing demographic profile and the central role played by informal caregivers throughout the continuum of long-term care, more public attention and resources are being directed to services and interventions that support family caregiving efforts.

THE EXPERIENCE OF GIVING AND RECEIVING CARE

A variety of characteristics of both the family caregiver and the person who requires care have an impact on the care experience. These characteristics range from an array of sociodemographic factors to family relationship dynamics and cultural values.

SOCIODEMOGRAPHIC CHARACTERISTICS

Gender

It is estimated that 59% to 75% of family caregivers in the United States are women (Arno, 2002), including caregivers who are wives or unmarried partners, daughters and daughters-in-law, nieces, and granddaughters. Female caregivers, regardless of employment status, spend as much as 50% more time providing care than male caregivers (Family Caregiver Alliance, 2001). Women and men differ in the types of tasks with which they help. Women are more likely to provide personal care assistance, whereas men are more likely to help with instrumental tasks such as decision making and financial management. Moreover, women often have multiple roles separate from but in addition to their family caregiving responsibilities such as hands-on health care provider, care/case manager, companion, surrogate decision maker, and advocate (Navaie-Waliser et al., 2002). Research also suggests that caregiving women report greater distress than men. This finding is consistent, regardless of caregiver employment status and whether the older adult has a diagnosis of cancer, dementia, stroke, head injury, physical impairment, or mental illness.

One explanation for these gender differences draws on studies of health and well-being in the general population, indicating that women commonly score higher than men on indicators of stress. As well, women may be more comfortable than men in expressing feelings of stress. It has also been suggested that the nurturant role developed by men in later life may be rewarding or act as a form of repayment for the care they received in the past, which in turn helps to counteract the otherwise negative effects of caregiving (Russell, 2007).

Age

The effects of age on a caregiver's ability to provide care or on how he or she responds to the stress of caregiving vary greatly depending on the caregiver's physical and mental health, coping skills, and socioeconomic resources. Indeed, the effects of age are nearly impossible to disentangle from the effects of other caregiver and older adult characteristics. A caregiver's age and kinship relationship are often identified as being confounded among spouse caregivers, who are typically older than adult children and other groups of caregivers. For older spouse caregivers, it is difficult to determine the origin of stress and whether the consequences of caregiving are related to age and chronic health conditions or to the specific experiences of caregiving. There is also inconsistent evidence about the effect of a caregiver's age on his or her levels and types of distress, with some evidence that older caregivers are more distressed, whereas other studies find younger caregivers to be the more distressed (Whitlatch & Noelker, 1996).

Ethnic, Cultural, and Class Diversity

A growing body of research documents the experience of family caregivers with diverse cultural and ethnic identities. Advances in cross-cultural research have demonstrated diversity among caregivers throughout the world, including differences between developing and developed countries, urban and rural settings, and social class structures. Research in the United States indicates both similarities and differences among caregivers of diverse cultural backgrounds and ethnicities (Aranda & Knight, 1997; Pinquart & Sorensen, 2005). Familial support networks for caregiving are common among Mexican Americans, African Americans, Asian Americans, and European Americans (Greek, Italian, Polish, Irish, etc.). Common across all cultures and ethnic groups is that family care is the most preferred and relied upon source of assistance.

An increasing number of research studies focus on culture and caregiving, yet research in the United States tends to focus on differences between European and non–European American caregivers, paying little attention to the great heterogeneity within different ethnic groups. For example, European American caregivers are frequently compared to Asian, Hispanic, or African American caregivers living in the United States. Growing evidence indicates that differences *among* these groups are less pronounced than differences *within* the groups. In addition, it has been suggested that group differences may be more related to the length of time since immigration rather than to a specific ethnic background. As a result, there has been a call to shift research efforts from intergroup study to intragroup differences.

The intersection of ethnicity and social class creates an interesting yet rarely studied phenomenon in caregiving. Research studies that report differences by cultural background or ethnicity often note that these differences could be compounded by or attributed to differences in class. For example, comparisons among different ethnic groups rarely include samples with diverse income, education, and employment categories (for exceptions, see the review by Dilworth-Anderson, Williams, & Gibson, 2002). Merrill (1997a) notes that, compared to caregivers from middle-class backgrounds, working-class family caregivers report lower usage of adult day programs, are less likely to place their relative in a nursing home, and are more likely to report being motivated by feelings of reciprocity (the desire to "pay parents back"). Additional research is needed to untangle the unique effects of race, ethnicity, and social class because existing research findings are limited and inconsistent.

Family Dynamics, Communication, and Decision Making in Family Care

The onset of providing care to an impaired family member takes many forms. A sudden illness or accident can quickly force a family member into the caregiving role. More slowly progressing illnesses may manifest with very few significant symptoms so that the onset of care goes almost unnoticed. Regardless of the nature and intensity of the onset of care provision, family caregiving is seen as "an evolving set of circumstances" that are dynamic and often unpredictable (Aneshensel, Pearlin, Mullan, Zarit, & Whitlatch, 1995). A period of reorganization is common for families as they work to restructure their lives to care for a family member. It is common for one individual, whether by choice or convenience, to take on the role of "**primary caregiver**" (i.e., the person responsible for the majority of hands on care for the older family member). This "primary" caregiver frequently seeks assistance from other family members, friends, or service providers. Within the family, there is often an unspoken understanding that the primary caregiver is the main person in charge of the care and service coordination for the impaired family member. In many families there is a naturally occurring hierarchy that determines who will become the primary caregiver. If a spouse is available and able to assist, then the spouse is the most likely person to assume the caregiving responsibilities. If a spouse is unavailable or unable to provide care, then a daughter or daughter-in-law often assumes care responsibilities. Among men, husbands are most likely to be caregivers; sons and sons-in-law are much less likely to take on the role. In fact, it is more common for an older woman to be cared for by her daughter-in-law than by her own son.

The quality of the caregiver's relationship with the care receiver is also associated with who will provide care. Family members with contentious or antagonistic relationships with the older adult, or relatives who are viewed as "irresponsible" or "unreliable," are less likely to provide care than those relatives who are more compatible. Unfortunately, when the caregiver and older relative are not compatible, it is common for both to experience heightened distress.

Yet, family caregivers differ in their levels of distress depending on the type of kinship tie they have to the older adult. Typically, caregiving wives report higher levels of emotional distress than do husbands. Differences between adult daughter and wife caregivers are also common, although some studies find daughters to be more distressed, whereas other studies report the reverse (Depp et al., 2005). Interestingly, there is evidence that daughters-in-law are less distressed than daughter caregivers (Merrill, 1997b). In addition, there are exceptions to these findings where no differences are found by kinship tie (Zarit, Todd, & Zarit, 1986). Clearly, further research is needed to determine the nature of kin group differences and how different kin groups might be helped by interventions targeted to their various needs.

Additional factors that influence whether or not a family member will become the primary caregiver include the health of family members, their proximity to the older adult, and the demands of their everyday life. Family members in poor health or at risk for worsening health are less likely to become caregivers. About one third of primary caregivers assume the role because they live closer to the care recipient than other family members. Employed relatives or those with multiple and/or competing family demands are also less likely to be caregivers. However, even under demanding and stressful conditions, family members are still more likely than service providers to care for impaired older persons.

TRANSITIONS IN THE CAREGIVER ROLE: FROM IN-HOME TO INSTITUTIONAL CARE

There is growing evidence that the tasks and responsibilities of caregivers continue, although in a manner that is somewhat altered, once an older relative moves to a residential setting. Current research indicates that caregivers continue to remain very active in the lives of their impaired family members once placement or entry into a residential setting becomes necessary. Family caregivers visit often and frequently travel great distances in order to spend time with their relatives. Caregivers of nursing home residents often perform many of the same tasks they did while caring at home, including assistance with eating, personal care, and walking. In fact, a large majority of caregivers remain very active in the lives of their placed relatives for many years after the initial change in residence has occurred (Zarit & Whitlatch, 1992).

Yet, this continued involvement in care has the potential to add stress to the lives of family caregivers. Once their family member is institutionalized, caregivers must restructure and redefine their lives and adjust to their new role. Thus, the stress of caregiving is not completely alleviated by placement. In fact, a major source of stress for caregivers of relatives in residential settings is guilt: guilt about needing to move their relative into residential care, guilt about visiting often enough or not visiting for longer periods of time. Although these caregivers are relieved of the day-to-day demands of in-home care, many continue to feel distress. Although some caregivers are less distressed, many exhibit symptoms well above their preplacement levels of distress. It appears that placement alters rather than eliminates the stresses of caregiving (Zarit & Whitlatch, 1992).

ETHICS, EXPLOITATION, AND ABUSE IN FAMILY CARE

Ethics are moral principles that influence the behavior of a person or group. Family members share a variety of principles or beliefs about their responsibilities toward each other that are shaped, in part, by the family's history and values. Some of these principles or beliefs are culturally based, whereas others are shaped by ascribed characteristics such as gender and birth order. Taken together, these beliefs and characteristics determine which family member will have primary responsibility for elder care. For example, although first-born males in some Asian cultures are expected to provide for older parents, it is typically the son's wife who ultimately provides the bulk of care for her in-laws. Expectations and perceived responsibilities also evolve over time and are influenced by a family's communication and negotiation styles, values, and history of support and caring. These responsibilities are referred to as "filial obligations" and reflect the family caregiver's perceptions of moral duties or demands regarding elder care. The underpinnings for filial obligations stem from traditions that command parental and elder reverence, the belief that one's parent or elder relative is owed a debt of gratitude, and as a means to express love for the older adult (McCarty et al., 2008).

Within some families, the members' expectations and preferences for care provision are not aligned. This can result in family conflict and an added sense of caregiving burden manifested in emotional disturbance, power struggles, stress, and burnout, as well as the potential for elder neglect and abuse. **Elder abuse** is defined as the infliction of physical, emotional, or psychological harm, financial exploitation, sexual abuse, or intentional or unintentional neglect.

Each year, an estimated 4 million older adults are victims of various forms of abuse and neglect (American Psychological Association, 2012); experts estimate that for every case of abuse or neglect reported to authorities 23 go unreported.

Elder abuse and neglect result from a complex interplay of factors related to familial, caregiver, and cultural issues. According to the American Psychological Association (2012), families more prone to abusive behaviors often have a history of violent interaction, social isolation, extreme stress on one or more members, and poor coping skills. Caregivers who are more likely to abuse or exploit the care receiver frequently report problems with substance abuse, mental or emotional illness such as depression, financial dependency on the care receiver, or feelings of helplessness and entrapment. Moreover, the caregiver of a person with a dementing or mental illness who is abusive is often abusive in return. Cultures with higher incidence rates of elder abuse often define family interactions as completely private, disrespect or devalue older persons, or allow for mistreatment of family members, especially women (American Psychological Association, 2012).

Elder abuse and neglect can be prevented, and the cornerstone is public awareness and education about this social problem. Information about elder abuse and domestic violence is available nationally through a variety of local and national organizations. There are resources available for families to help them reduce or manage care-related stress and burden that may lead to abuse, some of which includes actual and virtual support groups, education and training materials and classes, **respite services** (i.e., a break from providing care), and care management services. Additionally, the website of the National Adult Protective Services Association (NAPSA) provides information about elder abuse and contact information for local adult protective services (APS) organizations. NAPSA was formed in 1989 to provide state APS program administrators and staff with a forum for sharing information, solving problems, and improving the quality of services for victims of elder and vulnerable adult abuse. NAPSA maintains a working relationship with the National Center on Elder Abuse, is funded by the U.S. Administration on Aging, and is a founding member of the Elder Justice Coalition. (See Additional Resources listed at the end of this chapter for more information about elder abuse.)

KINSHIP CARE: MULTIGENERATIONAL HOUSEHOLDS AND GRANDPARENTS RAISING GRANDCHILDREN

Multigenerational households are increasing in number due to the effects of economic recessions, high divorce rates, and adult children returning with their own children to the parent's home. These family configurations are defined as households in which the "householder" lives with family members of different generations and not just with his or her own child (AARP, 2011). The number of multigenerational households is increasing at a dramatic rate. In 2008, there were 6.2 million multigenerational households in the United States (or 5.3% of all households). The economic downturn that began in 2008 is one explanation for the increase to 7.1 million in 2010 (or 6.1% of all U.S. households). This increase was greater than in the previous 8 years combined (AARP, 2011).

A related issue concerns older generations caring for younger generations. It is common for elderly parents to care for their disabled adult or chronically ill children or grandchildren. Within the African American community, increasing numbers of midlife and older women have primary responsibility for their grandchildren and great grandchildren. Typically, a family crisis precipitates grandparent caregiving. Often this occurs when the grandparent's child (whether as a teenager, young adult, or at midlife) becomes unable to care for his or her own child or children. Moreover, the circumstances that lead to a parent's inability to care for his or her own child are typically compounded for grandparents. Low or nonexistent rates of child support, issues with custody arrangements, low incomes, inadequate family leave policies, and a lack of social support as well as their own physical health problems often place grandparent caregivers at risk for developing further difficulties. Differences in this phenomenon are evident by cultural group, with 12% of African American children living with grandparents compared to 5.8% of Hispanics, and 3.6% of Whites.

Grandparents who provide care to a grandchild report a variety of stressors and benefits resulting from their caregiving role. Stressors often reported by kinship caregivers include worsening health, decreased financial resources, work conflict, negative changes to social interactions, and increased family conflict (Musil et al., 2000, 2008). Kinship caregivers also report many rewards, such as improved relationships with their grandchildren, the "second chance" to raise a child better than in the past, and increased social interactions resulting from engagement in their grandchild's school and social activities (Servaty-Seib & Wilkins, 2008). Unfortunately, few programs are designed to meet the specific needs of this vulnerable group of family caregivers.

One exception to this lack of targeted services is the Kinship Care program supported by funding through the Administration on Aging's **National Family Caregiver Support Program** (NFCSP; see the section "Public Policies Pertaining to Family Caregivers" for more information about the NFCSP). Local Area Agencies on Aging receive federal funding through State Units on Aging to provide supportive services to grandparent caregivers aged 60 and older. Services support the needs of grandparent caregivers and include health screenings, respite, socialization, permanency planning (i.e., developing a plan for the grandchild's permanent living situation), family counseling, financial support, and legal support. Kinship Care programs vary by region but attempt to meet the various needs of urban, rural, and suburban caregivers and caregivers of varying socioeconomic backgrounds.

IMPACT OF CAREGIVING

PHYSICAL AND MENTAL HEALTH CONSEQUENCES

There is substantial empirical evidence indicating that the stress of providing in-home care over the long term affects a caregiver's mental and physical health. Caregivers are more depressed than age-matched controls; exhibit deficits in physical health and depressed immunologic functioning as a result of caregiving; and use prescription drugs for depression, anxiety, and insomnia two to three times more often than the rest of the population (Adams, 2008; Dura, Stukenberg, & Kiecolt-Glaser, 1991; Haley, Levine, Brown, Berry, & Hughes, 1987;

Ho, Chan, Woo, Chong, & Sham, 2009; Pinquart & Sorensen, 2003). Caregivers have been found to have impaired immune functioning (Kiecolt-Glaser, Gravenstein, Malarkey, & Sheridan, 1996) and to be in worse physical health compared to family members who are not caregivers (Stone, Cafferata, & Sangl, 1987). (For a review of the physical and mental health effects that result from providing care to a relative, see Schulz & Sherwood, 2010.)

> *I want her to be my wife as long as possible. I don't want to burden her.*
>
> —Husband with early-stage dementia

FINANCES AND EMPLOYMENT CONSEQUENCES

Providing care to an impaired family member is associated with stress to a caregiver's finances, employment, and career. Compared to their age peers in the general population, caregivers are more likely to report adjusted family incomes below the poverty line. Family caregivers in general and caregivers of persons with dementia specifically incur very high out-of-pocket costs as they care for older relatives in the home and in institutional settings. These costs include Medicare premiums, health insurance premiums, and deductibles and copayments for services that are not covered by Medicare, Medicaid, or other sources. According to the Alzheimer's Association (2010b), out-of-pocket costs to people with Alzheimer's and their families will increase $30 billion in 2010 to $157 billion in 2050. Federal funds for health care, long-term care, and hospice for people with dementia are projected to increase dramatically over the next decades. It is estimated that dementia care costs will increase from $172 billion in 2011 to $1.1 trillion in 2050 (in 2011 dollars; Alzheimer's Association, 2010b).

Adding to this financial strain is the reality that the responsibilities of caregiving are associated with increased work stress and changes in work status. Male and female caregivers often decrease the number of hours they work, make the decision to retire early, or leave the workforce completely (Alzheimer's Association, 2010a). Caregivers of relatives with dementia report changing their work schedules or being forced to leave their jobs entirely because of poor performance. Well over half report getting to work late, leaving work early, taking time off, and/or taking a leave of absence (Alzheimer's Association, 2010a). Finally, for employed caregivers, especially those with both child- and adult-care responsibilities, younger caregivers are more likely to experience greater distress as well as absenteeism, interruptions at work, and difficulty in balancing work and family responsibilities.

POSITIVE EFFECTS OF CAREGIVING

Early conceptual models on the effects of caregiving tended to focus on the stress of care provision and the negative impact on caregiver well-being. This has been especially true for models and research examining the experiences of family caregivers of persons with memory loss (e.g., Alzheimer's disease, stroke, Parkinson's disease, frontal temporal dementia, MCI). Subsequently, the research findings related to caregiving stress were used to underscore the needs of caregivers for assistance and support and advocate for policy changes and new service programs. In response to this focus, calls were issued for a more balanced view of caregiving's effects with greater attention to models of adaptation to stress and the positive aspects of caregiving (PAC), often referred to as caregiver gain, satisfaction, and rewards (Miller & Lawton, 1997).

Subsequent studies validated the PAC measure that assesses the extent to which caregiving is viewed as personally satisfying and enriching and as enhancing connections to others (Tarlow et al., 2004). Positive appraisals of caregiving were found to be more commonly expressed by African American caregivers, compared with Caucasian, and they also expressed greater caregiving satisfaction and less burden. Among African American caregivers, the relationship between race and PAC was shown, in part, to be explained by higher religiosity, lower anxiety, and being less upset about care receivers' behaviors.

More recently, attention has turned to the quality of family care and how caregivers' perceptions of quality of care mediate the relationship between their appraisals of caregiving burden and PAC. Caregivers who report providing more "exemplary care" to older relatives with dementia had higher PAC and better emotional outcomes (Harris, Durkin, Allen, DeCoster, & Burgio, 2011). These findings suggest that educating and supporting caregivers to provide exemplary care, that is, person-centered respectful care, can positively affect appraisals of caregiving burden and emotional outcomes.

INTERVENTIONS FOR FAMILY CAREGIVERS

Given the variety, intensity, and duration of care provided by family caregivers, it is not surprising that many families seek assistance from **formal care** professionals. These professionals work with family caregivers to ensure that the older adult is receiving optimal care without the family caregiver sacrificing his or her well-being. The development and implementation of programs that provide care coordination between formal and informal community-based providers has been informed by a number of theoretical paradigms.

THEORETICAL PARADIGMS THAT INFORM THE DEVELOPMENT OF CARE COORDINATION BETWEEN FAMILY AND FORMAL CARE PROVIDERS

Family caregivers and paid providers typically develop personal and "care-related" relationships as they work to provide optimal care for older adults living in the community. The collaboration and coordination between family caregivers and paid providers can have a significant impact on service use and the mental and physical outcomes of family caregivers and older adults. Family caregivers are often the *gatekeepers* to and from the formal care system, influencing when, where, and from whom their older relative obtains services.

They function as *intermediaries* between the older adult and formal helpers by providing and interpreting information about care needs and service effectiveness. Informal caregivers can take the place of or assist professionals by serving as *care managers* seeking out and arranging services for the care receiver, helping to coordinate services and monitoring service quality. Existing service gaps and fragmentation along the long-term care continuum have also forced family caregivers to function as *facilitators*, smoothing transitions between care settings, such as from hospital to home or home to nursing home. Family caregivers who have close relationships with the older adult can be ideal *advocates* who work to coordinate high-quality care. Family caregivers who fill these roles are essential partners to service providers in the provision of care to chronically disabled persons (Noelker & Whitlatch, 2005).

Several theoretical models provide the foundation for understanding the connection between family and formal caregivers. First, the **hierarchical compensatory model** describes a preferred order as to who provides care. This order is typically based on the closeness of family relationships (Cantor, 1979). Family care is expected to be performed by the closest available and capable family member with spouses as first choice, followed by children, other kin, friends or neighbors, and formal helpers as the last option. For older adults who are more severely impaired and/or need more assistance, or when the availability of informal helpers is limited, there is more fluidity and overlap between family and paid helpers.

The **task-specific model** (Litwak, 1985) suggests that the appropriate provider of support is dictated by the type of task with which help is needed. Family is seen as best suited for assisting with nontechnical, nonmedical tasks and tasks that cannot be easily scheduled, such as toileting and transferring from chair to bed. Paid providers can best manage tasks requiring specialized knowledge and training that can be scheduled, such as wound care. The allocation of tasks reflects a clear division of labor with task segregation occurring between family and paid helpers. This arrangement minimizes the likelihood of conflict and other negative outcomes occurring between the family and paid helpers (Noelker & Whitlatch, 2005).

The **supplementation model** views formal care as supplementing the care provided by family, thus lessening the time-consuming and potentially exhausting demands on family caregivers (Edelman & Hughes, 1990). A large portion of the assistance needed by chronically ill and disabled elderly individuals is routine help with personal care and daily activities rather than technical and specialized care. Once the older adult requires more technical care, formal helpers step in to provide supplemental assistance.

Conversely, the **substitution model** assumes that given the option, families would choose or substitute formal care in place of providing care within the family (Greene, 1983). It is widely recognized that the public sector cannot assume the full cost of long-term care for disabled persons. Public planners and policy makers who advocate expanded reimbursement for community- and home-based services often discount the substitution model because it projects that the demand for and use of publically funded services would surpass the availability. However, little empirical evidence exists that suggests that families exit their role as the primary source of assistance to older impaired relatives once services become more available. When families have the financial resources and choose to purchase care from agencies or independent providers, they typically remain involved as care managers or overseers (Whitlatch & Noelker, 1996).

These conceptual models provide the foundation for understanding the coordination of care between family and formal helpers. The models have various degrees of empirical support, yet this support is inconsistent and limited in its application for improving the provision of long-term services to older adults and ensuring the well-being of family caregivers. The diverse experiences and needs of families make it unlikely that a single model will be able to capture the entire range of approaches that reflect the intersection of family and formal care. With improved understanding, we can develop more appropriate methods for supporting family caregivers and lessening the negative impact of providing care.

COGNITIVE BEHAVIORAL AND PSYCHOSOCIAL INTERVENTIONS

A variety of interventions have been developed and evaluated that target specific areas of caregiver stress. Many of these interventions have undergone rigorous evaluations and have resulted in a solid **evidence-based** array of programs that show promise for alleviating caregiver stress and negative outcomes (see Additional Resources for website information for the Rosalynn Carter Institute [2010] list of evidence-based family caregiver programs).

One landmark study of caregiver stress, the REACH project (Resources for Enhancing Alzheimer's Caregiver Health; see Schulz et al., 2003), evaluated the effectiveness of social and behavioral interventions for family caregivers. The findings from this longitudinal multisite study led to the development of a multicomponent intervention designed to alleviate stress of family caregivers of individuals with Alzheimer's disease or related conditions. The intervention (REACH II) utilized a risk-appraisal approach that identified a caregiver's level of risk in five areas: depression, burden, self-care, social support, and problem behaviors of the relative with dementia. Once risks were identified, intervention strategies were delivered, including education about the disease, the development of skills to manage troublesome care recipient behaviors, and enhancement of social support, as well as strategies for cognitively reframing negative emotional responses and enhancing healthy behaviors (Belle et al., 2006). Results of REACH II evaluations indicate that this targeted and structured multicomponent intervention improved caregiver self-reported health, while decreasing burden and "bother" in Hispanic or Latino, African American, and Caucasian caregiving populations (Elliott, Burgio, & DeCoster, 2010). REACH II investigators have developed related programs that have shown varied effectiveness, targeting a variety of populations and utilizing in-person and/or telephone intervention techniques (e.g., REACH OUT; Burgio, 2009; Care PRO, Coon, Thompson, Steffen, Sorocco, & Gallagher-Thompson, 2003; Gallagher-Thompson et al., 2003).

Additional innovative interventions that have been developed and tested include Reducing Disability in Alzheimer's Disease or RDAD (Teri et al.,

2003, pg. 87), the Savvy Caregiver (Hepburn, Lewis, Sherman, & Tornatore, 2003), and the Integrated Telephone-Linked Care intervention or TLC (Mahoney, Tarlow, & Jones, 2003). RDAD is an in-home education program delivered by trainers that combines teaching the caregiver how to manage dementia-related behavior problems with exercise training for the care receiver to improve strength, balance, and flexibility. Evaluation findings showed that care receivers in the program had better physical function, less depression, and were less likely to be institutionalized than those who did not. In contrast, the Savvy Caregiver is a 12-hour packaged training program that was shown to be effective in increasing caregivers' knowledge and skills and reducing stress and burden. It includes manuals, a videotape, and a CD-ROM and can be self-taught, making it well-suited for caregivers in geographically isolated areas. The TLC intervention, a third approach to educating caregivers of persons with dementing disorders, has been shown to increase mastery and reduce anxiety and depression. A telephone-based interactive voice response intervention helps family caregivers to manage disruptive behaviors related to dementia, to learn strategies for lowering stress levels, and to gain access to experts in Alzheimer's disease.

> *[The program] helped us make an effort to make exercise an important part of our life.*
>
> —Husband with dementia

RESPITE

Respite care is defined as any service or assistance that provides a family caregiver with the opportunity to take a break from care responsibilities. Respite takes many different forms and can be provided by an in-home care provider, family members or friends, an adult day program, or a residential facility that offers short- or long-term stays. These examples of respite care provide supervision for the impaired relative while the caregiver takes care of other responsibilities (e.g., goes to work) or takes care of him- or herself (e.g., visits with friends, goes on a trip, or takes time to be alone at home). In-home respite can be provided by a family member, friend, or paid provider who comes into the caregiver's home to provide custodial care for a few hours at a time during the week or on weekends. Adult day programs require the older adult to travel to the center where staff members monitor the older adult for longer periods of time. These programs offer a wide variety of recreational activities, field trips, a meal and snacks, personal care assistance, medical care management, and even transportation to and from the center (see Chapter 7). Residential facilities also offer respite options, but for more extended periods (e.g., weekends or several days). In this case, the older relative stays in the facility and is provided with round-the-clock care.

Respite care varies widely in cost, availability, accessibility, and flexibility. Some caregiver-focused programs provide financial compensation to relatives of caregivers who provide care and supervision to the older relative while the caregiver enjoys a variety of innovative forms of respite (see Family Caregiver Alliance and ARCH National Respite Network and Resource Center in the Additional Resources of this chapter for information on respite). This type of option allows a person who is familiar with the older relative to provide care (while the caregiver takes a break) and receive financial compensation for his/her time. The NFCSP provides funding through local Area Agencies on Aging for the provision of respite for family caregivers, including grandparents caring for grandchildren. These and other programs are examples of innovative and flexible forms of respite that meet the changing and diverse needs of caregivers (e.g., weekend and evening respite options, relaxation and healthy living "get-aways," and family-provided respite).

DYADIC INTERVENTIONS THAT TARGET BOTH THE FAMILY CAREGIVER AND THE OLDER ADULT

For the most part, interventions for families focus on assisting *either* the older adult with chronic health conditions, *or* the primary family caregiver. This separation of older adult and family caregiver has been the natural result of funding sources that recognize and reimburse for services that treat one but not the other or both persons in the "care dyad." Until recently, very few services simultaneously took into account both the older adult *and* the family caregiver. Increasingly, interventions that target both members of the care dyad have shown promise for improving outcomes.

One dyadic intervention, Acquiring New Skills While Enhancing Remaining Strengths (*ANSWERS*; Judge, Yarry, & Orsulic-Jeras, 2010; Yarry, Judge, & Orsulic-Jeras, 2010), is a six-session cognitive-rehabilitation and educational program that teaches care dyads a core set of skills related to effective communication, managing memory, staying active, and recognizing emotions and behaviors. Individuals with disabilities (IWDs) and their family caregivers have found the *ANSWERS* program highly acceptable and feasible (Judge et al., 2010) and IWDs have reported less distress in managing PADLs, decreased relationship strain with their primary caregiver (i.e., role strain), and less anxiety.

A second dyadic intervention is the SHARE program: Support, Health, Activities, Resources, and Education (previously referred to as EDDI: Early Diagnosis Dyadic Intervention; Whitlatch, Judge, Zarit, & Femia, 2006). This six-session program is conducted by trained clinicians who work with the IWD and family caregiver to help them understand dementia, discuss their values and preferences for care, improve communication, enhance healthy behaviors, and resolve conflicts about autonomy, social interactions, and quality of care. Preliminary findings suggest that the SHARE program is acceptable and feasible (Whitlatch et al., 2006) and leads to positive outcomes for both care partners (Whitlatch, 2007). SHARE is currently undergoing additional refining of techniques and materials through a randomized control trial funded by the U.S. Department of Health and Human Services Administration on Aging (see Case Study 3.1 for an example of how the SHARE program can support families).

Case Study 3.1: How the SHARE Program Can Help Families

Mr. Johnson is a 79-year-old caregiver to his 76-year-old wife with unspecified dementia. He is the sole provider of care for his wife, and he wants it to "stay that way." The couple has lived in their inner-ring suburban home for 45 years. Mr. Johnson reports himself to be in "good health," but attributes his good health to high blood pressure medication, a healthy diet, and daily walks around the neighborhood. Mr. Johnson does not identify as a "caregiver," but as a "devoted husband" who loves his wife and knows that if their situation was reversed, Mrs. Johnson would be taking care of him. Mrs. Johnson has not received a formal diagnosis, but their family physician believes she has some confusion related to her age, and poor vision and hearing.

The couple heard a radio announcement on their local station advertising help for families concerned about memory loss. They called the service agency connected to the announcement and learned about a program that was available to help people concerned about memory. The couple participated in a six-session SHARE program designed to help families facing the challenges of memory loss. The program helped the couple (a) improve their communication skills, (b) understand the importance of Mrs. Johnson receiving a thorough evaluation of her symptoms, (c) discuss their current and future care values and preferences, (d) engage in discussions about maintaining a healthy lifestyle and staying involved with family and friends, and (e) develop a potential plan of care that the couple can refer to in the future if Mrs. Johnson's symptoms worsen.

During the time that they were enrolled in the SHARE program, and at the suggestion of their intervention counselor, Mrs. Johnson was evaluated by a neurologist, who diagnosed her with MCI. The couple was able to discuss their concerns, fears, and expectations with their SHARE counselor. As a result of their discussions with their counselor, the couple's plan of care was more realistic and potentially more effective than had they postponed the evaluation until after they had completed the program. In addition, the intervention helped the couple understand the progressive nature of memory loss, which prompted them to develop a realistic plan of care that met their current and future care needs.

Care Consultation, a third dyadic intervention, is a telephone-based program that delivers information to caregivers and impaired older adults about health conditions, available resources, enhancing informal and formal support, and emotional support (Bass et al., 2013). Care consultants work with caregivers and older adults in an ongoing fashion, with the frequency of telephone contacts dependent on needs. Care consultation is modeled after empowerment and consumer-driven philosophies and is designed as a collaboration among caregivers, older adults, and care consultants who work together to develop a care plan. Care consultation is an excellent example of an **evidence-based intervention** because of its proven feasibility, efficacy, and effectiveness with many groups of persons with chronic health care issues and their caregivers. Outcomes that have been evaluated include psychosocial well-being and care-related strain; hospital, emergency department, and nursing home service use; and cost of care (Bass, personal communication, 2011; Rosalynn Carter Institute website, 2010).

PUBLIC POLICIES PERTAINING TO FAMILY CAREGIVERS

PUBLIC POLICY IN THE UNITED STATES

In the 1980s, an important shift in U.S. public policy occurred that presaged a growing emphasis on home- and community-based care and diminished reliance on institutional care. The first landmark piece of legislation passed in 1983 resulted in the Medicare hospital prospective payment system that effectively transferred 21 million hospital days to home and community (Harrington, Newcomer, & Estes, 1985). The more rapid hospital discharge of older persons "sicker and quicker" placed greater burdens on informal caregivers and also spurred the growth of home care agencies.

The second legislative breakthrough, the Americans with Disabilities Act (ADA), occurred in 1990. This wide-ranging civil rights law prohibited discrimination based on disability in employment and promoted the (re)design of physical environments to accommodate persons with disabilities. In 2009, this legislation was amended to include disability protections in all public entities (e.g., municipal, state) and public transportation requiring the provision of paratransit services by public entities.

NATIONAL FAMILY CAREGIVER SUPPORT PROGRAM

In 2000, the National Family Caregiver Support Program (NFCSP) was funded through the Older Americans Act reauthorization to address caregivers' needs for assistance. This legislation is the most comprehensive federal legislation supporting family caregivers to date. States are expected to work with the 56 State Units on Aging and 629 Area Agencies on Aging to implement caregiver services and support in five areas: (a) information about available caregiver services, (b) assistance in gaining access to services, (c) counseling and the organization of support groups and caregiver training, (d) respite care, and (e) other services that complement the assistance provided by caregivers. These services are designed to support caregivers of older relatives, grandparents, and other related caregivers of children age 18 and younger, and older adults caring for persons with developmental disabilities (Fox-Grage, Coleman, & Blancato, 2001).

CASH AND COUNSELING DEMONSTRATION AND REPLICATION

In 1998, the Cash and Counseling Program was launched in three states to help meet the personal care needs of older Medicaid consumers and their family caregivers. Under this program, older consumers had the option to manage a flexible budget and decide which services best meet their personal care needs and who should provide assistance, including hiring and paying family members to provide care. Since 2009, when the replication study within 12 states ended, states have continued to develop and expand participant-directed care options under state Medicaid-funded personal assistance services through new provisions in the 2005 Deficit Reduction Act and under the 2006 reauthorization of the Older Americans Act. Although more family caregivers now receive some financial compensation under participant-directed care programs, the wages are typically lower than average and do not cover all of the hours of care actually provided.

LOOKING TO THE FUTURE

Although the United States has made progress in the evolution of its public policies supporting family caregivers, there are a number of areas in which further advances are needed. Although the NFCSP provides a partial national caregiver strategy, support for family caregivers is highly variable across the 50 states. In March 2010, the Patient Protection and Affordable Care Act became public law. This legislation was designed primarily to expand health insurance coverage to all Americans, although it does include provisions that benefit family caregivers. Some of these provisions include training programs for family caregivers, incentives for states to increase access to home- and community-based services in Medicaid programs, and expanded access to care coordination and transitional care services. Additional provisions that are beneficial to caregivers include protection from having a health insurance policy cancelled if the policy holder gets sick, a ban on lifetime limits, no denial of coverage for pre-existing conditions, and the option of a free annual wellness checkup that can lead to a prevention plan to keep the caregiver and family member healthy.

SUMMARY

Family caregivers have and will continue to provide a significant portion of the long-term community-based care to the millions of older family members with chronic physical and mental health conditions. This care varies in its type, intensity, and duration, and its economic value is estimated to be nearly $450 billion. Family care is the preferred method of care provision for both the givers and receivers of care, across a variety of ethnic and socioeconomic groups.

Family caregivers report a variety of negative outcomes related to the care role, including depression; anxiety; anger; guilt; resentment; compromised immune functioning; social isolation; and stress related to employment, finances, and family conflict. Yet caregivers also report positive experiences and outcomes resulting from their care role, including personal gain, improved sense of identity, mastery, and feelings of reciprocity and competency. A variety of interventions target negative outcomes while enhancing the many strengths caregivers bring to their caregiving experience. There are a growing number of grandparent caregivers whose needs are both similar to and different from the needs of family members who provide assistance to older relatives. Targeted and evidence-based interventions and supportive services show great promise for meeting the changing and long-term needs of family caregivers.

An increasing number of public and private programs have been developed to meet the dynamic and long-term needs of family caregivers. These programs vary in their focus and eligibility criteria, which has resulted in a system of support that is disjointed and inconsistent across states and regions. Clearly, family caregivers are and will continue to play a significant role in the delivery of physical and mental health care to older adults in the United States and throughout the world. Improvements and innovations in caregiver support programs will help to ensure that family caregivers receive the assistance they need so that they can continue to provide the hands-on care their relatives require.

FOOD FOR THOUGHT

If you (or someone you loved) was experiencing memory loss, would you seek a medical diagnosis or would you want your loved one to seek a medical diagnosis? Why or why not?

DISCUSSION QUESTIONS

1. How does the type of care provided by a caregiver vary depending on the care recipient's diagnosis and care requirements? How does the type of care provided impact the caregiver's physical and mental health?
2. What is one of the most important strategies for preventing elder abuse and neglect? Why do so many cases of elder abuse and neglect go unreported each year?
3. What is "respite," and how can it help family caregivers?
4. Why would a "dyadic" intervention be a useful strategy for helping caregivers and the relatives for whom they provide care?

ADDITIONAL RESOURCES

ARCH National Respite Network and Resource Center http://archrespite.org
Eldercare Locator www.eldercare.gov
Family Caregiver Alliance www.caregiver.org
National Adult Protective Services Association www.apsnetwork.org

National Alliance on Caregiving www.caregiving.org
National Association of Area Agencies on Aging www.n4a.org
National Center on Elder Abuse www.ncea.aoa.gov
Rosalynn Carter Institute www.rosalynncarter.org

REFERENCES

AARP, Public Policy Institute. (2011). *Fact sheet: Multigenerational households are increasing*. Retrieved from http://assets.aarp.org/rgcenter/ppi/econ-sec/fs221-housing.pdf

Adams, K. B. (2008). Specific effects of caring for a spouse with dementia: Differences in depressive symptoms between caregiver and non-caregiver spouses. *International Psychogeriatrics, 20*, 508–520.

Administration on Aging. (2003). *Family caregiving*. Retrieved from http://www.aoa.gov

According to the Alzheimer's Association (2010), out-of-pocket costs to people with Alzheimer's and their families will increase $30 billion in 2010 to $157 billion in 2050.

Alzheimer's Association. (2010a). Alzheimer's disease facts and figures. *Alzheimer's & Dementia, 6*, 158–194.

Alzheimer's Association. (2010b). *Changing the trajectory of Alzheimer's disease: A national imperative* (p. 154). Retrieved from http://www.alz.org/documents_custom/alz_medicarecosts.pdf

Alzheimer's Association. (2011). Alzheimer's disease facts and figures. *Alzheimer's & Dementia, 7*, 298–244.

Alzheimer's Association. (2013). *Alzheimer's disease facts and figures*. Retrieved from www.alz.org/downloads/facts_figures_2013.pdf

American Psychological Association. (2012). *Elder abuse and neglect: In search of solutions*. Washington, DC: Author.

Aneshensel, C. S., Pearlin, L. I., Mullan, J. T., Zarit, S. H., & Whitlatch, C. J. (1995). *Profiles in caregiving: The unexpected career*. New York, NY: Academic Press.

Aranda, M. P., & Knight, B. G. (1997). The influence of ethnicity and culture on the caregiver stress and coping process: A sociocultural review and analysis. *The Gerontologist, 37*(3), 342–354.

Arno, P. S. (2002, February). *The economic value of informal caregiving, U.S. 2000*. Paper presented at the annual meeting of the American Association for Geriatric Psychiatry, Florida.

Bass, D. M., Judge, K. S., Snow, A. L., Wilson, N. L., Morgan, R., Looman, W. J., ... Kunik, M. E. (2013). Caregiver outcomes of Partners in Dementia Care: Effect of a care coordination program for veterans with dementia and their family members and friends. *Journal of the American Geriatrics Society, 61*(8), 1377–1386. doi: 10.1111/jgs.12362

Belle, S. H., Burgio, L., Burns, R., Coon, D., Czaja, S. J., Gallagher-Thompson, D., ... Zhang, S. (2006). Enhancing the quality of life of dementia caregivers from different ethnic or racial groups: A randomized, controlled trial. *Annals of Internal Medicine, 145*(10), 727–738.

Burgio, L. (2009). Translating the REACH caregiver intervention for use by area agency on aging personnel: The REACH OUT program. *The Gerontologist, 49*, 103–116.

Cantor, M. H. (1979). Neighbors and friends: An overlooked resource in the informal support system. *Research on Aging, 1*, 434–463.

Centers for Disease Control and Prevention. (2011). *Healthy aging: Helping people to live long and productive lives and enjoy a good quality of life*. Retrieved from http://www.cdc.gov/chronicdisease/resources/publications/aag/aging.htm

Coon, D. W., Thompson, L. W., Steffen. A., Sorocco, K., & Gallagher-Thompson, D. (2003). Anger and depression management: Psychoeducational skill training interventions for women caregivers of a relative with dementia. *The Gerontologist, 43*, 678–689.

Depp, C., Sorocco, K., Kasl-Godley, J., Thompson, L., Rabinowitz, Y., & Gallagher-Thompson, D. (2005). Caregiver self-efficacy, ethnicity, and kinship differences in dementia caregivers. *American Journal of Geriatric Psychiatry, 13*(9), 787–794.

Dilworth-Anderson, P., Williams, I. C., & Gibson, B. E. (2002). Issues of race, ethnicity, and culture in caregiving research: A 20-year review (1980–2000). *The Gerontologist, 42,* 237–272.

Dura, J. R., Stukenberg, K. W., & Kiecolt-Glaser, J. K. (1991). Anxiety and depressive disorders in adult children caring for demented parents. *Psychology and Aging, 6,* 467–473.

Edelman, P., & Hughes, S. (1990). The impact of community care on provision of informal care to homebound elderly persons. *Journal of Gerontology: Social Science, 45*(2), S74–S84.

Elliott, A. F., Burgio, L. D., & DeCoster, J. (2010). Enhancing caregiver health: Findings from the resources for enhancing Alzheimer's caregiver health II intervention. *Journal of the American Geriatrics Society, 58*(1), 30–37. doi: 10.1111/j.1532-5415.2009.02631x

Family Caregiver Alliance. (2001). *Incidence and prevalence of the major causes of adult-onset brain impairment* [Fact sheet]. San Francisco, CA: Family Caregiver Alliance.

Feinberg, L. F., Reinhard, S. C., Houser, A., & Choula, R. (2011). *Valuing the invaluable: 2011 update the growing contributions and costs of family caregiving.* Washington, DC: AARP, Public Policy Institute. Retrieved from http://assets.aarp.org/rgcenter/ppi/ltc/i51-caregiving.pdf

Fox-Grage, W., Coleman, B., & Blancato, R. B. (2001, October). *Federal and state policy in family caregiving: Recent victories but uncertain future (Executive Summary No. 2).* San Francisco, CA: Family Caregiver Alliance.

Gallagher-Thompson, D., Coon, D., Solano, N., Ambler, C., Rabinowitz, R., & Thompson, L. (2003). Change in indices of distress among Latina and Anglo female caregivers of elderly relatives with dementia: Site specific results from the REACH National Collaborative Study. *The Gerontologist, 43,* 580–591.

Greene, V. L. (1983). Substitution between formally and informally provided care for the impaired elderly in the community. *Medical Care, 21,* 609–619.

Haley, W. E., Levine, E. G., Brown, S. L., Berry, J. W., & Hughes, G. H. (1987). Psychological, social and health consequences of caring for a relative with senile dementia. *Journal of the American Geriatrics Society, 35,* 405–411.

Harrington, C., Newcomer, R. J., & Estes, C. L. (1985). *Long-term care of the elderly: Public policy issues.* Beverly Hills, CA: Sage.

Harris, G. M., Durkin, D. W., Allen, R. S., DeCoster, J., & Burgio, L. D. (2011). Exemplary care as a mediator of the effects of caregiver subjective appraisal and emotional outcomes. *The Gerontologist, 51*(3), 332–342.

Hepburn, K. W., Lewis, M., Sherman, C. W., & Tornatore, J. (2003). The Savvy Caregiver Program: Developing and testing a transportable dementia family caregiver training program. *The Gerontologist, 43*(6), 908–915.

Ho, S. C., Chan, C., Woo, J., Chong, P., & Sham, A. (2009). Impact of caregiving on health and quality of life: A comparative population-based study of caregivers for elderly persons and noncaregivers. *Journals of Gerontology: Biological Sciences, 64*(8), 873–879.

Hoyert, D. L., &. Rosenberg, H. M. (1999). *Mortality from Alzheimer's disease: An update* (National Vital Statistics Reports, Vol. 47, No. 20). Washington, DC: National Center for Health Statistics.

Judge, K. S., Yarry, S. J., & Orsulic-Jeras, S. (2010). Acceptability and feasibility results of a strength-based skills training program for dementia caregiving dyads. *The Gerontologist, 50*(3), 408–417.

Kiecolt-Glaser, J. K., Glaser, R., Gravenstein, S., Malarkey, W. B., & Sheridan, J. (1996). Chronic stress alters the immune response to influenza virus vaccine in older adults. *Proceedings of the National Academy of Sciences, USA, 93,* 3043–3047.

Levine, C. (2008). Family caregiving. In M. Crowley (Ed.), *From birth to death and bench to clinic: The Hastings Center bioethics briefing book for journalists, policymakers, and campaigns*. Garrison, NY: The Hastings Center.

Litwak, E. (1985). Complementary roles for formal and informal support groups: A study of nursing homes and mortality rates. *Journal of Applied Behavioral Sciences, 21*(4), 407–425.

Mahoney, D., Tarlow, B., & Jones, R. (2003). Effects of an automated telephone support system on caregiver burden and anxiety: Findings from the REACH for Telephone-Linked Care Intervention study. *The Gerontologist, 43*(4), 556–567.

McCarty, E. F., Hendricks, C. S., Hendricks, D. L., & McCarty, K. M. (2008). Ethical dimensions and filial caregiving. *Online Journal of Health Ethics, 5*(1), 81.

Merrill, D. M. (1997a). Just plain folk: Class, ethnicity, and gender. In D. M. Merill (Ed.) *Caring for elderly parents: Juggling work, family, and caregiving in middle and working class families* (pp. 147–157). Westport, CT: Auburn House.

Merrill, D. M. (1997b). Daughters-in-law as caregivers. In D. M. Merill (Ed.) *Caring for elderly parents: Juggling work, family, and caregiving in middle and working class families* (pp. 113–126). Westport, CT: Auburn House.

Miller, B., & Lawton, M. P. (1997). Positive aspects of caregiving: Finding balance in caregiver research. *The Gerontologist, 37*(2), 216–217.

Musil, C. M., Schrader, S., & Mutikani, J. (2000). Social support, stress and special coping tasks of grandmother caregivers. In C. Cox (Ed.), *To grandmother's house we go and stay: Perspectives on custodial grandparents* (pp. 56–70). New York, NY: Springer Publishing Company.

Musil, C. M., Warner, C. B., McNamara, M., Rokoff, S., & Turek, D. (2008). Parenting concerns of grandparents raising grandchildren: An insider's picture. In B. Hayslip, Jr. & P. Kaminski (Eds.), *Parenting the custodial grandchild: Implications for clinical practice* (pp. 101–114). New York, NY: Springer Publishing Company.

National Alliance for Caregiving in collaboration with American Association of Retired Persons. (2009). *Caregiving in the U.S.* Retrieved from http://www.caregiving.org/data/Caregiving_in_the_US_2009_full_report.pdf

National Alliance for Caregiving and the American Association of Retired Persons (NAC/AARP). (1997). *Family caregiving in the U.S.: Findings from a national survey*. Retrieved from http://www.caregiving.org/data/Family%20Caregiving%20in%20the%20US.pdf

National Family Caregivers Association. (2000). *National Family Caregivers Association survey 2000*. Retrieved from http://www.nfcacares.org/who_are_family_caregivers/2000_survey.cfm

National Institute on Aging. (1998). *Progress report on Alzheimer's disease, 1998*. Bethesda, MD: National Institutes of Health.

Navaie-Waliser, M., Feldman, P. H., Gould, D. A., Levine, C., Kuerbis, A. N., & Donelan, K. (2002). When the caregiver needs care: The plight of vulnerable family caregivers. *American Journal of Public Health, 92*(3), 409–413.

Noelker, L. S., & Whitlatch, C. J. (2005). Informal caregiving. In C. J. Evashwick (Ed.), *The continuum of long-term care* (3rd ed.). Stamford, CT: Delmar.

Pinquart, M., & Sorensen, S. (2003). Differences between caregivers and non-caregivers in psychological health and physical health: A meta-analysis. *Psychology and Aging, 18*(2), 250–267.

Pinquart, M., & Sorensen, S. (2005). Ethnic differences in stressors, resources, and psychological outcomes of family caregiving: A meta-analysis. *The Gerontologist, 45*(1), 90–106.

Russell, R. (2007). The work of elderly men caregivers: From public careers to an unseen world. *Men and Masculinities, 9*(3), 298–314.

Schulz, R., Burgio, L., Burns, R., Eisdorf, C., Gallagher-Thompson, D., Gitlin, L. N., & Mahoney, D. (2003). Resources for enhancing Alzheimer's caregiver health (REACH): Overview, site-specific outcomes, and future directions. *The Gerontologist, 43*(4), 514–520.

Schulz, R., & Sherwood, P. R. (2010). Mental and physical health effects of family caregivers. *Journal of Social Work Education, 44*(3), 105–113.

Servaty-Seib, H. L., & Wilkins, M. (2008). Examining the losses and gains experienced by grandparents raising grandchildren: A practical framework for intervention and research. In B. Hayslip & T. Kaminski (Eds.), *Parenting the custodial grandchild: Implications for clinical practice* (pp. 181–196). New York, NY: Springer Publishing Company.

Stone, R. I. (1995). Foreword. In R. A. Kane & J. D. Penrod (Eds.), *Family caregiving in an aging society*. Thousand Oaks, CA: Sage.

Stone, R. I. (2000). *Long-term care for the elderly with disabilities: Current policy, emerging trends, and implications for the twenty-first century*. New York, NY: Milbank Memorial Fund.

Stone, R. I., Cafferata, G. L., & Sangl, J. (1987). Caregivers of the frail elderly: A national profile. *The Gerontologist, 27*, 616–626.

Tarlow, B. J., Wisniewski, S. R., Belle, S. H., Rubert, M., Ory, M. G., & Gallagher-Thompson, D. (2004). Positive aspects of caregiving: Contributions of the REACH project to the development of new measures for Alzheimer's caregiving. *Research on Aging, 26*(4), 426–453.

Teri, L., Gibbons, L. E., McCurry, S. M., Logsdon, R. G., Buchner, D. M., Barlow, W. E., ... Larson, E. B. (2003). Exercise plus behavior management in patients with Alzheimer's disease: A randomized trial. *Journal of the American Medical Association, 290*(15), 2015–2022.

Whitlatch, C. J. (2007, March). *Early stage interventions for family caregivers and persons with dementia*. Paper presented at the Joint Conference of the American Society on Aging and the National Council on Aging, Chicago, IL.

Whitlatch, C. J., Judge, K., Zarit, S. H., & Femia, F. (2006). A dyadic intervention for family caregivers and care receivers in early stage dementia. *The Gerontologist, 46*(5), 688–694.

Whitlatch, C. J., & Noelker, L. S. (1996). Caregiving and caring. In J. E. Birren (Ed.), *The Encyclopedia of Gerontology*. New York, NY: Academic Press.

Wilson, R. S., Leurgans, S. E., Boyle, P. A., & Bennett, D. A. (2011). Cognitive decline in prodromal Alzheimer disease and mild cognitive impairment. *Archives of Neurology*, 68(3), 351–356.

Yarry, S. J., Judge, K. S., & Orsulic-Jeras, S. (2010). Applying a strength-based intervention for dyads with mild to moderate memory loss: Two case examples. *Dementia, 9*(4), 549–557.

Zarit, S. H., & Whitlatch, C. J. (1992). Institutional placement: Phases of the transition. *The Gerontologist, 32*, 665–672.

Zarit, S. H., Todd, P. A., & Zarit, J. M. (1986). Subjective burden of husbands and wives as caregivers: A longitudinal study. *The Gerontologist, 26*(3), 260–266.

Family Involvement in Residential Long-Term Care

MELANIE N. G. JACKSON
JOSEPH E. GAUGLER

CHAPTER OVERVIEW

This chapter focuses on family involvement in residential long-term care. We begin by providing background information on family caregiving with a focus on dementia caregiving. Against this backdrop, various types of family involvement in residential long-term care are defined and the role of family in long-term care in both nursing home and assisted living facilities is explored. Interventions for family involvement in residential settings are then considered. The chapter concludes with discussion of current limitations in creating interventions and policies for family involvement in residential long-term care.

LEARNING OBJECTIVES

The aim of this chapter is to provide the reader with a more in-depth understanding of how family involvement occurs in residential long-term care and how such involvement can be promoted. After completing this chapter, you should have an understanding of:

- Family involvement in residential long-term care, which consists of visiting, personal care, instrumental care, socioemotional support, monitoring, and advocacy
- Models of family involvement, including supplementation, substitution, kin dependence, and dual specialization
- The many factors that can influence family involvement in residential environments
- The philosophies guiding the culture change movement in nursing home environments and the implications this has for family involvement
- Interventions that promote and enhance family involvement in residential long-term care

KEY TERMS

Assisted living	Nursing home
Caregiving career	Preservative care
Culture change movement	Primary caregivers
Dual specialization	Progressive surrogacy
Eden Alternative	Secondary caregivers
Family involvement	Substitution model
Kin dependency	Supplementation model

INTRODUCTION

Long-term care for older adults with chronic illness is generally provided by two sources: informal, or unpaid, caregivers and/or formal (i.e., paid) caregivers. The term *informal/family caregiver* refers to individuals who care for family members or friends requiring assistance due to illness or disability, whereas the term *paid caregiver* refers to health care providers and other professionals who are trained and paid for their services (Family Caregiver Alliance, 2001; White House Conference on Aging, 2010). For the purposes of this chapter, the roles of informal caregivers are a primary focus. Informal caregivers are diverse in terms of their kin relationship to persons requiring care (e.g., spouse, adult child), the amount and type of care actually provided (personal care, medication management, help with shopping or appointments), and living arrangement (living in the same household as the person receiving care or living some distance away from the care recipient). Informal care providers are often categorized as "primary" or "secondary" caregivers. A **"primary" caregiver** is defined as the one family member who endures the most of the family caregiving obligations for the individual, including completing everyday tasks and errands (Gaugler, Kane, & Kane, 2002). **"Secondary" caregivers** are those who often provide support and assistance to primary caregivers by providing psychoemotional, instrumental, and financial support. Secondary caregivers may become involved in various types of assistance for the care recipient but not to the same extent as the primary caregivers (Bourgeois, Beach, Schulz, & Burgio, 1996).

In 2010, there were approximately 52 million family caregivers in the United States who were providing care to an adult with limitations in daily activities, with about 61.6 million persons providing care at some point during the prior year (Coughlin, 2010; Feinberg, Reinhard, Houser, & Choula, 2011). Within the dementia care context (a disease that has received considerable attention for its informal care requirements), approximately 14.9 million adults serve as family caregivers for someone who has Alzheimer's or a similar type of dementia (Alzheimer's Association, 2013). This care is currently valued at approximately $450 billion overall and $216 billion for dementia caregivers (Alzheimer's Association, 2013; Feinberg et al., 2011). Generally, there are more female caregivers than male caregivers, with the National Alliance for Caregiving and AARP

(2009) estimating that 66% of caregivers are female. This number is slightly higher in the dementia care literature, with Liu and Gallagher-Thompson (2009) estimating that 73% of dementia caregivers are female. On average, dementia caregivers are 48 years of age.

Informal caregivers often help with one or more personal activities of daily living (PADLs), which includes assistance with getting out bed, getting dressed, incontinence, bathing, and feeding. Family caregivers also help with instrumental activities of daily living (IADLs), such as managing medication, shopping, housework, meals, and managing finances. The number of hours families dedicate to informal care is also extensive; according to the National Alliance for Caregiving (2015), informal caregivers provide approximately 21 hours of assistance per week. Dementia caregivers spend an average of 40 or more hours per week providing informal care (Liu & Gallagher-Thompson, 2009). In addition to providing care to a relative, approximately 60% of informal caregivers are also employed on a full- or part-time basis and often suffer work-related difficulties because of these dual roles (Family Caregiver Alliance, 2001). Family caregivers frequently report having to rearrange their work schedules, decrease hours at their job, or take unpaid leave in order to meet caregiving responsibilities. Additionally, dementia caregivers suffer from more severe health complications, including an increased risk for hypertension and poorer immune responses, than nondementia caregivers (Liu & Gallagher-Thompson, 2009).

Assuming a caregiving role for a family member prompts feelings of burden, defined as "a multi-dimensional response to physical, psychological, emotional, social, and financial stressors associated with the caregiving experience" (Etters, Goodall, & Harrison, 2008, p. 119). Case Study 4.1a in this chapter

Case Study 4.1a: Caring for Robert

Pauline and her daughter, Mary, provide care to Mary's father, Robert, who has been suffering from Alzheimer's disease for the past 7 years. Robert and Pauline still live at home. As his spouse and the person who lives with him, Pauline is the primary caregiver for Robert, but Mary is living in the same town and visits to provide assistance two to three times a week on average as well as on weekends. The assistance Mary provides includes grocery shopping, setting up appointments, and spending time just talking to Robert so that Pauline can attend to other errands and get a break. Pauline feels unable to continue providing care for Robert on her own because his behaviors are becoming more challenging. Pauline and Mary have had to take away Robert's driver's license because he would frequently become confused on the road and get lost and had caused at least two minor accidents. He also gets lost in the neighborhood; luckily, neighbors usually see him and call Pauline. These events are happening more frequently, causing Pauline to feel as

(continued)

Case Study 4.1a: Caring for Robert (*continued*)

though Robert can no longer be left alone. His frequent wandering is making it difficult for Pauline to provide regular, routine care, and this is increasing her stress daily. With Pauline also being older, it is difficult for her to handle the physical demands that come with Robert's deteriorating health; for example, he now requires more assistance in getting out of bed, dressing, and taking a shower. He also shows increased aggression and has pushed Pauline before while she was caring for him. For these reasons, Pauline and Mary have discussed their options many times, and with Mary working full time, she is unable to provide further assistance in caring for her father outside of visiting, arranging appointments, and making sure Robert and Pauline's finances are in order. The decision to admit Robert to a nursing home is one that Pauline and Mary have struggled with for a very long time (both have promised Robert that they would never put him in "one of those places"), but as Robert's behaviors become more challenging, they have begun to consider placement more seriously. Pauline and Mary grapple with these decisions as they feel like they will be abandoning Robert if they put him in a nursing home. Pauline feels that her husband will give up his will to fight his Alzheimer's disease, or even live, if he is placed in a nursing home.

Case Study Discussion Questions:

1. Pauline is concerned about the level of care that Robert will receive at a nursing home. Are her concerns justified?
2. As a health care professional, what advice would you give this family to help their decision making?

provides an example of a family experiencing the caregiving role. Perceived burden on the part of caregivers is associated with poor outcomes, such as depression, illness, and decreased quality of life (Etters et al., 2008). More specific stressors that caregivers report experiencing, such as feeling overloaded by caregiving responsibilities and feelings of being captive in the caregiving role, are also associated with depressive symptoms over time. Additionally, depression in the caregiver can lead to depression in the relative with dementia, resulting in even more impaired functioning in the care recipient beyond that associated with the disease itself (Liu & Gallagher-Thompson, 2009).

THE CAREGIVING CAREER AND RESIDENTIAL CARE PLACEMENT

Many factors are involved in adopting the role of family caregiver, and the experience involves different stages and experiences. In the literature, informal caregiving is sometimes conceptualized as a "**caregiving career**" (Parminder et al., 2004). This conceptual framework attempts to provide a more complex understanding of caregiving and describes the family caregiving process as a dynamic one in which the caregiver experiences a number of "transitions," or turning points, as the chronic disability of the older care recipient progresses and generally worsens (Parminder et al., 2004). Various transitions include preparation for and acquisition of the caregiver role, enactment of the associated tasks and responsibilities, and eventual disengagement from the role.

Using Montgomery and Kosloski's (2000) model of caregiving transitions, we will explore the various ways that family members can experience the caregiving career through the case of Maryann. Maryann lives in the city neighboring that of her mother, Cathy. Maryann is one of four children, but she is the only one who still lives in the same state as their mother. Recently, Maryann has been helping her mother with various tasks. She has been taking her to her doctor appointments, helping her with chores in her home, and regularly does her shopping. Maryann is in the *first stage* of the caregiving career, as she is beginning to provide tasks associated with caregiving (i.e., she is caring for her mother in a way that is not typically associated with the role of adult child).

Maryann has been providing these tasks for a few months now, and during a discussion with one of her sisters about their mother, Maryann begins to acknowledge that her relationship with her mother is different compared to the relationship that her siblings have with their mother. In addition to her role as an adult child, she begins to think of herself as her mother's caregiver. Maryann is entering the *second stage* of the caregiving career. During this stage, Maryann begins to acknowledge that her activities go beyond the normal scope of familial roles and she begins to self-identify as a caregiver.

As time progresses, Cathy becomes increasingly dependent on Maryann for additional help. Maryann moves her mother into her home so that she can provide assistance with more personal care such as feeding and monitoring her mother. At this point, Maryann is providing a great deal of assistance to her mother and feels torn between her roles as child and caregiver to her mother. When the care needs of the care recipient intensify, relatives find themselves performing tasks that are significantly outside the realm of typical family relationship exchanges. At this point, Maryann may begin to identify herself as the primary caregiver; this shift in identity represents the *third stage* of the career.

Eventually, Maryann feels overwhelmed with the responsibility of caring for Cathy and begins considering other options for assistance. Maryann considers placing Cathy in an **assisted living** facility. The consideration of formal service use represents the fourth stage of the career, at which point the caregiver considers placement options such as assisted living facilities or **nursing homes.** *The fourth stage* can last for an extended period of time as the caregiver continues revisiting the idea of placement.

As shown in the example, residential care placement can become a more likely option as the care needs of a relative intensify (Montgomery, Rowe, & Kosloski, 2007). However, admitting a relative to a residential care facility is not a decision that families make easily. Family caregivers often express reluctance to place their older relative in a nursing home. The focus of this chapter is to examine this key transition point in the caregiving career.

Placing a relative in a long-term care facility is a very emotional experience for caregivers, and mixed feelings regarding the placement decision are common. Although many caregivers might express guilt, sadness, anger, and sense of failure and loss, others express feelings of relief and peace of mind. There can also be a great deal of uncertainty during the transition, with family members experiencing ambiguity regarding the shift from a direct care role to a more indirect supportive role (Reuss, Dupuis, & Whitfield, 2005; Specht, Reed, & Maas, 2005).

Caregivers report feelings of turmoil related to nursing home placement. Case Study 4.1b follows Pauline and Mary as they experience the transition of placing Robert in a nursing home facility. These feelings are associated with uncertainty regarding nursing home expectations, the actual process of placing a relative, and getting everything in order for the move. Some caregivers also experience distress when they feel that they have little control over the decision to place their relative, as health care professionals sometimes decide to admit an individual without **family involvement**. Once a relative has been placed, family

Case Study 4.1b: Placing Robert

Robert wanders away from home one night in the rain, becomes lost, falls, and breaks his hip and cannot be found for around 2 hours. The family decides that it is too difficult for Pauline to care for Robert at home because he is becoming a danger to himself and others, and it is time to place him in a nursing home. Because Robert needs almost immediate placement, Pauline and Mary visit several different homes within a few days. After several visits to various homes, Pauline and Mary feel frustrated. They felt unprepared for this decision and were not sure what to expect from their visits and what types of questions they should ask. They found it difficult to find a home that they felt could care for Robert the way they would prefer, and the few homes they found have extensive waiting lists. Finally, they are able to find an available bed at Serenity Nursing Home, which meets a few of their requirements: the staff appears to be friendly and caring, and there are many activities for residents; however, it is at least 35 miles away for Pauline and Mary to travel to visit Robert. They are still unsure that this is the right place for Robert.

Case Study Discussion Questions:

1. What factors should Pauline and Mary specifically consider before making a final decision?
2. Are there other questions they should ask the staff?

members often go through a period of adjustment. This adjustment can include letting go of previous ideas of what the nursing home experience would be like, accepting the fact that their relative will never return home, and adjusting expectations of what their relative's life would be like in a nursing home. Other relatives report feeling happy and relieved once their relative was placed, and they begin to accept that they made the best decision (Cheek & Ballantyne, 2001; Pearson, Nay, & Taylor, 2004; Ryan & Scullion, 2000). These conflicting emotions can be very challenging for families, and as a result, many caregivers make major personal sacrifices in order to keep family members at home for as long as possible (Strang, Koop, Dupuis-Blanchard, Nordstrom, & Thompson, 2006).

TYPES OF LONG-TERM CARE FACILITIES

In the context of this chapter, the interaction between "informal" (family involvement) and "formal" care (assistance provided by direct care workers) often operates in two distinct residential care settings: nursing homes and assisted living facilities. Nursing homes are a residence for people who are too frail or sick to live independently (Assisted Living Facilities). Nursing homes are likely to serve a chronically ill, functionally dependent segment of the population (Borson, Liptzin, Nininger, & Rabins, 1987). Residents suffering from multiple degenerative diseases and impairment in the capacity for self-care are common in nursing homes. Traditional models of nursing homes fit the description of an institution in many more ways than it fits the definition of a home. Nursing homes typically involve an emphasis on uniform treatment and medical issues, much like a hospital environment (Kahn, 1999). Residents and staff are usually on fixed schedules and can be very rigid in the services provided to residents. For example, nursing homes receiving funding from Medicaid are required to provide a range of services, including, but not limited to, dispensing and administering medication, room and bed maintenance, and routine personal hygiene items and services. Nursing homes can charge for other services such as a private room, unless it is required for medical purposes, telephone, television, and radio, and personal and cosmetic items and services in excess of what is included in basic service (Medicaid Program, 2012). The institutionalized setting of nursing homes has often been criticized for being less individualized and essentially stripping residents of their uniqueness as individuals (Drew, 2005).

The AARP proposed a definition of assisted living facility in 1992 as a group residential setting that is not licensed as a nursing home where personal care and routine nursing services are provided to meet the requirements of the resident. Definitions have continued to evolve because uniform standards across states do not exist and consensus could not be reached regarding which qualities of assisted living were required and which were recommended (Wilson, 2007). By 2008, Medicare defined assisted living facilities as a "general term for living arrangements in which some services are available to residents who still live independently within the assisted living complex" (Medicare Program, 2012). Assisted living settings are privately occupied apartments with features such as a full bathroom, kitchenettes, and locking doors where the residents control their space, furnishings, time of activities and care plans. Assisted living settings are recognized as residential options that bridge home care and more intensive skilled care provided in a nursing facility (Gaugler & Lindahl, 2011). These facilities vary according to size, services offered, and the degree of care residents require. Offering a mix of security and independence, assisted living facilities aim to provide supervision, assistance, and personal care services (Hawes, Phillips, Rose, Holan, & Sherman, 2003; Hawes, Rose, & Phillips, 1999; National Center for Assisted Living, 1998). Both nursing homes and assisted living facilities can come at high costs for families. Exhibit 4.1 describes how families fund long-term care.

According to the Centers for Disease Control (2010), there were approximately 1.5 million residents in nursing homes across the country, compared to an average of 733,000 residents in residential/assisted living facilities. In both facilities, the majority of residents are female and over the age of 65. Within nursing home facilities, approximately 52% of residents require care with at least four activities of daily living (ADLs, or help needed to bathe, eat, use the bathroom, get in and out of bed, or walk around), whereas approximately four in 10 residents within assisted living facilities required assistance with at least three ADLs (Caffrey et al., 2012; Centers for Disease Control and Prevention, 2004; Centers for Medicare & Medicaid Services, 2012).

EXHIBIT 4.1 How Do Families Fund Long-Term Care?

Medicare covers many of the costs of long-term care for the elderly and disabled. Medicaid is another funding option for covering long-term care, but this is only available for individuals who are poor, or become poor during the course of long-term care. These programs only cover some of the costs associated with care and with Medicaid the services covered varies by state (Feder, Komisar, & Niefeld, 2000). In 2005, nearly 49% of the $207 billion long-term care costs were covered by Medicaid, approximately 20% by Medicare, and 18% came out of pocket (Komisar & Thompson, 2007; E. A. Miller, Mor, & Clark, 2009).

This means that caregiving costs are often high for families who cover the remaining costs out of pocket. A 1996 survey of caregivers found that among employed caregivers, many had to sacrifice paid work hours, make adjustments to their work schedules, or even quit or retire early in order to perform caregiving tasks for a family member. Family caregivers have been neglected from long-term care policy because their services have been seen as personal obligation rather than service that should be paid for (Levine, Halper, Peist, & Gould, 2010). Government efforts to assist caregivers have stemmed largely from a desire to keep people out of nursing homes. In 2000, the first federal caregiver program was developed to assist caregivers. The National Family Caregiver Support Program provides services for caregivers, including information and referral and counseling. Researchers called for policies that address the needs of family caregivers and the relatives for whom they care.

FAMILY STRUCTURE

Although some differences exist in family structure across residential care settings, results from national surveys suggest that the typical resident of both nursing homes and assisted living facilities is White, female, and widowed (Hawes, Phillips, & Rose, 2000; Kasper & O'Malley, 2007). More recent studies that include data on key family variables (e.g., marital status, living children, and traveling distance of the nearest family member) also suggest that approximately 15% or more of residents had spouses, and 80% or more had adult children who remained involved in care. Additionally, a few assisted living residents resided with a spouse (around 7%). Having a spouse or adult children who live nearby may serve as sources of informal support. It is not clear whether residents who have no spouse or family members available have all of their care needs (which not only include care for ADLs but emotional support as well; see Exhibit 4.2) met through the formal support of the facility. It is important to note that these findings are dated, and updated demographic profiles are needed; given the changing nature of long-term care in the United States (particularly the rapid emergence of assisted living in many states), it is not clear how many potential family members current residents have available to provide help and support.

FAMILY INVOLVEMENT IN LONG-TERM CARE

Initially, researchers characterized the residential entry of a relative as a time of intensified isolation from families during which depression on the part of relatives was a common experience (Cath, 1972; Jones, 1972). Additional early research found the involvement of family members to be interfering and disruptive (Bates, 1968). Subsequent inquiry found, however, that family members remained meaningfully involved in the lives of their relatives after residential entry, although family care distinctly changes after a relative's move into a nursing home or assisted living facility.

Family involvement has been described as multidimensional and can include a range of components such as visiting, provision of personal or instrumental care, socioemotional support, monitoring, decision making, and advocacy (Gaugler, 2005; High & Rowles, 1995). *Visiting* refers to in-person contact with relatives in a residential care setting. Family members sometimes continue to provide *personal care* to their relatives, which includes ADL help such as grooming, helping the relative walk, helping the relative eat, although in many instances facility staff may assume the bulk of these responsibilities. Families may also provide instrumental care or assistance with laundry, cleaning, organizing space, and preparation of food and beverages. Another dimension of family involvement is socioemotional support. *Socioemotional support* can include talking with the resident, holding hands with the resident, and engaging in social activities (High & Rowles, 1995).

Family involvement in residential settings can interact in various ways with the formal care offered by direct care workers. **Supplementation** refers to the use of formal support to complement ongoing informal care tasks or activities but does not replace informal care provision (Edelman, 1986). Alternatively, **substitution** occurs when formal care (such as that provided by residential care facility staff) fully replaces certain dimensions of care once provided by informal/family caregivers (Greene, 1983). Another pattern of care that can occur is kin dependence. **Kin dependency** occurs when informal caregivers continue to provide the bulk of assistance even with the introduction of formal support (Lyons & Zarit, 1999). **Dual specialization** occurs when direct care staff provide personal, hands-on care, and family members remain responsible for psychosocial support (Dobrof & Litwak, 1977; Gaugler, 2005; Litwak, 1985).

Family members also provide additional types of assistance that are not directly provided to the relative but represent involvement on the part of family caregivers, such as monitoring, advocacy, and decision making. These types of assistance are based on "**preservative care**," in which the role of family members is to help maintain the identity of the relative via engagement with facility staff or other activities (Bowers, 1988). *Monitoring* may include supervising or collaborating with staff in order to maximize the quality of care provided to the relatives (e.g., sharing personal or historical information about the relative to the staff). *Advocacy* is defined as active support and recommendations for direct improvement of patient care (National Alliance for Caregiving, 2006). Some examples of this in the family caregiving literature include family members' reporting abuse to authorities, promoting family understanding of nursing home policies to other relatives, and initiating actions to ensure that good staff/family relations exist. Family members also continue to have high levels of involvement in the decision-making process of the relative. This has been defined in the literature as **progressive surrogacy** (High & Rowles, 1995), and refers to family members remaining involved in numerous decisions regarding daily living, such as decisions about physical environment and social environment, treatment and health care decisions, and crisis and end-of-life decisions. With progressive surrogacy, as decision-making ability declines, residents progressively cede some of these decisions, especially everyday decisions, to family members and to staff members who assume the role of surrogate family.

Visiting remains an important way to measure family involvement, and family members visit often and typically go to great efforts to visit, including traveling long distances (Chene, 2006; Ross, Rosenthal, & Dawson, 1997). The act of visiting a relative serves a multitude of purposes. Family members associate visiting their relative with showing love and devotion, assisting their relative, providing assistance to staff, and as an act of duty and obligation. Wives report that visiting their husbands provides a way to facilitate connectedness and to prevent them from feeling neglected at the facility. Visiting can be emotionally satisfying, but it can also be difficult for relatives. Some wives reported that visiting can be emotionally draining when they have to explain to husbands why they could not return home, thereby increasing their guilt (Ross et al., 1996).

Families visit frequently both in the beginning of residential placement and after their relative has been at the facility for some time. A study in 2001 by Port and colleagues found that 2 weeks following residential entry, significant others had contact with residents approximately 19.9 times. In other published research, Ross, Rosenthal, and Dawson (1997) conducted a longitudinal study of wives of nursing home residents and reported extensive visiting, with 80% visiting their husbands several times a week or more and 20% visiting every day, with visits lasting 2 to 4 hours. After 9 months, there was still no significant reduction in the number of visits.

While visiting, family members engage in various forms of socioemotional support, advocacy, monitoring, and even actual direct care in some instances (e.g., bathing, feeding, and dressing and grooming their relative). Because of a common shift in responsibilities away from most direct care tasks, family members have more time to devote to the relationship with their relative and to enhancing their quality of life. For example, family members may engage in conversations with their relatives about current events and about the stressors they experience. Family members may also take relatives out of the nursing home for social visits. Families may also assume the role of advocacy for the well-being of the relative in order to ensure that his or her needs are met. During visits, family members can represent the relative's unique contribution to the new home. They can ensure that staff is aware of their relative's preferences, personal history, and values and in so doing inform care staff of the most appropriate way to care for their relative. Additionally, family members may use their visiting time to monitor the standards of their relative's care and provide feedback to facility staff (Austin et al., 2009; Davies & Nolan, 2006).

Research on family involvement in assisted living examines many of the same types of family involvement as in nursing homes. Case Study 4.2 demonstrates some family experiences when visiting nursing homes. However, some of these behaviors look different in assisted living facilities. Exhibit 4.2 illustrates how family involvement differs in assisted living according to the various types of informal/formal care models described (see Gaugler & Kane, 2007). Residents in assisted living often receive frequent phone calls (often weekly or more) from family members. During visits, family members are engaged most frequently in providing socioemotional help. Families also provide some types of direct care but on a more modest basis than is provided to relatives in nursing homes (likely due in part to fewer care needs on the part of assisted living residents). Thus, either assisted living residents can conduct some of the daily living tasks themselves or perhaps family members were not as actively involved before the move to assisted living occurred. When comparing some of the differences between nursing homes and assisted living, family members of nursing home residents appeared more likely to engage in instrumental assistance (Gaugler & Kane, 2001, 2007; Leon et al., 2000), family interaction (Pruchno & Rose, 2002), and monitoring of cognitively impaired residents' medical, emotional, and financial well-being (Port et al., 2005).

Specifically, family members spend approximately 1 hour or less per month providing ADL care to their relatives in assisted living (Abbey, Schneider, & Mozley, 1999; Gaugler & Kane, 2001; Newcomer, Breuer, & Zhang, 1994; Stacey-Konnert & Pynoos, 1992). Additionally, when exploring behaviors in assisted living, researchers found that when couples are living together they do provide each other some assistance with both instrumental and socioemotional support,

Case Study 4.2: Visiting Robert

Pauline has tried to make contact with the nursing staff to discuss Robert's progress and health status. She has identified a nurse who works the early afternoon shift and who is very friendly and helpful and will take her concerns about Robert seriously. Pauline often shares stories about Robert with this nurse when she visits, sharing his general likes, dislikes, and the meanings behind certain behaviors. When this nurse is not around, Pauline finds that her concerns are often ignored, and this continues to be a source of frustration for her. For example, after consulting with Robert's primary care physician, Pauline asked the nurses to keep Robert on a bathroom schedule so that he does not soil himself. However, when she visits, she often finds Robert soiled, or when she is there during a scheduled bathroom break, she notices that no one comes around.

Mary lives some distance from the nursing home and is not able to visit as often as she used to because of her job. She visits her father on weekends and often brings the grandchildren. Mary is not as involved with the staff, but she does call in and speak to them on occasion if there is something her mother did not understand regarding facility policy or care practices. Mary's main contribution to Robert's care is financial; she has taken control of her parents' finances and is helping keep them in order for the family.

Case Study Discussion Questions:

1. What type of care is each relative providing?
2. What are some strategies that Pauline can use to get the staff to be more attentive to Robert's needs?

but they do not tend to rely only on each other for socioemotional support and negotiate separate social activities (Kemp, 2008). Little research exists that examines families' monitoring or advocacy behaviors in assisted living. The frequency of family visits, socioemotional support, and instrumental care provided by family members in assisted living are supplemental in nature to the care provided by staff in such settings (Newcomer et al., 1994).

Family involvement can vary across assisted living settings and nursing homes. These differences exist because, as noted previously, nursing homes and assisted living facilities cater to residents with diverse care needs. Assisted living facilities often become an option for older adults who are coping with some physical and cognitive decline and may need limited assistance with ADLs (Kelsey, Laditka, & Laditka, 2010; Wilson, 2007). Nursing homes often have residents who suffer from severe forms of dementia or degenerative brain diseases (Borson et al., 1987). Therefore, nursing home regulations may be more likely to discourage

EXHIBIT 4.2 Formal and Informal Care Provision in Residential Long-Term Care: Assisted Living and Nursing Homes

Type of Care	Assisted Living	Nursing Home
Personal care		
• Going to the bathroom	• Independence	• Substitution
• Eating	• Supplementation	• Substitution
• Grooming	• Independence	• Substitution
• Ambulation	• Supplementation	• Substitution[a]
• Bathing, dressing	• Substitution	• Substitution
Instrumental care		
• Transportation	• Supplementation	• Supplementation
• Shopping, finances	• Kin dependence	• Kin dependence
• Medication administration	• Supplementation	• Substitution[a]
• Laundry	• Substitution	• Substitution
Socioemotional support	Supplementation	Supplementation
Monitoring	Kin dependence	Kin dependence
Advocacy	Kin dependence	Kin dependence

[a]Family involvement is potentially discouraged.
Source: Reproduced from Gaugler & Kane (2007) with permission of Oxford University Press and The Gerontological Society of America.

families from engaging in the same types of care responsibilities, such as bathing or ambulation, due to potential risks (Gaugler & Kane, 2007). In addition, nursing home staff members are less likely to facilitate family involvement because of safety concerns and restrictions. In contrast, assisted living facilities foster a more independent lifestyle with an emphasis on control, privacy, and autonomy, and thus may be more likely to encourage family members to engage in care of their older relatives. In an assisted living facility, elders may rely on both the staff and their relatives to provide some of the daily care they request or require.

FAMILY OUTCOMES

Relationships between family and staff members at long-term care facilities can be very complex, and these complexities can have implications for how well the family and resident adjust to the placement.

Institutional practices affect the families' experience. The extensive waiting period that is often associated with finding an appropriate facility for their relative can result in additional stress and frustration for family caregivers. In addition, many placements occur in response to a crisis, leaving families feeling unprepared and lacking in sufficient information to make informed decisions. As in the case of Pauline and Mary, when families delay making placement choices until a crisis occurs, they may struggle to find a facility that meets the family's criteria.

The guilt family members often feel over the decision to move a care recipient to a residential facility may lead to difficulty in the family–staff relationship by causing them to become hyper vigilant and easily dissatisfied with care provided. In the case study described, Pauline struggled to get the staff to attend to Robert the way she wanted (Case Study 4.2). Pauline eventually only identified one staff member whom she really trusted with Robert's care. This hyper vigilance on behalf of the family can often be viewed as creating additional stress on the staff, who view frequent requests from family members to be disruptive to their workload, thus reducing their willingness to work with the family (Majerovitz, Mollott, & Rudder, 2009; Robison & Pillemer, 2005; Specht et al., 2005).

Additionally, some studies have found that the more time the resident spends in the nursing home, the more satisfied the family members are with the care their relative is receiving. This suggests that over time, families either adjust or begin to feel as though their family member's needs were met by the staff (Davies & Nolan, 2006; Natan, 2007). Typically, it appears that shifting to a more positive perspective is the result of a more collaborative relationship between family and staff. When family members feel that staff members are taking a vested interest in their relative and in their feelings, they report more positive feelings. Family members find it very helpful when staff members acknowledge their feelings of guilt surrounding the residential move, are available to answer questions, telephone with information or requests, provide information about changes in care, and involve family members in everyday decisions (Robinson, Reid, & Cooke, 2010). This collaborative approach on the part of staff is helpful in maintaining a positive relationship among the resident, family members, and staff.

Conflict also potentially exists between family members and staff in their view of their roles. Findings suggest that family members feel the need to maintain continuity, provide emotional support, and monitor standards of care for relatives in residential settings. Family members also feel that they can provide practical help by assisting the staff with aspects of care. However, staff members may not always be open to the family participating in care and sometimes see them as interlopers who should not be involved in the care of the resident (Davies & Nolan, 2006; Specht et al., 2005).

PROMOTING FAMILY INVOLVEMENT

FAMILY INVOLVEMENT IN CARE INTERVENTIONS

Family members typically report feeling more satisfied with the level of care provided when they feel as though they can interact with the staff regularly and are more involved in the care of their relative. An example of this is seen in Case Study 4.3. Family members report satisfaction with care if staff is friendly, make suggestions about care and treatment, and pass on information to family members spontaneously. Other research has shown that family members feel more satisfied with the residential setting when they believe that the staff show attentiveness and responsiveness to the resident and demonstrate an understanding of the resident as a person (Austin et al., 2009). Family members report being dissatisfied with care when staff members are detached and impersonal, fail

Case Study 4.3: Interacting With Staff

One year has passed since Pauline and Mary placed Robert at Serenity Nursing Home. Overall, they feel that the care he receives is acceptable, but they would still like him to receive more personalized care. Therefore, when the opportunity to participate in a statewide research study for family and staff communications arose, they accepted. During this study, Pauline and Mary met with two nurses and a doctor in charge of the care of Robert during which time they identified the interests of the resident, jointly discussed and developed care plans, and reviewed Pauline and Mary's concerns. After 10 weeks of involvement in the study, Pauline and Mary were asked to evaluate their experience. Both felt that the study was beneficial in shaping their relationship with the staff members, causing them to feel more likely to communicate and feel like their concerns were heard. They felt that the staff was willing to work with them. This made them more comfortable with the institution and they were more likely to enjoy visits with Robert.

Case Study Discussion Questions:

1. You are the primary investigator of the project in which Pauline and Mary are participants. You are required to present your findings to a group of nursing home directors regarding the most important points you believe they could implement to enhance the services they provide to their families. What do you suggest to them?
2. What additional suggestions do you have that you believe might help relationships between family members and staff?

to recognize the needs of the resident, and do not engage in personalized care unless it is initiated by the relatives (Davies & Nolan, 2006).

Family involvement and collaborative treatment between family members and health care professionals has been at the center of changes that policy makers are attempting to implement across the country. The **culture change movement** in long-term care facilities calls for a shift in focus from uniformity and medical issues to client-centered care and quality of life. The relationship between residents and care staff is a necessary component of this shift (White-Chu et al., 2009). Exhibit 4.3 provides additional information on the culture change movement. Consistent with this culture shift, in 2013, a white paper was released that emphasized the need for person-centered dementia care. The paper highlighted limitations of the biomedical approach with its narrow focus on the physical condition of the person with dementia rather than considering the psychosocial components that are also important for treatment and management. This type of care

EXHIBIT 4.3 The Culture Change Movement

The quality of care in nursing homes has been a topic of concern for families and researchers for decades. In the early 1990s William H. Thomas described a new perspective on nursing home care known as the Eden Alternative. In his book *Life Worth Living: How Someone You Love Can Still Enjoy Life in a Nursing Home*, Thomas critiqued the status quo of nursing homes for their focus on treatment through medical science and institutional policies instead of the care (i.e., the compassionate holistic treatment) of the residents. Thomas argued that the medical approach was creating more problems because residents learned to equate medical treatment with attention, which resulted in overmedicating (Thomas, 1994). Additionally, it led to residents becoming more subdued and showing decreased ability to care for themselves, which resulted in increased dependence on staff. Because of these philosophies, the nursing home culture change movement was started with the goal of deinstitutionalizing services and individualizing care (S. C. Miller, Miller, Jung, Sterns, Clark, & Mor, 2010).

A panel of nursing home experts created a document detailing the constructs they believed were pertinent to culture change. These constructs included: "(1) care and all resident-related activities are directed by residents; (2) a living environment designed to be a home rather than an institution; (3) close relationships between residents, family members, staff, and community; (4) work organized to support and empower all staff to respond to residents' needs and desires; (5) management enables collaborative and decentralized decision-making; and (6) systematic processes that are comprehensive and measurement-based and that are used for continuous quality improvement" (S. C. Miller et al., 2010, p. 675).

Findings regarding facilities utilizing this philosophy have been mixed. Some studies have found reductions in antipsychotic medications in comparison to traditional facilities. Some utilizing the Eden Alternative showed reduction in ulcer rates, increased staff and family satisfaction, and behavioral incidents as well, but another study of Eden Alternative nursing homes also found a higher incidence of falls and problems with nutrition (Coleman, Looney, O'Brien, Ziegler, Pastorino, & Turner, 2002; Ransom, 2000; Svarstad, Mount, & Bigelow, 2001; White-Chu, Graves, Godfrey, Bonner, & Sloane, 2009).

requires all stakeholders to be involved, such as the person with dementia, his or her family members, health care professionals, long-term care providers, advocates, policy makers, researchers, and scholars (The National Dementia Initiative, 2013). One of the ways that all stakeholders can engage in holistic treatment of persons with dementia is to more effectively involve both the family and health care professionals. In the next paragraph, we discuss some of the methods currently being explored, as well as potential ideas that may enhance this holistic approach.

Some models have been created and tested in response to the culture change movement. Examples of these models include (a) The Live Oak Institute, (b) Eden Alternative, (c) Wellspring Innovative Solutions, (d) Golden Gate National Senior Care, (e) Greenhouse, and (f) Holistic Approach to Transformational Change (HATCh). Of these, the Eden Alternative and Green House have received the most research attention.

The **Eden Alternative**, which has the potential to improve the quality of life for residents by creating a more homelike environment, the Eden Alternative settings or communities, fights against the traditional image of the "institutionalized" nursing home, which is conceived as sterile and regimented. Instead, the Eden Alternative aims to create a vibrant atmosphere where residents can interact with their surroundings (Thomas, 1994). To this end, animals are a regular part of the lives of the residents, and gardens are planted for both dietary benefits as well as social and spiritual reasons. Additionally, children play a large role in the Eden Alternative, and planned programs such as onsite childcare centers, and summer day camps are included. Some findings from the Eden Alternative show reductions in medication use, mortality rates, and infection in residents (Thomas, 1994). Since its inception, the Eden Alternative approach has been adopted at hundreds of long-term care settings. Although it is a promising solution, institutions still identify barriers to implementation. Some of these barriers/concerns include violating existing regulations, such as sanitation requirements, with the use of animals. Researchers also express concern that this model has not been rigorously evaluated and that some of the dramatic findings may be a result of leadership rather than other elements of the model (Wiener, 2003). Additionally, there are concerns regarding the costs to implement such a program on a large scale within the United States, as it requires more staff and incurs other additional costs. Currently, only New Jersey, New York, and Texas offer grant money for institutions to implement the Eden Alternative (Stone & Wiener, 2001; Wiener, 2003).

The engagement of family members is an important feature in the success of the Eden Alternative approach. Family members have many expectations and even fears regarding their view of a modern care facility. Family members expect homelike environments with a wide range of activities for residents but also fear potential threats to safety and health with the presence of animals and plants. Evaluations of family members' experience of the Eden Alternative indicated that family members were not satisfied with some aspects such as the food and laundry services. By engaging the family in the solutions to such concerns, family members may be able to offer ideas that the staff may not have considered, such as requesting recipes from the residents to incorporate into the menu. In one study, family and staff also began working together to solve the laundry problem (Drew, 2005). This collaborative approach uses family members as resources in care and has rich potential to evolve into a model for addressing other problems.

The **Green House model** is rooted in the Eden Alternative philosophy (Thomas, 1994). It is designed as a model for cultural change with nursing facilities, allowing these settings to feel like a real home while meeting regulatory requirements (The Green House Project, 2014). There are approximately 144 Green House homes open, with 120 more in development across 32 states. The operating costs for these homes are estimated to be around the same median cost as nursing homes (Jenkens, Sult, Lessell, Hammer, & Ortigara, 2011).

Family members of residents in Green Houses are more engaged than family members of residents remaining in nursing homes. When the facility feels like home, the quality of life of the resident is improved, and there are increased feelings of happiness, functional capacity, increased independence, increased involvement in everyday life, and fewer requests to "go home." Homelike qualities of the facility also lead to family members reporting diminished guilt, reduced worry, enhanced peace of mind and comfort with the process of entering the residential facility, as well as alleviation of some of the burden of care through reduced responsibility and fewer tasks (Lum, Kane, Cutler, & Yu, 2008; Robinson et al., 2010).

Several studies acknowledge the need for greater communication between family and staff, but few offer suggestions on how this can be accomplished. Researchers suggest that care staff should plan regular reviews of each resident's needs by involving the home manager, nurses, resident, family members, and any other individual involved in the resident's life (Davies & Nolan, 2006). Considering the significant emotions that families experience about having their relative in a residential living facility, it could be helpful to include a mental health professional to guide these meetings or to help deal with the emotions that will likely arise during these meetings. This would allow both family members and professionals to express their anxieties and concerns as they arise. This is consistent with other suggestions that have called for better relationships between family caregivers and health care professionals as well as providing training for caregivers that would allow them to provide high-quality care for their relatives. It is also suggested that health care professionals work in teams that provide holistic care and proactively engage family caregivers as partners (Levine et al., 2010). The success of these meetings may depend on the type of facility and may require diverse clinical content when considering each facility's environmental strengths. For example, it may be more challenging to conduct these meetings at a nursing home setting, in comparison to an assisted living facility, as the medical staff in a nursing home facility often does not have scheduled times for visiting residents, making it difficult for family and other staff to join. Additionally, physicians spend limited time in nursing home settings, making their availability for such meetings challenging at best.

In addition to system-wide efforts to change the culture of residential facilities, several specific interventions have been created to improve family and staff relationships and engage them in a more collaborative approach to care. The *Family Involvement in Care* (FIC) intervention is one such intervention. The goals of the FIC include developing partnerships between family caregivers and facility staff, clarifying each stakeholder's expectations and establishing mutually satisfying roles and relationships. In this approach, facility staff delivers the intervention. The staff is oriented to the rationale of the intervention, and they are made aware of problems faced by family members. The FIC educates family members on types of activities and approaches for relating with the resident and managing behaviors. Family caregivers are also guided in how to make their involvement in therapeutic activities meaningful and enjoyable. Family members and staff develop a partnership agreement for care activities, and this agreement is later evaluated and renegotiated (Specht et al., 2005).

Evaluations of the FIC show that upon completion of participation, family members often report positive changes in interactions and communications between family members and staff and generally feel more favorable about family visits. In addition to improved communication and interactions, families showed increased satisfaction with the physical care that their relatives were receiving. Facility staff may not receive as many benefits from interventions as family members. Findings from the FIC suggest that staff did not report a significant reduction in stress associated with caregiving, but this may be related to the level of ownership and compliance they had with the intervention.

Partners in Caregiving (PIC) is another intervention program that takes a collaborative approach to care. This intervention aims to develop partnerships among families, staff members, and nursing home administrators. Using communication techniques and meetings with all stakeholders, the intervention aims to change family's and staff's negative perceptions of the other's role and improve positive interactions between facility and family. The program also encourages family, staff, and administrators to collaboratively explore facility procedures and policies that affect their interactions. Evaluations of the PIC show improved attitudes for both family and staff, less conflict between family and staff, and reduced likelihood of staff to quit. Family members are also more likely to perceive staff as more empathic, whereas staff members experience family behaviors as supportive. This intervention even appears to improve resident behavior, and facility staff report a reduction in challenging resident behaviors such as aggressive behaviors, constant requests for attention, and wandering (Pillemer et al., 2003; Robison, Curry, Gruman, Porter, Henderson, & Pillemer, 2007).

Web-based interventions may be an option for engaging adult children who may not be able to physically invest in the care relationship. Web-based interventions can have many benefits such as providing educational opportunities and better quality of care and quality of life for the caregivers and care recipient while also being cost-effective and convenient. This approach is not without flaws. Developing Internet interventions can be very time-consuming and labor intensive, and it has legal and ethical implications not typically associated with face-to-face interventions (Tolbert & Basham, 2005). Further involvement between family members and health care professionals can lead to the person with dementia being seen in a more holistic manner instead of just being perceived through the lens of his or her illness.

A number of resources are available to caregivers to help them adjust to their role and guide them through the placement process. The Alzheimer's Association provides caregivers with a range of services, including educational resources and local support groups that help the caregiver transition through the role (Alzheimer's Association, 2013). Because the complex web of services available for older adults can be difficult to navigate, services are available to assist families in that process. An example of this is the Eldercare Locator. The Eldercare Locator is a public service provided by the

U.S. Department of Health and Human Services and provides older adults and caregivers with a wide range of information regarding available services nationwide. Services the Eldercare Locator can assist with include accessing meals, home care, transportation, and education and training resources for caregivers (Eldercare Locator, 2014).

Additionally, resources have been created to assist families in making informed and appropriate decisions regarding nursing home and assisted living placement. For example, the decision-making aid developed by the Ottawa Hospital Research Institute assists individuals with making important care decisions regarding the use of medications, the move of a relative into long-term care, and long-term care options that are available. Caregivers are provided with information about their options and outcomes of decisions regarding long-term care choices. The decision aid also incorporates an opportunity for caregivers to consider their personal values and feelings in the decision (Ottawa Hospital Research Institute, 2013).

For family members who decide that long-term placement is the best option, checklists exist to help them pick the facility best suited to their needs. Medicare provides caregivers with an opportunity to compare information regarding inspection results, staffing, and quality measures. Nursing homes are also given star ratings based on a combination of factors (Medicare Program, 2014).

Medicare also provides a nursing home checklist to assist families in assessing environmental and relational variables that affect satisfaction with the nursing home experience. Families are encouraged to consider the physical environment of the nursing home (e.g., whether the space is clean and comfortable) and resident factors (e.g., residents appear clean and groomed, residents are allowed to bring personal belongings with them, have their choice of menu, or are provided special dietary needs, and have their choice of roommates). Families are also encouraged to consider the level of staff involvement (e.g., interactions between staff and resident), safety plans, and activities available for residents (Medicare Program, 2013). A similar checklist also exists for assisted living facilities. However, because assisted living facilities focus more the continuing independence of the resident, questions from the assisted living checklist emphasize maintaining independence. For example, families are encouraged to ask questions regarding residents' automobiles, overnight guests, and more specific questions regarding privacy (American Health Care Association, 2014).

CONCLUSIONS

Family members are one of the main sources of support for elderly individuals in need of care. However, providing full-time caregiving for a relative is often a very burdensome experience that may result in emotional and physical challenges for the caregiver. Caregivers are often forced to renegotiate their personal and professional lives in order to continue providing assistance to elderly relatives. It is at this point that residential placement becomes a more likely option. Placing a relative in a residential long-term care facility can be emotionally difficult for family members. Residential placement marks a shift in caregiving responsibilities but seldom marks an end to caregiving. Family members still engage in a range of instrumental and socioemotional support, as well as engage in monitoring, advocacy, and progressive surrogacy on behalf of their relatives. The way that families are able to interact with residents as well as health care professionals may change in the ever-evolving system of long-term care.

Family involvement in residential long-term care has evolved over many decades. The traditional institutionalized settings of nursing home or similar facilities make it difficult for families to maintain involvement and connect with staff to provide the care they want for their relative. However, the culture change movement, with its emphasis on person-centered care, creates an important role for the family members of the residents. Many models have been created under this movement, and although results are mixed, there is some evidence that these models enhance resident autonomy and family and staff satisfaction. Further efforts are needed to implement programs and policies that will create meaningful partnerships between family members and residential staff in order to facilitate a more holistic approach to the lives and treatment of residents.

SUMMARY

This chapter describes in detail the types of family involvement that occur in residential facilities, highlighting the differences that exist between nursing home and assisted living facilities. We also discuss the culture change movement and how this may affect the future of residential living in the United States and the impact that it can have on residents, families, and health care professionals.

DISCUSSION QUESTIONS

1. What challenges do we still have to overcome with incorporating family care in the future? What methods can we implement to accomplish that?
2. We have discussed initiatives to improve long-term care, such as culture change. How might we expect long-term care to continue evolving in the future?
3. Throughout this chapter, we discuss traditional types of long-term care. Recently, concepts like the dementia village have been introduced in the Netherlands where residents with dementia are encouraged to live seemingly more independent lifestyles than they may experience in other long-term care facilities.
   a. What are some potential benefits and challenges for older adults and families with this model of care?
   b. Which models of family involvement would you expect to see in residential settings of this type?

ADDITIONAL RESOURCES

Caregiving Resource Center www.aarp.org/home-family/caregiving

Culture Change in Elder Care (Leading Principles & Practices in Elder Care Series) www.amazon.com/Culture-Change-Leading-Principles-Practices/dp/1932529861

The Eden Alternative www.edenalt.org

The Green House Project http://thegreenhouseproject.org

Long-Term Care by the U.S. Department of Health and Human Services http://longtermcare.gov

Medicare and Caregivers http://nihseniorhealth.gov/medicareandcaregivers/managingmedicalconditions/01.html

REFERENCES

Abbey, A., Schneider, J., & Mozley, C. (1999). Visitors' views on residential homes. *British Journal of Social Work, 29*, 567–579.

Alzheimer's Association. (2013). 2013 Alzheimer's disease facts and figures. *Alzheimer's and Dementia, 9*(2), 208–245. Retrieved from www.alz.org/downloads/facts_figures_2013.pdf

American Health Care Association, National Center for Assisted Living. (2014). *Choosing an assisted living residence: A consumer's guide.* Retrieved from www.ahcancal.org/ncal/resources/Documents/Choosing%20An%20Assisted%20Living%20Residence%202013.pdf

Assisted Living Facilities. (2015). *Assisted living compared to nursing homes.* Retrieved from http://www.assistedlivingfacilities.org/resources/quiz-what-type-of-care-is-right-for-me-/vs-nursing-homes/

Austin, W., Goble, E., Strang, V., Mitchell, A., Thompson, E., Lantz, H., ... Vass, K. (2009). Supporting relationships between family and staff in continuing care settings. *Journal of Family Nursing, 15*, 360–383.

Bates, R. C. (1968). *The fine art of understanding patients*. Oradell, NJ: Medical Economics Book Division.

Borson, S., Liptzin, B., Nininger, J., & Rabins, P. (1987). Psychiatry and the nursing home. *American Journal of Psychiatry*, 144, 1412–1418.

Bourgeois, M. S., Beach, S., Schulz, R., & Burgio, L. D. (1996). When primary and secondary caregivers disagree: Predictors and psychosocial consequences. *Psychology and Aging, 11*(3), 527–537.

Bowers, B. J. (1988). Family perceptions of care in a nursing home. *The Gerontologist, 28*, 361–368.

Caffrey, C., Sengupta, M., Park-Lee, E., Moss, A., Rosenoff, E., & Harris-Kojetin, L. (2012). Residents living in residential care facilities: United States, 2010. *NCHS Data Brief*, (91), 1-8.

Cath, S. H. (1972). The geriatric patient and his family. The institutionalization of a parent: A nadir of life. *Journal of Geriatric Psychiatry, 5*, 25–46.

Centers for Disease Control and Prevention. (2010). *Nursing home residents*. Retrieved from www.cdc.gov/nchs/data/nnhsd/Estimates/nnhs/Estimates_PaymentSource_Tables.pdf

Centers for Medicare & Medicaid Services. (2012). *Nursing home data compendium: 2012 edition.* Retrieved from www.cms.gov/Medicare/Provider-Enrollment-and-Certification/CertificationandComplianc/downloads/nursinghomedatacompendium_508.pdf

Cheek, J., & Ballantyne, A. (2001). Moving them on and in: The process of searching for and selecting an aged care facility. *Qualitative Health Research, 11*(2), 221–237.

Chene, B. (2006). Dementia and residential placement: A view from the carers' perspective. *Qualitative Social Work, 5*(2), 187–215.

Coleman, M. T., Looney, S., O'Brien, J., Ziegler, C., Pastorino, C. A., & Turner, C. (2002). The Eden Alternative findings after 1 year of implementation. *The Journals of Gerontology Series A: Biological Sciences and Medical Sciences, 57*(7), 422–427.

Coughlin, J., (2010). Estimating the impact of caregiving and employment on well-being. *Outcomes & Insights in Health Management*, 2(1), 1–7.

Davies, S., & Nolan, M. (2006). "Making it better": Self-perceived roles of family caregivers of older people living in care homes: A qualitative study. *International Journal of Nursing Studies*, *43*, 281–291.

Dobrof, R. D., & Litwak, E. (1977). Maintenance of family ties of long-term care patients. Bethesda, MD: National Institute of Mental Health.

Drew, J. C. (2005). Making the long-term care environment more like home, the Eden alternative: What families want and why. In J. E. Gaugler (Ed.), *Promoting family involvement in long-term care settings: A guide to programs that work* (pp. 71–89). Baltimore, MD: Health Professions Press.

Edelman, P. (1986). The impact of community care to the home-bound elderly on provision of informal care. *The Gerontologist*, *26*, 263.

Eldercare Locator. (2014). Retrieved from www.eldercare.gov/Eldercare.NET/Public/Index.aspx

Etters, L., Goodall, D., & Harrison, B. E. (2008). Caregiver burden among dementia patient caregivers: A review of the literature. *Journal of the American Academy of Nurse Practitioners*, *20*, 423–428. doi:10.1111/j.1745-7599.2008.00342.x

Family Caregiver Alliance. (2001). *National Center on Caregiving*. Retrieved from www.caregiver.org

Feder, J., Komisar, H. L., & Niefeld, M. (2000). Long-term care in the United States: An overview. *Health Affairs*, *19*(3), 40–56. doi: 10.1377/hlthaff.19.3.40

Feinberg, L., Reinhard, S. C., Houser, A., & Choula, R. (2011, July). Valuing the invaluable: 2011 update. The growing contributions and costs of family caregiving. AARP Public Policy Institute. Retrieved from http://hjweinbergfoundation.net/ficsp/documents/10/Caregivers-Save-the-System-Money-With-Uncompensated-Care.pdf

Gaugler, J. E. (2005). Family involvement in residential long-term care: A synthesis and critical review. *Aging and Mental Health*, *9*(2), 105–118.

Gaugler, J. E., & Kane, R. A. (2001). Informal help in the assisted living setting: A one-year analysis. *Family Relations*, *50*(4), 335–347.

Gaugler, J. E., & Kane, R. L. (2007). Families in assisted living. *The Gerontologist*, *47*(3), 83–99.

Gaugler, J. E., & Lindahl, D. M. (2011). Assisted living placement. In M. Craft-Rosenberg & S.-R. Pehler (Eds.), *Encyclopedia of family health*. Thousand Oaks, CA: Sage.

Gaugler, J. E., Kane, R. L., & Kane, R. A. (2002). Family care for older people with disabilities: Towards more targeted and interpretable research. *International Journal of Aging and Human Development*, *54*(3), 205–231.

The Green House Project. (2014). Retrieved from www.thegreenhouseproject.org/

Greene, V. (1983). Substitution between formally and informally provided care for the impaired elderly in the community. *Medical Care*, *21*, 609–619.

Hawes, C., Phillips, C. D., & Rose, M. (2000). *High service or high privacy assisted living facilities, their residents and staff: Results from a national survey*. Washington, DC: U.S. Department of Health and Human Services/Research Triangle Institute.

Hawes, C., Rose, M., & Phillips, C. D. (1999). *A national study of assisted living for the frail elderly: Executive summary: Results of a national survey of facilities*. Beachwood, OH: Meyers Research Institute.

Hawes, C., Phillips, C. D., Rose, M., Holan, S., & Sherman, M. (2003). A national survey of assisted living facilities. *The Gerontologist*, *43*, 875–882.

High, D. M., & Rowles, G. D. (1995). Nursing home residents, families, and decision making: Toward an understanding of progressive surrogacy. *Journal of Aging Studies*, *9*(2), 101–117.

Jenkens, R., Sult, T., Lessell, N., Hammer, D., and Ortigara, A. (2011). Financial implications of the green house model. *Seniors Housing and Care Journal*, *19*(1), 3–22.

Jones, D. C. (1972). Social isolation, interaction, and conflict in two nursing homes. *The Gerontologist, 12*, 230–234.

Kahn, D. L. (1999). Making the best of it: Adapting to the ambivalence of a nursing home environment. *Qualitative Health Research, 9*(1), 119–132.

Kasper, J., and O'Malley, M. (2007). *Changes in characteristics, needs, and payment for care of elderly nursing home residents: 1999 to 2004*. Washington, DC: Kaiser Commission on Medicaid and the Uninsured (Publication #7663). Retrieved from www.kff.org/medicaid/7663.cfm

Kelsey, S. G., Laditka, S. B, & Laditka, J. N. (2010). Caregiver perspectives on transitions to assisted living and memory care. *American Journal of Alzheimer's Disease and Other Dementi*as, *25*(3), 255–264.

Kemp, C. L. (2008). Negotiating transitions in later life: Married couples in assisted living. *Journal of Applied Gerontology, 27*, 231–251.

Komisar, H. L., & Thompson, L. S. (2007). *National spending for long-term care*. Washington, DC: Georgetown University Long-Term Care Financing Project. Retrieved from http://ltc.georgetown.edu/pdfs/natspendfeb07.pdf

Leon, J., Neumann, P. J., Hermann, R. C., Hsu, M., Cummings, J. L., Doraiswamy, P. M., & Marin, D. (2000). Health-related quality-of-life and service utilization in Alzheimer's disease: A cross-sectional study. *American Journal of Alzheimer's Disease & Other Dementias, 15*, 94–108.

Levine, C., Halper, D., Peist, A., & Gould, D. A. (2010). Bridging troubled waters: Family caregivers, transitions, and long-term care. *Health Affairs, 29*(1), 116–124. doi: 10.1377/hlthaff.2009.0520

Litwak, E. (1985). *Helping the elderly: The complimentary roles of informal networks and formal systems*. New York, NY: Guilford Press.

Liu, W., & Gallagher-Thompson, D. (2009). Impact of dementia caregiving: Risks, strains, and growth. In S. H. Qualls & S. H. Zarit (Eds.), *Aging families and caregiving* (pp. 85–111). Hoboken, NJ: John Wiley & Sons.

Lum, T. Y., Kane, R. A., Cutler, L. J., & Yu, T. C. (2008). Effects of greenhouse nursing homes on residents' families. *Health Care Financing Review, 30*(2), 35.

Lyons, K. S., & Zarit, S. H. (1999). Formal and informal support: The great divide. *International Journal of Geriatric Psychiatry, 14*, 183–196.

Majerovitz, S. D., Mollott, R. J., & Rudder, C. (2009). We're on the same side: Improving communication between nursing home and family. *Health Communication, 24*(1), 12–20.

Medicaid Program. (2012). *Nursing facilities*. Retrieved from www.medicaid.gov/Medicaid-CHIP-Program-Information/By-State/By-State.html

Medicare Program. (2012). *Nursing homes: Alternatives to nursing case*. Retrieved from www.medicare.gov/nursing/alternatives/other.asp?PrinterFriendly=true

Medicare Program. (2013). *Nursing home checklist*. Retrieved from www.medicare.gov/files/nursing-home-checklist.pdf

Medicare Program. (2014). *Nursing home compare*. Retrieved from www.medicare.gov/nursinghomecompare/search.html

Miller, E. A., Mor, V., & Clark, M. (2009). Reforming long-term care in the United States: Findings from a national survey of specialists. *The Gerontologist, 50*, 238–252. doi:10.1093/geront/gnp111

Miller, S. C., Miller, E. A., Jung, H. Y., Sterns, S., Clark, M., & Mor, V. (2010). Nursing home organizational change: The "culture change" movement as viewed by long-term care specialists. *Medical Care Research and Review, 67*(4), 65S–81S. doi: 10.1177/1077558710366862

Montgomery, R. J. V., & Kosloski, K. (2000). Family caregiving: Change, continuity, and diversity. In R. Rubinstein & M. Lawton (Eds.), *Alzheimer's disease and related dementias: Strategies in care and research* (pp. 143–171). New York: Springer.

Montgomery, R. J. V., Rowe, J. M., & Kosloski, K. (2007). Family caregiving. In J. A. Blackburn & C. N. Dulmus (Eds.), *Handbook of gerontology: Evidence-based approaches to theory, practice, and policy* (pp. 426–454). Hoboken, NJ: John Wiley & Sons.

Natan, M. B. (2007). Perceptions of nurses, families, and residents in nursing homes concerning residents' needs. *International Journal of Nursing Practice, 14*, 195–199.

The National Alliance for Caregiving. (2015). *Caregiving in the U.S.* Retrieved from http://www.caregiving.org/caregiving2015

The National Alliance for Caregiving and AARP. (2009). *Caregiving in the U.S. National Alliance for Caregiving*. Retrieved from www.cdc.gov/nchs/data/nnhsd/Estimates/nnhs/Estimates_PaymentSource_Tables.pdf

National Center for Assisted Living. (1998). *Facts and trends: The assisted living sourcebook*. Washington, DC: American Health Care Association.

The National Dementia Initiative. (2013). *Dementia care: The quality chasm (White paper)*. Retrieved from www.ccal.org/wp-content/uploads/DementiaCareTheQualityChasm_2-20-13-final.pdf

Newcomer, R., Breuer, W., & Zhang, X. (1994). *Residents and the appropriateness of placement in residential care for the elderly: A 1993 survey of California RCFE operators and residents*. San Francisco, CA: Institute for Health and Aging, University of California.

Ottawa Hospital Research Institute. (2013). *Patient decision aids*. Retrieved from http://decisionaid.ohri.ca/index.html

Parminder, R., O'Donnell, M., Schwellnus, H., Rosenbaum, P., King, G., Brehaut, J., ... Wood, E. (2004). Caregiving process and caregiver burden: Conceptual models to guide research and practice. *BMC Pediatrics, 4*, 1–13.

Pearson, A., Nay, R., & Taylor, B. (2004). Relatives' experience of nursing home admissions: Preliminary study. *Australasian Journal on Ageing, 23*(2), 86–90.

Pillemer, K., Suitor, J. J., Henderson, C. R., Meador, R., Schultz, L., Robison, J., & Hegeman, C. (2003). A cooperative communication intervention for nursing home staff and family members of residents. *The Gerontologist, 43*(Special Issue 2), 96–106.

Port, C. L., Zimmerman, S., Williams, C. S., Dobbs, D., Preisser, J. S., & Williams, S. W. (2005). Families filling the gap: Comparing family involvement for assisted living and nursing home residents with dementia. *The Gerontologist, 45*(Special Issue I), 87–95.

Pruchno, R. A., & Rose, M. S. (2002). Time use by frail older people in different care settings. *Journal of Applied Gerontology, 21*, 5–23.

Ransom, S. (2000). *Eden Alternative: The Texas project* (IQILTHC Monograph Series 2000–4, pp. 24–31). San Marcos, TX: Texas Long-Term Care Institute, Southwest Texas State University.

Reuss, G. F., Dupuis, S. L., & Whitfield, K. (2005). Understanding the experience of moving a loved one to a long-term care facility: Family members' perspectives. *Journal of Gerontological Social Work, 46*(1), 17–46.

Robinson, C. A., Reid, R. C., & Cooke, H. A. (2010). A home away from home: The meaning of home according to families of residents with dementia. *Dementia, 9*(4), 490–508.

Robison, J., Curry, L., Gruman, C., Porter, M., Henderson, C. R., & Pillemer, K. (2007). Partners in caregiving in a special care environment: Cooperative communication between staff and families on dementia units. *The Gerontologist, 47*(4), 504–515.

Robison, J., & Pillemer, K. (2005). Partners in caregiving: Cooperative communication between families and nursing homes. In J. Gaugler (Ed.), *Promoting family involvement in long-term care settings* (pp. 201–224). Baltimore, MD: Health Professions Press.

Ross, M. M., Rosenthal, C., & Dawson, P. (1997). Spousal caregiving in the institutional setting: Visiting. *Journal of Clinical Nursing, 6*, 473–483.

Ryan, A. A., & Scullion, H. F. (2000). Nursing home placement: An exploration of the experiences of family carers. *Journal of Advanced Nursing, 32*(5), 1187–1195.

Specht, J. K. P., Reed, D., & Maas, M. L. (2005). Family involvement in care of residents with dementia: An important resource for quality of life and care. In J. E. Gaugler (Ed.), *Promoting family involvement in long-term care settings: A guide to programs that work* (pp. 163–200). Baltimore, MD: Health Professions Press.

Stacey-Konnert, C., & Pynoos, J. (1992). Friendship and social networks in a continuing care retirement community. *Journal of Applied Gerontology, 11*, 298–313.

Stone, R. I., & Wiener, J. M. (2001). *Addressing the long-term care workforce crisis* (Report for US Department of Health and Human Services). Washington, DC: The Urban Institute.

Strang, V. R., Koop, P. M., Dupuis-Blanchard, S., Nordstrom, M., & Thompson, B. (2006). Family caregivers and transition to long-term care. *Clinical Nursing Research, 15*(1), 27–45. doi: 10.1177/1054773805282356

Svarstad, B. L., Mount, J. K., & Bigelow, W. (2001). Variations in the treatment culture of nursing homes and responses to regulations to reduce drug use. *Psychiatric Services, 52*(5), 666–672.

Thomas, W. H. (1994). *The Eden Alternative: Nature, hope, and nursing homes*. Sherburne, NY: Eden Alternative Foundation.

Tolbert, V. E., & Basham, J. G. (2005). Educating families and improving communication: A Web-based intervention program for families in nursing home residents with dementia. In J. E. Gaugler (Ed.), *Promoting family involvement in long-term care settings: A guide to programs that work* (pp. 227–248). Baltimore, MD: Health Professions Press.

White-Chu, E. F., Graves, W. J., Godfrey, S. M., Bonner, A., & Sloane, P. (2009). Beyond the medical model: The culture change revolution in long-term care. *Journal of the American Medical Directors Association, 10*(6), 370–378.

White House Conference on Aging. (2010). *Care for the family caregiver: A place to start.* Retrieved from http://www.caregiving.org/data/Emblem_CfC10_Final2.pdf

Wiener, J. M. (2003). An assessment of strategies for improving quality of care in nursing homes. *The Gerontologist, 43*(2), 19–27.

Wilson, K. B. (2007). Historical evolution of assisted living in the United States, 1979 to the present. *The Gerontologist, 47*(1), 8–22.

5

Home Health Care

SUSAN L. HUGHES
PANKAJA DESAI

CHAPTER OVERVIEW

The U.S. home health care industry grew rapidly during the latter part of the 20th century. At the end of the 1990s, reimbursement changes mandated by the Balanced Budget Act of 1997 (BBA 97, P.L. 105-33) caused substantial industry consolidation. Nevertheless, because of strong underlying trends that include demographics, technological advances that facilitate complex care in the home, and consumer demand, home health care is expected to continue growing considerably in the foreseeable future. This chapter examines the development of home care (overall market and Medicare model) in the United States, describes the payment and regulatory policies that have fostered our current complex array of home care services, details various sectors of the industry, and discusses challenges for maximizing the positive impact of home care in the 21st century.

LEARNING OBJECTIVES

After completing this chapter, you should have an understanding of:

- The complexity of the home care marketplace and forces that contributed to the development of three specific home care models
- The population, services, and quality assurances used for Medicare home health care
- The population, services, funding sources, and quality assurance mechanisms used for private home care, including Medicaid's Home and Community-Based Services (HCBS) waiver programs
- The population, services, funding sources, and quality mechanisms used for high-tech home care

- Technological advances that can improve the delivery and outcomes of all three home care models
- Initiatives in the Patient Protection and Affordable Care Act that can improve the coordination of care and care outcomes for persons served by home care programs who have chronic conditions

KEY TERMS

Affordable Care Act (ACA)
Capitation
Case mix
Conditions of participation
Consumer-directed home care
Home and community-based services (HCBS)
Home care
Home health care
Managed care plans
Medicaid waiver program 1915(c)
Medicare Advantage plans
Prospective payment system (PPS)
Telehealth

INTRODUCTION

HISTORICAL CONTEXT

Home care policy in the United States has developed in an incremental and disjointed way. The first formal home care programs began in the 1880s. Home health care programs emerged in significant numbers during the Progressive Era (1905–1915; Benjamin, 1993). At that time, knowledge about the role of bacteria, concerns about contagious disease and poor hygiene in crowded slums, and high infant mortality rates stimulated the development of public health nursing departments and Visiting Nurse Associations (VNAs) that still exist in many communities across the United States. For the most part, these agencies focused on maternal and child health and communicable disease.

Between 1915 and 1960, a number of hospitals began to provide post-discharge care at home, and occasionally a visionary provider advocated the expansion of care at home for chronically ill individuals. At the same time, social services agencies began providing homemaker services to families with young children whose mothers were incapacitated by illness. Finally, during the 1940s, the Joint Commission on Chronic Disease was established; it produced a groundbreaking report in 1956 (Benjamin, 1993).

Based on Commission members' site visits to outstanding programs, the Commission Report emphasized the importance of physician involvement in home care and advocated an expanded role for formal paid homemakers (Benjamin, 1993). The Commission also called for the development of *organized, full-service home care programs marked by centralized responsibility, coordinated care planning, and a team approach to care*. However, when the Commission Report was released in 1956, after 10 years of deliberations, it was paid scant attention because of concerns over growing costs of hospital care for older Americans. Although Social Security Administration policy analysts were favorably impressed by Blue Cross reports of savings achieved by hospital-based home care programs, analysts were more concerned about potential excess demand for home care, especially if the benefits were broadly defined to include homemaker services (Benjamin, 1993).

As a result of this concern, when Medicare was passed in 1965, the Part A Medicare home care benefit was purposefully configured as an adjunct to acute hospital care. Eligibility criteria were so stringent that they limited use of the benefit. A similar Part B benefit was also created that did not require a prior hospitalization; however, a 20% copayment served as a deterrent to its use.

When first established, Medicaid identified home health care as an optional service that states could provide to poor and medically indigent persons of all ages, using a combination of state and federal funding. One year later, in 1967, home health care was moved from the optional to the *mandatory* category of Medicaid benefits. The benefit included skilled care, as well as selected support services.

In the early 1970s, Medicare coverage was extended to persons with end-stage renal disease and adults with permanent disabilities. Social services funding for home care also increased in 1974 with the passage of the Social Security Act Social Services Block Grant Amendments (Title XX). This legislation encouraged states to consolidate social services and expand homemaker coverage to chronically ill adults. Meanwhile, Title III of the Older Americans Act established a network of Area Agencies on Aging to provide information and referral and chore/housekeeping services to persons 60 and older. Title VII of the Act provided funding for home-delivered and congregate meals. Two other developments of the 1970s also contributed to the complex composition of home care. First, appalled at the increased technological intensity, invasiveness, and emotional sterility of acute care for terminally ill persons, advocates of hospice care succeeded in mandating a national hospice demonstration and then enacted a Medicare hospice benefit for palliative care in 1982 (see Chapter 12). This benefit promoted care at home for terminally ill people. Second, aided by space-age technology, infusion pumps made "high-tech" care at home possible for persons requiring enteral and parental nutrition and intravenous antibiotics and chemotherapies.

In 1981, states could apply for **Medicaid 1915(c) waivers** to provide home- and community-based services (HCBS) to specific categories of Medicaid recipients who otherwise would require nursing home care. Services that could be provided included homemaker and personal care as well as others that states wished to provide to specific waiver populations. Shortly thereafter, the Medicare Tax Equity and Financial Responsibility Act (TEFRA; 1983) attempted to rein in rapid increases in hospital costs by mandating the prospective payment of Medicare hospital charges. The hospital **prospective payment system** (PPS) is a reimbursement system based on service categories with set payment amounts; fees are set for hospitals in advance for costs associated with care for a specific diagnosis as opposed to the prior practice of reimbursing for days of care irrespective of patient diagnosis. Under PPS, hospitals were paid a flat fee for an average stay for a hip replacement, for example. If a given hospital was able to discharge the patient earlier, the hospital could retain the savings as an efficiency "bonus." This new reimbursement system led hospitals to embark on systematic efforts to retain savings achieved by shortening patients' length of stay. Thus, PPS provided strong incentives for hospitals to enter the skilled/post-acute portion of the home care enterprise themselves or to transfer patients as soon as possible to home care or nursing home care for postacute care.

Within 20 years (1966–1986) and fueled by four basic trends (i.e., growth in older and disabled populations, increased technological capacity, popular demand, and federal funding), home care unintentionally evolved and became differentiated into four different models of care with multiple funding sources and differing eligibility criteria:

- Medicare-certified home health agencies
- Private or non-Medicare home care agencies
- High-tech home therapies and infusion
- Hospice

Three of these models are discussed in this chapter and the fourth, hospice care, is considered in Chapter 12.

Home health care is defined as services that are usually medical or clinical and are provided in the home, including various therapies and skilled nursing care. Some home health care services may also be classified as **home care** (non-medical services that are provided in the home, such as light housekeeping, meal preparation, and medication reminders). The primary philosophy of home health care today is to increase autonomy while improving functioning and quality of life and preventing hospital or nursing home admission (Ellenbecker et al., 2008). Benjamin (1999) describes goals of the Medicaid HCBS program. The goals are divided into client- and system-level goals. Client-level goals focus on enhancing the health, well-being, functioning, and independence of patients while helping them to remain in a safe home environment and to prevent health problems from occurring or detecting them early. Goals at the system level focus on providing effective and efficient access to comprehensive, affordable, and quality services to as many individuals as possible who are in need, while providing choice, tailoring services, and reinforcing informal networks. It is important to note that in many cases the home care option is only possible for persons having family members who can supplement these formal services with informal care. A whole body of literature has been devoted to understanding the impact of care provision on family members. This topic is addressed in Chapter 3.

NATIONAL PROFILE

In 2007, 2.6 million Americans were actively using some home health care or hospice care at any given time. This care was provided by approximately 14,500 home health and hospice agencies then reported in the United States (Park-Lee & Decker, 2010).

CLIENTS

On any given day in 2007, the year of the most recent National Home and Hospice Care Survey, part of an ongoing series of national surveys conducted by the Centers for Disease Control (CDC) with hospice and home health agencies, 1.46 million persons used home health care agencies (CDC, 2013). Home health care agencies included in the survey were certified by either Medicare or Medicaid or were licensed by a state to provide services to home health care users. Agencies were excluded if they provided only homemaker or housekeeping services, assistance with instrumental activities of daily living (IADLs), or durable medical equipment (DME) and supplies. Users of agencies surveyed tended to be aged 65 and older (69%), female (64%), and White (82%). More than one tenth (13%) had used care options in the 60 days before the survey interview, and more than one fifth (21%) of current home health care patients had at least one overnight hospital stay since admission to the home health care agency (NCHS, 2007a). On average, agencies served 178 current patients (NCHS, 2007b), 29% of whom had at least one advance directive on file.

AGENCIES

The number of home care organizations has grown markedly. In 1963 there were 1,100 home care agencies of record in the nation. By 1997, the U.S. Bureau of the Census estimated that this number had reached 19,690. The Census Bureau defined home care agencies as "firms that provide skilled nursing services exclusively or in combination with other services" (National Association for Home Care [NAHC], 2001). Because many private agencies do not provide skilled services but do provide homemaker/home health aide (HHA) services, this number substantially underestimates the total number of home care providers in the United States. Most recent numbers from the National Association for Home Care indicate that 33,000 organizations provide home care of some type (NAHC, 2010). The same National Home and Hospice Care Survey found that 14,500 agencies in the United States provided home health and/or hospice care. The majority (75%) provided home health care only. Of the home health only agencies, 76% were proprietary, 76% were located in a metropolitan area, 80% were certified by Medicare, and 79% were certified by Medicaid (NCHS, 2007b).

SERVICES

Largely as a result of funding streams and regulations, home care has evolved into four distinct models. The characteristics of each model differ. Exhibit 5.1 shows the services provided by the different home care models, which span a severity-of-need continuum. Although some health care services provide the full continuum of services, these are generally the exception, as multiple billing and regulatory mechanisms now in place discourage agencies from being full-service home care providers.

EXHIBIT 5.1 Home Services by Degree of Skill Intensity

TECHNOLOGIES INTENSITY	SERVICE	SKILLED (MEDICARE CERTIFIED)	SKILLED AND PERSONAL CARE (NOT MEDICARE CERTIFIED)	HIGH-TECH	HOSPICE
High	Enteral/parenteral nutrition			X	X
↑	Ventilation/respirator therapy			X	
	Antibiotic therapy			X	X
	Chemotherapy			X	X
	Renal dialysis			X	
	Pharmaceuticals				X
	Skilled nursing	X	X		X
	Physical therapy	X	X		
	Occupational therapy	X	X		
	Speech therapy	X	X		
	Medical social services	X	X		X
	Case management	X	X		X
	Nutrition service		X		X
	Full-time (24 hour) personal care		X		X
	Pastoral care				X
	Home health aide/personal care	X	X		
	Homemaker		X		
	Chore/housekeeping		X		
	Respite care		X		X
↓	Home-delivered meals		X		
Low	Durable medical equipment	X		X	X

Source: Hughes (1991).

Most people with chronic disabilities need flexible combinations of, and timely access to, the 21 services shown in Exhibit 5.1, especially as their conditions change over time. However, the organization and funding of these services in the United States has been fragmented, with no accountability across providers for the coordination and efficient management of care.

FUNDING

Home health care, very narrowly defined as free-standing programs (excluding hospital-based programs), was the fastest growing component of national health care expenditures during the last 40 years of the 20th century, increasing from $0.2 billion in 1970 to $34.5 billion in 1997 and then dropping to $32.4 billion in 2000, following the passage of the Balanced Budget Act of 1997 (BBA 97; Levit, Smith, Cowan, & Martin, 2002). Home care expenditures accounted for 0.3% of total health expenditures in 1970 but grew to account for 3.2% of expenditures in 1997 (Levit et al., 2002). The rate of growth was quickly reined in by BBA and the PPS for Medicare home health care that was implemented in 2000.

The magnitude of home care expenditures in 2009 ($68.3 billion) ranks far below expenditures for hospital, physician, and nursing home care, which accounted for 36%, 24%, and 9% of personal health care expenditures, respectively, in that same year (Martin, Lassman, Whittle, Catlin, & The National Health Expenditure Accounts Team, 2011). Between 2005 and 2009, home health expenditures increased on average by 8.8% per year, compared to average annual increases of 6.2% and 5.4% for hospital and physician services, respectively (see Chapter 17).

The major sources of payment for home care are public. Medicare and Medicaid paid for 65% of all formal home care services in 2009. Other public programs paying for home care include the Older Americans Act, Title XX Social Services block grants, the Department of Veterans Affairs, and the Civilian Health and Medical Program of the Uniformed Services (CHAMPUS). Ten percent of home care services are paid for out of pocket by care recipients and their families, and 8% is reimbursed by private insurance (NAHC, 2010).

Managed care plans provide health insurance by contracting with providers and facilities to develop a network that offers less expensive care to enrollees. There are three main kinds of managed care plans, which include health maintenance organizations (HMO), preferred provider organizations (PPO), and point of service plans (POS; Medline Plus, 2013a). Commercial insurance and managed care plans also pay for home care services. Although some may require home care agencies to be Medicare certified, others do not and are willing to cover care on an individual basis or to contract with an agency for coverage of eligible patients. A detailed description follows of agencies, users, and reimbursements associated with Medicare-certified skilled home care, private non-Medicare-certified home care, and high-tech home care.

MEDICARE-CERTIFIED HOME HEALTH AGENCIES

Medicare has been a driving force in the development of home health care. The 1965 legislation that established Medicare (Title XVIII of the Social Security Act) created two sources of payment for home care, one under Medicare Part A and another under Part B. Both were designed to provide skilled care for those recovering from an acute episode of illness. Medicare does not pay for home care on an indefinite basis or for those whose major problem is chronic illness or functional disability. The Medicare legislation also specified criteria with which home care agencies must comply to be "certified" to receive Medicare payment. These **conditions of participation** (COPs) specify staffing, reporting requirements, quality-assurance obligations, and structural characteristics, among other conditions. Compliance is expensive and requires strict adherence by all staff to Medicare policies and processes. Not all home care agencies choose to participate. As a result, a companion group of "non-Medicare-certified" home care agencies has emerged, which is described in the following section.

Data on Medicare-certified agencies are relatively good because they are maintained by the federal government, and agencies must submit information to be certified and be paid.

Traditionally, use of the Medicare home health care benefit was constrained by the review of claims done by designated regional fiscal intermediaries. These intermediaries were instructed to interpret the Medicare regulations regarding eligibility and benefits strictly in order to control use and cost. In 1989, a class action lawsuit protesting this practice (*Duggan v. Bowen*) was brought on behalf of beneficiaries, who argued that the practice violated the original intent of the Medicare legislation. The court found for the plaintiffs and mandated a broader interpretation of the definition of *homebound* and a broader limit on the number of covered visits. As a result, use of the Medicare home care benefit exploded, and the number of visits and reimbursements began increasing *at an annual rate of 30%*. In an effort to staunch this fiscal hemorrhage, Congress passed the Balanced Budget Act of 1997. BBA 97 mandated development of a *case-mix-based PPS* and an *interim payment system (IPS)* for use while the prospective system was in development. It is important to note that the IPS contained new per-beneficiary reimbursement limits that had a major negative effect on the number of agencies participating in the Medicare program and on home health care payments. The new PPS for Medicare home health care was implemented in October 2000, which served to stabilize the industry.

CLIENTS

To be eligible for Medicare payment of home care, a person must be enrolled in Medicare, be homebound (i.e., unable to leave the house as certified by a physician), require skilled nursing care or physical therapy, and need intermittent as opposed to continuous care. Although criteria have been modified somewhat over the years, they remain focused on recovery from acute illness, not long-term maintenance or assistance with functional disability.

In 1996, the number of clients served per year peaked at roughly 3.6 million; it declined to 2.4 million in 2001 shortly after the implementation of prospective payment (NAHC, 2010), a decline of 1.2 million users or 33%. However, by 2008, the number of persons served per year rebounded to 3.4 million, reflecting the longer term impact of more stable funding under PPS.

Home health care is also a mandatory benefit that states must provide under Medicaid. States establish their own criteria for acceptance as a Medicaid provider. States typically accept home health agencies certified to participate in Medicare as providers for Medicaid as well. Persons who receive care must be eligible for Medicaid because of low income or because they have met their state's spend-down requirements. Between 1999 and 2007, clients served by Medicaid home health increased from 680,000 to 814,000, an increase of 20% (Kaiser Commission on Medicaid and the Uninsured, 2011). In 2007, 826,000 persons were served by the Medicaid personal care benefit, which is optional on the part of the states. Close to 1.2 million were served through the HCBS waiver, discussed later in this chapter.

The top three principal diagnoses among Medicare home health care users in 2008 were diseases of the circulatory system (about 26%), heart disease (12.6%), and diseases of the musculoskeletal system (12.6%; NAHC, 2010).

The early Medicare home care reimbursement regulations attempted to ensure that the benefit would be used only by persons recovering from an acute bout of illness who required skilled care. Beneficiaries were required to undergo a 3-day hospitalization prior to referral to home care. Although this requirement was discontinued, the majority of users of Medicare-certified home health services are people who are discharged from the hospital.

AGENCIES

The number of Medicare-certified home health agencies grew from 1,753 in 1967, one year after the implementation of Medicare, to an all-time high of 10,444 in 1997 (NAHC, 1999). BBA 97 resulted in the closure of roughly one third of all Medicare-certified agencies, with the number declining to 7,152 in 2000, a reduction of 31.5% (NAHC, 2001). With the implementation of prospective payment, the number of agencies has recovered to reach 10,581 in 2009 (NAHC, 2010).

In addition to their numbers, the organizational auspices of home health care agencies have changed markedly. Figure 5.1 contrasts the prevalence of organizational arrangements over time. In 1966, the VNA and public health departments accounted for 90% of all certified home health agencies. The Omnibus Reconciliation Act of 1980 changed the Medicare COPs to permit proprietary providers in states without home care licensure requirements to provide Medicare-reimbursed care. Then, in 1983, Medicare prospective payment for

FIGURE 5.1 Number of Medicare-certified home care agencies, by auspice, by selected years, 1967–2009.

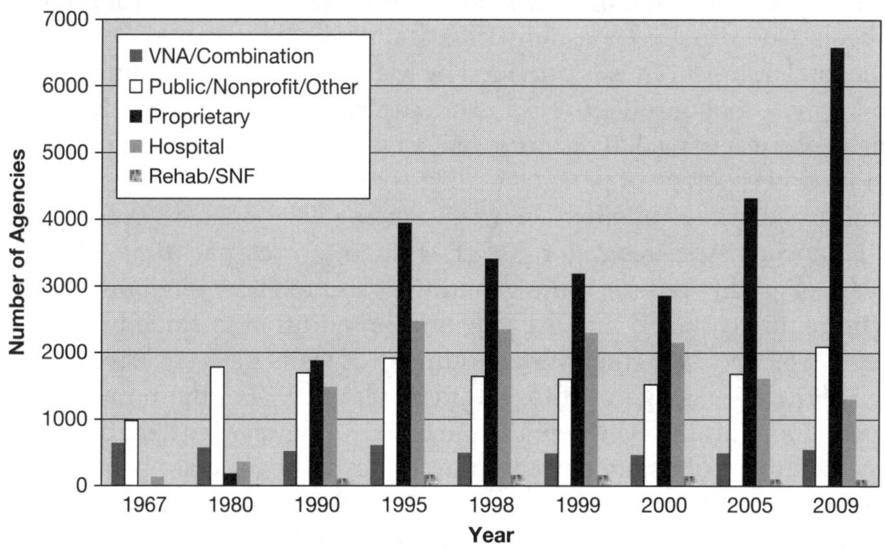

Sources: National Association of Home Care (2001, 2010).

hospital care encouraged hospitals to develop their own hospital-based or linked programs in order to streamline discharge planning and maximize patient care revenues. As a result, by 2000, VNA and public health providers dropped to 19.2% of total home care providers, whereas proprietary agencies increased from 0% to 40%, and hospital-based providers rose from 6% to 30% of all Medicare-certified providers (NAHC, 2001). By 2009, this trend continued to accelerate such that more than 62% of providers were freestanding proprietary agencies, and an additional 12% were hospital based. This shift meant that far fewer providers were willing to accept patients whose eligibility for reimbursement was unclear and far fewer providers were willing to provide care beyond the episodes covered by payers. It is unclear whether these shifts were accompanied by simultaneous growth in the use of Medicaid home health care by persons of low income or those who are medically indigent.

SERVICES

Services provided by skilled home health agencies include skilled nursing, skilled therapies (physical, occupational, and speech), medical social work, and HHA. Three services constituted 97% of total reimbursable visits in 1996: skilled nursing (41%), HHA (49%), and physical therapy (7%; U.S. Department of Health and Human Services, 1998). To be eligible for Medicare reimbursement, Medicare clients must be certified by a physician as needing skilled nursing or physical therapy. Other skilled services and HHA care are then also allowable. Because of federal regulations, Medicare-certified agencies tend to offer only those services paid for by Medicare. Noncertified private agencies may offer skilled as well as support services.

Skilled personnel coordinate with staff of other organizations providing care to the client. The nurse, for example, may function as a case manager and contact a company providing DME and a community agency providing Meals on Wheels. Coordination is usually informal rather than formal.

The total number of visits provided by Medicare-certified home health agencies by year is shown in Figure 5.2. Annual visits rose precipitously, especially among those receiving 100 or more visits, reflecting a significant expansion in eligibility and coverage of persons with chronic care needs.

This growth occurred after *Duggan v. Bowen* (1986), which forced the Health Care Financing Administration (HCFA) to interpret part-time/intermittent Medicare eligibility criteria more generously and to allow eligibility for enrollees who required skilled nursing *judgment*, in addition to skilled nursing *care*. Between 1989 and 1996, the average number of visits per year tripled, from 27 to 76. Following passage of BBA 97, under the new IPS, the number of visits dropped dramatically. Between 1996 and 1998, the median length of stay on Medicare home health care decreased by 16 days, the decrease being especially pronounced among proprietary providers (Murkofsky, Phillips, McCarthy, Davis, & Hamel, 2003). Up to this point in time Medicare home health care was reimbursed on a retrospective cost-per-visit basis. Therefore, participating

FIGURE 5.2 Medicare home care visits, 1984–2008.

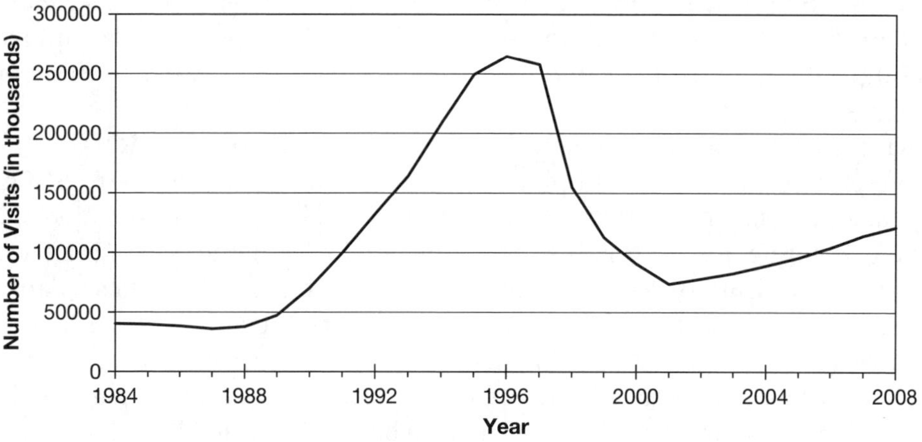

Sources: National Association of Home Care (2001, 2010).

agencies had no incentives to economize on number of visits provided and every incentive to do the reverse. The new PPS implemented in October 2000 attempted to remove this incentive by reimbursing *prospectively* for a *case-mix-based episode* of care. As data in Figure 5.2 demonstrate, the number of visits has rebounded somewhat from a nadir of 73,698 visits in 2001 to 121,026 visits in 2008. However, 2008 visits still constituted only 46% of visits provided in 1996. Although few studies have examined the impact of PPS on client outcomes, research examining the impact of the IPS indicates that access to home health care services was constrained among the poorest Medicare beneficiaries, especially among those who were not eligible for Medicaid-reimbursed services (McCall, Komisar, Petersons, & Moore, 2001; Zhu, 2004). The Medicare Payment Advisory Commission (MedPAC) calculated a total reduction of 1.3 million beneficiaries between 1997 and 2001 and in June 2003 issued a report indicating that skilled nursing facility (SNF) care is now substituting for home health care for some patients, most likely at a much higher cost to Medicare (Medicare Payment Advisory Commission, 2003; NAHC, 2010).

To further constrain rapidly increasing Medicare home health care costs, BBA 97 also mandated that, as of January 1, 1998, home health coverage under Medicare Part A would be limited to a maximum of 100 visits during an illness, after a hospitalization, or after receiving covered services in an SNF. All other home health coverage would be rendered under Part B. This shift was phased in gradually over time, at the rate of one sixth of beneficiaries per year through January 1, 2002.

STAFFING

Of 290,000 full-time equivalent (FTE) Medicare home health workers in 2009, 92,113 (32%) were registered nurses (RNs), 44,646 (15%) were licensed practical nurses (LPNs), and 65,146 (23%) were home care aides (NAHC, 2010). Social workers, occupational and speech therapists, and homemakers also may be on staff. By Medicare regulation, the majority of staff are salaried employees, although some professional staff may be on contract for a specified number of hours per month.

Home health agencies depend heavily on the availability of RNs and, to a growing degree, LPNs, in addition to HHAs. At present, the industry is highly regulated. Thus, opportunities for experiments involving the substitution of less skilled personnel for more skilled personnel are limited, unless care is provided through a **Medicare Advantage** (Medicare-managed care) plan. These plans are provided by organizations that contract with Centers for Medicare & Medicaid Services (CMS) to provide health insurance in the form of coordinated care plans or traditional managed care plans, medical savings account plans, private fee-for-service plans, and religious fraternal benefit plans (CMS, 2011).

Although the medical complexity of Medicare home care clients is increasing, the physician's role in home health care has been limited, with the notable exception of the Veterans Affairs (VA) Home Based Primary Care (HBPC) program, in which physicians work closely with a home care team as primary care managers. Until the early 1990s, physician visits were reimbursed at a lower rate than HHAs. A randomized study of the VA home care model found that home health teams that included active physician participation reduced hospital readmission costs by 29% (Cummings et al., 1990). The issue of physician involvement in home care is being reconsidered at present. An American Academy of Home Care Physicians has been established and the American Medical Association (AMA) has developed physician home care practice guidelines. In 1995 the HCFA increased the reimbursement for physician home visits and allowed physicians to bill for case management functions on behalf of clients. However, a national survey of 600 physicians who signed Medicare home health care plans of care in 2000 found that less than 3% of total home health claims were submitted for this service, because physicians reported that the reimbursement provided was too low to offset the costs of completing the paperwork required for billing (Office of the Inspector General, 2001).

Recent studies have examined rehospitalizations among patients in the Medicare fee-for-service program and found that almost one fifth (19.6%) of beneficiaries who had been discharged from a hospital were rehospitalized within 30 days and 34.0% were rehospitalized within 90 days (Jencks, Williams, & Coleman, 2009). The annual cost of Medicare hospital readmissions, 80% of which are potentially avoidable, is $415 billion (Miller, Ramsland, & Harrington, 1999). As of October 1, 2012, for the first time hospitals were held accountable for the quality of their discharge planning when Medicare began reducing payments to hospitals with high readmission rates for three high-volume, high-cost conditions. At present, the conditions targeted include heart attack, pneumonia, and heart failure that together account for 18% of 30-day readmissions (Thorpe & Ogden, 2010). It is important to note that several initiatives of the Patient Protection and Affordable Care Act (ACA) address preventable hospital readmissions. These include the Community Care Transitions Program, which targets improved discharge planning and follow-up care in the community for persons at high risk of readmission and the Medicare Independence at Home Demonstration Program, which will test the use of interdisciplinary teams in the home for persons with chronic conditions and disabilities. Other reimbursement reforms under the ACA that address this issue include the accountable care organizations, which seek to integrate the care of enrollees across all providers and the bundling of acute and postacute care payments into one overall rate to a pre-established group of providers (Thorpe & Ogden, 2010).

Medicare home health care agencies have the potential to play a very important role by partnering with hospitals to prevent readmissions. For example, a randomized trial by Naylor and colleagues has shown that Medicare patients hospitalized for congestive heart failure who received advanced practice nurse–directed discharge planning and a home care follow-up protocol experienced an increased length of time between hospital discharge and readmission that was accompanied by a reduction in the total number of rehospitalizations and decreased cost (Naylor et al., 2004), indicating substantial potential to improve clinical and economic outcomes for this group of patients.

FUNDING

Total reimbursements for Medicare-certified home health agencies expanded gradually between 1974 and 1989. As regulatory restraints on the number of visits were relaxed, the number of visits and concomitant reimbursements expanded markedly before peaking in 1997 and then dropping precipitously following the passage of BBA 97 (Figure 5.3). It is important to note that trend data through 2008 now indicate that reimbursement under PPS has returned to the same high seen in 1996.

In dollar terms, expenditures for Medicare-certified home care increased from $2.5 billion in 1989 to $16.7 billion in 1997 (an annual rate of increase

FIGURE 5.3 Medicare home care reimbursement, 1984–2008.

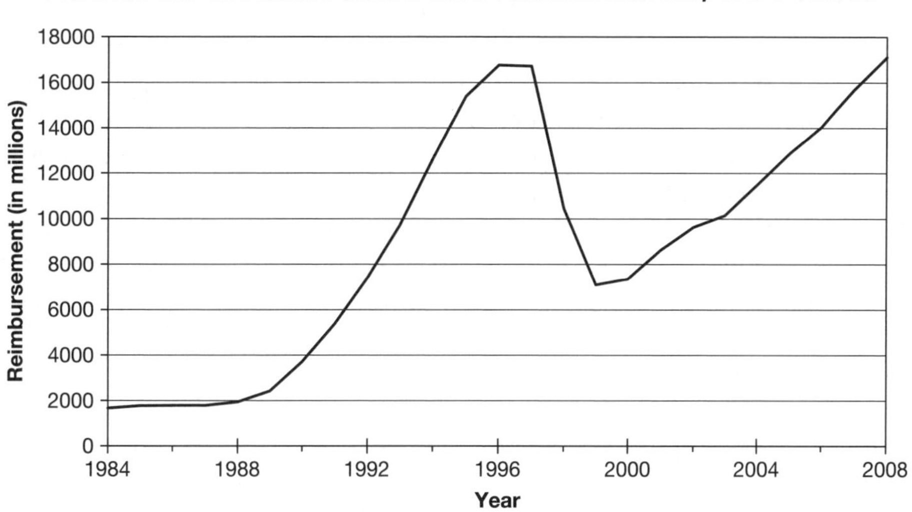

Sources: National Association of Home Care (2001, 2010).

of 33%). As described earlier, BBA 97 attempted to mitigate this rate of increase by mandating a change from fee-for-service/retrospective reimbursement based on cost to prospective payment based on per-beneficiary episodes of care. While the new PPS was being developed, agencies were reimbursed under an IPS that precipitously reduced expenditures to $14 billion in 2000—a decrease of 16.2% between 1997 and 2000.

The goal of the PPS is to reward efficient providers and to encourage inefficient providers to change their behaviors. Although PPS decreased the use of the home health benefit among beneficiaries age 85 and older (McCall, Petersons, Moore, & Korb, 2003), the impact of PPS reimbursement is not yet known. The PPS system relies on a 153-category **case-mix** adjuster to set payment rates based on patient characteristics, including clinical severity, functional status, and use of rehabilitative services; it includes payment for unexpectedly high-use cases through an outlier adjustment, as well as adjustment for area wages indices. In this system, agencies are reimbursed based on a 60-day episode of care for a specific condition. The agency has the latitude to decide when to discharge a patient within each 60-day episode, but is held accountable for care outcomes. A review of PPS by the General Accounting Office (GAO) identified several areas of concern, including the 60-day episode for payment, which may be too long for some clients; the impact of payment on different types of providers in different geographic locations; and the adequacy of the case-mix adjustment method with respect to accurate assessments of resource needs. As a result of these concerns, GAO urged that the impact of the new system be carefully studied by the Centers for Medicare and Medicaid Services (CMS; GAO, 2000). Meanwhile, it is important to note that the dollar value of reimbursements ($17 million in 2008) was very similar to the $16.8 million figure seen in 1996 (NAHC, 2010). Provisions of the 2010 Affordable Care Act (ACA) may reverse this trend. Because Congress perceived that home health care agencies and skilled nursing facilities experienced high profit margins in the recent past (estimated by the MedPAC to be 10.3% in 2008 for nursing homes and 17.4% for home health), they wrote into law that ACA will achieve health reform savings by reducing the annual update for inflation for these providers. Specifically, provisions of the Act project that savings of $61.1 billion will be generated across skilled nursing facilities, home health, and hospice providers through 2019 (Wiener, 2010). The impact of reduced inflation adjustments on providers, access, and outcomes is currently unknown.

Medicaid also reimburses for skilled home health care. In 1975, hospital and nursing home payments combined to account for 62% of national Medicaid expenditures. By 2007, these payments had dropped to 34% of total expenditures, whereas home health payments increased from 0.6% of Medicaid to 20.2% ($55.9 million), reflecting the same trends toward shortened hospital length of stay, reduction of hospital admissions, and increased capacity to provide technologically complex care in the home as well as growing expenditures under the Medicaid HCBS waiver programs.

Commercial insurance companies and managed health plans typically provide a benefit for skilled home care in conjunction with an acute episode of illness. Private insurance paid for 12.3% of home care provided in 2007, compared to 55.7% of payments from Medicare and 22.4% from Medicaid (Park-Lee & Decker, 2010). Although these payers can establish their own policies, they tend to mirror federal Medicare policies. Thus, the services covered and the rates allowed are usually quite similar to those of Medicare. Since 1994, Medicare payments to managed care plans do not distinguish home care. As a result, CMS utilization and expenditures data do not reflect home care used by managed care enrollees.

LICENSURE, CERTIFICATION, AND ACCREDITATION

Licensure

Most states license a Medicare-certified home health agency as a health provider. This is typically done under the jurisdiction of the state's health department.

Certification

Home health care agencies must be certified if they are to obtain Medicare reimbursement. Similarly, most states certify agencies as eligible to participate in Medicaid based on their certification by Medicare. Certification for Medicare is based on compliance with the federally mandated COPs, which, until the late 1990s, relied mainly on compliance with structure and process standards.

The Omnibus Budget Reconciliation Act of 1989 (OBRA '89) mandated the development and testing of client outcomes for home health care and the inclusion of client home visits in the quality-assurance survey conducted by state licensing agencies. Beginning in January 1999, CMS (formerly HCFA) required all Medicare-certified providers to implement the Outcome Assessment and Information Set (OASIS) system. OASIS is a uniform set of indicators of client outcomes. OASIS data are collected at multiple points in time during the course of each patient's treatment, including admission, follow-up, or recertification; when a patient is admitted to a hospital for any reason; when a patient returns to an agency following a hospitalization; upon discharge; or if the patient dies at home. Different pieces of data are collected at specified time points by either a staff nurse or a therapist. CMS requires that data be gathered and submitted electronically on all Medicare, Medicaid, managed care, private pay, and personal care–only patients. Data are then forwarded at regular intervals to a designated state agency, where they are further processed, forwarded to the state home care regulatory agency, and sent to CMS. In 2003, CMS established a website called Home Health Compare: www.medicare.gov/homehealthcompare/search.html that provides information directly to consumers. The website is searchable and provides rankings for all home care agencies serving a specific zip code. Rankings are shown for the agency and compared to the average ranking on the same item for the state and also for the country.

Accreditation

Home health agencies can seek accreditation from either The Joint Commission (TJC; www.joint commission.org) or the Community Health Accreditation Partner (CHAP; www.chapinc.org). TJC and CHAP have also developed voluntary quality-assurance programs for home health care providers that incorporate the OASIS data set. Participation in TJC's ORYX® program is mandatory for home care programs that are hospital based or owned and have an average monthly census of 10 or more patients. Participating agencies select measures from listed performance measurement systems, apply the measures, and submit the data regularly to TJC, which uses controls and comparison charts to identify performance trends and patterns that are then discussed during on-site surveys (www.jointcommission.org/). Although participation in these voluntary programs can be expensive, if providers meet certification requirements of either of these programs, they are "deemed" to comply with the Medicare COPs and are exempt from state-sponsored regulatory surveys.

PRIVATE OR NON-MEDICARE HOME CARE AGENCIES

Private home care agencies offer a broad range of home care services, from skilled services available through Medicare-certified agencies to personal support provided by paraprofessionals, including personal care and homemaker/chore services. Services can be provided separately or in conjunction with any of the other models of home care. Home care is provided to persons with chronic functional disabilities who wish to remain in their homes, rather than enter an institution, as well as to those recovering from an acute illness.

AGENCIES

Skilled nursing and therapies can be provided by home care agencies that are licensed by the state but not certified to receive reimbursements from Medicare or Medicaid. Because providers are not required to be certified, no complete listing is currently available at the national level; however, data are available in each of the states. NAHC reports that there were over 33,000 home care providers in the United States in 2010 (NAHC, 2010). This number also may substantially underestimate the true supply, because not all providers are known.

CLIENTS

Clients receiving care from noncertified agencies have a wider range of needs than those who are eligible for Medicare reimbursement. Clients' needs may range from around-the-clock skilled nursing to a weekly "bathe and shave" service. Those using homemaker and chore services tend to be people with functional disabilities who need assistance with activities of daily living (ADLs) and/or IADLs rather than skilled nursing care or therapies. Medicaid Section 2176

Community Care Waiver and Medicaid Section 1915(c) waivers can be applied to older adults, to younger persons with physical disabilities, to persons with AIDS, and to persons with developmental disabilities who have impairment levels that would render them eligible for nursing home care if community-based care were not available. Currently, federal regulations mandate that the average cost of Medicaid waiver services not exceed average Medicaid reimbursements for nursing home care.

Services

Services provided vary but may include case management, homemaker/chore services, and personal care, as well as the full range of skilled home care services provided by nurses and therapists. Capital funding, start-up, and operating costs for noncertified home care services are less than for Medicare-certified agencies because the agencies do not need to meet Medicare requirements for personnel or financial solvency. However, because of the low rates paid by the Medicaid waiver programs in many states, many noncertified programs have found that the best way to survive in this segment of the home care field is by building volume, which entails the development of a multiunit, if not multistate, chain capacity. Private home care agencies may also exist in parallel with a Medicare-certified agency, with an exchange of appropriate referrals. Under Medicare regulations, the two agencies must be operated by the same corporation or health care delivery system.

STAFFING

In contrast to Medicare-certified agencies, noncertified agencies typically do not employ staff on a full-time basis. Rather, they maintain a registry of people who are willing to work on an on-call basis for an hourly fee. Skilled personnel, such as RNs and therapists, work on an hourly, rather than salaried basis as they do for Medicare-certified agencies. Functional support services are primarily provided by paraprofessional workers: nurse's aides (NAs), HHAs, and licensed vocational or practical nurses (LVNs, LPNs). In 2008, approximately 800,000 direct care workers did not have health care coverage. Many workers are paid less than workers in the fast-food industry and have less than full-time employment, with minimal, if any, benefits prior to 2011. With the passage of ACA, employers with more than 50 workers will have to pay a penalty if any employee receives a premium tax credit; the fee is higher if the employer does not offer health insurance. Persons for whom health insurance is too expensive will be required to obtain health insurance through Medicaid or through new health insurance exchanges (Wiener, 2010). These reforms may help reduce staff turnover in this sector of the home care industry.

Home care workers value autonomy in their jobs and enjoy their caregiving roles. However, they want to have more input into client care plans. They need opportunities for further training and career advancement, as well as better pay and benefits. Thus, the main challenge facing noncertified home care providers is the recruitment and retention of trained personnel. At present, noncompetitive wages, low benefits, and the challenging nature of the work are believed to be the cause of high staff turnover rates in this sector of the home care industry. Ensuring quality is difficult when staff are parttime and on the registry of several agencies.

One possible solution to this urgent manpower issue is **consumer-directed home care**, a new model of care that was recently tested by researchers at Mathematica Policy Research, Inc. As its name implies, consumer-directed care (also known as cash and counseling) enables home care consumers to recruit and manage their personal care helpers, who may be paid family members (Benjamin, 2001). This model of care has been the standard for younger persons with disability who are accustomed to directing their own personal care attendants. It has only recently been tested with an elderly population. Findings from a multisite randomized test of the model in three states indicate that older adults who participate in the model receive services promptly and report greater satisfaction with care. Because clients receive services rather than languishing on waiting lists, the initial costs of their care is higher. However, this cost is offset by reduced rates of nursing home admission (Doty, Mahoney, & Sciegaj, 2010). The Medicaid Deficit Reduction Act of 2005 allowed all states to offer consumer-directed care and currently 12 "second generation" states are implementing it, having served 15,000 participants by 2009 (Doty et al., 2010).

FUNDING

Charges for home care services are roughly equivalent to those for Medicare services. Charges are typically per hour rather than per visit. Some services may establish a minimum or flat rate. Although private home care agencies cannot receive payment from Medicare, they may be authorized providers for other public programs, particularly those offered by states and counties. Hence, private home care services are reimbursed by a variety of sources, including Medicaid 2176 Community Care Waivers, state block grants (Title XX), Older Americans Act Title III funds, state and local revenues, and private out-of-pocket payment. Although Title XX and OAA funding remained relatively constant during the 1990s, substantial growth has occurred in Medicaid and state funding of home care services.

The Medicaid Section 2176 Home and Community-Based Care Waiver (HCBCW) was created by the Omnibus Budget Reconciliation Act of 1981 (OBRA '81) in an attempt to decrease the use of nursing homes by Medicaid-eligible and low-income older adults and persons with physical or developmental disabilities. A modification of Social Security Act Title XIX, Section 2176, allows states to apply for and receive a waiver from the federal government to modify the benefits required for Medicaid. States may expand the services covered, the eligibility criteria, or the geographic area of eligibility for increased benefits. In 1982, six states participated in the waiver, with expenditures of $3.8 million. The program has since grown to encompass all but two states, with expenditures of $42 billion in 2007, representing a doubling from 1999 (Kaiser Commission on Medicaid and the Uninsured, 2011).

FIGURE 5.4 Medicaid 1915(c) home and community-based services waiver enrollees and expenditures by enrollment group, 2007.

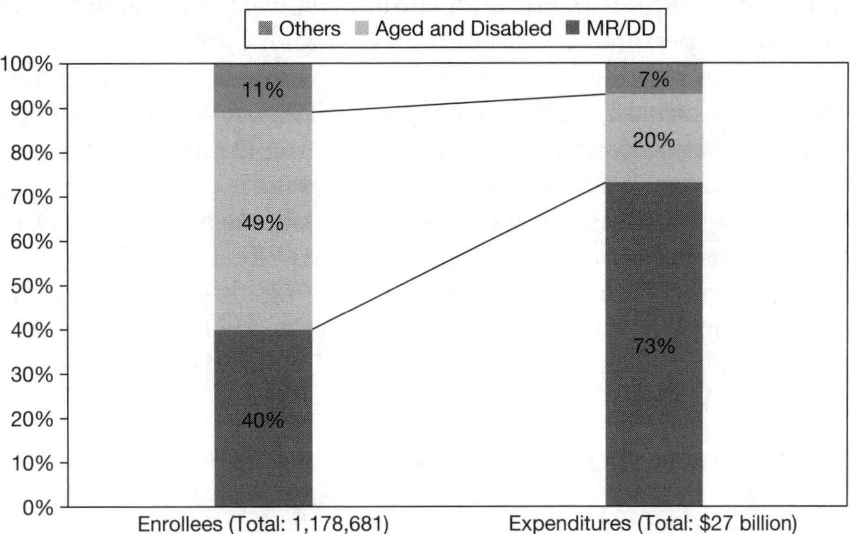

Source: Kaiser Commission on Medicaid and the Uninsured (2011).

Medicaid waiver spending for individuals with developmental disabilities has accounted for the majority of expenditures, accounting for about 73% of total waiver expenditures in 2007 (Figure 5.4), mainly because many people with developmental disabilities receive 24-hour support (Coleman, Fox-Grage, & Folkemer, 2003). In the past, Medicaid programs in most states preferentially funded institutional rather than HCBS long-term care services. In an effort to rebalance their efforts, states are now redirecting funding to HCBS. As a result, the national percentage of Medicaid spending on HCBS has more than doubled from 19% in 1995 to 42% in 2008 (Kaiser Commission on Medicaid and the Uninsured, 2011). However, the generosity of the waivers varies greatly within states, depending on the population targeted as well as among states. The number of participants in each waiver is capped by states at a level they can afford. Because of participant caps, many states have long waiting lists for approval if available participant slots are filled. Specifically in 2009, 39 states reported waiting lists with a national average wait time of 21 months (Kaiser Commission on Medicaid and the Uninsured, 2011). Finally, approved service plans are also capped by case managers to ensure that the cost of the care provided remains comparable to the cost of nursing home care in each state. Both participant and service caps increase the predictability of expenses that states incur in offering the waiver programs.

It is important to note that the new ACA includes additional options that states can pursue to enhance their waiver programs. Under a State Balancing Incentive Payments Program, a time-limited increase in federal match can be provided to states that currently spend less than 50% of Medicaid long-term care dollars on HCBS. States that apply to exercise this option must agree to provide a single point of entry to care and standardized needs assessments.

The Community First Choice State Plan Option for Attendant Services and Supports removes the current mandate that expenditures for community care be less than what Medicaid spends on institutional care. States cannot set ceilings on the number of persons served nor limit geographic areas of the state served. In return, services provided will receive 6% increase in federal matching funds.

Under the Medicare Deficit Reduction Act of 2005, states were invited to participate in a Money Follows the Person Rebalancing Demonstration. This demonstration provides substantially enhanced federal Medicaid match dollars for states to transition persons in nursing homes back to the community. Originally, nursing home residents targeted by this demonstration had to have been in the home a minimum of 6 months prior to transitioning; this requirement has now been shortened to 3 months, with enhanced federal match for services provided during the client's first year in the community (Reinhard, 2010).

LICENSURE, CERTIFICATION, AND ACCREDITATION

Licensure

Very few states license non-Medicare-certified providers, except for business licenses. However, most states have developed mandatory quality-assurance/improvement programs for private providers who participate in waiver and state-revenue-funded community care programs. In most cases, structure standards are used to assess quality and process, and outcome measures are conspicuously absent.

Certification

Private home care agencies may be certified by public programs other than Medicare to be authorized providers. Certification criteria are determined by the specific program. Examples include state or county mental health departments, Veterans Affairs Medical Centers, and Older American Act providers selected by the local Area Agency on Aging. An agency that meets certification requirements is entitled to bill for the care provided but must also comply with the operating regulations of the funder.

Accreditation

The Accreditation Commission for Health Care (ACHC) currently accredits many private home care providers, including high-tech providers. In addition, many national home care chains have developed their own internal quality-assurance systems, including the initiation of continuous quality-improvement programs. In large part, participation in quality-assurance programs across providers is voluntary and variable. Moreover, findings are not made available to consumers. Proponents of the cash and counseling model of HCBS believe that the client's ability to hire and fire homemakers and personal care aides has injected direct consumer quality control over that segment of the industry (Simon-Rusinowitz, Loughlin, Ruben, & Mahoney, 2010).

HIGH-TECH HOME CARE

High-tech home therapy combines skilled home care professionals, advanced technology medical equipment, and pharmaceuticals. In 1968, patients without functioning digestive organs were sustained for the first time through total parenteral nutrition (TPN) provided intravenously. TPN is now prescribed routinely for those who are unable to or should not obtain nutrition through eating or drinking. TPN usually consists of carbohydrates and sugars, proteins, lipids, electrolytes, and trace elements that are administered by needle or through a catheter (Medline Plus, 2013b). Initially, these treatments required 24-hour-a-day hospital care. The invention of pumps in the early 1970s permitted more rapid infusion of solutions, freeing patients from tubes and bottles for up to 16 hours a day. High-tech home care has expanded to include respirator/ventilation therapy, intravenous (IV) antibiotics, chemotherapy treatments, and home-based renal dialysis, in addition to enteral and parenteral nutrition. As a result of advances in this technology, this care is now provided in the home, where it enables people to maintain normal lives, including resumption of work or school.

Original projections of growth in high-tech home care were glowing. The American Society for Parental and Enteral Nutrition estimated in 1983 that 150,000 to 200,000 home parental patients alone would be treated in 1990, at expenditures of up to $1.6 billion per year (Donlan, 1983). Current data indicate that these projections for growth in numbers of users and expenditures were not too far from the mark. For example:

- In 1997, an estimated 250,000 Americans used outpatient intravenous antibiotics, and this number is expected to increase annually by 15% to 20%. New technology has enabled the dosage of antibiotics to be timed for maximum effect with home infusion systems.
- The development of plastic polymer catheters as replacements for steel has enabled catheters to remain in place for up to a year, an important feature for patients with long-term chronic conditions such as AIDS, cancer, cystic fibrosis, or Lyme disease.
- Electric left ventricular assist devices (LVADS) and other advances enable patients with end-stage heart disease to be sustained at home on battery-operated pumps while awaiting a heart transplant.
- Advances in respiratory therapy technology have enabled chronic obstructive pulmonary disease and asthma patients to be maintained at home with oxygen concentrators and portable ultrasonic nebulizers.
- Developments in telemedicine include digitized devices such as blood glucose meters, pulse oximeters, blood pressure cuffs, CT scanners, and MRI machines, which collect and transmit patient information electronically through use of telemedicine applications. Some products are designed for patient use and others are for health professionals (Hein, 2009).

Although Medicare-certified and private home health care agencies described previously account for 75% of the total home care industry and are estimated to generate approximately $30 billion in health care spending, high-tech home care accounts for the remaining 25% of the home health care market. Altogether, this segment of the industry, which includes respiratory therapy, infusion therapy, and DME, accounts for another $10 billion in home care expenditures (CMS, 2002).

CLIENTS

High-tech home care is used in the treatment of a wide variety of disease conditions that require enteral or parental nutrition, ventilator therapy, IV antibiotics, chemotherapy, or renal dialysis. Users span all age groups, including "technology-dependent" children, many of whom have been able to receive care at home rather than in a hospital as a result of this technology. An early study of high-tech home care users at 150 home health care agencies across the United States found that one in 10 home care patients uses high-tech care, with hospices serving the largest proportion of patients (Kaye & Davitt, 1995). Complex regimens using equipment and pharmaceuticals often require that a caregiver be involved to help clients manage their care.

SERVICES

High-tech home care combines skilled home care professionals, medical equipment, and pharmaceuticals. The patient's physician must initially authorize care at home. An RN is often involved to educate the patient and family about all aspects of care, as well as to monitor care. A specially trained technician may be involved to establish the initial setup of equipment and supplies. Pharmacists offsite organize and monitor drug use. Equipment may be simple or quite complex. Initial education and ongoing commitment of the patient and family are essential to successful use of high-tech therapy; patients may have multiple conditions that require monitoring or treatment beyond the high-tech therapy, for which other home care providers and the patient's regular physician continue to be involved.

STRUCTURE

Approximately 4,500 infusion companies exist nationally. These include pharmacies, hospital-affiliated organizations, regional infusion providers, and home infusion organizations. At present, this segment of the home care industry is extremely fragmented and typically is composed of small local and regional operators. Because of increased billing complexity, limited access to capital, and payment cuts included in BBA 97, an estimated 3,000 home care agencies either closed or merged by 2000. The Medicare Home Health Prospective Payment System (PPS) was implemented in October 2000 and contributed to the stabilization of the home health care industry, which is anticipated to grow at a 5% to 10% rate because of demographic trends, cost benefits, and other efficiencies under the PPS (CMS, 2003).

Home care providers who wish to provide high-tech care can pursue several different options. They can start their own in-house pharmacy, they can also contract with local retail pharmacies, or they can form joint ventures with a national home care chain that has expertise in this area.

A primary consideration in high-tech home care is the status of clients' homes and the capacity of clients or informal caregivers to be involved in care. Clients must have adequate space to store medical supplies, the capacity to refrigerate solutions, and the ability to learn and adhere to a detailed care regimen.

STAFFING

High-tech home care requires close collaboration of the physician, the pharmacist, the RN, and, depending on the type of therapy, possibly the medical supply company. Skilled home health agencies may also participate in the client's care. The high-tech home care patient places a greater demand on traditional home care agencies in terms of staff and technology. Patients may require both more time and a greater level of skilled care. Both patient and family need to be trained in care techniques, and family concerns must be accommodated by staff. The provision of high-tech care may also demand greater physician involvement than traditional home care services. In addition, if the home care agency contracts with a separate equipment provider, services must be coordinated with emergency backup plans and plans for equipment maintenance. Pharmacists may be involved in cases for which drugs must be specifically mixed and carefully monitored.

FUNDING

At present, some or all components of high-tech home care are reimbursed by Medicare, Medicaid, Medicaid waivers for technologically dependent children, and most private insurance. Nursing visits to provide skilled care, patient education, supplies, and DME are covered by Medicare; however, drugs are not covered. Because of its perceived cost-effectiveness, the use of high-tech home care is increasing among both private insurance carriers and large employer-administered benefit plans. Such insurance can be more flexible than Medicare in covering the total cost of care. However, awareness is growing among these groups that the benefit must be very carefully managed to produce cost savings. This management may include negotiated contracts based on discounted charges with home health care agencies and medical equipment suppliers. The billing for a high-tech client can be complex, involving up to four separate bills: one each for the home health agency skilled nurse, the pharmaceuticals, the initial equipment setup, and the ongoing equipment monitoring.

LICENSURE, CERTIFICATION, AND ACCREDITATION

Licensure

Each service provider must meet state requirements for licensure as a distinct service. For example, home care agencies seeking Medicaid certification must be licensed by the state department of health. Pharmacies must be licensed as pharmacies, and DME companies must have a business license. No single encompassing license exists for a "high-tech" provider.

Certification

High-tech home care agencies that wish to seek reimbursement from Medicare must meet Medicare COPs. Agencies can also be certified by Medicaid and select other government programs. Medical supply companies can bill Medicare Part B, which has no required COPs.

Accreditation

Participation in accreditation programs is voluntary but advisable if a provider seeks to contract with managed care plans. TJC has accredited more than 5,600 organizations under its home care accreditation program, which also includes high-tech providers (TJC, 2015). Other organizations that accredit high-tech home care providers are CHAP and ACHC.

TECHNOLOGICAL ADVANCES IN THE CARE OF HOME CARE PATIENTS

The development of recently emergent technological tools can substantially improve the management of home care patients (Case Study 5.1). These

Case Study 5.1: Providing Home Health Care for Mrs. Walker

Mabel Walker is a 73-year-old widow who lives alone. She has a son who also lives alone about an hour away from her. He provides her with transportation to medical appointments and assists her with grocery shopping, home maintenance, and bill paying. Mrs. Walker has congestive heart failure, arthritis, and poor vision from developing cataracts. She has been hospitalized multiple times with exacerbations of heart failure, and this is her second transition from St. Bartholomew Hospital to Sunshine Home Care, a certified Medicare home health care provider, within 60 days. Mrs. Walker's physician has ordered that she receive skilled nursing and HHA services. She also has a medical alert bracelet.

Staff at Sunshine are concerned about her risk for hospital readmission and do a complete reassessment of her care needs and opportunities to support them using new technologies in which the firm has recently invested to monitor patients at home in-between visits, such as blood pressure and glucose monitoring. Prior to visiting Mrs. Walker at home, a nurse from Sunshine obtains Mrs. Walker's most recent diagnostic and treatment data electronically from St. Bartholomew

(*continued*)

Case Study 5.1: Providing Home Health Care for Mrs. Walker (*continued*)

and from the physician and discusses her case in a virtual case conference that examines factors related to this most recent hospitalization. The nurse arranges a first visit with Mrs. Walker and her son in order to conduct a comprehensive assessment of Mrs. Walker's needs. The nurse uses a tablet and voice recognition software on the home visit to complete her assessment and record her notes. These notes are transmitted to both the Sunshine Home Care physician and to Mrs. Walker's attending physician and are accessible to the home care aide in Mrs. Walker's home.

The nurse alerts the HHA to Mrs. Walker's risk for readmission and instructs the aide to monitor Mrs. Walker's diet and weight carefully during home visits. During her visits the aide observes that Mrs. Walker is ordering and eating a lot of take-out food that is high in calories and salt, that Mrs. Walker is also mixing up her medications because she is having difficulty reading the labels on the medication bottles and has difficulty opening the bottles because of arthritis in her hands. With her poor vision and unsteady gait and many scatter rugs, Mrs. Walker is also at risk for falls. She also has difficulty bathing. The aide notifies the nurse regarding these problems using a smartphone. The nurse uses the agency's discretionary patient care fund to purchase a large-print digital scale for Mrs. Walker and instructs her in its use. She also reviews the need for a lower salt diet and asks the physician to reinforce this instruction with Mrs. Walker by phone. She also asks the physician to authorize occupational therapist (OT) visits to assess the home environment for falls, potential home modifications, and safer medication management. The home care social worker also meets with Mrs. Walker and her son to develop a plan for grocery shopping and refers Mrs. Walker to the local Area Agency on Aging for low-salt home-delivered meals. The nurse also helps Mrs. Walker to organize her medications and the OT helps Mrs. Walker and her son to pack up some of the rugs, arranges for the installation of grab bars in the tub, and calls the local pharmacy to ask that her medications be set up in a large-print daily presorted medication dispenser. Daily transmittal of information on weight and vital signs over the next few weeks indicates that Mrs. Walker's condition has stabilized. As a result, the nurse contacts the home care social worker and asks her to begin discharge planning for Mrs. Walker.

Knowing that it can take weeks for the local Medicaid HCBS program to complete client assessments, the Sunshine Home Care social worker immediately contacts the local case management office to arrange for follow-up care in the form of a home care aide and transfers a complete

(*continued*)

Case Study 5.1: Providing Home Health Care for Mrs. Walker (*continued*)

electronic summary of Mrs. Walker's history to the HCBS case manager, who also reviews it with the new aide. Sunshine also transmits an electronic summary of Mrs. Walker's care to the physician, along with information on the future role of the HCBS program in her care and contact information for the case manager.

Mrs. Walker is maintained at home without further exacerbation of her condition for the next 2 years.

Case Study Discussion Questions:

1. What factors should be considered when developing a care plan for Mrs. Walker?
2. How can technology be used to help Mrs. Walker maintain her independence?
3. How can the agency assure that her ongoing chronic care needs will be met postdischarge?

technologies include telehealth, digital imaging, microdiagnostics, wireless connectivity, web-based data access, and voice recognition. **Telehealth** allows the monitoring of a patient's condition through remote computer access and updating a central nursing station through a wireless network. Digital-imaging technology is becoming more sophisticated and will enable certain medical testing to be administered from the patient's home. Diagnostic tools have been reduced in size, are less expensive, and more user friendly. Wireless connectivity and web-based data access now allow health care professionals to find and communicate information and data about their patients quickly and securely. Voice recognition software is also improving and may eventually replace typing by deciphering spoken words into text. These new and developing technologies offer an opportunity to significantly enhance current home health care operations by improving communication and information access for both health care professionals and patients (Tweed, 2003).

INTEGRATING MECHANISMS

STRUCTURE

The diversity of home care programs is reflected in the wide variation of organizational arrangements for its provision. Many agencies provide only one model of home care, are freestanding, and relate to other providers of all types through informal relationships. At the other extreme is the large multiorganizational health care system that owns all types of home care services. Under the latter scenario, services may be well coordinated or operate as independently as if they were separate community-based agencies.

Because financing and regulations have fragmented home care delivery in a way that is not consistent with client care needs, all home care providers face the challenge of coordinating their care with that rendered by other providers (see Case Study 5.1). Primarily because of stringent federal regulations, home care providers must structure their operations in specified ways. Even within publicly funded home care, Medicare home health programs have no jurisdiction over Medicaid waiver- or Older Americans Act–funded home care services, and vice versa. Thus, the synergies, enhancements to quality, and efficiencies that could be gained by close collaboration are seldom realized.

Home care agencies are the one provider (other than assisted living providers) that is in a client's home on a regular basis and can observe the environment and social dynamics. Home care workers have the opportunity to assist the family in accessing the full range of health and social services needed to maximize independence at home. At the same time, home care may exemplify lack of clinical coordination because several people helping a client at home may come from different agencies having no formal relationship. At present, if a person requires more than one type of home care at a time, no single individual or agency is officially in charge of that care. Home care personnel set their own schedules, and so all may arrive on the same day at the same time or too far apart. A strong and involved family may assume an active role in coordinating care providers, but an ill individual living alone may be unable to do so.

As noted earlier, physician involvement in home care is minimal. Although skilled services must continue to seek physician certification, nonskilled service providers, of those who have paid privately, have no obligation to inform the client's physician of routine care or noted problems.

Hospital admissions and nursing home placements usually result from decisions made jointly by patients and physicians. Historically, physicians have been actively discouraged from assuming a leadership role in home care, with physician home visits reimbursed at a level below that for an HHA until 1992. To maximize patient outcomes, communication and coordination are essential but happen on an informal and episodic basis. The ACA makes care coordination and reduction of unnecessary rehospitalizations a major policy focus for the first time and also promotes enhanced coordination and management for persons with chronic conditions through the specific initiatives listed in Exhibit 5.2.

MANAGED CARE AND HOME CARE

Managed care is a logical source to assume both coordination and reimbursement; however, experience with managed home care is quite limited at present. Medicare Advantage plans are paid by Medicare on a **capitation** rate (reimbursement at a specific amount annually by the insurer for each patient enrolled in the plan) that encompasses the full spectrum of required services, including home health care. However, Medicare does not require the plans to report the details of service actually provided. Thus, the number of people using home

EXHIBIT 5.2 ACA Initiatives

CMS OFFICES	DEMONSTRATIONS
Federal Coordinated Health Care Office	*Medicare Independence at Home Demonstration Program*
This new office within CMS is charged by ACA to improve coordination between Medicare and Medicaid programs for beneficiaries dually eligible for both programs.	This demonstration will test the use of medical practices consisting of primary care teams of physicians, nurse practitioners, and others to coordinate care and deliver care to chronically ill and disabled populations in their homes.
Center for Medicare and Medicaid Innovation	*Community Care Transitions Program*
Also located within CMS, this new office will test innovative payment and delivery arrangements that can be expected to enhance the coordination of care.	This demonstration will provide transition services to Medicare beneficiaries at high risk of rehospitalization or poor transition from hospital to postacute care.

care, the number and type of visits, and other data about home care that are available for fee-for-service Medicare enrollees are not reported for Medicare Advantage enrollees. This results in an underreporting of the use of Medicare-certified home health services by older adults and makes analysis for policy or management purposes challenging.

Of particular relevance to home care are *Medicare Special Needs Plans*. These plans are Medicare Advantage plans that target the enrollment of beneficiaries who are dually eligible, reside in nursing homes, or have chronic disabling conditions. The ACA reauthorizes these plans and requires them for the first time to contract with both Medicare and Medicaid, authorizes a new risk-adjustment payment for fully integrated plans, and requires their accreditation through the National Committee for Quality Assurance (Wiener, 2010). This new incarnation of these plans holds significant promise to improve the coordination of care and care outcomes for the dually eligible.

ONE-STOP HOME CARE PROVIDERS

At present, the home care industry is divided into four home care models. The past 30 years have seen dramatic increases in the number of home care providers and clients, and the current political environment suggests that this trend will continue for the foreseeable future. Most analysts agree that home care is here to stay and believe that the major policy questions concern how to manage home care to improve its effectiveness. A major unanswered question is, "How can we streamline the delivery and management of care to maximize its efficiency and effectiveness?" Methods of integrating home care services with those of acute care and other long-term care providers are badly needed as are methods of reimbursing care that promotes efficiency across home care types.

In a landmark decision (*Olmstead v L.C.*, 1999), the Supreme Court ruled that individuals with disabilities must be enabled by states to live in the most integrated setting appropriate to their needs and that "unjustifiable institutionalization of persons with disabilities is a form of discrimination" (Rosenbaum, 2000, p. 5). This ruling has very important policy implications for community care. It sent a clear message to the states that care should begin at home and that institutionalization is an option of last resort. All states are currently developing plans in response to this ruling. The *Olmstead* ruling is a major driver of states' efforts to rebalance the provision of long-term care through the dedication of increased resources to HCBS. As HCBS continue to grow, it will be even more important for home care agencies to consider the advantages of becoming full-service home care providers as opposed to targeting an isolated niche of the home care marketplace.

INFORMATION SYSTEMS

Information systems for home care have evolved separately from those of hospitals, nursing homes, or any other providers. Home care systems tend to be standalone and do not interface with other public or private systems. This characteristic has been exacerbated by Medicare's requirements that Medicare-certified agencies establish direct electronic billing and complete the OASIS clinical reporting. As home care enters the 21st century, it is well entrenched in management mechanisms that set it apart rather than allow it to function as an integrated service component of a continuum of care.

In order to achieve advances in care coordination and enhance outcomes for the chronically ill, agencies must have 21st-century technology. This armamentarium of tools is necessary to improve transition and readmission outcomes, while also contributing to improving operational efficiency. These tools should include the technological developments described earlier in the chapter (Tweed, 2003).

ADMINISTRATIVE CHALLENGES

All sectors of the home care field have undergone nearly constant change during the past few decades. Such a demanding and volatile environment brings numerous daily challenges to administrators. The most significant issues faced by managers at this point include:

- *Nursing shortage.* The current shortage of nurses across the nation makes it difficult for administrators to identify qualified nurses and retain them in the home care field.
- *Payment lag times.* Both Medicare and Medicaid payments are frequently delayed, requiring all agencies dealing with the government as payer to have sufficient cash flow to meet payroll and other needs despite delayed payments.

- *Mergers and acquisitions.* Although the rate of closure of Medicare-certified agencies that was rampant immediately after BBA 97 has slowed, mergers are still occurring. Mergers are challenging for both the agency that is being acquired and for the agency that is doing the acquiring, with respect to staffing, billing, name recognition, maintenance of referral and patient bases, and recordkeeping. They are also challenging for clients, and potentially affect client and family loyalty and satisfaction.
- *Outcomes.* Home Care Compare is a "report card" for Medicare home care agencies being made available to the public by CMS. Its purpose is to offer a suitable set of stable and relevant outcome indicators by which to compare Medicare-certified home care agencies. Other home care providers will be challenged to develop or respond to the demand for consumer-oriented performance measures.
- *Regulatory issues.* Directors of all types of home care agencies spend a great deal of time dealing with regulatory requirements imposed by federal, state, and local governments, as well as by consumer and accreditation organizations. Compliance with new patient privacy regulations is a recent example. In an evolving field there is always some new external pressure that requires adjustment of the home care agency's internal operations. Home care programs that participate in the Medicaid waiver programs can be at the mercy of external case managers in their state who determine which agencies receive client referrals. In this case it is very important for agency managers to be aware of this issue and cultivate good working relationships with these gatekeepers.

SUMMARY

A number of questions persist regarding the organization and delivery of home care in the United States. Home care has grown prodigiously in terms of providers, users, and costs. The relationship between the use of home care and the use of other health care services remains unclear. Basic issues, such as geographic variations in supply, utilization, and cost, determinants of scope of services provided, and organizational/management practices that maximize outcomes for specific patient groups, remain to be explored. Home care has arrived and is here to stay. It is a prevalent and essential component of the continuum of long-term care. The challenges of the future are to achieve integration and to demonstrate cost-effective outcomes.

DISCUSSION QUESTIONS

1. What is the focus of Medicare home health care and why?
2. Where is growth occurring in the home health market and why?
3. What are the implications for patient care and outcomes of the Balkanization of home care into different models?

4. How can this fragmentation be overcome? What tools or structural changes might be needed?
5. What provisions of the ACA foster the better coordination of home care with other providers of care for persons with chronic conditions?

ADDITIONAL RESOURCES

ADDITIONAL USEFUL PUBLICATIONS OR REPORTS

National Association for Home Care (NAHC). *Basic statistics about home care, updated 2010.* www.nahc.org/assets/1/7/10HC_Stats.pdf

National Center for Health Statistics (NCHS). Home health care patients and hospice care discharges. *2007 National Center for Health Statistics Home and Hospice Care Survey.* www.cdc.gov/nchs/data/nhhcs/2007hospicecaredischarges.pdf

National Center for Health Statistics (NCHS). Home health and hospice care agencies. *2007 National Center for Health Statistics Home and Hospice Care Survey.* www.cdc.gov/nchs/data/nhhcs/2007hospicecaresurvey.pdf

KEY WEBSITES

Joint Commission: Accreditation, Health Care, Certification www.jointcommission.org

Medicare.gov Home Health Care Compare www.medicare.gov/homehealthcompare/About/What-Is-HHC.html

Medicaid.gov Waivers www.medicaid.gov/Medicaid-CHIP-Program-Information/By-Topics/Waivers/Waivers.html

National Association of Home Care & Hospice www.nahc.org

REFERENCES

Benjamin, A. E. (1993). An historical perspective on home care. *Milbank Quarterly, 71*(1), 129–166.

Benjamin, A. E. (1999). A normative analysis of home care goals. *Journal of Aging and Health, 11*(3), 445–468.

Benjamin, A. E. (2001). Consumer-directed services at home. *Health Affairs, 20*(6), 80–95.

Centers for Disease Control and Prevention. National Home and Hospice Care Survey. (2013). *Home health care patients and hospital discharges fact sheet*. Retrieved from www.cdc.gov/nchs/nhhcs.htm and www.cdc.gov/nchs/data/nhhcs/2007hospicecaredischarges.pdf

Centers for Medicare and Medicaid Services. (2002). *Health care industry market update, home health*. Retrieved from www.cms.hhs.gov/marketplace

Centers for Medicare and Medicaid Services. (2003). *Health care industry market update, home health*. Retrieved from www.cms.gov/CapMarketUpdates/Downloads/hcimu92203.pdf

Centers for Medicare and Medicaid Services. (2011). General provisions. Chapter 1 in *Medicare managed care manual*. Retrieved from www.cms.gov/Regulations-and-Guidance/Guidance/Manuals/downloads/mc86c01.pdf

Coleman, B., Fox-Grage, W., & Folkemer, D. (2003). *2003 State long-term care: Recent developments and policy directions*. Retrieved from http://nasuad.org/sites/nasuad/files/hcbs/files/7/318/LTC2003.pdf

Community Health Accreditation Partner. (2011). Retrieved from http://www.chapinc.org/what-we-do/chap-accreditation.aspx

Cummings, J., Hughes, S. L., Weaver, F., Manheim, L. M., Conrad, K., Nash, K., ... Adelman, J. (1990). Cost-effectiveness of V.A. hospital-based home care: A randomized clinical trial. *Archives of Internal Medicine, 150*, 1274–1280.

Department of Health and Human Services. (2001). *Letter to state Medicaid directors (Olmstead decision)*. Retrieved from www.hhs.gov/ocr/olms0114.htm

Donlan, T. (1983). No place like home. *Barron's, 6*, 21.

Doty, P., Mahoney, K. J., & Sciegaj, M. (2010). New state strategies to meet long-term care needs. *Health Affairs, 29*(1), 49–56.

Ellenbecker, C. H., Samia, L., Cushman, M. J., & Alster, K. (2008). Patient safety and quality in home health care. In R. G. Hughes (Ed.), *Patient safety and quality: An evidence-based handbook for nurses* (pp. 301–304). Rockville, MD: Agency for Healthcare Research and Quality.

General Accounting Office. (2000). *Medicare home health care: Prospective payment system will need refinement as data become available (GAO/HEHS-00-9)*. Washington, DC: U.S. General Accounting Office. Retrieved from www.gao.gov/assets/230/229024.pdf

Hein, M. A. (2009). *Telemedicine: An important force in the transformation of healthcare*. Washington, DC: U.S. Department of Commerce International Trade Administration.

Hughes, S. L. (1991). Home care: Where we are and where we need to go. In M. G. Ory & A. P. Duncker (Eds.), *In-home care for older people*. Newbury Park, CA: Sage.

Jencks, S. F., Williams, M. V., & Coleman, E. A. (2009). Rehospitalizations among patients in the Medicare fee-for-service program. *New England Journal of Medicine, 360*, 1418–1428.

Kaiser Commission on Medicaid and the Uninsured. (2011, February). *Medicaid home and community-based service programs: Data update.* Retrieved from www.kff.org/medicaid/upload/7720-04.pdf

Kaye, L. W., & Davitt, J. K. (1995). Provider and consumer profiles of traditional and high-tech home health care: The issue of differential access. *Health and Social Work, 20*(4), 262–271.

Levit, K., Smith, C., Cowan, C., & Martin, A. (2002). Inflation spurs health spending in 2000. *Health Affairs, 21*(1), 172–181.

Martin, A., Lassman, D., Whittle, L., Catlin, A., & The National Health Expenditure Accounts Team. (2011). Recession contributes to slowest annual rate of increase in health spending in five decades. *Health Affairs, 30*(1), 11–22.

McCall, N., Komisar, H. L., Petersons, A., & Moore, S. (2001). Medicare home health before and after the BBA. *Health Affairs, 20*(3), 189–198.

McCall, N., Petersons, A., Moore, S., & Korb, J. (2003). Utilization of home health services before and after the Balanced Budget Act of 1997: What were the initial effects? *HSR: Health Services Research, 38*(1), 85–106.

Medicare.gov Home Health Care Compare. Retrieved from www.medicare.gov/homehealthcompare/About/What-Is-HHC.html

Medicare Payment Advisory Commission. (2003, June). *Report to the Congress: Variation and innovation in Medicare*. Washington, DC: MedPAC.

Medline Plus. (2013a). *Definition: Managed care*. Retrieved from www.nlm.nih.gov/medlineplus/managedcare.html

Medline Plus. (2013b). *Definition: Total parenteral nutrition (TPN)*. Retrieved from www.nlm.nih.gov/medlineplus/druginfo/meds/a601166.html

Miller, N. A., Ramsland, S., & Harrington, C. (1999). Trends and issues in the Medicaid 1915(c) Waiver Program. *Health Care Financing Review, 20*(4), 139–160.

Murkofsky, R. L., Phillips, R. S., McCarthy, E. B., Davis, R. B., & Hamel, M. B. (2003). Length of stay in home care before and after the Balanced Budget Act. *Journal of the American Medical Association, 289*(21), 2284–2848.

National Association for Home Care. (1999). *Basic statistics about home care, 1999*. Retrieved from www.nahc.org

National Association for Home Care. (2001). *Basic statistics about home care, 2001*. Retrieved from www.nahc.org/Consumer.hestats.html

National Association for Home Care. (2010). *Basic statistics about home care, updated 2010*. Retrieved from www.nahc.org/assets/1/7/10HC_Stats.pdf

National Center for Health Statistics. (2007a). Home health care patients and hospice care discharges. *2007 National Center for Health Statistics home and hospice care survey*. Retrieved from www.cdc.gov/nchs/data/nhhcs/2007hospicecaredischarges.pdf

National Center for Health Statistics. (2007b). Home health and hospice care agencies. *2007 National Center for Health Statistics home and hospice care survey*. Retrieved from www.cdc.gov/nchs/data/nhhcs/2007hospicecaresurvey.pdf

Naylor, M. D., Brooten, D. A., Campbell, R. L., Maislin, G., McCauley, K. M., & Schwartz, J. S. (2004). Transitional care of older adults hospitalized with heart failure: A randomized, controlled trial. *Journal of the American Geriatrics Society, 52*, 675–684.

Office of the Inspector General, U.S. Department of Health and Human Services. (2001). *The physician's role in Medicare home health 2001 (OEI-02-00-00620)*. Washington, DC: U.S. Office of the Inspector General. Retrieved from oig.hhs.gov/oei/reports/oei-02-00-00620.pdf

Olmstead, v. L. C., 527 U.S. 581 (1999).

Park-Lee, E. Y., & Decker, F. H. (2010). Comparison of home health and hospice care agencies by organizational characteristics and services provided: United States, 2007. In *National Health Statistics Reports, U.S. Department of Health and Human Services, Centers for Disease Control and Prevention, National Center for Health Statistics, number 30*. Retrieved from www.cdc.gov/nchs/data/nhsr/nhsr030.pdf

Reinhard, S. C. (2010). Diversion, transition programs target nursing homes' status quo. *Health Affairs, 29*(1), 44–48.

Rosenbaum, S. (2000). *Olmstead v. L. C.: Implications for older persons with mental and physical disabilities (AARP Public Policy Institute, INB#30 and #2000-21)*. Washington, DC: AARP.

Simon-Rusinowitz, L., Loughlin, D. M., Ruben, K., & Mahoney, K. J. (2010). What does research tell us about a policy option to hire relatives as caregivers? *Public Policy & Aging Report, 20*(1), 32–37.

The Joint Commission. (2015). Facts about home care accreditation. Retrieved from http://www.jointcommission.org/accreditation/accreditation_main.aspx

Thorpe, K. E., & Ogden, L. L. (2010). The foundation that health reform lays for improved payment, care coordination, and prevention. *Health Affairs, 29*(6), 1183–1187.

Tweed, S. C. (2003). Performance-accelerating technologies that will shape the future of home care. *Home Healthcare Nurse, 21*(10), 647–650.

U.S. Department of Health and Human Services, Health Care Financing Administration Office of Strategic Planning. (1998). *Health care financing review, Medicare and Medicaid statistical supplement*. Baltimore, MD: Author.

Wiener, J. M. (2010). What does health reform mean for long-term care? *Public Policy & Aging Report, 20*(2), 8–15.

Zhu, C. W. (2004). Effects of the Balanced Budget Act on Medicare home health utilization. *Journal of the American Geriatrics Society, 52*, 989–994.

6

Rehabilitation

DEBRA J. SHEETS

CHAPTER OVERVIEW

Geriatric rehabilitation is an increasingly important intervention in the continuum of long-term care. The purpose of rehabilitation is to restore or enhance function to maximize independence. In older adults, disability is often multicausal, reflecting a higher burden of comorbid disease. An interdisciplinary team is required to manage complex medical issues and rehabilitation needs. Older adults are high users of health services, and studies indicate that appropriate rehabilitation can decrease hospital costs, reduce hospital readmissions, lower mortality, and improve morale and functional status (Wells, Seabrook, Stolee, Borrie, & Knoefel, 2003b). This chapter focuses on rehabilitation in postacute care (PAC) settings that include long-term acute-care hospitals (LTACHs), inpatient rehabilitation facilities (IRFs), skilled nursing facilities (SNFs), and home health agencies (HHAs). The chapter begins with an overview of the development of the field of rehabilitation and a discussion of two conceptual models for disability. Next is a description of clients, providers, rehabilitation settings, and levels of care for geriatric rehabilitation. Additionally, interventions and modalities are discussed to support function in older adults. The chapter concludes with an examination of Medicare funding for rehabilitation service.

LEARNING OBJECTIVES

After reading this chapter, you will be able to:

- Identify two conceptual models for disability and analyze how they inform our understanding of rehabilitation
- Describe the rehabilitation team and the roles of individual members in establishing rehabilitation goals and coordinating care
- Discuss inpatient and outpatient rehabilitation settings for postacute care
- Describe rehabilitation interventions and modalities
- Discuss Medicare funding for rehabilitation services for older adults

KEY TERMS

- Activities of daily living (ADLs)
- Centers for Medicare & Medicaid Services (CMS)
- Comorbidity
- Disability
- Durable medical equipment (DME)
- Functional Independence Measure (FIM®)
- Inpatient rehabilitation facility (IRF)
- Instrumental activities of daily living (IADLs)
- International Classification of Function, Disability, and Health (ICF)
- Medicare Advantage (Part C)
- Original Medicare (Part A)
- Physiatrist
- Postacute care (PAC)
- Prospective payment system (PPS)
- Rehabilitation
- Skilled nursing facility (SNF)

INTRODUCTION

Rehabilitation is designed to facilitate the process of recovery from injury, illness, or disease to as normal a condition as possible. Because of population aging, older adults (persons aged 65 and over) are the fastest growing age group needing rehabilitation services. The goal of geriatric rehabilitation is to enable older adults to function at the highest possible level despite physical **disability** and disease. Geriatric rehabilitation involves an interdisciplinary team that uses a comprehensive geriatric assessment to inform the development of a plan of care to improve or restore function. Rehabilitative services are offered in a variety of settings across the continuum of care, but are most commonly offered in the **postacute care (PAC)** phase, following an acute illness or hospitalization. Several systematic reviews indicate that appropriate use of geriatric rehabilitation can reduce health care costs while leading to better outcomes that include improved function, reduced admissions to nursing homes, and lower mortality rates (Bachmann et al., 2010; Wells, Seabrook, Stolee, Borrie, & Knoefel, 2003a).

Although advances in medicine and rehabilitative science have reduced the prevalence of disability in old age, these have also contributed to rising health care costs (Schoeni, Freedman, & Martin, 2008). Unfortunately, these gains in health and disability may not extend to the future as the baby boom generation begins to enter the retirement years. Recent trends in disability among persons ages 50 to 65 show significant increases in mobility-related disabilities linked to musculoskeletal disorders, as well as increases in disability related to depression, diabetes, and nervous system conditions (e.g., Parkinson's disease, multiple sclerosis; Martin, Freedman, Schoeni, & Andreski, 2010). As the numbers of older adults (ages 65 and older) double in the next two decades, these trends will likely drive increases in the need for rehabilitation.

Using rehabilitation resources effectively requires knowing how disability occurs and what is needed to achieve effective rehabilitation outcomes (Hoeing &

Kortebein, 2012). It is critical to know who provides rehabilitation, what is available, in what settings, for whom, and how such rehabilitation is funded. This chapter reviews these aspects of geriatric rehabilitation. First is an overview of the evolution of rehabilitation and a discussion of two well-known conceptual models for disability. Next is a description of clients, providers, rehabilitation settings, and levels of care for geriatric rehabilitation. Additionally, interventions and modalities are discussed to support function in older adults. The chapter concludes with an examination of Medicare funding for rehabilitation services.

DEVELOPMENT OF THE FIELD OF REHABILITATION

The field of rehabilitation initially emerged in response to two major world wars. In 1917, reconstruction units were set up in 35 general hospitals and 18 base hospitals in the United States to address the needs of wounded soldiers returning from the battlefields. The programs were regarded positively because they allowed injured soldiers to recover and return to full duty. Strategically, rehabilitation was referred to as the third branch of medicine, which would complement specialties within the primary (i.e., diagnosis and treatment) or secondary branches (i.e., health promotion/disease prevention) of medicine. In the 1920s, the field was developed by physical therapy (PT) physicians. One may be surprised to learn that radiologists were the first to use physiotherapy to treat patients. However, by 1938, the radiologists and PT doctors recognized their different interests. In 1939, the term "physiatry" was coined, which recognized some of the similarities of physical rehabilitation to psychiatry. A **physiatrist** is a physician who specializes in physical medicine and rehabilitation (also called PM&R) and focuses on the prevention, diagnosis, and treatment of disease or injury.

During World War II, rehabilitation experienced tremendous growth. Bernard Baruch, a philanthropist, contributed funds to develop physiatry programs at selected universities and to award training fellowships to selected physicians in PM&R. This effort resulted in a core cadre of well-trained academicians to direct residencies and PM&R programs. By 1945, the American Medical Association (AMA) had established a section on PM&R, and in 1947, the AMA recognized physiatry as a separate medical specialty. The concept of rehabilitation involved a team's approach to care led by the physiatrist, and this team included physical therapists (PTs), occupational therapists (OTs), vocational education specialists, and recreation personnel.

Medical rehabilitation got another boost in 1952 with the polio epidemics that affected more than 21,200 Americans of all ages. Until 1955, with the invention of the Salk vaccine, the polio epidemic dominated the attention of PM&R physicians. In 1958, the Vocational Rehabilitation Act added training funds for resident stipends in PM&R. Unfortunately, the 1965 enactment of Medicare and Medicaid did not provide funding for rehabilitation, but in 1972, Medicare coverage expanded to include inpatient rehabilitation.

Medical rehabilitation services and programs grew rapidly during the 1980s and 1990s, driven largely by the Medicare payment system. Prior to the

Balanced Budget Act (BBA) of 1997, Medicare reimbursed all allowable charges for rehabilitation services and programs, although payments to a facility were capped at an annual maximum. This payment system served as an incentive for growth, and between 1985 and 1999, the total number of rehabilitation facilities (i.e., rehabilitation hospitals, rehabilitation units, long-term care hospitals [LTCHs], and comprehensive outpatient rehabilitation facilities [CORFs]) grew three-fold from 626 to 1,863 facilities. By 2002, the growth stalled out with implementation of a **prospective payment system (PPS)** in **inpatient rehabilitation facilities (IRFs)**. IRFs are rehabilitation hospitals or rehabilitation units in an acute-care hospital that are licensed under state laws to provide intensive rehabilitative services. IRFs decreased to 1,165 by 2011 when they served about 371,000 Original Medicare (Part B) beneficiaries at a cost of $6.46 billion (Medicare Payment Advisory Commission [MedPAC], 2012a).

DISABILITY RIGHTS AND THE *OLMSTEAD* DECISION

In recent decades, vocational rehabilitation has received growing attention as the prevalence of disability has increased and disability has become more visible in society. Many older adults are "aging into disability" in later life because of chronic disabling conditions. In addition, more people are surviving with congenital disabilities (e.g., cerebral palsy) or with disability acquired in adulthood (e.g., spinal cord injury) because of accidents or trauma (Kemp & Mosqueda, 2004). People of all ages are benefiting from assistive technologies (ATs; e.g., electric wheelchairs, augmentative communication devices) that provide mobility and allow them to be mainstreamed into our society. The passage of the Americans with Disabilities Act (ADA) in 1990 assured civil rights protections for persons with disabilities against discrimination and required "reasonable accommodations" to allow full participation in society. In 1993, amendments to the Rehabilitation Act increased access to vocational rehabilitation by requiring "presumption of ability" and offering necessary services and supports, including AT, for employment. Another pivotal moment in disability rights occurred with the *Olmstead v. L.C.* decision in 1999, when the United States Supreme Court held that the ADA requires that states provide the necessary community-based services to persons with disabilities to allow them to live in the least restrictive setting available. In the years since this ruling, the *Olmstead* decision has been used to improve the lives of thousands of persons with disabilities of all ages by assuring them of their right to rehabilitation and to continue living in the community rather than being institutionalized.

CONCEPTUAL MODELS FOR DISABILITY

Conceptual models are useful in gaining a clearer understanding of the underlying processes that lead to disability and for which rehabilitative interventions are possible, which can change outcomes by improving function. In the last several

FIGURE 6.1 WHO ICF model of disability.

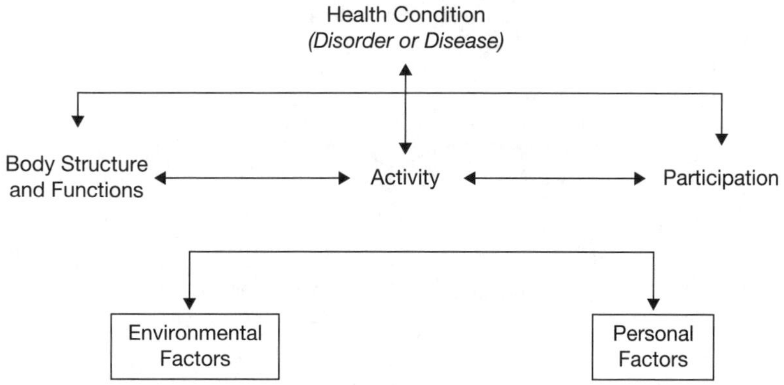

Health Condition
(Disorder or Disease)

Body Structure and Functions
Activity
Participation

Environmental Factors
Personal Factors

decades, our understanding of the causes of disability has changed. Two well-known and widely used conceptual models are described in the following sections.

INTERNATIONAL CLASSIFICATION OF FUNCTIONING, DISABILITY, AND HEALTH

The **International Classification of Functioning, Disability, and Health** (ICF) model, developed by the World Health Organization (2001), is a classification framework for assessing health and functioning at both the individual and population level. The framework proposes that health conditions (e.g., spinal injury) can cause impairments (e.g., paralysis) that affect the individual's level of function (i.e., body function, ability to do a task, and participate in activities) within the context of environmental and personal factors (see Figure 6.1). Medical interventions (e.g., medication, surgery) address the underlying health conditions, and rehabilitation services target the impairment, activities, and participation. Personal (e.g., preferences) and environmental factors (e.g., assistive devices, personal assistance) also influence activity and participation. What this means for older adults is that the disablement process will be highly influenced by the number and type of comorbidities and the resulting impairments. Multiple strategies are needed for effective treatment of late-life disability (Hoenig & Kotebein, 2013).

INSTITUTE OF MEDICINE ENABLING–DISABLING MODEL

The Institute of Medicine (IOM) proposed a disability model to illustrate the enabling–disabling process (Brandt & Pope, 1997). The IOM Model draws from the social model of disability that emerged as an alternative to the dominant medical model of disability in which disability was viewed as a deficit that needs to be "fixed." The social model suggests that although physical, sensory, intellectual, and psychological factors can cause functional limitations, it is environmental and societal barriers that cause disability. According to the enabling–disabling process, disability results when there is a gap between individual capacity and the demands of the environment. For example, an older person

FIGURE 6.2 The IOM enabling–disabling model of disability.

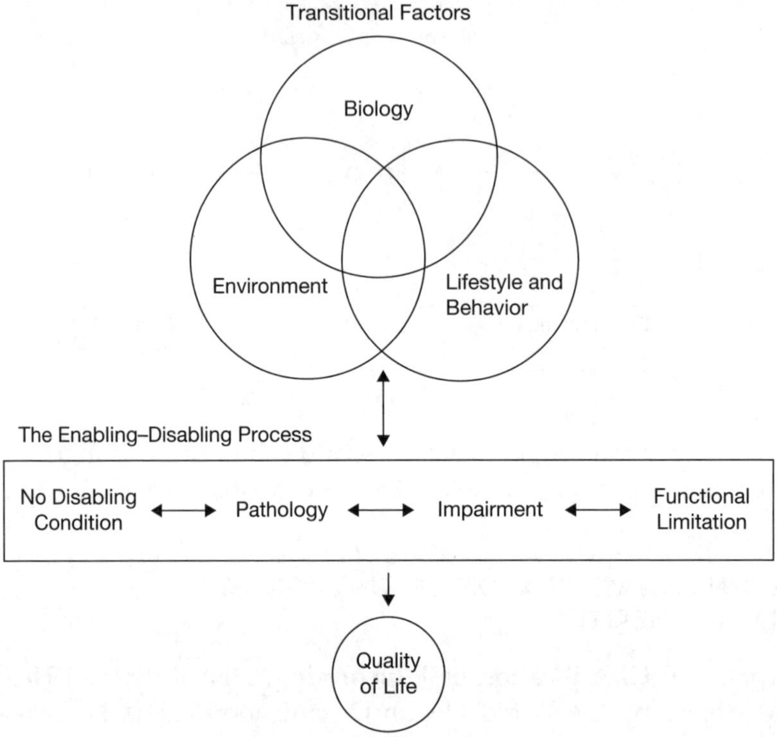

with presbyopia is disabled in a restaurant if he or she lacks corrective glasses to allow reading the menu. According to the ecological model, disability can be addressed through interventions that increase the individual capacity or reduce task demand. Returning to the former example, reading glasses can be provided to increase individual capacity. Alternatively, the environment can also be modified by providing a food menu with larger print (Figure 6.2).

GERIATRIC REHABILITATION

CLIENTS

Traditionally, rehabilitation programs were designed for young adults or children. Today, the majority of rehabilitation clients are older adults with an average age of 66 years; only 10% of rehabilitation patients are 44 years of age or younger (Nelson et al., 2007). Women comprise 57% of rehabilitation clients. About 90% of patients who need rehabilitation are discharged from an acute-care hospital to a PAC setting (i.e., inpatient rehabilitation hospital/unit [IRH/U], home health care, or **skilled nursing facility [SNF]**). The key areas of focus in the rehabilitation process are identified in Exhibit 6.1.

The most common conditions in old age that require rehabilitation are stroke, hip fracture, and limb amputation. Another group of conditions includes patients who have been deconditioned because of serious illness (e.g., heart attack,

EXHIBIT 6.1 Key Areas of Focus with Geriatric Rehabilitation

1. Preventing, recognizing, and managing comorbid illness and medical complications.
2. Training to maximize independence in self-care and daily activities.
3. Facilitating psychosocial coping and adaptation by patient and family.
4. Preventing secondary disability (e.g., depression, pressure ulcers) by supporting resumption of home, recreational, and family activities.
5. Enhancing quality of life with accommodations (e.g., AT, home modifications) to address any residual disability.
6. Promoting health to prevent other disabling conditions.

surgery). One caution is that older adults can become discouraged if they compare themselves to younger clients. In addition, older adults often have different treatment goals (e.g., **activities of daily living [ADLs]** and **instrumental activities of daily living [IADLs]**), need a lower intensity of rehabilitation, and require different types of care (e.g., cardiac monitoring). The very old and even cognitively impaired elders can benefit from rehabilitation, although progress may occur more slowly than with younger populations. Unfortunately, many older adults who could benefit from rehabilitation do not receive it and suffer a marked decline in quality of life. For example, a survey by the National Stroke Association (2006) found that only 15% of stroke survivors see a physiatrist for poststroke care; 38% said they lacked information on rehabilitation and recovery after stroke.

REHABILITATION PROVIDERS

The cornerstone of effective rehabilitation is an interdisciplinary team providing a comprehensive approach to care (Prvu Bettger & Stineman, 2007). Most geriatric patients have complex and multiple interacting problems and contextual factors that require interventions from several disciplines (Hoenig & Kortebein, 2013). The rehabilitation team typically includes a physician, nurse, social worker, physical therapist, and occupational therapist. Other disciplines, such as speech pathology, clinical psychology, pharmacology, or nutrition, may be requested for consultation as needed.

Members of the rehabilitation team bring expertise that overlaps and supports the interventions of each other. Team members complete a comprehensive geriatric assessment with patients using standardized tools to aid diagnosis, assessment, and outcome measurement (Wells et al., 2003a). Typically, geriatric clients must be medically stable and able to actively participate in a rehabilitation program. The client must also have sufficient cognitive function to allow participation in rehabilitation programs or have a caregiver who can prompt and support rehabilitation. On the basis of the initial assessment, the rehabilitation team must be able to identify achievable rehabilitation goals that improve or maintain the client's self-care, function, and mobility. Typically, the geriatric client must

EXHIBIT 6.2 Common Short-Term Rehabilitation Goals for a Geriatric Client and Team Member

REHABILITATION GOALS	TEAM MEMBER
Smooth transition from acute facilities to outpatient rehabilitation	Nursing
Full assessment and supportive interventions to promote independence in ADLs	OT/PT/Nursing
Assessment for mobility aids to support mobility and prevent falls	PT
Perform a comprehensive physical exam and functional assessment that includes mental status, cognition, social support, and nutrition	Nursing
Assessment of safety risks	PT/Nursing
Medication and pain management education	Nursing
Caregiver education and support	OT/PT/Nursing
Assessment and intervention for home/environmental accommodations/adaptation	OT/PT/Nursing

require at least two or more team members to achieve therapeutic goals. Older adults often have complex health needs, such as impaired balance, inactivity, depression, dementia, lack of endurance or strength, limited joint mobility, poor coordination, and reduced agility, which must also be identified and addressed in order to make progress in achieving rehabilitation goals. Thus, a specialized team approach is essential to be effective. An example of a typical rehabilitation teams' (e.g., nursing, PT, and OT) short-term goals for a geriatric client is provided in Exhibit 6.2.

Coordination of care is managed through team conferences and by updating each other through routine charting or by leaving e-mail or voice mail messages. Each member of the team is responsible for the interventions appropriate to his or her skills and area of specialization (see Exhibit 6.3).

Physicians

As noted previously, physiatrists are physicians who specialize in PM&R. They focus on restoring function to patients who have experienced catastrophic events resulting in paraplegia, quadriplegia, or traumatic brain injury, as well as individuals who have suffered strokes, orthopedic injuries, or neurologic disorders such as multiple sclerosis or polio. Physiatrists also treat patients with acute and chronic pain and musculoskeletal problems, such as back and neck pain, tendinitis, pinched nerves, and fibromyalgia. Orthopedic surgeons may supervise the rehabilitation of patients with musculoskeletal problems that have been corrected by surgery, such as hip fractures, knee and other joint replacements, and broken backs. Neurologists may manage the rehabilitation of patients recovering from a stroke, spinal cord injury, or traumatic brain injury.

EXHIBIT 6.3 Primary Roles and Functions of Members of the Multidisciplinary Rehabilitation Team

DISCIPLINE	TYPICAL CREDENTIAL	ROLE/RESPONSIBILITIES
Physiatrist	MD, 4-year residency in PM&R and board certification	• Assess and treat medical conditions, establishment of rehabilitation goals
Nurse	Associate, baccalaureate, or graduate degree; current license; may seek credentialing as a certified rehabilitation registered nurse (CRRN)	• Medication management and wound care, develops patient care plan; coordinates the team; monitors the patient and progress toward rehabilitation goals; evaluates self-care and provides self-care training, patient and family education
Physical therapist (PT)	Clinical doctorate, licensed	• Assessment of range of motion and strength • Assessment of gait and mobility • Treatment with physical modalities (heat, cold, ultrasound, massage, electrical stimulation) • Training on safe transfers, spasticity, and adaptive equipment
Occupational therapist (OT)	Master's or doctoral degree, licensed	• Evaluate self-care skills and other ADLs • Home safety evaluation • Recommend AT • Fabricate splints • Treatment of upper extremity deficits • Assess leisure skills and interests
Speech/Language therapist (SLP)	Master's or doctoral degree in communication sciences and disorders; licensed	• Assessment of all aspects of communication • Assessment of swallowing disorders; recommendations for dietary alterations and positioning to treat dysphagia

Nurses

Nursing staff members conduct the initial assessment of the patient, implement the rehabilitation plan, monitor the course of treatment, and chart the progress of the patient. They coordinate the team and ensure that care is appropriate for the patient who usually has other medical problems. The nurse reinforces the goals and techniques of therapy, provides patient and family education, and is responsible for ensuring continuity of care. Nurses are licensed by the state in which they work and may have a specialized certification in rehabilitation. Registered nurses are generally trained at the baccalaureate level.

Physical Therapists

Physical therapists evaluate and treat people with limitations in gross motor function. The goal of treatment is to restore or maximize functional capacity by improving muscle strength, joint motion, and endurance. PTs use hot or cold compresses, ultrasound, or electrical stimulation to relieve pain, reduce swelling, and improve muscle tone. PTs also teach clients how to use crutches, prostheses, and wheelchairs for mobility. PT practice requires a clinical doctorate from an accredited PT program, passing a national registry exam, and obtaining state board licensure. Reflecting this advanced professional training and expertise, 32 states allow PTs to provide services to clients without requiring a physician referral.

Occupational Therapists

Occupational therapists evaluate and assess functioning in self-care, work, or leisure/play activities. Clients may have cognitive–perceptual difficulties, visual limitations, or social dysfunction that interferes with carrying out life skills. OTs teach clients how to perform essential daily activities such as dressing, bathing, and eating. They help individuals develop skills important for living independently, obtaining an education, maintaining employment, and participating in leisure. OTs conduct home safety assessments and teach clients how to use adaptive equipment (e.g., splints, aids for eating, and dressing) to perform ADLs. OTs must complete a master's degree from an accredited OT program and pass a state board licensing exam.

Speech–Language Pathologists

Speech–language pathologists (SLPs), informally speech therapists, are trained in the diagnosis of speech, voice, and language disorders. Speech therapists help patients relearn language skills. Disorders may result from hearing loss, stroke, cerebral palsy, mental disability, or brain injury. Speech therapists also help patients with difficulty in swallowing or dysphagia to regain their ability to take foods orally. Speech therapists complete a master's degree from an accredited speech and language pathology program and take a state licensing examination. Speech therapy programs are moving toward requiring a clinical doctorate for entry-level practice. Entry-level practice for an audiologist requires a doctoral (e.g., AuD) or other graduate degree.

REHABILITATION CONSULTANTS

Rehabilitation teams include other specialists (e.g., social workers, nutritionists) as needed to consult on specific problems (Exhibit 6.4).

EXHIBIT 6.4 Rehabilitation Consultants

HEALTH CARE PROFESSIONAL	TYPICAL CREDENTIAL	ROLE/RESPONSIBILITIES
Social worker (SW)	Baccalaureate or postbaccalaureate (master's or doctoral) degree in social work, current license	• Evaluation of family and home care needs • Assessment of psychosocial factors • Counseling • Liaison with community resources
Psychologist/ psychiatrist (PsyD or PhD)	Doctoral degree, current license	• Assessment of mental and emotional health • Evaluation of coping skills • Treatment of mental health disorders (e.g., counseling, medication)
Pharmacist (PharmD)	Doctoral degree, license	• Assessment of drug therapy and response • Evaluation of adverse drug reactions • Recommend changes in drug therapy • Patient and family education
Dietitian (RD)	Baccalaureate or postbaccalaureate (master's) degree, current license	• Assess nutritional status • Alter diet to maximize nutrition.

Social Workers

Social workers assess the patient's social and psychological behaviors, living situation, financial resources, and availability of family support. They often function as case managers or discharge planners to help to ensure that a patient's course of treatment is appropriate and cost-effective. Social workers arrange for community-based services as needed and may provide counseling to patients and/or family members. Social workers may have a baccalaureate or master's degree in social work (MSW). Clinical social workers (e.g., licensed clinical social workers, LCSWs) are licensed by the state.

Clinical Psychologists

Clinical psychologists assist the patient in coping with behavioral and emotional issues that arise in adjusting to a disability. They are trained to assess intelligence, personality, cognitive skills, and perceptual–motor skills. Clinical psychologists play an important role in the rehabilitation of individuals with impaired cognitive ability and behavioral changes because of traumatic brain injury, stroke, or spinal cord injury. Psychotherapy can help a patient cope more effectively during the course of the treatment process, which increases the effectiveness of rehabilitation. Clinical psychologists are trained at the doctoral level and are licensed by the state in which they work.

Pharmacists

Older adults are often on numerous medications after an acute illness—many of them new. The role of the consulting pharmacist is to review medications, identify medication problems, and convey recommendations for changes to the physician and the rest of the team. Pharmacists can ensure that older adults are taking their medications correctly and consistently. Pharmacists can also screen for and reduce risks of drug interactions.

Dietitians

The nutritional status of older adults can range from being undernourished and debilitated to situations in which there are complications from obesity (e.g., coronary artery disease, stroke). In addition, older adults often have special nutritional issues such as poor intake, poor chewing abilities, and swallowing difficulties. A dietitian can assess nutritional status and make recommendations to optimize a person's diet.

REHABILITATION SETTINGS

Rehabilitation is delivered across the care continuum in a variety of settings. The intensity and nature of rehabilitative services differ depending on the setting. Postacute settings include rehabilitation hospitals and units, LTCHs, SNFs, outpatient facilities, and the patient's home. Rehabilitative services often begin in the hospital with a focus on early mobilization starting on the first day and involve the integration of activities with a focus on discharge planning. The purpose of rehabilitation is to help maximize recovery for older adults. Early and intensive PT/OT is particularly beneficial in improving functional outcomes (e.g., toileting independently, walking) as well as in lowering mortality (Horn et al., 2005; Siu et al., 2006) for patients with a stroke or a total joint replacement or hip fracture.

INPATIENT REHABILITATION FACILITIES

IRFs include rehabilitation hospitals and units, LTCHs, and SNFs. In 2012, there were about 1,166 IRFs in the United States. The types of clients needing rehabilitation in IRFs are shown in Table 6.1. Over the past decade, the patient mix for IRFs has changed significantly with increases in clients with stroke, brain injuries, and neurological disorders. A significant decrease in inpatient rehabilitation for major joint replacement of lower extremities is also evident.

TABLE 6.1 Changes in Patient Mix for Inpatient Rehabilitation Facilities (2004–2013)

TYPE OF CASE	2004 (%)	2013 (%)	PERCENTAGE POINT CHANGE
Stroke	16.6	19.4	2.8
Fracture of lower extremity	13.1	12.6	−0.5
Major joint replacement of lower extremity	24.0	8.8	−15.2
Debility	6.1	10.3	4.2
Neurological disorders	5.2	12.5	7.3
Brain injury	3.9	8.1	4.2
Other orthopedic conditions	5.1	7.6	2.5
Cardiac conditions	5.3	5.4	0.1
Spinal cord injury	4.2	4.5	0.3
Other	16.4	10.7	−5.7

Source: Medicare Payment Advisory Commission (MedPAC; 2013).

Rehabilitation Hospitals and Units

Intensive inpatient rehabilitation programs are provided by rehabilitation hospitals and units. A typical rehabilitation hospital has 60 to 100 beds, whereas units have 10 to 40 beds. Patients must be capable of participating in a high-intensity (generally more than 3 hours per day) program. Some rehabilitation hospitals or units specialize in specific kinds of impairments, such as spinal cord injury or stroke.

Long-Term Care Hospitals

LTCHs focus on patients who need more than 25 days of medical and rehabilitative care. They are certified as acute-care hospitals, and the majority of LTCH patients transfer from an intensive or critical care unit. Common LTCH services include comprehensive rehabilitation, respiratory therapy, head trauma treatment, and pain management. In 2011, Medicare recognized the existence of 436 LTCHs.

Skilled Nursing Facilities

Most SNFs are part of a nursing home that provides custodial care to long-term residents whom Medicare does not cover (see Chapter 11). Medicare-covered SNF patients usually represent a small share of an SNF's total patient census (e.g., 12% of total patient days in 2010), but represent a larger share of facility revenues (e.g., 23% of payments; MedPAC, 2012b). SNFs offer Medicare-certified therapy services (e.g., PT, OT, and speech–language pathology) through less intensive rehabilitative programs that average 1 to 3 hours of therapy per day up to 5 days a week.

COMMUNITY-BASED REHABILITATION

Home Health Care

Home care has become a major setting for rehabilitation services (i.e., PT, OT, and speech–language pathology) in the past decade, and home care agencies employ a significant number of rehabilitation professionals. Original Medicare (Part A) covers services from a Medicare-certified home health agency for a 60-day period, called an "episode of care." Therapy services must be reasonable and necessary with the expectation of improvement in the identified condition. Rehabilitation in the home is preferred by older adults and is often more effective because the therapist can assess the performance of the individual in the environment in which he or she actually lives. Seeing the home care setting makes it easier to determine the appropriate mix of home modifications (e.g., ramps, grab bars), AT (e.g., walkers, shower chairs), and therapeutic exercise (e.g., strengthening activities). However, Medicare will only cover 80% of Medicare-approved **durable medical equipment** (under Part B) that has been ordered by a doctor, such as a wheelchair, walker, or oxygen equipment.

Most licensed HHAs provide physical, occupational, and speech therapy services. Medicare authorizes PT as a stand-alone service; however, occupational and speech therapy may be ordered in conjunction with nursing services. The most common rehabilitation diagnoses seen by home health care providers include congestive heart failure, hip and knee surgeries, open heart surgery, and stroke. For a fuller discussion of home health care, see Chapter 5.

Outpatient Therapy

Outpatient therapy is appropriate for stable patients who can travel to outpatient rehabilitation clinics, doctors' offices, or other community-based settings. These patients often have uncomplicated conditions or present with minimal disability. Outpatient rehabilitation programs have traditionally served patients with orthopedic, neurological, or back conditions. More recently, outpatient rehabilitation services for older adults include pain management and incontinence. Outpatient therapy is provided in private practice, CORFs, adult day health care, and hospital outpatient departments. Adult day health care is a new setting for outpatient rehabilitation that targets services to frail older adults and those with disabilities (see Chapter 7). Older adults attending adult day health care arrive in the morning and participate in several hours of intensive rehabilitation therapy. At the end of the day, patients return to their homes. Some adult day health care programs qualify for reimbursement from Medicaid waiver programs designed to maximize the independence of those who are "at risk" for institutionalization.

REHABILITATION INTERVENTIONS

EXERCISE

After an injury or surgery, an exercise conditioning program can help older adults regain their independence and return to daily activities. Exercise programs are commonly implemented in rehabilitation recovery programs for heart conditions, orthopedic, and neurosurgery procedures. PTs and physiatrists can tailor an exercise program to address the needs of each patient. Specific patient populations, such as those who are frail, can benefit from certain types of exercise. For example, a systematic review of research on strength training found significantly improved muscle strength and function in frail older adults (Liu & Latham, 2009). As noted previously, early mobilization of patients during hospitalization can improve outcomes for most, including those with hip fracture, acute pneumonia, or stroke.

ASSISTIVE TECHNOLOGY

Assistive technology refers to any item or equipment used to increase, maintain, or improve functional capacity. AT services help people select, acquire, or use AT by providing functional evaluations, training, demonstration, and purchasing or leasing of devices. A growing body of literature supports the effectiveness of technology; AT may reduce decline associated with disability by one-half (Hoenig, Taylor, & Sloan, 2003; Schoeni et al., 2008; Verbrugge, Rennert, & Madans, 1997). An excellent resource on assistive devices is AbleData (www.abledata.com), which provides information on almost 40,000 assistive devices and rehabilitation equipment. Other good resources are the State Assistive Technology Programs (www.resnaprojects.org/nattap/at/stateprograms.html), funded under the Assistive Technology Act of 1998, which works to improve access to AT (see Chapter 8). Exhibit 6.5 offers an overview of the types of AT, their purpose, and specific examples of equipment and devices.

Mobility Aids

Mobility aids are one of the most common types of ATs used by older adults. In 2000, 10% of older adults used canes, and 4.6% used walkers (Bradley & Hernandez, 2011). Canes are light and versatile, but are most useful for a mild gait problem, as they require upper extremity strength and cannot support more than 20% of body weight (Hoenig, 2004). A quad cane can provide more support, but is often harder to use. Canes can help improve balance or reduce pain from an arthritic joint. Improper fit or incorrect use of a cane can increase an older adult's risk of falls. Canes should be used in the hand opposite the impaired leg.

Walkers are used for gait problems when more support is needed than can be safely provided with a cane. Two-wheeled (front-wheel) walkers are the most common. Four-wheel walkers are increasingly fit with brakes and other

EXHIBIT 6.5 Examples of Assistive Technology

TYPE	PURPOSE	EXAMPLES
Aids for daily living	Self-help aids for use in activities	Modified eating utensils, adapted books, pencil holders, dressing aids, self-care devices
Aids for hearing impairment	Deaf and hard-of-hearing population	Assistive listening devices (FM loop systems, infrared), hearing aids, Text Telephone (TTY), visual and tactile alerting systems, closed captioning
Aids for vision impairment	Visually impaired or blind population	Magnifiers, Braille or speech output devices, large-print screens,
Augmentative and alternative communication (AAC)	Speech and/or hearing disabilities	Communication boards, speech synthesizers, modified typewriters, head pointers, text-to-voice software
Computer access aids	Make computers accessible	Headsticks; light pointers; modified or alternate keyboards; switches activated by pressure, sound, or voice; touch screens; special software; voice-to-text software; speech recognition software
Environmental controls	Allow control over various appliances	Switches for telephone, TV, or other appliances that are activated by pressure, eyebrows, or breath
Home/workplace modifications	Structural adaptions to remove or reduce physical barriers	Ramps, lifts, bathroom changes, automatic door openers, expanded doorways
Mobility aids	Help move within environment	Electric or manual wheelchairs, modifications of vehicles for travel, scooters, crutches, canes and walkers
Prostheses and orthoses	Prostheses replace a body part; orthoses provide support to a weak or injured part	Prostheses include artificial limbs or breast implants; orthoses include splints or braces
Recreation	Enable participation in sports, social, and cultural events	Audio description for movies, adaptive controls for video games, adaptive fishing rods, etc.
Seating and positioning	Provide body support to help maintain posture and perform daily tasks	Adapted seating, cushions, standing tables, positioning belts, braces, cushions, and wedges
Service animals	Any animal individually trained to provide assistance	A guide dog (for visually impaired and blind individuals), signal dog (for hearing impaired or deaf individuals)
Vehicle modifications	Personal transportation	Adaptive driving aids, hand controls, wheelchair and other lifts, modified vans or other motor vehicles

options such as a seat or a basket. Though these options are more expensive and require coordination to use, the seat is particularly useful for patients with limited endurance.

Wheelchairs are used for older adults who have significant mobility impairments due to lower extremity weakness, impaired balance, or motor coordination problems. Manual wheelchairs are the most common. Ill-fitting wheelchairs are uncomfortable and increase risk of pressure ulcers. Patients and health care providers may be concerned about the idea of "use it or lose it" with a wheelchair, but there is no evidence that wheelchairs contribute to functional decline and deconditioning (Hoenig, Pieper, Branch, & Cohen, 2007).

Older adults with arthritis or weak upper extremities are at risk of developing shoulder pain or rotator cuff tendinitis with manual wheelchair use (Finley & Rodgers, 2004). Specialized wheelchairs are available to address unique needs. Increasingly, motorized wheelchairs and scooters are being used in the community to address mobility limitations, although they can be difficult to maneuver in the home. Scooters can be expensive, because in addition to the cost of the device, older adults need a home ramp and a car lift for transporting them. Evidence on best practices to follow when obtaining a wheelchair is limited, but there is some evidence that expert assistance, fitting, and training can be helpful in ensuring an optimal wheelchair selection (Greer, Brasure, & Wilt, 2012).

All mobility aids are considered DME by Medicare and are eligible for coverage if guidelines are followed. Documentation must show that lower level devices do not compensate for the problem. Usually, Medicare reimbursement is limited to one type of aid (e.g., both a wheelchair and a quad cane are not provided). Power mobility devices require substantial medical justification. Medicare covers an OT or PT consultation for fitting and training in the use of any DME. After 13 months of rental of a manual wheelchair, the Medicare beneficiary owns it. The Veterans Health Administration (VHA) has more comprehensive DME and AT coverage, and as long as it is a medical necessity, will cover more than one type of mobility aid.

Bathroom and Self-Care Aids

Self-care tasks, especially those in the bathroom, are easier and safer with AT and home modifications. Assistive devices for self-care have been shown to improve clinical outcomes (e.g., reduce falls, improve balance; Gitlin et al., 2006). Common bathroom equipments and modifications include raised toilet seats, tub/shower seats, handheld showers, and grab bars. Raised toilet seats make it easier for persons with weak legs or poor balance to stand. Tub/shower bench makes is easier and safer to bathe. Handheld showers add to comfort and ease of bathing. Grab bars can increase safety in the bathroom, but must be placed correctly and be securely attached to the wall or they can be dangerous. The Center for Universal Design (www.ncsu.edu/ncsu/design/cud/) has a useful brochure: "Residential Rehabilitation, Remodeling and Universal Design" (www.ncsu.edu/ncsu/design/cud/pubs_p/docs/residential_remodelinl.pdf).

Prosthetics and Orthoses

A prosthesis is an artificial body part (e.g., leg, breast implant), whereas an orthosis is an externally applied device (e.g., brace, splint) used to support or assist function. Diabetes accounts for 90% of lower leg amputations. The disease process of diabetes can limit the ability of an older adult to use a prosthesis. Other comorbid conditions, such as dementia, arthritis, stroke, or pulmonary disease, can also affect the use of a prosthesis by older adults. Mobility using a manual or power wheelchair may provide the most functional option. Both low-tech and high-tech prostheses are available and depend on the unique needs of the patient. Amputee clinics can provide the most comprehensive approach to the problem, but if this is not available, then a certified prosthetist and PT are needed. Orthoses are available off the shelf or can be custom fabricated by an orthotist or an OT. Common braces for older adults include those for the knee (e.g., knee sleeve, knee unloader braces), ankle/foot orthoses for foot drop, and heel cushions for plantar fasciitis/heel pain. Knee sleeves are often used for knee osteoarthritis (OA). Foot drop occurs most commonly after a stroke, and ankle/foot orthoses (AFOs) can improve gait speed by maintaining the foot in a neutral position during ambulation. Medicare covers the cost for many prosthetic and orthotic devices, although a 20% copayment is typically required.

Environmental Modification

Universal design refers to a set of principles that lead to environments that are usable and effective for everyone, including persons with disabilities. Environmental modifications focus on making the physical environment more accessible. OTs have expertise in assessing the person–environment fit within the home and making recommendations for devices and modifications. PTs are specialists in mobility issues. Low-vision specialists can help older adults with low vision (e.g., glaucoma, macular degeneration; see Chapter 8 for elaboration on these themes).

MODALITIES

HEAT/COLD

The most common therapeutic modality for treating pain is application of heat or cold. Both can be delivered in several ways. Thermal transfer can occur through conduction (e.g., hot or cold pack, heat lamp), convection (e.g., hot tub/whirlpool bath, paraffin baths), and conversion (e.g., ultrasound). Heat is usually avoided initially after acute injury. Application of cold is avoided if the patient has insensitive skin.

TRANSCUTANEOUS ELECTRICAL NERVE STIMULATION

Transcutaneous electrical nerve stimulation (TENS) is an electrotherapy that can provide relief from musculoskeletal pain. It involves putting electrodes on the skin that deliver intermittent electrical stimulation to surface nerves that block the transmission of pain signals. TENS is often used to treat back pain.

ULTRASOUND

Ultrasound transmits high- or low-frequency sound waves to the muscles to cause deep tissue/muscle warming. It promotes tissue relaxation and is useful in treating muscle tightness and spasms.

SWALLOWING STUDIES

Older adults with dysphagia, which often occurs poststroke, may need special feeding techniques and/or dietary modifications (e.g., use of gelatin to thicken liquids). An SLP can perform swallowing studies (e.g., endoscopic or radiographic) to assess the extent of the dysphagia and to make recommendations for appropriate remedies.

MEDICARE REIMBURSEMENT FOR REHABILITATION

MEDICARE (PART A; ACUTE/POSTACUTE CARE)

Medicare has implemented PPS in acute and postacute settings to limit overutilization of services and to motivate providers to deliver patient care effectively and efficiently. With PPS, the provider receives a flat dollar amount and is responsible for providing services that the patient needs. PPS creates an incentive for providers to develop systems that facilitate efficient diagnosis and treatment of patients. Medicare (Part A) covers all rehabilitation services provided in hospitals, IRFs, SNFs, and HHAs (see Exhibit 6.6).

Inpatient Rehabilitation Facilities

Implementation of the IRF-PPS began in 2003 (MedPAC, 2014). Under the IRF-PPS, Medicare reimburses for rehabilitation service based on the IRF patient assessment instrument (PAI). PAIs are converted through a **CMS** formula into a case-mix group (CMG) that has a reimbursement rate attached. Each patient falls into a certain CMG, which has a specific reimbursement rate assigned regardless of what services the patient receives. The PAI is calculated for each patient on admission and at discharge and is based on the **Functional Independence Measure** (**FIM**). The FIM is a well-validated tool based on the International Classification of Impairments, Disabilities and Handicaps (ICIDH; Uniform Data System for Medical Rehabilitation, 2013), which provides a systematic way to measure disability and determine how much assistance is required with ADLs. The FIM instrument consists of 18 items: 13 measure motor function and five measure cognitive tasks. Tasks are rated on a 7-point ordinal scale, and scores range from 18 to 128. Higher scores indicate greater independence.

EXHIBIT 6.6 Summary of Medicare (Part A): Prospective Payment Systems by Rehabilitation Provider Settings

PROVIDER SETTING	CLASSIFICATION SYSTEM	SUMMARY DESCRIPTION
Acute-care hospital	Diagnosis-related groups (DRGs)	• Primary diagnosis determines assignment to one of 535 DRGs • DRG payment is adjusted on the basis of age, sex, secondary diagnosis, and major procedures; DRG payment is per stay • Outlier payment made only if length of stay far exceeds the norm
Inpatient rehabilitation facility (i.e., rehabilitation hospital or unit)	CMGs	• PAI determines assignment to one of 95 CMGs; CMG determines payment rate per stay • Rehabilitation impairment categories (RICs) are based on diagnosis; CMG is based on RIC, motor and cognition scores, and age • PAI includes comprehension, expression, and swallowing • Must meet 60% rule
Skilled nursing facility	Resource Utilization Groups, 3rd version (RUG-III)	• 58 groups • Beneficiaries assigned per diem payment based on Minimum Data Set (MDS) comprehensive assessment • Specified minimum number of minutes per week is established for each rehabilitation RUG based on MDS score and rehabilitation team estimates
Home health agency (HHA)	Home health resource groups (HHRGs)	• 80 HHRGs • The Outcome and Assessment Information Set (OASIS) determines the HHRG and is completed for each 60-day period • A predetermined base payment for each 60-day episode of care is adjusted according to the patient's HHRG • No limit to number of 60-day episodes • Payment is adjusted if patient condition significantly changes

Source: American Speech-Language-Hearing Association.

For an IRF to qualify to receive payment under Medicare's IRF-PPS, at least 60% of a facility's total inpatient population must have at least one of 13 conditions listed in Exhibit 6.7. Facilities that fail to meet the 60% rule risk losing all reimbursement from Medicare for all hospital admissions to the IRF in that fiscal year (Centers for Medicare and Medicaid Services, 2013).

MEDICARE (PART B; OUTPATIENT THERAPY)

The Medicare Physician Fee Schedule (MPFS) is the method of payment for outpatient therapy services provided through Medicare (Part B), which include the following: CORFs, outpatient PT providers (OPTs; e.g., private practice), outpatient hospital departments, SNFs (for residents not covered in a Part A stay), and HHAs (for individuals who are not homebound). As of 2014, the therapy cap no longer applies to hospital outpatient departments unless Congress passes additional legislation. Since 1999, an annual per beneficiary limit has been applied to PT and speech–language pathology combined. A separate limit was applied to all OT services. These limits are indexed each year. In 2013, the therapy cap for PT and speech–language pathology services combined was $1,900 and a separate $1,900 amount was allotted for OT services. Therapists can apply for an

EXHIBIT 6.7 Thirteen Medical Conditions that Qualify for the 60% Rule

1. Stroke
2. Spinal cord injury
3. Congenital deformity
4. Amputation
5. Major multiple trauma
6. Hip fracture
7. Brain injury
8. Neurological disorders (e.g., multiple sclerosis, motor neuron diseases, polyneuropathy, muscular dystrophy, Parkinson's disease)
9. Burns
10. Active polyarticular rheumatoid arthritis and psoriatic arthritis
11. Systemic vasculidities with joint inflammation causing functional impairment
12. Severe or advanced osteoarthritis involving two or more weight-bearing joints (e.g., elbow, shoulders, hips, or knees) with joint deformity and substantial loss of range of motion and significant disability
13. Knee or hip replacement, or both, during and acute-care hospitalization, which meets one or more of the following criteria: (a) bilateral knee or bilateral hip replacement, (b) extremely obese with body mass index ≥50; or (c) patient age 85 or older

"automatic exception" for claims between $1,900 to $3,700 when a patient's condition can be justified by documentation indicating that the beneficiary required continued skilled therapy. Many **Medicare Advantage (Part C)** plans have chosen not to apply a therapy cap, but plans vary (Kaiser Family Foundation [KFF], 2013).

OTHER REIMBURSEMENT ISSUES

Medicare, Observation Status, and SNF Eligibility

Original Medicare (Part A), in which 75% of older adults are enrolled, covers up to 100 days of SNF care if an older adult has had a hospital stay of at least 3 days and the SNF admission occurs within 30 days of the acute hospital discharge. Of all Medicare beneficiaries using PAC (e.g., home health, inpatient rehabilitation, LTCHs, or SNF after a hospitalization), 29% use SNF services. Medicare pays 100% of payment rates for the first 20 days of care. For days 21 to 100, Medicare requires a daily copayment. In 2013, the copayment for an SNF was $148 per day. Most SNFs (90%) are dually certified as an SNF and as a nursing facility that provides custodial long-term care.

Generally, patients who are in the hospital for a few days assume that they have been admitted and have inpatient status. However, in recent years, hospitals have begun placing older patients on "observation status," meaning that technically, they are still outpatients. In 2012, the American Hospital Association (AHA) and four health systems filed a lawsuit against the U.S. Department of Health and Human Services (HHS) to challenge the use of observation status. The use of observation status became common as Medicare began conducting recovery audits that looked back 3 years. If auditors decided that a hospital should have classified a patient as an outpatient rather than an inpatient, then the hospitals had to return funding and would get little or no reimbursement. Hospitals began keeping patients "under observation" rather than admitting them in order to make sure that Medicare paid them some compensation that they would not have to return. Over the past 6 years, the number of Medicare patients under "observation" doubled and reached 1.6 million in 2011 (Advisory Board Company, 2013). In 2012, more than 600,000 Medicare patients were in the hospital for at least 3 days, but they could not qualify for coverage of nursing home care (Jaffe, 2013). Patients discharged from the hospital to an SNF were often shocked to find out that they were not eligible for SNF coverage even if they had been in the hospital for 3 or more days, because they had been on "observation" rather than being admitted.

In March 2013, CMS proposed a rule for the proposed inpatient PPS (IPPS) to limit the growing length of observation visits. The proposed rule requires that Medicare patients be admitted if the physician expects a hospital stay for 3 or more days. However, patients will be considered an outpatient under observation if they are expected to be discharged within 2 days. The rule does not require hospitals to inform patients of their observation status or give patients the right to appeal. The Center for Medicare

Advocacy, Inc. (CMA; 2013) has filed a lawsuit against CMS to remove the observation designation.

REPRESENTATION, LICENSURE, AND ACCREDITATION

REPRESENTATION

Representation for rehabilitation professionals is provided by discipline-specific as well as cross-cutting (e.g., medical rehabilitation providers) associations. Rehabilitation associations are a major force in furthering the development and evolution of rehabilitation as an important part of the health care continuum. Some of the more prominent organizations are described briefly in the following sections. Additional information on many of the organizations is provided in the Additional Resources at the end of this chapter.

PROFESSIONAL ASSOCIATIONS

Each discipline in rehabilitation has a professional association and many are active at the national, regional, state, and local levels (see Exhibit 6.8). Most associations have established standards of practice and a code of ethics. Several provide discipline-specific accreditation for graduate degree programs.

CROSS-CUTTING ASSOCIATIONS

Cross-cutting associations include trade associations, research societies, and interdisciplinary organizations. The American Medical Rehabilitation Providers Association (AMRPA) is the primary national organization and lobbying association for rehabilitation providers, including rehabilitation hospitals,

EXHIBIT 6.8 Professional Associations for Rehabilitation Disciplines

ASSOCIATION	DISCIPLINE
American Academy of Physical Medicine and Rehabilitation (AAPM&R)	Physiatry
Association of Rehabilitation Nurses (ARN)	Rehabilitation nurses
American Occupational Therapy Association (AOTA)	Occupational therapists Occupational therapy assistants
American Physical Therapy Association (APTA)	Physical therapists Physical therapy assistants
American Speech Language and Hearing Association (ASHA)	Audiologists and speech–language pathologists

outpatient rehabilitation facilities, and SNFs. Another national organization that attracts rehabilitation providers is the AHA. The AHA is a national lobbying organization that represents hospitals, health care networks, and patients. The Long-Term Care and Rehabilitation Constituency section of AHA is working to ensure adequate financing for postacute rehabilitation providers and to improve the continuity of care among acute, postacute, and long-term care services. The National Association for Home Care (NAHC) is a trade association representing home care agencies, hospices, and home care aide organizations that offer individual memberships to professionals, such as nurses or PTs, who are involved in home care.

One of the leading organizations for rehabilitation research is the American Congress of Rehabilitation Medicine (ACRM). This organization of rehabilitation professionals supports research that promotes health, independence, productivity and quality of life, and the advancement of patient care. It also focuses on meeting the needs of rehabilitation clinicians and people with disabilities. Other specializations in rehabilitation are represented in interdisciplinary organizations such as the Rehabilitation Engineering Society of North America (RESNA), which represents individuals and organizations interested in technology and disability. Similarly, the National Rehabilitation Association (NRA) is a national organization that represents rehabilitation professionals involved in advocacy and services for people with disabilities.

LICENSURE

The authority and responsibility for establishing licensing requirements for hospital units, facilities, and outpatient programs is held by each state. States have the right to expand on The Joint Commission's (TJC's) federal regulations and to establish additional requirements for practice, quality assurance, credentialing, and other areas. For example, a state may require that a program maintains a specific staff-to-patient ratio when providing therapy, which accreditation organizations do not require. Some states require that a provider facility be accredited at regular intervals by TJC or the Commission for Accreditation of Rehabilitation Facilities (CARF). Other states may accept accreditation in lieu of conducting their own surveys. This limits the number of surveys a provider must undergo and saves states money.

CERTIFICATION

To participate in Medicare and Medicaid programs, a rehabilitation provider must be "certified." A provider must apply for a provider number and maintain licensure in his or her state, which may require the appropriate accreditation. (A facility that is accredited has *deemed* status; it has met the requirements of the federal government for participation in the Medicare program.)

ACCREDITATION

Accreditation for acute and PAC rehabilitation settings is shared by TJC and the CARF. In 1997, TJC and the CARF began offering a combined accreditation survey process to rehabilitation hospitals. A year later, TJC expanded recognition of CARF accreditation to include medical rehabilitation programs that are units of larger entities and no longer require that they be included in TJC surveys.

The CARF develops specific programmatic standards for providing rehabilitation services to ensure quality. The CARF has responded to the rapid growth of inpatient rehabilitation services by developing specific program standards for offering comprehensive integrated inpatient rehabilitation programs (CIIRP). A CIIRP is a "program of coordinated and integrated medical and rehabilitation services that is provided 24 hours per day" (CARF, 2013) that can be provided in a hospital, SNF, or LTCH. The preadmission assessment of the patient determines the program and setting that will best meet the needs and the scope and intensity of care provided. The basic idea here is that an older adult collaborates with the rehabilitation team to identify and address his or her medical and rehabilitation needs. The CARF accredits medical rehabilitation programs in a wide variety of specialty areas as well as establishing care standards for aging services for persons of age 60 and older (see Exhibit 6.9).

EXHIBIT 6.9 CARF Rehabilitation Accreditation Areas and Standards for Aging Services

CARF ACCREDITATION OF MEDICAL REHABILITATION PROGRAMS

- Inpatient rehabilitation
- Outpatient rehabilitation
- Home and community services
- Residential
- Vocational
- Brain injury
- Spinal cord system of care
- Stroke specialty
- Amputation specialty
- Interdisciplinary pain rehabilitation
- Occupational rehabilitation programs
- Case management
- Pediatric specialty programs
- Independent evaluation services

CONTINUUM OF CARE STANDARDS FOR AGING SERVICES/CARF-CCAC

- Continuing care retirement communities (CCRC)
- Adult day services
- Assisted living
- Aging services networks
- Dementia care specialty program
- Stroke specialty program
- Home and community services

INTEGRATING MECHANISMS

The interdisciplinary nature of rehabilitation makes integrating mechanisms particularly important for the effective delivery of services. Key mechanisms include case management and information systems.

CASE MANAGEMENT

The rehabilitation team works together to plan the course of treatment for each patient, chart progress in reaching goals, and plan for a successful discharge or transition (Case Study 6.1). The team may have a specific person who functions only as a case manager (usually a nurse or a social worker), or the team member representing the primary services that a patient requires may assume the care coordinator/case management function. The case manager coordinates the functional assessment of the patient, the evaluation of rehabilitation potential, and the assignment of support systems. The case manager monitors and evaluates patient needs, and the team recommends and revises treatment protocols as the patient moves through the rehabilitation continuum utilizing inpatient, outpatient, and home care services. Communication among the case manager and family, primary care and specialty physicians, insurance case managers, and employers contributes to the team effort that maximizes patient outcomes.

Case Study 6.1: Rehabilitation for Mrs. Klein

Mrs. Klein is a frail 80-year-old female who was hospitalized with bleeding and acute blood loss anemia. She has functional decline after 6 days in the hospital. She is alert and oriented, but appears depressed. Her medical history includes congestive heart failure, coronary artery disease, high blood pressure, diabetes, and obesity. Prior to hospitalization, Mrs. Klein was independent with transfers and able to walk using a walker in the nursing home where she has lived for the past 2 years. She lost 10 pounds during her hospital stay. Upon admission to the rehabilitation facility, the patient required assistance for transfers and was able to walk only three steps using a walker. She could tolerate standing for only 1 minute.

Case Study Discussions Questions:

1. Can you identify three rehabilitation goals for this patient?
2. What members of the rehabilitation team should evaluate this patient and what will their role be in addressing the functional declines Mrs. Klein has experienced?

INFORMATION SYSTEMS

The development of sophisticated intrahospital computer systems is helping integrate rehabilitation into the continuum of health care delivery. Technological breakthroughs in security systems allow rehabilitation team members to share information more easily and quickly than ever before. Because a rehabilitation provider depends on information from others in planning interventions, information systems are essential to maximizing function efficiently. By the end of 2013, more than 50% of doctors' offices and 80% of hospitals had electronic health records (EHRs; USHHS, 2013). In 2008, only 17% of physicians and 9% of hospitals were using an EHR system. The adoption of health information IT is an integral element of health care quality and efficiency improvements. Health IT systems make it easier for health care providers to coordinate and deliver high-quality care to patients.

SUMMARY

These are challenging times for rehabilitation providers who face pressures to improve services, provide more efficient treatments, and produce better outcomes, within a PPS that limits reimbursement. As the U.S. health care system becomes more vertically integrated and different levels of care (e.g., acute care, SNFs, home care) are provided under one organization, rehabilitation providers must respond proactively and strategically to ensure their place in the continuum of care. In many parts of the nation, the rapid penetration of managed care organizations, such as Kaiser Permanente, has had a tremendous impact on the pricing and delivery of health care services. Finally, rehabilitation expertise in managing patients will be increasingly vital in the managed care environment and is key to ensuring that rehabilitation is valued as an essential service. Geriatric rehabilitation has traditionally been viewed as less essential than other specialties, even though it has the potential to significantly reduce health care costs (American Medical Rehabilitation Providers Association [AMRPA], 2013). In an era of increasing accountability and reform, tracking outcomes is key to demonstrating the value of rehabilitation and its contribution to affordable and efficacious treatment.

DISCUSSION QUESTIONS

1. Why is an interdisciplinary team necessary for effective rehabilitation with geriatric clients?
2. What are some examples of rehabilitation goals for a geriatric client who has had a stroke that has left him with right-sided paralysis and difficulty in speaking and swallowing? Which member of the rehabilitation team would address which goals?
3. What do the ICF and IOM models of disability focus our attention on in thinking about rehabilitative services? How are they similar and different?

4. What are the gaps in coverage for rehabilitative services through Medicare?
5. Why does Medicare cover DME, but typically not cover AT?
6. Will EHRs integrate the delivery of rehabilitation services across the continuum of care?
7. How can we assure a high quality of care in rehabilitation? How does CMS try to do this?
8. Develop a short case example of an older adult with a significant disability. Give an example of two AT devices that would be helpful and analyze the impact on function.

ADDITIONAL RESOURCES

REPORTS, ARTICLES, BOOKS

Field, M., & Jette, A. (Eds). (2011). *Future of disability in America*. Washington, DC: National Academies Press.

Hoenig, H., & Siebens, H. (2004). Geriatric rehabilitation. In D. H. Solomon, J. LoCicero III, & R. A. Rosenthal (Eds.), *New frontiers in geriatric research* (pp. 339–368). New York, NY: American Greiatrics Society. Retrieved from http://newfrontiers.americangeriatrics.org/chapters/pdf/rasp_25.pdf

Kauffman, T., Barr, J., & Moran, M. (2007). *Geriatric rehabilitation manual*. (2nd ed.). New York, NY: Elsevier.

Kemp, B.J., & Mosqueda, L. (Eds.). (2004). *Aging with a disability: What the clinician needs to know*. Baltimore, MD: The Johns Hopkins University Press.

Medicare Payment Advisory Commission. (2013). *Report to the Congress: Medicare and the health care delivery system*. Retrieved from www.medpac.gov/documents/Jun13_EntireReport.pdf

World Health Organization. *Towards a common language for functioning, disability, and health*. Geneva, Switzerland: Author. Retrieved from www.who.int/classifications/icf/training/icfbeginnersguide.pdf

KEY WEBSITES

www.aapmr.org **American Academy of Physical Medicine and Rehabilitation (AAPM&R)**

The AAPM&R is a national medical society representing 6,000 physiatrists, that is, physicians who are specialists in the field of PM&R. The organization works to advance the field of PM&R, promoting excellence in physiatric practice, and advocating on public policy issues related to disability.

www.acrm.org **American Congress of Rehabilitation Medicine (ACRM)**

The ACRM is a research and advocacy organization that promotes rehabilitation research. The ACRM seeks to address issues that include outcomes, efficacy of treatment, managed care, best practices, and reimbursement for the field of rehabilitation.

www.aha.org **American Hospital Association (AHA)**

The AHA is a national trade and advocacy organization that represents and serves all types of hospitals, health care networks, and their patients and communities. It has approximately 5,000 institutional, 600 associate, and 40,000 personal members. It has a division that focuses on long-term care and rehabilitation.

www.amrpa.org **American Medical Rehabilitation Providers Association (AMRPA)**

This is the primary national organization and lobbying association for rehabilitation providers, including rehab hospitals, outpatient rehabilitation facilities, and SNFs.

www.aota.org **American Occupational Therapy Association (AOTA)**

The AOTA is a national professional association representing 60,000 occupational therapists and OT assistants. The AOTA has established standards for the profession that have been adopted by many states in their laws and regulations. The AOTA also has accredited the nation's OT educational programs since 1935.

www.apta.org **American Physical Therapy Association (APTA)**

The APTA is a national professional association representing more than 70,000 physical therapists, physical therapist assistants, and students of PT. The APTA has established standards of practice as well as a code of ethics.

www.asha.org **American Speech Language and Hearing Association (ASHA)**

The ASHA is a professional, advocacy, and credentialing association for more than 96,000 audiologists; SLPs; and speech, language, and hearing scientists. The ASHA offers voluntary accreditation to graduate degree programs in speech–language pathology and/or audiology.

www.carf.org **Commission for Accreditation of Rehabilitation Facilities (CARF)**

The CARF is an accreditation organization that develops and maintains current, field-driven standards for rehabilitation programs and services. It also conducts accreditation research, emphasizing outcomes measurement and management, and provides consultation, education, training, and publications that support the accreditation process.

www.nahc.org **National Association for Home Care (NAHC)**

The NAHC is a trade association representing more than 6,000 home care agencies, hospices, and home care aide organizations. Its members are primarily corporations or other organizational entities in addition to state home care associations, medical equipment suppliers, and schools. The NAHC also offers individual memberships to professionals, such as social workers, nurses, and physical therapists, who are employed by home care agencies or are interested in home care.

http://silk.nih.gov/silk/NCMRR **National Center for Medical Rehabilitation Research (NCMRR)**

The NCMRR is a component of the National Institute of Child Health and Human Development (NICHD) at the National Institutes of Health (NIH). The NCMRR supports rehabilitation research that enhances the health, productivity, independence, and quality of life of persons with disabilities.

www.nationalrehab.org/website/index.html **National Rehabilitation Association (NRA)**

The NRA is a national organization representing professionals in the field of rehabilitation, particularly vocational rehabilitation. The membership includes rehab counselors, physical, speech and occupational therapists, job trainers, consultants, independent living instructors, and other professionals involved in the advocacy of programs and services for people with disabilities.

www.naric.com **National Rehabilitation Information Center (NARIC)**

The NARIC is a library service, funded by the National Institute on Disability and Rehabilitation Research (NIDRR), which collects and disseminates the results of federally funded research projects. The NARIC collection averages around 200 new documents per month and includes commercially published books, journal articles, and audiovisuals.

www.resna.org **Rehabilitation Engineering Society of North America (RESNA)**

The RESNA is an interdisciplinary professional organization representing 1,600 individuals and 150 organizations who are interested in technology and disability. The RESNA promotes research, development, education, advocacy, and the provision of technology.

www.udsmr.org **Uniform Data System for Medical Rehabilitation (UDSMR)**

The UDSMR is an instrument that was created by a national task force to document the severity of patient disability and the outcomes of medical rehabilitation. Today, it is used by over 1,400 facilities in the United States, Canada, Hong Kong, Finland, the United Kingdom, and Australia.

REFERENCES

Advisory Board Company. (2013). Medicare tries to limit the use of observation status. *The Daily Briefing*. Retrieved from www.advisory.com/Daily-Briefing/2013/05/06/Medicare-tries-to-limit-the-use-of-observation-status

American Medical Rehabilitation Providers Association. (2013). *Rehabilitation Is Not a Medicare Cost-Driver.* Retrieved from www.amrpa.org/uploads/docuploads/Spring%20Meeting/Rehabilitation%20is%20not%20a%20Medicare%20Cost-Driver.pdf

American Speech-Language-Hearing Association. (2015). *Medicare reimbursement of speech-language pathology services*. Retrieved from http://www.asha.org/practice/reimbursement/medicare/SLPMcareReimbursement

Bachmann, S., Finger, C., Huss, A., Egger, M., Stuck, A., & Clough-Gorr, K. (2010). Inpatient rehabilitation specifically designed for geriatric patients: Systematic review and meta-analysis of randomized controlled trials. *British Medical Journal, 340*(2), 1719–1729.

Bradley, S. M., & Hernandez, C. R. (2011). Geriatric assistive devices. *American Family Physician, 84*, 405.

Brandt, E., & Pope, A. (Eds.). (1997). *Enabling America: Assessing the role of rehabilitation science and engineering*. Washington, DC: Institute of Medicine.

Center for Medicare Advocacy, Inc. (2013). *Observation status & Bagnal v. Sebelius*. Retrieved from www.medicareadvocacy.org/medicare-info/observation-status

Centers for Medicare and Medicaid Services. (2013). *IRF classification criteria*. Retrieved from www.cms.gov/Medicare/Medicare-Fee-for-Service-Payment/InpatientRehabFacPPS/Criteria.html

Commission for Accreditation of Rehabilitation Facilities. (2013). *Comprehensive integrated inpatient rehabilitation programs*. Retrieved from www.carf.org/Programs/ProgramDescriptions/MED-Inpatient-Rehab-Hospital

Finley, M. A., & Rodgers, M. M. (2004). Prevalence and identification of shoulder pathology in athletic and nonathletic wheelchair users with shoulder pain: A pilot study. *Journal of Rehabilitation Research and Development, 41*, 395.

Gitlin, L. N., Winter, L., Dennis, M. P., Corcoran, M., Schinfeld, S., & Hauck, W. W. (2006). A randomized trial of a multicomponent home intervention to reduce functional difficulties in older adults. *Journal of the American Geriatrics Society*. 54, 809–816.

Greer, N., Brasure, M., & Wilt, T. J. (2012). Wheeled mobility (wheelchair) service delivery: Scope of the evidence. *Annals of Internal Medicine, 156*, 141.

Hoenig, H. (2004). Assistive technology and mobility aids for the older patient with disability. *Annals of Long-Term Care*. Retrieved from www.annalsoflongtermcare.com/article/3403

Hoenig, H. (2014, November). Overview of geriatric rehabilitation: Program components and settings for rehabilitation. UpToDate. Wolters Kluwer. Topic 16852 Version 9.0.

Hoenig, H., Pieper, C., Branch, L. G., & Cohen, H.J. (2007). Effect of motorized scooters on physical performance and mobility: A randomized clinical trial. *Archives of Physical Medicine Rehabilitation, 88*, 279.

Hoenig, H., Taylor, D. H., Jr., & Sloan, F. A. (2003). Does assistive technology substitute for personal assistance among the disabled elderly? *American Journal of Public Health, 93*, 330.

Horn, S. D., DeJong, G., Smout, R. J., Gassaway, J., James, R., & Conroy, B. (2005). Stroke rehabilitation patients, practice, and outcomes: Is earlier and more aggressive therapy better? *Archives of Physical Medicine Rehabilitation, 86*, S101–S114.

Jaffe, I. (2013). *For hospital patients, observation status can prove costly*. National Public Radio. Retrieved from, www.npr.org/blogs/health/ 2013/09/04/218633011/for-hospital-patients-observation-status-can-prove-costly

Kaiser Family Foundation. (2013). *Medicare Advantage 2013 spotlight: Enrollment market update*. Retrieved from http://kff.org/medicare/issue-brief/medicare-advantage-2013-spotlight-enrollment-market-update

Kemp, B. J., & Mosqueda, L. (Eds.). (2004). *Aging with a disability: What the clinician needs to know*. Baltimore, MD: Johns Hopkins University Press.

Liu, C. J., & Latham, N. K. (2009). Progressive resistance strength training for improving physical function in older adults. *Cochrane Database Systems Review, 3*, 267, Retrieved from http://web.a.ebscohost.com.ezproxy.library.uvic.ca/ehost/detail/detail?sid=4e353af4-d4a1-42cc-b6e9-f3ea00d6b391%40sessionmgr4003&vid=2&hid=4209&bdata=JnNpdGU9ZWhvc3QtbGl2ZSZzY29wZT1zaXRl#db=chh&AN=CD002759.

Martin, L. G., Freedman V. A., Schoeni, R. F., & Andreski, P. M. (2010). Trends in disability and related chronic conditions among people ages fifty to sixty-four. *Health Affairs, 29*, 725.

Medicare Payment Advisory Commission. (2012a). Skilled nursing facility services. In *Report to the Congress: Medicare Payment Policy* (Chapter 7, pp. 171–208). Washington, DC: Author. Retrieved from http://www.medpac.gov/documents/reports/march-2012-report-to-the-congress-medicare-payment-policy.pdf?sfvrsn=0

Medicare Payment Advisory Commission. (2012b). Inpatient rehabilitation facility services. In *Report to the Congress: Medicare Payment Policy* (Chapter 9, pp. 233–255). Retrieved from http://www.medpac.gov/documents/reports/march-2012-report-to-the-congress-medicare-payment-policy.pdf?sfvrsn=0

Medicare Payment Advisory Commission (MedPac). (2014). Inpatient rehabilitation facility services. In *Report to the Congress: Medicare payment policy* (Chapter 10, pp. 257–279). Washington, DC: Author. Retrieved from http://www.medpac.gov/documents/reports/march-2012-report-to-the-congress-medicare-payment-policy.pdf?sfvrsn=0

National Stroke Association. (2006). *Lack of adequate post-stroke care unveiled*. Retrieved from www.stroke.org/site/DocServer/NSA_Stroke_Perceptions_Survey_Highlights_final.pdf

Nelson, A., Powell-Cope, G., Palacios, P., Luther, S., Black, T., Hillman, T., … Gross, J. (2007). Nurse staffing and patient outcomes in inpatient rehabilitation settings. *Rehabilitation Nursing, 32*(5), 179–202.

Prvu Bettger, J. A., & Stineman, M. G. (2007). Effectiveness of multidisciplinary rehabilitation services in postacute care: State-of-the-science: A review. *Archives of Physical Medicine Rehabilitation, 88*, 1526.

Schoeni, R. F., Freedman, V.A., & Martin, L. G. (2008). Why is late-life disability declining? *Milbank Quarterly, 86*, 47.

Siu, A. L., Penrod, J. D., Boockvar, K. S., Koval, K., Strauss, E., & Morrison, R. S. (2006). Early ambulation after hip fracture: Effects on function and mortality. *Archives of Internal Medicine, 166*, 766–771.

Uniform Data System for Medical Rehabilitation (UDSMR). (2013). *Rehab measures: Functional Independence Measure*. Retrieved from http://www.rehabmeasures.org/Lists/RehabMeasures/DispForm.aspx?ID=889

U.S. Health and Human Services. (2013). *Doctors and hospitals' use of health IT more than doubles since 2012*. Retrieved from www.hhs.gov/news/press/2013pres/05/20130522a.html

Verbrugge, L. M., Rennert, C., & Madans, J. H. (1997). The great efficacy of personal and equipment assistance in reducing disability. *American Journal of Public Health, 87*, 384.

Wells, J. Seabrook, J., Stolee, P., Borrie, M., & Knoefel, F. (2003a). State of the art in geriatric rehabilitation. Part I: Review of frailty and comprehensive geriatric assessment. *Archives of Physical Medicine Rehabilitation, 84*, 890–897.

Wells, J. Seabrook, J., Stolee, P., Borrie, M., & Knoefel, F. (2003b). State of the art in geriatric rehabilitation. Part II: Clinical challenges. *Archives of Physical Medicine Rehabilitation, 84*, 898–903.

World Health Organization. (2001). International Classification of Function, Disability, and Health (ICF). Retrieved from www.who.int/classifications/icf/en

Adult Day Services

HOLLY DABELKO-SCHOENY
KEITH A. ANDERSON
JEE HOON PARK

CHAPTER OVERVIEW

Adult day services (ADS) provide individuals with cognitive and physical disabilities community-based long-term care services in a group setting during daytime hours. ADS provide respite and support services for their family caregivers. The majority of ADS participants are older adult White women. Participants often have chronic diseases such as dementia, heart disease, and diabetes. ADS centers offer a wide range and combination of services contributing to the health and well-being of participants, including socialization, personal care, and meals. The majority of centers are private, nonprofit operations. Public/government funding has been the largest source of revenue for ADS centers. ADS centers are increasingly offering therapeutic and specialized medical services. Staffing in ADS often consists of a combination of RNs, licensed practical nurses (LPNs), direct care workers (DCWs; such as nursing assistants and nurse aides), social workers, activity/recreation therapists, and support personnel. ADS centers are well positioned to become the "hub" for caregiver support services in the communities they serve, helping family caregivers support family members with functional limitations maintain the highest possible level of independence for as long as possible.

LEARNING OBJECTIVES

After completing this chapter, you should have an understanding of:

- The history and development of adult day services as a component of the long-term care spectrum
- The demographic characteristics of the population served by ADS, the organizational and operational structure of ADS, the services offered in ADS, and the funding of ADS

- Existing research on the impact and effectiveness of ADS for participants, family members, and society
- Future directions and potential functions of ADS in meeting the growing need and desire for home- and community-based services

KEY TERMS

Adult day services (ADS)
Adult day services plus (ADS plus)
Aging in place
Area Agencies on Aging (AAA)
Combined models of care
Intellectual and developmental disabilities (IDD)
Intergenerational programming
Medicaid Home and Community-Based Services waiver programs
Medical model
Older Americans Act (OAA)
Programs of All-Inclusive Care for the Elderly (PACE)
Respite
Social model

INTRODUCTION

Adult day services (ADS), also referred to as adult day care, support the health, nutritional, social, and daily living needs of adults with functional limitations in a group setting during daytime hours. ADS also support family caregivers by enabling them to remain in the workforce and receive **respite**, a break from providing support for individuals with cognitive and physical limitations. Efforts have been made by groups, such as the National Adult Day Services Association, to encourage providers, consumers, and policy makers to use the term *ADS* instead of *adult day care* to distinguish the adult programs from child day-care programs. ADS are not babysitting programs for adults, but instead are important providers of long-term care services in the United States. ADS centers do not operate under a federal definition of care as nursing homes do. Licensure and certification requirements vary from state to state, resulting in considerable differences in programs, participants, and funding sources among centers.

Historically, ADS have been characterized in three ways, as **medical models**, **social models,** or **combined models of care** (Weissert, 1976, 1977). Centers operating medical programs emphasized skilled assessment, treatment, and rehabilitation. Social models focused on socialization and preventive services, and combined models had elements of both social and medical models, depending on individual participant needs. This typology was expanded in 1989 to include special purpose centers that served a single type of participant, such as an individual with dementia, developmental disability, or mental illness (Weissert et al., 1989). Increasing evidence suggests that these distinct models of care no longer exist and that ADS centers are increasingly becoming more medically focused, providing comprehensive care by professionals to individuals with more complex health care needs (Anderson, Dabelko-Schoeny, & Johnson, 2013). These medically focused centers are sometimes referred to as **adult day health care centers** and are staffed by nurses, social workers, and activity professionals.

The purpose of ADS is to provide individuals with cognitive and physical limitations community-based long-term care services where they can get their health and social needs met in the least restrictive environment possible. The ADS care model is dependent on strong family caregiving support. Participants return to their homes to receive care from family caregivers at night and on weekends, depending on the hours of operation of their particular center. ADS centers support independence and choice for participants.

The intent of ADS largely follows the concept of "aging in place." **Aging in place** refers to older adults' ability to remain in their homes and communities as they face the challenges often associated with growing older. Researchers have found that there is typically a strong attachment to the physical, social, and emotional notions of "home," and the vast majority of middle-age and older adults would prefer to grow old in their communities and, if possible, their own homes. There is also evidence that aging in place is associated with aspects of successful aging, such as increased socialization and community engagement (Keenan, 2010). A sense of home can also provide meaning and security for older adults, further contributing to their well-being (Rowles & Bernard, 2013). Aging in place also means that older adults and their families can avoid the stress and expense associated with placement into long-term care. The cost of long-term care is also a significant issue for payer sources, such as Medicaid.

BACKGROUND

The ADS sector is in its infancy compared with other long-term care service providers in the United States, such as nursing homes and home health care, which began providing services as far back as the mid-1850s. Originally based on Britain's model of geriatric day hospitals, ADS did not emerge as a provider of long-term care in the United States until the 1972 amendments to the Social Security Act, which funded about a dozen ADS demonstration programs (Dabelko, Koenig, & Danso, 2008).

As the concern for the high cost of nursing home care grew in the mid-1980s, funding for ADS increased as new sources of government dollars for home- and community-based services (HCBS) were established. Title XX of the Social Security Act and Title III of the **Older Americans Act (OAA)** provided block grant funding to states for supportive and nutritional services, including

ADS. Section 2176 of the **Medicaid Home and Community-Based Services waiver program** allowed states to receive matching federal funds for poor, nursing home–eligible individuals to receive HCBS at lower costs than institutional care (Dabelko et al., 2008).

The 1980s and 1990s also marked the beginning of growth in the number of providers and of a shift in ADS from "mom and pop shops" delivering socialization services in the basement of churches to medical service providers relying on public funding for services (Dabelko et al., 2008). Also during this time, the **Programs of All-Inclusive Care for the Elderly (PACE)** became more popular. PACE programs integrate acute (short-term) and long-term care services for persons 55 years and older who meet eligibility criteria for both Medicare and Medicaid. In an effort to control costs, a menu of services is provided at a set rate per person within an adult day setting. In 2010, there were 75 PACE sites in the United States. Not only have PACE sites been successful in managing costs, but programs have also demonstrated a reduction in nursing home and hospital utilization; support for family caregivers; and are associated with improved health, quality of live, and overall life satisfaction for consumers (Chatterji, Burstein, Kidder, & White, 1998; Wieland et al., 2000).

Increases in public funding for HCBS led to growth in the number of ADS programs from 15 in 1972 to approximately 1,200 by the mid-1990s (Dabelko et al., 2008). Public funding for ADS continued to grow in the 1990s and 2000s as public awareness was raised about the devastating effects of Alzheimer's disease and related dementias and the financial, physical, and emotional burden of family caregiving. As the number of baby boomers reaching older age increased, consumers began to want more choice in long-term care services and to receive care in the least restrictive environment possible. The Alzheimer's Disease Demonstration Grants Program and the National Family Caregiver Support Program funneled additional dollars into adult day programs to support respite services, relief for family caregivers from providing support for individuals with functional limitations (see Case Study 7.1). A census conducted in 2002 identified 3,400 centers in the United States (Partners in Caregiving [PIC]; 2001–2002). In a 2010, large-scale national survey, the number of ADS centers was estimated at over 4,600. Serving over a quarter of a million individuals, ADS are a growing source of long-term care for individuals with functional limitations (Anderson et al., 2013). (Note: In the following discussion of the characteristics of ADS participants, centers, and services, 2002 statistics were drawn from the Partners in Caregiving Study, and 2010 statistics were drawn from the MetLife National Study of ADS (MetLife Mature Market Institute, 2010b)

PARTICIPANT PROFILE

ADS typically provide programs and services to individuals with physical and/or cognitive limitations. Although most participants have such limitations, diversity exists in terms of age, gender, race/ethnicity, health status, ability and disability, care needs, and home life. As a result, presenting an aggregate picture of the "average ADS participant" can be rather misleading. It is critical to note

Case Study 7.1: Mary Baker

Mrs. Mary Baker is a 72-year-old African American woman who recently moved in with her daughter after her husband of 55 years died. She is a retired elementary school teacher's aide and lives off a modest pension. Mrs. Baker has diabetes and has been experiencing cognitive decline over the past few years. Recently, her daughter came home from work to find her mother sitting in her backyard confused about how to get back into the house. On the recommendation of one of her friends at church, Mrs. Baker's daughter contacted the local Area Agency on Aging for help. The Area Agency on Aging sent a licensed social worker out to assess Mrs. Baker. The social worker found her to have significant cognitive impairment and recommended that she be evaluated by a neurologist. The neurologist diagnosed Mrs. Baker with early-stage Alzheimer's disease. Mrs. Baker enrolled in a Medicaid Home and Community-Based Services waiver program and now attends ADS 5 days a week. Mrs. Baker enjoys participating in the center's choir and bible study group. She receives medication administration, blood pressure checks, and participates weekly in an early memory loss group. Mrs. Baker's daughter attends the monthly caregiving education series offered by the center. Mrs. Baker seems to enjoy her time at the center and feels as though she is less of a burden to her daughter. Now her daughter does not worry about her during the day and can concentrate more on her work.

that this is not a homogeneous group. More differences than similarities exist among individuals participating in ADS.

ADS participants have traditionally been divided into two groups: younger adults with **intellectual and developmental disabilities (IDD)** and older adults with care needs primarily related to physical and/or cognitive limitations. In the 2010 MetLife study, 69% of ADS participants were aged 65 and older, 21% were age 41 to 64, and 9% were age 40 and younger. These statistics indicate that ADS continue to serve a distinct group of older adults. Statistics also suggest that the younger adult profile may be becoming more diverse in terms of age, reflective of the increased life expectancy for younger adults with IDD (Long & Kavarian, 2008). It may be the case that younger adults with disability are aging in place in ADS.

Reflective of the general population, particularly the older adult population, women constitute a majority of ADS participants (58%). The race/ethnicity of ADS participants, however, does not directly reflect that of the general population. In 2010, 61% of participants were White, 16% were Black, 9% were Asian, 9% were Hispanic, and 4% were either a combination of races or listed as "other race." On the other hand, a 5-year estimate of race/ethnicity in the United States lists the general population as approximately 75% White, 12% Black, 4% Asian, and 15% Hispanic (U.S. Census Bureau, 2009). Several reasons help to explain

FIGURE 7.1 Health status of participants.

Condition	Percentage
TBI	4%
Cancer	6%
Parkinson's Disease	6%
Stroke	14%
Development Disability	20%
Chronic MH	25%
Diabetes	31%
Cardiovascular Disease	34%
Physical Disability	42%
HTN/High BP	46%
Dementia	47%

0% 5% 10% 15% 20% 25% 30% 35% 40% 45% 50%

Source: MetLife Mature Market Institute (2010a).

these disparities. First, ADS traditionally have served individuals and families with fewer resources, and Blacks and non-Hispanics are over-represented in this group. Second, there is greater availability of ADS in urban areas where minority populations tend to have the highest concentrations. In addition, ADS have grown from models of care in the Asian community and are a widely accepted care option for this group. Finally, nursing homes, a care alternative, have historically served a greater proportion of White individuals as compared to Black. ADS participants may have grown more diverse since the 2002 PIC study, when 76% of participants were White and non-Hispanic.

As indicated in Figure 7.1, physical and cognitive disability levels remain high among the ADS population. In 2010, approximately half of ADS participants had some form of dementia, and 42% had some form of physical disability. Chronic disease was also prevalent, largely reflective of the growing problem of chronic illness in the general population. Approximately 46% of participants had hypertension, 34% had cardiovascular disease, and 31% had diabetes. Certain conditions have become more prevalent since the 2002 PIC study, including a near doubling of the rate of physical disability and a 70% increase in chronic mental illness. Overall, it appears that the acuity level of ADS participants is increasing. As expected, high levels of acuity are closely correlated with high levels of assistance needed. Just under half of ADS participants required assistance with toileting (45%) and medications (44%). Assistance with other activities of daily living (ADLs) and instrumental ADLs (IADLs) also remained relatively high (bathing, 30%; transferring, 25%; walking or using wheelchairs, 18%; eating, 16%).

Living arrangements and individuals who provide care in the home setting are also important to consider, as both factors influence service usage by ADS participants. In 2010, 27% of ADS participants lived with an adult child, 21% lived with a spouse, 20% lived alone, 18% lived in a communal setting (e.g., group housing, assisted living), and 11% lived with another relative, such as a parent (Anderson et al., 2013). Living arrangements appear to have changed somewhat, with fewer ADS participants living with adult children (35% in 2002) and more ADS participants living alone (11% in 2002). These changes suggest that the improved quality and availability of HCBS may support independent living for ADS participants—an important determinant of quality of life for both the care recipient and the caregiver. In terms of caregiving, over one third of ADS participants listed an adult child as their primary caregiver, 23% listed their spouse, and 13% listed another relative (e.g., parent, sibling, grandchild). Interestingly, 19% of ADS participants listed their primary caregiver as a paid professional, such as a home health aide, and 9% reported that they did not have a primary caregiver. Again, these percentages point to the growing importance and use of HCBS in maintaining the independence of ADS participants. ADS appear to be an important resource within the spectrum of HCBS.

Understanding the precise reasons of how and why participants enroll and eventually leave ADS are also important considerations, particularly from the standpoint of measuring the effectiveness of ADS. Participants and family members take a variety of routes in finding their way to ADS. In the 2010 MetLife study, ADS centers ranked **Area Agencies on Aging (AAA)** as their primary referral source. AAAs provide information and referral services as established through the OAA to link older adults and families with services. Family and friends, self-referral, and physicians were also listed as important sources of referral. Although it is promising that physicians would understand the benefits of ADS, it is surprising that hospital discharge planners were not mentioned as important referral sources. It may be that ADS have yet to establish or market themselves as a platform for medical care and that the medical community continues to view ADS solely as providers of social services. Alternatively, ADS providers may not be able to enroll individuals as quickly as nursing homes or other alternative care providers, as required by discharge planners.

ENROLLMENT IN ADS

Primary reasons for enrollment in ADS included increased functional needs and increased behavioral problems. Both factors are closely related to caregiver burden and institutional placement (Gaugler, Duval, Anderson, & Kane, 2007). ADS centers also listed caregiver respite and declines in caregiver abilities as primary reasons for enrollment. These reasons may represent the downward cascade that aging, physical decline, and increased care needs can have on the home care situation for both care recipient and caregiver. On average, ADS participants remain enrolled for approximately 2 years. This figure has remained relatively constant since 2002 (Anderson et al., 2013).

Primary reasons for disenrollment from ADS identified in the MetLife study included: (a) placement into a nursing home; (b) death of the participant; and (c) mismatches between the services offered in ADS and the needs of participants (i.e., health declines in participants), an indication that there are limitations to the services that can be effectively provided in the community. Nursing home placement may be necessary and, in some cases, is in the best interest of both care recipient and caregiver. The death of participants could be viewed as a success in allowing a participant to both live and die in a community setting.

ADS CENTER PROFILE

The number of ADS centers has increased dramatically—a 35% growth rate since 2002. Within this growth, there have been significant changes in characteristics of ADS centers. There appears to be diversity in the location, administrative structure, and operating characteristics of ADS centers. Much of the change that has occurred is related to changes in demographics of the United States and policies that determine funding for ADS.

In the past, ADS centers have been characterized as conforming to a medical model, social model, or a combination of both. In 2002, approximately 37% of ADS centers were based on the medical model, 21% on the social model, and 42% on a combination of the medical and social models (PIC, 2001–2002). Though it may be convenient to classify ADS centers in this way, the large majority of centers offer a combination of social and health-related services. For example, in 2010, over 95% of ADS centers offered assistance with toileting, and 89% offered blood pressure monitoring—certainly health-related services (Anderson et al., 2013). Rather than continuing this classification system, it is best to consider ADS centers as facilities that offer a wide range and combination of services contributing to the health and well-being of participants.

ADS centers are often affiliated or located within parent organizations although an increasing number of centers are stand-alone entities. For instance, in 2010, approximately 10% of centers were affiliated with nursing homes, 9% with senior service organizations, 7% with IDD organizations, and 4% with hospitals. At the same time, a considerable percentage of ADS centers (39%) reported that they were not affiliated with a parent organization. Almost one third of ADS centers were a part of multiple-center organizations, a decrease of 9% since 2002. In terms of profit status, the majority of centers were private, nonprofit operations; over one quarter were private, for profit; and the remainder were either public or government operated. Most centers (86%) were state certified; it should be noted that there is variability in the certification standards across the states. This variability results in different centers providing different services, which can make it difficult for consumers to understand what ADS provide. Once again, diversity seems to be the hallmark of ADS centers, which may be indicative of the flexibility and responsiveness of the industry to adapt to the diverse needs of the communities they serve.

PARTICIPANTS AND MEETING THEIR NEEDS

Participation and enrollment rates provide some indication of the size and capacity of ADS centers. ADS centers have grown in capacity, enrollment, and daily participation since 2002 (PIC, 2001–2002). The total capacity (e.g., the maximum number of participants that a center can physically hold) was approximately 51 participants in 2010 (up from 38 in 2002), the total average enrollment was 57 (up from 42 in 2002), and daily participation averaged 34 (up from 25 in 2002). ADS centers are bigger and serve more people than before. In terms of physical space, most centers were between 1,000 and 5,000 square feet of indoor programming space (office spaces not included) plus an average of almost 200 square feet of outdoor space.

Almost all ADS centers operate from Monday through Friday, approximately 15% are open on Saturday, and approximately 4% are open all weekend. Most centers open between 6:30 to 8:30 a.m. and close between 4:00 and 6:00 p.m. These schedules appear to be closely aligned with typical working hours, thus providing family caregivers with the respite they need to remain employed. Interestingly, a small number of centers are open on a 24-hour schedule, which may be aligned with the working hours of certain industries (e.g., factory workers, service industries). Most ADS participants attend full days, and nearly 50% attend 5 days per week. Those attending 5 days per week may have family caregivers who work fulltime, whereas those attending on partial-week schedules likely have family caregivers who either work parttime or need respite for only a few days per week.

The administrative structure and staffing of ADS centers also contributes to the functioning, capabilities, and overall quality of services offered. Almost 60% of ADS directors have backgrounds and education in the helping disciplines (e.g., nursing, social work, and activities/recreation therapy; Anderson et al., 2013). Approximately 30% of ADS directors came from the business and health care management and administration disciplines. Staffing in ADS often consists of a combination of registered nurses, licensed practical nurses, direct care workers (such as nursing assistants and nurse aides), social workers, activity/recreation therapists, and support personnel. In 2010, almost 80% of ADS centers had either an RN or an LPN on staff. Breaking this down further, 65% reported having at least one RN on staff, and 48% had an LPN on staff. In comparing these staffing levels with past data, professional nursing staff has grown substantially in ADS (53% with an RN and 33% with an LPN in 2002). This increase suggests that ADS centers have an increased capacity to deliver health-related services. In terms of DCWs, the ratio of worker to participant improved from one DCW for every eight participants in 2002 to one DCW for every six participants in 2010. Again, this points toward increased capacity to care for the needs of participants. This trend also allows for more personalized care and for the care of participants with multiple or complex care needs. Other disciplines are also well represented in ADS. Over 90% of ADS centers had activity professionals on staff, and almost 50% employ professional social workers (Anderson et al., 2013; PIC, 2001–2002).

SERVICES OFFERED IN ADS

ADS centers offer a variety of services to meet the needs of participants and their family members. Initially, ADS centers focused on social services, such as monitoring frail older adults and providing sheltered work opportunities for younger adults with IDD. As the ADS model of care evolved, centers began to offer expanded services to meet the social, health, nutritional, and emotional needs of

Adult Day Participants Involved in Activities.

Source: Pictures used with permission from Heritage Day Health Centers, Columbus, Ohio.

a wide array of participants. Today, most ADS centers offer services that address the holistic needs of participants and family caregivers. Programs work to adapt services to the individual needs of participants and their family caregivers.

Care plans are the blueprints that outline individual care needs and treatment of ADS participants. As expected, almost every center offered care planning in 2010, and these plans are updated on a regular basis, typically every 3 to 6 months. The most basic care generally revolves around ADLs and IADLs, those activities that occur within the fabric of daily life. Over 90% of ADS centers provided assistance with walking, toileting, transferring and sit-to-stand movements, and meals. These types of services were generally included in the daily rate for care and extra fees are not typically charged. Other basic services, such as bathing, were offered at over half of all ADS centers (see Case Study 7.2). As this type of service is more labor intensive, almost half of facilities charged an extra fee. As indicated in Figure 7.2, most ADS centers also provided nursing and health-related services

Case Study 7.2: James King

Mr. James King is a 58-year-old man with Down syndrome. He has heart disease and an unsteady gait. He has been attending an ADC program for the last 24 years. Over the years, he participated in job training programs offered in the community and received transportation to and from a local sheltered workshop where he put together ink pens. Mr. King started to reduce his working hours over the past few years until he stopped working altogether because of his failing eyesight and lack of energy. His mother and father are now in their 80s and have mobility challenges. Historically, they have been able to assist Mr. King with his bathing and grooming. Over the past few months, the adult day center has started to provide Mr. King with a bath two times a week to reduce the physical burden on his parents. Mr. King receives ongoing physical therapy at the center to increase his strength and balance, which have been challenges over the years because of his heart disease. Though Mr. King enjoyed helping serve lunch at the day program and was a long-time member of the men's discussion group, over the past few months he has refused to participate. ADS staff have become concerned about him. Though the day program has provided important support to Mr. King and his parents, his parents worry about what will happen to Mr. King when they will die.

FIGURE 7.2 Health and nursing-related services.

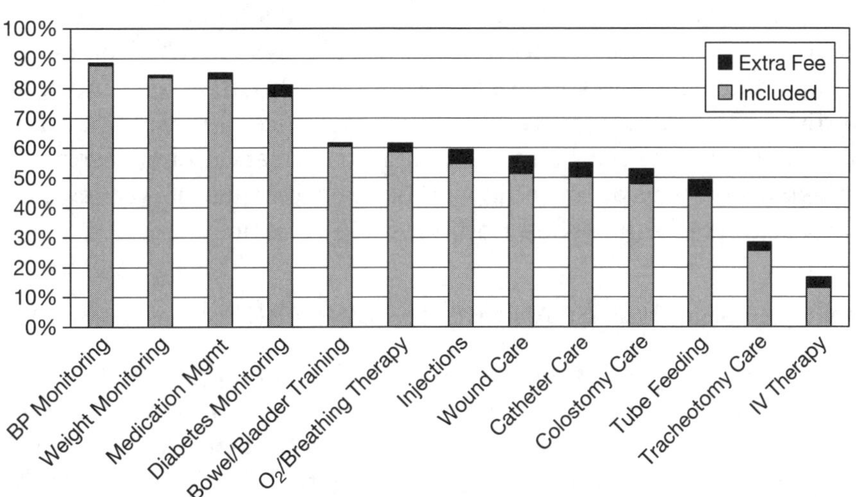

Source: MetLife Mature Market Institute (2010a).

in addition to basic care services. For instance, over 80% of centers offered blood pressure monitoring, weight monitoring, medication management, and diabetes monitoring. Such services are critical for many participants, particularly those with complicated medical conditions that require frequent monitoring. Other commonly offered services included bowel and bladder training for incontinence and oxygen and breathing therapies. Reflective of the growing capacity of ADS centers to address complex care needs, approximately half of centers offered medication injections, wound care, catheter and colostomy care, and tube feeding. The provision of such services almost invariably requires both advanced clinical skills and licensure, such as those held by RNs. The availability of such services speaks to a number of factors, including the increased prevalence of chronic illness in society, the higher levels of trained health care professionals working in ADS, and the growing desire and expectation of individuals and families to "age in place" and avoid institutionalization.

ADS centers are increasingly offering therapeutic and specialized medical services. Almost half of ADS centers offered physical, occupational, and speech therapies in 2010, and, in some cases, at no extra cost to participants. Some centers also provided on-site podiatry, hearing, dental, and vision services. By offering these services on-site, ADS centers help meet the comprehensive needs of participants and alleviate the often arduous process of transporting fragile or disabled participants to off-site appointments. The emotional well-being and needs of participants is also accounted for in ADS, with the majority of centers providing psychosocial assessments and social services from trained professionals (e.g., social workers).

Nutrition services have long been a staple in ADS centers. In 2010, almost every ADS center offered meals to participants and most (85%) at no extra cost. Over three quarters of ADS centers offer transportation to and from the facility. Given the prohibitive cost of such services, particularly in rural areas, 35% of centers offering transportation charge an additional fee to participants. Another basic feature in ADS is recreational and social programming. Over 75% offer music, art, and pet therapies, and over 70% offer **intergenerational programming** (e.g., activities that bring different age groups together). Caregiver support is also an important service offered in ADS. Most ADS centers provided educational programs and support groups for family caregivers, and some even offer individual counseling. Several additional services appear to be offered in a growing number of ADS centers, including hospice and in-home services. This service expansion may be an indication of the expansion of ADS as a comprehensive service platform beyond traditional expectations.

ADS AND CHRONIC DISEASE AND HEALTH CONDITIONS

As ADS continue to grow, it is important to understand how and to what extent such centers address specific diseases and health conditions. The Centers for Disease Control and Prevention (CDC) and the National Institutes of Health (NIH) have identified priorities for preventing and treating some of the most prevalent and costly health conditions. In the 2010 MetLife study (Metlife Mature Market Institute, 2010b), ADS centers provided information regarding programs, activities, and services that targeted specific diseases and health conditions common to the ADS population, including arthritis, cancer, cardiovascular disease, communicable diseases, dementia, depression, developmental disabilities, diabetes, and falls. As expected, many ADS centers offered programs targeted at the prevention and management of many of these conditions and diseases. Although there is considerable variability in services offered across ADS centers, a large proportion offer disease-specific educational programs, diet and weight management programs, medication management, physical activities, and referrals when needs cannot be met by center staff.

Diabetes offers a good example of a problematic chronic condition that ADS is able to address. Diabetes affects 26.3 million individuals in the United States or almost 8% of the overall population. This chronic condition is especially prevalent in those over the age of 60, affecting 12.2 million older adults or 23.1% of this segment of the population. Diabetes is the seventh leading cause of death in the United States and is associated with heart disease, stroke, high blood pressure, blindness, and amputation. In 2012, it was estimated that the treatment of diabetes costs the country approximately $245 billion annually (American Diabetes Association, 2013). The prevention and management of diabetes call for regular practices, all of which are amenable to the ADS platform. In 2010, approximately three quarters of ADS centers offered blood sugar monitoring, medication management, diet programs, and physical exercise programs. Over half offered educational programs about diabetes, weight control programs, and referrals to specialists, such as endocrinologists and podiatrists.

ADS centers provide services to younger people as well as older adults. In particular, a significant portion of centers target their services to younger adults with IDD or traumatic brain injury. The services offered to this group often include the social and health programs typical of most ADS centers; however, many of these centers also offer specific services geared toward the needs of this population. In 2010, almost one quarter of all ADS centers offered community engagement programs and independent living skill-building programs. Over one in 10 centers offered job training programs, and over 7% provided sheltered workshops. These types of services are critical for adults with IDD and brain injury, as they provide opportunities to engage in meaningful activity and to learn work and life skills. These programs may help this group remain independent and live in the community for longer periods of time than would be the case without these services.

FUNDING ADS

ADS centers rely on a patchwork of public and private funding to keep programs operating. Fee structures vary from hourly charges, half-day, or full-day charges to flat rates regardless of how many hours a participant attends. Participant fees do not typically cover the cost of delivering care, and many providers must rely on supplemental funding from grants or donations to cover costs. The average full-day fee for ADS was $61.71 in 2010, but the cost

FIGURE 7.3 Sources of revenue.

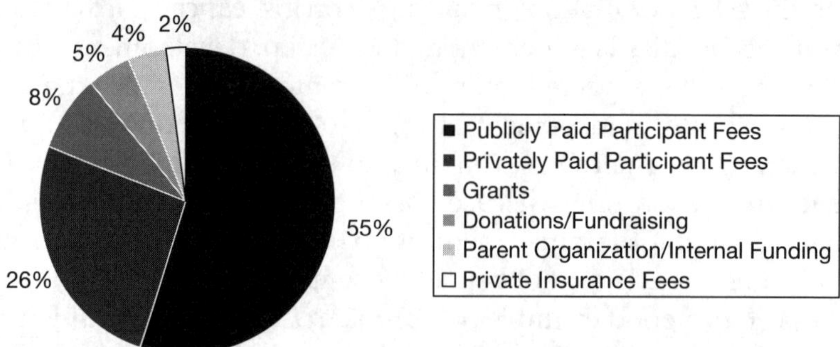

Source: MetLife Mature Market Institute (2010a).

of delivering care was $68.89 (MetLife, 2010b). Comparing data from 2009 and 2010, there was no apparent increase of cost of ADS. This contrasts with nursing home semiprivate rooms for which fees increased by 4.6% and assisted living for which the increase was 5.2% during that same time period. In 2010, approximately 80% of ADS centers offered transportation with fees ranging up to $20 per round trip. Geographic location and distance likely drive the fees charged to participants for this service.

Public/government funding has been the largest source of revenue for ADS centers (55%; Anderson et al., 2013). In 2010, private pay participant fees on average made up 26% of revenues, whereas private insurance reimbursement made up only 2% (Anderson et al., 2013). The private pay participants and private insurance reimbursement remain untapped markets for ADS centers. As government funders continue to seek out avenues for reducing costs of long-term care, ADS centers will need to learn how to market and provide services to participants who can pay privately for services. ADS centers are financially vulnerable by relying so heavily on public sources of funding (Figure 7.3).

Since 2002, the Veterans Administration (VA) has increased its commitment to provide funding for ADS for veterans. In 2010, the VA was identified as the second most common source of public funding, after the Medicaid Home and Community-Based Services waiver programs, by the 2010 MetLife study respondents (Anderson et al., 2013). It is likely that more ADS centers are going to see young veterans who have been injured in international conflicts and need support that ADS programs can provide. ADS centers are well positioned to adapt their services to meet the needs of this special population.

With shortfalls between fee-based revenues and costs, most ADS centers are finely balanced between operating in a deficit or at a profit. In 2010, the majority of centers (70%) reported operating on a balanced budget, whereas 17% reported a deficit and 13% a profit (Anderson et al., 2013). ADS administrators and advocates need to expand existing funding sources, such as long-term care insurance and private pay consumers, and to seek out alternative sources of funding for services, such as Medicare, to ensure financial viability in the future.

IMPACT OF ADS

The impact of ADS attendance can be divided into three primary areas: (a) improvement of caregiver's health and well-being, (b) improvement of participant's health and well-being, and (c) change in health care utilization (Fields, Anderson, & Dabelko-Schoeny, 2014; Gaugler & Zarit, 2001). Researchers have found that caregivers who utilize ADS for at least 8 hours a week experience a reduction in subjective care burden, perceived role overload, worry, anger, and depression (Gaugler et al., 2003; Lawton, Brody, & Saperstein, 1989; Montgomery & Borgatta, 1989; Zarit, Stephens, Townsend, & Greene, 1998; Zarit, Stephens, Townsend, Greene, & Leitsch, 1999). Adding more intensive case management supports for family caregivers to available ADS, including face-to-face and telephone education and counseling and referral services, seems to result in even better caregiver outcomes. Caregivers who participated in **ADS plus** programs, programs that provide case management services for family caregivers, reported less depression, more confidence in managing participant behaviors, and fewer nursing home placements after 1 year compared to those who only used ADS (Gitlin, Reever, Dennis, Mathieu, & Hauck, 2006).

ADS centers are well positioned to become the "hub" for caregiver support services in the communities they serve, helping family caregivers who support family members with functional limitations maintain the highest possible level of independence for as long as possible. Recently, ADS programs have started to experiment with providing primary care to family caregivers onsite through nurse practitioners. As ADS centers are the only community-based provider of services for individuals with Alzheimer's and related dementias, partnerships with the local Alzheimer's Association chapters to provide caregiver support and resources could result in innovative collaborations.

Benefits for individuals attending ADS centers have been more difficult to document. Because of a lack of federal guidelines, significant variation exists in service delivery on programmatic and individual levels, making it more difficult to connect services with particular outcomes (Dabelko & Zimmerman, 2008). In addition, many of the individuals served by ADS are facing chronic progressive conditions, resulting in steady declines in functioning over time. Most of the improvements experienced by participants seem to be in emotional well-being such as morale, mood, and satisfaction (Baumgarten, Lebel, Laprise, Leclerc, & Quinn, 2002; Dabelko-Schoeny & King, 2010; Zank & Schacke, 2002). Overall quality of life also seems to improve with ADS utilization. When compared to similar community-dwelling older adults, adult day health care participants showed improvement in how their physical and emotional limitations affected their functioning in daily life (Schmitt, Sands, Weisee, Dowling, & Covinsky, 2010). Some of the most promising outcomes for participants in ADS may be found by measuring the impact of disease-specific support being offered in centers (Fields et al., 2014). Programs providing diet, exercise, medication management, and other support to treat hypertension, diabetes, and heart disease may be in the best position to document positive changes in their participants. Another promising area of research examines the impact of attendance on behavior of individuals with dementia while they are at home with their caregivers (Fields et al., 2014). Femia, Zarit, Stephens, and Greene (2007) found that the duration of sleep disturbances among individuals with dementia who attended ADS was shorter when compared to community-dwelling individuals who did not attend ADS. Getting plenty of sleep is an important element for maintaining the physical health of both caregivers and participants.

Finally, delay in institutionalization is an outcome that has been difficult to document. This outcome is of particular interest to public policy makers who look to HCBS as a less expensive alternative to nursing home care to support long-term care needs of the growing number of older adults. At this point, studies that have examined rates of institutionalization among ADS participants have not demonstrated a delay in nursing home placement as the result of attendance (Weissert, Lesnick, Musliner, & Foley, 1997; Weissert, Wan, Livieratos, & Katz, 1980). However, the overall rates of institutionalization and the amount of service in these studies (number of days of attendance) were low, perhaps resulting in difficulties in detecting an effect of ADS attendance on institutionalization rates. More recent work suggests that the risk of nursing home placement actually increases for individuals with dementia with the number of days individuals with Alzheimer's disease attend ADS programs (McCann et al., 2005). This may reflect caregivers using ADS as an intermediary step to institutionalization. Some evidence suggests that proclivity to institutionalize family members may be dependent on the caregiver's familial relationship with the participant. Researchers found that wives of participants of ADS place their husbands into nursing homes at higher rates than their counterparts who do not use ADS (Cho, Zarit, & Chiriboga, 2009). Adult daughters using ADS were more likely to postpone institutionalization compared to other caregivers who do not utilize ADS.

Research on the impact of ADS on caregivers and participants has lagged behind the growth in the number of programs and individuals served. It is important to note that unanswered questions remain about the individual and financial benefits of ADS programs. Teasing out what services make a difference to whom and under what kinds of situations is critical for the future development of ADS as a key provider of long-term care services. Special attention to programs serving particular groups of individuals, such as veterans, those with IDD, and individuals with dementia, need to be carefully evaluated to have a better understanding of how they work and the benefits they provide.

FUTURE OF ADS

The future of ADS will be dependent on the ability to diversify funding sources and to establish leadership in managing expensive chronic diseases such as diabetes and Alzheimer's disease. This effort will require raising public awareness about ADS and documenting participant and caregiver benefits. ADS can no longer be viewed as "the best kept secret." Public education campaigns about what ADS can offer and building partnerships with other community agencies, long-term care insurance providers, and academic institutions will be crucial to the success of these activities. Testing disease-specific interventions that are tied to a reduction of more costly health care options, such as hospitalization or emergency room visits, will be important to secure future funding.

Recent efforts to add ADS as a Medicare service provider through the Medicare Prescription Drug, Improvement, and Modernization Act of 2003 and the proposed Medicare Adult Day Services Act are important vehicles for expanding funding for services. The Medicare Prescription Drug, Improvement and Modernization Act of 2003 provides funding for pilot programs to explore using home health agencies to deliver services traditionally delivered in the homes of elders within ADS. The proposed Medicare Adult Day Services Act would fund ADS to provide postacute services after a hospital stay. ADS advocates, such as the National Adult Day Services Association (NADSA) and the American Association of Homes and Services for the Aging (AAHSA), will likely continue to push for such a law. The Patient Protection and Affordable Care Act (ACA), or health care reform of 2010, demonstrates that commitment to HCBS and ADS has the possibility of capitalizing on the opportunities presented in this legislation. Finally, the need for this support will likely be increasingly recognized as overwhelmed caregivers seek out a "hub" for resources and support while juggling employment and their own well-being.

ADS may be dramatically affected by the ACA of 2010. The ACA promises quality health care for all Americans, with emphasis on community living assistance services (Title I, II, and VIII). According to the community first choice option (Title II, Subtitle E), a new optional Medicaid benefit offers community-based services for individuals with disabilities requiring care in a hospital, nursing home, or any medical care facilities for mental disabilities (Somers & Mahadevan, 2010). This would enable ADS centers to receive another source of public funding for care provided. The ACA emphasizes the importance of prevention programs for chronic illness (Title IV), and also enhancing workforce and health care education and training (Title V) as well as requiring improved diverse medical therapies (Title VII).

As the society ages, the rate of chronic disease, such as dementia, diabetes, hypertension, cardiovascular disease, and other physical disability, will increase, encouraging demand for ADS. The ACA supports routine checkups and screenings of diabetes and heart disease without copays or deductibles. The ACA (Title V, Subtitle D) enhances health care workforce education and training. It supports training for DCWs in family medicine and physician assistantship, on cultural competency, prevention, and public health, and on working with individuals with disabilities. All of these are significant areas of interest to ADS providers.

In terms of facilitating aging in place, ADS may play an even greater role in the future. The development of "livable communities" has recently been an area of focus for community planners and advocates for older adults. Livable communities foster aging in place by providing environments that are congruent with the abilities and needs of older adults in terms of housing, services, transportation, and mobility. The ADS of the future may be an integral part of these livable communities. Unfortunately, policies and practices that support livable communities are lagging or lacking. Researchers have identified a number of deficiencies, including "unsupportive community design, unaffordable and inaccessible housing, and a lack of access to needed services" (Farber, Shinkle, Lynott, Fox-Grage, & Harrell, 2011, p. vii). It appears that many existing communities are far from livable for older adults and that to date, practice has not followed policy. Until the widespread actualization of such livable communities, it remains to be seen how the ADS of the future will look in terms of design, purpose, and community integration.

SUMMARY

ADS support the health, nutritional, social, and daily living needs of adults with functional limitations in a group setting during daytime hours. ADS also provide critical respite and support services for caregivers and family members, often helping them to remain employed and providing the opportunity for extending their time as primary caregivers. The majority of ADS participants are older adults, although a significant portion of participants are younger adults with IDD. Reflective of the general population, ADS participants are a diverse group in terms of demographic characteristics, backgrounds, abilities, and needs. ADS centers provide an array of services, from socialization and skills training to the prevention and treatment of both acute and chronic health care conditions (e.g., short-term rehabilitation, diabetes, and dementia). ADS is growing (35% increase in the number of centers since 2002) and evolving as individuals and families increasingly desire and expect to be able to age in place.

As with other areas of health care, the future of ADS largely depends on evidence of the effectiveness of the services provided. Although researchers have begun to identify benefits related to ADS, such as gains in overall well-being and quality of life, more research is needed to fully understand the benefits of the service. The future of ADS is also largely determined by legislative initiatives and subsequent funding. Finding new and effective ways to care for the aging baby boom generation will undoubtedly shape the development of ADS in the coming years.

DISCUSSION QUESTIONS

1. What are the primary factors that have driven the evolution and development of ADS in the United States?
2. Diversity seems to be the hallmark of both the participants and the services offered in ADS. Should ADS be regulated by the federal government like nursing homes? How might this change the services offered and participants served?
3. In Case Study 7.1, Mrs. Baker readily agreed to attend ADS. What if she refused to enroll? What strategies might her daughter and the ADS program employ to assist her with the transition?

4. Take a closer look at the health care priorities set forth by the CDC (www.cdc.gov). Identify specific areas where ADS might be able to provide services to address these priorities.
5. In Case Study 7.2, Mr. King has lost interest in participating in his favorite activities at ADS. What might be going on with Mr. King? How might the ADS staff assess his current condition?
6. What are some of the difficulties that researchers face as they investigate whether or not ADS contributes to the prevention or delay of nursing home placement?

ADDITIONAL RESOURCES

www.aahsa.org **The American Association of Homes and Services for the Aging (AAHSA)**

The AAHSA is an organization dedicated to advancing policy, programs, and research related to housing and community-based services for older adults. This site is particularly useful for information on policy related to ADS.

www.aoa.gov **The Administration on Aging (AoA)**

The AoA is a government agency that helps to develop HCBS for older adults. The site contains useful information regarding AAA as well.

www.cdc.gov **The Centers for Disease Control and Prevention (CDC)**

The CDC is a government agency aimed at the treatment and prevention of disease and the promotion of health. This site is a clearinghouse of information on health, including statistics and national priorities and initiatives.

www.easterseals.org **Easter Seals**

Easter Seals provides services and advocacy for individuals with IDD. This site contains information regarding ADS centers and programs that serve this specific population.

www.hcbs.org **Home and Community-Based Services (HCBS)**

The HCBS is a clearinghouse of information on HCBS for older adults and persons with disability. This site is particularly useful for up-to-date information on policy related to ADS.

www.nadsa.org The **National Adult Day Services Association (NADSA)**

The NADSA is an organization that provides education, services, advocacy, and research on ADS across the United States. This site provides information and resources focusing exclusively on ADS.

REFERENCES

American Diabetes Association. (2013). *Resources*. Retrieved from www.diabetes.org/advocate/resources/

Anderson, K. A., Dabelko-Schoeny, H., & Johnson, T. D. (2013). The state of adult day services: Findings and implications from the MetLife National Study of Adult Day Services. *Journal of Applied Gerontology*, *32*(6), 729–748.

Baumgarten, M., Lebel, P., Laprise, H., Leclerc, C., & Quinn, C. (2002). Adult day care for the frail elderly. *Journal of Aging and Health*, *14*(2), 237–259.

Chatterji, P., Burstein, N. R., Kidder, D., & White, A. J. (1998). *Evaluation of the program for all-inclusive care for the elderly (PACE)*. Cambridge, MA: Abt Associates.

Cho, S., Zarit, S. H., & Chiriboga, D. A. (2009). Wives and daughters: The differential role of day care use in nursing home placement of cognitively impaired family members. *The Gerontologist*, *49*(1), 57–67.

Dabelko, H. I., Koenig, T. L., & Danso, K. (2008). An examination of the adult day services industry using the resource dependence model within a values context. *Journal of Aging & Social Policy, 20*(2), 201–217.

Dabelko, H. I., & Zimmerman, J. (2008). Outcomes of adult day health services for participants: A conceptual model. *Journal of Applied Gerontology, 27*(1), 78–92.

Dabelko-Schoeny, H., & King, S. (2010). In their own words: Participants' perceptions of the impact of adult day services. *Journal of Gerontological Social Work, 53*(2), 1–17.

Farber, N., Shinkle, D., Lynott, J., Fox-Grage, W., & Harrell, R. (2011). *Aging in place: A state survey of livability policies and practices*. Retrieved from http://assets.aarp.org/rgcenter/ppi/liv-com/aging-in-place-2011-full.pdf

Femia, E. E., Zarit, S. H., Stephens, M. A. P., & Greene, R. (2007). Impact of adult day services on behavioral and psychological symptoms of dementia. *The Gerontologist, 47*, 775–788.

Fields, N. L., Anderson, K. A., & Dabelko-Schoeny, H. (2014). The effectiveness of adult day services for older adults: A review of the literature from 2000 to 2011. *Journal of Applied Gerontology, 33*(2), 130–163.

Gaugler, J. E., Duval, S., Anderson, K. A., & Kane, R. L. (2007). Predicting nursing home admission: A meta-analysis. *BMC Geriatrics, 7*(13), 1–14.

Gaugler, J. E., Jarrott, S. E., Zarit, S. H., Stephens, M. A. P., Townsend, A., & Greene, R. (2003). Adult day service use and reduction in caregiver hours: Effect on stress and psychological well-being for dementia caregivers. *International Journal of Geriatric Psychiatry, 18*, 55–62.

Gaugler, J. E., & Zarit, S. H. (2001). The effectiveness of adult day services for disabled older people. *Journal of Aging & Social Policy, 12*(2), 23–47.

Gitlin, L. N., Reever, K., Dennis, M. P., Mathieu, E., & Hauck, W. W. (2006). Enhancing quality of life of families who use adult day services: Short- and long-term effects of the adult day services plus program. *The Gerontologist, 46*(5), 630–639.

Keenan, T. A. (2010). *Home and community preferences of the 45+ population*. Retrieved from http://assets.aarp.org/rgcenter/general/home-community-services-10.pdf

Lawton, M. P., Brody, E. M., & Saperstein, A. R. (1989). A controlled study of respite service for caregivers of Alzheimer's patients. *The Gerontologist, 29*(1), 8–16.

Long, T., & Kavarian, S. (2008). Aging with developmental disabilities: An overview. *Topics in Geriatric Rehabilitation, 24*(1), 2–11.

McCann, J. J., Hebert, L. E., Yi, Y., Wolinsky, F. D., Gilley, D. W., Aggarwal, N. T., ... Evans, D. A. (2005). The effect of adult day care services on time to nursing home placement in older adults with Alzheimer's disease. *The Gerontologist, 45*(6), 754–763.

MetLife Mature Market Institute. (2010a). *The MetLife national study of adult day services*. Retrieved from www.metlife.com/assets/cao/mmi/publications/studies/2010/mmi-adult-day-services.pdf

MetLife Mature Market Institute. (2010b). *The 2010 MetLife market survey of nursing home, assisted living, adult day services, and home care costs*. Retrieved from www.metlife.com/assets/cao/mmi/publications/studies/2010/mmi-2010-market-survey-long-term-care-costs.pdf

Montgomery, R. J. V., & Borgatta, E. F. (1989). The effectiveness of alternative support strategies on family caregiving. *The Gerontologist, 29*, 457–464.

Partners in Caregiving. (2001–2002). *National study of adult day services*. Retrieved from www.rwjf.org/pr/product.jsp?id=20940

Rowles, G. D., & Bernard, M. (2013). The meaning and significance of place in old age. In G. D. Rowles & M. Bernard (Eds.), *Environmental gerontology: Making meaningful places in old age* (pp. 3–24). New York, NY: Springer Publishing Company.

Schmitt, E. M., Sands, L. P., Weisee, S., Dowling, G., & Covinsky, K. (2010). Adult day health care participation and health-related quality of life. *The Gerontologist, 50*(4), 531–540.

Somers, S. A., & Mahadevan, R. (2010). *Health literacy implications of the Affordable Care Act.* Hamilton, NJ: Center for Health Care Strategies, Inc. Retrieved from www.iom.edu/~/media/Files/Activity%20Files/PublicHealth/HealthLiteracy/Commissioned%20Papers/Health%20Literacy%20Implications%20of%20Health%20Care%20Reform.pdf

U.S. Census Bureau. (2009). *2005–2009 American Community Survey (ACS).* Retrieved from http://factfinder.census.gov

U.S. Census Bureau. (2008). *Projected population of the United States, by age, sex, race, and Hispanic origin: 2000 to 2050.* Retrieved from http://www.census.gov/population/projections/files/methodstatement.pdf.

Weissert, W. G. (1976). Two models of geriatric day care. *The Gerontologist, 16*(5), 420–427.

Weissert, W. G. (1977). Adult day care programs in the United States: Current research projects and a survey of 10 centers. *Public Health Reports, 92*(1), 49–56.

Weissert, W. G., Elston, J. M., Bolda, E. J., Cready, C. M., Zelman, W. N., Sloane, P. D., … Koch, G. G. (1989). Models of adult day care: Findings from a national study. *The Gerontologist, 29*(5), 640–649.

Weissert, W. G., Lesnick, T., Musliner, M., & Foley, K. A. (1997). Cost savings from home and community-based services: Cost savings from Arizona's Medicaid long-term care program. *Journal of Health Politics, Policy & Law, 22*(6), 1329–1357.

Weissert, W. G., Wan, T., Livieratos, B., & Katz, B. (1980). Effects and costs of day-care services for chronically ill. *Medical Care, 18*, 567–584.

Wieland, D., Lamb, V. L., Sutton, S. R., Boland, R., Clark, M., Friedman, S., … Eleazer, G. P. (2000). Hospitalization in the Program for All-Inclusive Care for the Elderly (PACE): Rates, concomitants and predictors. *Journal of the American Geriatrics Society, 48*, 1373–1380.

Zank, S., & Schacke, C. (2002). Evaluation of geriatric day care units: Effects on patients and caregivers. *Journals of Gerontology: Psychological Sciences, 57B*(4), 348–357.

Zarit, S. H., Stephens, M. A. P., Townsend, A., & Greene, R. (1998). Stress reduction for family caregivers: Effects of adult day care use. *Journal of Gerontology, 53B*(5), S267–S277.

Zarit, S. H., Stephens, M. A. P., Townsend, A., Greene, R., & Leitsch, S. A. (1999). Patterns of adult day service use by family caregivers: A comparison of brief versus sustained use. *Family Relations, 48*, 361–533.

Transitional Long-Term Care

8

Environmental Design and Assistive Technologies

JULIE A. BROWN
GRAHAM D. ROWLES
AMBER S. MCILWAIN

CHAPTER OVERVIEW

Framed within a transactional ecological perspective, this chapter considers the role of environmental design and the use of assistive technologies (AT) in contemporary long-term care. The ability to age in place and delay or prevent the need for institutional long-term care can be enhanced by thoughtful and supportive environmental design at scales ranging from the community at large to the individual residence. In combination with supportive environmental design, the emergence and use of an array of AT is becoming an important component of the arsenal of resources available to support long-term care, facilitate aging in place, and reduce the need for relocation. The use of increasingly sophisticated technologies is becoming an integral part of modern long-term care. This trend is likely to accelerate as more advanced monitoring and surveillance technologies become available and as the prospect of ambient living environments becomes a reality. The chapter concludes by considering practical and ethical dilemmas associated with the use of technology in long-term care.

LEARNING OBJECTIVES

After reading this chapter, you should have an understanding of:

- The role of the built environment in shaping the need for and delivery of long-term care
- Assistive technologies that facilitate aging in place

- Age-friendly communities
- The principles of universal design and smart home technologies
- Practical and ethical dilemmas associated with environmental design interventions and assistive technology in long-term care

KEY TERMS

Age-friendly communities	Environmental design
Aging in place	Gerontechnology
Ambient assisted living (AAL)	Smart home
Assistive technology (AT)	Universal design

INTRODUCTION

Long-term care is provided at a variety of levels and in physical settings that include neighborhoods and communities, individual residences, housing for elderly persons, assisted living facilities, skilled nursing facilities, rehabilitation environments, adult day centers, and comprehensive continuing-care communities. These environments provide a continuum of more or less supportive living situations. With the emergence of environmental gerontology over the past three decades (Scheidt & Windley, 2006; Wahl & Weisman, 2003) and the growth of **gerontechnology** (the study of older adult use and interaction with technology; Bouma, Fozard, & van Bronswijk, 2009), it has become increasingly apparent that the design of living environments and the use of assistive technologies is strongly related to individual well-being and the ability to **age in place** (sustain residence in a specific location while experiencing changes associated with aging).

The majority of people prefer to age in place (Callahan, 1992; Greenfield, 2012; Pynoos, 1990; Rowles, 1993), but with advancing age and declining physical and sensory capabilities, it becomes difficult for many people to maintain themselves in accustomed surroundings. There are two responses to this situation. One is to move to a more supportive setting; often this is accompanied by considerable stress. A sizable literature exists, dating back more than half a century, which details the increased morbidity and mortality that can result from involuntary relocation (Aldrich & Mendkoff, 1963; Danermark, Ekstrom, & Bodin, 1996). There is also a growing literature on the stresses involved in having to give up possessions accumulated over a lifetime in order to move into a smaller and more manageable environment (Ekerdt, Luborsky, & Lysack, 2011; Ekerdt, Sergeant, Dingle, & Bowen, 2004). A second option is to delay the need to move through supportive **environmental design** (the physical configuration of built environments) and the use of AT (Freedman, Agree, Martin, & Cornman,

2005; McCreadie & Tinker, 2005). This chapter focuses on such strategies as approaches to facilitating long-term care in familiar settings.

THEORETICAL PERSPECTIVE

A long history of research, stemming from Kurt Lewin's classic "equation," $B = f(P, E)$ framing the person–environment relationship, provides a theoretical context for considering the role of environmental design and the use of AT in long-term care (Lewin, 1935). Lewin argued that behavior (B) is a function of the evolving relationship between person (P) and environment (E). In gerontology, a series of theoretical perspectives was developed on the basis of this fundamental proposition (Kahana, 1982; Lawton & Nahemow, 1973; Pastalan, 1970). It was suggested that the physical and social environment shapes the behavior of the individual. In turn, each individual modifies his or her environment, creating a continual transactional process of person → environment → person → environment feedback. In recent years, acknowledgment that the separation of person from environment is somewhat artificial has led to transactional perspectives that emphasize the intimate reciprocity of the relationship and the arbitrariness of the separation (Cutchin, 2004; Dickie, Cutchin, & Humphrey, 2006).

The best-known perspective is the ecological model (Figure 8.1; Lawton & Nahemow, 1973). Lawton and Nahemow conceptualized the

FIGURE 8.1 Lawton and Nahemow's ecological model.

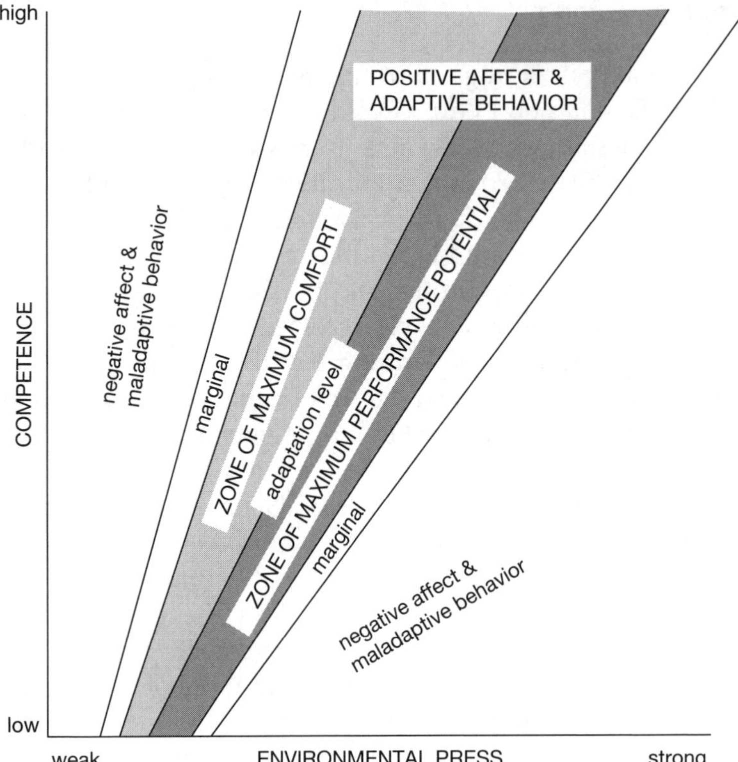

person–environment relationship within a *needs/press* framework. A person's needs were expressed in terms of his or her level of physiological and psychological *competence*; for example, physical strength and flexibility and cognitive ability to climb stairs. The environment was considered in terms of the amount of *press* it exerted; for example, the presence of physical barriers, such as stairs, and context-related challenges to successfully meeting needs. Lawton and Nahemow argued that there was an *adaptation level* that reflected balance between a given level of competence and level of press. Lawton and Nahemow suggested that a situation of complete adaptation was not necessarily optimal for the individual, as it provided no stimulation or challenge. Their model identified a zone of *maximum performance potential* for each level of competence (represented by the dark shaded area in Figure 8.1). The lower the individual's competence, the less environmental press can be tolerated by that individual without maladaptive or negative consequences.

The ecological model provides a framework in which the trajectory of each individual's situation with respect to long-term care can be characterized within four interwoven dimensions: (a) personal competence, (b) environmental press, (c) adaptation (personal accommodation or environmental modification), and (d) relocation. These dimensions can be considered on multiple scales and in many different environments. Here, the focus is on neighborhood planning, environmental design, and AT in allowing older adults to sustain the highest possible adaptation level.

HISTORICAL CONTEXT

Enhancing the quality of living environments through environmental design and technology is not new. Our cave-dwelling ancestors almost certainly modified their immediate surroundings to maximize their comfort and safety. Throughout history, the design of communities, neighborhoods, and residences has constantly evolved in relation to local climatic conditions, terrain, perceived comfort needs of inhabitants, and local culture (Rapoport, 1990).

Optimal planning of communities and the design of accessible and people-friendly neighborhoods and residences received a boost in the early 20th century with the emergence of town planning. In 1917, the American City Planning Institute was incorporated (renamed the American Institute of Planners in 1939), and in 1934 the American Society of Planning Officials was incorporated. These organizations thrived during an era of urban renewal and new town planning (Gans, 1968; Osborn & Whittick, 1970; Wilson, 1966) and merged in 1978 to form the American Planning Association.

Focus on a smaller, more local, and intimate scale and concern with the design of individual residences was boosted in the post-World War II era through a growing environmental design movement. This movement came together with the development of environmental psychology as a discipline in the 1970s, the emergence of organizations such as the Environmental Design Research Association, founded in 1968, and the initial publications of the scientific journals *Environment and Behavior*, first issue published in 1969, and the *Journal of Environmental Psychology*, first issue published in 1981.

Growing sophistication of community planning and environmental design (in parallel with increasing recognition of the needs of an aging population) stimulated interest in environmental design for older adults. Concern with providing special housing options resulted in federal intervention and an era, spanning the 1950s through the 1970s, of construction of age-segregated housing. Much of this housing was developed in the inner city on space vacated by urban renewal. High-rise residential complexes, such as Victoria Plaza in San Antonio, Texas, the subject of Frances Carp's seminal treatise, became major features of the urban landscape (Carp, 1972; Jephcott, 1971).

There was also increased interest in the way individual dwellings were designed to accommodate the special needs of older adults. This focus resulted in a corpus of knowledge on the construction or adaptation of residences to accommodate the declining physical capabilities of older adults (Lawton, Newcomer, & Byerts, 1976; Regnier, 2003; Regnier & Pynoos, 1987). Simple modifications, such as ensuring that shelves are low enough for older adults to reach without fear of falling, that window sills facilitate easy visual access to the outside by persons in a wheelchair, that door knobs are replaced by levers, and that supportive rails are provided to minimize the risk of falls, have been supplemented by increasingly sophisticated design strategies, including universal design and smart homes (Fisk, 2001; Sanford, 2012; Story, 1998). Many of these innovations enable older adults to age in place far longer than might otherwise be the case. Published guidelines for environmental safety in the home by organizations such as AARP have been accompanied by the formation of companies that provide home environmental assessments; for example, Eval-U-Safe, a company based in Louisville, Kentucky, offers a three-step comprehensive evaluation to help make home environments safer and more comfortable for residents.

THE ROLE OF COMMUNITY ENVIRONMENTS IN FACILITATING LONG-TERM CARE

Designing, building, and maintaining age-friendly environments is central to addressing the needs, challenges, and preferences of an aging and/or disabled population. In this section, we examine elements of environmental design as a resource for making the environmental setting an implicit component of long-term care through the support it provides to maintaining independence.

AGE-FRIENDLY COMMUNITIES

Enabling older adults and persons with disabilities to successfully age in place in community settings is no easy task. A range of environmental barriers limit the ability of those who are frail to remain engaged in their communities; such barriers reinforce segregation and exclusion. The possibility of social isolation, especially for older adults and persons with disabilities who live alone, can be increased by the lack of access to the exterior environment and is linked to poor health, decreased life quality and well-being, and even mortality. Common barriers include a lack of appropriately sited and designed affordable housing options, poor physical access to resources and services, and inadequate mobility alternatives, including public transportation and well-maintained sidewalks. The timing brevity of many "Walk"/"Don't Walk" signs, difficulties with escalators, doors to public buildings that require Herculean strength to open, the prevalence of unnecessary steps and high curbs, long distances that must be negotiated in airports, and the cognitively overloaded environments of shopping malls are also well-known barriers. Comprehensive community planning and age-friendly design can remove such barriers (Kochera & Bright, 2006). With the adoption of aging in place as a public policy goal, *"governments and international organizations now agree that supporting older people to continue to live in the community for as long as possible makes both economic and social sense"* (Lui, Everingham, Warburton, Cuthill, & Bartlett, 2009, p. 116).

Age-friendly communities (sometimes called "livable communities") improve the lives of community-dwelling older adults. A growing literature on **age-friendly communities** (enabling and supportive community environments for all age groups and abilities) suggests that communities should have adequate and affordable housing options for all residents and should include a variety of senior apartments, assisted living alternatives, and quality skilled nursing facilities that facilitate aging in place in a familiar neighborhood (Alley, Liebig, Pynoos, Banergee, & Hee Choi, 2007; Pynoos, Caraviello, & Cicero, 2009). There should be options for downsizing by moving into smaller accommodations or care facilities within familiar communities of residence. Age-friendly communities should be accessible through the provision of older adult-friendly transportation options, well-placed and well-designed sidewalks, sufficient handicapped parking, and easily accessible health and social services resources. Indeed, cities should provide additional supportive services to neighborhoods with high densities of older adults, such as naturally occurring retirement communities (NORCs).

In their review of different characteristics of age-friendly communities, Lui et al. (2009) discuss integration of the physical and social environment through policies, structures, and services intended to develop environments that meet the challenges and needs of older adult and disabled populations (Table 8.1). A survey conducted by AARP Public Policy Institute asked community-dwelling respondents to grade their communities on a number of features and opportunities (AARP, 2003). Respondents most often gave poor grades for dependable public transportation, nearby grocery stores and drugstores, available entertainment opportunities, and well-planned sidewalks. Communities were also marked down if they lacked community hospitals, affordable housing, and sufficient variety in housing options (AARP, 2003). A livable community would, therefore, have affordable and appropriate housing, supportive community features and services, and sufficient mobility options—all of which would work together to facilitate the independence and civic and social engagement of older adults (Kochera & Bright, 2006).

TABLE 8.1 Key Features of an Age-Friendly Community

	AGE-FRIENDLY CITY (WORLD HEALTH ORGANIZATION [WHO])	LIFETIME NEIGHBORHOOD (DEPARTMENT FOR COMMUNITIES & LOCAL GOVERNMENT, UK)	LIVABLE COMMUNITY (AARP)	LIVABLE COMMUNITY (NATIONAL ASSOCIATION OF AREA AGENCIES ON AGING, USA)	ELDER-FRIENDLY COMMUNITY (UNIVERSITY OF CALGARY, CANADA)	ELDER-FRIENDLY COMMUNITY (THE ADVANTAGE INITIATIVE, USA)
Physical Infrastructure	Outdoor spaces and buildings	Built environment	Land use	Planning and zoning	–	–
	Transportation	–	Transport and mobility	Transportation	Being mobile	Maximizing independence
	Housing	Housing	Housing	Housing	–	–
	Communication and information	–	Cooperation and communication	–	Ready access to information and services	–
Social Environment	Social participation	Social cohesion and sense of place	–	–	Maintain independence and involvement in activities	Promotes social and civic engagement
	Respect and social inclusion	Social inclusion	–	Public safety	The importance of being valued and respected/ Financial security and personal safety	Addresses basic needs
	Civic participation and employment	–	Public education and involvement in community planning	Culture and lifelong learning	–	Promotes social and civic engagement
	–	Innovation and cross-sectorial planning	Leadership	–	Community development work	–

Source: Reproduced from Lui et al. (2009) p. 118.

The World Health Organization defines an age-friendly city as an inclusive and accessible urban environment that promotes active aging and has developed an extensive guide that cities can use to evaluate their age friendliness, plan for age-friendly community development, and track progress as changes are implemented (World Health Organization, 2007a, 2007b; see also, Chapter 1). New York City was the first city to be certified by the WHO as age friendly and it serves as a model for other cities, both nationally and internationally. As part of New York's age-friendly initiative, approximately 1,000 benches were proposed to be installed at bus stops and in commercial districts and neighborhoods with high concentrations of older adults. The goal was to reinvigorate the city's sidewalks, making the city more walkable and livable for its older citizens (Mays, 2011). Other city initiatives include improving the reliability of elevator and escalator service to increase accessibility to subway stations, installing public restrooms at key citywide locations, redesigning major street intersections to boost crossing safety for older pedestrians, and providing bus service for easier access to grocery stores (Age-Friendly NYC, 2011).

Community Facilities

Key elements of age-friendly communities that are supportive of long-term care are the community facilities they sustain. Support resources, such as senior centers and adult day service centers, are increasingly essential features of community-based long-term care (see Chapter 7). A senior center is a place where older adults in a community can gather for physical activities, socialization, and a wide array of medical and social services (Pardasani, Sporre, & Thompson, 2009). Senior centers help many older adults remain engaged in their communities while interacting as part of a community. Adult day centers provide social and health services to adults in need of supervised day care outside of the home environment. In the United States, adult day centers have been promoted by the National Adult Day Services Association as "a viable community-based care option for people with disabilities within the larger constellation of long-term care services" (www.nadsa.org). Senior centers and adult day centers cater to individuals with different needs and requirements. Senior centers target older adults who want to remain engaged, whereas adult day service centers provide care for adults with functional impairments who require supervised care.

Flexibility is fundamental to both senior center and adult day service center design. In particular, the need for design that is responsive to the needs of different age cohorts with diverse capabilities and expectations has resulted in a transformation of the design and functionality of senior centers, as centers increasingly cater to more active older populations (Hostetler, 2011). Spaces designed for quilting and crocheting are being complemented by gymnasia, computer rooms, and coffee shops providing lattes, which fulfill the needs of new generations of older adults (Gallow, 2012). Complementing these needs with those of frail older adults with significant physical and cognitive impairment is fast becoming the focus of the design of contemporary senior centers and adult day centers.

AGE-FRIENDLY RESIDENCES

As individuals transition into old age, their residence becomes an increasingly meaningful space as an increasing proportion of each day, often in excess of 80%, is spent in this location (Oswald & Wahl, 2005). For many older adults, particularly those having spent lengthy residence in a single dwelling, this location becomes the physical locus of life and a place that, because of its familiarity, can be easily negotiated as capabilities decline. The residence also becomes a repository of meaning, as it transforms into a "home," providing a sense of centering, ownership, privacy, security, refuge, control, familiarity, and comfort in a world that is increasingly difficult to negotiate (Rowles & Chaudhury, 2005; Zingmark, Norberg, & Sandman, 1995).

The design of home space and the possessions it contains become critical elements in the preservation of identity (Rowles & Watkins, 2003; Rubinstein & de Medeiros, 2005). It is increasingly acknowledged that the physical internal design and layout of residences for older adults can facilitate the process of making the "spaces" of residences into "places" (Rowles & Bernard, 2013). Places that hold significant meaning facilitate extended ability to remain in a familiar residence, sometimes for far longer that objective measures of physical capability would indicate are possible (Rowles, Oswald, & Hunter, 2003; Rowles & Watkins, 2003). As people become frail, competence declines, environmental press increases, and the disruption of an intimate physical and psychological familiarity with a home and the objects it contains can become quite stressful (Ekerdt et al., 2012).

Environmental Design and Home Modification

Given the significance of a residence as home, it is important for the physical design and layout of spaces where older adults live to be accommodating of both normative and disease-related physical and cognitive changes that occur with advancing age. Many individuals live in residences that were not designed to accommodate mobility limitations. Indeed, there is increasing concern that the spacious two-story "McMansions" that characterize many affluent contemporary American suburban landscapes represent "Peter Pan" housing, residences designed on the assumption that people never grow old.

A variety of design innovations and accommodations make dwellings more age friendly and suitable for persons with disabilities. The WHO summarizes essential features for elder-friendly housing in its guide to global age-friendly cities, and similar design recommendations are provided in a number of other guides and publications (Danziger & Chaudhury, 2009; Kim, Ahn, Steinhoff, & Lee, 2014; Kochera, 2002; Sanford, Pynoos, Tejral, & Browne, 2002; World Health Organization, 2007a). In general, housing should be designed to be consistent with and equipped to withstand local environmental conditions. There should be adequate space to move about freely—space adaptable to the changing needs of older adults that includes level surfaces, wide passages accessible to wheelchairs, and appropriately designed bathrooms and kitchens. A plethora of specific home modifications are possible, including removing door thresholds, discarding

FIGURE 8.2 Home modification to facilitate aging in place.

Source: Rob Caswell © 2009, www.alliswell.com Used with permission.

throw rugs, providing accessible shelves, installing lazy Susans, adjusting the height of countertops, providing chairs with arms that make rising easy, removing hazardous items from stairs to reduce the risk of tripping, improving lighting, using levers rather than rounded door knobs, installing grab bars in bathrooms, providing elevated toilet seats and portable shower seats, adding handrails on stairs and on outside steps, and installing stair elevators (Figure 8.2).

The WHO also identifies a set of contextual prerequisites for ensuring that appropriate housing modification can be achieved, noting that housing should be modified as needed, modifications should be affordable, equipment for modifications should be readily available, and financial assistance should be provided to those who need to make modifications. Finally, resources should be available to educate everyone involved about the ways in which housing can be modified to meet the specific needs of older adults (WHO, 2007a).

Of course, the optimum solution to the dilemma of making residences age friendly and supportive of long-term care is to ensure that dwellings are constructed in the first place to ensure the needs of individuals with reduced abilities. **Universal design**—design that is accessible to all users, regardless of age or ability—is intended to achieve this outcome (Sanford, 2012; Steinfeld, & Maisel, 2012). The development of universal design can be traced to the barrier-free movement of the 1950s that brought designing for people with disabilities to the attention of public policy and design practices. An example of barrier-free, or accessible, design would be a wheelchair ramp installed alongside the steps of a building entrance. Although barrier-free design remained focused on design for people with moderate to severe physical disabilities, universal design emerged as design for all people regardless of ability.

In the late 1990s, advocates of universal design, specifically a working group of architects, product designers, engineers, and environmental design researchers at North Carolina State University's Center for Universal Design, developed seven principles of universal design (Connell et al., 1997; Steinfeld & Maisel, 2012; Story, 1998). These principles formalized a language for talking about universal design that is becoming increasingly utilized throughout the world.

The first principle, *equitable use*, means the design must be useful and marketable to people with diverse abilities. An example of equitable use would be step-free level entrances into a residence. The second principle, *flexibility in use*, requires that designs accommodate a wide range of individual preferences and abilities. An example of flexibility in use would be kitchen countertops adjustable to provide easy access at both sitting and standing heights. The third principle is *simple and intuitive use*. Design features must be easy to understand, regardless of the user's experience, knowledge, language skills, or current concentration level. An example of simple and intuitive use would be lever handles on door knobs and faucets. The fourth principle, *perceptible information*, focuses on communication. Designs must communicate necessary information effectively to the user, regardless of ambient conditions or the user's sensory ability. An example of perceptible information would be a thermostat providing tactile, visual, and audible instructions. The fifth principle of universal design is high *tolerance for error*. Universal design minimizes hazards and the adverse consequences of accidental or unintended actions. An example of tolerance for error would be antiscald temperature and pressure-balanced shower valves. Designs that can be used efficiently and comfortably with minimal effort and minimum potential for fatigue exemplify the sixth principle, *low physical effort*. Examples of low physical effort would be touch lamps and rocker light switches. Finally, universal design mandates accessibility—sufficient *size and space for approach and use*. This principle mandates appropriate space for reach, manipulation, and use regardless of the user's body size, posture, or mobility. For example, doorways and hallways must be wide enough to accommodate wheelchairs and walkers.

Increased interest in universal design is one aspect of a gradual transformation in the construction of dwellings that is making them increasingly supportive of sustained long-term care. Over time, advances in technology are allowing us to reduce the "press" of the environment and make residences supportive of persons with reduced levels of competence, thus enabling them to age in place for far longer than would otherwise be the case. A key element of this process has been harnessing AT.

THE EXPANDING ROLE OF ASSISTIVE TECHNOLOGIES

The word *technology* often brings to mind visions of sophisticated electronic devices, and although this may be accurate in many instances, technology has broad and varied applications. AT encompasses a wide range of devices used in everyday life to aid in the execution of specific tasks. Humans have been using AT for thousands of years, millennia before the invention of the computer chip. The composition of the assistive device is not important; rather, function and purpose determine whether a device can be classified as AT. For example, one of the most common AT devices is the cane. This simple tool can aid an individual with mobility or stability problems. AT can also be quite complicated, such as sensors embedded in the home environment to monitor a resident's every move so that the environment can adjust to the particular needs of the individual.

The Technology Related Assistance for Individuals with Disabilities Act of 1992 defines AT as *"any device or piece of equipment, whether acquired commercially off the shelf, modified, or customized, that is used to increase, maintain, or improve functional capabilities of individuals with disabilities"* (20 U.S.C. Chapter 33, Section 1401 [250]). Examples of AT, as described in this broad definition, include devices used in the daily lives of many people such as hearing aids, walkers, and prescription glasses. Less obvious, but no less important, are grab bars in a shower, daily-labeled pill dispensers, and closed-captioned television programming. At a higher level of sophistication are electronic-based devices, such as medical-alert call devices, that can be worn by persons who are medically vulnerable or living alone.

The rapid advancement and proliferation of new technologies, coupled with the demographic trend toward increase in the numbers of persons in need of long-term care assistance, means that AT is becoming a significant component of the long-term care landscape. And, in the future, the attractiveness of AT is likely to be magnified as a component of long-term care in view of the anticipated decline in the availability of caregivers, both in the workforce and in families (Fleming, Evans, & Chutka, 2003; Lee et al., 2006).

ASSISTIVE TECHNOLOGY: FOR WHOM?

AT devices can compensate for minor physical or mental deficiencies or serve as a means of accident prevention. For example, balance tends to wane with age and is the cause of one of the leading problems for older adults within their home—fall-related injuries (Stevens, Mahoney, & Ehrenreich, 2014). Therefore, it is important for devices to be placed within the home or with the person to help prevent falls or notify caregivers that a fall has occurred (Hawley-Hague, Boulton, Hall, Pfeiffer, & Todd, 2014). In this case, AT might be in the form of a rail along the stairs, a rubber slip mat placed beneath a rug, or a call device to alert a caregiver.

If a disability affects a person to the extent that he or she is no longer able to adequately care for him- or herself, then independent living is at risk. Although a caregiver may monitor health status or assist the individual with daily activities, not everyone may have someone at his or her disposal or even want personal care. In this case, a variety of AT devices, from monitoring technologies to home modifications, may be an option for the older adult, yet there are a number of factors to consider, such as the user's level of self-efficacy with the product.

With each generation, there is a proliferation and advancement in the sophistication of technology; with exposure and use comes a corresponding comfort level with that technology. Because of earlier exposure to and lifelong familiarity with technology, younger people are likely to be more receptive to the most current technology than someone from an older generation. For example, the younger members of the baby boom generation are more likely to feel at ease with sophisticated forms of AT than older adults from previous generations. Nonetheless, it is important to be cautious about generalized assumptions of technological self-efficacy with any population. Some older adults view the acceptance of assistive devices as an insult or weakness, whereas others come to embrace the opportunity to resume or continue a life of independence. For example, some older adults are reluctant to use hearing aids because they feel that they symbolize aging and personal decline, whereas others have no concerns about employing such a technology (Jenstad & Moon, 2011).

Even if an older adult is open to the concept of incorporating AT into his or her life, there may be a financial issue that inhibits use. Affordability is a primary consideration for many older adults, even for devices that are on the lower end of the cost spectrum. In addition, insurance may not cover the cost of devices that would aid the older adult. Yet, this does not necessarily deter an individual from achieving a desired goal. Instead of relying on an off-the-shelf product, compensation for a compromised capability may derive from a "homemade" product. For example, something as simple as a kitchen drawer can serve as an AT. An older adult who has arthritic hands may have difficulty gripping a bowl for mixing purposes. In this case, it can be wedged in a top drawer to provide stability for the task. Another example includes hanging a cord or tassel on the switch of a lamp. This can be both a visual and tactile cue for an individual who may otherwise have a difficult time locating the exact location of or gripping the switch.

CLASSIFYING ASSISTIVE TECHNOLOGY

Numerous approaches have been attempted in classifying AT for older adults and other vulnerable populations (Bougie, 2008; Bouma et al., 2009; Schulz et al., 2014). One way is to group items based on type of impairment or compromised function. Another is to consider the environment in which the technology is used. Yet another, introduced by Bouma et al. (2009), pioneers in the emergent field of gerontechnology, focused on the overall goal or life domain in which the technology is used. Taking additional aspects of technological progress into account, such as elder-friendly communities, universally designed residences, and smart homes, makes classification even more complex because such holistic environments may not make individual impairments as noticeable and make it difficult to explicitly distinguish among diverse elements of assistive support due to more multifaceted and accommodating overall design (Hammel, 2004).

The most recent classification focuses on two major themes: **life domains** (physical and mental health, mobility, social connectedness, safety, and everyday activities and leisure) and the **functional purposes** of technologies "*monitoring or measuring the environment or the individual, ... diagnosing or screening to identify problems, needs or desires, ... and ... treating or intervening to address identified problems, needs or desires*" (Table 8.2; Schulz et al., 2014, p. 4). As the authors note, it is possible to identify specific technologies that would be applicable to every cell within this matrix and there are few, if any, technologies that would not be embraced by the model.

Most consumers of supportive technologies—older adults, persons with disabilities, and caregivers—are not familiar with the intricacies of academic

TABLE 8.2 Technology Applications to Important Life Domains

TECHNOLOGY FUNCTIONS	LIFE DOMAINS				
	PHYSICAL AND MENTAL HEALTH	MOBILITY	SOCIAL CONNECTEDNESS	SAFETY	EVERYDAY ACTIVITIES AND LEISURE
Monitoring/ measurement (person, environment)	Physiological functioning (e.g., heart rate, blood pressure, and oximetry) affect health behaviors	Speed and variability of gait, distance covered, vestibular functioning, driving behavior, daily exercise	Frequency and duration of mobile and fixed communication device uses, frequency and duration of time in direct communication with other humans, frequency and time spent in social settings	Frequency of falls, location, driving ability	Frequency, accuracy, and speed of daily task performance, frequency and duration of leisure activities
Diagnosis, screening	Clinical conditions, risk status for clinical conditions	Risk for falling; ambulatory ability, adequacy of daily physical exercise	Social isolation, social integration	Emergency situation, being lost, at risk for driving accidents	Critical cognitive functioning, critical ADL/ IADL status
Treatment, intervention (compensation, prevention, enhancement)	Remote behavioral treatment, chronic disease management, prevention and wellness interventions, clinical decision support	Guidance assistance, risk mitigation (e.g., risk of falling), encouragement and support for exercise	Enhanced social integration, connectivity through computers/ communication technologies	Emergency response systems, computerized driving assistance, alert systems	Task assistance or training, entertainment, education

ADL, activities of daily living; IADL, instrumental activities of daily living.

Source: Reproduced from Schulz et al. (2014).

taxonomies. In most cases, with little awareness of the full array of options available, how does one begin to identify and procure an appropriate AT? For example, if an older adult with moderate vision loss needs a stove with a large display to indicate burner levels (assuming an awareness of this need), there would be at least three possibilities for this circumstance within AT classification. First, the decrease of visual acuity would constitute impairment. Second, the item under consideration is within the kitchen (environment). Finally, the act of cooking (function and goal) would be regarded as an activity of daily living. One consumer-oriented way of simplifying this issue is by considering the physical composition of the device. **Low-** and **high-assistive technology** (also known as low technology and high technology) refers to the level of sophistication of the aid. Low AT would include many of the common tools used by older adults and persons with disabilities that can be found in everyday environments: railings, ergonomically designed tools, T-faucets, and straws, for example. Because these items require the user to manipulate the device, these technologies are regarded as *active.* In contrast, high AT indicates a component of modern or cutting-edge technology, such as a light timer, a voice-activated remote control, or even a house embedded with sensors to monitor movement. A user may not directly interact with these devices, much less be aware of these technologies, if they are seamlessly incorporated within the environment; these are considered to be *passive* technologies. Whether a device is regarded as low or high technology, active or passive, is not of primary importance. Rather, the availability of these items and willingness of the older adult to adopt these devices into regular use within his or her daily life is the paramount consideration.

ADVANCING AT THE SPEED OF LIGHT

Once an item of high status, the cell phone is now so common that it rivals the traditional landline; it is used by persons across the age spectrum. Although the sleek lines of modern fashion dominate the interface design of these devices, there are a number of cell phones that have been designed with the unique needs of less able users in mind. Some now have larger displays, textured buttons, vibrations to alert the user, or an emergency button that transmits a signal to a designated receiver. Computers and even digital games are becoming more commonplace within the personal environment of older adults (Brown, 2014). Tools such as these can be regarded as AT depending on their purpose and use. For example, the use of communicating or generating a document via a computer may be more comfortable as compared to writing by hand, especially when utilizing a feature such as speech-to-text. Yet, there are high-tech devices on the market now that do more for the older adult than just serve as a means to communicate (computers) or engage in exercise/physical therapy (digital games).

By no means ubiquitous, but slowly generating attention, the use of robots is increasing and can serve to assist older adults with basic functions such as reading documents, retrieving an item, or even serving as a source of companionship (Brose et al., 2010). One of the key issues in the use of such technologies is the degree to which they will achieve acceptance by older adults and populations of persons with disabilities (Flandorfer, 2012; Neven, 2010). Even more fundamental are questions regarding the social and emotional consequences of the use of robots. There is concern that as economic pressures to harness this option increase, it would *"most likely ensure that the result was a decrease in the amount of human contact experienced by older persons being cared for, which itself would be detrimental to their wellbeing"* (Sparrow & Sparrow, 2006, p. 141).

Modern forms of AT are increasingly incorporating sensors, which are becoming a building block for advanced passive systems designed to monitor the individual and assess functional needs on a regular basis. A common sensor found within many homes today is an alarm system. When activated, it alerts the homeowner that a sensor has been tripped, possibly indicating an intruder. Over the years, similar technology has been modified to alert the homeowner of potentially dangerous situations, such as stove settings that indicate prolonged use. In addition, sensors can now be embedded within the home to serve a variety of alternate functions. This includes sensors that help eliminate or simplify difficult tasks within the home, warn the individual or his or her caregiver of a specific need, or monitor activities for health purposes. Such sensors can range from options as "simple" as an automatic water faucet for a person with arthritis of the hand, or self-dimming lights, pressure mats, or sensing devices that remotely indicate to a caregiver that the adult is out of bed. These are often referred to as **smart home** technologies.

Smart home technology is wide ranging and has the potential to help keep older adults and persons with disabilities in their private residences even after the onset of cognitive and physical decline. Although smart homes support the health, safety, and independence of older adults, they may also transform their lives to being constantly monitored and managed, as well as motivated to maintain health and wellness (Coughlin, D'Ambrosio, Reimer, & Pratt, 2007). Smart home sensors, for example, can be placed in the floor, in walls, in furniture, and in appliances. Sensors can monitor an older adult's activities of daily living without intrusive cameras or microphones, thereby protecting privacy. Examples of practical uses of smart home technologies include motion sensors that can monitor mobility patterns within the home environment, gait monitors that can detect ambulatory changes and detect falls, pressure sensors that can determine how long a person sits or lies in the same position, temperature sensors that can detect whether the stove is left on or the refrigerator is left open, and humidity sensors that can monitor how often the shower is used. We anticipate that as these technologies become more widely employed, they will become relatively inexpensive in comparison to other forms of direct interpersonal caregiving. Not only will they save time and resources for both the older or disabled adult, but also they will save on travel to and from the home and enable formal caregivers to simultaneously monitor multiple individuals in different locations.

Monitoring systems, particularly those that provide health feedback to a caregiver, may be the deciding factor in whether an older adult is able to remain in his or her home if declining health becomes an issue (Sixsmith et al., 2007).

There are now sensors that can be attached to "everyday use" items or locations: if a sensor is not triggered in a device, a toothbrush, for example, the caregiver knows the care receiver has not used it and can intervene. In addition, a sensor that is not triggered, or is triggered at an atypical time, can be charted to identify potential problematic patterns of behavior, which can be a signal for other health issues, including cognitive decline.

The use of sensing technologies to alert health care professionals via a remote system began in the 1970s with the personal emergency response system (PERS) and rose to popularity among older adults in the 1980s (Parker & Sabata, 2004). The technology entailed an older adult wearing a remote device with a call button that he or she could press if there was a perceived need. This alerted a monitoring station and allowed a two-way conversation via a speakerphone in the home. Although this form of AT offered a sense of security for many, technology advance has produced systems exponentially more sophisticated. For example, the traditional cane has come a long way, it can now be outfitted with a GPS to assist the adult with navigation in his or her community, or to send signals of that location to a caregiver. The same is also being done with devices designed to appear as jewelry worn on the adult; these serve a dual purpose: fashion statement and GPS tracking device that can be activated if help is needed.

The technologies found in smart homes have become commonplace within the AT market and now include devices that serve an array of functions of benefit to aging and disabled individuals: as safety alarms, as informational sensors, as mechanisms for remote monitoring, and as sources for telecommunication for health maintenance and socialization. The use of these technologies in combination has resulted in initiatives to create model smart homes that are fully automated and push the boundaries of technological support (Chan, Campo, Esteve, & Fourniols, 2009; Park et al., 2007). The ultimate expression of such composite technology aspirations is the recent exploration of the potential for creating **ambient assisted living** (AAL) environments (Cardinaux, Bhowmik, Abhayaratne, & Hawley, 2011). Such environments move beyond the components of smart homes because they create a residence in which the environment is embedded with a single integrated system of networked sensors throughout the dwelling programmed specifically to the needs and preferences of the user(s) (Sixsmith & Müller, 2008). This sophisticated passive form of AT not only monitors the user, but *anticipates* his or her needs and automatically adjusts devices within the home to meet those needs without immediate direction from the user. In addition, the system can be programmed to interact with the user so that adjustments within the home can alter individual settings in accordance with the user's preference; settings such as the height of a cabinet, the temperature of a room, or the amount of light within an area.

We can envisage a future scenario of smart homes and AAL. Upon awakening, appropriate lighting illuminates 89-year-old Connie's bedroom while her vital signs are recorded and transmitted to a caregiver 12 miles away. As she gets out of bed and moves to her bathroom, sensors in the floor simultaneously measure speed and gait while the lights automatically adjust for safe navigation.

Meanwhile, her coffee begins to brew in the kitchen and the temperature in this room adjusts automatically to the level she prefers when she is sitting by the window and having her breakfast. Her vitamins and medications are automatically dispensed into a small weight-sensored cup with a visual or audible alarm that goes off until it registers as empty. When this has occurred, her caregiver is informed through an automatic text to her cell phone.

This kind of monitoring activity and environmental adjustment would continue throughout Connie's day to ensure her well-being while maintaining her independence without the need for direct contact with a caregiver. Connie's robot, designed to assist her with key movements, such as rising from her chair and giving her something to hold on to as she is guided across the room, allows her to navigate her home with ease and autonomy. Later in the day, she is able to participate in a "*telehealth*" consultation with her physician's assistant who is able to monitor her status via her in-home camera. And, as evening approaches, Connie spends a couple of hours interacting with her friends through the sophisticated telecommunication and conferencing resources that are built into her living room (see Case Study 8.1).

Case Study 8.1: Belinda's Day

Today is an important day for Belinda. Now an 87-year-old widow, Belinda Marshall has lived at 231 Corunda Drive since 1967 when, together with her husband (now deceased) and her two children, Ralph (now 56) and Ester (now 52), she moved into the two-story suburban residence that was to become the family home and the place where her children grew up. Belinda vividly remembers Esther's wedding day, her daughter was violently sick in the dining room, shortly before she was to leave for the church with her father. Her husband had his fatal heart attack here, in the hallway. Her home is a repository for memories. Over the years, Belinda has surrounded herself with photographs of her grandchildren, proudly displayed on the mantle. There are the pictures on the wall. Each tells a story. The one over the fireplace was given to her by her husband on the couple's 25th wedding anniversary (she always had thought of it as a rather strange gift, but she had grown to like it). In the corner, on a wall tucked behind the Tiffany-style lamp she obtained from a yard sale in 1984, are the paintings that Ralph created when he was in high school. They are not very good, but she loves them anyway, particularly the one of the dog they had at the time. The small table on which she piles her sewing projects goes back to the time of her grandmother, and she remembers the tensions with her siblings when the decision was being made as to who should inherit the piece. There is a story to everything in her home. Now, she lives alone, surrounded by her life.

(*continued*)

Case Study 8.1: Belinda's Day (*continued*)

Today is an important day for Belinda. In a few hours, Ralph and his new wife and one of her step-grandchildren will be coming to help Belinda sort through her things so that she can decide what to keep and what she must discard as she moves into the new apartment. She has been thinking about this day with dread for many weeks, and it has been in the back of her mind for far longer. In some ways, she has prepared for it. During family visits, she has often asked the children and the grandchildren what they would like when she is gone. Her grandson, Timmy, will inherit the large vase decorated with the somewhat abstract purple irises that she has noticed he likes so much. She has taped a label under the vase indicating that it is to go to him. As she glances around the room, she notices many similar items discretely marked with intended recipients.

Today is an important day for Belinda. She has had Toby for 12 years. A poodle–terrier mix, he appeared on her doorstep one snowy Christmas Eve looking bedraggled and forlorn. Contacts with animal control, visits to vets, notices in the paper and posted throughout the community, and Ralph's posts on Facebook had all failed to locate the owner. Ralph thought the dog had simply been dropped off at the end of her driveway. She had come to love Toby and found him to be good company, especially on some of the lonelier nights. Later tonight, Ester is coming to take him to his new home. She tears up at the thought. Welton Manor does not allow pets.

Today is an important day for Belinda. It is her last day in this residence. Tomorrow, she will be moving to a small apartment. Welton Manor is nice enough. The two rooms are relatively spacious, and she will have a panoramic view from the living room over hillsides that she has been told have breathtaking color in the fall. She will have many elderly neighbors, and so she will probably make new friends. There are lots of things to do each day, but she worries whether she will fit in. She hopes that they will not be forcing her to partake in all sorts of activities. These days, she likes to be left alone. Yes, she knows that the move is for the best. There will be a call button and help if she falls again. The staff will help her remember to take her medicine. She will not have to cook. And Ralph and Ester will know she is safe. But she wishes she did not have to go.

Today is an important day for Belinda.

Case Study Discussion Questions:

1. How would you go about helping Belinda prioritize what she should take and what she should abandon, store or bequeath, as later today she goes through her stuff with Ralph?
2. In what ways can you help Belinda cope with the loss of her dog?
3. Place yourself in Ralph's position. How will you handle this day?
4. What role could modern assistive technologies play in helping Belinda put off this day?

CHALLENGES AND CONCERNS

There is some distance between the creation of elder-friendly communities and the brave new world of AAL on the continuum of long-term care. Both ends of the continuum are highly relevant to long-term care in contemporary society. Achieving elder-friendly communities delays and reduces the likelihood of physical and social barriers, resulting in the need for long-term care intervention. At the other extreme, the prospect of AAL offers the hope of technologies that will allow persons who are frail or disabled to remain at home in a familiar environment. In moving in these directions, it is important to temper enthusiasm with acknowledgment that a variety of challenges and concerns remain.

Fundamental ethical questions must be addressed in using monitoring and surveillance technologies. A key issue is one of privacy, especially with respect to the use of video surveillance. For some older adults, cameras or visual surveillance are not acceptable in any form (Steele, Lo, Secomb, & Wong, 2009). However, many are comfortable with such surveillance if it means that they can retain their independence (Van Hoof, Kort, Rutten, & Duijnstee, 2011). Acceptance of such technologies alters the context in which people lead their lives, thereby placing them potentially under constant scrutiny. Maintaining a level of control over the utilization of such technologies becomes a key issue. Under what circumstances, at what times, and in what locations within the residence should older adults and those who are disabled be enabled to turn off part or all of the technology? This dilemma becomes particularly important with respect to those who are cognitively impaired.

At what point does AT impede communication and societal engagement? Does employing such technologies run the risk of creating a barrier rather than a facilitator of ongoing contact (Sparrow & Sparrow, 2006)? What is the risk that caregivers, including adult children, will use the technology as an excuse for less frequent visits, causing a transformation, perhaps a distancing, in the emotional quality of their relationship with the care recipient? To what extent are those who are designing, manufacturing, and marketing AT reinforcing an ageist culture of learned dependence? There is a need to probe more deeply into philosophical and moral questions raised by new forms of caregiving.

A second set of issues pertains to the economics of technology-based long-term care. Although low-technology interventions often cost little, high-technology interventions can be quite expensive. Currently, and for the foreseeable future, many of the most advanced technological interventions, including sophisticated smart homes and AAL, are beyond the financial means of most families. Thus, though there appear to be many options, in reality, there may be few choices. In addition, it is important to be mindful of the potential for systems of technology-based care that further separate those with means from those with few resources in a dual long-term care culture. Within such a system, there will be those who are affluent, who have knowledge of the range of options, and who are able to pay for the latest technologies; they will be able to ease the burden of their caregiving. On the other hand, there will be those without sufficient financial resources and with limited knowledge of the possibilities who will remain fully reliant on energy-sapping and time-consuming traditional models of long-term care provision based on direct person-to-person care.

It is important to remain mindful of a potential paradox here for the recipients of long-term care—a paradox of some poignancy. Those whose families are able to afford the very latest in caregiving technologies may be at risk of finding themselves increasingly isolated and separated from those they love while those whose families cannot afford such advanced support systems remain within the physical embrace of their loved ones.

SUMMARY

The past few decades have seen the rapid expansion of environmental design and assistive technology interventions that assist older adults and persons with disabilities to age in place in familiar communities and dwellings. Against the backdrop of historical context and using the ecological model as an organizing framework, we have explored some of these trends. In environmental design, a burgeoning interest in age-friendly communities, new types of community facilities, advances in residential design, universal design, and smart homes have provided an ever-widening array of options for delaying the need for relocation to more institutional environments. A major factor in this trend has been the rapidly expanding role of assistive technologies. Such technologies, ranging from simple aids to daily living to the most advanced forms of computer technology and robotics, may eventually lead us to the prospect of ambient assisted living. While such advances are to be welcomed because they enhance individual's ability to remain in a known and familiar environment, it is important to acknowledge a variety of issues that are raised by current trends ranging from ethical issues of surveillance, through the unequal distribution of new technologies, to the fundamental question of the potential for sophisticated technologies to lead, paradoxically, to increased social isolation.

DISCUSSION QUESTIONS

1. What is being done in your community to make it more elder friendly? How might you become more personally involved in making your community more elder friendly?
2. What changes would you make in the residence where you currently live to make it more elder friendly? How much do you think it would cost to make the changes you come up with?
3. How do you feel about the prospect of having a robot, perhaps a robot maid, to maximize your independence when you are old? What would be the benefits? What would be the costs?

ADDITIONAL RESOURCES

REPORTS, ARTICLES, BOOKS

Golant, S. M. (2015). *Aging in the right place.* Baltimore, MD: Health Professions Press.

Rowles, G. D., & Bernard, M. (Eds.). (2013). *Environmental gerontology: Making meaningful places in old age.* New York, NY: Springer Publishing Company.

Sanford, J. A. (2012). *Universal design as a rehabilitation strategy.* New York, NY: Springer Publishing Company.

KEY WEBSITES

AARP Livable Communities www.aarp.org/livable-communities/network-age-friendly-communities/info-2014/an-introduction.html

World Health Organization Age Friendly Cities Initiative www.who.int/ageing/publications/Global_age_friendly_cities_Guide_English.pdf

REFERENCES

AARP. (2003). *Beyond 50.03: A report to the nation on independent living and disability.* Washington, DC: Author.

Age-Friendly NYC. (2011). *Age-friendly NYC: A progress report.* New York, NY: Office of the Mayor and New York Academy of Medicine.

Aldrich, C., & Mendkoff, E. (1963). Relocation of the aged and disabled, a mortality study. *Journal of the American Geriatrics Society, 11,* 185–194.

Alley, D., Liebig, P., Pynoos, J., Banergee, T., & Hee Choi, I. (2007). Creating elder-friendly communities. *Journal of Gerontological Social Work, 49*(1–2), 1–18.

Bougie, I. T. (2008). ISO 999 assistive products for persons with disability—Classification and terminology. In A. Helal, M. Mokhtari, & B. Abdulrazak (Eds.), *The engineering handbook of smart technology for aging, disability and independence* (pp. 117–126). Hoboken, NJ: John Wiley & Sons.

Bouma, H., Fozard, J. L., & van Bronswijk, J. E. M. H. (2009). Gerontechnology as a field of endeavor. *Gerontechnology, 8*(2), 68–75.

Brose, S. W., Weber, D. J., Salatin, B. A., Grindle, G. G., Wang, H., Vazquez, J. J., & Cooper, R. A. (2010). The role of assistive robotics in the lives of persons with disability. *American Journal of Physical Medicine and Rehabilitation, 89,* 509–521.

Brown, J. A. (2014). *Let's play: Understanding the role and significance of digital gaming in old age.* Doctoral dissertation, University of Kentucky, Lexington, Kentucky.

Callahan, J. J. (1992). Aging in place. *Generations, 16*(2), 5–6.

Cardinaux, F., Bhowmik, D., Abhayaratne, C., & Hawley, M. S. (2011). Video based technology for ambient assisted living: A review of the literature. *Journal of Ambient Intelligence and Smart Environments, 3*(3), 253–269.

Carp, F. M. (1972). *A future for the aged: Victoria Plaza and its residents.* Austin, TX: University of Texas Press.

Chan, M., Campo, E., Esteve, D., & Fourniols, J. (2009). Smart homes—Current features and future perspectives. *Maturitas, 64,* 90–97.

Connell, B. R., Jones, M., Mace, R., Mueller, J., Mullick, A., Ostroff, E., … Vanderheiden, G. (1997). *The principles of universal design.* Raleigh, NC: Center for Universal Design, North Carolina State University.

Coughlin, J. F., D'Ambrosio, L. A., Reimer, B., & Pratt, M. R. (2007). Older adult perceptions of smart home technologies: Implications for research, policy & market innovations in healthcare. In *Engineering in Medicine and Biology Society, 2007.* France: EMBS

Lyon. Symposium conducted at the 29th Annual International Conference of the IEEE, August 23–26, 2007, Lyon, France.

Cutchin, M. P. (2004). Using Deweyan philosophy to rename and reframe adaptation-to-environment. *American Journal of Occupational Therapy, 58*(3), 303–312.

Danermark, B. D., Ekstrom, M. E., & Bodin, L. L. (1996). Effects of residential relocation on mortality and morbidity among elderly people. *European Journal of Public Health, 6*(3), 212–217.

Danziger, S., & Chaudhury, H. (2009). Older adults' use of adaptable housing features in housing units: An exploratory study. *Journal of Housing for the Elderly, 23*, 134–148.

Dickie, V., Cutchin, M. P., & Humphry, R. (2006). Occupation as transactional experience: A critique of individualism in occupational science. *Journal of Occupational Science, 13*(1), 83–93.

Ekerdt, D. J., Luborsky, M., & Lysck, C. (2012). Safe passage of goods and self during residential relocation in later life. *Ageing and Society, 32*(5), 833–850.

Ekerdt, D. J., Sergeant, J. F., Dingle, M., & Bowen, M. E. (2004). Household disbandment in later life. *Journals of Gerontology, Social Science, 59*(5), S265–S273.

Fisk, M. J. (2001). The implications of smart home technologies. In S. M. Peace & C. Holland (Eds.), *Inclusive housing in an aging society: Innovative approaches* (pp. 101–124). Bristol, UK: The Policy Press.

Flandorfer, P. (2012). Population aging and socially assistive robots for elderly persons: The importance of sociodemographic factors for user acceptance. *International Journal of Population Research, 2012*, 1–13.

Fleming, K. C., Evans, J. M., & Chutka, D. S. (2003). Caregiver and clinician shortages in an aging nation. *Mayo Clinic Proceedings, 78*, 1026–1040.

Freedman, V. A., Agree, E. M., Martin, L. G., & Cornman, J. C. (2005). Trends in the use of assistive technology and personal care for late-life disability, 1992–2001. *The Gerontologist, 46*(1), 124–127.

Gallow, D., Jr. (2012). *Design and renovation of senior centers—Fundamental issues*. National Council on Aging. Retrieved from www.ncoa.org/national-institute-of-senior-centers/research-promising-practices/design-and-renovation-of.html.

Gans, H. (1968). *People and plans*. New York, NY: Basic Books.

Greenfield, E. A. (2012). Using ecological frameworks to advance a field of research, practice, and policy on aging-in-place initiatives. *The Gerontologist, 52*(1), 1–12.

Hammel, J. (2004). Assistive technology as tools for everyday living and community participation while aging. In D. C. Burdick & S. Kwon (Eds.), *Gerotechnology: Research and practice in technology and aging* (pp. 119–131). New York, NY: Springer Publishing Company.

Hawley-Hague, H., Boulton, E., Hall, A., Pfeiffer, K., & Todd, C. (2014). Older adults perceptions of technologies aimed at falls prevention, detection or monitoring: A systematic review. *International Journal of Medical Informatics, 83*(6), 416–426.

Hostetler, A. J. (2011). Senior centers in the era of the "Third Age": Country clubs, community centers, or something else? *Journal of Aging Studies, 25*, 166–176.

Jenstad, L., & Moon, J. (2011). Systematic review of barriers and facilitators to hearing aid uptake in older adults. *Audiology Research, 1*(1), 91–96.

Jephcott, P. (1971). *Homes in high flats*. Edinburgh, UK: Oliver & Boyd.

Kahana, E. (1982). A congruence model of person-environment interaction. In M. P. Lawton, P. G. Windley, & T. O. Byerts (Eds.), *Aging and the environment: Theoretical approaches* (pp. 97–121). New York, NY: Springer Publishing Company.

Kim, H., Ahn, Y. H., Steinhoff, A., & Lee, K. H. (2014). Home modification by older adults and their informal caregivers. *Archives of Gerontology and Geriatrics, 59*, 648–656.

Kochera, A. (2002). *Accessibility and visitability features in single-family homes: A review of state and local activity*. Washington, DC: AARP Public Policy Institute.

Kochera, A., & Bright, K. (2006). Livable communities for older people. *Generations, 29*(4), 32–36.

Lawton, M. P., & Nahemow, L. (1973). Ecology and the aging process. In C. Eisdorfer & M. P. Lawton (Eds.), *The psychology of adult development and aging* (pp. 619–674). Washington, DC: American Psychological Association.

Lawton, M. P., Newcomer, R. J., & Byerts, T. O. (Eds.). (1976). *Community planning for an aging society*. Stroudsburg, PA: Dowden, Hutchinson & Ross.

Lee, I., Pappas G. J., Cleaveland, R., Hatcliff, J., Krogh, B. H., Lee, P., ... Sha, L. (2006). High-confidence medical device software and systems. *Computer, 39*(4), 33–38.

Lewin, K. (1935). *A dynamic theory of personality: Selected papers*. New York, NY: McGraw-Hill.

Lui, C-W., Everingham, J.-A., Warburton, J., Cuthill, M., & Bartlett, H. (2009). What makes a community age-friendly: A review of international literature. *Australasian Journal of Ageing, 28*(3), 116–121.

Mays, J. (2011). *1,000 new benches coming to city streets*. Retrieved from www.dnainfo.com/20111020/harlem/1000-new-benches-coming-city-streets

McCreadie, C., & Tinker, A. (2005). The acceptability of assistive technology to older people. *Age & Society, 25*, 91–110.

Neven, L. (2010). 'But obviously not for me': Robots, laboratories and the defiant identity of elder test users. *Sociology of Health and Illness, 32*(2), 335–347.

Osborn, F. J., & Whittick, A. (1970). *The new towns: The answer to megalopolis*. Cambridge, MA: MIT Press.

Oswald, F., & Wahl, H.-W. (2005). Dimensions of the meaning of home in later life. In G. D. Rowles & H. Chaudhury (Eds.), *Home and identity in late life* (pp. 21–45). New York, NY: Springer Publishing Company.

Pardasani, M., Sporre, K., & Thompson, P. M. (2009). *New models of senior centers taskforce final report*. Washington, DC: National Institute of Senior Centers (NISC).

Park, K.-H., Bien, Z., Lee, J.-J., Kim, B. K., Lim, J.-T., Kim, J. O., ... Lee, W.-J. (2007). Robotic smart house to assist people with movement disabilities. *Auton Robot, 22*, 183–198.

Parker, M. H., & Sabata, D. (2004). Home, safe home: Household and safety assistive technology. In D. C. Burdick & S. Kwon (Eds.), *Gerotechnology: Research and practice in technology and aging* (pp. 145–160). New York, NY: Springer Publishing Company.

Pastalan, L. A. (1970). Privacy as an expression of human territoriality. In L. A. Pastalan & D. H. Carlson (Eds.), *Spatial behavior of older people* (pp. 88–101). Ann Arbor, MI: Wayne State University.

Pynoos, J. (1990). Public policy and aging in place: Identifying the problems and potential solutions. In D. Tilson (Ed.), *Aging in place: Supporting the frail elderly in residential environments* (pp. 167–208.). Glenview, IL: Scott, Foresman.

Pynoos, J., Caraviello, R., & Cicero, C. (2009). Lifelong housing: The anchor in age-friendly communities. *Generations, 33*(2), 26–32.

Rapoport, A. (1990). *History and precedent in environmental design*. New York, NY: Plenum Press.

Regnier, V. (2003). Purpose built housing and home adaptations for older adults: The American perspective. In K. W. Schaie, H.-W. Wahl, H. Mollenkopf, & F. Oswald (Eds.), *Aging independently: Living arrangements and mobility* (pp. 99–117). New York, NY: Springer Publishing Company.

Regnier, V., & Pynoos, J. (Eds.). (1987). *Housing for the aged: Design directives and policy considerations*. New York, NY: Elsevier.

Rowles, G. D. (1993). Evolving images of place in aging and "aging in place." *Generations, 17*(2), 65–70.

Rowles, G. D., & Bernard, M. (Eds.). (2013). *Environmental gerontology: Making meaningful places in old age*. New York, NY: Springer Publishing Company.

Rowles, G. D., & Chaudhury, H. (2005). *Home and identity in late life*. New York, NY: Springer Publishing Company.

Rowles, G. D., Oswald, F., & Hunter, E. G. (2004). Interior living environments in old age. In H.-W. Wahl, R. J. Scheidt, & P. G. Windley (Eds.), *Aging in context: Socio-physical environments. Annual review of gerontology and geriatrics* (Vol. 23, pp. 167–194). New York, NY: Springer Publishing Company.

Rowles, G. D., & Watkins, J. F. (2003). History, habit, heart and hearth: On making spaces into places. In K. W. Schaie, H.-W. Wahl, H. Mollenkopf, & F. Oswald (Eds.), *Aging independently: Living arrangements and mobility* (pp. 77–96). New York, NY: Springer Publishing Company.

Rubinstein, R. L., & de Medeiros, K. (2005). Home, self and identity. In G. D. Rowles & H. Chaudhury (Eds.), *Home and identity in late life* (pp. 47–62). New York, NY: Springer Publishing Company.

Sanford, J. A. (2012). *Universal design as a rehabilitation strategy*. New York, NY: Springer Publishing Company.

Sanford, J. A., Pynoos, J., Tejral, A., & Browne, A. (2002). Development of a comprehensive assessment for delivery of home modifications. *Physical and Occupational Therapy in Geriatrics, 20*(2), 43–55.

Scheidt, R. J., & Windley, P. G. (2006). Environmental gerontology: Progress in the post-Lawton era. In J. E. Birren & K. W. Schaie (Eds.), *Handbook of the psychology of aging* (pp. 105–125). New York, NY: Academic Press.

Schulz, R., Wahl, H.-W., Matthews, J. T., de Vito Dabbs, A., Beach, S. R., & Czaja, S. J. (2014). Advancing the aging and technology agenda in gerontology. *The Gerontologist*, August 27. [Epub ahead of print].

Sixsmith, A., Hine, N., Neild, I., Clarke, N., Brown, S., & Garner, P. (2007). Monitoring the wellbeing of older people. *Topics in Geriatric Rehabilitation, 23*(1), 9–23.

Sixsmith, A., & Müller, S. (2008). *User requirements for ambient assisted living: Results of the SOPRANO project*. Paper prepared for the 6th International Conference of the International Society for Gerontology 2008, Pisa, Italy.

Sparrow, R., & Sparrow, S. (2006). In the hands of machines? The future of aged care. *Minds and Machines, 16*, 141–161. doi: 10.1007/s11023-006-9030-6

Steele, R., Lo, A., Secombe, C., & Wong, Y. K. (2009). Elderly persons' perception and acceptance of using wireless sensor networks to assist health care. *International Journal of Medical Informatics, 78*, 788–801.

Steinfeld, E., & Maisel, J. (2012). *Universal design: Designing inclusive environments*. Hoboken, NJ: John Wiley & Sons.

Stevens, J. A., Mahoney, J. E., & Ehrenreich, H. (2014). Circumstances and outcomes of falls among high risk community-dwelling older adults. *Injury Epidemiology, 1*(5), 1–9.

Story, M. F. (1998). Maximizing usability: The principles of universal design. *Assistive Technology, 10*, 4–12.

Van Hoof, J., Kort, H. S. M., Rutten, P. G. S., & Duijnstee, M. S. H. (2011). Ageing-in place with the use of ambient intelligence technology: Perspectives of older users. *International Journal of Medical Informatics, 80*, 310–331.

Wahl, H.-W., & Weisman, G. D. (2003). Environmental gerontology at the beginning of the new millennium: Reflections on its historical, empirical, and theoretical development. *The Gerontologist, 43*(5), 616–627.

Wilson, J. Q. (1966). Urban renewal: The record and the controversy. Cambridge, MA: MIT Press.

World Health Organization. (2007a). *Global age-friendly cities: A guide*. Geneva, Switzerland: WHO Press.

World Health Organization. (2007b). *Checklist of essential features of age-friendly cities*. Geneva, Switzerland: WHO Press.

Zingmark, K., Norberg, A., & Sandman, P.-O. (1995). The experience of being at home throughout the life span: Investigation of persons aged from 2 to 102. *International Journal of Aging and Human Development, 41*, 47–62.

9

Housing's Role in the Long-Term Care Continuum

CAROLINE CICERO
JON PYNOOS

CHAPTER OVERVIEW

Picture your parents and grandparents growing older. They will likely tell you of their strong preference to age in their lifelong communities, where they have memories of both of the interior and exteriors of their homes, neighborhood streets, restaurants, community parks, and shops. Now imagine their possible changing physical needs. Do the changes they are experiencing as they age necessitate a move into a retirement community or nursing home? For some older adults with physical or cognitive issues, relocation is necessary, but for the majority of older people, increased services and home modifications can make it possible for them to stay in their homes for many years.

LEARNING OBJECTIVES

After completing this chapter, you should have an understanding of:

- Where, how, and why older adults age in place
- Home modification programs that allow people with functional decline to adapt to their environments
- Innovative models that allow for long-term care to be delivered in the home through shared housing, and through shared community experiences
- Public program and service options in housing that contribute to the long-term care continuum and are alternatives to assisted living and skilled nursing facilities
- Zoning, neighborhood design, and housing design that provide an aging-friendly built environment

KEY TERMS

Accessory dwelling units (ADUs)
Aging in place
Attachment to place
Elder-friendly communities
Home modifications
Intentional community
Naturally occurring retirement communities (NORCs)
Reverse mortgage
Smart growth
Universal design
Village model
Visitability

INTRODUCTION

Housing is an integral component in the development of a comprehensive, community-based long-term care system. The home environment plays an integral role in the maintenance and improvement of older adults' daily functioning (Wahl, Fänge, Oswald, Gitlin, & Iwarsson, 2009) and the management of chronic care and rehabilitation. The independent living environment is the cornerstone on which the continuum of long-term care is built, with community-based services existing to keep people living in their homes as long as possible. Long-term care is delivered to most Americans in their own homes or apartment units as they age in place with the support of informal caregiving, home health, rehabilitation, hospice, and other community-based services such as nutrition programs, social services, and transportation.

THE NEED FOR LONG-TERM CARE IN THE HOME

The need for community-based long-term care can occur suddenly in response to an acute medical condition or a traumatic event. More common, it occurs in response to an older adult's gradual decline in cognitive and/or physical functioning. In some instances, long-term care in the home occurs after a discharge following acute care in a hospital or emergency room or in a nursing home following a serious health care incident such as an accidental fall, stroke, or heart attack.

Such conditions require assistance with activities of daily living (ADLs) and independent activities of daily living (IADLs) as well as accompanying modifications to the environment that support self-care, social engagement, and caregiving assistance from others. Both services and home modifications respond to the strong preference of persons with disabilities of all ages to live in independent housing in the community rather than in other settings such as an assisted living facility or nursing home. **Aging in place** refers to both the preference and the phenomenon of older adults living in their own homes for as long as possible, without relocating to a retirement community, assisted living facility, or nursing home. For older persons, in particular, the longing to age in place reflects a strong desire to keep living in familiar homes and communities, often in proximity to immediate and extended family and friends. In some instances, modifying housing to allow for aging in place may be a one-time event, but more likely for those with chronic diseases such as arthritis, multiple sclerosis, Parkinson's, or Alzheimer's, it is an intermittent or continuous process over a period of years during which the environment and individual lifestyle are adapted to changing needs.

Whether older adults suffer from fall-related injuries, cognitive decline, and/or chronic health problems and diseases, the issue of how long or whether they can age in place is a complex one. Finding the balance between older adults' right to self-determination and realistic assessment of their ability to safely age in place is a dilemma in the provision of community-based long-term care and in senior housing policy, as portrayed in Figure 9.1. Practitioners and policy makers must weigh that balance as they seek to provide an appropriate continuum of care.

Policy makers influence the balance not only when they authorize and legislate programs, but also when they appropriate and reappropriate funds. For example, if the federal government and the states reduce Medicaid spending for in-home support programs aimed to prevent unnecessary institutionalization, older adults with functional disabilities might lose their ability to live in their own homes and be forced into other settings such as skilled nursing facilities. By default, policy may deem them unable to live at home because of the lack of available resources allocated on their behalf. Apart from policy that pits rights to self-determination against realistic assessments of functional abilities, the role of housing in the long-term care continuum depends on residents' psychological, functional, and financial attributes and resources, the physical condition of the home and neighborhoods in which older people live, and the availability of alternative living settings.

FIGURE 9.1 Creating a supportive housing environment in which an older person can age in place with community-based long-term care can be a balancing act.

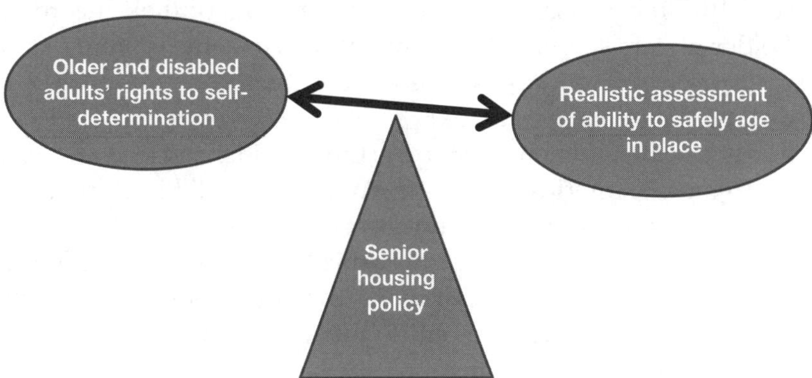

AGING IN PLACE

WHERE DO OLDER PEOPLE LIVE?

Americans prefer to age in place in their lifelong homes rather than relocating to assisted living or skilled nursing institutions. Indeed, very small numbers of older people actually relocate each year. Census data indicates that 99% of older people live in the same house as they did one year prior. Those who move do not relocate very far—usually within the same county (American Housing Survey, 2011, Table C-08-A0). Despite the common perception that older people often move into an "old folks home" to live out their final years, the vast majority of older adults stay living at home, even when long-term care is necessary, because of psychological attachments, financial considerations, and fear of institutionalization. This pattern is reflected in high rates of home ownership among older adults; almost 74% of housing units occupied by older adults are owned (American Community Survey, 2011, Tables C-01-00 and C-01-A0). By the year 2030, 34 million homeowners will be aged 65+, with more than 4 million aged 85+ (Pendall et al. 2012).

In order to understand how older person's housing can support them in the long-term care continuum, it is important to understand their housing profiles. Living in rental or owned housing, residing alone, having disabilities, or living in housing that has been adapted with supportive features are all characteristics that can affect the ability to age in place and obtain long-term care provision at home. In addition, the geographical locations in which older adults live, and their access to supportive services, shape the challenges they face and the opportunities for accessing community-based long-term care available to them.

OWNERS OR RENTERS

Large differences exist between older homeowners' and older renters' housing. The disparities influence Americans' resources, options, and need for community-based long-term care. More than 21 million housing units are occupied by homeowners age 65+. Less than 8 million housing units are occupied by older renters who pay a median rent of $671 per month (American Housing Survey, 2011, Table C-01-RO). Most older renters live in rental units that do not meet housing policy standards for affordability (American Housing Survey, 2011, Table C-10-R0) because they spend 30% or more of their income on rent. A third of older renters spend half or more of their income on rent, leaving few resources left to pay for other basic necessities, including supportive services that could allow them to age in place.

Two thirds of older homeowners own their residences free and clear with no home mortgages (American Housing Survey, 2011, Table C-10-00). The one third of older homeowners who do not own their homes free and clear pay a median of $643 per month on mortgage costs (American Housing Survey, 2011, Table C-10-00). Thirty-four percent of older homeowners who have mortgages pay more than one third of their monthly income on mortgage costs, and 18% spend more than half of their income.

WHERE DO OLDER PEOPLE LIVE AND WITH WHOM?

The locations where older people live influence their access to long-term care services and affect their ability to safely age in place. Nearly 16 million older households live in single family, detached homes (American Housing Survey, 2009, Table 2-1), which in low-density areas, such as suburbs, may make it difficult to access services. However, more than one million older-renter households are in buildings with 50 or more rental units (American Housing Survey, 2009, Table 4-1), where proximity to other older adults and economies of scale could be an advantage in accessing long-term care services.

Most older people live in suburbs. Depending on their design and planning, many of these areas can negatively affect their ability to access transportation, local services, and age in place. Figure 9.2 shows where older people live. Nearly an equal number of older households reside in central cities and rural areas; they face different issues in accessing community-based long-term care.

Twenty percent of all older people in America are women who live alone. In all, nearly 11 million older adults live alone; more than 75% of whom are women. More than 7 million older homeowners live alone (American Housing Survey, 2011, Table C-08-A0). Older adults who live alone may have greater needs than their cohabiting peers in accessing the community-based long-term care services continuum. Those in single-family homes may be especially isolated

FIGURE 9.2 Where older adults live.

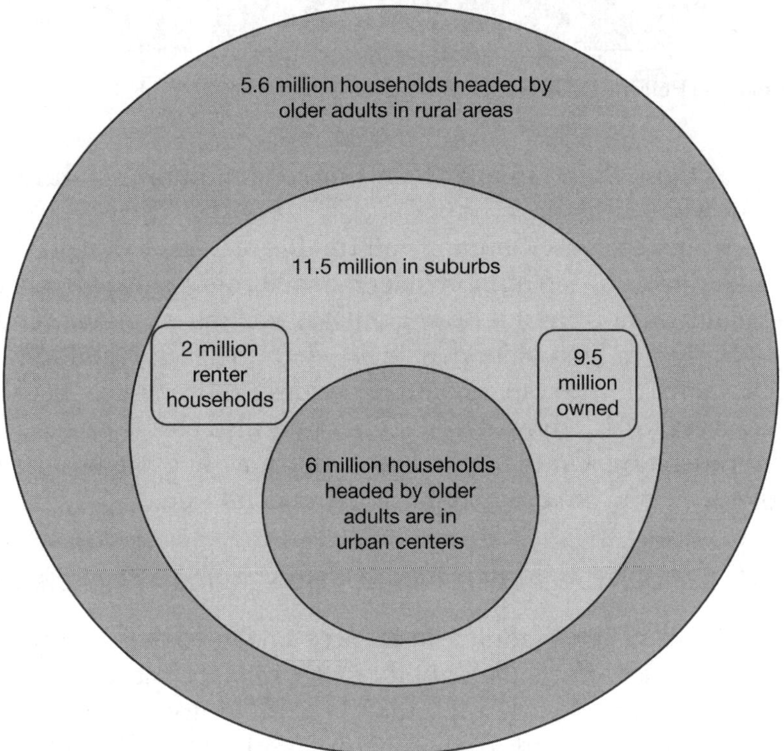

Source: American Community Survey (2009, Table 2-1).

FIGURE 9.3 Older adults living alone.

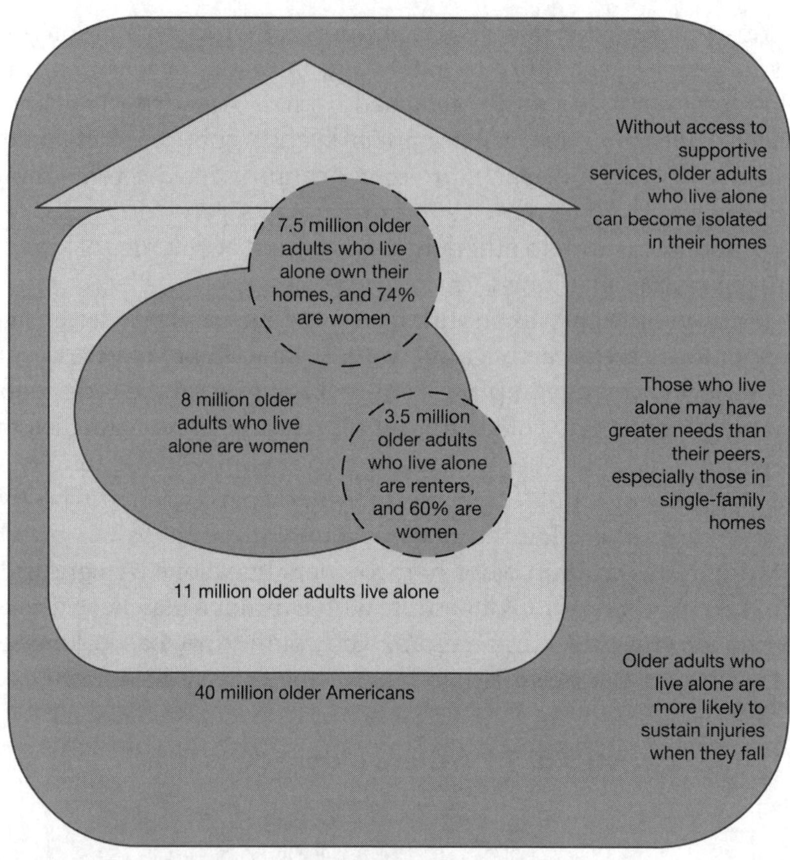

Source: American Housing Survey (2011, Table C-08-A0).

compared to those living in apartments or condominiums. Figure 9.3 depicts older adults who live alone.

Spouses are the most common informal caregivers for older adults with functional limitations. Ten million older married couples live together and have the potential benefit of mutual caregiving as well as emotional and financial support. Nearly 3 million older people live with their adult children, and more than 3.5 million live with other relatives besides children or spouses (American Housing Survey, 2011, Table C-08-A0). They may also be advantaged in terms of obtaining caregiving. On the other hand, they may find themselves in the role of caregivers, even to the extent of raising grandchildren.

DISABILITY, RESIDENTIAL ACCESSIBILITY, AND SERVICE AVAILABILITY

The accessibility of older adults' residences in the context of their changing physical capabilities affects their ability to age in place and utilize community-based long-term care. Nearly nine million community-dwelling older people report disabilities; two thirds of those with disabilities live in settings in which the housing environment may negatively impact their lives (American Housing

Survey, 2009, Table 2-9). For example, 3 million report disabilities that reduce the ability to leave the house, and 1.5 million have self-care disabilities. Nine million older homeowner households report that they need to use steps to enter their single-family house from outside (American Housing Survey, 2009, Table 3-7) as do 1.5 million older renter households in multiunit buildings. Another 750,000 in detached rental houses must navigate steps to access their home (American Housing Survey, 2009, Table 4-1). Such accessibility problems are significant, as nearly 40% of older people report problems going up and down stairs, making accessing their homes difficult and putting them at risk of injurious falls.

Organized long-term care services are available to some older people who live in rental housing, especially those who reside in government-subsidized rental housing, described later in this chapter. More than 800,000 households report that IADL assistance services are available to them, with more than half a million having access to transportation and meal services. Nearly 500,000 older households have housekeeping available to them, 370,000 can access shopping assistance, and 200,000 have access to financial management help and telephone assistance (American Housing Survey, 2009, Table 4-7). In addition, 200,000 to 300,000 renter households indicate that they have ADL assistance available to them in their rental units (American Housing Survey, 2009, Table 4-7).

ATTACHMENT TO PLACE

In addition to the economic investments that the majority of older people have made in their homes, a major reason that older adults desire to age in place is because of their psychological attachment to their homes and the communities in which they live. **Attachment to place** is indicated by the large percentage of older persons who have stayed in their homes for long periods of time. It is at the core of people's housing preferences and a significant influence on their views about long-term care.

Attachment to place even extends to the end of life, as many older people prefer to die in place in their own homes. Studies in Asia, Europe, and North America indicate that, across the globe, patients prefer to die at home (Beccaro et al., 2006; Brazil, Howell, Bedard, Krueger, & Heidebrecht, 2005; Tang & McCorkle, 2003; Tang, Liu, Lai, & McCorkle, 2005). Most terminal patients want to die at home so that during their final days they live in a familiar setting with the presence of family caregivers. For some older adults, attachment to home is intensified because this is the place where loved ones have also died (Shenk, Kuwahara, & Zablotsky, 2004). Both socioemotional meaning and number of years of residence in one place can contribute to residents' attachment and desire to live out their lives in their own homes.

Over the life course, specific landscapes, cities, neighborhoods, houses, and rooms form the foundation for personal stories and identities. For people who have lived in the same home for long periods of time, the home itself can have strong personal importance, cultural significance, and even spiritual meaning (Cooper Marcus, 2006; Golant, 2003; Rowles & Watkins, 2003). The home is often the place where older adults have raised their own families and represents ties to the wider neighborhood and community. For many, the house is much more than a physical structure; it is a Jungian metaphor—a mirror of one's ego (Cooper Marcus, 2006; Rowles, 2008).

Over 110,000 older Americans have occupied the same house for 70 or more years. Although 84% of them own their home, 16% of those who have lived in the same place for 70 years are renters. Another 308,000 have lived in the same house for 60 years, nearly 1.5 million have lived in their house for 50 years, and 2.9 million older homeowners have lived in the same place for 40 years (American Housing Survey, 2009, Table 2-9). Homes that have been passed down through generations may have especially significant meaning within extended families. Furthermore, in America's diverse cultures, place attachment may have even more long-lasting and significant meaning such as that of an ancestral or spiritual home.

Understanding attachment to place provides an important explanation for older adults' motivation for aging in place (Rowles & Bernard, 2013). It is important for long-term care and aging-industry professionals to convey the power of place attachment to policy makers and other professionals, such as health care workers or public safety workers, so that they understand older adults' behaviors and motivations for staying in their homes. Lack of awareness of older adults' reasons for staying put can lead to ageism and the belief that older people are too set in their ways and unable to accept change. These misunderstandings arise not only in chronic care situations and evaluations of a housing unit's physical adequacy, but also in emergency scenarios, such as weather-related events or natural disasters, in which older adults may be reluctant to evacuate their homes.

LAWS THAT FACILITATE COMMUNITY-BASED LONG-TERM CARE AND SUPPORT AGING IN PLACE

FEDERAL LAW

Disabled and older adults' right to age in place and live in the community is sanctioned by federal law. Exhibit 9.1 shows Federal Programs and Laws Benefitting Older Adults Housed in Their Own Communities. In 1999, the Supreme Court ruled in the *Olmstead v. L.C.* (United States Department of Justice Civil Rights Division, n.d.) decision, that states must administer programs and services to disabled persons, including older adults in the "most integrated setting appropriate" to their needs. This ruling came in response to a lawsuit by two disabled persons against the state of Georgia, which had forced them to live in institutions despite their preferences to live in the community (Pynoos, Nishita, Cicero, & Caraviello, 2008). The *Olmstead* decision is the impetus for several recent community-based long-term care service programs created by the federal government, such as "Money Follows the Person" and "Assisted Living Waivers," which will be described later in this chapter.

The Fair Housing Amendments Act (FHAA) of 1988, which is essentially a residential counterpart to the Americans with Disabilities Act of 1990 (ADA), requires landlords of existing multiunit buildings of four or more units to make "reasonable" modifications to public spaces, including entryways, if requested by residents who have disabilities. The term "reasonable" modification is subject to interpretation, as the FHAA has its roots in civil rights legislation with the courts interpreting it in terms of costs. The FHAA does not require that landlords pay for adaptations in individual units but does allow tenants to make modifications, subject to the provision that the tenant may have to remove them when he or she leaves if the landlord makes such a request (Pynoos et al., 2008). In addition, the FHAA requires new multiunit residential buildings to provide

EXHIBIT 9.1 Federal Programs and Laws Benefitting Older Adults Housed in Their Own Communities

NAME OF PROGRAM	DESCRIPTION	QUALIFICATIONS
Public and Assisted Housing	Rental units financed by the U.S. Department of Housing and Urban Development (HUD). Families or individuals pay no more than 30% of their income in rent.	Low-income families or individuals of all ages
Section 8 Certificates/ Vouchers	Provides a voucher that family or individual can take to approved apartment of their choosing. Covers the difference in rent above 30% household income and market value.	Low-income families or individuals of all ages
Section 202	Provides developers with funding for construction. Provides rental units and may provide income-supportive services, such as meals and transportation, and access to other federal service programs.	Developer benefitting from 202 program must provide rentals to very low-income older adults and disabled adults.
Congregate Housing Services Program	Provides independent older adults in 202 units and public housing with services, including meals and transportation.	Very low-income older adults with ADL limitations
HOPE	Combines Section 8 rental assistance with case management and supportive services.	Low-income older adults with ADL limitations
Service Coordinator Program	Links older adults in Section 202 or public housing with services.	Very low-income older adults
Naturally Occurring Retirement Community Services Program	Provides supportive services, health promotion.	Residents of qualified NORCS

(*continued*)

EXHIBIT 9.1 Federal Programs and Laws Benefitting Older Adults Housed in Their Own Communities (*continued*)

NAME OF PROGRAM	DESCRIPTION	QUALIFICATIONS
Programs of All-Inclusive Care for the Elderly (PACE)	Provides meals and supportive services.	Medicare and Medicaid residents age 55+ at risk of institutionalization
Money Follows the Person	Provides medical and social services.	Medicaid recipients who were institutionalized but desire to move back into community
Assisted Living Waivers	Provides medical and social services.	Medicaid recipients at risk of institutionalization
Medicare Medical Home Program	Provides physician house calls.	Medicare recipients, only available in some states
Low-Income Housing Tax Credits (LIHTC)	Provides developers with incentives for building low-income housing for families and seniors.	A developer benefitting from an LIHTC must in turn provide subsidized rental units to tenants.
Fair Housing Amendments Act of 1988	Requires landlords of multiunit buildings to make reasonable modifications for disabled tenants.	Applies to buildings with more than four units.
Olmstead v. L.C. 1999 Supreme Court Ruling	Requires states to administer programs and services to disabled persons in "most integrated setting appropriate" to need.	Resulting from original lawsuit in Georgia in which disabled adults were forced into institutionalization

basic accessibility features in public spaces and residential units (the ADA covers employment, public accommodations and entities, and telecommunications).

LOCAL ORDINANCES

The FHAA is an important law that supports renters in apartment buildings; however, most Americans live in single-family residences. In lieu of federal legislation, state and local laws and regulations have been created to facilitate aging in place in single-family homes, as described in Exhibit 9.2. For example, some states stipulate that their local governments allow for the development

EXHIBIT 9.2 Local Ordinances and Design Facilitating Housing Supportive of Community-Based Long-Term Care

NAME OF PROGRAM	DESCRIPTION	IMPLICATIONS
Accessory Dwelling Units and Flexibility in Land Use and Zoning	Zoning that allows second units to be developed on single-family lots or shared communal spaces between existing lots.	An elder can have a caregiver or other family members living in proximity. Or, a group of elders can choose to live in proximity, forming an intentional community.
Conditions, Covenants, and Restrictions and Homeowners Association Allowances	Flexible allowances for interior and exterior home modifications	Restrictive communities that prohibit ramps, handrails, lighting, and other home modifications can hinder ability to age in place.
Visitability and Universal Design Ordinances	Ordinances that suggest, recommend, or require developers and designers use elder-friendly design in construction and renovations	Encouraging designers to use universal design and visitability can provide an elder-friendly environment.
Smart Growth/Elder-Friendly Community	Urban design with mixed land uses that combine transportation, commercial, and residential uses	Design that allows residents to walk to services and utilize public transport instead of dependence on cars

of second units on singlefamily home properties. Cities and counties can allow for flexible zoning and housing density bonuses, whereby they permit the legal habitation and construction of second units. These small housing units, also known as granny flats, mother-in-law units, guest houses, and **accessory dwelling units (ADUs)** are important parts of the continuum of care (Cicero & Pynoos, 2008). Residents in need of supportive care can live either in the main house or an ADU, next to their caregivers, who can help provide them with needed long-term care services. Additionally, older homeowners could rent out such units in order to supplement their income and use it for purposes such as paying for in-home care (see Case Study 9.1; Liebig & Cicero, 2008).

Other governing regulations that can affect residents' ability to age in place in their single-family homes include homeowner association (HOA) covenants, conditions, and restrictions (CC&Rs). CC&Rs are regulations established by HOAs that stipulate design features that residents are allowed to include in their home. For example, some HOAs may not allow wheelchair ramps on the front of a home or alterations to the structure of the physical environment such as interior ramps, elevator-type lifts, or stair modifications.

Case Study 9.1: Spotlight on Aging in Place

Mr. and Mrs. Carney have owned their suburban, one story, three-bedroom, two-bath ranch style home for 50 years. Mr. Carney, age 80, has Parkinson's disease and walks with a shuffling gait. A retired government worker, he leaves the house rarely, but when he goes out for appointments, he has to enter the house through the back door, where there is a slight incline leading to the driveway where they park, instead of through the front door where there are a few steps. Mrs. Carney, age 78, has been caregiving for many years. Recently, Mrs. Carney fell, broke her pelvic bone, and was hospitalized for several weeks before being discharged to a rehabilitative facility. Mr. and Mrs. Carney's adult children, who live out of town, hired a full-time caregiver for their father.

Mrs. Carney is now home from rehabilitation and wants to make her house more suitable for herself and her husband. The discharge planner gave her a big packet of materials, but she cannot sort it all out. Their hired caregiver has been sleeping in an extra bedroom. Mrs. Carney would like to find a student from the nearby university to live in their other extra bedroom at the back of their house. She figures that he or she can help around the house in exchange for a reduced rent. The room she wants to rent has its own entrance so the student could come and go as he or she pleases, but the bathroom is down the hall in the main part of the house. She would like to install an extra door to shut off the hallway and create a private suite or wing for her boarder that would include a bathroom and bedroom, but she is not sure she should spend any savings to make that change. She is also not sure she wants to share the other bathroom with their hired caregiver.

Mrs. Carney goes online regularly and orders food to be delivered from the local "mom and pop" grocery store, but the store is going out of business soon. She asks her local church to send someone to talk to her, as she has not been able to drive herself to church since being discharged back to her home. She figures that once she recovers, she will drive herself to do the shopping.

Mrs. Carney's mind is sharp, and she has always been a great idea person, having started several small businesses when she was younger and raising her kids. Because several of her widowed friends live nearby in houses that are too big for them to take care of, she poses the idea to her minister that several older parishioners should move in together and share resources. Because her house has only one story, she wonders if adapting it would be more feasible than her friends' houses, or if the city would allow them to share housing. She is not even sure how to start this process, as she knows city regulations can be tough. Years ago, Mr. and Mrs. Carney illegally converted their garage into an office, and she doesn't want to raise eyebrows or get in trouble.

(*continued*)

Case Study 9.1: Spotlight on Aging in Place (*continued*)

Case Study Discussion Questions:

1. Why don't Mr. and Mrs. Carney move to a nursing home?
2. What would you do if Mr. and Mrs. Carney were your grandparents?
3. What would happen to Mrs. Carney if Mr. Carney dies?
4. What would happen to Mr. Carney if Mrs. Carney dies?
5. What design concepts and features would make Mr. and Mrs. Carney's home more livable?
6. What resources are available to Mr. and Mrs. Carney that would allow them to live safely in their home right now?
7. What resources will help them in the future?

HOME MODIFICATIONS THAT ALLOW FOR AGING IN PLACE AND LONG-TERM CARE IN THE HOME

Home modifications are physical adaptations to home environments in areas such as entryways, kitchens, bathrooms, and stairwells that can make it safer and easier to perform tasks and carry out ADLs. Home modifications can be simple, inexpensive changes or more expensive adaptations. Examples include repairs, such as fixing loose stairs, removing hazards such as clutter, exposed electrical cords and throw rugs; adding special features or assistive devices such as grab bars; rearranging furniture to facilitate easier negotiation of residential space; and renovations such as installing a barrier free shower or an elevator. As their physical capabilities change, people generally adapt their behaviors to the environment. These behavior changes also can facilitate aging in place such as adjusting where activities occur (e.g., sleeping near an accessible bathroom or on the ground floor instead of on the second floor).

WHY DOESN'T EVERYONE HAVE HOME MODIFICATIONS?

Home modifications are important to the ability of chronically ill or disabled residents to live independently. Many older people who could benefit from home modifications do not have them, owing to the choices they make, lack of skilled providers, and affordability. For example, some residents exercise their right to self-determination and simply do not want to alter their homes. Their attachment to place and identification of its features with their own lifestyle or even lost loved ones may make them reluctant to make changes (Shenk et al., 2004). In other cases, older people fear that modifying their home is an acknowledgment that they are losing their independence, and by admitting the need for support, they will subsequently end up in a nursing facility. Ironically and paradoxically, without home modifications many people put themselves at greater risk of accidents or relocation.

Costs and implementation are barriers to home modification. Some modifications may be unaffordable, and finding reliable contractors or remodelers to install them can be problematic (AARP, 2003). Because they are generally not covered by standard health insurance or Medicare, most residents pay for home modifications themselves. Simple changes that residents can make by themselves to improve safety and maximize their independence at home include adding night lights and nonslip surfaces in bathrooms or on steps, removing throw rugs, taping down carpets, and increasing the brightness of lighting throughout the house. Changing faucets and door knobs (AARP, 2003), installing light switches, handrails, grab bars, and ramps, and mounting new light fixtures may require hiring a handyman, a remodeler, an electrician, or a contractor. The cost of some of these features combined with the need to find and hire a building professional can prevent older people from making needed adaptations. Moreover, many professionals and older residents are simply not well informed about potential hazards and possible mitigating features in the home environment. Instructing older persons as well as their health care providers is critical, as is informing residents and housing staff alike.

EXAMPLES OF HOME MODIFICATION PROGRAMS

Even though the cost of home modifications may deter people from installing them, with appropriate installation and in conjunction with guidance on how to use them properly as a strategy in independent living, they have been demonstrated to play an effective role in delaying or preventing institutionalization and reducing the risk of injuries (Gitlin, 2003, Gitlin et al., 2006; Lord, Menz, & Sherrington, 2006). Accordingly, there are programs that pay for home modification and employ them as an overall strategy of community care. For example, in Pennsylvania, a Medicare HMO, Health Partners Medicare Silver Plan, offers a Home Safety benefit that covers up to $1,500 in home safety modifications for eligible recipients who have signed their Medicare over to the HMO. Many local governments have used Older Americans Act (OAA) funds along with a U.S. Department of Housing and Urban Development (HUD) Community Development Block Grant (CDBG) to pay for repairs and home modifications for low-income residents.

The Home Secure Program of the City of Los Angeles, funded through the city's Department of Aging, pays for the installation of grab bars, handheld showers, night lights, and nonslip surfaces for older and disabled low-income residents who qualify. Residents apply through local senior or independent living centers, and typically, a case manager refers them to the program. Similarly, the Philadelphia Corporation on Aging (PCA), a private nonprofit organization, operates a Senior Housing Assistance Repair Program (SHARP) that can make repairs such as fixing a roof and modifying older adults' homes, including stair railings, entryways, and bathrooms. PCA is able to integrate SHARP with its Home- and Community-Based Aging Services Waiver for individuals age 60 and older and to provide low-income skilled nursing facility (SNF)–eligible residents with in-home supports and services. Also, in the OPTIONS program, older residents whose income is not low enough to qualify for the waiver program pay for services, such as transportation, home-delivered means, in-home care, and telephone monitoring, on a sliding scale (www.pcacares.org). Unfortunately, such care management programs serve a limited number of people and many communities do not offer home modifications on their menu of services. In order to fill this gap, some communities piece together funds from the OAA, CDBG, Medicaid Waivers, and the Department of Energy. For older people who are unlikely to qualify or seek out publicly funded programs or live in places where programs are unavailable, cities, can nonetheless encourage them to install supportive features in the home to allow for aging in place. An increasing number of cities, along with religious institutions and community colleges, have made an effort to spread the word—beyond senior center and parks and recreation programs—about the need for home modifications and a more accessible, supportive housing stock.

PREVENTING FALLS WITH HOME MODIFICATIONS

One third of older adults fall each year, and most falls occur inside or near the home. Especially among adults over age 80, falls can result in serious injuries—including hip fractures and brain injuries. Often, injurious falls lead to a need for long-term care. Falls are expensive. By 2020, the direct costs of falls among older adults are expected to reach $55 billion (Stevens, Corso, Finkelstein, & Miller, 2006). Even though strategies are complicated, there is increasing evidence that the risk of falls can be reduced through multifactorial approaches that include medication management, strength training, balance training, vision assessment, and home modification. A recent study found that, among the five methods of fall prevention, home modifications provided the best cost value (Frick, Kung, Parrish, & Narrett, 2010).

Home modifications are an important component of a discharge plan for persons who have been hospitalized for falling. In the Los Angeles region, for example, although 46% of older adults hospitalized after falling were discharged to an SNF following an acute hospital stay in 2006, 37% were discharged home (OSHPD, 2006). There has been a trend toward increased discharges to homes and fewer to SNFs: in 2000, 49% were discharged to an SNF, whereas 34% were discharged home (OSHPD, 2000). People hospitalized for fall-related injuries are at high risk of falling again, and home modifications can reduce potential hazards.

AGING IN PLACE IS NOT FOR EVERYONE

Aging in place is the most prevalent way people grow old in America. However, it is often idealized beyond sound logic (Golant, 2008; Thomas, 2004). Considerations that can affect the ability to age in place include realistic assessments of older adults' physical abilities to safely age in place given the condition of their home and the community where they live. Nearly one million older adult households report moderate to severe deficiencies in their kitchens, plumbing, heating, and electrical systems (American Housing Survey, 2009, Table 2-7). The lowest income older and disabled residents are the most vulnerable to living in inferior housing stock and inhospitable neighborhoods (Golant, 2008). When such substandard conditions cannot be rectified through repair, the home cannot as easily incorporate home modifications, or a resident's functional disabilities cannot be adapted to the home environment, other options must be considered.

If the home environment is not suitable, aging in the same home for 50 or 70 years may be infeasible. Experts in place attachment suggest that when older adults are no longer able to age in place and must transfer to an alternative setting, long-term care workers and housing professionals can ease the transition by validating feelings about the loss of one's home and encouraging people to bring with them personal belongings that trigger memories and symbolize past relationships (Golant, 2003; Oswald & Rowles, 2007). An increasingly acknowledged and difficult part of this process is the need to give up belongings in order to move to a smaller space, a process of breaking up a home that can be highly stressful (Ekerdt, Sergeant, Dingel, & Bowen, 2004). Recognizing and validating the strength of attachment to place assists when residential transitions are necessary, whether older people are selling their house and moving to a smaller apartment nearby, moving in with a relative, or relocating to a long-term care facility.

PROGRAMS AND SERVICES THAT CREATE SUPPORTIVE HOUSING

"AGING IN COMMUNITY" AND THE VILLAGE MODEL

Intentional Communities

Two growing trends in housing that support people with differing levels of service needs without institutionalization are the Aging in Community movement and the Village Model. The Aging in Community movement is based on the proposition that Americans must get past the idealization of the private home and the individualization and potential isolation that it supports (Thomas, 2004). Therefore, older adults and/or disabled adults should be able to live in an **intentional community** as an alternative to aging in place in their lifelong home. In an intentional community, residents commit to living together with a shared common purpose or goal. Although older adults may have to relocate from their homes in these models, they can remain in their own communities, accessing familiar services, maintaining meaningful relationships, and maximizing their financial resources. Intentional communities that provide for supportive aging include cohousing and shared housing. One form of such a community is the Green House, which can provide an independent, shared housing experience for older people, or a more supportive version can replace a traditional nursing facility while providing long-term care in a homelike environment (Thomas, 2004). Seeking to change the culture of long-term care, visionary geriatrician Dr. William Thomas developed the model for the Green House. There are now 150 across the country with an equal number in development. St. Martin in the Pines in Alabama is one Green House created under the model.

The **Village Model** offers an approach to aging in place that allows for communal experience, resource sharing, and care provision without physical relocation. The flagship community for the Village Model is Beacon Hill Village in Boston. Started in 2001, it has been replicated in at least 50 American cities. Older adults join the village for a small fee (approximately $400 to $800 per year). This option provides members with information and referral to a network of vetted services intended to support their ability to stay in the community. Beacon Hill Village addresses three main areas of need: community building through social activities; transportation; and member services, including information and referral to providers such as remodelers, handy workers, and home health professionals (McWhinney-Morse, 2009). A Village is similar to living in an independent living retirement community without walls—the benefits are included without the relocation.

NORCs AND SERVICE CLUSTERING

Clustering services in areas with high concentrations of older people is a strategy to capitalize on economies of scale and more easily coordinate otherwise fragmented services so that older persons can age in place. **Naturally occurring retirement communities** are neighborhoods where high concentrations of older people have moved or have aged in place, but they were not planned as retirement communities. An NORC could be in an urban high-rise condominium complex, a low-income apartment building, a suburban village of townhomes, or an exurban single-family neighborhood—anywhere that people have aged in place and/or other older people have decided to move due to proximity to services they desire.

Although NORCs originally sprung up in communities without intentional planning or oversight, today the federal government and local service providers acknowledge their efficacy as a community-based long-term care model. Because of the concentration of older people with similar needs, the provision of services in an NORC setting provides economies of scale. Therefore, an NORC program can provide the services of the Village Model and can often be focused in a specific, smaller, geographic locale, creating a village unto itself that offers social services and health care. The NORC model builds community by empowering adults, fostering personal connections, and maximizing health. Features include nursing and social services, community engagement, socialization, education, recreation, and medical diagnosis, treatment, and disease management (Enguidanos, Pynoos, Denton, Alexman, & Diepenbrock, 2010; Vladeck, Segel, Oberlink, Gursen, & Rudin, 2010).

The first NORC program began in an affordable-housing complex in New York City in 1986. Today, the federal Administration on Aging recognizes NORC programs in over 25 states (www.norcblueprint.org; Vladeck et al., 2010). Both public and private funding are used to operate the programs. In the State of New York, there are 54 service-enriched NORCs, including 34 NORC service programs funded by New York City located in large and small public and private housing complexes that contain single-family homes and garden apartments. Ten are located in New York's public housing developments (Vladeck et al., 2010).

PUBLIC PROGRAMS THAT LINK SERVICES TO HOUSING

SUBSIDIZED RENTAL HOUSING

The federal HUD supports a variety of housing programs that support older persons, including Section 202 housing and public housing, both are for qualified low-income older adults and for disabled persons. There are more than 20,000 government-assisted apartment buildings housing over 1 million older and disabled renters across the United States. In most cases, private and nonprofit developers, including community-development corporations, faith-based groups, and social service agencies, utilize HUD funding to build low-income senior and disabled housing, coordinating funding, such as Section 202, low-income housing tax credits, state redevelopment funds, and private grants.

Public funding sources stipulate that rental apartments be provided for low-income older adults for a specified number of years, usually 30 to 40. In some cases, these affordability restrictions are expiring, and private developers are allowed to convert these units to market-rate apartments and/or condominiums, displacing long-time low-income residents. For the 67% of older renters who spend more than a third of their income on rent (American Housing Survey, 2009, Table 4-13), the supply of 202 units and other affordable apartments is far below the need. Low-income units for older people have long waiting lists, especially in the nation's major cities. HUD estimates that more than 365,000 of the older and disabled residents in their buildings are frail. In order to provide service-enriched housing that will help subsidized-housing residents to avoid institutionalization, HUD funds the Service Coordinator Program. Owners of HUD-subsidized housing apply to fund service coordinators who help arrange for ADL assistance, monitor services, educate residents about resources, and build social support networks among residents' family and friends (www.hud.gov).

There are residents of public housing who move into their units as younger adults and age in place over decades. Similarly, a Section 202 resident could move into a building and live there for 30 to 40 years. Although public and Section 202 housing programs are tied to the specific building, the HUD Section 8 voucher program allows residents to live in a broader range of housing settings. In cities that take advantage of the program, low-income residents apply for a voucher, and once granted, they can use it at an approved rental unit. The resident pays one third of his or her income in rent, and the voucher pays the difference between the market rate and one third of the recipient's income. The advantage of a Section 8 voucher is personal choice. Low-income older adults can use it at a building of their choice, subject to the stipulation that the rental units meet HUD's criteria in terms of condition and cost.

SERVICE LINKAGES

In order to access community-based long-term care and avoid moving to an SNF, retirement community, or assisted living facility, residents in subsidized apartment buildings often utilize other publicly funded service programs, including

OAA-funded case management—typically through a senior center; transportation; home-delivered meals and nutrition; in-home supportive services or other in-home aides; and Medicaid Home and Community-Based Services long-term care waiver case management programs, whose goals are to provide long-term care services in the home and avoid institutionalization (Exhibits 9.1 and 9.3). Individual states and local Area Agencies on Aging (AAAs) determine how to utilize funds and implement these programs to meet their populations' needs. Serving low-income people who live in market-rate apartments and privately owned homes as well as subsidized housing, these community-based programs allow older adults to age in place and are consistent with the *Olmstead* decision of 1999. Case managers who work in community-based long-term care programs are typically social workers and professionals trained in gerontology. They provide helpful services to older adults and their caregiving family members, easing a burden on both. Such assistance for caregiving family members can help reduce their stress and number of hours they might need to take off from work, school, or caring for their own children to help their aging parent or relative.

ALTERNATIVES TO INSTITUTIONALIZATION

Institutionalized Medicaid beneficiaries who desire to integrate back into community living can access the Centers for Medicare and Medicaid Services (CMS) federal Money Follows the Person Program (MFPP). MFPP provides medical and rehabilitation services, home health, transportation, emergency response, and case management. For older adults whose family members still have

EXHIBIT 9.3 Programs and Services that Create or Link with Supportive Housing

	INCOME ELIGIBILITY	GOVERNMENT OPERATED	FOR RENTERS	FOR OWNERS
Assisted Living Waivers	X	X	X	
HUD Service Coordinator	X	X	X	
Intentional Communities			X	X
Medicaid Waiver	X	X	X	
Medicare Medical		X	X	X
Money Follows the Person	X	X	X	X
NORCs			X	X
PACE	X	X	X	X
Village Model			X	X

Note: Income eligibility requires that residents be low or very low income. Definitions of those categories depend on the state and county in which the resident and housing is located.

maintained their homes, this process may be more feasible than for those who require placement in a subsidized rental apartment.

CMS-funded Assisted Living Waivers (ALW) are another approach through which community-based long-term care services can be provided in publicly subsidized housing, thereby avoiding institutional care. ALW program eligibility includes functional status that would otherwise require nursing home care, as well as Medicaid eligibility. Recipients have access to assisted care services provided by a home health agency, care coordination, environmental accessibility adaptations, and nursing facility transition care coordination to help move residents out of nursing homes (California Department of Health Care Services, 2007).

The Medicare Medical Home program, an additional federally funded innovative health care program that allows older adults to age in place, has been tested in a few states, and is being implemented more widely. This program is based on the old-fashioned idea of doctors' house calls, in which the primary care physician visits older adults in their homes, thereby reducing emergency room and hospital visits. Such visits also allow the doctor to better understand the circumstances in which people actually live, with the possibility of making recommendations for home modifications.

The Programs of All-Inclusive Care for the Elderly is a benefit provided under both Medicare and Medicaid for residents who are age 55+ and are at risk of institutionalization. A team of physicians, nurses, and other health professionals provide long-term care, usually in an adult day center or at home or, less often, in an in-patient facility during daytime hours. Participation in the program allows community-dwelling older adults to age in place while accessing meals, primary care, social services, restorative therapy, personal supportive care, and nutritional counseling (www.medicare.gov). Having a home environment with supportive home modifications is an important component of making PACE a successful community-based long-term care option. In addition, a number of PACE programs have found it advantageous to develop associated subsidized senior housing near the core service site to assist older frail persons who need more supervision and services than can be delivered to their own home or apartment.

There are three main reasons why the Medicare and Medicaid programs provide community-based long-term care in the home. The Supreme Court's *Olmstead* decision requires states to provide home-based living if residents prefer it. CMS programs have been found to be cost-effective (Doty, 2000) based on studies that have found that the provision of in-home care and related services is less expensive than the cost of nursing home care. Finally, people prefer to age in place in their own homes, with proximity to family members and the resources of their communities.

TAPPING INTO THE AMERICAN DREAM

USING HOME EQUITY TO AGE IN PLACE

Most older Americans are homeowners. Two thirds of the nation's 18.5 million older owner-occupied households have no mortgages or loans (American Housing Survey, 2009, Table 3-15). The downturn in the national housing resale market that began in 2008 has had an impact on aging in place. Some older homeowners who may have planned to sell their homes, downsizing into a smaller house or a retirement community may have changed their plans and are instead staying put. However, without moving or selling their home, they can utilize their home equity to make aging in place possible.

Reverse Mortgages

An increasingly common way to age in place and maximize investment in a home while still living there is the **reverse mortgage**. A reverse mortgage is a loan that allows homeowners age 62 and over with high equity (i.e., a relatively small or no loan on the home)—to convert part of that investment into cash. No payment is required until the homeowner dies or no longer uses the home as a principal residence. There are few restrictions on the use of the funds generated from a reverse mortgage, and they are often used to purchase in-home care, to upgrade the home to accommodate a caregiver, and/or to finance costly supportive features such as a fully accessible bathroom or an elevator.

Approximately 250,000 older households utilize reverse mortgages (American Housing Survey, 2009, Table 3-15). However, 12 to 13 million older households are candidates for reverse mortgages that could be used to help pay for long-term care within their homes (American Housing Survey, 2009; Stucki, 2005). Older homeowners in all income categories could benefit from a reverse mortgage to access in home care services. They include 400,000 Medicaid beneficiaries; nearly 1.5 million low-income non-Medicaid homeowners; 3.3 million households at risk of spending down their assets; and 8 million affluent homeowners, who have the greatest amount of home equity. Nearly 75% of reverse-mortgage-eligible older households have functional limitations or need assistance with ADLs and/or IADLs (NCOA, 2005).

The down side to reverse mortgages include relatively high fees and interest rates, and reduction of potential inheritance for the older adult's children and grandchildren. The reverse mortgage is paid back when the older adult dies or moves out of the home permanently and the house is sold. As with all loans, it is important that the borrower understands all risks and fine print. AARP has worked closely with the federal government to assure that legitimate reverse mortgages are a viable option for older adults, especially those seeking to age in place.

Paying for Health Care With Home Equity Conversion Mortgages

In 1987, Congress authorized the Federal Housing Administration (FHA) to create the Home Equity Conversion Mortgage (HECM) program, and since then, over 345,000 federally insured reverse mortgages have been issued. Borrowers' average age decreased from 76.7 years in 1990 to 72.9 years in 2010. At the start of the HECM program, more than 57% of borrowers were single females. However, in 2010 single females accounted for only 41%, whereas couples constituted 37% of borrowers, up 11 percentage points from 1990 (Trawinski, 2013).

An AARP Public Policy Institute Survey (Trawinski, 2013) found that one quarter of borrowers used their reverse mortgage to pay for health care or needs related to disability. Forty percent of those homeowners indicated that payment for prescription drug costs was the main reason they sought a reverse mortgage, in addition to home care, equipment and devices, and hospital stays. Other borrowers stated that they wanted to pay off debts, including 20% who identified owing money for health care. In addition, 11% of borrowers who used a reverse mortgage to pay for home improvements indicated they were planning to help someone with a disability (Trawinski, 2013). Recent changes have reduced the upfront costs that previously were an impediment to older people applying for these mortgages. Uncertainties in the housing market and declining home values have limited more widespread use of HECMs in recent years.

DESIGN CONSIDERATIONS TO SUPPORT AGING IN PLACE

In order to implement Americans' desire to age in their own homes, living spaces can be built and redesigned with functional change in mind. Building better new housing in the first place would be ideal. However, retrofitting housing with inclusive design is vital as well. Two main design concepts that accommodate disability and age-related changes are **visitability** and **universal design.**

Visitability

Visitability consists of three main components to make a home accessible to residents, friends, and relatives who have limited functioning: zero-step entrances to the home, wide interior doors, and at least a half bathroom on the ground floor (toilet and sink). Visitability is aimed toward single-family homes, duplexes, and triplexes, and is not expected to provide a totally accessible living space. Advocates of visitability would like all new homes to include inclusive design features. For example, Pima County, Arizona, home to Tucson, has an inclusive home design ordinance and more than 11,000 visitable homes (retrieved December 17, 2010, www.visitability.org).

Universal Design

Universal design is a more all-encompassing concept promoting design in homes and public spaces that is accessible, adaptable, and usable by persons of all ages and abilities. The seven principles of universal design are presented in Chapter 8. Examples of universal design include door handles that are levers, which are easier for all people to use than a round knob and a halting image of a red hand on a crosswalk sign that is more widely understood than the traditional words "Don't Walk." Universal design in the home applies to the entire residence and can be implemented through such features as variable-height counters, supportive bars in bathroom and shower, rocker light switches, large-font thermostats and screens, appliances that are reachable from a chair, and wheelchair and walker-accessible kitchens and bathrooms.

In addition to structural design features, other important design elements support independent living. People with vision impairments can be helped by strong color contrasts on walls and ample lighting choices. Round configurations and symmetrical shapes can help orient cognitively impaired people, and objects such as art, plants, and conspicuous doors can help people orient themselves.

Housing in Elder-Friendly Communities

In recent years, urban planners, public health officials, and aging experts have teamed up to envision aging-friendly cities, also referred to as **elder-friendly communities**, which combine the design features inherent in universal design along with the neighborhood-based service models of NORCs or the Village Model. A crucial component of elder-friendly communities that link well-designed home and streets with surrounding accessible services is pedestrian friendliness. As with universal design, an elder-friendly community is intended for everyone across all stages of the life span, including parents pushing strollers, children riding bicycles, adults with shopping carts, and wheelchair users. Readable signs, curb cuts leading to smart crosswalks, respite benches, and well-maintained, wide sidewalks are imperative. In addition, larger scale components such as transit-oriented development with housing in proximity to public transportation, commercial and service uses immediately adjacent to residential use, and green recreational spaces are features of elder-friendly communities.

In the urban planning field, such desirable neighborhood components are known as **smart growth**. Smart growth features a town-centered approach focused on transit and pedestrian convenience. Zoning is crucial. Housing and commercial uses are mixed together in the same neighborhoods, on the same block, or in the same buildings, providing usability to people of all ages and abilities. Another characteristic of smart growth is adding in-fill housing in pre-existing neighborhoods, where single vacant lots can be developed to meet the needs of the neighborhood. In areas zoned for single-family homes, flexibility of uses and zoning variances can accommodate the changing needs of an aging society. As described earlier in this chapter, an Aging in Community approach allows older adults to intentionally live together in their own de facto group home, in Green Houses or in cohousing (Thomas, 2004). In addition, zoning that allows for second units, such as ADUs, can be implemented to provide more aging-friendly neighborhoods (Cicero & Pynoos, 2008), allowing residents to age in place in proximity to caregivers and extended family members. Zoning, which permits a variety of housing types, can offer residents choices for the kind of built environment in which they prefer to age in place. With the aging of the baby boom population, it is important that these concepts be codified in zoning ordinances and translated into widespread, universal use in order to provide a complete, community-based continuum of care.

SUMMARY

Most long-term care is delivered in the home. This chapter has described where older people live, what kinds of housing they live in, how long they have lived there, and how they pay for it. Older people's strong psychological attachments to their homes and communities motivate them to age in place. Whether facing chronic functional decline or acute loss of physical abilities following a hospitalization, older people can benefit from home modifications that allow them to adapt to their built environment. Programs providing supportive housing alternatives to assisted living and skilled nursing are a key element that can allow persons to live in community housing settings. These include innovative community-building alternatives, such as physician house calls, naturally occurring retirement communities, and Villages and intentional communities where people share their resources.

In addition, subsidized rental housing and service linkages can allow lower income adults to age in the community and avoid institutionalization. For older adults who own their homes, reverse mortgages can be used to both upgrade the housing and help pay for community-based long-term care services. In addition, more broadly based and inclusive approaches, such as visitability, universal design, elder-friendly communities, and smart growth can allow older people and those with functional disabilities to exercise their preferences for living in their own homes and accessing community-based long-term care. Supportive housing that allows for aging in place and the delivery of in-home long-term care needs to be accessible, affordable, and adaptable.

DISCUSSION QUESTIONS

1. Can you construct an argument in opposition to the *Olmstead* decision?
2. Explain your argument and offer examples.
3. There are so many nice-looking retirement communities! Why do older people want to age in place?
4. What features do the Village Model, NORCs, and elder-friendly communities share?
5. What housing and service programs are available to low-income older adults to help them age in the community?
6. Are there many older people living in your neighborhood? Why or why not?

ADDITIONAL RESOURCES

http://beaconhillvillage.org **Beacon Hill Village** provides information about accessing or starting a village.

http://stopfalls.org **The Fall Prevention Center of Excellence** provides extensive resources on preventing falls in the home environment.

www.thegreenhouseproject.org **The Green House Project** provides extensive information about innovative shared housing options and intentional communities.

www.homemods.org **The National Resource Center on Supportive Housing and Home Modification** offers further information on home modification research, products, and programs.

www.norcblueprint.org **Naturally Occurring Retirement Communities (NORC)** provides information about NORCs and their solutions for aging in place.

www.medicare.gov **Medicare** includes detailed information on the Programs of All-Inclusive Care for the Elderly.

www.aarp.org and www.ncoa.org **AARP** and the **National Council on Aging** provide more information on reverse mortgages.

http://smartgrowth.org **The Smart Growth Information Clearinghouse** website describes the components of design promoting smart growth.

Udeworld.com and ncsu.edu **The Center for Inclusive Design and Environmental Access** and **North Carolina State University** both provide information on universal design.

http://concretechange.org and www.visitability.org **Concrete Change** and **Visitability** both contain information on visitability's origins and tenets.

www.who.int **World Health Organization** is an important source for information on the WHO Age-Friendly Environments Program.

REFERENCES

AARP. (2003). *These four walls*. Washington, DC: AARP.

American Community Survey. (2009). Retrieved from www.factfinder.census.gov

American Housing Survey for the United States. (2011). Retrieved from http://factfinder2.census.gov/

American Housing Survey for the United States. (2009, Series H150/09). Retrieved from www.census.gov

Beccaro, M., Costantini, M., Giorgi Rossi, P., Miccinesi, G., Grimaldi, M., & Bruzzi, P. (2006). Actual and preferred place of death of cancer patients. Results from the Italian survey of the dying of cancer (ISDOC). *Journal of Epidemiology Community Health, 60*(5), 412–416.

Brazil, K., Howell, D., Bedard, M., Krueger, P., & Heidebrecht, C. (2005). Preferences for place of care and place of death among informal caregivers of the terminally ill. *Palliative Medicine, 19*(6), 492–499.

California Department of Health Care Services. (2007). Retrieved from www.dhcs.ca.gov

Cicero, C., & Pynoos, J. (2008, Jan–Feb). Housing opportunities within current and proposed zoning practices. *Aging Today, 7*, 10.

Cooper Marcus, C. (2006). *House as a mirror of self*. Lake Worth, FL: Nicolas-Hays.

Doty, P. (2000). *Cost-effectiveness of home and community-based long-term care services*. Washington, DC: U.S. Department of Health and Human Services/Office of Disability, Aging and Long-Term Care Policy. Retrieved from http://aspe.hhs.gov

Ekerdt, D. J., Sergeant, J. F., Dingel, M., & Bowen, M. E. (2004). Household disbandment in later life. *Journals of Gerontology, Series B, Psychological Sciences, 59*(5), S265–S273.

Enguidanos, S., Pynoos, J., Denton, A., Alexman, S., & Diepenbrock, L. (2010). Comparison of barriers and facilitators in developing NORC programs. *Journal of Housing for the Elderly, 24*(3/4), 291–303.

Frick, K., Kung, J., Parrish, J., & Narrett, M. (2010). Evaluating the cost-effectiveness of fall prevention programs that reduce fall-related hip fractures in older adults. *Journal of the American Geriatrics Society, 58*, 136–141.

Gitlin, L. N. (2003). Conducting research on home environments: Lessons learned and new directions. *The Gerontologist, 43*, 628–637.

Gitlin, L. N., Winter, L., Dennis, M. P., Corcoran, M., Schinfeld, S., & Hauck, W. W. (2006). A randomized trial of a multicomponent home intervention to reduce functional difficulties in older adults. *Journal of the American Geriatrics Society, 54*, 809–816.

Golant, S. M. (2003). Conceptualizing time and behavior in environmental gerontology: A pair of old issues deserving new thought. *The Gerontologist, 43*, 638–648.

Golant, S. M. (2008). Commentary: Irrational exuberance for the aging in place of vulnerable low-income older homeowners. *Journal of Aging and Social Policy, 20*(4), 379–397.

Liebig, P., & Cicero, C. (2008). Economic well-being and security of older Americans: State approaches and innovations. *Generations, 32*(3), 27–33.

Lord, S. R., Menz, H. B., & Sherrington, C. (2006). Home environment risk factors for falls in older people and the efficacy of home modifications. *Age and Ageing, 35*, ii55–ii59.

McWhinney-Morse, S. (2009). Beacon Hill Village. *Generations, 33*(2), 85–86.

Office of Statewide Health Planning and Development. (2000). *California hospital patient discharge data*. Retrieved from www.oshpd.ca.gov

Office of Statewide Health Planning and Development. (2006). *California hospital patient discharge data*. Retrieved from www.oshpd.ca.gov

Oswald, F., & Rowles, G. D. (2007). Beyond the relocation trauma in old age: New trends in elders' residential decisions. In H.-W. Wahl, C. Tesch-Romer, & A. Hoff (Eds.), *New dynamics in old age: Individual, environmental and societal perspectives* (pp. 127–152). Amityville, NY: Baywood Publishing Company.

Pendall, R., Freiman, L., Myers, D., & Hepp, S. (2012). *Demographic challenges and opportunities for U.S. housing markets*. Washington, DC: Bipartisan Policy Center. Retrieved from http://www.urban.org/research/publication/demographic-challenges-and-opportunities-us-housing-markets/view/full_report

Pynoos, J., Nishita, C., Cicero, C., & Caraviello, R. (2008). Aging in place, housing, and the law. *University of Illinois Elder Law Journal, 16*(1), 77–107.

Redfoot, D., Scholen, K., & Brown, S. (2007). *Reverse mortgages: Niche product or mainstream solution*? (Report on the 2006 AARP National Survey of Reverse Mortgage Shoppers. AARP Public Policy Institute Paper #2007-22). Washington, DC: AARP. Retrieved from https://assets.aarp.org/rgcenter/consume/2007_22_revmortgage.pdf

Rowles, G. D. (2008). Place in occupational science: A life course perspective on the role of environmental context in the quest for meaning. *Journal of Occupational Science, 15*(3), 127–135.

Rowles, G. D., & Bernard, M. (2013). The meaning and significance of place in old age. In G. D. Rowles & M. Bernard (Eds.), *Environmental gerontology: Making meaningful places in old age* (pp. 3–24). New York, NY: Springer Publishing Company.

Rowles, G. D., & Watkins, J. F. (2003). History, habit, heart and hearth: On making spaces into places. In K. W. Schaie, H.-W. Wahl, H. Mollenkopf, & F. Oswald (Eds.), *Aging independently: Living arrangements and mobility* (pp. 77–96). New York, NY: Springer Publishing Company.

Shenk, D., Kuwahara, K., & Zablotsky, D. (2004). Older women's attachments to their home and possessions. *Journal of Aging Studies, 18*, 157–169.

Stevens, J. A., Corso, P. S., Finkelstein, E. A., & Miller, T. R. (2006). The costs of fatal and nonfatal falls among older adults. *Injury Prevention, 12*, 290–295.

Stucki, B. (2005). *Use your home to stay at home.* Arlington, VA: National Council on Aging. Retrieved from http://www.ncoa.org/news-ncoa-publications/publications/reversemortgagereportpublications.pdf

Tang, S. T., Liu, T. W., Lai, M. S., McCorkle, R. (2005). Discrepancy in the preferences of place of death between terminally ill cancer patients and their primary family caregivers in Taiwan. *Social Science & Medicine, 61*(7), 1560–1566.

Tang, S. T., & McCorkle, R. (2003). Determinants of congruence between the preferred and actual place of death for terminally ill cancer patients. *Journal of Palliative Care, 19*(4), 230–237.

Thomas, W. (2004). *What are old people for?* Acton, MA: Vander Wyk and Burnham.

Trawinski, L. (2013, June 18). Long term sustainability for reverse mortgages: HECM's impact on the mutual mortgage insurance fund (written testimony). Committee on Banking, Housing, and Urban Affairs Subcommittee on Housing, Transportation, and Community Development.

United States Department of Justice Civil Rights Division. (n.d.). *Olmstead: Community integration for everyone.* Retrieved from http://www.ada.gov/olmstead/olmstead_about.htm

Vladeck, F., Segel, R., Oberlink, M., Gursen, M., & Rudin, D. (2010). Health indicators: A proactive and systematic approach to healthy aging. *Cityscape: A Journal of Policy Development and Research, 12*(2), 67–85.

Wahl, H.-W., Fänge, A., Oswald, F., Gitlin, L. N., & Iwarsson, S. (2009). The home environment and disability-related outcomes in aging individuals: What is the empirical evidence? *The Gerontologist, 49*, 355–367.

Assisted Living

STEPHEN M. GOLANT
JOAN HYDE

CHAPTER OVERVIEW

This chapter considers the range of places that call themselves assisted living residences in the United States in the first part of the 21st century. It focuses on the following: (a) defining assisted living and the sources of our knowledge about this option; (b) providing a brief history of assisted living; (c) presenting a typology of assisted living models; (d) explaining how assisted living differs from other housing-care options; (e) considering the occupancy costs of assisted living; (f) specifying the demographics, health, and impairment profiles of assisted living residents; (g) exploring the regulatory environment of assisted living communities and its provision of supportive- and nursing-related services; (h) identifying the challenges of achieving both a good quality of life and a good quality of care; (i) describing the characteristics of small assisted living properties: board and care and adult foster care; (j) explaining the role of Medicaid in making assisted living affordable; and (k) discussing the future prospects of assisted living as a long-term care alternative.

LEARNING OBJECTIVES

After completing this chapter, you should have an understanding of:

- The occupants of assisted living properties
- The philosophy of care associated with assisted living
- The variability of assisted living settings
- How assisted living compares to other long-term care options
- How the regulatory environment influences the look and operation of assisted living properties

KEY TERMS

Board and care/adult foster care
Continuing-care retirement communities
Housing and services model
Independent living communities
Medicaid
Negotiated risk agreements
New-model assisted living properties
Old-model assisted living properties
Person-centered principles
Residential normalcy
Social model
Special care units (memory support neighborhoods)

INTRODUCTION

Older Americans dread the prospect of spending the last years of their lives in a nursing home with its institutional-like physical ambience and hospital-like service environment. Since the mid-1980s, older adults who have difficulties living independently in their own homes have enjoyed another option. They can receive assistance coping with their impairments or managing their health care problems in a long-term care alternative that is now widely known as assisted living (Ball, Perkins, Hollingsworth, Whittington, & King, 2009; Wilson, 2007). Most experts believe that the emergence of assisted living is, at least partly, responsible for the decline in the rate of nursing home use—even by the most physically and cognitively vulnerable population in their mid-80s and over (The Lewin Group, 2007).

Most researchers and professionals now describe assisted living as a group-oriented residential care setting not licensed as a nursing home that provides on both a scheduled and an unscheduled basis the housekeeping, meals, personal assistance, medication management, and health/nursing-related services required by older persons who have experienced physical and/or cognitive health declines. Assisted living subscribes to a social model of care in contrast to the institutional or medical model associated with nursing homes.

DEFINING *ASSISTED LIVING*

A COMPLEX LONG-TERM CARE OPTION

Although we initially offered a basic definition of assisted living, any such description greatly oversimplifies the complexities of this long-term care option with its many variations. Definitions of assisted living share more commonalities than differences, but even advocates of this long-term care alternative have difficulty agreeing on how to define it. This is not a homogeneous product. If you have seen one assisted living community, you have seen one assisted living community.

A major reason for this diversity is that each state regulates its assisted living properties differently. State governments have different standards and requirements for the physical design and infrastructure of their buildings, which consider the maximum severity of residents' impairments, staffing levels and qualifications, the levels and operating standards of personal and health-related care provided, and admitting and discharge criteria (Assisted Living Workgroup Steering Committee, 2003; Brown, 2007; Mollica, Sims-Kastelein, & O'Keeffe, 2007).

Experts are more likely to agree that assisted living is distinguished because of its **social model** of care. This philosophy emphasizes that older people—whatever their level of vulnerability—should be accommodated in a setting that uses "residential architectural styles and scale, providing privacy and control of a resident's personal space" (Hernandez, 2006, p. 17). Here, the residents should be treated as valued customers and made to feel "at home" (Wylde, 2008, p. 191). Even as residents receive high-acuity care, the operators of assisted living should treat them in a dignified manner and respect their personal autonomy. Like consumers of other services, they should be given the right to make choices—even bad ones—about how they live and about how and when to receive services and assistance. Foremost, proponents of a social model of care believe that these goals are achievable without excessive government regulation, which they believe has contributed to the medicalization of nursing homes. The bottom line is that they do not believe that the implementation of this philosophy of care compromises in any way the safety of the residents or the quality of their professionally delivered health-related and chronic care services. Indeed, many believe that assisted living can accommodate residents with the same severity of needs as found in nursing homes.

SOURCES OF DATA

Making accurate generalizations about this important long-term care alternative depends on good sources of information. The diversity of assisted living properties, however, makes it more difficult to obtain reliable and comprehensive data. The last statistically representative national survey of assisted living providers was conducted in 2010 by the Centers for Disease Control and Prevention's National Center for Health Statistics, Division of Health Care Statistics. It included licensed or certified properties with at least four dwelling units or beds that provided room and board, at least two meals a day, around-the-clock on-site supervision, and help with personal care (such as bathing or dressing) or health-related services such as medication management (Caffrey et al., 2012; Park-Lee et al., 2011).

Other data about the national supply of assisted living residences come from surveys of state regulatory agencies. Two professional organizations, the National Academy for State Health Policy and the National Center for Assisted Living, currently offer summaries of how each state licenses or certifies its assisted living option (Mollica et al., 2007; Polzer, 2013). These agency data were used in a 2007 study of the locations and market area characteristics of a national cross-section of state-licensed assisted living properties (Stevenson & Grabowski, 2010). An overview of the current and future status of assisted living in the United States was also the subject of a book by the authors of this chapter (Golant & Hyde, 2008).

Three major insurance companies have conducted market surveys that report on what it costs elderly consumers to occupy assisted living properties, but they do not provide information about their sampling procedures (Genworth Financial, 2013; Metlife Mature Market Institute, 2012; Prudential Insurance Company of America, 2010). Five major trade associations (LeadingAge, American Seniors Housing Association, Assisted Living Federation of America, National Center for Assisted Living, and the National Investment Center for the Seniors Housing & Care Industry) regularly poll their assisted living/senior housing memberships of providers and managers, but their participation in these surveys is voluntary (American Association of Homes and Services for the Aging, 2009; American Seniors Housing Association, 2010). These surveys also differ in several ways: the size and statistical representativeness of their samples, the extent that they include licensed as opposed to unlicensed properties, the scope of their questions, and the extent that they include smaller sized assisted living properties.

A BRIEF HISTORY OF ASSISTED LIVING

Assisted living as we know it today is a relatively new concept. During the 19th and the early decades of the 20th century, only small percentages of people lived to an advanced old age and rarely survived for long periods with extensive care needs. Consequently, older people usually lived on their own or relied on assistance from their extended families. "Homes for the aged"—sometimes called almshouses or poor farms—were operated by municipal or county governments, churches, or community-based charities and primarily served elders who were destitute or had no family supports. Elders who had dementia were often housed in state mental hospitals (Doty, 2008; see Chapter 2).

After the Great Depression of the 1930s, changing demographics, the advent of the Medicare and **Medicaid** programs, and the institution of regulation led to the creation of the nursing home industry (see Chapters 2 and 13). The less medically intensive old-age homes—variously called "board and care," "rest homes," or other comparable names continued to operate. These were sometimes family homes that took in older adults as boarders, or buildings operated by nonprofit or religious organizations. Also available since the 1900s were **continuing-care retirement communities** (CCRCs), originally known as life care communities. These age-restricted properties accommodate older persons with all levels of assistance and care needs in independent living, assisted living, and skilled nursing facilities found on a campus-like setting.

The mid-1980s first witnessed the availability of stand-alone assisted living communities. Initially, they were located in Virginia and Oregon, primarily due to the efforts of visionary people—Paul and Terri Klassen in Virginia and Keren Brown Wilson in Oregon. These founders were idealists who knew there had to be a better way to serve people who needed some care, but who neither needed nor wanted to live out their lives in the highly regulated atmosphere of the nursing home. The growth of assisted living in Oregon was further aided by its being the first state, under the leadership of Richard Ladd, to provide funding under the Medicaid community-based waiver model (Wilson, 2007).

This residential option soon expanded to other states. Sixty percent of the current supply of units opened their doors between 1990 and 2001 (Wilson, 2007). The for-profit sector—disproportionately privately owned as opposed to publicly held companies—mostly developed these properties, usually without the help of government financing. Only about a dozen states imposed any controls on how many units could be built (such as certificate-of-need requirements) (Stevenson & Grabowski, 2010).

By 2010, there were over 51,000 assisted living properties with over 1.2 million beds/dwelling units in the United States (Mollica, Houser, & Ujvari, 2012). However, the size of this industry depends on how one defines this alternative. These numbers include small board and care/foster care properties (with as few as two beds/dwelling units). If we restrict the universe to larger properties (four or more units/beds), there were over 31,000 properties with about 970,000 units/beds (Park-Lee et al., 2011).

The 11 states with the highest older population penetration rates (assisted living units divided by number of people age 65 and over) included Minnesota, Virginia, Oregon, Nebraska, Washington, Pennsylvania, North Carolina, California, Illinois, Maine, and Iowa (Stevenson & Grabowski, 2010). These states are more likely to be occupied by older populations with higher incomes, educational status, and housing wealth. They are also in locations where providers, regulators, and consumers appear to value community-based long-term care alternatives over institution-like nursing home options (Stevenson & Grabowski, 2010).

Although the assisted living industry has experienced much growth since its beginnings, it has witnessed several periods of rapid expansion alternating with spells of sparse development. Similar to other economic activities, it has been susceptible to the vagaries of consumer demand, overbuilding leading to excessive supply, and the vicissitudes of the U.S. economy. During the Great Recession and housing meltdown in the United States (2007–2009), for example, assisted living building and occupancy rates dropped sharply because of tight construction-lending standards, because prospective older consumers could not sell their homes and the accompanying stock market decline resulted in serious losses to their wealth—thereby reducing their spending. As the economy subsequently recovered, occupancy rates again moved higher.

TYPOLOGY OF ASSISTED LIVING MODELS

There have been several attempts to classify the different types of assisted living residences. One useful typology used a statistical procedure known as cluster analysis to distinguish assisted living properties based on their ownership, size, years in business, resident characteristics—level of frailty, dementia, and socioeconomic status—and the level of services and privacy of accommodations offered to residents (Park, Zimmerman, Sloane, Gruber-Baldini, & Eckert, 2006; Zimmerman & Sloane, 2007). The study labeled one of the largest groups of facilities as **new-model assisted living**. These were typically corporate-owned facilities, occupied by a relatively large number of residents, and found in modern buildings that offered greater resident privacy. They accommodated persons with a wide range of impairments, but, because of costs, were less likely to accept residents dependent on Medicaid. This group contrasted with two other facility clusters that tended to be smaller, older, often "mom and pop" establishments that served lower income elders who were more likely to share their units.

Even among the new-model assisted living category there is much diversity. The average new-model assisted living building contains about 50 units, although some of the largest properties have over 120 units (Assisted Living Federation of America, 2009). Their buildings variously encompass Victorian mansions, boxy multiunit apartment-style structures, luxurious Trump Towers-like high-rise apartment structures, and resort-like two- or three-story buildings. Interior architectural designs sometime resemble the décor of luxurious hotels, but (sadly) in some cases are more similar to the medical-like interiors of nursing homes. Most have predominantly one-bedroom and studio apartments, but some assisted living properties have a wider mixture of one-, two- and even three-bedroom apartments. Some features are more widespread among new-model assisted living properties. Most living units have their own self-contained kitchens, full bathroom facilities, doors that lock, and individual temperature controls. Residents can fill them with their own furnishings. Most occupants (90%) do not share their apartments or rooms (Figure 10.1).

FIGURE 10.1 Examples of assisted living properties.

(*continued*)

FIGURE 10.1 (*continued*)

With thanks to James A. Antonucci, Executive Director of The Village, Gainesville, Florida.

About 37% of new-model assisted living properties consist of freestanding buildings. Another 19% are in buildings that also have separate floors or sections (or are on a campus setting) with independent living units (see in the following sections). Fewer than 10% of assisted living properties are part of CCRCs. Finally, about 7% consist of buildings that also include a nursing home (Assisted Living Federation of America, 2009).

To accommodate the growing share of older occupants who have some form of dementia, particularly Alzheimer's disease, an additional 28% of assisted living properties have a physically separated area dedicated to serving persons with dementia. These dedicated floors, sections, or wings are usually referred to as **special care units** (SCUs; Hyde, Perez, & Forester, 2007), or more recently, **memory support neighborhoods**. The residential units tend to be smaller in these specialized dementia wings and may consist of only studio or bedroom units as opposed to an apartment. Shared occupancy is more common. Entry and exit doors of these living areas are often secured by locks, alarms, or passcode systems to prevent residents from wandering. Some, although not all SCUs, also have "safe and interesting walkways, and appropriate levels of auditory and visual stimulation, to yield improved outcomes, such as reduced agitation and enhanced quality of life" (Hyde et al., 2007, p. 56).

In contrast, **old-model assisted living properties**, now also usually subsumed under the general "assisted living" label—but often referred to as board and care/adult foster care—are more likely to be in smaller buildings. Their accommodations are more likely to consist of bedroom-like units. Multiple residents may have to share toilet facilities and/or bathing areas found in another part of the building. The oldest assisted living properties, some of which were converted from nursing home wings, are more likely to offer these more institutional-like accommodations (Hernandez, 2006). This category of assisted living is occupied by higher percentages of residents with dementia and/or psychiatric diagnoses, but unlike the new-model assisted living properties, these residents are often mixed in with the other residents.

ASSISTED LIVING: DIFFERENT FROM OTHER HOUSING CARE OPTIONS

Many advocates and consumers describe assisted living by emphasizing its differences from other supportive housing and care arrangements. In physical appearance, assisted living residences resemble what the senior housing industry now refers to as **independent living communities**, once labeled as congregate housing. Like assisted living communities, these residential-like settings provide hotel-like hospitality services such as meals, housekeeping, laundry, transportation, and recreational activities (Case Study 10.1).

Independent living communities are less likely than assisted living residences to accommodate physically or cognitively impaired residents (Hyde, Perez, & Reed, 2008). When older occupants receive personal assistance and health-related services to cope with their functional limitations, they rely on family members or professionals who are often employed with licensed home care agencies.

Case Study 10.1: So You Want to Be an Assisted Living Developer?

As is true for most businesses, would-be assisted living developers must obtain a large amount of start-up capital to develop a new property and to fund operations. They will have to address a myriad of issues for a successful launch: obtaining zoning approvals sometimes in the restrictive suburban locations favored by older residents, developing a business plan that takes into consideration continual and unpredictable competition, navigating the vagaries of the economy and changing market demand, ongoing difficulties hiring and retaining high-quality staff, the ever-changing needs and preferences of older consumers and their families, and complying with an ever-changing and expensive regulatory environment. Despite these challenges, many assisted living providers find this a deeply satisfying industry in which to work. They estimate that there will be an insufficient supply of long-term care options for the exploding population of very old. They believe that assisted living will fill this void and will represent an indispensable long-term care strategy to keep tomorrow's older population out of nursing homes.

In 1995, an ambitious young nursing home administrator who was frustrated with the constraints she experienced operating in a highly regulated nursing home and dealing with the bureaucratic demands and low bed-operating reimbursements of the Medicaid program—enabling the poor to occupy her facility—joined forces with a multifamily housing developer to form the ABC Assisted Living Company. Together, Jill and Tim identified a rare high-quality 4-acre site in a suburban community and spent 2 years obtaining zoning approvals. Financing came from a combination of investing their own capital and a Department of Housing and Urban Development (HUD) Section 232 insured loan that required some of the units to be available for lower income residents. In 1997, construction started, and by 1999, they obtained a license from their state government and began operating their first building. ABC on Main Street offered 80 studio and one-bedroom apartments, including a 25 unit (30 bed) dementia unit. The total cost to obtain the land, get all the approvals, develop the building, and fund the marketing and start-up was just over $16,000,000.

The first year at ABC was stressful. The executive director they hired, though a seasoned professional, had personal problems and left after 4 months. Ironing out policies and procedures to meet ever-changing regulations while meeting needs and preferences of the residents was challenging. Hiring and training nearly 100 full- and part-time staff was also time-consuming and difficult. Moving in seven or eight new residents every month was sometimes chaotic. However, by late 2000, they were able to achieve 90% occupancy and begin to break even on the operating costs and carrying costs for the mortgage.

(*continued*)

Case Study 10.1: So You Want to Be an Assisted Living Developer? (*continued*)

A year later, in the wake of 9/11, fill-up rates significantly slowed. Older adults hesitated to make life-changing decisions and an increase in the availability of private home care agencies making aging in place more feasible reduced the urgency of their moves. The opening of another assisted living property just 2 miles away further stalled resident interest. With aggressive and consumer-friendly marketing techniques, they weathered these challenges, and their occupancy rate crept up to 94% by late 2002. The operation continued to break even and eventually made a small profit. In 2003, the ABC Assisted Living Company was approached by a real estate investment trust (REIT) that encouraged them to build several other facilities, and by 2007, they had a total of six buildings in operation in the Northeast. These were heady times, and the future looked rosy.

The U.S. recession and widespread decline in the housing market all but eliminated new move-ins, and occupancy fell below the break-even point in two of their buildings. Their state government cut their Medicaid reimbursement rate by 2% for the 10% of their units set aside for lower income residents. This occurred even as costs and resident needs continued to increase. Unregulated "independent" housing-with-services options started up in their marketing area and offered prospective seniors more flexible service delivery at a lower price. A few nursing homes in their region started participating in the culture change movement and offered private rooms and person-centered care. These were unsettling times for operators of assisted living facilities. Recently, while still committed to their ideal of offering services that respect the wishes of their residents, the management team of the ABC Assisted Living Company is less evangelical about assisted living and has begun to explore new options for providing services to the coming wave of older Americans. It plans to introduce new smart home technologies that will more quickly detect and respond to changes in the self-care needs of their residents.

Case Study Discussion Questions:

1. How should the Center for Medicare & Medicaid Services (CMS) treat assisted living for the purposes of Medicaid reimbursement—that is, as an institution or as a community-based setting?
2. As the public and regulators become concerned about safety and the quality of health-related service delivery in assisted living settings, states have increased the regulatory requirements for these providers. How has this restricted the ability of providers to give their residents more control over their care decisions?

In contrast, assisted living residences are usually licensed by state governments to offer in-house services. Twenty-four-hour on-duty staff provides scheduled and unscheduled personal assistance and protective oversight. They sometimes offer residents health- or nursing-related services, such as medication and incontinence management. Staff may also monitor the chronic health problems of older residents and coordinate their care after they have a hospital stay. Increasingly, staff members are available to responsively and reassuringly assist older persons who suffer from dementia-related cognitive declines or behavioral problems, and they operate social/recreational activity programs tailored specifically to these occupants.

OFTEN COMPARED WITH NURSING HOMES

Assisted living communities differ in important ways from nursing homes. The more institutional-like setting of the nursing home is more focused "on the delivery of appropriate health care services," (Polivka & Salmon, 2008, p. 400) with the result that nursing homes have a much stronger medical or hospital ambience about them and tend to have a more rigid set of rules and regulations governing every aspect of their physical design and operations. In contrast, assisted living properties are far more likely to offer supportive- and health-related services relying on a person-centered or social model of care.

Proponents of nursing homes argue that they are different from assisted living because they serve a sicker and more impaired older population who require 24-hour nursing services (Golant, 2004). This is generally true, but some states allow assisted living properties to accept residents meeting their nursing homes' minimum level of care occupancy criteria. Thus, they can serve older persons who require discreet skilled nursing services, but "no states allow persons who need a skilled level of nursing home care to be served in [assisted living] (e.g., individuals who require 24-hour-a-day skilled nursing oversight or daily skilled nursing services)" (Mollica et al., 2007, p. 19). Even this generalization must be qualified because states do not have uniform nursing home admitting criteria. Thus, assisted living properties in some states will admit older occupants when they need more assistance than will others. Many states also permit assisted living providers to offer hospice care for terminally ill residents (Cartwright, Miller, & Volpin, 2009).

OCCUPANCY COSTS

Older persons typically rent new-model assisted living units on a monthly basis. The number of services offered by these facilities partly drives their pricing plans. These can include care management and monitoring, personal assistance with everyday activities, housekeeping and laundry, medication management, recreational facilities, security, transportation, and two or more meals a day (Metlife Mature Market Institute, 2010). In 2013, the median annual cost of new-model assisted living properties (one-bedroom single occupancy) was $41,400. Even these averages may understate occupancy costs. Older persons will pay more to occupy architecturally luxurious assisted living properties and when they receive services that require more hands-on care by staff. As a rule of thumb, the more demanding the physical or cognitive impairments of the resident, the higher the occupancy costs. As an example, in 2012, the national average monthly base rate for dementia care was $4,807 (or $57,684 annually; Metlife Mature Market Institute, 2012). Assisted living properties will also charge more for private than semiprivate units. Location also matters. As examples showing the range, in 2013, the median annual cost for assisted living in Missouri was $27,450, whereas in Delaware it was $66,396. To put all these prices in perspective, it still costs less to occupy assisted living residences than nursing homes. Older persons paid on average $95,265 ($261 daily) a year for a private room in an Alzheimer's disease wing of a nursing home (Metlife Mature Market Institute, 2012).

WHO OCCUPIES ASSISTED LIVING RESIDENCES?

PAST RESIDENTIAL HISTORIES AND DEMOGRAPHICS

About 70% of older adults who live in new-model assisted living properties moved from their own homes or apartments, whereas 7% came from their family's dwelling. About 9% had earlier resided in an independent living community and 5% in another assisted living property, whereas 9% moved from a nursing home. Most had previously lived within a 10-mile (62%) or at least a 25-mile (80%) radius of their current assisted living property (American Association of Homes and Services for the Aging, 2009). Between 20% and 25% of assisted living occupants decided mainly on their own to occupy these places. These proactive older persons tended to have higher income and education levels (Ball et al., 2009). In contrast, family members or professionals had a major say in the decisions of the others.

On average, assisted living residents occupy their accommodations just over 2 years, but many have shorter and longer stays. About a third of the residents in assisted living die at the end of their occupancy. Median annual resident turnover (move-outs divided by average occupancy during the year) is high and ranges from 40% to 50% (American Seniors Housing Association, 2010). Among residents who relocate to other housing and care settings, well over 70% move to a nursing home or hospital setting because they require a higher level of care. The remainder move for financial or other personal reasons and variously relocate to their former residences, the homes of a family member, or to another senior housing option such as another assisted living residence or an independent living community (Assisted Living Federation of America, 2009).

The typical person who occupies new-model assisted living is White, widowed, female, and in her mid-80s (Hernandez & Newcomer, 2007). To be more specific, the average age of assisted living residents is 87; three quarters are female, just over three quarters are widowed, just over 12% are still married, and the remainder are divorced or separated. When older persons first move into assisted living properties, they are on average a somewhat younger 84.6 years.

Non-White older persons, particularly African Americans, are underrepresented in new-model assisted living (Ball et al., 2009). Rather, these and other racial and ethnic minorities are more likely to occupy "the smaller, older, and lower priced [board-and-care] homes that have fewer residential and safety enhancing architectural design features" (Hernandez & Newcomer, 2007, p. 113).

Many older occupants of the new-model corporate owned or operated assisted living residences have high incomes, but about half have modest incomes that would appear to make their accommodations unaffordable. These seniors made up their income gap either by drawing on the cash proceeds from the sale of their homes or other assets or by receiving financial help from their families. A recent survey estimated that about 11% of older adults identified family as their primary payment source and another 24% as their secondary payment source (Assisted Living Federation of America, 2009).

A second group of low-income older persons is able to occupy assisted living residences because they have income and asset levels low enough to qualify for means-tested government support programs. As of 2010, Medicaid covered at least some of the costs for 19% of assisted living occupants (Caffrey et al., 2012).

Conspicuously absent from assisted living are another group of older persons with low incomes. Not only are they unable to afford the costs of assisted living, but also they do not have low-enough incomes to qualify for assistance from most government programs. Academics and professionals have referred to this group as the *Tweeners* (Knickman, Hunt, Snell, Alecxih, & Kennell, 2003) or the *Gap Income Group* (Moore, 2009). Experts estimate the incomes of this group range from $12,000 to $30,000 and that they represent about 35% of all U.S. households over the age of 75.

IMPAIRMENT AND HEALTH PROFILES

After they turn 65, about seven out of 10 persons will need long-term care (either from family or paid workers) at some point before they die. On average, they will be in their homes for two thirds of their years of need, and in nursing or assisted living properties for the remainder (Kemper, Komisar, & Alecxih, 2005). When they need such care, it generally means that they will require hands-on or standby assistance from another person to perform their activities of daily living (ADLs) or instrumental ADLs (IADLs; Kemper et al., 2005). ADLs include bathing, dressing, eating, using the toilet, and getting into and out of a bed or chair (transferring). IADLs include preparing meals, managing money, shopping for necessities, getting around outside the home, light housework, and using the telephone.

On average, residents in assisted living communities need help with over four IADLs. In particular, over 80% need assistance with light housework, personal laundry, preparing meals, using transportation, and managing their medications. They also need assistance with an average of 1.6 to 2.6 ADLs (American Association of Homes and Services for the Aging, 2009; Cohen, Shi, & Miller, 2009). In particular, over 60% require assistance with bathing, 40% with dressing, 26% with toileting, and almost 20% need assistance with transferring. Although about 23% could walk unaided, 54% depend on some assistive device (e.g., cane, walker), over 22% use a wheelchair at least part of the time, and 10% are bedfast (American Association of Homes and Services for the Aging, 2009).

Studies offer a wide range of estimates of the share of assisted living residents diagnosed as having some form of dementia, including Alzheimer's disease. Numbers range from as low as 40% to as high as 67% (American Association of Homes and Services for the Aging, 2009; Cohen et al., 2009; Hyde et al., 2007). These residents experience severe memory loss and manifest disoriented behaviors. Consequently, they require cueing assistance to perform their everyday activities, need a physically secure building to prevent them from wandering, and need staff with the ability to deal with disruptive or aggressive behaviors. Tragically, these cognitive declines often afflict older persons who are still in relatively good physical health.

Even as older persons enter assisted living properties mainly to address their long-term care needs, they often must rely on these settings to help them coordinate care for their acute and chronic health care problems. A 2009 study found that a large percentage of the occupants of assisted living in the United States suffered from one or more chronic health problems, usually high blood pressure, arthritis, coronary heart disease, osteoporosis, and/or depression. Consistent with the presence of these health problems, about 42% of residents were treated in a hospital emergency room in the past year, and about 35% were treated in a hospital overnight or longer (Assisted Living Federation of America, 2009).

CHANGING DEMOGRAPHICS OF ASSISTED LIVING RESIDENCES

Assisted living providers must continually adjust their operations to conform to the changing demographics of older consumers. Providers are finding that they must accommodate older persons who are more impaired and require higher acuity services and care than in the past. Today's older adults only enter these residences after extensive periods of aging in place in their own homes and at ever higher chronological ages. These trends explain why a growing share of assisted living properties has SCUs for their older residents with Alzheimer's disease or a related disorder (Hyde et al., 2007). The competitive environment is also a factor. Older persons can now remain longer in independent living communities because they receive personal assistance and health services from the flourishing home care industry.

Assisted living providers must continually change their business models to keep up with the continually changing preferences of prospective residents.

One expert noted that assisted living residences are increasingly tailoring their properties to accommodate very different niche subgroups: Asian Americans; gay, lesbian, and transgender populations; nudists in Florida; and intellectually striving university-based retirees (Carle, 2010).

THE REGULATORY ENVIRONMENT OF ASSISTED LIVING

MUCH STATE DIVERSITY

Regulatory agencies in more than two thirds of the states use the term *assisted living*. Other state governments refer to long-term care facilities as residential care, boarding homes, board-and-care facilities, basic care facilities, homes for the aged, personal care homes, adult care homes, and adult foster care (Mollica, 2008; Polzer, 2013). Adding to the confusion is that many state regulatory agencies have multiple licensing standards and recognize three or four different assisted living categories, each with distinctive physical infrastructure and service requirements. This helps explain the proliferation of 200-plus page manuals outlining how each state's assisted living program differs from the others (Mollica et al., 2007; Polzer, 2013).

Even within any given state, assisted living properties may not look or operate the same. Most state regulatory agencies give assisted living providers the discretion of admitting a less impaired population than allowed by their requirements, and they may involuntarily discharge residents when they cannot meet their needs (Carlson, 2005; Hernandez, 2006). On the other hand, some assisted living properties accommodate older persons who are as physically or cognitively impaired as their state regulations allow.

Regulations governing assisting living are in continual flux. Between 2012 and 2013, the National Center for Assisted Living—an advocacy group for the American Health Care Association (AHCA)—reported that 18 states had made statutory, regulatory, or policy changes that influenced the appearance or operation of their assisted living properties (Polzer, 2013).

Opinions vary as to whether this diverse and changing regulatory environment is a bane or blessing. Critics charge that "the state regulatory scheme is chaotic, disorderly, and largely ineffective" (Bruce, 2006, p. 82) "and that the current assisted living regulatory scheme, implemented state-by-state, is ineffective due to the piecemeal and varied state regulation" (Bruce, 2006, pp. 62–63). They argue for the increased role of federal regulation as a way to achieve more uniformity. Some providers, especially those who own and operate properties in multiple states, argue that this diversity hampers their ability to communicate a standardized marketing message. A diverse product line can also confuse older consumers, who are often unclear about a property's admitting policies, services, and costs.

Other experts are quick to counter these criticisms. They argue that this regulatory diversity and provider flexibility are strong plusses. A uniform assisted living product would fail to recognize the failings of a one-size-fits-all shelter-and-care environment (Mollica et al., 2007). Older consumers want to have more long-term care choices, providers want to implement different business models and serve distinctive niche markets, and state governments want their assisted living residences to serve older persons with different vulnerability profiles and satisfy different requirements and regulations—some more stringent than others (Golant, 2008b).

STATE REGULATORY ENVIRONMENTS

State regulation of assisted living residences contains two main categories of requirements. The first establishes standards for physical infrastructure, appearance, and design attributes. State regulatory agencies usually require that assisted living properties meet minimum building and unit designs. Some require that assisted living properties have apartment-like units with self-contained kitchens and bathrooms, although they will require different minimum area sizes for these spaces. Some states allow only one person to occupy these physical accommodations. Other states, following what is labeled as an "institutional model" (Mollica et al., 2007), allow multiple-occupancy bedrooms, shared by up to four people, without attached baths, and with shared toilets and bathing areas. These regulatory differences are often very detailed. For example, Connecticut requires that each resident's unit includes a full bath and equipment for the preparation and storage of food, and residents are not required to share a unit. In contrast, New York allows shared units, and includes units that do not have their own toilets, and depending on the facility category, only requires one toilet for every three or six residents, and one tub/shower for three to 10 residents (Polzer, 2013).

The second category of regulatory requirements identifies the allowable supportive- and nursing-related services, staffing responsibilities, and admitting and discharge criteria that take into account the residents' chronic health problems, physical and cognitive functioning, and behavioral problems.

Most states view assisted living as a "**housing and services model**," whereby they license or certify both the appearance of new-model apartment-like properties and their long-term care assistance. Fewer states regulate assisted living as a "*service model*." They do not regulate the building or shelter arrangement itself, but "allow existing building codes and requirements—rather than new licensing standards—to address the housing structure" (Mollica et al., 2007, p. 1–8). However, they license either the assisted living provider or outside community-based service providers (e.g., home health agency or an adult day care center) to control the types and levels of offered care.

ALLOWABLE IMPAIRMENTS OF RESIDENTS AND LEVEL OF SERVICES

States differ substantially regarding the types and level of allowable supportive and health-related services (Mollica et al., 2007). Some allow properties to only offer light care and minimal medical or nursing services with the result that they accommodate less physically or cognitively limited older persons. Other states mandate that assisted living properties accommodate some minimum percentage of residents who are very frail. These are typically persons having difficulties performing four or more ADLs and requiring the services of a nurse or equivalent health care professional several times a week.

Regulations also specify minimum levels of staffing and their qualifications and training requirements. These regulations may restrict who can administer nursing-related services such as catheterization, ostomy care, care of skin wounds, and oxygen therapy. They may specify whether licensed health personnel, such as registered nurses, can delegate certain nursing procedures, such as administering medications, to unlicensed staff, such as nurses' aides or certified nurse assistants. They also will specify under what circumstances assisted living providers can contract or outsource services from other agencies or organizations (for example, certified home health agencies), thereby enabling their residents to receive higher acuity care than provided by in-house staff.

New Jersey is an example of a state that allows assisted living properties to serve more severely impaired older persons. Although they cannot serve residents "who require a respirator or mechanical ventilator or people with severe behavior management problems" (Mollica et al., 2007, p. 21), they can accommodate residents if they have the following impairments or care needs (Mollica et al., 2007, p. 21):

- Require 24-hour, seven day a week nursing supervision
- Are bedridden longer than 14 days
- Are consistently and totally dependent in four or more ADLs
- Have cognitive decline that interferes with simple decisions
- Require treatment of Stage III or IV pressure sores or multiple Stage II sores
- Are a danger to self or others
- Have a medically unstable condition and/or special health problems.

States may also impose more stringent physical infrastructure and care requirements on assisted living communities providing dementia care. Cognitively impaired older adults, particularly those with Alzheimer's disease, typically need extensive cueing or reminders to reach their rooms or the congregate dining areas. Staff must also monitor resident behaviors to keep them from wandering or bothering other residents. These persons will sometimes remove items from other people's rooms, enjoy a nap in a neighbor's unit, or walk around disrobed. Consequently, state regulations may include specific language regarding exit controls, alarm systems, staffing levels, training, medication management practices, ability to evacuate independently in a fire and "disclosure of what is special about the SCU"

EXHIBIT 10.1 Virginia's Requirements for Alzheimer's Disease Units and Care

Alzheimer's Unit Requirements

"The regulations cover facilities caring for adults with serious cognitive impairments due to a primary psychiatric diagnosis of dementia who cannot recognize danger or protect their own safety and welfare. At least two direct care staff members must be in the special care unit at all times, with an exception allowing one staff person in the unit under specified circumstances. Doors leading to the outside are required to be monitored or secured. There must be protective devices on bedroom and bathroom windows and on common area windows that are accessible to residents with dementia. Free access to an indoor walking corridor or other indoor area that may be used for walking must be provided. There are other specific requirements for special care units and who may be in them" (Polzer, 2013, p. 223).

Staff Training for Alzheimer's Care

"The administrator and direct care staff must complete four hours of training in cognitive impairments due to dementia within two months of employment. The administrator and direct care staff must also complete at least six more hours of training in caring for residents with cognitive impairment due to dementia within the first year of employment. Topics that must be included in the training are specified. There are annual training requirements for direct care staff and for the administrator."

(Hyde et al., 2007, p. 61). As an example, Exhibit 10.1 shows the specific requirements for Virginia.

BALANCING QUALITY OF LIFE WITH QUALITY-OF-CARE GOALS

We earlier emphasized that advocates consider the social model of care as the centerpiece of the ideal assisted living community. Older persons should live and be cared for in a home-like and less regulated place that maximizes their autonomy, dignity, independence, and quality of life (Kane, Kane, & Ladd, 1998; Polivka & Salmon, 2008). Exhibit 10.2 offers an abbreviated summary of four sets of **person-centered principles** that would be recommended by advocates of a social model of care. This would increase the likelihood of assisted living residents experiencing "**residential normalcy**" (Golant, 2011b). That is, they occupy places where they enjoy comfortable and pleasurable surroundings (not unlike their original homes) and despite their physical or cognitive limitations still feel like they are competent individuals who are in control of their lives and environment. A summary of how older residents experience their assisted living accommodations is found in Exhibit 10.3.

EXHIBIT 10.2 Person-Centered Principles of a Social Model of Care

Individual Experiences and Activities

✓ Give older adults as much choice as their capabilities allow to conduct activities that are consistent with their past lifestyles, current social and recreational interests.
✓ Give them choices about how to spend their time and when to eat, sleep, and be bathed.
✓ Mimic as much as possible the features and ambience of the conventional residence—maintain the individual's personal possessions, duplicate aromas, smells, and dining experiences.
✓ Assure their privacy not just in their own dwellings, but also in a property's common areas (e.g., dining and recreational areas).
✓ Reinforce a person's self-esteem—that is, how he or she feels about him- or herself.

Physical Design of Residence and Its Surroundings

✓ Break down larger 40- to 60-bed units into smaller clusters—sometimes referred to "neighborhoods."
✓ Increase the availability of specialized common areas—kitchens, dining rooms, living rooms—instead of the "ubiquitous multipurpose day room."
✓ Create smaller scaled more intimate and friendly spaces.
✓ Create spaces that are aesthetically different—colors, textures, furniture, and decorating styles.
✓ Create living areas that maximize the residents' sense of orientation—signs, directions, meaningful cues, overall sense of location.
✓ Eliminate or minimize institution-like paraphernalia—e.g., nursing stations, medication/food carts.
✓ Offer easy access to the outdoors

Staffing Environment

✓ Assure as much as possible that the staff include older persons and their family members when making decisions affecting their activities, routines, and care.
✓ Assure the staff persons have as strong interpersonal skills as possible and are sensitive to the idiosyncratic needs of individuals and their need for independence.
✓ Offer staff more training and continually monitor their performance to realize these goals.

Connections With Family and Community

✓ Maintain linkages (outings, visits, recreational activities) with the surrounding community.
✓ Encourage family members to participate as much as possible in the lives of their loved ones and in the activities of the assisted living community.

Source: Adapted from Calkins and Keane (2008, pp. 114–115).

EXHIBIT 10.3 Experiencing Assisted Living: Resident Views

- A majority of older residents rate their assisted living properties as excellent or good or report that they are satisfied with the quality of life offered in their communities. Key to their positive assessments was feeling safe and being served by staff who were friendly, respectful, qualified, and courteous. They less favorably assessed food appeal and the ability to grow as persons (Assisted Living Federation of America, 2013; National Research Corporation, 2012).
- Such above ratings must be tempered by other evidence revealing that a small share of assisted living residences offer their residents poor-quality residential and care environments and inadequately trained or inexperienced staff (Eisenberg, 2013; Rosenfeld, 2010; The Florida Senate, 2011). Reports on averages and overall response distributions often hide this variation (Robison et al., 2011).
- Residents want the physical environment of their assisted living properties—private rooms/dwellings and common areas—to have architectural design features and furnishings that resemble their prior homes more than institutional environments, such as nursing homes (Kemp, Ball, Hollingsworth, & Perkins, 2012)
- They value management of assisted living properties who respect their individuality, show an interest in their personal needs, and give them choices as to how to conduct their activities and receive their care. They want to live with dignity and respect (Hyde et al., 2008; Park, Zimmerman, Kinslow, Shin, & Roff, 2012).
- They want to live in a place that offers quality daily living (Wylde, 2008) where they can enjoy the activities and celebrate the life events that are important to them—as they did in their previous homes (Fienberg, 2012; Yamasaki & Shari, 2011).
- They want privacy—the ability to control who they see and with whom they interact (Polivka & Salmon, 2008).
- They do not want overreaching rules that prevent them having a drink with dinner, becoming romantically involved with another resident, or dictate when they must retire to their rooms and sleep (Hedrick et al., 2009; Park et al., 2012).
- Residents want to maintain strong connections with their families and keep in contact with their past friends (Hyde et al., 2007; Perkins, Ball, Kemp, & Hollingsworth, 2013; Perkins, Ball, Whittington, & Hollingsworth, 2012; Yamasaki & Shari, 2011).
- However, the social contacts of assisted living residents that influence their emotional well-being the most are the other residents with whom they spend so much time (Perkins et al., 2013).
- Social compatibility is greater when the other residents share the same socioeconomic, ethnic, racial, religious, and political backgrounds (Perkins et al., 2012, 2013).
- The eating experience of older persons can be linked to the design features of their central dining room setting—size, home-like atmosphere,

(*continued*)

EXHIBIT 10.3 Experiencing Assisted Living: Resident Views (*continued*)

lighting and color contrast, minimized noise, music, orientation cues, and furniture grouping (Chaudhury, Hung, & Badger, 2013).

- Eating in a dining area with compatible and friendly persons is especially important for the social well-being of older residents (Eckert et al., 2009; Frankowski, Roth, Eckert, & Harris-Wallace, 2011; Kemp et al., 2012; Park et al., 2012).
- Assisted living residents usually do not enjoy being surrounded by other residents who are more physically or cognitively frail than themselves. They remind them of their own vulnerable futures and their closeness to death. Furthermore, these persons are unable to participate fully in the same activities because of their limitations (Gubrium, 1973; Park et al., 2012; Shippee, 2012; Street & Burge, 2012; Street, Burge, Quadagno, & Barrett, 2007; Wylde, 2008).

ADVANTAGES AND DISADVANTAGES OF A SOCIAL MODEL OF CARE

The social model of care stands in stark contrast to the medical model of the nursing home. Most state governments regulate nursing homes far more rigidly than assisted living properties. As a consequence, operators must micromanage all aspects of care practices by "setting eligibility standards, monitoring everything from medical equipment and personal care to safety, cleanliness, and other physical aspects of the care setting" (Collopy, 1995, p. 65). States believe these are necessary practices to ensure that older persons occupy a sufficiently protected and safe place to receive long-term care. The occupants of nursing homes, however, view them as physically unattractive and inflexible hospital-like institutional environments.

Proponents of the medical model respond that older persons occupying less regulated assisted living properties are far more likely to receive poorer quality care. As one of the authors of this chapter summarized elsewhere (Golant, 1998, p. 45):

> They question whether assisted-living providers can deal with a very frail population's complex health care needs, including their use of medications, the management of their chronic physical conditions, the detection of threatening medical conditions, and the diagnosis and treatment of depression and other cognitive disorders.

Most advocates of assisted living reject the need for the medical model's strong and restrictive oversight. They fear that it would not take "the application of very many nursing home style regulations to make assisted living substantially less affordable and far less attractive than it has proven to be during the past ten years" (Polivka & Salmon, 2008, p. 415). They have palpable concerns about the prospects of increased regulation and worry that state governments will primarily determine "success" by measuring resident health outcomes. As one expert puts it, "If quality in assisted living is measured in the same terms as quality in nursing homes, assisted living communities will come to look and feel like nursing homes" (Zimmerman, Sloane, & Fletcher, 2008, p. 120).

Advocates of nursing homes question the correctness of this position, especially now that many assisted living communities are caring for physically and cognitively impaired older persons who in the past would have occupied nursing homes. They further point out this is happening more often. To maintain their consumer market share—especially in economic downturns when vacancy rates are higher—assisted living providers are keeping older residents in their properties as long as possible. Critics argue that this reluctance to discharge makes it more likely that assisted living providers are retaining residents for whom they cannot provide adequate care. As one expert observed, "The too-late discharge is the source of many serious assisted living problems. The most horrific incidents in assisted living often are the result of a facility retaining a resident for whom the facility is incapable of providing care" (Carlson, 2005, p. 9). Unfortunately, critics are continually able to point to visible examples of poor quality care offered by today's assisted living properties (The Florida Senate, 2011; Rosenfeld, 2010).

TRADE-OFFS OF A SOCIAL MODEL OF CARE

Critics also argue that in an effort to follow person-centered principles, assisted living providers continually confront situations in which they must make difficult trade-offs between the quality of life and quality of care of their residents. A resident with diabetes may choose a less-restrictive diet to increase her dining pleasure contrary to her doctor's prescription, even though she risks shortening her life. A physically impaired resident may choose to preserve her privacy and dignity by showering alone despite a high risk of falling.

Assisted living providers acknowledge that well-trained and licensed full-time nurses predictably contribute to better health outcomes (Chou, Boldy, & Lee, 2003). They worry that their presence can also contribute to a hospital-like environment. Instead, they argue that with proper supervision, unlicensed and less medical-like staff can perform the same nursing procedures. Many state regulatory agencies concur. Currently, about three fifths of states allow some degree of delegated nurse supervision of unlicensed staff or trained aides to administer oral medications and sometimes to administer injections (Polivka & Salmon, 2008).

Because of their more laissez faire care environment, assisted living providers may have greater legal liability exposure. For example, a disgruntled family member sued the provider after her mother fell, even as the mother engaged in a risky behavior. Some states (as of 2007, about 15 states and the District of Columbia) have responded by recognizing legal instruments known as **negotiated risk agreements** in their assisted living regulations (Mollica et al., 2007).

They are also found in other states where the regulations do not explicitly prohibit their use (Jenkens, O'Keefe, Carder, & Wilson, 2006).

Negotiated risk agreements formally express the care preferences of older residents and document how assisted living providers plan to accommodate them. It is one of several mechanisms used by assisted living providers and residents to clarify how they will handle complex health- and safety-related issues. They codify the risks the resident is willing to tolerate in return for enjoying a more accustomed way of life. For example, despite their risk of falling, older persons may insist on not receiving staff assistance when showering with the caveat that the resident and family understand that if the resident continues to fall, and there are three more falls, or one more fall with injury, the resident may need to move to another setting. These agreements would also be used to negotiate other care issues associated with diabetes management, dietary needs, bed sores, and wandering (Yee-Melichar, Boyle, & Flores, 2011). Residents agree to excuse the property from liability in such risky situations (Bruce, 2006).

Opponents of these agreements argue that occupants of assisted living "already have the right to act autonomously and that there is therefore no necessity to negotiate about it" (Mitty & Flores, 2008, p. 98). Furthermore, they risk lowering "the standard of care below state minimums" (Yee-Melichar et al., 2011, p. 262). Critics also argue that these instruments are unenforceable and do not reliably limit a provider's legal liability, especially when residents are purposively exposed to dangerous practices—that is, the harm was foreseeable (Carlson, 2005). Consequently, "negotiated risk agreements are quite controversial and their legality is dubious" (Yee-Melichar et al., 2011, p. 262). Other experts, however, believe that these agreements help educate residents and their family members about possible risks connected with their assisted living occupancy. In turn, they ensure that management and staff are clear as to how they are supposed to respond in different care situations. Thus, these agreements may be conducive to better communication among all parties.

Some providers question the desirability of a social model of care for another reason. The ideal assisted living residence is supposed to offer older persons their own apartment units or rooms in order to guarantee their needs for privacy. Many advocates consider shared accommodations to be a major violation of this model (Cutler, 2007). Some providers retort that were it not for their ability to offer shared accommodations (two or four persons to a unit/bedroom), it would be financially infeasible for them to charge lower rents and thus they would have to exclude lower income applicants. This results in an ethical dilemma. If lower income older persons in assisted living residences are overall enjoying a better quality of life and care than they would in other settings, does it not justify sacrificing their privacy?

The current operating dynamics of assisted living create other difficulties in achieving the social model of care. Older persons undoubtedly enjoy a better quality of life when staff members treat them as individuals and in a dignified and respectful manner (Mitchell & Kemp, 2000; Wylde, 2008).

But achieving this outcome turns out to be difficult because assisted living residences have high staff turnover, which annually averages 42% (Sikorska-Simmons, 2005; Zimmerman et al., 2008). Such turnover disrupts established resident–staff relationships and can result in workers who are not adequately prepared to respond to specific resident care needs or establish warm relationships.

The adoption of new information-gathering and transmission technologies by assisted living providers presents other challenges. These variously consist of integrated sensors and wireless technologies built within the walls and floors of a dwelling, wearable technologies, activity monitors, spatial and temporal pattern-detection devices that measure all types of modalities: video, audio, light, motion, acceleration, temperature, moisture, sound, odors, physiology, vibration, kinematics, and piezoelectricity (Bharucha et al., 2009; Demiris & Hensel, 2008; Kutzik, Glascock, Lundberg, & York, 2008; Mann & Milton, 2005). These new devices (often encompassed under the category of smart home technologies) unquestionably help assisted living providers respond more effectively to residents' care needs (see Chapter 8). To the extent that they eliminate more intrusive staff interventions, they may be consistent with a social model of care. Yet, understandably, critics of these new technologies argue that they pose a new threat to older persons' rights to privacy and autonomy. Again, operators confront a dilemma—do they realize *quality of care* gains only by sacrificing the *quality of life* of their older occupants?

BOARD AND CARE/ADULT FOSTER CARE

A variety of old-style assisted care settings are more appropriately labeled as **board and care/adult foster care**, adult residential care homes, small group homes, or domiciliary care. Some state agencies or county-based governments license or certify these residences no differently than their assisted living properties (sometime depending on their size), whereas others regulate them as separate programs. Other states do not directly license or certify these residences, whereas still others monitor their care standards through their Medicaid programs (Carder, Morgan, & Eckert, 2006; Mollica et al., 2009).

MAJOR PHYSICAL FEATURES AND OPERATING CHARACTERISTICS

There are about 19,000 properties in this category with a capacity to serve over 64,000 residents (Mollica et al., 2009). Compared with the previously examined new-model assisted living communities, these properties tend to be older and smaller with most accommodating fewer than seven persons (Mollica et al., 2009). Many are located in buildings that owners converted from single-family dwellings. Consequently, they consist of bedroom units that require their residents not only to share their private living quarters and their bathrooms, but also to eat and socialize with the rest of the residents in common dining and living room areas. They are also located in residential-zoned neighborhoods and are often not easily distinguishable as group homes for older people.

Researchers warn about making simple generalizations about assisted living and note that "distinctions are neither clear-cut nor consistent" (Carder, Morgan, & Eckert, 2008, p. 148). This category also includes larger and purposely built group homes (not licensed as nursing homes) that look more like dormitory or ward-type facilities and have more of an institutional appearance (Stevenson & Grabowski, 2010). Here, three to four persons may share bedrooms and as many as eight to 10 residents may use the same bathroom.

Researchers have mostly studied the smaller homes (Eckert, Morgan, Carder, Frankowski, & Roth, 2009) that are typically privately owned "mom and pop" family operations. Many of their owners were formerly human service professionals (Mollica et al., 2009). They often live on the premises and function as the primary caregivers with assistance from a small rotating shift of paid employees (Carder et al., 2008; Hedrick, Sullivan, Sales, & Gray, 2009). Some (a smaller share) of these small residences may be corporately owned and managed as commercial chains.

Compared with their professionally managed corporate assisted living counterparts, higher percentages of the very poor occupy board-and-care homes. They are typically less educated minorities (especially African Americans; Ball et al., 2009) and tend to be both more physically and cognitively impaired. Consequently, they are more likely to rely on mobility devices, such as walkers and wheelchairs, and require more supervisory and personal care (Carder et al., 2006, 2008; Hedrick et al., 2009). Younger (under age 65) developmentally disabled and chronically mentally ill persons are also more likely to be residents.

ADVANTAGES AND DISADVANTAGES

The typically smaller size and homeownership flavor of board-and-care homes can result in a more desirable close-knit family and home-like atmosphere where residents and caregivers feel emotionally connected (Carder et al., 2006, 2008). These benefits are not achieved without trade-offs. Many older persons do not enjoy the prospect of spending their days in these more public, group-oriented living and dining areas. Because they are living in close quarters, there is always the possibility of conflicts between incompatible residents. Operators may seek to avoid such problems by having curfews, not allowing liquor in the rooms, and having a "set time for bathing and lights out" (Hedrick et al., 2009, p. 47), thus infringing on everyday freedoms. Because these smaller places operate with few staff, it is simply not feasible to offer 24-hour care, 7 days a week (Bruce, 2006). They also are only able to offer their residents a limited selection of recreation and social activities.

The operators of small group homes face formidable challenges that explain why a good many go out of business (Golant, 2008b). As with assisted living communities, they must compete with other properties for residents, hire and retain high-quality workers, and cope with rising health care and insurance liability costs. Yet, they usually must charge lower rents than corporate-operated assisted living residences in order to remain competitive. This results in few providers making large profits and most only breaking even (Mollica et al., 2009).

Board-and-care homes confront other disadvantages because of their smaller size and less professional operating environments. Older occupants needing assistance may overlook them as care alternatives because they have limited marketing budgets and, consequently, lower visibility. They also do not benefit from the economies of scale enjoyed by larger properties that would allow them to keep operating costs lower (per resident) for everything from food to personal care. Their tight budgets also make it less likely for them to benefit from expensive new care-related technologies. For example, they are less likely to record and exchange health information electronically (Caffrey & Park-Lee, 2013).

Some small group homes are further disadvantaged when states do not regulate them any differently than larger properties. This uniform regulatory approach allows for standardization, but it may fail to recognize the unique operating challenges faced by small-scale operators and the difficulties they have complying with their states' requirements.

The operators of board-and-care homes confront the same care dilemmas as their larger corporate counterparts. Because of efforts to accommodate lower income occupants and allow them to age in place as long as possible, they run the risk of inadequately addressing their higher impairment levels and greater care needs. This leads critics to charge that these older persons would be better served if they occupied new-model corporate-operated assisted living accommodations that have more services and professional staff (Carder et al., 2008; Mollica et al., 2009). Studies have not substantiated these concerns but rather report that small homes do not offer inferior-quality care and contend that residents do not have poorer health outcomes (Zimmerman et al., 2005). Hedrick et al. (2009) also point out that these care environments offer advantages over larger assisted living properties. In particular, they have a greater potential to offer personalized assistance, and their often foreign-born owners have more respect for their elder occupants than do their Caucasian counterparts. Thus, they are able to cater more effectively to the preferences of their older residents and can more readily and flexibly monitor and respond to their changing care needs and problems.

Finally, it is important to acknowledge that not all small group home operators confront these challenges. A small share of these small group homes has adopted a very different business model. They market their accommodations to very wealthy older persons. Like the patrons of small cruise ships, small hotels, and small luxurious private retail stores, these older consumers are attracted to a "high-end, boutique model of long-term care" (Golant, 2008b, p. 40), offering private suite accommodations in a residential setting that more resembles a luxurious bed-and-breakfast hotel.

MEDICAID: MAKING PRIVATE-PAY ASSISTED LIVING AFFORDABLE

A small share of assisted living properties—mainly board-and-care and adult foster care residences—will accept **Medicaid**-eligible older occupants. Persons age 65 and older can generally qualify if they have very low incomes or are medically needy (have large enough medical expenses) and if they have limited financial assets, not counting home equity, auto values, and clothing.

By 2013, most states participated in Medicaid programs to subsidize the costs of assisted living for their low-income older adults. They relied on one or two main funding approaches to make their assisted living properties affordable: the Medicaid State Plan Personal Care Option and Section 1951(c) Home and Community-Based Services (HCBS) Waiver (Carlson, Coffey, Fecondo, & Newcomer, 2010; Mollica, 2009; The Lewin Group, 2007). The majority used the HCBS Waiver program.

States are motivated to subsidize assisted living costs through Medicaid programs. In the absence of such funding, they fear that a significant share of older persons needing affordable long-term care will have no other choice but to end up in more costly Medicaid-reimbursed nursing home beds. Additionally, since the 1999 U.S. Supreme Court *Olmstead v. L.C.* decision, states must avoid unnecessarily segregating people with disabilities in institutions, such as nursing homes, (the integration mandate of the Americans with Disabilities Act) and must have plans to accommodate them in the least restrictive living environments found in community-based settings (Mollica, 2009). Although the CMS considers assisted living a noninstitutional "community" setting for purposes of classifying reimbursement to states through their Medicaid Waivers or State Plans, the courts are increasingly (and confusingly) treating assisted living as an "institutional" setting under the aforementioned *Olmstead* decision.

MAJOR PROGRAM FEATURES

Medicaid State plans cover costs of offering personal care services to assist older persons with ADLs and IADLs, but not the costs of nursing services or medical care. As an entitlement program, State Plans must provide services to all qualified applicants, although the eligibility criteria are up to state governments. For example, personal care services may be limited to residents of group living arrangements or to people living in their own home (The Lewin Group, 2007). Applicants must meet Medicaid's relatively restrictive community-based income-level eligibility standards. This requires that they can have incomes only up to 100% of the federal government's Supplemental Security Income (SSI) Program (Title XVI of the Social Security Act), up to 100% of the federal poverty level, or meet the state's medically needy income standard (Mollica, 2009).

The 2005 Deficit Reduction Act offered a variation of this plan, the Section 1915(i) HCBS State Plan Option. It gave states greater flexibility to cover assisted living by allowing applicants to have higher incomes (up to 150% of the poverty level). It further allowed them to offer services covered under their Section 1915(c) Waiver programs (Mollica, 2009). As of 2009, no states had yet used this option.

Since 1981, HCBS Waivers have allowed states to apply to the CMS to waive federal requirements preventing them from offering services not covered by their Medicaid State Plans. Applicants must be eligible to enter a nursing home because of their level of care needs, but as noted earlier, these are not everywhere the same and "states vary a great deal in their thresholds for nursing home admission" (The Lewin Group, 2007, p. 5). Under the State Plan, older persons do not have to demonstrate that they require the care offered in nursing homes.

HCBS Waivers cover a broad range of services: case management, homemaker/home health aides, personal care services, adult day health services, rehabilitation services, respite care, day treatment or partial hospitalization, psychosocial rehabilitation services, and clinic services for individuals with chronic mental illness. The waivers also include any other services requested by a state deemed necessary to keep an older person from entering institutions, such as nursing homes. These might include in-home supports, minor home modifications, and transportation for nonmedical services (The Lewin Group, 2007).

Along with being able to offer more services, states have other incentives to apply for these waivers. They can serve higher income older persons—those with incomes up to 300% of the maximum SSI benefit—thereby giving a larger population of seniors access to assisted living. The monthly maximum SSI amounts for 2013 were $710 for an eligible individual and $1,066 for an eligible individual with a spouse. They can also limit the number of participants, serving only those in certain counties or regions and members of certain groups (e.g., older persons vs. younger disabled; Mollica, 2009). In return for this flexibility, states must demonstrate that their waivers are "budget neutral," that is, that their funding costs would not exceed what it would cost them to provide the same services in a nursing home. This cost neutrality is not required when they provide services under their state plan.

MAJOR LIMITATIONS OF MEDICAID

As a source of funding to cover costs of assisted living, the Medicaid program has important limitations. The increase in state regulatory oversight that comes with accepting Medicaid occupants discourages potential operators. In some states, moreover, the number of budgeted Medicaid Waiver slots is in short supply. When available, Medicaid programs can also only reimburse assisted living providers for their service costs. Unlike nursing home coverage, Medicaid cannot reimburse providers for their room-and-board expenses (that is, hotel or shelter-like expenses such as debt service, maintenance, utilities, and taxes, and food). Moreover, most providers consider this reimbursement amount inadequate; over time, they do not keep pace with rising operator costs. Furthermore, Medicaid can also restrict how much an assisted living property charges for its room and board (Carlson et al., 2010; Hernandez & Newcomer, 2007; Mollica et al., 2007).

Most assisted living properties, even the small board-and-care and adult foster care properties, cannot afford to accommodate low-income seniors based on these Medicaid reimbursement rates, which are usually far below what they charge their private-pay occupants. These low reimbursements are especially prohibitive when providers are accommodating older persons requiring heavy care (because of their more serious physical or cognitive limitations). To reimburse assisted living providers for their higher occupancy costs, state governments have relied on an array of strategies (Exhibit 10.4).

Despite the downsides of accepting Medicaid-eligible older occupants, assisted living operators "must decide which is worse: letting a bed remain empty for a month or more or accepting a very poor resident who may remain for a long time" (Carder et al., 2008, p. 160). They have to decide whether filling their units compensates for the lower Medicaid reimbursements (as opposed to private pay rates) that they receive to provide shelter and care and the extra paperwork and expense of satisfying more demanding and ever-changing regulations.

EXHIBIT 10.4 State Strategies to Compensate Assisted Living Providers for Accommodating Medicaid-Eligible Older Persons

- Provide a state supplement to the federal SSI payment (State Supplemental Payment program—SSP) of the older occupant and limit the amount that assisted living residences can charge to not more than the combined SSI plus SSP payment. These supplements are state determined and vary widely (Mollica et al., 2007).
- Use the more liberal income-eligibility criteria for the Waiver program—up to 300% of the federal SSI payment—to enable beneficiaries to better afford their room-and-board costs. States must also allow Medicaid Waiver residents to retain sufficient income to pay for their room and board (The Lewin Group, 2007).
- Allow family members to contribute income to the older occupant (or directly to the assisted living property) to help defray their loved one's room-and-board costs. About half of the states allow family supplementation. These contributions are not without serious downsides, because they may result in a reduction in the older person's SSI benefit and jeopardize their financial eligibility for Medicaid. Some states, however, can exempt this income as a basis to determine eligibility when it is required to pay for room and board (Mollica, 2009).
- Use the federal Food Stamp Program to reduce board costs, by offsetting the meal costs charged by the assisted living residence (Mollica et al., 2007).
- Identify any room-and-board charges that might be reimbursed as a service—such as laundry assistance, light housekeeping, or food preparation (The Lewin Group, 2007).

THE FUTURE PROSPECTS OF ASSISTED LIVING

Assisted living communities have offered older Americans a way to cope with their long-term care needs and to avoid or postpone a nursing home stay. This would bode well for a bright future for this form of accommodation. Making this prediction is less than straightforward, however, considering all the factors that are likely to influence future demand (Golant, 2008b).

The least ambiguous and most positive factor will be tomorrow's demographics. All projections for the next two decades point to strong expected population growth of older persons, especially those in their mid-70s and older, the most likely candidates for assisted living. Experts do not agree, however, on whether this future older generation will have the same prevalence of need for long-term care as the current generation of older adults. On the one hand, there is evidence suggesting that baby boomers entering old age will have fewer functional limitations; on the other hand, Americans are also entering old age with a higher prevalence of health problems such as obesity, diabetes, and high blood pressure.

Much will certainly depend on major new advances in disease prevention and management (e.g., new assistive and monitoring devices, pharmaceuticals) that could make it substantially easier for older people to live independently. As an example, a major medical breakthrough in arresting or preventing Alzheimer's disease would profoundly change long-term care need estimates.

Even if we could forecast the long-term care needs of future generations of older people, housing and care strategies that they will use to cope with their frailties is uncertain. Most of today's impaired older population can deal with their frailties in their homes and apartments. Future technological advances may make it even more feasible for older adults to age in place and avoid the assisted living option. Many experts predict that health care professionals will be better able to monitor and respond to chronic illnesses and impairment restrictions, even from distant locations (see Chapter 8). A higher share of older people is also able to age in place in independent living communities. The latest competitive challenge is surprisingly coming from nursing homes, which are undergoing their own transformation. They are subscribing to the *culture-change movement* (referred to by labels such as Pioneer Network, the Eden Alternative, and Green Houses) that calls for changes in physical appearance and staffing behaviors to parallel the social model of care found in assisted living (see Chapter 11). Such unexpected developments emphasize the difficulty of predicting what long-term care will look like over the next two decades.

The future role of families of older persons will be crucial because caregiving assistance has traditionally been the first line of defense. A less available informal support network would increase the demand for care settings such as assisted living. However, some predict that tomorrow's elders will be less able to rely on their spouses and adult children (Stone, 2011; Wolff & Kasper, 2006). They point to the relatively high past divorce rates and smaller families of tomorrow's elderly population. When they do have children, they may be living in different states or regions. Future generations of women, by far the most important caregivers, may also be less available (Golant, 2009). They may not feel as motivated or obligated to assist their frail spouses or older parents because they will want to pursue their own independent lifestyles and careers. They may also be less willing to endure the tremendous physical and psychological toll of caregiving, especially if they have confidence in other care options.

A dampened demand for assisted living may result from tomorrow's elders viewing less favorably the prospects of occupying age-segregated settings (Golant, 2008a). This generation of old persons is continually hearing the message that they should remain as young as possible (the Botox generation) and maintain as much control as possible over their lives. A possible consequence is that they will want to dissociate themselves from people or places that lead others to identify them as old. They may especially avoid places, such as assisted living, that are negatively stigmatized as a residential arrangement dominated by frail and vulnerable older adults. An alternative scenario is that a significant share of tomorrow's old will be positively disposed to living in residential settings occupied by people the same age as themselves because they associate getting old with "positive attributes such as maturity, competence, sophistication, and self-reliance" (Golant, 2008b, p. 23). They will also remember their many past positive experiences living in other age-homogenous enclaves, such as student dormitories, singles' buildings, active adult communities, and independent living communities.

Future demand for assisted living will also depend on its affordability. Few predicted that the deep U.S. economic recession in 2008 and 2009 would so reduce the wealth—from owned homes to stock portfolios—of millions of U.S. older adults. Few anticipated that older homeowners would have difficulties selling their homes and would not be able to rely on this equity to help pay for their assisted living accommodations. Nor was it foreseeable that the children of these elders would themselves be facing hard economic times and unable to help their mothers and fathers pay for their long-term care. Long-term care insurance offers a pathway to making assisted living affordable, but only small numbers of older baby boomers—the next generation of older adults—have purchased this coverage. One might vainly hope that public programs will be more available to lower income seniors—especially minorities—to subsidize the costs of this long-term care alternative, but this scenario appears unlikely in the current economic climate.

Just over two decades ago, assisted living did not exist. The future long-term care landscape may contain some other unforeseen housing-care innovation. The only certainty is that change will occur. The hope, rather than the prediction, is that tomorrow's versions of assisted living accommodations will allow older Americans to receive long-term care in places where they can achieve the aforementioned **residential normalcy** (Golant, 2011a).

SUMMARY

Assisted living residence is a mainstream long-term care option that offers group-oriented residential care to physically and cognitively frail older persons in the United States. This chapter has focused mainly on facilities that are corporately owned and professionally managed and to a lesser extent on family owned "mom and pop" small board-and-care and foster care homes. State governments regulate assisted living properties and each has its own set of standards and requirements. The chapter included the history of this living alternative and described its costs, occupants, physical appearance, operating characteristics, services and social model of care, and how it differs from other shelter-and-care options. Although predominately catering to higher income older adults, the Medicaid program enables a small proportion of facilities to offer affordable accommodations to very low-income older adults. The chapter considered the challenges faced by assisted living operators seeking to offer both good-quality care and a good quality of life and concludes with discussion of what the future holds for this important long-term care alternative.

DISCUSSION QUESTIONS

1. What are the pros and cons of the diversity of assisted living settings and regulatory structures?
2. Discuss the challenges involved in offering high levels of resident control while providing high-quality health-related services.
3. How has the overall business climate and changing demographics effected the growth of the assisted living industry?
4. To what extent may future changes in Medicare and Medicaid support or challenge the expansion of the assisted living option?

ADDITIONAL RESOURCES

www.leadingage.org **LeadingAge** Senior housing professional organization

www.seniorshousing.org **American Seniors Housing Association** Senior housing professional organization

www.ahcancal.org/ncal **National Center for Assisted Living** Assisted living professional organization

www.nic.org **National Investment Center for Seniors Housing & Care (NIC)** Assisted living professional organization

www.alfa.org/alfa **Assisted Living Federation of America (ALFA)** Assisted living professional organization

www.yearsahead.com **Years Ahead** Consumer oriented site for assisted living

http://justiceinaging.org **Justice in Aging** Consumer oriented site specializing in legal issues affecting older people

http://aspe.hhs.gov/topics0.cfm **U.S. Department of Health and Human Services, Office of the Assistant Secretary for Planning and Evaluation (ASPE)** Government site that is source of long-term care studies

www.assistedlivingconsumers.org/advocacy **The Assisted Living Consumer Alliance (ALCA)** Consumer oriented site for assisted living

www.caring.com **Caring.com** Consumer oriented site for assisted living

www.ccal.org **CCAL** Consumer oriented site for assisted living

www.retirement-living.com/about **Guide to Retirement Living SourceBook** Consumer oriented site for assisted living

REFERENCES

American Association of Homes and Services for the Aging. (2009). *2009 Overview of assisted living*. Washington, DC: American Association of Homes and Services for the Aging.

American Seniors Housing Association. (2010). *The state of senior housing 2010*. Washington, DC: Author.

Assisted Living Federation of America. (2009). *2009 Overview of assisted living*. Washington, DC: Author.

Assisted Living Federation of America. (2013). *2013 Survey of assisted living residents*. Washington, DC: Author.

Assisted Living Workgroup Steering Committee. (2003). *Assuring quality in assisted living: Guidelines for federal and state policy, state regulations, and operations: A report to the U.S. Special Committee on Aging from the Assisted Living Group*. Washington, DC: American Association of Homes and Services for the Aging.

Ball, M. M., Perkins, M. M., Hollingsworth, C., Whittington, F. J., & King, S. V. (2009). Pathways to assisted living: The influence of race and class. *Journal of Applied Gerontology, 28*(1), 81–108.

Bharucha, A. J., Anand, V., Forlizzi, J., Dew, M. A., Reynolds, C. F., III, Stevens, S., & Wactlar, H. (2009). Intelligent assistive technology applications to dementia care: Current capabilities, limitations, and future challenges. *American Journal of Geriatric Psychiatry, 17*(2), 88–104.

Brown, K. W. (2007). Historical evolution of assisted living in the United States, 1979 to the Present. *The Gerontologist, 47*(Special Issue III), 8–22.

Bruce, P. A. (2006). The ascendancy of assisted living: The case for federal regulation. *Elder Law Journal, 14*, 61–90.

Caffrey, C., & Park-Lee, E. (2013). Use of electric health records residential care communities. *NCHS Data Brief, 128*, 1–7.

Caffrey, C., Sengupta, M., Park-Lee, E., Moss, A., Rosenoff, E., & Harris-Kojetin, L. (2012). Residents living in residential care facilities: United States, 2010. *NCHS Data Brief, 91*, 1–8.

Calkins, M., & Keane, W. (2008). Tomorrow's assisted living and nursing homes: The converging worlds of residential long-term care. In S. M. Golant & J. Hyde (Eds.), *The assisted living residence: A vision for the future* (pp. 86–118). Baltimore, MD: The John Hopkins University Press.

Carder, P. C., Morgan, L. A., & Eckert, J. K. (2006). Small board-and-care homes in the age of assisted living. *Generations, 29*(4), 24–31.

Carder, P. C., Morgan, L. A., & Eckert, J. K. (2008). Small board-and-care homes: A fragile future. In S. M. Golant & J. Hyde (Eds.), *The assisted living residence: A vision for the future* (pp. 143–168). Baltimore, MD: The John Hopkins University Press.

Carle, A. (2010, Sept./Oct.). Academic outlook. *Assisted Living Executive*, pp. 34–36.

Carlson, E., Coffey, G., Fecondo, J., & Newcomer, R. (2010). Medicaid funding for assisted living care: A five-state examination. *Journal of Housing for the Elderly, 24*, 5–27.

Carlson, E. M. (2005). *Critical issues in assisted living*. Washington, DC: National Senior Citizens Law Center.

Cartwright, J. C., Miller, L., & Volpin, M. (2009). Hospice in assisted living: Promoting good quality care at end of life. *The Gerontologist, 49*(4), 508–516.

Chaudhury, H., Hung, L., & Badger, M. (2013). The role of physical environment in supporting person-centered dining in long-term care: A review of the literature. *American Journal of Alzheimer's Disease and Other Dementias, 28*(5), 491–500.

Chou, S. C., Boldy, D. P., & Lee, A. H. (2003). Factors influencing residents' satisfaction in residential aged care. *The Gerontologist, 43*(4), 459–472.

Cohen, M. A., Shi, X., & Miller, J. S. (2009). *Cognitive and functional disability trends for assisted living facilty residents*. Waltham, MA: LifePlans.

Collopy, B. J. (1995). Home versus nursing home: Getting beyond the differences. In E. Olson, E. R. Chichin, & L. S. Libow (Eds.), *Controversies in ethics in long-term care* (pp. 57–72). New York, NY: Springer Publishing Co.

Cutler, L. J. (2007). Physical environments of assisted living: Research needs and challenges. *The Gerontologist, 47*(Special Issue III), 68–82.

Demiris, G., & Hensel, B. K. (2008). Technologies for an aging society: A systematic review of "smart home" applications. *IMIA Yearbook of Medical Informatics*, *47*(Suppl.), 33–40.

Doty, P. (2008). The influence of public and private financing on assisted living and nursing home care: The past, present, and possible futures. In S. M. Golant & J. Hyde (Eds.), *The assisted living residence: A vision for the future* (pp. 299–328). Baltimore, MD: The John Hopkins University Press.

Eckert, J. K., Morgan, L. A., Carder, P. C., Frankowski, A. C., & Roth, E. G. (2009). *Inside assisted living*. Baltimore, MD: The John Hopkins University Press.

Eisenberg, R. (2013, July 29). PBS' powerful assisted living exposé. *Forbes*. Retrieved from http://www.forbes.com/sites/nextavenue/2013/07/29/dont-miss-pbs-assisted-living-expose

Fienberg, L. (2012). *Moving toward person- and family-centered care*. Washington, DC: AARP Public Policy.

Frankowski, A. C., Roth, E. G., Eckert, J. E., & Harris-Wallace, B. (2011). The dining room as the locus of ritual in assisted living. *Generations*, *35*(1), 41–46.

Genworth Financial. (2013). *Genworth 2013, cost of care survey*. New York, NY: Author.

Golant, S. M. (1998). The promise of assisted living as a shelter and care alternative for frail American elders: A cautionary essay. In B. Schwarz & R. Brent (Eds.), *Aging, autonomy, and architecture: Advances in assisted living* (pp. 32–59). Baltimore, MD: The John Hopkins University Press.

Golant, S. M. (2004). Do impaired older persons with health care needs occupy U.S. assisted living facilities? *Journal of Gerontology: Social Sciences*, *59*(2), S68–S79.

Golant, S. M. (2008a). Commentary: Irrational exuberance for the aging in place of vulnerable low-income older homeowners. *Journal of Aging and Social Policy*, *20*(4), 379–397.

Golant, S. M. (2008b). The future of assisted living residences: A response to uncertainty. In S. M. Golant & J. Hyde (Eds.), *The assisted living residence: A vision for the future* (pp. 3–45). Baltimore, MD: The John Hopkins University Press.

Golant, S. M. (2009). The gender inequalities of eldercare. *Aging Today*, *30*(2), 2.

Golant, S. M. (2011a). The changing residential environments of older people. In R. H. Binstock & L. K. George (Eds.), *Handbook of aging and the social sciences* (7th ed., pp. 207–220). New York, NY: Academic Press.

Golant, S. M. (2011b). The quest for residential normalcy by older adults: Relocation but one pathway. *Journal of Aging Studies*, *25*(3), 193–205.

Golant, S. M., & Hyde, J. (Eds.). (2008). *The assisted living residence: A vision for the future*. Baltimore, MD: The John Hopkins University Press.

Gubrium, J. F. (1973). *The myth of the golden years*. Springfield, NJ: Charles C Thomas.

Hedrick, S. C., Sullivan, J. H., Sales, A. E., & Gray, S. L. (2009). Mom and pop versus the big boys: Adult family homes as providers of Medicaid-funded residential care. *Journal of Aging and Social Policy*, *21*(1), 31–51.

Hernandez, M. (2006). Assisted living in all of its guises. *Generations*, *29*(4), 16–22.

Hernandez, M., & Newcomer, R. (2007). Assisted living and special populations: What do we know about differences in use and potential access barriers? *The Gerontologist*, *47*(Special Issue III), 110–117.

Hyde, J., Perez, R., & Forester, B. (2007). Dementia and assisted living. *The Gerontologist*, *47*(Special Issue III), 51–67.

Hyde, J., Perez, R., & Reed, P. S. (2008). The old road is rapidly aging: A social model for cognitively or physically impaired elders in assisted living's future. In S. M. Golant & J. Hyde (Eds.), *The assisted living residence: A vision for the future* (pp. 46–85). Baltimore, MD: The John Hopkins University Press.

Jenkens, R., O'Keefe, J., Carder, P. C., & Wilson, K. B. (2006). *A study of negotiated risk agreements in assisted living: Final report*. Washington, DC: U.S. Department of Health and Human Services, Office of Disability, Aging and Long-Term Care Policy.

Kane, R., Kane, R. L., & Ladd, R. C. (1998). *The heart of long-term care*. New York, NY: Oxford University Press.

Kemp, C. L., Ball, M. M., Hollingsworth, C., & Perkins, M. M. (2012). Strangers and friends: Residents' social careers in assisted living. *The Journals of Gerontology Series B: Psychological Sciences and Social Sciences, 67*(4), 491–502.

Kemper, P., Komisar, H. L., & Alecxih, L. (2005). Long-term care over an uncertain future: What can current retirees expect? *Inquiry, 42*(4), 335–350.

Knickman, J. R., Hunt, K. A., Snell, E. K., Alecxih, L. M., & Kennell, D. L. (2003). Wealth patterns among elderly Americans: Implications for health care affordability. *Health Affairs, 22*(3), 168–174.

Kutzik, D., Glascock, A. P., Lundberg, L., & York, J. (2008). Techological tools of the future: Contributing to appropriate care in assisted living. In S. M. Golant & J. Hyde (Eds.), *The assisted living residence: A vision for the future* (pp. 223–247). Baltimore, MD: The John Hopkins University Press.

Mann, W. C., & Milton, B. R. (2005). Home automation and smart homes to support independence. In W. C. Mann (Ed.), *Smart technology for aging, disability, and independence* (pp. 33–66). Hoboken, NJ: John Wiley & Sons.

Metlife Mature Market Institute. (2010). *The 2010 MetLife market survey of nursing home, assisted living, adult day services, and home care costs*. Westport, CT: Author.

Metlife Mature Market Institute. (2012). *The 2012 MetLife market survey of nursing home, assisted living, adult day services, and home care costs*. Westport, CT: Author.

Mitchell, J. M., & Kemp, B. J. (2000). Quality of life in assisted living homes: A multidimensional analysis. *Journal of Gerontology: Social Sciences, 55*(2), P117–P127.

Mitty, E., & Flores, S. (2008). Aging in place and negotiated risk agreements. *Geriatric Nursing, 29*(2), 94–101.

Mollica, R. (2008). Foreword. In S. M. Golant & J. Hyde (Eds.), *The assisted living residence: A vision for the future* (pp. vi–xv). Baltimore, MD: The John Hopkins University Press.

Mollica, R. L. (2009). *State Medicaid reimbursement policies and practices in assisted living*. Washington, DC: National Center for Assisted Living, American Health Care Association.

Mollica, R., Houser, A., & Ujvari, K. (2012). *Assisted living and residential care in the states in 2010*. Washington, DC: AARP Public Policy Institute.

Mollica, R. L., Sims-Kastelein, K., Cheek, M., Baldwin, C., Farnham, J., Reinhard, S., & Accius, J. (2009). *Building adult foster care: What states can do*. Washington, DC: AARP.

Mollica, R. L., Sims-Kastelein, K., & O'Keeffe, J. (2007). *Residential care and assisted living compendium*. Washington: U.S. Department of Health and Human Services, Office of Disability, Aging and Long-Term Care Policy.

Moore, J. (2009). *Independent living and CCRCs*. Fort Worth, TX: Westridge Publishing.

National Research Corporation. (2012). *2011–2012 National survey of customer and employee satisfaction in assisted living communities*. Lincoln, NE: Author.

Park, N. S., Zimmerman, S., Kinslow, K., Shin, H. J., & Roff, L. L. (2012). Social engagement in assisted living and implications for practice. *Journal of Applied Gerontology, 31*(2), 215–238.

Park, N. S., Zimmerman, S., Sloane, P. D., Gruber-Baldini, A. L., & Eckert, J. K. (2006). An empirical typology of residential care/assisted living based on a four-state study. *Gerontologist, 46*(2), 238–248.

Park-Lee, E., Caffrey, C., Sengupta, M., Moss, A. J., Rosenoff, E., & Harris-Kojetin, L. D. (2011). Residential care facilities: A key sector in the spectrum of long-term care providers in the United States. *NCHS Data Brief, 78*, 1–8.

Perkins, M. M., Ball, M. M., Kemp, C. L., & Hollingsworth, C. (2013). Social relations and resident health in assisted living: An application of the convoy model. *The Gerontologist, 53*(3), 495–507.

Perkins, M. M., Ball, M. M., Whittington, F. J., & Hollingsworth, C. (2012). Relational autonomy in assisted living: A focus on diverse care settings for older adults. *Journal of Aging Studies*, *26*(2), 214–225.

Polivka, L., & Salmon, J. R. (2008). Assisted living: What it should be and why. In S. M. Golant & J. Hyde (Eds.), *The assisted living residence: A vision for the future* (pp. 397–418). Baltimore, MD: The John Hopkins University Press.

Polzer, K. (2013). *Assisted living state regulatory review, 2013*. Washington, DC: National Center for Assisted Living.

Prudential Insurance Company of America. (2010). *Long-term care cost study*. Newark, NJ: Author.

Robison, J., Shugrue, N., Reed, I., Thompson, N., Smith, P., & Gruman, C. (2011). Community-based versus institutional supportive housing: Perceived quality of care, quality of life, emotional well-being, and social interaction. *Journal of Applied Gerontology*, *30*(3), 275–303.

Rosenfeld, J. (2010). Sunrise cited for neglect after assisted living facility fails to provide timely treatment for an injured resident. *Nursing Homes Abuse Blog*. Retrieved from http://www.nursinghomesabuseblog.com/

Shippee, T. P. (2012). On the edge: Balancing health, participation, and autonomy to maintain active independent living in two retirement facilities. *Journal of Aging Studies*, *26*(1), 1–15.

Sikorska-Simmons, E. (2005). Predictors of organizational commitment among staff in assisted living. *The Gerontologist*, *45*(2), 196–205.

Stevenson, D. G., & Grabowski, D. C. (2010). Sizing up the market for assisted living. *Health Affairs*, *29*(1), 35–43.

Stone, R. (2011). *Long-term care for the elderly*. Washington, DC: The Urban Institute Press.

Street, D., & Burge, S. W. (2012). Residential context, social relationships, and subjective well-being in assisted living. *Research on Aging*, *34*(3), 365–394.

Street, D., Burge, S., Quadagno, J., & Barrett, A. (2007). The salience of social relationships for resident well-being in assisted living. *Journal of Gerontology: Social Sciences*, *62*(2), S129–S134.

The Florida Senate. (2011). *Interim report 2012-138, review regulatory oversight of assisted living facilities in Florida*. Tallahassee, FL: Author.

The Lewin Group. (2007). *Medicaid and assisted living: Opportunities and challenges*. Washington, DC: American Seniors Housing Association.

Wilson, K. B. (2007). Historical evolution of assisted living in the United States, 1979 to the present. *The Gerontologist*, *47*(Special Issue III), 8–22.

Wolff, J. L., & Kasper, J. D. (2006). Caregivers of frail elders: Updating a national profile. *Gerontologist*, *46*(3), 344–356.

Wylde, M. A. (2008). The future of assisted living: Residents' perspectives. In S. M. Golant & J. Hyde (Eds.), *The assisted living residence: A vision for the future* (pp. 169–197). Baltimore, MD: The John Hopkins University Press.

Yamasaki, J., & Shari, B. F. (2011). Opting out while fitting in: How residents make sense of assisted living and cope with community life. *Journal of Aging Studies*, *25*(1), 13–21.

Yee-Melichar, D., Boyle, A. R., & Flores, C. (2011). *Assisted living administration and management: Effective practices and model programs in elder care*. New York, NY: Springer Publishing Company.

Zimmerman, S., & Sloane, P. D. (2007). Definition and classification of assisted living. *The Gerontologist*, *47*(Spec No 3), 33–39.

Zimmerman, S., Sloane, P. D., Eckert, J. K., Gruber-Baldini, A. L., Morgan, L. A., Hebel, J. R., … Chen, C. K. (2005). How good is assisted living? Findings and implications from an outcomes study. *Journal of Gerontology: Social Sciences*, *60*(4), S195–S204.

Zimmerman, S., Sloane, P. D., & Fletcher, S. K. (2008). The measurement and importance of quality: A collaborative effort. In S. M. Golant & J. Hyde (Eds.), *The assisted living residence: A vision for the future* (pp. 119–142). Baltimore, MD: The John Hopkins University Press.

Facility-Based Long-Term Care

Nursing Facilities

JESSICA DORNIN
JAMIE FERGUSON-ROME
NICHOLAS G. CASTLE

CHAPTER OVERVIEW

Nursing facilities are an integral part of the health care system. In this chapter, a history of the development and growth of nursing facilities in the United States is provided. Then the structural characteristics of current nursing facilities, including ownership characteristics, location, and staffing levels, are described. Information on the services provided in nursing facilities is given. This includes services such as special care units and rehabilitation. The types of residents receiving services from nursing facilities are described. This includes the average age and typical health conditions of residents. Common payment mechanisms for receiving nursing facility care (including the Medicare and Medicaid programs) are discussed. Finally, the challenges and opportunities for nursing facilities of payment reform, health care reorganizations, and changing demographics are addressed.

LEARNING OBJECTIVES

After completing this chapter, you should have an understanding of:

- The history of the development and growth of nursing facilities
- Structural characteristics
- The services provided in nursing homes
- Resident demographics
- Reimbursement by Medicare and Medicaid programs

KEY TERMS

Certification
Dual eligiblility
Nursing facility
Nursing home
Person-centered care
Spend down

INTRODUCTION

The National Nursing Home Survey defines **nursing homes** as "facilities with three or more beds that routinely provide nursing care services" (Jones, 2002, p. 1). Nursing homes typically act as short-term rehabilitative facilities (most often, but not necessarily exclusively the clientele is elderly) and/or serve as an individual's permanent residence home; (Castle, Ferguson, & Hughes, 2009). The majority of nursing homes are certified by Medicare and/or Medicaid, whereas others are licensed by individual states (Fairchild & Knebl, 2002). Approximately 1.5 million people reside in the nation's 16,100 nursing homes each day (Centers for Disease Control and Prevention [CDC], 2013).

As noted later in the text, complements and alternatives to nursing homes exist, including home- and community-based service (HCBS) initiatives. The aging baby boomers will continue to increase the demand for nursing homes and their services (Kaiser Family Foundation [KFF], 2013). It is estimated that by 2030 almost 20% of the U.S. population will be over the age of 65 (Federal Interagency Forum on Aging-Related Statistics, 2012). As the number of aging individuals increases, the burden of care on nursing homes and health care spending will increase (Bohm, 2001).

Nursing homes have been and continue to be an integral part of American society and the American health care system, and it is likely that they will remain so in the foreseeable future. In this chapter, we provide a brief history of the development of nursing homes, review operation of nursing homes today, and elaborate on current and future challenges and opportunities nursing homes face.

HISTORICAL DEVELOPMENT OF NURSING HOMES

Historically, the burden of caring for elderly people fell to individuals' relatives or willing neighbors, thereby allowing individuals to maintain their standard of living (Lidz, Fischer, & Arnold, 1992). This type of community-based assistance was referred to as "outdoor relief" because those in need were allowed to remain in the home environment (Bohm, 2001). In accordance with the English Poor Law of 1601, government aid was only provided to those individuals whose family or friends were incapable of providing for them (Bohm, 2001). Assistance was provided to those deemed worthy of government aid in the form of "money, wood, or clothes" (Haber, 2002, p. 1006). As the number of older adults began to rise, so did the need for establishments capable of housing such individuals (see also Chapter 2).

In order to meet the needs of the growing number of older adults and keep up with the evolving complexity of society, larger facilities were erected to care for them, and the switch from "outdoor relief" to "indoor relief" began (Lidz et al., 1992). During this time, "indoor relief," or care in the form of institutions (such as almshouses or poorhouses), became a focus in caring for older adults (Lidz et al., 1992). Almshouses were not originally developed to house the elderly population (Bohm, 2001). Furthermore, there were negative connotations associated with residing in almshouses due in part to the deplorable conditions of these facilities (Bohm, 2001).

The 20th century brought with it the Great Depression and increased questioning of the nature of almshouses and the propriety of institutionalizing older adults (Lidz et al., 1992). As an overwhelming number of individuals began inundating the almshouses, the burden became more than the institutions could bear (Watson, 2009). Horrible living conditions in the almshouses were revealed, evoking sympathy for older adults and fueling increasing demand for public pensions (Lidz et al., 1992; Watson, 2009). Gradually, the almshouses were replaced by public nursing homes (Bohm, 2001).

With the passage of the Social Security Act in 1935, the nursing home environment, as well as attitudes toward older adults, began to change (Bohm, 2001). Qualified individuals were able to obtain unemployment insurance, old-age insurance, and take part in welfare programs after the passage of the Social Security Act (Social Security Administration [SSA], 2005). In an effort to discourage the use of public nursing homes, Social Security specified that public institutions were not eligible to receive federal funds (Watson, 2009). This stipulation was put in place under the Old Age Assistance (OAA) program, which was created under Title I of the Social Security Act (Emerzian & Stampp, 1993). The resulting action spurred an increase in the number of private care homes, and the shift from public nursing homes and almshouses to private nursing homes began (Bohm, 2001).

The transition from public to private institutions did not necessarily improve the quality of care residents were receiving (Bohm, 2001). Numerous quality complaints went unaddressed, leading to the demand for more medicalized care (Lidz et al., 1992). With the passage of the Hill–Burton Act in 1946, an increase in the number of hospitals constructed was realized as federal funds were set aside for this purpose (Lidz et al., 1992). The Hill–Burton Act provided funds for the improvement of existing nursing homes as well (Health Resources and Services Administration [HRSA], n.d.). However, it was not until the 1960s, with the passage of the Kerr–Mills Act and subsequently, the development of Medicare and Medicaid, that the growth of nursing homes increased (Watson, 2009). The implementation of Medicare and Medicaid not only spurred an increase in government (federal and state) funds provided to nursing homes, but also developed regulations and standards that participating facilities were required to follow (Emerzian & Stampp, 1993). To ensure that the various facets of Medicare and Medicaid ran smoothly, the Health Care Financing Administration (HCFA) (later renamed the Centers for Medicare & Medicaid Services [CMS]) was developed in 1977. The HCFA became responsible for the **certification** process required for nursing homes as well as the creation of certification standards (Castle & Ferguson, 2010).

The 1987 passage of the Omnibus Budget Reconciliation Act (OBRA '87) further reformed the nursing home environment by increasing the standards that participating facilities had to maintain to qualify for Medicare and Medicaid reimbursement (Emerzian & Stampp, 1993). Although the implementation of the improved standards and enforcement was slow, the quality standards currently in place in certified nursing facilities can be attributed to OBRA '87 (Castle & Ferguson, 2010).

NURSING HOMES TODAY

The term *nursing home* has been replaced in recent years with the term *nursing facility*. The use of the term *nursing facility* is predominantly regulatory in nature and came about with the passage of OBRA '87 (Pratt, 1999). To be more specific, **nursing facilities** are defined as "health care facilities licensed by the state offering room, board, nursing care, and some therapies" (Pratt, 1999). Also included in this term are skilled nursing facilities (SNFs), which provide around-the-clock nursing care and other specialized services such as speech pathology and physical therapy (Pratt, 1999).

Nursing facilities continue to play a vital role in the provision of long-term care services for the elderly. Although facilities themselves have undergone major changes since their conception, the following section provides statistics about the current structural characteristics of nursing facilities, the staff who provide care, resident characteristics, payments and reimbursements, and challenges nursing homes currently face.

STRUCTURAL CHARACTERISTICS OF NURSING FACILITIES

According to the Nursing Home Data Compendium, there was a decline in the number of nursing facilities in operation during the first decade of the 21st century, with a slight increase in 2011 (CMS, Department of Health and Human Services, 2012b). In 2011, 15,683 nursing facilities were in operation (CMS, Department of Health and Human Services, 2012b). California has the most nursing homes of all states, with a total of 1,232 facilities. The largest concentration of certified nursing home beds is located in central United States, with 56.1 to 68.7 beds per thousand persons aged 65 and older (CMS, Department of Health and Human Services, 2012b).

A majority of today's nursing facilities are private, for-profit facilities owned by an "individual, partnership, or corporation," with the remaining portion of nursing homes being nonprofit or government owned (Grabowski & Stevenson, 2008). In essence, for-profit organizations exist to generate revenue; excess earnings are then distributed among the company's investors (Miller & Hutton, 2000). Conversely, nonprofit organizations are generally exempt from paying taxes and are prohibited from distributing their earnings (Scalesse, 2013).

FIGURE 11.1 Nursing facility ownership and affiliation in 2011.

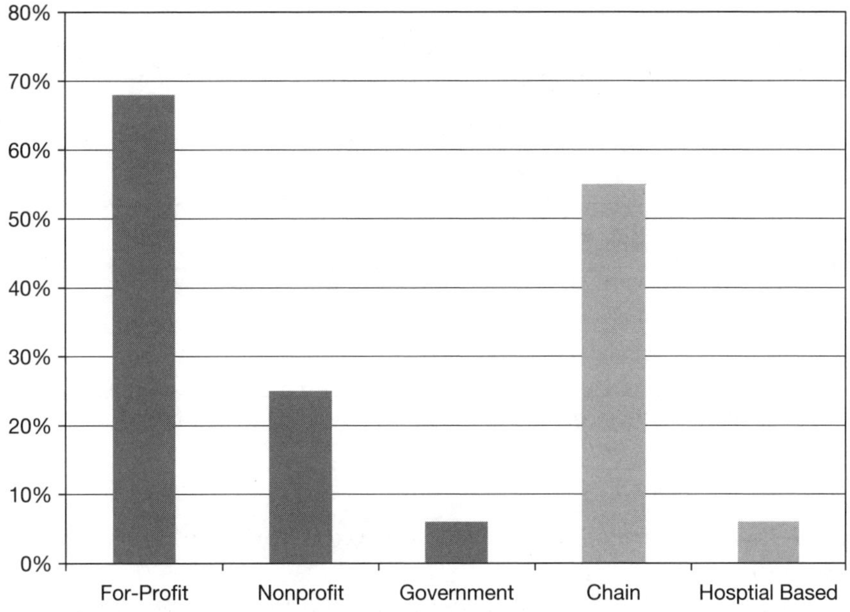

Source: KFF (2013).

In government-owned organizations, operational monies are generated through taxes or fees coming from state or federal resources (Pratt, 1999). Beyond these three ownership types (i.e., for-profit, not-for-profit, and government run), controlling entities are varied and include limited partnerships (LPs), limited liability partnerships (LLPs) and limited liability corporations (LLCs), general partnerships (GPs), and sole proprietorships (Stevenson, Bramson, & Grabowski, 2013).

Statistics show that for-profit facilities have increased in number, whereas nonprofit and government-owned facilities have decreased in number (CMS, Department of Health and Human Services, 2012b). For-profit facilities account for 69% of today's nursing homes, whereas nonprofit and government-owned facilities account for the remaining 31% (see Figure 11.1), or, 25.3% and 5.7%, respectively (CMS, Department of Health and Human Services, 2012b).

It is important to point out that multifacility chain ownership (often shortened to "chain ownership") and hospital-based affiliation also exist. Chains are defined as two or more homes under one ownership (*State Operations Manual*, 2012) and are typically large businesses that own multiple nursing facilities. Many chains are for-profit (KFF, 2013). Overall, chain ownership accounts for about 55% of U.S. nursing facilities (KFF, 2013). Hospital-based nursing homes are defined as having an affiliation with a hospital (*State Operations Manual*, 2012). Approximately, 6% of nursing homes are hospital based (KFF, 2013).

Bed size refers to the number of beds in a given facility (KFF, 2013). In 2011, the average number of certified beds in U.S. nursing facilities was 108.5 (see Figure 11.2; KFF, 2013). This number reflects a slight increase from previous years, with 108.4 beds in 2010, 108.3 in 2008, and 107.8 in 2006 (KFF, 2013). The average number of beds varies significantly across states with Alaska

FIGURE 11.2 Average number of certified nursing facility beds.

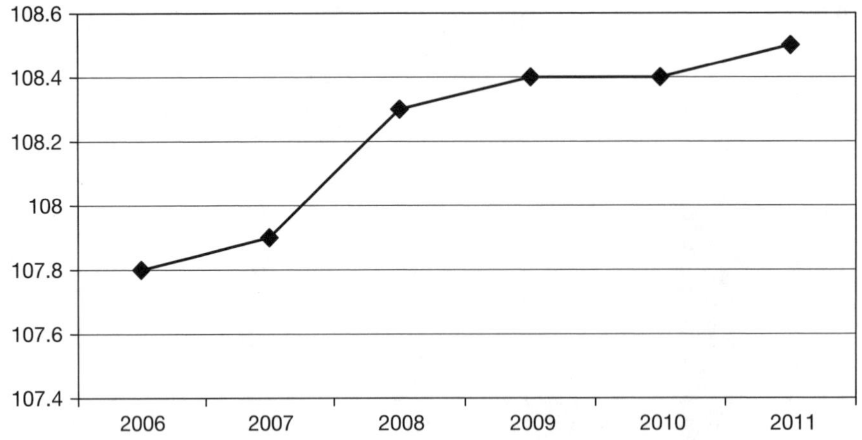

Source: KFF (2013).

having the lowest average at 42.5 beds and New York having the highest with 186 beds (KFF, 2013).

The beds in nursing facilities are often divided into sections called units. A typical 108-bed facility has four units. Units are defined as a number of rooms or even a section of a facility devoted to providing specific care (*State Operations Manual*, 2012). That is, units are typically set up to provide a multitude of different services, ranging from basic caregiving to rehabilitative services (KFF, 2013). Typically seen in SNFs, rehabilitation units (i.e., rehabunits) are devoted to providing rehabilitation to postoperative patients or those recovering from a stroke (Rau, 2013; Skillednursingfacilities.org, 2010). These units are noteworthy because they most often provide care for Medicare patients. The patient's length of stay is usually brief (National Stroke Association, 2006; Skillednursingfacilities.org, 2010). These patients are often termed "short-stay residents" (with an average length of stay of 27 days) and account for approximately half of all residents (Grabowski, 2010).

Specific units within a nursing home are called special care units (SCUs) and are created to provide care for a particular group of residents with unique needs or medical conditions (Pratt, 1999). SCUs typically require specific licensure or certification requirements (e.g., those providing dementia-related care; Estabrooks, Morgan, Squires et al., 2011). SCUs in nursing homes exist for conditions including, but not limited to, dementia, Parkinson's disease, wound care, and brain injuries (Pratt, 1999).

STAFFING

Federal government regulations address staffing standards in nursing homes (primarily coming from The Nursing Home Reform Act [NHRA], which was included in the 1987 Omnibus Budget Reconciliation Act). Government regulations (for Medicare/Medicaid-certified facilities) require that a "facility provide services by a sufficient number of nursing personnel on a 24-hour basis to provide the required care in accordance with care plans. A nursing home must have (a) a licensed nurse who functions as a charge nurse on each shift, (b) a registered nurse (RN) on duty at least eight consecutive hours per day, seven days a week, and (c) an RN designated as the director of nursing on a full-time basis who can also serve as the charge nurse when the average daily occupancy is 60 or fewer patients" (Decker et al., 2001, p. 17). In addition, minimum hours per resident day staffing-level standards also exist in many states, ranging from 3.6 hours per resident day (in Florida) to 1.76 hours per resident day (in Oregon; Mueller et al., 2006). These staffing standards are noted by many to be inadequate (Harrington et al., 2000).

In reality, much of the physical care in nursing facilities is administered by certified nursing assistants (CNAs). Of the 952,100 full-time employees (FTEs) in U.S. nursing facilities in 2012, CNAs accounted for 65.4%, or the majority (Harris-Kojetin, Sengupta, Park-Lee, & Valverde, 2013). The remaining percentage comprised RNs at 11.7% and licensed practical nurses (LPNs) or licensed vocational nurses (LVNs) at 22.9% (Harris-Kojetin et al., 2013). On average, residents received 3.83 hours of direct care a day from a combination of these caregivers, although most care was provided by CNAs (Harris-Kojetin et al., 2013). Other staff employed by nursing homes include administrative and support personnel, social workers, dietitians and food services staff, pharmacists, therapists, activity directors, housekeeping, and maintenance staff (Table 11.1; Pratt, 1999).

TABLE 11.1 Number and Percentage Distribution of Staffing Characteristics in Nursing Homes, 2012

CHARACTERISTIC	NURSING HOME	STANDARD ERROR
Total number of nursing employee FTEs	952,100	4,235.39
Percentage of total nursing employee FTEs		
Registered nurse	11.7	0.06
Licensed practical nurse or licensed vocational nurse	22.9	0.07
Aide	65.4	0.07
Hours per resident or participant per day		
Registered nurse	0.52	0.01
Licensed practical nurse or licensed vocational nurse	0.85	0.01
Aide	2.46	0.02
Social worker	0.08	–

Source: Harris-Kojetin et al. (2013).

According to 2004 to 2005 data from the National Nursing Home Assistant Survey, the average hourly wage rate for CNAs was $10.36 (National Nursing Home Assistant Survey [NNHAS], 2008). Data from this survey also demonstrates that women constitute the majority of CNAs with 646,100 employed as compared to 56,300 men (CDC, 2008). The largest age group for CNAs was those aged 35 to 44 years followed closely by workers aged 25 to 34 years (NNHAS, 2008). The majority of these employees had only a high school diploma and a family income of less than $20,000 a year (NNHAS, 2008).

All CNAs working in Medicare- and/or Medicaid-certified facilities are required by federal regulations to "complete a State-approved training program, pass a competency exam, and receive certification from the State in which they are employed" (Health and Human Services: Office of Inspector General [OIG], 2002, p. 5). These training programs "must be a minimum of 75 hours and include 16 hours of supervised clinical training" (OIG, 2002, p. 5). Additionally, "all NAs must complete 12 hours of continuing education annually" in order to maintain certification (OIG, 2002, p. 5).

The adequacy of the training that nursing assistants (NAs) receive in training programs is widely debated. It is noted that numerous state officials perceive the initial training hours required of NAs to be insufficient (Sengupta, Harris-Kojetin, & Ejaz, 2010). Similarly, various national organizations have advocated for an increase in the number of hours of federally mandated training, suggesting upwards of 150 to 160 hours as opposed to the currently mandated 75 hours (Harrington, Kovener, Mezey, et al., 2000; Sengupta et al., 2010). These concerns are not unwarranted, as the federally mandated training requirements have remained unchanged since their inception in 1987 (Sengupta et al., 2010) and in subsequent years nursing homes have seen an increase in the complexity of residents care needs (Paraprofessional Healthcare Institute [PHI], 2012). Another concern centers on the disparity between in-class training and hands-on training, with hands-on training typically receiving fewer hours in many training programs (Sengupta et al., 2010) resulting in "a divide between the classroom and the workplace" (PHI, 2012, p. 2).

RESIDENT CHARACTERISTICS

According to information gathered from the 2012 Nursing Home Data Compendium, the vast majority of nursing facility residents are non-Hispanic Whites (78.9%), with women comprising a large percentage (67.2%) of the resident population (CMS, Department of Health and Human Services, 2012b). Furthermore, of the 1.5 million residents in nursing facilities at the end of 2011, residents age 65 and older accounted for approximately 42.1% of the resident population, whereas those ages 85 and older accounted for approximately 42.9% (CMS, Department of Health and Human Services, 2012b). Thus, roughly 85% of the residents in nursing facilities are age 65 and older (see Table 11.2; CMS, Department of Health and Human Services, 2012b).

Residents live in nursing facilities for a variety of different reasons. An overwhelming number suffer from Alzheimer's disease or another form

TABLE 11.2 Characteristics of Nursing Home Residents

RESIDENT CHARACTERISTIC	ALL RESIDENTS	
	NUMBER	PERCENTAGE
	1,431,730	100
Gender		
Male	469,454	32.8
Female	962,129	67.2
Age		
0–21 years	3,027	0.2
22–30 years	4,705	0.3
31–64 years	206,719	14.4
65–74 years	209,209	14.6
75–84 years	393,983	27.5
85–95 years	504,799	35.3
95+ years	109,279	7.6
Race/Ethnicity		
American Indian/Alaska Native	5,499	0.4
Asian	21,743	1.6
Black, not Hispanic origin	193,700	13.8
Hispanic or Latino	68,216	4.9
Native Hawaiian/Pacific Islander	1,865	0.1
White, not Hispanic Origin	1,103,978	78.9
More than one Race	4,439	0.3

Source: CMS (2012b).

of dementia (51%) or have been diagnosed with depression (35%; Moore, Boscardin, Steinman, & Schwartz, 2012). Others suffer from conditions such as high blood pressure, heart disease, arthritis, stroke, and cancer (Zanfardino, 2012).

Conditions such as these (dementia and depression) can make performing activities of daily living (ADLs) difficult. ADLs include functions such as bathing, toileting, and dressing. Caregivers provide varying degrees of help/care for residents with these ADL difficulties. ADLs are also commonly used to assess a resident's physical or cognitive function (Harris-Kojetin et al., 2013). Information from 2011 and 2012 found that 96.1% of residents needed assistance with bathing, dressing (90.9%), toileting (86.6%), and eating (56.0%; Harris-Kojetin et al., 2013).

Short stay or postacute care (PAC) services are available for those needing continuing specialized care or rehabilitation for a short duration, typically between 1 and 90 days, following a hospital stay (American Hospital Association [AHA], 2010; Gassoums, Fike, Rahman, Enguidanos, & Wilber, 2013). These services are provided by SNFs as well as inpatient rehabilitation facilities (IRFs), home health agencies (HHAs), and long-term care hospitals (LTCHs)—with SNFs being the most frequently utilized PAC setting (Grabowski, 2010; MedPAC, 2011). Furthermore, 93% of SNFs operate as Medicaid-certified nursing facilities (Grabowski, 2010).

PAYMENTS AND REIMBURSEMENTS

Health care spending accounted for 17.9% of the U.S. gross domestic product (GDP) in 2011 (The World Bank, 2014). Spending on nursing care facilities and continuing care retirement communities (CCRCs) across all payers in 2011 was $149 billion (CMS, 2013a).

There are two major payers for nursing homes, the government (through either Medicare or Medicaid) and what is known as *private pay* (KFF, 2013). Medicare is defined as "the federal health insurance program for people who are 65 or older, certain younger people with disabilities, and people with End-Stage Renal Disease (permanent kidney failure requiring dialysis or a transplant, sometimes called ESRD)" (Medicare.gov, n.d.-d). Medicaid is "a joint federal and state program that helps with medical costs for some people with limited income and resources" (Medicare.gov, n.d.-b). Medicaid provides coverage for nursing home admissions and personal care services; services are typically only covered under Medicare if they are deemed medically necessary for a short duration (CMS, 2014a; Medicare.gov, n.d.-a).

Medicare will cover inpatient rehabilitation costs following a medically necessary hospital stay and pay the costs in full for a period of 20 days, provided the rehabilitation facility is Medicare certified (Linehan, 2012; Mullin, 2013). For days 21 to 100, the patient is responsible for a daily copay (currently $152 per day), with Medicare covering the remaining costs (CMS, 2014a; Linehan, 2012). After 100 days, the patient is solely responsible for the costs of care (CMS, 2014b). Medicare does not provide coverage for long-term care services (Mullin, 2013). Instead, Medicaid is the major financier of long-term care services (MedPAC, 2012; Table 11.3).

To assist with costs, Medicaid is available to individuals whose liquid assets are below a specific amount as determined by each state (Medicare.gov, n.d.-a). Individuals with substantial medical bills may be able to qualify for Medicaid by spending down their assets or transferring them to a spouse (Wilson, 2006). **Spend down** is the process of reducing assets in order to qualify for programs and services. This is possible in situations in which a person's medical expenses exceed or greatly diminish his or her available income (Medicare.gov, n.d.-c). When this occurs, the individual uses his or her disposable income to pay for medical bills, and Medicaid covers the remaining portion (Wilson, 2006). However, an individual must follow the appropriate procedures for spending down assets, as there is a 5-year look-back period for Medicaid (Wilson, 2006). Prior to the

TABLE 11.3 Unit of Payment, Average Payment Amount, and Length of Stay in Postacute Care Settings, 2011

	SKILLED NURSING FACILITY	HOME HEALTH AGENCY	INPATIENT REHABILITATION FACILITY	LONG-TERM CARE HOSPITAL
Unit of payment	Day	60-day episode	Discharge	Discharge
Average payment per unit	$11,707 per stay	$2,691 per episode	$17,398 per discharge	$38,664 Per discharge
Average length of stay	27 days	2 episodes	13.0 days	26.3 days

Sources: Linehan (2012; chart updated by authors to reflect 2011 data); CMS (2012a); MedPAC (2013, June).

Medicaid eligibility period, an individual cannot gift sums of money or assets ("for less than fair market value") to his or her child or other family members in order to expedite the spend-down process (Wilson, 2006), with certain transfers between spouses allowable (Wilson, 2006).

Those who qualify for both Medicare and Medicaid are considered "**dually eligible**" (CMS, 2014b). Specifically, the term *dual eligiblility* refers to those utilizing "Medicare Part A and/or Part B and eligible for some form of Medicaid benefit" (CMS, 2013a). For example, Medicare pays days 1 to 20 in an SNF, and Medicaid may cover the daily copay for days 21 to 100, depending on the individual's beneficiary group (MedPAC, 2012). There are four beneficiary groups for dual eligibles: qualified Medicare beneficiaries (QMB), specified low-income Medicare beneficiaries (SLMB), qualifying individuals (QI), and qualified disabled working individuals (QDWI; CMS, 2013c). Each group covers a specific facet of Part A, Part B, or both (CMS, 2014a). Additionally, individuals considered full-benefit dual eligibles (FBDE) "are those eligible for full Medicaid benefits" (CMS, 2013a, 2013b, 2013c) in addition to Medicare benefits, and typically have the majority of their medical costs covered (CMS, 2013a, 2014b).

A number of residents pay for the cost of nursing care out-of-pocket (i.e., private pay) when they are admitted to a nursing home (Medicare.gov, n.d.-d). A majority pays out-of-pocket until eligible for Medicaid, whereas others rely on long-term care insurance, life insurance, or continue to use personal funds (Medicare.gov, n.d.-c). In 2011, private-pay residents accounted for 22% of nursing facility occupants (KFF, 2013).

Medicare and/or Medicaid certification is required for reimbursement. Certification for one or both programs is recommended by the State Survey Agency, which conducts an inspection of the facility in question and provides its findings to a CMS Regional Office (CMS, 2012c). The vast majority of nursing homes are dually certified, accepting both Medicare and Medicaid (KFF, 2013). Because Medicare is regulated by the federal government, the CMS Regional

Office makes the final determination regarding certification (CMS, 2012b). When the decision concerns certification for Medicaid only, the State Survey Agency is simply reporting its own certification determination (CMS, 2012c). It is important to note that participation in one or both of these programs is completely voluntary, but (as noted) a majority of residents use Medicare or Medicaid as a payer source, and so most facilities look to be certified to accept these residents/payments (KFF, 2013). Of the 15,683 nursing homes surveyed in 2012, 14,330 were dually eligible, 571 were Medicaid only, and the remaining 782 were Medicare only (CMS, Department of Health and Human Services, 2012b).

CHALLENGES AND OPPORTUNITIES FOR NURSING FACILITIES

Nursing facilities will face numerous challenges in the coming years. One prominent challenge is related to the new forms of caregiving facilities that have emerged in the long-term care sector—assisted living facilities (ALFs). ALFs are facilities in which individuals reside within an apartment or homelike structure. Such facilities hire personal care staff to assist residents throughout the day and are becoming an increasingly popular alternative to nursing facilities (Assisted Living Federation of America [ALFA], 2013; see Chapter 10, this volume). These establishments are generally more affordable than nursing facilities, although prices vary widely, and some ALFs are even more expensive than nursing facilities (MedlinePlus, 2014). In addition, the financial burden of paying for ALF residence falls on the resident or his or her family, as Medicare does not cover these particular costs (MedlinePlus), although, in some cases Medicaid can pay some costs. That is, in some states Medicaid will pay the per day rate for an ALF stay. In 2012, there were approximately 22,220 such facilities (Harris-Kojetin et al., 2013).

Another alternative to nursing facilities is HCBS (see Chapter 5). HCBS offer Medicaid recipients the ability to receive services that they would normally receive in a nursing facility in their home or in a community setting (Medicaid.gov, n.d.). The provision of Medicaid HCBS is optional and left to the discretion of individual states (Watson, 2009). Research has demonstrated that HCBS is less costly than care a recipient would receive in a facility (KFF, 2013). Another initiative that supports HCBS is the Money Follows the Person Program (MFPP; Medicaid.gov, n.d.-c). MFPP aids states in rebalancing "their Medicaid long-term care systems" and has assisted over 31,000 people in shifting from institutional care to community-based services (Medicaid.gov, n.d.).

With more people choosing to reside in their homes as long as possible, there has been an increase in the number of residents choosing ALFs or HCBS in recent years (Harris-Kojetin et al., 2013). Moreover, with the number of nursing facility alternatives, nursing facilities have seen an increase in the acuity of their residents as well as a decrease in residents' length of stay (Mor, Caswell, Littlehale, Niemi, & Fogel, 2009).

The quality of care residents receive has been an ongoing challenge for the nursing home industry. Structural quality indicators (i.e., staffing levels), process quality indicators (i.e., pain control), outcome quality indicators (i.e., infections), as well as deficiency citations can all be used to measure quality (Castle & Ferguson, 2010). It is important to note that CMS determines quality based on 18 quality measures given on a web-based report card (Nursing Home Compare). These quality measures include resident pain, falls, and pressure ulcers (CMS, 2013a). Many facilities perform poorly on these measures. Furthermore, quality has been associated with staffing levels and turnover. One study showed that high staff turnover in nursing facilities resulted in decreased quality of care for residents (Castle & Engberg, 2006).

Person-centered care may alter the quality of care and quality of life for nursing facility residents. Person-centered care is part of the culture change movement occurring in nursing facilities. The movement strives to personalize the residents' environment in an attempt to individualize and deinstitutionalize care (Koren, 2010). Other such initiatives include the Eden Alternative, which uses environmental and social stimulation to prevent depression in residents, and Green Houses, which "use free-standing small group homes, not large facilities, where residents are cared for by a consistent group of direct care staff" (Koren, 2010, p. 312). Studies involving Green Houses found residents' quality of life markedly higher than that of residents in traditional facilities with lower turnover rates among staff due to increased job satisfaction (Koren, 2010; see Case Study 11.1).

Case Study 11.1: A Resident Transitions to Nursing Facility Care

Miss Betty Spiels was a plucky member of her garden club and a prominent member of her community. Having remained in her hometown for most of her life, she was an independent, well-heeled, and well-educated woman. Influential because of "family money" and supposed reputation, she never married and was considered rather self-promoting when it came to subjugating her needs over those of others. As a matter of fact, her often-dismissed but rather unsavory traits, such as taking credit for the work and ideas of others in the town, did nothing but exacerbate with age, and her supposed friendship network eroded over time as Miss Betty became more demanding, less trustworthy, and increasingly apt to speak her mind, regardless of the fallout. She lived alone in her lovely two-story home and was assisted by her personal assistant, Rhiana Jaster. All went well in the small town until Miss Betty took an unfortunate fall down the steps of her home that left her with broken bones and mental confusion. A neighbor called adult protective services (APS), because she strongly suspected that Miss Betty had been pushed by Rhiana. APS determined that the best placement for Miss Betty was the local nursing home as a private-pay resident. Trouble was, when the paperwork was being prepared, an

(*continued*)

Case Study 11.1: A Resident Transitions to Nursing Facility Care

assessment of her assets revealed that her accounts had been drained. It was under these circumstances that Louis Acres received its newest resident.

Case Study Discussion Questions:

1. How will the facility address Miss Betty's notorious personality traits?
2. How will the facility address Miss Betty's lack of funds?
3. What are the implications of person-centered care for Miss Betty?

There are a number of additional challenges and opportunities that nursing homes will confront in the coming years, including pay-for-performance, culture-change initiatives, and workforce hurdles. Nursing facilities are integral components of health care and will continue to face ongoing issues alongside acute care facilities. Currently, payment reform, health care reorganizations, and changing demographics (such as increased obesity) all represent challenges and opportunities for nursing facilities.

SUMMARY

As the number of aging individuals grows, the burden of care on nursing facilities will increase. Nursing facilities are integral components of health care and will continue to face ongoing issues alongside acute care facilities. Currently, payment reform, health care reorganizations, and changing demographics all represent challenges and opportunities for nursing facilities. This will likely increase spending on nursing facilities. The operation of nursing facilities will likely change substantially.

DISCUSSION QUESTIONS

1. What resources should be available for consumers to pick a nursing home? What characteristics of nursing homes should be included in these resources?
2. With alternatives to nursing facilities, such as home- and community-based services (HCBS), how should nursing facilities adapt to remain viable?
3. The quality of care residents receive has been an ongoing challenge for the nursing home industry. What can be done to improve quality? In

particular, what can regulators do and what can facilities do to improve quality?

4. Medicaid pays for a substantial portion of nursing home care. What are the implications of this payment system, and what reforms may be necessary for nursing home reimbursement?

ADDITIONAL RESOURCES

PUBLICATIONS

American Health Care Association. (2014, June). *Trends in nursing facility characteristics.* Washington, DC: Author.

Centers for Medicare & Medicaid Services. (2008). *Action plan for (further improvement of) nursing home quality.* Retrieved from www.cms.hhs.gov/certificationandcomplianc/downloads/sfflist.pdf

Centers for Medicare & Medicaid Services. (2009). *Skilled nursing facilities nonswing bed: Medicare national summary.* Retrieved from www.cms.hhs.gov/MedicareFeeforSvcPartsAB/Downloads/NationalSum2007.pdf

General Accounting Office. (1987). *Medicare and Medicaid: Stronger enforcement of nursing home requirements needed* (GAO-87-113). Washington, DC: Author.

General Accounting Office. (1999). *Nursing homes: Additional steps needed to strengthen enforcement of federal quality standards* (GAO/HEHS-99-46). Washington, DC: Author.

Institute of Medicine. (1986). *Improving the quality of care in nursing homes.* Washington, DC: National Academy Press.

Institute of Medicine. (1996). *Committee on the adequacy of nurse staffing in hospitals and nursing homes. Nursing staff in hospitals and nursing homes: Is it adequate*? Washington, DC: National Academy Press.

Institute of Medicine. (2001). *Crossing the quality chasm: a new health system for the 21st century.* Washington, DC: National Academy Press.

Institute of Medicine. (2004). *Keeping patients safe: Transforming the work environment of nurses.* Washington, DC: National Academy Press.

National Nursing Home Survey. (2004). *National Center for Health Statistics.* Hyattsville, MD: Public Health Service.

KEY WEBSITES

AARP www.aarp.org
Advancing Excellence in Americas Nursing Homes (AE) www.nhqualitycampaign.org
Agency for Healthcare Research and Quality (AHRQ) AHRQ.gov
American College of Health Care Administrators (ACHCA) www.achca.org
American Hospital Association (AHA) www.aha.org
Centers for Disease Control and Prevention (CDC) www.cdc.gov
Centers for Medicare and Medicaid Services (CMS) www.cms.gov
Department of Health and Human Services (DHHS) http://aspe.hhs.gov
Institute of Medicine (IOM) www.iom.org
Kaiser Family Foundation (KFF) http://kff.org
LeadingAge (American Association of Homes and Services for the Aging) LeadingAge.org
National Center for Health Statistics (NCHS) www.cdc.gov/nchs
National Citizen's Coalition for Nursing Home Reform http://theconsumervoice.org

National Health Policy Forum (NHPF) www.nhpf.org
Nursing Home Compare www.medicare.gov/nursinghomecompare
Office of Inspector General (OIG) http://oig.hhs.gov

REFERENCES

American Hospital Association (AHA). (2010). *TrendWatch: Maximizing the value of post-acute care*. Retrieved from www.aha.org/research/reports/tw/10nov-tw-postacute.pdf

Assisted Living Federation of America (ALFA). (2013). *Senior living options*. Retrieved from www.alfa.org/alfa/Assisted_Living_Information.asp

Bohm, D. A. (2001). Striving for quality care in America's nursing homes: Tracing the history of nursing homes and noting the effect of recent federal government initiatives to ensure quality care in the nursing home setting. *DePaul Journal of Health Care Law*, *4*, 317–362.

Castle, N. G., & Engberg, J. (2006). Organizational characteristics associated with staff turnover in nursing homes. *The Gerontologist*, *46*, 62–73.

Castle, N. G., & Ferguson, J. (2010). What is nursing home quality and how is it measured? *The Gerontologist*, *50*(4), 426–442.

Castle, N. G., Ferguson, J., & Hughes, K. (2009). Humanism in nursing homes: The impact of top management. *Journal of Health and Human Services Administration*, *31*(4), 483–508.

Centers for Disease Control and Prevention. (2008). *National Nursing Home Survey (NNHS) 2004–2005. Nursing assistant tables—Estimates*. Retrieved from www.cdc.gov/nchs/data/nnhsd/Estimates/nnas/Estimates_PayBenefits_Tables.pdf#21

Centers for Disease Control and Prevention. (2013). *Nursing home care*. Retrieved from www.cdc.gov/nchs/fastats/nursingh.htm

Centers for Medicare & Medicaid Services, Department of Health and Human Services. (2012a). *Medicare and Medicaid statistical supplement, 2012 edition* (Table 6.2). Retrieved from www.cms.gov/Research-Statistics-Data-and-Systems/Statistics-Trends-and-Reports/MedicareMedicaidStatSupp/2012.html

Centers for Medicare & Medicaid Services, Department of Health and Human Services. (2012b). *Nursing home data compendium, 2012 edition*. Retrieved from www.cms.gov/Medicare/Provider-Enrollment-and-Certification/CertificationandComplianc/downloads/nursinghomedatacompendium_508.pdf

Centers for Medicare & Medicaid Services, Department of Health and Human Services. (2012c). *Survey & certification—Certification and compliance*. Retrieved from www.cms.gov/Medicare/Provider-Enrollment-and-Certification/CertificationandComplianc/index.html?redirect=/Certificationandcomplianc/18_RHCs.asp

Centers for Medicare & Medicaid Services, Department of Health and Human Services. (2013a). *National health expenditure data (historical)*. Retrieved from www.cms.gov/Research-Statistics-Data-and-Systems/Statistics-Trends-and-Reports/NationalHealthExpendData/NationalHealthAccountsHistorical.html

Centers for Medicare & Medicaid Services, Department of Health and Human Services. (2013b). *Medicaid coverage of Medicare beneficiaries (dual eligibles) at a glance*. Retrieved from www.cms.gov/Outreach-and-Education/Medicare-Learning-Network-MLN/MLNProducts/downloads/medicare_beneficiaries_dual_eligibles_at_a_glance.pdf

Centers for Medicare & Medicaid Services, Department of Health and Human Services. (2013c). *Quality measures*. Retrieved from www.cms.gov/Medicare/Quality-Initiatives-Patient-Assessment-Instruments/NursingHomeQualityInits/NHQIQualityMeasures.html

Centers for Medicare & Medicaid Services, Department of Health and Human Services. (2014a). *Medicare & you 2014*. Retrieved from www.medicare.gov/Pubs/pdf/10050.pdf

Centers for Medicare & Medicaid Services, Department of Health and Human Services. (2014b). *Medicare coverage of skilled nursing facility care*. Retrieved from www.medicare.gov/pubs/pdf/10153.pdf

Decker, F. H. (2006). Nursing staff and the outcomes of nursing home stays. *Medical Care, 44*, 812–821.

Decker, F., Dollard, K. J., & Guterman, S. (2001). *Staffing of nursing services in long-term care: Present issues and prospects for the future*. Washington, DC: American Health Care Association—Health Services Research and Evaluation.

Emerzian, A. D. J., & Stampp, T. (1993). Nursing home reform: Its legislative history and economic impact upon nursing homes. *Benefits Quarterly, 9*(1), 19–28.

Estabrooks, C. A., Morgan, D., Squires, J. E., Boström, A. M., Slaughter, S. E., Cummings, G. G., & Norton, P. G. (2011). The care unit in nursing home research: Evidence in support of a definition. *BMC Medical Research Methodology, 11*, 46.

Fairchild, T. J., & Knebl, J. A. (2002). Nursing homes. In D. J. Ekerdt (Ed.), *Encyclopedia of Aging*. (Vol. 3., pp. 999–1002). New York, NY: Macmillan Reference, USA.

Federal Interagency Forum on Aging-Related Statistics. (2012). *Older Americans 2012: Key indicators of well-being*. Washington, DC: Federal Interagency Forum on Aging-Related Statistics. Retrieved from http://agingstats.gov/agingstatsdotnet/Main_Site/Data/2012_Documents/Docs/EntireChartbook.pdf

Gassoums, Z., Fike, K., Rahman, A., Enguidanos, S., & Wilber, K. (2013). Who transitions to the community from nursing homes? Comparing patterns and predictors for short-stay and long-stay residents. *Home Health Care Services Quarterly, 32*(2), 75–91.

Grabowski, D. (2010). *Post-acute and long-term care: A primer on services, expenditures and payment methods*. Washington, DC: U.S. Department of Health and Human Services. Retrieved from http://aspe.hhs.gov/daltcp/reports/2010/paltc.htm

Grabowski, D. C., & Stevenson, D. G. (2008). Ownership conversions and nursing home performance. *Health Services Research, 43*(4), 1184–1203.

Haber, C. (2002). Nursing homes: History. In D. J. Ekerdt (Ed.), *Encyclopedia of aging* (pp. 1005–1008). New York, NY: Macmillan Reference USA.

Harrington, C., Kovner, C., Kayser-Jones, J., Burger, S., Mohler, M., Burke, R., & Zimmerman, D. (2000). Experts recommend minimum nurse staffing standards for nursing facilities in the United Sates. *The Gerontologist, 40*(1), 1–12.

Harrington, C., Kovner, C., Mezey, M., Kayser-Jones, J., Burger, S., Mohler, M., Burke, R., & Zimmerman, D. (2000). Experts recommend minimum nurse staffing standards for nursing facilities in the United Sates. *The Gerontologist, 40*(1), 5–16.

Harris-Kojetin, L., Sengupta, M., Park-Lee, E., & Valverde, R. (2013). *Long-term care services in the United States: 2013 overview*. Hyattsville, MD: National Center for Health Statistics. Retrieved from www.cdc.gov/nchs/data/nsltcp/long_term_care_services_2013.pdf

Health and Human Services: Office of Inspector General. (2002). *Nurse aide training*. Retrieved from http://oig.hhs.gov/oei/reports/oei-05-01-00030.pdf

Health Resources and Services Administration. (n.d.). *Hill-Burton free and reduced-cost health care*. Retrieved from www.hrsa.gov/gethealthcare/affordable/hillburton/

Jones, A. (2002). The National Nursing Home Survey: 1999 summary. *Vital and Health Statistics, 152*(13). Retrieved from www.cdc.gov/nchs/data/series/sr_13/sr13_152.pdf

Kaiser Family Foundation. (2013). *Overview of nursing facility capacity, financing, and ownership in the United States in 2011*. Retrieved from http://kff.org/medicaid/fact-sheet/overview-of-nursing-facility-capacity-financing-and-ownership-in-the-united-states-in-2011

Koren, M. (2010). Person-centered care for nursing home residents: The culture-change movement. *Health Affairs, 29*(2), 312–317.

Lidz, C., Fischer, L., & Arnold, R. M. (1992). *The erosion of autonomy in long-term care*. New York, NY: Oxford University Press.

Linehan, K., & National Health Policy Forum. (2012). *Medicare's post-acute payment: A review of the issues and policy proposals* (Issue Brief 847). Retrieved from www.nhpf.org/library/issue-briefs/IB847_PostAcutePayment_12-07-12.pdf

Medicaid.gov. (n.d.). *Home and community based services*. Retrieved from www.medicaid.gov/Medicaid-CHIP-Program-Information/By-Topics/Long-Term-Services-and-Support/Home-and-Community-Based-Services/Home-and-Community-Based-Services.html

Medicare.gov. (n.d.-a). *How can I pay for nursing home care?* Retrieved from www.medicare.gov/what-medicare-covers/part-a/paying-for-nursing-home-care.html

Medicare.gov. (n.d.-b). *Medicaid*. Retrieved from www.medicare.gov/your-medicare-costs/help-paying-costs/medicaid/medicaid.html

Medicare.gov. (n.d.-c). *Money Follows the Person (MFP)*. Retrieved from www.medicaid.gov/Medicaid-CHIP-Program-Information/By-Topics/Long-Term-Services-and-Support/Balancing/Money-Follows-the-Person.html

Medicare.gov. (n.d.-d). *What is medicare*? Retrieved from www.medicare.gov/sign-up-change-plans/decide-how-to-get-medicare/whats-medicare/what-is-medicare.html

Medicare Payment Advisory Commission. (2011). *Payment basics: Skilled nursing facility services payment system*. Washington, DC: Author. Retrieved from www.medpac.gov/documents/MedPAC_Payment_Basics_11_SNF.pdf

Medicare Payment Advisory Commission. (2012). *Skilled nursing facility services* (Chapter 7, pp. 181–209). Washington DC: MedPac. Retrieved from www.medpac.gov/chapters/Mar12_Ch07.pdf

Medicare Payment Advisory Commission. (2013, June). *A data book: Health care spending and the Medicare program* (p. 6, program spending; p. 130, HHA; p. 133, IRF; p. 137, LTCH). Retrieved from www.medpac.gov/documents/Jun13DataBookEntireReport.pdf

MedlinePlus. (2014). *Nursing homes*. Retrieved from www.nlm.nih.gov/medlineplus/nursinghomes.html

Miller, R. D., & Hutton, R. C. (2000). *Problems in health care law* (8th ed., p. 21). New York, NY: Aspen.

Moore, K., Boscardin, J., Steinman, M., & Schwartz, J. (2012). Age and sex variation in prevalence of chronic medical conditions in older residents of US nursing homes. *Journal of the American Geriatrics Society*, *60*(4), 756–764.

Mor, V., Caswell, C., Littlehale, S., Niemi, J., & Fogel, B. (2009). *Changes in the quality of nursing homes in the US: A review and data update*. Retrieved from www.ahcancal.org/research_data/quality/Documents/ChangesinNursingHomeQuality.pdf

Mueller, C., Arling, G., Kane, R., Bershadsky, J., Holland, D., & Joy, A. (2006). Nursing home staffing standards: Their relationship to nurse staffing levels. *The Gerontologist*, *46*(1), 74–80.

Mullin, E. (2013). *How to pay for nursing home costs. US News*. Retrieved from http://health.usnews.com/health-news/best-nursing-homes/articles/2013/02/26/how-to-pay-for-nursing-home-costs

National Nursing Assistant Survey. (2008). *National Nursing Assistant Survey. Long-Term Care Statistics Branch Division of Health Care Statistics,* National Center for Health Statistics, Hyattsville, MD.

National Stroke Association. (2006). *National Stroke Association's guide to choosing stroke rehabilitation services*. Retrieved from www.stroke.org/site/DocServer/Choose_Rehab.pdf?docID=1101

Paraprofessional Healthcare Institute. (2012). *PHI national policy agenda: Training and support*. Retrieved from http://phinational.org/sites/phinational.org/files/wp-content/uploads/2008/11/policyagendatraining.pdf

Pratt, J. R. (1999). Long-term care managing across the continuum (pp. 21, 79–104, 123–127, 308–310, 445–446). New York, NY: Aspen.

Rau, J. (2013). *Medicare seeks to curb spending on post-hospital care. Kaiser Health News (KHN)*. Retrieved from www.kaiserhealthnews.org/stories/2013/december/01/post-acute-care-medicare-cost-quality.aspx

Scalesse, M. (2013). The great healthcare debate: For-profit vs. not-for-profit. *Nursing Management*, *44*(11), 38–43.

Sengupta, M., Harris-Kojetin, L., & Ejaz, F. (2010). A national overview of the training received by certified nursing assistants working in the U.S. nursing homes. *Gerontology & Geriatrics Education*, *31*(3), 201–219.

Skillednursingfacilities.org. (2010). *Rehabilitation units in skilled nursing facilities*. Retrieved from www.skillednursingfacilities.org/blog/life-in-nursing-homes/rehabilitation-units-skilled-nursing-facilities

State Operations Manual. (2012). Washington, DC: Centers for Medicare and Medicaid Services. Retrieved from www.cms.hhs.gov/manuals

Stevenson, D. G., Bramson, J. S., & Grabowski, D. C. (2013). Nursing home ownership trends and their impacts on quality of care: A study using detailed ownership data from Texas. *Journal of Aging and Social Policy*, *25*(1), 30–47.

U.S. Social Security Administration. (2005). Social Security: A program and policy history. *Social Security Bulletin*, *66*(1). Retrieved from www.ssa.gov/policy/docs/ssb/v66n1/v66n1p1.html

Watson, S. D. (2009). From almshouses to nursing homes and community care: Lessons from Medicaid's history. *Georgia State University Law Review*, *26*(3), 937–969.

Wilson, J. (2006, February). *Deficit Reduction Act of 2005 Summary of Medicaid/Medicare/Health Provisions*. Washington, DC: National Conference of State Legislatures. Retrieved from www.ncsl.org/print/health/SumS1932Jan3106.pdf

The World Bank. (2014). *Health expenditure, total (% of GDP)*. Retrieved from http://data.worldbank.org/indicator/SH.XPD.TOTL.ZS

Zanfardino, R. (2012). Ten most common medical conditions among nursing home patients uncovered. *Health News Observer*. Retrieved from www.healthnewsobserver.com/articles/detail/ten-most-common-medical-conditions-among-nursing-home-patients-uncovered

Hospice and Providing Palliative Care

AMY M. WESTCOTT
SUSAN LYSAGHT HURLEY
KAREN B. HIRSCHMAN

CHAPTER OVERVIEW

In our aging society, increasing numbers of adults with advanced illness receive long-term care services and support in a variety of settings (Medicare, 2009). Long-term care services and support can be provided at home or in the community (i.e., in senior centers, in Programs of All-Inclusive Care for the Elderly [PACE]), in assisted living facilities, in personal care homes, or in nursing homes. Thus, older adults who wish to age in place or die in place may take advantage of various models of care from diagnosis of an advanced illness through death, and health care providers need to rise to the challenge of providing the best possible care. In this chapter, we consider ways in which this care is provided by hospice, palliative care, and the integration of good end-of-life care into existing long-term care services and supports.

LEARNING OBJECTIVES

After completing this chapter, you should have an understanding of:

- The history and development of hospice and palliative care
- The various settings that deliver hospice and palliative care
- The benefits and challenges of delivering hospice and palliative care

KEY TERMS

Collaborative care
End-of-life care
Hospice
Hospice-Supported Consult Model
Long-Term Care Community-Based Model
Palliative care
Palliative Care Consult Model
Plan of care

INTRODUCTION

The concept of a formal program for hospice care originated with Cicely Saunders, a British physician with prior experience as a nurse and social worker. Dr. Saunders is often credited with being the pioneer of the modern hospice movement. She founded St. Christopher's hospice in England 1967 (Clark & Foley, 2003; St. Christopher's Hospice, 1967; Storey, 1990).

Formal hospice care actually preceded formal palliative care in the United States. In 1982, the Medicare Hospice Benefit (MHB) was created to provide comprehensive care to patients who have a terminal illness and wish to die at home. **Hospice** is defined as a program that *focuses on caring, not curing* and is "considered the model for quality compassionate care for people facing a life-limiting illness … hospice provides expert medical care, pain management, and emotional and spiritual support expressly tailored to the patient's needs and wishes" (National Hospice and Palliative Care Organization, 2012, p. 3). A terminal illness was defined as one in which someone would have a life expectancy of 6 months or less, should a disease run its natural course. The MHB requires that the patient forego curative treatment and opt for more aggressive palliative symptom management (Centers for Medicare & Medicaid Services, 2010).

Hospice delivers care using an interdisciplinary team generally consisting of a nurse, social worker, chaplain, bereavement specialist physician, volunteers, home health aides, and therapists who work in partnership with the patient and family and with existing long-term care services. Each team member brings a discipline-specific expertise as well as superior communication skills to develop and implement an individualized **plan of care** to meet the needs of the patient and/or family. **Collaborative care** among all team members is key to success (Figure 12.1).

Of the 2.5 million Americans who died in 2009, 42% or just over 1 million died under hospice care (National Hospice and Palliative Care Organization, 2012). Hospice patients tend to be older (aged 65 or older), female, and White (Connor, Elwert, Spence, & Christakis, 2007, 2008). The older population using hospice services tends to have a noncancer primary diagnosis (62% in 2011), such as debility, dementia, heart disease, lung disease, and end-stage organ failure (National Hospice and Palliative Care Organization, 2012). Approximately 42% of patients enrolled in hospice receive care at a private residence, but a growing number of hospice patients are receiving care in nursing homes (18%) and

FIGURE 12.1 Components of collaborative care.

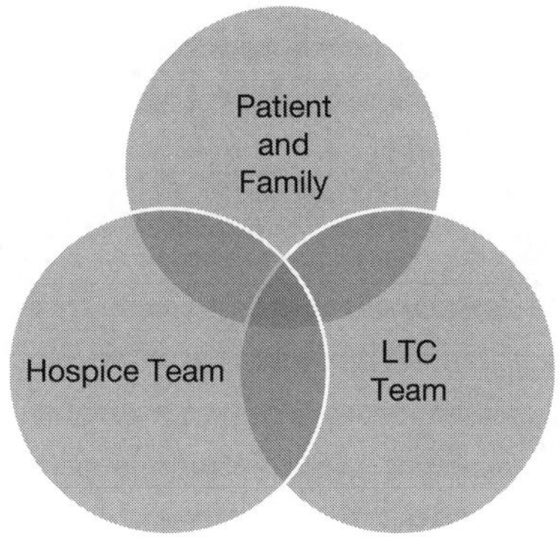

in residential care communities (7%; National Hospice and Palliative Care Organization, 2012). Hospice care in the United States is largely provided through the Medicare Hospice Benefit (MHB).

MEDICARE HOSPICE BENEFIT

The MHB is funded through the U.S. government Medicare program (Part A). In general, Part A covers care provided by a hospital, skilled nursing facility (SNF), nursing home, hospice, and home health services (Centers for Medicare & Medicaid Services, 2010, 2012a, 2012b), whereas Part B primarily covers preventive and outpatient services. Originally, hospice was created for care of someone with a life-limiting illness, such as cancer, in the home with a primary caregiver providing a majority of the care. In 1986, Congress extended the MHB to cover those with life-limiting illnesses residing in nursing homes, and state Medicaid programs were given the option to include the hospice benefit as well, which allowed greater access to the MHB (Medicare, 2009; National Hospice and Palliative Care Organization, 2012). One important consideration for many nursing home residents who may be receiving the Medicare skilled nursing benefit, which covers room and board, is that when the MHB is selected, everything related to the terminal diagnosis is covered except room and board, which is often covered out-of-pocket or by Medicaid.

Care provided by either the primary caregiver in the home or staff in a nursing home or assisted living facility is supplemented by a hospice interdisciplinary team 24 hours a day and 7 days a week with visits, medical equipment, medications related to the hospice diagnosis, an on-call telephone hotline service, and bereavement support to loved ones for 13 months after the death. As of 2012, the MHB is a capitated reimbursement structure, with a *per diem* rate (depending on the site of care and geographic region) for routine home care (approximately $140), continuous home care (approximately $830), inpatient respite care (approximately $150), and general inpatient care (approximately $640). This means that the hospice organization received a set payment to provide all of the hospice services (Centers for Medicare & Medicaid Services, 2012b).

FIGURE 12.2 Interface of hospice and palliative care.

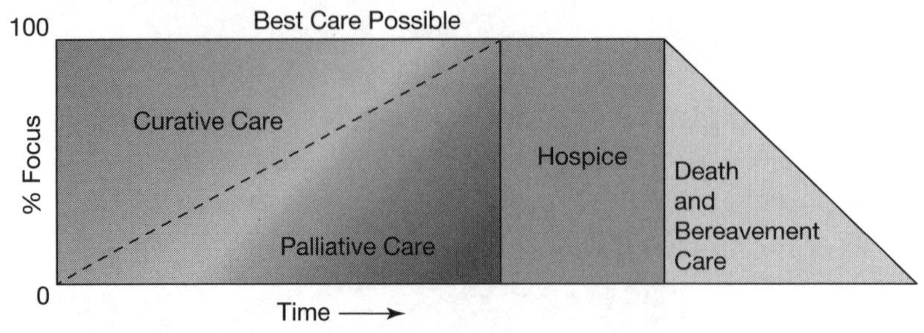

Source: Adapted from Lynn (2005).

In addition to the MHB, hospice may be paid for in other ways. For instance, most private insurance plans currently offer a hospice benefit. Some private insurance companies are exploring open-access hospice programs that will provide ongoing treatment in conjunction with hospice management or programs that extend the prognosis to more than 6 months (i.e., 1 year). Also, many hospices will provide charity care for those who don't have insurance or cannot afford parts of their care. Although hospice is the most commonly utilized model to provide palliative care, in Figure 12.2, we depict that it only reaches a small portion of the ill, specifically those who have a prognosis of 6 months or less. The hope is for palliative care to be integrated much earlier.

PALLIATIVE CARE

Palliative care is an approach to care as well as a formal specialty in many health-related disciplines. Although the palliation of symptoms can occur during the course of any illness (i.e., when we are treating an infection but give acetaminophen to relieve the discomfort of fever), formal palliative care usually refers to supportive care of those with life-limiting illness. The World Health Organization defines **palliative care** as "an approach that improves the quality of life of patients and their families facing the problem associated with life-threatening illness, through the prevention and relief of suffering by means of early identification and impeccable assessment and treatment of pain and other problems, physical, psychosocial and spiritual" (World Health Organization, 2010). For older adults with progressive and advanced illness, goals of care may change from curative treatment to a palliative approach. Palliative care focuses on the goals of care, a patient's wishes, and aggressive symptom management.

Although the notion of palliative care is much older, in the United States the first medical palliative care program was established at the Cleveland Clinic by Declan Walsh in 1987 (Meier, Isaacs, & Hughes, 2010). The Institute of Medicine took notice in 1997 with a report titled *Approaching Death: Improving Care at the End of Life* (Board on Health Care Services, 1997). This report was followed by the establishment of the National Consensus Project for Quality

Palliative Care in 2001, which led to the 2004 consensus guidelines and the most recent 2013 third edition of *Clinical Practice Guidelines for Quality Palliative Care* (National Consensus Project for Quality Care, 2013).

Today, palliative medicine is a board-certified field for physicians in the United States. Nurse practitioners, nurses, and social workers can also achieve additional certification for providing palliative care (Center to Advance Palliative Care, 2011). Now, hospital-based palliative care programs can also be credentialed (The Joint Commission, 2011). Other models exist for providing palliative care for patients living in the community or in nursing homes. For the purpose of this chapter, *community* will be defined broadly as the patient's home. However, we acknowledge that the community at large often plays a role in providing palliative care, especially in rural areas and within certain subgroups in the United States. Home-based palliative care models are usually provided through a home care agency to those with a skilled nursing need. In addition, some of the PACE (Program of All-Inclusive Care for the Elderly) models may incorporate a palliative care approach into their model through staff education or a designated team. Currently, the most utilized model for palliative care is delivered through hospice models either through the MHB, which is paid for by Medicare and sometimes Medicaid, or via private insurances, volunteers, private pay, or charity care.

INSTITUTION-BASED MODELS

In this chapter, institutional settings include nursing homes, residential, assisted living, and personal care homes. The hospice model allows institutional communities to contract and collaborate with a hospice provider to care for eligible residents with life-limiting conditions. Hospice is often considered the gold standard for delivering comprehensive **end-of-life care**. End-of-life care is defined primarily by the regulatory environment rather than by scientific data due to the lack of reliable prognostic scientific evidence. Components of the definition of end-of-life care include (a) presence of a chronic disease(s) or symptoms or functional impairments and (b) irreversible/progressive disease causing symptoms or impairments that may lead to death (National Institutes of Health, 2004). More recently, the National Consensus Project and the National Quality Forum outlined eight domains for palliative care: (a) structure and processes of care; (b) physical aspects of care; (c) psychosocial and psychiatric aspects of care; (d) social aspects of care; (e) spiritual, religious, and existential aspects of care; (f) cultural aspects of care; (g) care of the patient at end of life; and (h) ethical and legal aspects of care (National Consensus Project for Quality Care, 2013).

The hospice model sets a high standard for palliative care by fusing the strengths of the interdisciplinary team (i.e., nursing home, assisted living, or community-based long-term care services) with those of the hospice interdisciplinary team to care for the older adult and family. Both teams have mutual goals to provide quality care, symptom management, and dignity to dying residents and their families (Hirschman et al., 2005). For example, the nursing home team or assisted living staff bring prior knowledge about the resident/family,

EXHIBIT 12.1 Barriers to Hospice Care in Nursing Homes

Type of Barrier	Examples
Cultural	• Ethnic differences • Focus on rehabilitation and restoration of function
Financial	• Declining reimbursements from Medicaid • Room and board not paid for by hospice for routine level of care
Regulatory	• Federal regulations focus on maintaining weight, preventing falls, and preventing skin breakdown
Organizational	• Transitions between acute care and nursing home • Inadequate staffing • Training and education gaps • Commitment from leadership

Source: Center to Advance Palliative Care (2008).

ongoing relationships, and personal care needs. The hospice team brings expertise in pain and symptom management, spiritual care, and bereavement support. Ideally, the collaboration between hospice and long-term support and services provides complementary care through effective leadership and communication (Miller, 2007; Zerzan, Stearns, & Hanson, 2000); however, some barriers do exist (Exhibit 12.1). These barriers include cultural, financial, regulatory, and organizational challenges for hospice to provide care in the long-term care residences and to the families of residents.

Over the past two decades, the benefits of the integration of formal end-of-life care into nursing homes has been supported by research into evidence-based practices amid concern for the quality of care and quality of life of terminally ill older adults (Center to Advance Palliative Care, 2008). This approach has been demonstrated in studies about the education and training of staff, advance directives for residents, comparison of hospice and nonhospice patients in long-term care, and the influence of hospice on the care of every nursing home resident (Oliver, Porock, & Zweig, 2005; Stevenson & Bramson, 2009).

The general characteristics of hospice patients residing in a nursing home differ from hospice patients receiving care at home. Hospice patients in the nursing home are more likely to have a noncancer diagnosis as their documented terminal illness, use more physician and specialty services, and are more dependent in activities of daily living (Han, Tiggle, & Remsburg, 2007). Noncommunity (i.e., nursing home) hospice users are also more likely to be older, female, "dually" eligible (for Medicare and Medicaid), and have a shorter length of hospice enrollment (Stevenson, Huskamp, Grabowski, & Keating, 2007).

Barriers to Providing Hospice in Long-Term Care Settings

There are a number of barriers to providing hospice and palliative care services in institutional communities. Continuing-care retirement communities, nursing homes, assisted living, and residential care facilities that care for older adults at the end of life each have their own set of cultural norms related to the operations within each community.

Financial incentives and the regulatory environment may also play an important role in constraining the provision of palliative care. Most nursing homes provide a skilled nursing facility (SNF) care benefit, with a focus on rehabilitation or restoration of function. The SNF care is traditionally provided in the nursing home setting with physical therapy, occupational therapy, speech therapy, skilled nursing care, and other services. The focus on rehabilitation or maintenance of function is reinforced by state and federal regulations that monitor for decline, such as weight loss, falls, and pressure ulcers. It is financially more profitable for a nursing home to provide skilled care than hospice care because room and board needs to be paid privately or by Medicaid, depending on the state. An example would be sending a nursing home resident to be hospitalized in order to obtain a 3-day hospital stay that will then qualify the resident to return to the facility under the Skilled Medicare Benefit (Center to Advance Palliative Care, 2008). Case Study 12.1 highlights these issues.

Case Study 12.1: Robert Smith

Mr. Robert Smith is a 92-year-old gentleman with end-stage dementia who requires assistance for all personal care needs, careful hand-feeding by nursing home staff; it has been noted that he is declining. The nursing home team thinks that he needs a feeding tube placed and the nursing home administrator agrees, knowing that the reimbursement will be better for an SNF bed. However, Mr. Smith's only son, who lives 500 miles away, elected not to have tube feeding after a recent episode of pneumonia, and reports feeling tremendous guilt ever since he put his father into a nursing home. The son asks for hospice after a friend recommends it because the friend recently went through a similar experience. The hospice team and nursing home team together coordinate support for both the resident and his son. After Mr. Smith's death, the son is followed for 13 months by a bereavement specialist to assist in processing his guilt.

Case Study Discussion Questions:

1. What incentive does the nursing home have to recommend the feeding tube placement?
2. How can the hospice better partner with the nursing home to provide care for residents with end-stage dementia?
3. What are the benefits of including hospice in the care of Mr. Robert Smith?

Finally, from an organizational standpoint, nursing homes may lack the support of leadership or staffing to provide adequate palliative care. Leadership may or may not support ongoing education for staff and collaborative relationships with hospice or palliative care providers.

Other Palliative Care Models

Other nonhospice models that offer end-of-life expertise for residents in long-term care settings have evolved over time (Carlson, Lim, & Meier, 2011; Center to Advance Palliative Care, 2008). One of these collaborative models is the **Hospice-Supported Consult Model**. This model allows palliative care consultant providers from a contracted hospice provider to consult upon the request of the resident's attending physician. This model often draws on the existing hospice–community relationship. A second nonhospice model is called the **Palliative Care Consult Model**. This model allows nonhospice-affiliated palliative care consult providers to complete assessments upon request of the resident's attending physician. Palliative consultants bill separately and are usually not employed by the long-term care community. Palliative care consultants may be physicians, nurse practitioners, or physician assistants. One of the advantages to this model is that patients have access to specialty palliative care providers, even if they are using their Skilled Nursing Benefit. Finally, there is the **Long-Term Care Community-Based Model** in which nursing homes integrate palliative care best practices through education and/or a designated team that operates within the community setting (Carlson et al., 2011; Center to Advance Palliative Care, 2008). This model is often executed through a nursing home designated team, including a nursing assistant, nurse, social worker, and physician or nurse practitioner who work with residents with goals of comfort care. Case Study 12.2 provides further discussion on this topic.

Challenges

Specialized hospice and palliative care education for long-term care staff have demonstrated considerable gains in providing quality end-of-life care for patients and residents. Providing end-of-life care in long-term care settings requires unique needs and the education of staff in those areas should also be tailored to address these needs (Ersek & Wilson, 2003). There are good educational programs aimed at long-term care nursing and nursing assistant staff to improve staff satisfaction and confidence in providing end-of-life care, for example, the Palliative Care Educational Research Team or PERT project (Ersek, Grant, & Kraybill, 2005). Another example is the End of Life Nursing Education Curriculum-Geriatric Project (Kelly, Ersek, Virani, Malloy, & Ferrell, 2008). It will be helpful in the future to explore the resident outcomes of enhanced provider education.

Impact of Hospice on Long-Term Care Recipients

There are better outcomes for residents utilizing the MHB in nursing homes than those who did not use it. Hospice use in the nursing home has been associated with lower costs, fewer hospitalizations, better pain management, and

Case Study 12.2: Ellen White

Ms. Ellen White is an 86-year-old woman with end-stage congestive heart failure. She lives in an assisted living community and has had multiple recent admissions to the hospital. She has difficulty breathing with minimal exertion and has worsening lower extremity swelling despite medication management of her congestive heart failure. She is followed by a visiting nurse and mentions that she is tired of going to the hospital. Her visiting nurse discusses hospice services and how the services are provided jointly with the staff at the assisted living community. When Ms. White started to decline, the assisted living community recommended that she transition to a nursing home to meet her care needs but Ms. White wished to stay in her own residence. She had the funding to pay for 24/7 home health aides to assist with personal care, but there were issues as to how her medications were going to be administered. The hospice was able to teach the assisted living nursing staff (who are allowed to administer medications on a state-by-state basis) and family how to administer medications, contributed more home health aide support, and provided telephone response at all hours to support the family and staff members caring for her. The family stepped up their presence and worked with the nursing staff from the assisted living community and hospice to provide the care needed for her to die in place.

Case Study Discussion Questions:

1. Why would an assisted living community be apprehensive about providing hospice care?
2. How could the assisted living center better prepare to allow its residents to die in place?
3. What is unique about Ms. Ellen White's case vignette?

increased family satisfaction (Baer & Hanson, 2000; Gozalo, Miller, Intrator, Barber, & Mor, 2008; Miller, Gozalo, & Mor, 2001; Miller, Mor, & Teno, 2003). To increase the use of hospice, some nursing homes have employed screening tools to increase referrals to hospice, thereby improving family evaluation of the quality of end-of-life care for those residents enrolled in hospice (Casarett et al., 2005). However, Munn, Hanson, Zimmerman, Sloane, and Mitchell (2006) found no significant differences in end-of-life care for hospice and nonhospice residents of nursing homes and assisted living facilities when death was expected. Additionally, other evidence suggests that appropriate and timely hospice referrals were related to nursing home staff's ability to recognize terminal decline (Welch, Miller, Martin, & Nanda, 2008). There is also limited information available on assisted living communities and other long-term care support services programs in relation to hospice and palliative care. Finally, hospice does not just benefit an individual patient and his or her family. An indirect effect on the entire facility has been described when hospice services are provided for any number of residents leading to reduced risk of hospitalization (Miller et al., 2001).

DEDICATED HOSPICE UNITS

Hospice can also be provided in a facility dedicated solely to providing care to hospice patients, which is usually owned by a hospice agency. These facilities are licensed to provide care on either a community or inpatient level. Approximately 20% of hospice agencies nationwide now operate an inpatient unit or freestanding facility that may or may not be physically connected to a health system or nursing home community (National Hospice and Palliative Care Organization, 2012). Although the original hospice in the United States in Connecticut began with a dedicated hospice facility, the growth of hospice facilities across the country has been most significant in the past 5 to 10 years. Patients are admitted to these facilities contingent on their eligibility for hospice services. For facilities providing inpatient care, the units must be staffed around the clock with an RN with usual have daily visits by a physician or an advanced practice nurse. Facilities caring for patients on the community level have supplemental nursing, physician, social work, and chaplain services from a hospice team just as a patient would in a private residence (Exhibit 12.2).

EXHIBIT 12.2 Long-Term Care Models of Palliative Care

Model	Expertise	Service Highlights
Community with hospice	Hospice interdisciplinary team collaborative care	24-hour directed health care via telephone and home visits; intermittent physician visits; home health aides to assist with personal care; bereavement
Noncommunity (i.e., nursing home) based with hospice	Hospice interdisciplinary team collaborative care	24-hour directed health care via telephone and home visits; intermittent physician visits; home health aides to assist with personal care; bereavement
Noncommunity (i.e., nursing home) based with palliative care	Community interdisciplinary team	Highly variable depending on regional availability of services (i.e., palliative care consult service)
Dedicated hospice unit	Hospice interdisciplinary team collaborative care	24-hour directed care provided in a hospice unit; intermittent physician visits; all personal and medical care provided

Sources: Carlson et al. (2011); Mcphee, Winker, Rabow, Pantilat, and Markowitz (2011).

ETHICAL CONSIDERATIONS

Profound ethical considerations are involved in access to good palliative care. Most hospice programs require enrollees to forfeit potentially curative or life-prolonging treatments to focus on aggressive symptom management and comfort care. Most patients and families find shifting to a noncurative focus a very difficult decision to make. Patients may desire to continue expensive therapies, such as radiation or chemotherapy, that may have palliative benefits, but choosing these may preclude access to the MHB. This is challenging, particularly as more innovative therapies become available. Those enrolled in hospice may have to forego access to aggressive pain or symptom management.

Compounding this shift in goals for treatment, physicians are poor prognosticators and report feeling inadequately trained in prognostication and often overestimate how much time a patient may have (Christakis & Iwashyna, 1998; Forster & Lynn, 1988; Parkes, 1972). For a noncancer diagnosis, this is even more difficult, because end-stage organ failure (i.e., renal, lung, heart) has very different disease trajectories, thus making the noncancer diagnosis challenging to predict to better prepare patients/families. There are prognostic tools available based on limited research and usually generated by consensus; however, the reality is that they are not always useful in identifying those who are eligible for hospice (Fox et al., 1999).

CONCLUSIONS

As our society cares for an increasing number of older adults with chronic and life-limiting illnesses, hospice and other palliative care programs must continue to evolve to meet the unique palliative care needs of those at the end of life. One option will be to increase the accessibility to hospice programs that will allow patients and families to continue palliative therapies and possibly curative ones while receiving comprehensive pain, symptom, and psychological management by a skilled interdisciplinary team. Another option would be to take away the 6-month prognosis requirement for the MHB eligibility and open the program to all individuals with a life-limiting illness. Finally, the reimbursement for both hospice and palliative care services will need to be transformed in the future in order to address the needs for those older adults with chronic and life-limiting illnesses.

SUMMARY

Hospice and palliative care programs are integral for caring for those older adults with life-limiting illness residing in long-term care. Hospice and hospice-supported consult models are the primary programs accessible to most who reside in long-term care. The hope is to have more long-term care community-based models in the future with reimbursement models for sustainability. There are various challenges to implementing and integrating hospice and palliative care programs; however, the benefits far outweigh the challenges.

DISCUSSION QUESTIONS

1. What disciplines participate as part of the hospice team?
2. What are the different settings where hospice care may be delivered?
3. What are some of the benefits and barriers to providing hospice and palliative care?

ADDITIONAL RESOURCES

USEFUL BOOKS AND REPORTS

Doyle, D., Hanks, G., Cherny, N., & Calman, K. (Eds.) (2005). *Oxford textbook of palliative medicine* (3rd Ed.). Oxford, UK: Oxford University Press.

Henderson, M. L., Hanson, L. C., & Reynolds, K. S. (2003). *Improving nursing home care of the dying. A training manual for nursing home staff.* New York, NY: Springer Publishing Company.

Robert Wood Johnson Foundation Series on Health Policy. (2010). In D. E. Meier, S. L. Isaacs, & R. G. Hughes (Eds.), *Palliative care: Transforming the care of serious illness*. San Francisco, CA: Jossey-Bass.

Smucker, W., Cefalu, C., Keay, T. J., Levenson, S., Pandya, N., Schamp, R., & Sperling, D. (2008). *Palliative care in the long-term care setting* (LTC Physician Information Tool Kit Series). Washington, DC: American Medical Directors Association.

KEY WEBSITES

www.capc.org **Center to Advance Palliative Care (CAPC)**
CAPC is the resource for palliative care program development, growth, and education.

www.geripal.org **GeriPal: Geriatrics and Palliative Care Blog**
GeriPal is a geriatric and palliative medicine blog.

www.nhpco.org **National Hospice and Palliative Care Organization (NHPCO)**
NHPCO focuses on advocacy, regulations, and education.

www.pallimed.org **Pallimed: A Hospice & Palliative Medicine Blog**
Pallimed is a hospice and palliative medicine blog.

REFERENCES

Baer, W. M., & Hanson, L. C. (2000). Families' perception of the added value of hospice in the nursing home. *Journal of the American Geriatrics Society*, *48*(8), 879–882.

Board on Health Care Services. (1997). *Approaching death: improving care at the end of life.* Washington, DC: National Academy Press, Institute of Medicine.

Carlson, M. D., Lim, B., & Meier, D. E. (2011). Strategies and innovative models for delivering palliative care in nursing homes. *Journal of the American Medical Directors Association*, *12*(2), 91–98.

Casarett, D., Karlawish, J., Morales, K., Crowley, R., Mirsch, T., & Asch, D. A. (2005). Improving the use of hospice services in nursing homes: A randomized controlled trial. *Journal of the American Medical Association*, *294*(2), 211–217.

Center to Advance Palliative Care. (2008). *Improving palliative care in nursing homes*. Retrieved from www.Capc.Org/Support-From-Capc/Capc_Publications/Nursing_Home_Report.pdf

Center to Advance Palliative Care. (2011). *Licensing and certification*. Retrieved from www.Capc.Org/Palliative-Care-Professional-Development/Licensing/

Centers for Medicare & Medicaid Services. (2010). *Electronic code of Federal Regulations, title 42: Public health; part 418-hospice care*. Retrieved from www.Ecfr.Gov/Cgi-Bin/Text-Idx?C=Ecfr&Rgn=Div5&View=Text&Node=42:3.0.1.1.5&Idno=42

Centers for Medicare & Medicaid Services. (2012a). *Medicare benefit policy manual* (Chapter 9).

Centers for Medicare & Medicaid Services. (2012b). *Payment system fact sheet: Hospice payment system*. Retrieved from www.Cms.Gov/Outreach-And-Education/Medicare-Learning-Network-Mln/Mlnproducts/Downloads/Hospice_Pay_Sys_Fs.Pdf

Christakis, N. A., & Iwashyna, T. J. (1998). Attitude and self-reported practice regarding prognostication in a national sample of internists. *Archives of Internal Medicine, 158*(21), 2389–2395.

Clark, D., & Foley, K. M. (2003). Dame cicely saunders. *Pharos of Alpha Omega Alpha Honor Medical Society, 66*(3), 8–10.

Connor, S. R., Elwert, F., Spence, C., & Christakis, N. A. (2007). Geographic variation in hospice use in the united states in 2002. *Journal of Pain & Symptom Management, 34*(3), 277–285.

Connor, S. R., Elwert, F., Spence, C., & Christakis, N. A. (2008). Racial disparity in hospice use in the united states in 2002. *Palliative Medicine, 22*(3), 205–213.

Ersek, M., & Wilson, S. A. (2003). The challenges and opportunities in providing end-of-life care in nursing homes. *Journal of Palliative Medicine, 6*(1), 45–57.

Ersek, M., Grant, M. M., & Kraybill, B. M. (2005). Enhancing end-of-life care in nursing homes: Palliative care educational resource team (PERT) program. *Journal of Palliative Medicine, 8*(3), 556–566.

Forster, L. E., & Lynn, J. (1988). Predicting life span for applicants to inpatient hospice. *Archives of Internal Medicine, 148*(12), 2540–2543.

Fox, E., Landrum-Mcniff, K., Zhong, Z., Dawson, N. V., Wu, A. W., & Lynn, J. (1999). Evaluation of prognostic criteria for determining hospice eligibility in patients with advanced lung, heart, or liver disease. support investigators' study to understand prognoses and preferences for outcomes and risks of treatments. *Journal of the American Medical Association, 282*(17), 1638–1645.

Gozalo, P. L., Miller, S. C., Intrator, O., Barber, J. P., & Mor, V. (2008). Hospice effect on government expenditures among nursing home residents. *Health Services Research*, 43(1 Pt 1), 134–153.

Han, B., Tiggle, R. B., & Remsburg, R. E. (2007). Characteristics of patients receiving hospice care at home versus in nursing homes: results from the national home and hospice care survey and the national nursing home survey. *American Journal of Hospice & Palliative Medicine, 24*(6), 479–486.

Hanson, L., & Ersek, M. (2011). Meeting palliative care needs in post-acute care settings: "To help them live until they die." In S. J. McPhee, M. A. Winker, M. W. Rabow, S. Z. Pantilet, & A. Z. Markowitx (Eds.), *Care at the close of life: Evidence and experience (JAMA evidence)* (Chapter 39). New York, NY: McGraw Hill.

Hirschman, K. B., Kapo, J. M., Stratton, J., Stanley, L., Strumpf, N. E., & Casarett, D. J. (2005). Hospice in long term care. *Annals of Long-Term Care, 13*(10), 25.

The Joint Commission. (2011). *The Joint Commission launches advanced certification in palliative care program*. Retrieved from www.Pwrnewmedia.Com/2011/Joint_Commission/Palliative_Care/

Kelly, K., Ersek, M., Virani, R., Malloy, P., & Ferrell, B. (2008). End-of-life nursing education consortium. geriatric training program: Improving palliative care in community geriatric care settings. *Journal of Gerontological Nursing, 34*(5), 28–35.

Lynn, J. (2005). *Living long in fragile health: The new demographics shape end of life care*. Garrison, NY: Hastings Center. Hastings Center Report Spec. No.S14-18.

Medicare. (2009). *Medicare.Gov*. Retrieved from www.Medicare.Gov/Longtermcare/Static/Home.Asp

Meier, D. E., Isaacs, S. L., & Hughes, R. G. (Eds.). (2010). *Palliative care: Transforming the care of serious illness*. San Francisco, Ca: Jossey-Bass.

Miller, S. C. (2007). *Nursing home/hospice partnerships: A model for collaborative success—through collaborative solutions*. Providence, RI: Brown Medical School Center for Gerontology and Healthcare Research.

Miller, S. C., Gozalo, P., & Mor, V. (2001). Hospice enrollment and hospitalization of dying nursing home patients. *American Journal of Medicine, 111*(1), 38–44.

Miller, S. C., Mor, V., & Teno, J. (2003). Hospice enrollment and pain assessment and management in nursing homes. *Journal of Pain & Symptom Management, 26*(3), 791–799.

Munn, J. C., Hanson, L. C., Zimmerman, S., Sloane, P. D., & Mitchell, C. M. (2006). Is hospice associated with improved end-of-life care in nursing homes and assisted living facilities? *Journal of the American Geriatrics Society, 54*(3), 490–495.

National Consensus Project for Quality Care. (2013). *Clinical practice guidelines for quality palliative care* (3rd Ed.). Pittsburgh, PA: National Consensus Project for Quality Palliative Care. Retrieved from www.Nationalconsensusproject.Org/Ncp_Clinical_Practice_Guidelines_3rd_Edition.Pdf

National Hospice and Palliative Care Organization. (2010). *History of hospice care*. Alexandria, VA: NHPCO. Retrieved from www.Nhpco.Org/I4a/Pages/Index.Cfm?Pageid=3285

National Hospice and Palliative Care Organization. (2012). *NHPCO facts and figures: Hospice Care in America* (2011 edition).

National Institutes of Health. (2004). *National Institutes of Health state-of-the-science conference: Statement on improving end-of-life care*. Retrieved from http://consensus.nih.gov/2004/2004EndOfLifeCareSOS024Program.pdf

Oliver, D. P., Porock, D., & Zweig, S. (2005). End-of-life care in u.s. nursing homes: A review of the evidence. *Journal of the American Medical Directors Association, 6*(3 Suppl.), S21–30.

Parkes, C. M. (1972). Accuracy of predictions of survival in later stages of cancer. *British Medical Journal, 2*(5804), 29–31.

St. Christopher's Hospice. (1967). Self-help in the hospital. *British Medical Journal, 3*(5558), 169–170.

Stevenson, D. G., & Bramson, J. S. (2009). Hospice care in the nursing home setting: A review of the literature. *Journal of Pain & Symptom Management, 38*(3), 440–451.

Stevenson, D. G., Huskamp, H. A., Grabowski, D. C., & Keating, N. L. (2007). Differences in hospice care between home and institutional settings. *Journal of Palliative Medicine, 10*(5), 1040–1047.

Storey, P. (1990). Goals of hospice care. *Texas Medicine, 86*(2), 50–54.

Welch, L. C., Miller, S. C., Martin, E. W., & Nanda, A. (2008). Referral and timing of referral to hospice care in nursing homes: The significant role of staff members. *The Gerontologist, 48*(4), 477–484.

World Health Organization. (2010). *WHO definition of palliative care*. Retrieved from www.Who.Int/Cancer/Palliative/Definition/En

Zerzan, J., Stearns, S., & Hanson, L. (2000). Access to palliative care and hospice in nursing homes. *Journal of the American Medical Association, 284*(19), 2489–2494.

Contemporary Issues in Long-Term Care

13

Long-Term Care Populations: Persons With Mental Illness

FAIKA ZANJANI
AMY F. HOSIER

CHAPTER OVERVIEW

A breakdown in mental/cognitive processes causing significant impairment is considered mental illness. This includes an array of conditions such as depression, anxiety, and dementia. Mental illness at any life stage presents an impediment that needs to be overcome through detection, treatment, and management. In late life, mental illness has life stage-specific consequences such as morbidity, disability, and even mortality. Appropriate mental health management can keep older adults outside of institutional care or even help older adults transition out of institutional care. In order to prevent the serious negative consequences of mental illness in old age there is a need for improved clinical and societal knowledge and action for mental health improvement.

LEARNING OBJECTIVES

After completing this chapter, you should have an understanding of:

- The importance of addressing the mental health of older adults as a key factor in preventing or delaying a move into residential long-term care
- The areas needing improvement for enhanced mental health management (e.g., screening, detection/diagnosis, treatment, and referral) at all levels of existing settings along the continuum of long-term care
- The future areas of inquiry and intervention needed, including the development of a better understanding of managing severe mental illness and psychiatric comorbidities in late life in both institutional and community care settings

KEY TERMS

Age in place
Assisted living
Community living
Comorbidity
Dementia
Depression
Fall
Mental illness
Olmstead decision
Serious mental illness
Skilled nursing facilities (SNFs)

INTRODUCTION

Mental illness is a process described as decline in mental health status, traits, and ability, which leads to impairment in everyday functioning that can be characterized as diagnosable medical conditions (mental health disorders); entailed as a disruption in a person's thinking, feeling, mood, ability to relate to others, and daily functioning; and often results in a diminished capacity for coping with ordinary demands of life (National Alliance on Mental Health [NAMI], 2010). Approximately 26% of the U.S. population suffers from some form of mental illness at some point along the life course (Kessler, Chiu, Demler, Merikangas, & Walters, 2005). Mental illness can be particularly detrimental to older adults because it often goes under recognized and is misrepresented as a normal part of aging (A. J. Mitchell, Rao, & Vaze, 2010; Substance Abuse and Mental Health Services Administration [SAMHSA], 2003). Regardless of age, recovery from many mental illnesses is generally possible through pharmacological and behavioral treatment, and recovery creates longer life spans for individuals who are suffering from mental illness (NAMI, 2010).

Variations in mental health disorders are based on a characteristic mental/cognitive breakdown and the presence and outcomes of the disorder. For example, depression is characterized by a low mood and inability to carry out everyday activities that had normally once been conducted. On the other hand, anxiety is characterized by excessive worry above and beyond functional levels that can impair productivity and ability to relate to others. In general, according to the *Diagnostic and Statistical Manual of Mental Disorders*, Fifth Edition (*DSM-5*; American Psychiatric Association, 2013) mental health disorders are categorized as Neurodevelopmental, Schizophrenia Spectrum, Bipolar, Depressive, Anxiety, Obsessive-Compulsive, Trauma- and Stressor-, Dissociative, Somatic, Feeding and Eating, Elimination, Sleep–Wake, Sexual Dysfunction, Gender Dysphoria, Disruptive/ Impulse-Control/Conduct, Substance-Related/Addictive, Neurocognitive, Personality, Paraphilic, and Medication-Induced/Adverse Effects of Medication Disorders. Many of these disorders are extremely rare in older adults. Common mental health disorders among older adults include anxiety, dementia, depression, posttraumatic stress, schizophrenia, and substance abuse/dependence (Exhibit 13.1; Blazer & Steffens, 2009).

EXHIBIT 13.1 Prevalent Late-Life Mental Health Conditions

MENTAL HEALTH CONDITIONS	BRIEF DESCRIPTION
Anxiety	Significant impairment characterized by excess worry about specific objects/situations or across life domains that inhibit productivity and life engagement. Can be behaviorally characterized by avoidance and panic.
Bipolar	Significant impairment characterized by fluctuating high and low moods.
Dementia	Significant impairment characterized by cognitive breakdown in problem solving, memory, and learning.
Depression	Significant impairment characterized by low affect and negative moods inhibiting ability to be productive and engaged.
Posttraumatic stress disorder	Significant impairment characterized by reliving, remembering, and consequently being disabled by a stressful past event.
Schizophrenia	Significant impairment characterized by psychosis (losing touch with reality), delusions (grandiose or bizarre beliefs), and hallucinations (hearing or seeing things that are not present).
Substance abuse/ dependence	Significant impairment characterized by any chemical substance, such as tobacco, alcohol, illicit drugs, prescription drugs.

This chapter focuses on the interrelationship between one type of mental illness, depression, and long-term care, as this interrelationship has been extensively examined. **Depression** (a mental health disorder that includes a prolonged state of feeling hopeless and unhappy) is one of the most common mental health illnesses. The *DSM-5* (American Psychiatric Association, 2013) characterizes depression as involving presence of sad, empty, or irritable mood, accompanied by somatic and cognitive changes that significantly affect the individual's capacity to function. Depressive symptoms affect approximately 27% of community residing adults over the age of 60 (Blazer, Hughes, & George, 1987) and approximately 30% of adults living in long-term care (Seitz, Purandare, & Conn, 2010). In **skilled nursing facilities** (**SNFs**; facilities that provide long-term care services to assist with limitations that significantly impair self-care and activities of independent living), where memory impairment rates often soar, more residents are admitted with depression than **dementia** (a mental health disorder indicating significant cognitive impairment in memory, reasoning, and thinking abilities), comprising approximately 18% versus 12% of admissions (Fullerton, McGuire, Reng, Mor, & Grabowski, 2009).

The World Health Organization (2010) recognizes depression as one of the leading causes of disability and contributors to the burden of disease. **Serious mental illness** (a diagnosable mental, behavioral, or emotional disorder that meets criteria in the *DSM 5* (APA, 2013) and that results in functional impairment that substantially interferes with or limits one or more major life activities), including major depression, can reduce life expectancy by nearly 25 years and is attributable to poor health behaviors and the presence of preventable diseases (National Association of State Mental Health Program Directors [NASMHPD], 2006). Known risk factors for depression in older adults include functional impairment, loneliness, and a family history of depression and neuroticism (Eisses et al., 2004). Depression can lead to poor health trajectories in morbidity, physical and mental functioning, and reduced time to death (Benton, Staab, & Evans, 2007; Evans et al., 1999), particularly among older adults (Roberts, Kaplan, Shema, & Strawbridge, 1997).

DEPRESSION AND HEALTHY AGING

Depression can be detrimental to aging individuals in various ways. For instance, depression can increase disease/disability (Barry, Allore, Bruce, & Gill, 2009), which can directly and indirectly have a negative effect on all aspects of individual life quality. Depression can also increase the risk for ischemic events: fatal or nonfatal myocardial infarction or angina pectoris (Bremmer et al., 2006), cardiovascular conditions (Frasure-Smith & Lesperance, 2006), stroke (House, Knapp, Bamford , & Vail, 2001), cancer (Lemogne & Consoli, 2010), pain (Landi et al., 2005), and mortality (Frasure-Smith & Lesperance, 2006; House et al., 2001).

Health outcomes of depressed individuals are relatively poor when compared to individuals without depression (Leas & McCabe, 2007). Allgower, Wardle, and Steptoe (2001) found that depressive symptoms are associated with unhealthy behavioral patterns, including obesity, smoking, not exercising, not using a seat belt, not having regular sleep hours, and poor breakfast habits. The literature also confirms a correlation between depression and alcohol consumption, indicating a greater prevalence of depression when unhealthy alcohol patterns are present (Choi & Dinitto, 2010). Over time, depression can lead to increased smoking and decreased physical activity among middle-aged and older adults ages 55 to 85 (van Gool et al., 2003).

Poor health outcomes often create comorbidities among adults with depression and a need for high levels of medical service use, including the use of nonmental health services (Braune & Berger, 2005). Individuals with depression tend to have increased incidence of impaired psychosocial functioning, such as poor well-being (Smalbrugge et al., 2006). Social interaction and activity, important aspects of well-being and the caregiving relationship, can be impaired when depression is present (Achterberg et al., 2003).

Although depression affects both men and women, in some instances, depressed women are at higher risk for disease/disability and poor quality of life. One explanation for negative health outcomes are reports of women with depression experiencing more difficulty in comparison to men recovering from illness, specifically stroke (Lai, Duncan, Dew, & Keighley, 2005). Also, in the area of recovery, Onder et al. (2003) found that older hospitalized women with depression have a higher probability of adverse drug interactions as compared to male counterparts. In women, there is evidence that depression also leads to poor physical functioning (Hollenberg, Haight, & Tager, 2003) and cognitive deficits (Pálsson et al., 2001), with depression having higher predictive value than physical functioning with respect to long-term cognitive functioning (van Hooren et al., 2005). In sum, depression, especially in women, decreases older adults' total and active life expectancy, even when accounting for chronic conditions (e.g., heart disease, cancer, diabetes, and stroke; Reynolds, Haley, & Kozlenko, 2008).

The combination of depressive symptoms, poor health behaviors, gender, and age jeopardizes an older individual's ability to safely **age in place** (i.e., sustain residence in a specific location at home or within the community while experiencing changes associated with aging) and consequently creates an increased need for long-term care. Older adults who live in the community with untreated depression are at increased risk of nursing home admission (Fullerton et al., 2009). Identifying and addressing individual mental health impairment may be one of the most important factors in delaying long-term care placement of older adults and maintaining independence in later life (Cohen-Mansfield & Wirtz, 2007).

SPECIAL CONSIDERATIONS IN LONG-TERM CARE

In 1999, the United States Supreme Court passed a landmark case that has come to be known as the ***Olmstead* decision** (*Olmstead v. L.C.*), a ruling that made it discriminatory to institutionalize a person with a disability, including those with mental illness, who wish to live in the community as long as the person is capable of benefitting from the setting. The Olmstead decision impelled states to address the residential preferences of those with disabilities, including older adults with mental illness (Bartels, Miles, Dums, & Levine, 2003). Findings from Bartels et al. (2003) revealed that **community living** (living in one's own home or in a community-based home-like setting) versus institutionalized care settings (e.g., psychiatric unit, hospital, or SNF) is the optimal setting for older adults living with mental illness. The same study recognized that those with severe behavior problems, physical impairment, greater medical illness burden, and those with a diagnosis of dementia were better suited for and safer in institutional care settings. Interestingly, age and need for assistance with self-care or community living skills were not significant determinants of nursing home placement, reflecting the view that community-based options and services should be provided regardless of age or ability.

Because of the numbers of older adults living with depression and other mental illnesses/disorders, the Olmstead decision, and the current demographics indicating a growing older population (Hyman, 2001), an increased need exists for mental health services, mental health care provider training, and overall mental health awareness along the entire long-term care continuum. Therefore, it is important to consider how different levels of long-term care can interact with the presence of depression. The remainder of this chapter examines the relationship of depression with three different levels of long-term care (community-based services, **assisted living** facilities, and SNFs), within the overriding rubric of recognition that depression decreases a person's ability to age in place and escalates his or her need for increased levels of care in facility-based long-term care settings (Aud & Rantz, 2005). Because depression is one of the strongest life quality predictors among both community dwellers and institutionalized older adults (Borowiak & Kostka, 2004), special consideration across the long-term care spectrum for older adults living with depression is imperative.

MENTAL ILLNESS CONSIDERATIONS FOR INFORMAL CARE AND BASIC COMMUNITY-BASED LONG-TERM CARE: LIVING AT HOME

With age, older adults face increasing challenges and losses (Gill & Morgan, 2011), including retirement, health worries, death of family members and friends, increased risk for disease/disability, mobility limitations, loss of independence, and possible need for downsizing or relocating to long-term care facilities. Throughout the challenges of aging, many older adults strive to remain in their home for as long as possible, where they feel autonomous and secure and in control of their life. Individual losses and the accumulation of losses can be stressful and precipitate risk factors that lead to depression. Risk factors include loneliness and isolation, reduced sense of purpose, physical illness and disability, polypharmacy, fear, enforced dependency, abuse, instability, and recent bereavement (Bell & Goss, 2001; Glass, De Leon, & Bassuk, 2006; McAllister & Matarasso, 2007). Risk factors for depression can also contribute to eventual nursing home placement. Harris and Cooper (2006) evaluated depressive systems in older adults to predict nursing home admissions. They found three interwoven means by which depressive symptoms could be associated with risk for nursing home admission: (a) an increase in disease manifestations, including diseases of the heart and brain; (b) less motivation to maintain a healthy lifestyle; and (c) the presence of another condition, such as dementia.

When left untreated, depression can take its toll on health, independence, and the ability to safely function within one's home (Bell & Goss, 2001). Depression can also impair individual decision making (van Randenborgh, de Jong-Meyer, & Hüffmeier, 2010), which can undermine an adult's ability to make decisions necessary to remain independent, including decisions relating to health and finances. Impaired decision making, combined with the other risk factors associated with depression, can place older adults with mental illness at greater risk for long-term care placement, as informal caregivers and various community-based services eventually can no longer fulfill their care needs, especially if a strong informal and/or formal support system does not exist (McAllister & Matarasso, 2007).

In order to successfully age in place at home, especially with major depression, an older adult needs social contact and, generally, support from informal caregivers who provide unpaid care out of love, respect, obligation, or friendship (e.g., family, friends, neighbors, or church members), and from formal care (e.g., volunteers or paid care providers associated with a service system) or a combination of both (Maulik, Eaton, & Bradshaw, 2011). Unfortunately, only a small percentage of older adults reach out for the help they need and few caregivers are sufficiently prepared to identify or help someone with depression. Some individuals believe that feeling blue is a "normal" part of aging, whereas others are unwilling to talk about their feelings or ask for help (Bartels, 2003; SAMHSA, 2003). Concentrating on misperceptions and age-related decline and physical complaints, caregivers, including physicians, can overlook signs of depression. Untreated depression challenges the ability to age in place because it places older adults at greater risk for polypharmacy (Harris, 2007), environmental challenges (Bell & Gross, 2001), alcohol and drug use (Lemke & Schaefer, 2010), suicide (Conwell & Brent, 1995; National Institute of Mental Health [NIMH], 2007), and nursing home placement (Fullerton et al., 2009).

Seventy-eight percent of older adults living in the community who ultimately need long-term care services depend on family and friends as their only source of help (Thompson, 2004). Informal caregivers are crucial to helping older adults safely age in place in their homes. Informal caregiving may come with a price, especially as the emotional, physical, and financial demands of caregiving increase (Schulz, Belle, Czaja, McGinnis, Stevens, & Zhang, 2004). Twenty-three percent of family members caring for vulnerable family members for 5 years or more report fair or poor health (National Alliance for Caregiving and AARP, 2009). Twenty percent of employed female caregivers over 50 years old report symptoms of depression compared to 8% of their non-caregiving peers (National Alliance for Caregiving and MetLife Mature Market Institute, 2010) and 40% to 70% of family caregivers have clinically significant symptoms of depression with approximately a quarter to half of these caregivers meeting the diagnostic criteria for major depression (Zarit, 2006). As constraints on the ability of an informal caregiver increase, a caregiver's physical and mental health can deteriorate (Center on Aging Society, 2005), and the stress can cause premature aging (Epel, 2004).

If a caregiver has a good understanding of mental illness and the classic symptoms of major depression, but knows how best to deal with them, then appropriate mental health management can be implemented, and consequently, many barriers that depression creates can be overcome. Unfortunately, in many cases, informal caregivers try to provide care beyond their ability or expertise. This is usually done "out of love" or from a sense of obligation, even though a better or safer solution for everyone involved might be the use of formal services (Gonyea, Paris, & de Saxe Zerden, 2008).

MENTAL ILLNESS CONSIDERATIONS FOR TRANSITIONAL LONG-TERM CARE: ASSISTED LIVING FACILITIES

Assisted living facilities (ALFs) are often promoted as an intermediate level or transitional type of care between independent living and skilled nursing care; such facilities encourage autonomy and promote privacy and dignity beyond what is available in a nursing facility (see Chapter 10; Golant, 2005). They also support the need for residents to remain part of their social network (Golant, 2008; Kane, 2004). In the United States, approximately 38,000 ALFs (Mollica, Houser, & Ujvari, 2012) provide care and housing to an estimated 1 million Americans who can no longer manage to live on their own (Chen, Zimmerman, Sloane, & Barrick, 2007; Hyde, Perez, & Reed, 2008). Of these older adults, approximately 24% live with mental illness, primarily depression, and about half have some form of dementia (Hyde et al., 2008; National Center for Assisted Living [NCAL], 2001).

According to Chen, Zimmerman, et al., (2007), studies vary in the reported prevalence of depression among ALF residents. Two studies reported that ALF residents experienced significant depressive symptoms (Ball et al., 2000) or were severely depressed (Watson, Garrett, Sloane, Gruber-Baldini, & Zimmerman, 2003). Chen, Zimmerman, et al., (2007) associated depression with a person's inability to control his or her environment. In a study based on residents' views of life quality, Ball et al. (2000) found that 54% of their sample (n = 55) noted depression as a common health problem that required care, followed by pain (48%), high blood pressure (38%), and anxiety (34%). Participants in the study associated their depression with the loss of physical and cognitive functioning, in addition to the loss of their home, independence, loved ones, and former routines. Residents also reported feeling lonely (44%) and bored (36%). Social isolation and boredom are strongly connected with depression. Watson et al. (2003) associated depression in ALFs with hospitalization, dependence in more than three areas of activities of daily living, medical comorbidity, cognitive impairment, psychosis, agitation, and social withdrawal.

ALFs are attractive to people with mental illness for a variety of reasons. People living with depression may no longer be able to function safely at home, but they are not so dependent that they need to rely on the intensive medical services of nursing home care. People with mental illness remain aware of their environment and continue to benefit from their surroundings. ALFs promote privacy and autonomy in their "home-like" settings, providing residents with a sense of control over their lives (Polivka & Salmon, 2008). People with mental illness can thrive as a result of being able to harness an ALF's range of medical, psychosocial, and rehabilitation services and opportunities that encourage social autonomy, dignity, social activity, decision making, privacy, and well-being (Chen, Zimmerman, et al., 2007; Pruchno & Rose, 2000).

Because ALFs are less regulated than SNFs, service provision and clientele served can vary from facility to facility. Some ALFs offer high-acuity care and staff that can manage cognitive and physical impairments similar to those found in nursing homes. Other ALFs provide low-acuity or light care to individuals who need minimal assistance (Golant, 2008). With ALF social models of care, family members and informal caregivers have greater opportunities for involvement in a person's care. Such involvement can positively influence a person's mental health and ability to age in place in the ALF (Ball et al., 2004; J. M. Mitchell & Kemp, 2000).

The average length of stay in an ALF ranges from approximately 2.5 to 3 years (Hawes, Phillips, & Rose, 2000; NCAL, 2001). Residents may be discharged if they need assistance with transfers, have a high level of medical comorbidity, display increased cognitive impairment, or exhibit negative behavioral symptoms (Hawes, Phillips, Rose, Holan, & Sherman, 2003). Unfortunately, many symptoms of major depression mirror ALF discharge criteria, reflecting the need for the improved identification and management of depression in ALFs to help individuals avoid an unnecessary relocation. AFLs are not required to screen residents for depression. Therefore, many residents go untreated, and their conditions are wrongly associated with dementia or other age-related conditions. Some might expect that depression among ALF residents is likely to be detected. To the contrary, research demonstrates that staff member's ability to recognize depression is limited. In some instances, less than one third to one half of those with depression received treatment (Davison et al., 2007).

Untreated depression can lead to discharge from an ALF. Watson et al. (2003) reported that depressed residents were discharged to nursing homes at 1.5 times the rate of nondepressed residents and that mortality rates were also higher for depressed residents. Depression in ALFs has been associated with transfer into a nursing home or hospital for higher levels of care (Davison et al., 2007; Watson et al., 2003). Depression rates in residential care/ALF are nearly equivalent to those in formal nursing home long-term care, at approximately 30% (Gruber-Baldini et al., 2005). Although residents of nursing homes have a greater number of disabilities than those in ALFs, due to higher percentages of heart disease and stroke, the populations look similar when comparing physical and cognitive/mental health diagnoses. Data from the 2004 National Nursing Home Survey and from an industry-sponsored survey of assisted living indicate considerable overlap with those living in ALFs and those receiving long-term care in nursing homes in terms of age, cognitive status, chronic medical illnesses, disability, mental illness, depression, and care needs (Table 13.1; Ruckdeschel & Katz, 2004; Zimmerman et al., 2003). With regard to mental illness besides depression, more nursing home residents live with affective disorders, schizophrenia, bipolar disorders, and other mental disorders that affect behavior, also reflected in Table 13.1, than do those in ALFs (Redfoot, 2007).

ALFs strive to support life quality and prevent mental illness, including depression (Ball et al., 2000; Chen, Zimmerman, et al., 2007), but ALF workers

TABLE 13.1 Rates for Cognitive and Mental Health Conditions in Long-Term Care

COGNITIVE/MENTAL CONDITIONS	ASSISTED LIVING RESIDENTS (%)	NURSING HOME RESIDENTS (%)
Depression	38	37
Dementia	33	23
Mental Disorder*	9	26

*Includes affective disorders, schizophrenia, bipolar disorders, and other mental disorders.
Source: National Nursing Home Survey (2004).

need more training in order to be fully confident and comfortable in providing such care. "A key element in enabling more cognitively and physically impaired residents to remain in assisted living is the availability of appropriate personal care and health-related services, along with social and recreational activities" (Hyde et al., 2008, p. 68). Inability to properly identify and treat mental illness in ALFs remains a problem. Depending on a state's regulations, care-related services can be contracted with outside agencies, including mental health services. Typically, visiting nurses and home health agencies can be called to take care of services beyond the capabilities of ALFs (Hyde et al., 2008). The number of people moving in and out of ALFs supports the interaction and interdependence of the types of settings along the long-term care continuum required to meet the dynamic needs, including mental health needs, of residents (Golant & Hyde, 2008; NCAL, 2001).

MENTAL ILLNESS CONSIDERATIONS FOR FORMAL SKILLED NURSING CARE

SNFs, known to most people as nursing homes, provide a broad range of long-term care services, including personal, social, and medical services designed to assist people who have functional or cognitive limitations in their ability to perform self-care and other activities necessary to live independently (see Chapter 11). Although nursing facilities are often the "last stop" in the long-term care continuum, length of stay varies widely from brief stays for short-term rehabilitation and postacute care following hospitalization to medical care that will last for many years (Houser, 2007). Nursing home residents are at greater risk of becoming long-stay residents if they demonstrate cognitive impairment, limitations in activities of daily living, and social isolation (Fullerton et al., 2009). Longer nursing home stays are also associated with depression (Webber et al., 2005). Many residents spend their first few weeks in a facility feeling abandoned, vulnerable, and displaced (Bagley et al., 2000; Kao, Travis, & Acton, 2004). During this "disorganization phase" (Brooke, 1989), in particular, it is important for caregivers to differentiate between grief and depression and to recognize symptoms of mental illness in order to make appropriate referrals and provide proper support.

If depression is not already present, older adults who transition to skilled nursing are at increased risk for experiencing mental health problems (Bagley et al., 2000). Choi, Ransom, and Wyllie (2008) noted that prevalence rates of depressive symptoms among nursing home residents range from 9% to 75%, and prevalence rates for major depressive disorders range from 5% to 31%. Some estimate the numbers to be even higher when residents with dementia are included, for depression is often a secondary diagnosis to dementia (Choi et al., 2008; Snowden, Sato, & Roy-Byrne, 2003). Major themes related to the onset of depression in older nursing home residents include loss of physical independence, freedom, and continuity with their past lives; feelings of social isolation and loneliness; lack of privacy and frustration at the inconvenience of having a roommate and sharing a bathroom; loss of autonomy due to institutional regimens and regulations; ambivalence toward cognitively impaired residents; ever-present death and grief; staff turnover and shortage; and stale programming and lack of meaningful in-house activities (Choi et al., 2008; Dahle & Ploeg, 2009).

According to Houser (2007), nearly all nursing homes provide mental health services, either on or off site, especially as nursing homes have become the primary institutional setting for older adults with serious mental illness (Bartels, Miles et al., 2003). Approximately 80% of newly admitted residents undergo some form of depression treatment (Boyle et al., 2004). Similar to ALFs, very few nursing home staff members recognize depressive symptoms. In fact, less than 2% of nursing home staff receives any kind of in-service training on depression (Bagley et al., 2000). Cohen, Hyland, and Kimhy (2003) found that fewer than one fourth of depressed residents were identified and treated by nursing home physicians.

With nursing staff spending on average only 3.7 hours per day in direct nursing care (Harrington, Carrillo, & LaCava, 2006), it is crucial that nursing and frontline staff members are properly trained to recognize symptoms of mental illness in order to prevent underdiagnosis and inadequate mental health treatment. It is often difficult to identify signs of depression in the nursing home. Even though symptoms of depression among older adults have been classified as being no different than in younger populations, identifying depression can be challenging because depression conditions often coexist in other medical conditions, including dementia (Kales, Chen, Blow, Welsh, & Mellow, 2005). For example, for persons with major depression, significant risk indicators for older nursing home patients have been identified as pain, functional limitations, visual impairment, stroke, loneliness, lack of social support, negative life events, and perceived inadequacy of care (Jongenelis et al., 2004). Signs and symptoms of depression in nursing home residents can include excessive use of services, decreased socialization, apathy/flat affect behavior, combative/resistive behavior, delusions, paranoia, sleep problems, and weight loss/poor appetite (Quality Partner of Rhode Island [QPRI], 2004). Suicide risk can also increase with relocation into a nursing home (Davis, Kenarney, Murdell, & Zabak, 2001). The incidence of mortality increases among depressed nursing home residents, but this can be combated through appropriate psychiatric treatment (Sutcliffe et al., 2007).

HEALTH OUTCOME CONSIDERATIONS FOR FORMAL LONG-TERM CARE

COMORBIDITY

When two or more disorders or illnesses occur in the same person, simultaneously or sequentially, the occurrence is called **comorbidity**. A hallmark of depression in older people is its comorbidity with medical illness (Lyness, Niculescu, Xin, Reynolds, & Caine, 2006; Scott et al., 2007). With impaired decision making and health practices as a part of depression come increases in medical comorbidity, which can increase the need for greater care along the long-term care continuum (Alexopoulos et al., 2002; see Case Study 13.1). For instance, older adults hospitalized for heart failure who also present with depression have a 50% increased risk of a nursing home admission, compared to nondepressed older adults (Ahmed,

Case Study 13.1: Sunny Days Ahead: Marilyn's Battle With Depression and Long-Term Care

Due to a stroke that left 86-year-old Marilyn in a wheelchair with slurred speech and partial right-side paralysis, her family assumed they understood her disinterest in favorite pastimes, lower energy level, poor concentration, and increasing time spent in bed. Unable to offer or hire help to properly manage her medical condition, her family concluded that she needed to move to a long-term care facility. Relocated against her will from the home in which she had lived for 50 years, Marilyn was moved to the Sunny Days Retirement Center. This ALF assured Marilyn of "all the comforts of home," including privacy, dignity and respect. In addition, she was promised social activity; nutritious meals; and assistance with bathing, dressing, and toileting. Despite the care she received and the friendly environment, Marilyn did not thrive in her new home. Her health began to deteriorate. She became increasingly dependent and frail, falling, and forgetting things. The facility prescribed medications to treat her conditions and reassured Marilyn's family that this was "normal" behavior for someone her age with her disability. The family was told that Marilyn needed time to "adjust." But after a year, Marilyn, quite uncharacteristically, grew increasingly combative, refused needed assistance with personal care, and slept through the majority of her days. As her health declined and functional impairments worsened, Marilyn's family was asked to either contract additional care to support her medical and personal needs or move Marilyn into a more supportive facility. Neither the staff nor family recognized that Marilyn's condition was significantly exacerbated due to severe depression. Meanwhile, feeling purposeless, helpless, and lonely, and taking nine medications daily, Marilyn spent her days wondering why she was still alive.

Case Study Discussion Question:

How could Marilyn's life have been different if someone who loved and/or cared for her had working knowledge of mental illness in older adults? What should these people have done?

Ali, Lefante, Mullick, & Kinney, 2006). Persons admitted with depression have higher rates of comorbid conditions than those admitted with dementia and individuals free of dementia and mental illness (Fullerton et al., 2009).

Depression can interact with existing comorbidity through drug interactions. There has been a two-fold increase in older nursing home residents, in antidepressant prescribing, from 22% to 48% (Hanlon, Handler, & Castle, 2010). Data from the Centers for Medicare & Medicaid Services Online Survey, Certification, and Reporting indicate that 52% of nursing home residents were diagnosed with depression, with 83% receiving an antidepressant (Gaboda, Lucas, Siegel, Kalay, & Crystal, 2011). Antidepressant medications can worsen comorbidities through side effects (e.g., dizziness, insomnia, and nausea) and major to minor drug and disease interactions (Mark et al., 2011).

FALLS

A **fall**, defined as an inadvertent and sudden postural change toward the ground, is often the sign of other health problems or environmental hazards. In a long-term care facility, depression can increase a resident's risk of falling (Kose, Cuvalci, Ekici, Otman, & Karakaya, 2005). Older adults living in nursing homes who reported a greater fear of falling tended to report depressive symptoms more frequently, regardless of sociodemographic and physical health status (Chou, Yeung, & Wong, 2005).

Medications can also increase the risk of falls and fall-related injuries. In addition to drugs that affect the central nervous system, such as sedatives and antianxiety drugs (Centers for Disease Control and Prevention [CDC], 2008; Ray, Thapa, & Gideon, 2000), tricyclic and other heterocyclic antidepressants are associated with an increased risk of falling (Darowski, Chambers, & Chambers, 2009). Sedation, insomnia/impaired sleep, nocturia, impaired postural reflexes, increased reaction times, head rushes/dizzy spells, cardiac rhythm and conduction disorders, and movement disorders appear to be contributing factors to falls in patients taking antidepressants (Darowski et al., 2009). Because nursing home residents are more prone to physical disability, depression, day-time drowsiness, and multiple medications, they may not physically or emotionally be prepared to exercise their muscles to maintain their strength, leaving them especially physically and mentally susceptible to falls.

DEMENTIA

Dementia rates among nursing home residents are reported to be as high as 46.4% (Redfoot, 2007). The onset of dementia is complicated by the presence of depressive disorders because depression becomes a challenge to diagnose as signs of depression can mirror the signs of dementia, and as dementia makes detection of depression more difficult (Kales et al., 2005). Dementia patients can be screened for depression and successfully treated, but diagnostic and treatment issues need to be considered (Cohen et al., 2003; Peskind, 2003). Treating depression can reduce cognitive impairment (Kenefick, 2004). Untreated depression in dementia patients leads to early nursing home placement (Dorenlot, Harboun, Bige, Henrard, & Ankri, 2005). Dementia complicated by mixed agitation and depression accounts for over one third of complicated dementia and is associated with multiple psychiatric and medical needs, intensive pharmacological treatment, and use of high-cost services (Bartels, 2003). Irritability with dementia is a strong indicator that depression might be present (Verkaik, Francke, van Meijel, Ribbe, & Bensing, 2009).

STRATEGIES TO CONSIDER FOR FORMAL LONG-TERM CARE

Regardless of setting, low rates of mental health treatment lead to poor health outcomes for older adults. Strategies can be implemented throughout the long-term care continuum to combat the unnecessary negative outcomes of mental illness, such as training staff to recognize and manage mental illness, implementing regular mental health screenings, and increasing access to mental health treatment and/or referral capabilities for use when needed.

TRAINING

With high depression rates in both ALFs and nursing homes, statistics that demonstrate untreated and undertreated depression can be as high as 75% (Choi et al., 2008). Older nursing home patients are consistently undertreated for depression (Davison et al., 2007). Consequently, it is critical to combat the negative effects of mental illness. One suggestion is to equip caregivers, at all levels of long-term care, with skills and knowledge necessary to recognize and manage mental illness (Glaister & Blair, 2008) and to have sufficient staff to care for individual mental health needs (Lenhoff, 2003). Research indicates that knowledge about mental illness in long-term care personnel is less than ideal, leading to insufficient care and poor health of older residents (Brühl, Luijendijk, & Muller, 2007; Davison, McCabe, Mellor, Karantzas, & George 2009). Caregiver training can be geared toward improving knowledge about mental illness, mental illness detection, and proper mental health care (Chopra & Owen, 2006; Davidson, Koritsas, O'Connnor, & Clarke 2006; Meeks & Burton, 2004; Meeks, Looney, Van Haitsman, & Teri, 2008). In addition, properly trained staff can reduce rates of caregiver mental illness and its negative effects (Chen, Sabir, Zimmerman, Suitor, & Pillemer, 2007) and improve mental health detection (Chopra & Owen, 2006; Davidson et al., 2006). After initial educational and skill-building mental health training, additional training and continual monitoring is necessary to ensure adequate mental health management (Watson, Zimmerman, Cohen, & Dominik, 2009).

SCREENING/DIAGNOSIS

Programs, such as the Preadmission Screening and Resident Review (PASRR), and tools, including the Minimum Data Set (MDS), have been implemented to better understand and track mental illness in the long-term care system. Although neither are ideal tools for improving mental health treatment and management by themselves (Anderson, Buckwalter, Buchanan, Maas, & Imhof, 2003), there are tools that can be used to complement existing screening assessments (American Geriatrics Society & American Association for Geriatric Psychiatry [AGS & AAGP], 2003; Hendrix, Sakauye, Karabatsos, & Daigle, 2003;

Linkins, Lucca, Housman, & Smith, 2006). Mental health screening is recommended 2 to 4 weeks following a long-term care admission and repeated at least every 6 months. In addition, a new onset or worsening of mental health symptoms should prompt an assessment that includes psychological, situational, and medical evaluations (AGS & AAGP, 2003). Nursing home residents with behavioral problems and agitation are most likely to receive psychiatric consultation; however, a resident who is depressed and quiet, lethargic, or socially withdrawn may be overlooked (Fenton et al., 2004).

A mixture of assessments is ideal for detecting mental illness (Johnston, Reid, Wilson, Levesque, & Driver 2007; Koehler et al., 2005). Depression screening instruments can be used for identification and assessing depressed residents and evaluating treatment effectiveness (AGS & AAGP, 2003; Brühl et al., 2007). Self-report scales, including the Geriatric Depression Scale or Beck Depression Inventory, are recommended only for residents with mild to moderate impairment, whereas observer-rated scales, such as the Cornell Scale for Depression in Dementia, are indicated for residents with moderate to severe dementia (AGS & AAGP, 2003; Greenberg et al., 2004). To screen across the spectrum of mental health disorders, the MINI International Neuropsychiatric Interview can be used to detect depression in addition to disorders such as anxiety, posttraumatic stress disorder, and substance abuse (Sheehan et al., 1998; Exhibit 13.2).

Assessments conducted by a specialized geriatric clinician can result in optimal mental health diagnosis (Hickie, Burke, Tobin, & Mutch, 2000). In order to reduce the burden and responsibility on geriatric clinicians, effectiveness for alternative forms of mental health assessment needs to be improved (Kerber, Dyck, Culp, & Buckwalter, 2008). Furthermore, disadvantaged groups, including African Americans, residents with physical and cognitive impairments, and those residing in deficient institutions are less likely to be diagnosed and treated for mental illness (Levin et al., 2007). For improved mental health management, effective screening tools need to be identified and implemented among disadvantaged groups.

TREATMENT

Across the mental health disorder spectrum, the best line of treatment is a combination of pharmacological and psychosocial interventions to manage chemical, cognitive, and lifestyle imbalances. The American Geriatrics Society and the American Association for Geriatric Psychiatry panel (2003) agreed that the first-line treatment of major depression should include antidepressant medications. When antidepressant medications are prescribed in nursing home populations, medications, such as selective serotonin–re-uptake inhibitors (SSRIs), which are medications that increase the neurotransmitter serotonin, are the most appropriate first-line treatment. Some antidepressant medications need to be generally avoided in treating nursing home residents, including strong anticholinergics (medications that increase the availability of neurotransmitter acetylcholine) and monoamine oxidase inhibitors (medication that increases the monoamine neurotransmitters), due to negative side effects. Overuse and unjustified use

EXHIBIT 13.2: The MINI International Psychiatric Interview Screens

Depressive disorder
Suicidality
Bipolar disorder
Panic disorder
Agoraphobia disorder
Social phobia (social anxiety disorder)
Obsessive-compulsive disorder
Posttraumatic stress disorder
Alcohol dependence/abuse
Substance dependence/abuse
Psychotic disorders
Anorexia
Bulimia
Generalized anxiety disorder
Antisocial personality disorder

Discussion Questions:
Knowing that depression is most prevalent in the older population, while anorexia and bulimia is rare in the older population, including those living in institutional care, how should screening for other mental health disorders, outside of depression, be managed?

1. How should screening, such as the MINI, be given in its entirety?
2. How should screening, such as the MINI, be given for selected components?
3. What is the cost of regularly implementing the MINI in its entirety?
4. What is the cost of implementing the MINI on an as-needed basis, and/or for specific common components only, such as depression and anxiety?

of psychotropic medication in nursing homes has been documented (Gobert & D'hoore, 2005; Grabowski, Aschbrenner, Rome, & Bartels, 2010), making the need for appropriate medication practices even more important. In addition, there needs to be an awareness that disparities in pharmacological treatment may exist. For example, African Americans may be receiving less pharmacological treatment than other populations (Hudson, Cody, Armitage, Curtis, & Sullivan, 2005). Careless institutional practices and disparities can result in further under treatment or nontreatment, or even mistreatment (Lapane & Hughes, 2004).

Use of nonpharmacological interventions in combination with antidepressant medications for treating major depression can also be effective (AGS & AAGP, 2003). Psychotherapeutic modalities, including group and individual cognitive behavioral psychotherapy, can be helpful. Other nonpharmacological interventions to consider include increasing social activities and providing meaningful activities, such as sheltered workshops, volunteering, religious activities, or activities that maintain past roles (AGS & AAGP, 2003). Reminiscence therapy (Jones, 2003) and electroconvulsive therapy (Kallenbach & Rigler, 2006) are other therapies to consider for older adults, with reminiscence therapy appearing more effective in institutionalized adults as compared to community-dwelling older adults (Wang, 2004). Personnel and resource barriers to offering combination therapies and nonpharmacological therapies often exist in long-term care; these need to be overcome to ensure availability and effectiveness (Wagenaar et al., 2003).

For persons with minor depression, treatment alternatives include nonpharmacological interventions, antidepressants, and watchful waiting (i.e., evaluate and monitor). The choice among these options depends on factors such as severity, previous history, and preferences of the resident, family, or legal representative (AGS & AAGP, 2003). Depressed older nursing home residents appear to prefer nursing home programs that reduce their isolation over group or individual psychotherapy (Choi et al., 2008). Some residents also prefer self-management strategies such as taking a walk (Tsai, 2006). Depression treatment has also been known to alleviate other behavioral problems such as agitation (Heeren et al., 2003). Brief intervention treatment (a briefer form of mental health treatment that can be done over the telephone and that has motivational interviewing underpinnings) for depression is also a viable option (Cole & Dendukuri 2004; Jonkers et al., 2007). A comparative analysis of depression management is necessary to determine which treatments are most effective (Snowden et al., 2003). Along with effective treatment, continued monitoring is necessary to ensure the effectiveness of treatment over time (Kaldyand & Tarnove, 2003). Strategies that have often been discussed, which can be used to prevent and manage mental health, include lifestyle strategies such as mental/physical exercise, socialization, learning, reading, working/volunteering, healthy nutrition, self-efficacy, self-mastery, life resolution, stress management, spirituality, goal setting, and ensuring safety (Zanjani, Kruger, & Murray, 2012). For example, it is very important in institutional settings to create a sense of community through friendships and bonds for support and companionship. In addition, technology can be used to foster the suggested lifestyle strategies by fostering online social communications and facilitating mental and intellectual engagement.

REFERRAL

Residents in long-term care settings who demonstrate mental illness symptoms with psychotic features (i.e., symptoms that indicate hallucinations, delusions, or not being in touch with reality) or have not responded to 6 or more weeks of treatment are recommended for referral to a mental health professional. Because access to qualified mental health professionals may be limited for some facilities, qualified primary care providers may be able to perform such services when mental health providers are not available. Residents with suicidal ideation, with or without verbalization of a plan to harm themselves, should be considered for immediate referral to a mental health professional for treatment (AGS & AAGP, 2003; Suominen et al., 2003). The determination of

FIGURE 13.1 Psychiatric comorbidity with depression.

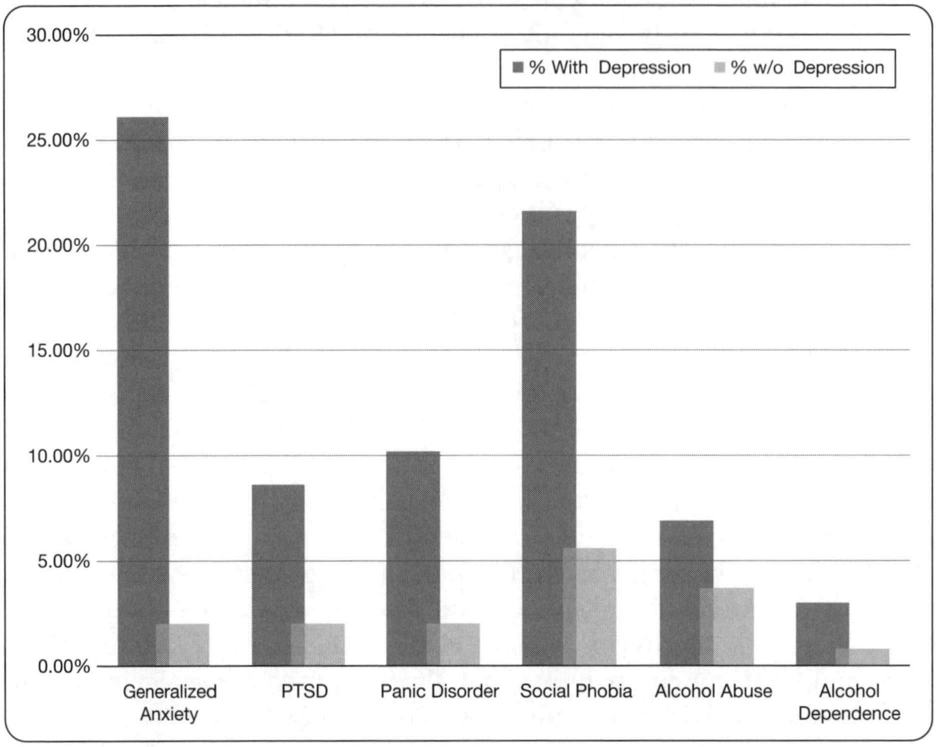

Note: Rates based on Collaborative Psychiatric Epidemiology Surveys, 2001–2003 [United States], age 65+, *N* = 2,626.

need for immediate referral should be based on the particular circumstances, including intent, and likelihood of harm to self. The need for screening, referral, and treatment should not be based on the availability of staff.

FUTURE DIRECTIONS IN LONG-TERM CARE RESEARCH

Currently, it is not very well known how mental health disorders other than depression affect transitions in long-term care. When investigating other mental health disorders, it is critical to acknowledge that comorbid depression symptoms often exist. Research has indicated that depressive disorders often co-occur with anxiety disorders and substance abuse (Kessler, Berglund, et al., 2005). For instance, a secondary data analysis of the U.S. Collaborative Psychiatric Epidemiology Surveys, 2001–2003, of community-dwelling adults age 65+ (*N* = 2,626) indicated a significantly higher prevalence rate of generalized anxiety (26% vs. 2%), posttraumatic stress syndrome (9% vs. 2%), panic disorder (10% vs. 2%), social phobia (22% vs. 6%), alcohol abuse (7% vs. 4%), alcohol dependence (3% vs. 1%), and cognitive disability (3.4 vs. 1.1 mean level of cognitive impairment) in individuals with depression, as compared to individuals without depression (Figure 13.1). Figure 13.2 details that depression is associated with

FIGURE 13.2 Cognitive impairment with depression.

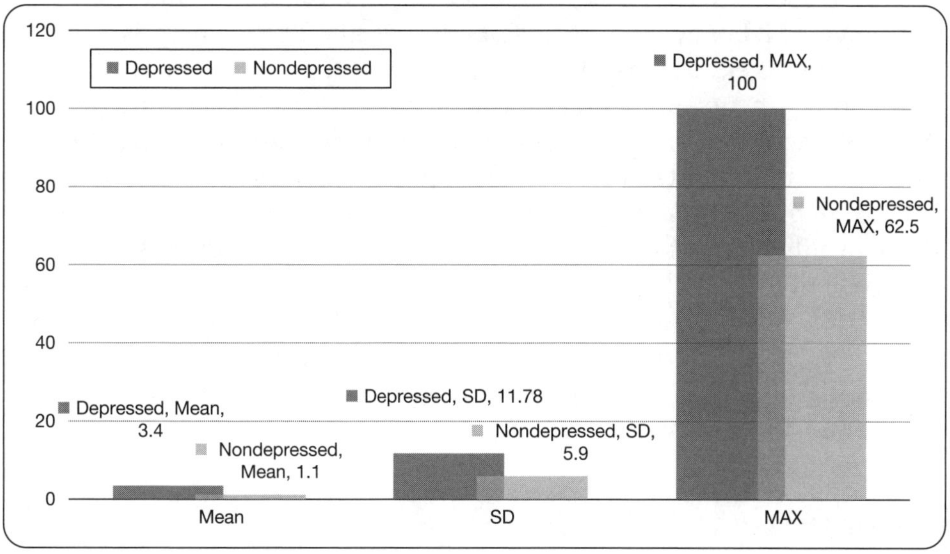

120
100
80
60
40
20
0
Depressed Nondepressed
Depressed, MAX, 100
Nondepressed, MAX, 62.5
Depressed, Mean, 3.4
Nondepressed, Mean, 1.1
Depressed, SD, 11.78
Nondepressed, SD, 5.9
Mean
SD
MAX

Note: Levels of cognitive disability based on Collaborative Psychiatric Epidemiology Surveys, 2001–2003 [United States], age 65+, *N* = 2,626.

higher levels of cognitive impairment, and greater variance and range in cognitive impairment is associated with depression. Therefore, understanding the detrimental effects of depression, when investigating other mental health disorders, is needed to fully comprehend the negative effects of other mental health disorders on the transitions of long-term care. Because individuals with serious mental illness, including schizophrenia and bipolar disorders, also have high rates of cognitive impairment and social isolation, they, too, are at greater risk of nursing home admission and long-term stay according to Fullerton et al. (2009).

It is also important to consider the impact of technology and the growth in the baby boom population. We have yet to understand how developments and advances in technology will affect mental health in old age. For example, it is possible that because of technological advances in creating and implementing programs to detect and monitor mental illness, there can be a vast improvement in mental health. This vast increase could imply that mental health can be a more pressing public health concern, but the aging of the baby boomers can also be an impetus for improvements in mental health care in older age if older adults demand routine, timely, and appropriate treatment.

CONSIDERATIONS FOR MENTAL HEALTH MANAGEMENT IN LONG-TERM CARE

When attempting to aid older adults in long-term care settings with mental health management, an ethical stance focused on not undermining the autonomy of the individual is crucial. Gaining a better understanding of the mental health experience (Phillips, 2008), and promotion of consumer-directed care is a priority (AGS & AAGP, 2003; Shen, Smyer, Mahoney, Loughlin, et al., 2008; Shen, Smyer, Mahoney, Simon-Rusinowitz, et al., 2008). There is a growing need for more geriatric psychiatric specialists (Carlson & Snowden, 2007). Furthermore, a better understanding is needed for the detection and mental health treatment outcomes of both community-dwelling and long-term care facility residents in rural settings because up to 50% of older adults living in rural areas face depression (Dobalian, Tsao, & Radcliff, 2003; Fisher & Copenhaver, 2006). Consideration of older persons in long-term care settings with severe and persistent mental illness, including major depression, schizophrenia, bipolar disorder, obsessive-compulsive disorder, panic disorder, posttraumatic stress disorder, and borderline personality disorder, should be a priority, as these populations are beginning to live longer into old age (Bartels et al., 2003; O'Connor, Little, & McManus, 2009).

SUMMARY

Mental illness is not a normal part of aging. Most forms of mental illness can be treated at any stage of life, including old age. The key lies in family and staff training to recognize symptoms, diligent screening and referral, and the provision of appropriate treatment interventions ranging from medication to an array of nonpharmacological approaches, including group and individual cognitive behavioral psychotherapy, reminiscence therapy, emphasis on social activities, and providing meaningful occupation such as sheltered workshops, volunteering, religious activities, or activities that maintain past roles (AGS & AAGP, 2003). Experiencing all levels of the long-term care continuum is not inevitable for all older adults, but knowing how to identity and manage symptoms of mental illness can potentially delay or even prevent long-term facility placement. When long-term care is needed, treating mental illness can significantly improve the chances that older adults and their families can continue to flourish with a high quality of life in whatever setting they are residing.

DISCUSSION QUESTIONS

1. What is the best way for dealing with an older adult showing changes in personality or thinking?
2. How does depression affect aging?
3. What are some effective treatment strategies for mental illness in old age?
4. When is mental referral needed?
5. What are some future directions for inquiry concerning long-term care and mental illness?
6. What would you do if you suspect mental illness in an older-aged loved one?
7. Consider a mental illness other than depression and discuss the degree to which its manifestations are similar to or different from those of depression.

ADDITIONAL RESOURCES

American Association for Geriatric Psychiatry (AAGP) www.aagponline.org
National Alliance on Mental Illness (NAMI) www.nami.org
National Institute of Mental Health (NIMH) www.nimh.nih.gov/index.shtml
Substance Abuse and Mental Health Services Administration (SAMHSA) www.samhsa.gov
U.S. Collaborative Psychiatric Epidemiology Surveys www.icpsr.umich.edu/icpsrweb/ICPSR/studies/20240

REFERENCES

Achterberg, W., Pot, A. M., Kerkstra, A., Ooms, M., Muller, M., & Ribbe, M. (2003). The effect of depression on social engagement in newly admitted Dutch nursing home residents. *The Gerontologist*, *43*(2), 213–218.

Ahmed, A., Ali, M., Lefante, C. M., Mullick, M. S., & Kinney, F. C. (2006). Geriatric heart failure, depression, and nursing home admission: An observational study using propensity score analysis. *American Journal of Geriatric Psychiatry*, *14*(10), 867–875.

Alexopoulos, G. S., Buckwalter, K., Olin, J., Martinez, R., Wainscott, C., & Krishnan, K. R. (2002). Comorbidity of late life depression: An opportunity for research on mechanisms and treatment. *Biological Psychiatry*, *52*(60), 543–558.

Allgower, A., Wardle, J., & Steptoe, A. (2001). Depressive symptoms, social support, and personal health behaviors in young men and women. *Journal of Health Psychology*, *20*(3), 223–227.

American Geriatrics Society & American Association for Geriatric Psychiatry. (2003). Consensus statement on improving the quality of mental health care in U.S. nursing homes: Management of depression and behavioral symptoms associated with dementia. *Journal of the American Geriatrics Society*, *51*(9), 1287–1298.

American Psychiatric Association. (2013). *Diagnostic and statistical manual of mental disorders* (5th ed.). Arlington, VA: American Psychiatric Press.

Anderson, R. L., Buckwalter, K. C., Buchanan, R. J., Maas, M. L., & Imhof, S. L. (2003). Validity and reliability of the Minimum Data Set Depression Rating Scale (MDSDRS) for older adults in nursing homes. *Age and Ageing*, *32*(4), 435–438.

Aud, M. A., & Rantz, M. J. (2005). Admissions to skilled nursing facilities from assisted living facilities. *Journal of Nursing Care Quality*, *20*(1), 16–25.

Bagley, H., Cordingley, L., Alistair, B., Mozley, C. G., Challis, D., & Huxley, P. (2000). Recognition of depression by staff in nursing and residential homes. *Journal of Clinical Nursing*, *9*, 445–450.

Ball, M. M., Perkins, M. M., Whittington, F. J., Connell, B. R., Hollingsworth, C., King, S. V., Elrod, C. L., & Combs, B. L. (2004). Managing decline in assisted living: The key to aging in place. *Journals of Gerontology B: Psychological Sciences and Social Sciences*, *59*(4), S202–S212.

Ball, M. M., Whittington, F. J., Perkins, M. M., Patterson, V. L., Hollingsworth, C., King, S.V., & Combs, B.L. (2000). Quality of life in assisted living facilities: Viewpoints of residents. *Journal of Applied Gerontology*, *19*, 304–325.

Barry, L. C., Allore, H. G., Bruce, M. L., & Gill, T. M. (2009). Longitudinal association between depressive symptoms and disability burden among older persons. *Journal of Gerontology: Biological Sciences/Medical Sciences*, *64*(12), 1325–1332.

Bartels, S. J. (2003). Improving the system of care for older adults with mental illness in the United States: Findings and recommendations for the president's new freedom commission on mental health. *American Journal of Geriatric Psychiatry, 11*(5), 486–497.

Bartels, S. J., Horn, S. D., Smout, R. J., Dums, A. R., Flaherty, E., Jones, J. K., ... Voss, A. C. (2003). Agitation and depression in frail nursing home elderly patients with dementia: Treatment characteristics and service use. *American Journal of Geriatric Psychiatry, 11*(2), 231–238.

Bartels, S. J, Miles, K. M., Dums, A. R., & Levine, K. J. (2003). Are nursing homes appropriate for older adults with severe mental illness? Conflicting consumer and clinician views and implications for the Olmstead decision. *Journal of the American Geriatrics Society, 51*(11), 1571–1579.

Bell, M., & Goss, A. J. (2001). Recognition, assessment and treatment of depression in geriatric nursing homes. *Clinical Excellence in Nursing Practice, 5*(1), 26–36.

Benton, T., Staab, J., & Evans, D. L. (2007). Medical co-morbidity in depressive disorders. *Annals of Clinical Psychiatry, 19*(4), 289–303.

Blazer, D. G., & Steffens, D. C. (Eds.). (2009). *The American psychiatric publishing textbook of geriatric psychiatry*. Washington, DC: American Psychiatric Publishing.

Blazer, D., Hughes, D. C., & George, L. K. (1987). The epidemiology of depression in an elderly community population. *The Gerontologist, 27*(3), 281–287.

Borowiak, E., & Kostka, T. (2004). Predictors of quality of life in older people living at home and in institutions. *Aging Clinical and Experimental Research, 16*(3), 212–220.

Boyle, V. L., Roychoudhury, C., Beniak, R., Cohn, L., Bayer, A., & Katz, I. (2004). Recognition and management of depression in skilled-nursing and long-term care settings. *American Journal of Geriatric Psychiatry, 12*(3), 288–295.

Braune, B. T., & Berger, K. (2005). The influence of depressive mood on activities of daily living and health care utilization in the elderly—The MEMO study on the KORA platform Augsburg. *Gesundheitswesen, 67*(Suppl. 1), S176S–S179S.

Bremmer, M. A., Hoogendijk, W. J., Deeg, D. J., Schoevers, R. A., Schalk, B. W., & Beekman, A. T. (2006). Depression in older age is a risk factor for first ischemic cardiac events. *American Journal of Geriatric Psychiatry, 14*(6), 523–530.

Brooke, V. (1989). How elders adjust: Through what phases do newly admitted residents pass? *Geriatric Nursing, 10*(2), 66–68.

Brühl, K. G., Luijendijk, H. J., & Muller, M. T. (2007). Nurses' and nursing assistants' recognition of depression in elderly who depend on long-term care. *Journal of the American Medical Directors, 8*(7), 441–445.

Carlson, W. L., & Snowden, M. (2007). Improving treatment for depression in the nursing home population: Integrating the model of the depression care manager. *Harvard Review of Psychiatry, 15*(3), 128–132.

Centers for Disease Control and Prevention. (2008). *Falls in nursing homes*. Retrieved from www.cdc.gov/ncipc/factsheets/nursing.htm

Center on Aging Society. (2005). How do family caregivers fare? *Caregivers of Older Persons: Data Profile*. Retrieved from http://ihcrp.georgetown.edu/agingsociety/pubhtml/caregiver3/caregiver3.html#5

Chen, C. K., Sabir, M., Zimmerman, S., Suitor, J., & Pillemer, K. (2007). The importance of family relationships with nursing facility staff for family caregiver burden and depression. *Journals of Gerontology Series B, 62*(5), 253–260.

Chen, C. K., Zimmerman, S., Sloane, P. D., & Barrick, A. L. (2007). Assisting living policies promoting autonomy and their relationship to resident depressive symptoms. *American Journal of Geriatric Psychiatry, 15*, 122–129.

Choi, N. G., & Dinitto, D. M. (2010). Heavy/binge drinking and depressive symptoms in older adults: Gender differences. *International Journal of Geriatric Psychiatry, 26*(8), 860–868.

Choi, N. G., Ransom, S., & Wyllie, R. J. (2008). Depression in older nursing home residents: The influence of nursing home environmental stressors, coping, and acceptance of group and individual therapy. *Aging and Mental Health, 12*(5), 536–547.

Chopra, M. P., & Owen, R. R. (2006). Assessment and treatment of depression in long-term care: Tools and options help reduce morbidity and potential mortality. *Journal of the Arkansas Medical Society, 102*(8), 220–221.

Chou, K. L., Yeung, F. K., & Wong, E. C. (2005). Fear of falling and depressive symptoms in Chinese elderly living in nursing homes: Fall efficacy and activity level as mediator or moderator? *Aging and Mental Health, 9*(3), 255–261.

Cohen, C. I., Hyland, K., & Kimhy, D. (2003). The utility of mandatory depression screening of dementia patients in nursing homes. *American Journal of Psychiatry, 160*(11), 2012–2017.

Cohen-Mansfield, J., & Wirtz, P. W. (2007). Characteristics of adult day care participants who enter a nursing home. *Psychology and Aging, 22*(2), 354–360.

Cole, M. G., & Dendukuri, N. (2004). The feasibility and effectiveness of brief interventions to prevent depression in older subjects: A systematic review. *International Journal of Geriatric Psychiatry, 19*(11), 1019–1025.

Conwell, Y., & Brent, D. (1995). Suicide and aging. I: Patterns of psychiatric diagnosis. *International Psychogeriatrics, 7*(2), 149–164.

Dahle, R., & Ploeg, J. (2009). On the outside looking in: Nurses in gerontology: A qualitative descriptive study of the lived experiences of older women with depression living in long-term care. *Perspectives, 33*(1), 5–12.

Darowski, A., Chambers, S. A., & Chambers, D. J., (2009). Antidepressants and falls in the elderly. *Drugs Aging, 26*(5), 381–394.

Davidson, S., Koritsas S., O'Connnor, D. W., & Clarke, D. (2006). The feasibility of a GP led screening intervention for depression among nursing home residents. *International Journal of Geriatric Psychiatry, 21*(11), 1026–1030.

Davis, P., Kenarney, K., Murdell, D., & Zabak, K. (2001). The potential for elderly suicide. Is health care missing it? *Director, 9*(4), 122–125.

Davison, T. E., McCabe, M. P., Mellor, D., Karantzas, G., & George, K. (2009). Knowledge of late-life depression: An empirical investigation of aged care staff. *Aging and Mental Health, 13*(4), 577–586.

Davison, T. E., McCabe, M. P., Mellor, D., Ski C., George, K., & Moore, K. A. (2007). The prevalence and recognition of major depression among low-level aged care residents with and without cognitive impairment. *Aging and Mental Health, 11*(1), 82–88.

Dobalian, A., Tsao, J. C., & Radcliff, T. A. (2003). Diagnosed mental and physical health conditions in the United States nursing home population: Differences between urban and rural facilities. *Journal of Rural Health, 19*(4), 477–483.

Dorenlot, P., Harboun, M., Bige, V., Henrard, J. C., & Ankri, J. (2005). Major depression as a risk factor for early institutionalization of dementia patients living in the community. *International Journal of Geriatric Psychiatry, 20*(5), 471–478.

Eisses, A. M., Kluiter, H., Jongenelis, K., Pot, A. M., Beekman, A. T., & Ormel, J. (2004). Risk indicators of depression in residential homes. *International Journal of Geriatric Psychiatry, 19*(7), 634–640.

Epel, E. S., Blackburn, E. H., Lin, J., Dhabhar, F. S., Adler, N. E., Morrow, J. D., & Cawthon, R. M. (2004). Accelerated telomere shortening in response to life stress. *Proceedings of the National Academy of Sciences, 101*(49), 17312–17315.

Evans, D. L., Staab, J. P., Petitto, J. M., Morrison, M. F., Szuba, M. P., Ward, H. E., … O'Reardon, J. P. (1999). Depression in the medical setting: Biopsychological interactions and treatment considerations. *Journal of Clinical Psychiatry, 60*(4)(Suppl.), S40–S55.

Fenton, J., Raskin A., Gruber-Baldini, A. L., Menon, A. S., Zimmerman, S., Kaup, B., … Magaziner, J. (2004). Some predictors of psychiatric consultation in nursing home residents. *American Journal of Geriatric Psychiatry, 12*(3), 297–304.

Fisher, K. M., & Copenhaver, V. (2006). Assessing the mental health of rural older adults in public housing facilities: A comparison of screening tools. *Journal of Gerontological Nursing*, *32*(9), 26–33.

Frasure-Smith, N., & Lesperance, F. (2006). Depression and other psychological risks following myocardial infarction. *Archives of General Psychiatry*, *60*, 627–636.

Fullerton, C. A., McGuire, T. G., Reng, Z., Mor, V., & Grabowski, D. C. (2009). Trends in mental health admissions to nursing homes, 1999–2005. *Psychiatric Services*, *60*(7), 965–971.

Gaboda, D., Lucas, J., Siegel, M., Kalay, E., & Crystal, S. (2011). No longer undertreated? Depression diagnosis and antidepressant therapy in elderly long-stay nursing home residents, 1999 to 2007. *Journal of the American Geriatrics Society*, *59*(4), 673–680.

Gill, E. A., & Morgan, M. (2011). Home sweet home: Conceptualizing and coping with the challenges of aging and the move to a care facility. *Health Communication*, *14*, 1–11.

Glaister, J. A., & Blair, C. (2008). Improved education and training for nursing assistants: Keys to promoting the mental health of nursing home residents. *Issues in Mental Health Nursing*, *29*(8), 863–872.

Glass, T., De Leon, C., & Bassuk, S. (2006). Social engagement and depressive symptoms in late life: Longitudinal finings. *Journal of Aging Health*, *18*, 604–628.

Gobert, M., & D'hoore, W. (2005). Prevalence of psychotropic drug use in nursing homes for the aged in Quebec and in the French-speaking area of Switzerland. *International Journal of Geriatric Psychiatry*, *20*(8), 712–721.

Golant, S. M. (2005). Do impaired older persons with health care needs occupy US assisted living facilities? An analysis of six national studies. *Journal of Gerontology, B Psychosocial Sciences*, *60*, S191–S192.

Golant, S. M. (2008). The future of assisted living residences: A response to uncertainty. In S. M. Golant & J. Hyde (Eds.), *The assisted living residence: A vision for the future* (pp. 3–45). Baltimore, MD: Johns Hopkins University Press.

Golant, S. M., & Hyde, J. (2008). *The assisted living residence: A vision for the future*. Baltimore, MD: The Johns Hopkins University Press.

Gonyea, J. G., Paris, R., & de Saxe Zerden, L. (2008). Adult daughters and aging mothers: The role of guilt in the experience of caregiver burden. *Aging & Mental Health*, *12*(5), 559–567.

Grabowski, D. C., Aschbrenner, K. A., Rome, V. F, & Bartels, S. J. (2010). Quality of mental health care for nursing home residents: A literature review. *Medical Care Research Review*, *67*(6), 627–656.

Greenberg, L., Lantz, M. S., Likourezos, A., Burack, O. R., Chichin, E., & Carter, J. (2004). Screening for depression in nursing home palliative care patients. *Journal of Geriatric Psychiatry and Neurology*, *17*(4), 212–218.

Gruber-Baldini, A. L., Zimmerman, S., Boustani, M., Watson, L. C., Williams, C. S., & Reed, P. S. (2005). Characteristics associated with depression in long-term care residents with dementia. *The Gerontologist*, *45* Spec No *1*(1), 50–55.

Hanlon, J. T., Handler, S. M., & Castle, N. G. (2010). Antidepressant prescribing in US nursing homes between 1996 and 2006 and its relationship to staffing patterns and use of other psychotropic medications. *Journal of the American Medical Directors Association*, *11*(5), 320–324.

Harrington, C., Carrillo, H., & LaCava, C. (2006). Nursing facilities, staffing, residents and facility deficiencies 1999–2005. *Center for Personal Assistance Services*. San Francisco, CA: University of California. Retrieved from www.pascenter.org/nursing_homes/nursing_trends_2005.php

Harris, Y. (2007). Depression as a risk factor for nursing home admission among older individuals. *Journal of the American Medical Directors*, *8*(1), 14–20.

Harris, Y., & Cooper, J. K. (2006). Depressive symptoms in older people predict nursing home admission. *Journal of the American Geriatrics Society*, *54*(4), 593–597.

Hawes, C., Phillips, C. D., & Rose, M. (2000). *High service or high privacy assisted living facilities, their residents and staff: Results from a national survey*. Beachwood, OH: Myers Research Institute. Retrieved from http://aspe.hhs.gov/daltcp/reports/hshp.htm

Hawes, C., Phillips, C. D., Rose, M., Holan, S., & Sherman, M. (2003). A national survey of assisted living facilities. *The Gerontologist, 43*(6), 875–882.

Heeren, O., Borin, L., Raskin, A., Gruber-Baldini, A. L., Menon, A. S., Kaup, B., ... Magaziner, J. (2003). Association of depression with agitation in elderly nursing home residents. *Journal of Geriatric Psychiatry and Neurology, 16*(1), 4–7.

Hendrix, C. C., Sakauye, K. M., Karabatsos, G., & Daigle, D. (2003). The use of the minimum data set to identify depression in the elderly. *Journal of the American Medical Directors, 4*(6), 308–312.

Hickie, I., Burke, D., Tobin, M., & Mutch, C. (2000). The impact of the organization of mental health services on the quality of assessment provided to older patients with depression. *Australian and New Zealand Journal of Psychiatry, 34*(5), 748–754.

Hollenberg, M., Haight, T., & Tager, I. B. (2003). Depression decreases cardiorespiratory fitness in older women. *Journal of Clinical Epidemiology, 56*(11), 1111–1117.

House, A., Knapp, P., Bamford, J., & Vail, A. (2001). Mortality at 2 and 24 months after stroke may be associated with depressive symptoms at 1 month. *Stroke, 32*, 696–701.

Houser, A. (2007). AARP Public Policy Institute analysis of 2004 National Nursing Home Survey. *Public Policy Institute*. Retrieved from www.aarp.org/home-garden/livable-communities/info-2007/fs10r_homes.html

Hudson, T. J., Cody, M., Armitage, T. L., Curtis, M. A., & Sullivan, G. (2005). Disparities in use of antipsychotic medications among nursing home residents in Arkansas. *Psychiatric Services, 56*(6), 749–751.

Hyde, J., Perez, R., & Reed, P. S. (2008). The old road is rapidly aging: A social model for cognitively or physically impaired elders in assisted living's future. In S. M. Golant & J. Hyde (Eds.), *The assisted living residence: A vision for the future* (pp. 46–85). Baltimore, MD: The Johns Hopkins University Press.

Hyman, S. E. (2001). Mental health in an aging population: The NIMH perspective. *American Journal of Geriatric Psychiatry, 9*(4), 330–339.

Johnston, L., Reid, A., Wilson, J., Levesque, J., & Driver, B. (2007). Detecting depression in the aged: Is there concordance between screening tools and the perceptions of nursing home staff and residents? A pilot study in a rural aged care facility. *Australian Journal of Rural Health, 15*(4), 252–256.

Jones, A. L., Dwyer, L. L., Bercovitz, A. R., & Strahan, G. W. (2009). *The National Nursing Home Survey: 2004 overview*. National Center for Health Statistics. *Vital and Health Statistics, 13*(167).

Jones, E. D. (2003). Reminiscence therapy for older women with depression. Effects of nursing intervention classification in assisted-living long-term care. *Journal of Gerontological Nursing, 29*(7), 26–33, 56–57.

Jongenelis, K., Pot, A. M., Eisses, A. M., Beekman, A. T., Kluiter, H., & Ribbe, M. W. (2004). Prevalence and risk indicators of depression in elderly nursing home patients: The AGED study. *Journal of Affective Disorders, 83*(2–3), 135–142.

Jonkers, C., Lamers, F., Bosma, H., Metsemakers, J., Kempen, G., & Van Eijk, J. (2007). Process evaluation of a minimal psychological intervention to reduce depression in chronically ill elderly persons. *Patient Education and Counseling, 68*(3), 252–257.

Kaldyand, J., & Tarnove, L. (2003). A clinical practice guideline approach to treating depression in long-term care. *Journal of the American Directors Association*, 4(2 Suppl.), S60–S68.

Kales, H. C., Chen P., Blow, F. C., Welsh, D. E., & Mellow, A. M. (2005). Rates of clinical depression diagnosis, functional impairment, and nursing home placement in coexisting dementia and depression. *American Journal of Geriatric Psychiatry, 13*(6), 441–449.

Kallenbach, L. E., & Rigler, S. K. (2006). Identification and management of depression in nursing facility residents. *Journal of the American Medical Directors Association*, *7*(7), 448–455.

Kane, R. A. (2004). *Assisted living as a long-term care option: Transition, continuity, and community*. Fairfax, VA: Assisted Living Research Institute.

Kao, H. F., Travis, S. S., & Acton, G. J. (2004). Relocation to a long-term care facility: Working with patients and families before, during, and after. *Journal of Psychosocial Nursing and Mental Health Services*, *42*(3), 10–16.

Kenefick, A. L. (2004) Pain treatment and quality of life: Reducing depression and improving cognitive impairment. *Journal of Gerontological Nursing*, *30*(5), 22–29.

Kerber, C. S., Dyck, M. J., Culp, K. R., & Buckwalter, K. (2008). Antidepressant treatment of depression in rural nursing home residents. *Issues in Mental Health Nursing*, *29*(9), 959–973.

Kessler, R. C., Berglund, P. A., Demler, O., Jin, R., Merikangas, K. R., & Walters, E. E. (2005). Lifetime prevalence and age-of-onset distributions of DSM-IV disorders in the National Comorbidity Survey Replication (NCS-R). *Archives of General Psychiatry*, *62*(6), 593–602.

Kessler, R. C., Chiu, W. T., Demler, O., Merikangas, K. R., & Walters, E. E. (2005). Prevalence, severity, and comorbidity of 12-month DSM-IV disorders in the National Comorbidity Survey Replication. *Archives of General Psychiatry*, *62*(6), 617–627.

Koehler, M., Rabinowitz, T., Hirdes, J., Stones, M., Carpenter, G. I., Fries, B. E., … Jones, R. N. (2005). Measuring depression in nursing home residents with the MDS and GDS: An observational psychometric study. *BMC Geriatrics*, *5*(1), 1–8.

Kose, N., Cuvalci, S., Ekici, G., Otman, A. S., & Karakaya, M. G. (2005). The risk factors of fall and their correlation with balance, depression, cognitive impairment and mobility skills in elderly nursing home residents. *Saudi Medical Journal*, *26*(6), 978–981.

Lai, S. M., Duncan, P. W., Dew, P., & Keighley, J. (2005). Sex differences in stroke recovery. *Preventing Chronic Disease*, *2*(3), 1–11.

Landi, F., Onder, G., Cesari, M., Russo, A., Barillaro, C., Bernabei, R., & SILVERNET-HC Study Group. (2005). Pain and its relation to depressive symptoms in frail older people living in the community: An observational study. *Journal of Pain Symptom Management*, *29*(3), 255–262.

Lapane, K. L., & Hughes, C. M. (2004). Which organizational characteristics are associated with increased management of depression using antidepressants in US nursing homes? *Medical Care*, *42*(10), 992–1000.

Leas, L., & McCabe, M. (2007). Health behaviors among individuals with schizophrenia and depression. *Journal of Health Psychology*, *12*(4), 563–579.

Lemke, S., & Schaefer, J. A. (2010). VA nursing home residents with substance use disorders: Mental health comorbidities, functioning, and problem behaviors. *Journal of Aging and Mental Health*, *14*(5), 593–602.

Lemogne, C., & Consoli, S. M. (2010). Depression and cancer: Challenging the myth through epidemiology. *Psycho-Oncologie*, *4*(1), 22–27.

Lenhoff, D. R. (2003). The American Geriatrics Society/American Association for Geriatric Psychiatry mental health in nursing homes consensus statement. *Journal of the American Geriatrics Society*, *51*(9), 1287–1298.

Levin, C. A., Wei W., Akincigil A., Lucas J. A., Bilder S., & Crystal S. (2007). Prevalence and treatment of diagnosed depression among elderly nursing home residents in Ohio. *Journal of the American Medical Directors Association*, *8*(9), 585–594.

Linkins, K. W., Lucca, A. M., Housman, M., & Smith, S. A. (2006). Use of PASRR programs to assess serious mental illness and service access in nursing homes. *Psychiatric Services*, *57*(3), 325–332.

Lyness, J. M., Niculescu, A., Xin, T., Reynolds, C. F., & Caine, E. D. (2006). The relationship of medical comorbidity and depression in older, primary care patients. *Psychosomatics*, *47*, 435–439.

Mark, T. L., Joish, V. N., Hay, J. W., Sheehan, D. V., Johnston, S. S., & Cao, Z. (2011). Antidepressant use in geriatric populations: The burden of side effects and interactions and their impact on adherence and costs. *American Journal of Geriatric Psychiatry, 19*(3), 211–221.

Maulik, P. K., Eaton, W. W., & Bradshaw, C. P. (2011). The effect of social networks and social support on mental health services use, following a life event, among the Baltimore Epidemiologic Catchment Area cohort. *Journal of Behavioral Health Services & Research, 38*(1), 29–50.

McAllister, M., & Matarasso, B. (2007). Mental health community liaison in aged care: A service of value to all. *International Journal of Older People Nursing, 2*, 148–154.

Meeks, S., & Burton E. G. (2004). Nursing home staff characteristics and knowledge gain from a didactic workshop on depression and behavior management. *Gerontology and Geriatrics Association, 25*(2), 57–66.

Meeks, S., Looney, S. W., Van Haitsma, K., & Teri, L. (2008). BE-ACTIV: A staff-assisted behavioral intervention for depression in nursing homes. *The Gerontologist, 48*(1), 105–114.

Mitchell, A. J., Rao, S., & Vaze, A. (2010). Do primary care physicians have particular difficulty identifying late-life depression? A meta-analysis stratified by age. *Psychotherapy and Psychosomatics, 79*(5), 285–294.

Mitchell, J. M., & Kemp, B. K. (2000). Quality of life in assisted living homes: A multidisciplinary analysis. *Journals of Gerontology B Psychological Sciences and Social Sciences, 55*, 117–127.

Mollica, R., Houser, A., & Ujvari, K. (2012). *Assisted living and residential care in the states in 2010*. Washington, DC: AARP Public Policy Institute.

National Alliance for Caregiving and AARP. (2009). *Caregiving in the US*. Retrieved from www.caregiving.org/data/04finalreport.pdf

National Alliance for Caregiving and MetLife Mature Market Institute. (2010). New insights and innovations for reducing health care costs for employers. *The MetLife study of working caregivers and employer health costs*. Retrieved from www.metlife.com/assets/cao/mmi/publications/studies/2010/mmi-working-caregivers-employers-health-care-costs.pdf

National Alliance on Mental Health. (2010). *What is mental illness: Mental illness facts*. Retrieved from www.nami.org/Content/NavigationMenu/Inform_Yourself/About_Mental_Illness/About_Mental_Illness.htm

National Association of State Mental Health Program Directors. (2006). Morbidity and mortality in people with serious mental illness. *Medical Directors Council: Thirteenth in a Series of Technical Reports*. Retrieved from www.nasmhpd.org/

National Center for Assisted Living. (2001). Facts and trends. In *The assisted living sourcebook*. Washington, DC: NCAL. Retrieved from http://www.ahcancal.org/research_data/trends_statistics/Documents/Assisted_Living_Sourcebook_2001.pdf

National Institute of Mental Health. (2007). *Older adults: Depression and suicide facts (fact sheet)* (NIH Publication No. 4593). Washington, DC: Health and Human Services, NIH. Retrieved from www.nimh.nih.gov/health/publications/older-adults-depression-and-suicide-facts-fact-sheet/index.shtml

O'Connor, D., Little, F., & McManus, R. (2009). Elders with serious mental illness: Lost opportunities and new policy options. *Journal of Aging and Social Policy, 21*(2), 144–158.

Onder, G., Penninx, B. W., Landi, F., Atkinson, H., Cesari, M., Bernabei, R., … Investigators of the Gruppo Italiano di Farmacoepidemiologia nell'Anziano Study. (2003). Depression and adverse drug reactions among hospitalized older adults. *Archives of Internal Medicine, 163*(3), 301–305.

Older Americans Act of 1965. Public Law 89-73, 79 Stat. 218 (1965).

Olmstead v. L.C. (98-536) 527 U.S. 581 (1999).

Pálsson, S., Larsson, L., Tengelin, E., Waern, M., Samuelsson, S., Hällstro, T., & Skoog, I. (2001). The prevalence of depression in relation to cerebral atrophy and cognitive performance in 70- and 74-year-old women in Gothenburg. The Women's Health Study. *Psychological Medicine, 31*(1), 39–49.

Peskind, E. R. (2003). Management of depression in long-term care of patients with Alzheimer's disease. *Journal of the American Medical Directors Association*, *4*(6 Suppl.), S141–S145.

Phillips, L. J. (2008). Advancing depression research in nursing home residents. *Western Journal of Nursing Research*, *30*(6), 651–652.

Polivka, L., & Salmon, J. R. (2008). Assisted living: What it should be and why. In S. M. Golant & J. Hyde (Eds.), *The assisted living residence: A vision for the future* (pp. 397–418). Baltimore, MD: The Johns Hopkins University Press.

Pruchno, R. A., & Rose, M. S. (2000). The effects of long-term care environments on health outcomes. *The Gerontologist*, *40*, 422–428.

Quality Partner of Rhode Island. (2004). Recognition and treatment of depression in long-term care facilities. *Rhode Island Medical Society*, *87*(8), 247–248.

Ray, W. A., Thapa, P. B., & Gideon, P. (2000). Benzodiazepenes and the risk of falls in nursing home residents. *Journal of the American Geriatrics Society*, *48*(6), 682–685.

Redfoot, D. (2007). *How do the residents in assisted living and nursing homes compare?* Center for Excellence in Assisted Living. Retrieved from www.theceal.org/column.php?ID=16

Reynolds, S. L., Haley, W. E., & Kozlenko, N. (2008). The impact of depressive symptoms and chronic diseases on active life expectancy in older Americans. *American Journal of Geriatric Psychiatry*, *16*(5), 425–432.

Roberts, R. E., Kaplan, G. A., Shema, S. J., & Strawbridge, W. J. (1997). Does growing old increase risk for depression? *American Journal of Psychiatry*, *154*, 1384–1390.

Ruckdeschel, K., & Katz, I. R. (2004). Care of dementia and other mental disorders in assisted living facilities: New research and borrowed knowledge. *Journal of the American Geriatrics Society*, *52*(10), 1771–1773.

Schulz, R., Belle, S. H., Czaja, S. J., McGinnis, K. A., Stevens, A., & Zhang, S. (2004). Long-term care placement of dementia patients and caregiver health and well-being. *Journal of the American Medical Association*, *292*(8), 961–967.

Scott, K. M., Bruffaerts, R., Tsang, A., Ormel, J., Alonso, J., Angermeyer, M. C., ... Von Korff, M. (2007). Depression–anxiety relationships with chronic physical conditions: Results from the World Mental Health Surveys. *Journal of Affective Disorders*, *103*(1–3), 113–120.

Seitz, D., Purandare, N., & Conn, D. (2010). Prevalence of psychiatric disorders among older adults in long-term care homes: A systematic review. *International Psychogeriatrics*, *22*(7), 1025–1039.

Sheehan, D. V., Lecrubier, Y., Sheehan, K. H., Amorim, P., Janavs, J., Weiller, E., ... Dunbar, G. C. (1998). The Mini-International Neuropsychiatric Interview (M.I.N.I.): The development and validation of a structured diagnostic psychiatric interview for DSM-IV and ICD-10. *Journal of Clinical Psychiatry*, *59*(Suppl. 20), 22–33; quiz 34–57.

Shen, C., Smyer, M. A., Mahoney, K. J., Loughlin, D. M., Simon-Rusinowitz, L., & Mahoney, E. K. (2008). Does mental illness affect consumer direction of community-based care? Lessons from the Arkansas Cash and Counseling program. *The Gerontologist*, *48*(1), 93–104.

Shen, C., Smyer, M., Mahoney, K. J., Simon-Rusinowitz, L., Shinogle, J., Norstrand, J., ... del Vecchio P. (2008). Consumer-directed care for beneficiaries with mental illness: Lessons from New Jersey's Cash and Counseling program. *Psychiatric Services*, *59*(11), 1299–1306.

Smalbrugge, M., Pot, A. M., Jongenelis, L., Gundy, C. M., Beekman, A. T., & Eefsting, J. A. (2006). The impact of depression and anxiety on well being, disability and use of health care services in nursing home patients. *International Journal of Geriatric Psychiatry*, *21*(4), 25–32.

Snowden, M., Sato, K., & Roy-Byrne, P. (2003). Assessment and treatment of nursing home residents with depression or behavioral symptoms associated with dementia: A review of the literature. *Journal of the American Geriatrics Society*, *51*(9), 1305–1317.

Substance Abuse and Mental Health Services Administration. (2003). *Get connected: Linking older American with medication, alcohol, and mental health resources* (DHHS Publication No., (SMA) 03-3824). Rockville, MD: Center for Substance Abuse Treatment, Substance Abuse and Mental Health Services Administration.

Suominen, K., Henriksson, M., Isometsä, E., Conwell, Y., Heilä, H., & Lönnqvist, J. (2003). Nursing home suicides-a psychological autopsy study. *International Journal of Geriatric Psychiatry, 18*(12), 1095–1101.

Sutcliffe, C., Burns, A., Challis, D., Mozley, C. G., Cordingley, L., Bagley, H., & Huxley, P. (2007). Depressed mood, cognitive impairment, and survival in older people admitted to care homes in England. *American Journal of Geriatric Psychiatry, 15*(8), 708–715.

Thompson, L. (2004). Long-term care: Support for family caregivers. *Long term care financing project issue brief.* Washington, DC: University of Georgetown. Retrieved from http://ltc.georgetown.edu/pdfs/caregivers.pdf

Tsai, Y. F. (2006). Self-care management and risk factors for depressive symptoms among elderly nursing home residents in Taiwan. *Journal of Pain and Symptom Management, 32*(2), 140–147.

van Gool, C. H., Kempen, G. I. J. M., Penninx, B. W. J. H., Deeg, D. J. H., Beekman, A. T. F., & vanEijk, J. T. M. (2003). Relationship between changes in depressive symptoms and unhealthy lifestyles in late middle aged and older persons: Results from the Longitudinal Aging Study Amsterdam. *Age and Ageing, 32*, 81–87.

van Hooren, S. A., Valentijn, S. A., Bosma, H, Ponds, R. W., van Boxtel, M. P., & Jolles, J. (2005). Relation between health status and cognitive functioning: A 6-year follow-up of the Maastricht Aging Study. *Journal of Gerontology Psychological Sciences Series B, 60*(1), 57–60.

van Randenborgh, A., de Jong-Meyer, R., & Hüffmeier, J. (2010). Decision making in depression: Differences in decisional conflict between healthy and depressed individuals. *Clinical Psychology & Psychotherapy, 17*(4), 285–298.

Verkaik, R., Francke, A. L., van Meijel, B., Ribbe, M. W., & Bensing, J. M. (2009). Comorbid depression in dementia on psychogeriatric nursing home wards: Which symptoms are prominent? *American Journal of Geriatric Psychiatry, 17*(7), 565–573.

Wagenaar, D., Colenda, C. C., Kreft, M., Sawade, J., Gardiner, J., & Poverejan, E. (2003). Treating depression in nursing homes: Practice guidelines in the real world. *Journal of the American Osteopathic Association, 103*(10), 465–469.

Wang, J. J. (2004). The comparative effectiveness among institutionalized and non-institutionalized elderly people in Taiwan of reminiscence therapy as a psychological measure. *Journal of Nursing Research, 12*(3), 237–245.

Watson, L. C., Garrett, J. M., Sloane, P. D., Gruber-Baldini, A. L., & Zimmerman, S. (2003). Depression in assisted living: Results from a four-state study. *American Journal of Geriatric Psychiatry, 11*(5), 534–542.

Watson, L. C., Zimmerman, S., Cohen, L. W., & Dominik, R. (2009). Practical depression screening in residential care/assisted living: Five methods compared with gold standard diagnoses. *American Journal of Geriatric Psychiatry, 17*(7), 556–564.

Webber, A. P., Martin, J. L., Harker, J. O., Josephson, K. R., Rubenstein, L. Z., & Alessi, C. A. (2005). Depression in older patients admitted for postacute nursing home rehabilitation. *Journal of the American Geriatrics Society, 53*(6), 1017–1012.

World Health Organization. (2010). *Depression: What is depression? Mental health.* Geneva, Switzerland: World Health Organization. Retrieved from www.who.int/mental_health/management/depression/definition/en/

Zanjani, F., Kruger T., & Murray, D. (2012). Evaluation of the mental healthiness aging initiative: Community program to promote awareness about mental health and aging issues. *Community Mental Health Journal, 48*, 193–201.

Zarit, S. (2006). Assessment of family caregivers: A research perspective. In Family Caregiver Alliance (Eds.), *Caregiver assessment: Voices and views from the field. Report from a National Consensus Development Conference* (Vol. II, pp. 12–37). San Francisco, CA: Family Caregiver Alliance.

Zimmerman, S., Gruber-Baldini, A. L., Sloane, P. D., Eckert, J. K., Hebel, J. R., Morgan, L. A., … Konrad, T. R. (2003). Assisted living and nursing homes: Apples and oranges? *The Gerontologist, 43*, 107–117.

Ethics, Aging, and Long-Term Care: Questioning What "Everyone Knows"

MARTHA B. HOLSTEIN

CHAPTER OVERVIEW

The purpose of this chapter is to frame ethical concepts, particularly feminist ethics of care, within the context of long-term care. This chapter explores what it means to be a practitioner, a resident, or both in long-term care settings; how these notions influence conceptions of autonomy; and how a different way of understanding autonomy, as well as the ethical principles of beneficence, nonmaleficence, and justice, broaden the scope of justifiable action. The chapter suggests how injustices fester in long-term care policy and practice and critiques the standard paradigm for analyzing ethical problems in long-term care.

LEARNING OBJECTIVES

After completing this chapter, you should have an understanding of:

- General ethical concepts
- The application of ethical concepts to long-term care
- Examples of ethical conundrums that long-term care facilities face

KEY TERMS

Autonomy
Critical gerontology
Ethical analysis
Ethical dilemma
Feminist ethics
Household issues
Informed consent
Negotiated consent
Preventive ethics
Principalism

Moral reflection requires that we examine different ways of being moral agents and work toward teachable and livable moralities that are sensitive to the socio-political contexts in which people need to live well and sustain their relationships.

—A. Baier

INTRODUCTION

Ethics is a disciplined and systematized reflection on moral practices (Walker, 2003). It offers a means to expose taken-for-granted values, judgments, responsibilities, aims, and actions to critical scrutiny while also inviting the ability to address new or emergent areas of concern. Contemporary attention to ethics, aging, and long-term care traces its beginnings to the mid-1980s with the path-breaking initiatives of The Retirement Research Foundation. Encompassing the approach developed to analyze moral problems, the core values that ethical thinking then relied on, and the areas deemed appropriate for ethical consideration, an examination in 2015 is part of the "critical turn" that we are witnessing in so many fields today (see Holstein, Parks, & Waymack, 2011). With this chapter's grounding in the meanings of autonomy, readers are less likely to raise questions about what autonomy means in practice or how attending so exclusively to that principle has often effaced social justice concerns.

This chapter explores what it means to be a practitioner, a resident (in a nursing home or other congregate living site), or both, how these notions influence conceptions of autonomy, and how a different way of understanding autonomy, as well as how the ethical principles of beneficence, nonmaleficence, and justice are by themselves inadequate to address the questions that arise in long-term care. The chapter suggests how injustices fester in long-term care policy and practice and critiques what has become the standard paradigm for analyzing ethical problems in long-term care. First, it is important to ground these viewpoints both conceptually and personally because there is no neutral starting place from which to consider ethical concerns (Walker, 2003).

PERSPECTIVE: A CONCEPTUAL AND PERSONAL ORIENTATION

Who we are affects what we see, how we think, judgments we reach, and hence, actions that become possibilities. This author addresses issues seen from a commitment to **feminist ethics** (concerned with care and responsibility and invested in action to remedy injustice) and **critical gerontology** (scientific understanding cannot be divorced from either values or subjective aspects of the lived experience of the older person). These commitments mean that ethical primacy is placed on the ways in which gender, race, and/or class create situations of unequal power that subtly but consistently disadvantage individuals by virtue of these characteristics. They inform long-term care constructs such as giving and receiving care, justice within families, and end-of-life care. "Doing ethical work" using a feminist ethics approach means that emotion counts, context matters, and that abstract principles and rules are to be borne in mind but are not the sole arbiters of what counts in particular relationships among people. It means thinking about an autonomous person not as an isolated individual who closely guards a zone of freedom, but rather as a person who is interdependent and enmeshed in relationships of care that deserve support and protection (MacKenzie & Stoljar, 2000). It means acknowledging inevitable ambiguities and accepting that good ethical work may be described as the process whereby "reasonable people struggle together to reach judgments" (Pritchard, 2006, p. 7). For this reason, no one approach to addressing ethical dilemmas is sufficient to respond to the issues and people who are involved. An approach related to feminist ethics is communicative ethics (Cooper, 2004; Hugman, 2005; Johnson, 1999; Moody, 1992), which invites information gathering, deliberation, and negotiation (Johnson, 1999) among equal participants who strive to reach an agreement that all can accept, even if the agreement constructed is not their first choice. Moral compromise is often necessary, especially in situations of factual uncertainty typical in long-term settings, legitimate ethical differences, and the need to continue working together (Goodstein, 2000). It might call for a *narrative approach* (use of personal stories or interpretations: See Case Study 14.1) in which participants try to understand the values and motives of all the people involved

Case Study 14.1: Finding Common Ground

Imagine for a moment exposing your body that does not meet cultural norms of beauty or attractiveness to the eyes of a stranger as she is helping you with your bath. In this asymmetrical relationship, where trust is so essential and the potential for power abuse so possible, trust, an elemental moral value, raises the task of bathing to forming a deeply moral relationship (Twigg, 2004).

To consider this situation, let us stipulate that Mrs. Smith, who is getting the bath, is competent but has Parkinson's disease and severe osteoarthritis and so has limited ability to maneuver in space. Mrs. Foster is a caregiver in the nursing home where Mrs. Smith lives. Mrs. Foster is rushed every morning because of all the women she needs to help bathe and dress. Mrs. Smith tries to be generous to her caregivers but she feels so disempowered when Mrs. Foster assists her with her bath that she has started to resist bathing even though throughout her life, her morning shower was essential to her way of life.

For the nursing home and for Mrs. Foster, Mrs. Smith's resistance to taking a bath makes her a "problem" patient because she impedes the time-based schedule of the nursing home. The ethical dilemma in this situation is the clash between what the nursing home defines as efficient operational methods and the special needs that Mrs. Smith seems to have about bathing.

(*continued*)

Case Study 14.1: Finding Common Ground (*continued*)

Case Study Discussion Questions:

1. Rather than think of Mrs. Smith as a problem, what story might she want to tell about how she experiences bathing?
2. How might that story (narrative) be elicited?
3. Who is responsible for listening to the story?
4. Imagine a conversation between the two women: What would they say to one another? How might you learn what is important to her and what she finds so problematic in regard to her bath?
5. Expand the conversation to include an administrator: What would they say to one another?
6. Assume that Mrs. Smith wants greater privacy during her bath and doesn't want to be rushed, assume that she is uncomfortable with more than one set of eyes looking at her body, assume that she argues that she can be left alone for the time it takes to wash and relax in the tub (she's in a seat); make any other assumptions that you think would explain her resistance. Once you know why she is so resistant, what ethical problems do you confront? At what level can they be addressed? What are the nursing home's moral obligations and what are the moral obligations of Mrs. Foster, the caregiver? In turn, what are Mrs. Smith's moral obligations? What values seem critically important in this situation? Are there any moral rules that apply in this situation? What are the consequences of acting in different ways? What actions can you take? What actions will you take and why?

and devise an answer that responds to these often different perspectives and values. There is less certainty about right and good actions than common introductions to ethics and aging might suggest. Finally, in the tradition of feminist scholarship, a critically based ethic "links conclusions about how to live with attempts to put those conclusions into practice" (Nussbaum, 1997, p. 208), thus joining the political and the ethical (Lloyd, 2006).

JOURNEY TO THE PRESENT: AN OVERVIEW AND CRITIQUE OF ETHICS AND AGING

For older people, ethical work that has been undertaken during the past two decades has placed certain values at the forefront; for example, in the long-term care setting, this involves values about keeping confidences, telling the truth, and respecting older people as important decision makers in their own lives. The principle of **autonomy**, or self-governance and self-direction, most often serves as the preeminent value, enacted in the practice setting through informed consent. Discussed in the text that follows, autonomy and informed consent can retain their importance as values, but they are being reinterpreted in the light of a different understanding of what it means to be an older resident or staff member in a long-term care setting and the role of families in decision making.

For generations, the moral point of view—one that was detached, universal, impartial—remained unchallenged. It was at the heart of ethical theories that are now so familiar—Kantianism, utilitarianism, and the social contract, but most familiar, it gave rise to the *principlism* or "doing ethics" using four principles—autonomy, beneficence, nonmaleficence, and justice—that have played such an important role in the evolution of the field (Beauchamp & Childress, 2001). "Doing" ethics was organized around the notion of an **ethical dilemma**, in which values conflicted and the possibility of a solution was promised (Jennings, 2006). **Ethical analysis** or ethical consideration of an issue or problem focused on patient competency and self-determination; on the nature and limits of caregiver obligation; and on threats posed by professional paternalism, institutional self-interest, and the imperatives of high-tech medicine. Though efforts were made to address the demands placed on others as the result of patient or client choices, in practice, client choice reigned relatively unchallenged (Collopy, Dubler, & Zuckerman, 1990).

As experience would show, this impartial, universal, and largely individualistic approach to "doing" ethics was not well suited to address **"household" issues**, problems that arose in the everyday worlds of older people, family members, the community, and long-term care settings. Household issues for residents and staff in long-term care settings included who was to care for whom, what to do when family members disagreed, or what to do when the responsibility for care fell completely on one person. **Principlism** did not account for the moral claims of caregivers or for moral obligations that transcended decision making, including meaning making and identity preservation. Nonetheless, this mind-set carried a particular authority to engage in ethical analysis, which meant applying relatively few abstract principles and the rules derived from them, such as confidentiality or truth telling, in specific situations. In many ways it makes sense to order, weigh, or reconcile conflicting values and interests held by individuals who are autonomous, rational, and competent individuals (Cole & Holstein, 1996). This focus on the individual, although a welcome antidote to paternalism (or behaviors by an individual, organization, or the state, which restrict the autonomy of a person or group because of a perceived best interest), has meant that far less attention has been devoted to changing the context, such as public policies that limit choices that are possible, than on encouraging the older person to choose within those limits (Capitman & Sciegaj, 1995; Lloyd, 2006). An activist agenda that focused on modifying the social or economic conditions that made actual autonomy (Agich, 1990; Kittay, 1999) very nearly impossible for large numbers of older people in long-term care settings took second or third place to the narrow understanding of choice that prevailed.

Another difficulty was that the "subject" of traditional ethical thinking—an older adult freely able to choose his or her obligations and needing protection from the interference of others—differed dramatically from the "subject" of long-term care, most often, people whose infirmities and complicated lives embedded them in multiple relationships that both mattered to them and affected them deeply. Because traditional ethics offered no account of dependency or vulnerability and the moral relationships that these human conditions called for, much that is ethically important for the actual people in long-term care settings received little or no attention. Instead, the focus on free and equal moral agents obscured "the moral significance of our day-to-day relationships, ones that are frequently involuntary and unequal and thus [we have] failed to see how those attributes apply in the ... wider society" (Held, 2006, p. 13). Problems that arise in long-term care—dependency, vulnerability, daily relationships of care, and unavoidable unequal relationships—are real and cannot be evaded in efforts to reverse the once-dominant decline and loss paradigm. More appropriately, "doing ethics" as understood from a feminist ethics approach, confronts head-on the moral dimensions of the frailties and dependencies that are often unavoidable conditions of advancing age.

It is not surprising that, the individualistic notion of autonomy was, in time, extended to people who had lost decisional capacity. Through assigning decision making to a proxy, individuals, at least in theory, were able to extend their autonomy until they died (see critique of advance directives in Holstein et al., 2011). In practice, many older people in long-term care settings do not focus on their own autonomous choices but remain deeply concerned about their families, worry about being a burden, and often want family decision makers to decide in ways that are good for them too (High, 1988, 1991). Older adults want some say in the broad goals of treatment but not necessarily control over individual treatments. Yet, the focus on individual autonomy, defined as self-governing choice, has often led health professionals to view families skeptically, as less than trustworthy transmitters of the interests of their loved ones (Levine & Zuckerman, 1999). The problem, however, seems not to be selfish concerns for themselves but rather deep confusion about what to do when physicians present choices that are potentially beneficial.

In the United States, The Retirement Research Foundation's ground-breaking initiative Enhancing Autonomy in Long-Term Care, launched in 1984, almost single-handedly defined the work to come. Researchers uncovered multiple ways in which nursing homes disregarded client/patient autonomy (Lidz, Fischer, & Arnold, 1992). Collopy (1988) contributed a fine-grained, conceptual analysis of autonomy, particularly recognizing that an individual's inability to act on his or her choices did not mean denying the right to choose. In what remains a classic account of autonomy in long-term care, Collopy called attention to issues that are still inadequately addressed, such as the interrelation between competency (or incapacitated choice) and autonomy, the right to be left alone against the need for positive action that makes real choice possible, and the distinction between short-term and long-term autonomy.

One result of the new thinking is that American nursing homes now post a Patient Bill of Rights. They less often address the companion piece—responsibilities of living in the closed and intimate communities of long-term care. Admissions agreements are improved (Ambrogi & Leonard, 1988), and patients are invited to participate in "care planning." In community-based care, autonomy is also the most frequently articulated value. This commitment sets the stage for common ethical conundrums, such as individual choice versus safety, causing Kane and Levin (2001) to ask how one avoids interfering with life goals while meeting one's professional obligation to promote health and safety. As they observe, the "rights of a consumer to take informed risks are modified by the moral, legal, and regulatory responsibilities of health professionals and care organizations" (Kane & Levin, 2001, p. 221). In an effort to address these concerns, strategies for assessing risk were developed (Fireman, Dornberg-Lee, & Moss, 2001) while negotiated risk agreements (Kane & Levin, 2001) permit facilities, usually in assisted living options, to protect themselves from litigation while granting considerable freedom to individuals.

The preceding text suggests that a gap in ethical thinking exists in the area of "self-neglect." Such dilemmas pertain to the person who seemingly—and often dangerously—disregards his or her well-being but refuses any intervention. The standard response has been that if the person has decisional capacity, beyond trying to persuade him or her to accept help, a social service provider must accept the choices the person makes. This issue requires further study and analysis, focusing on compromised capacity, longer and shorter term autonomy, long-term care choices that we actually have to offer people, and the role of emotions, such as compassion in working with an individual to determine the most appropriate action, all things considered. In an effort to address the seemingly unbridgeable divide between paternalism and autonomy (one way of framing the situation of "self-neglect"), Kittay (1999) suggests a common search for goals that both the patient/client and the provider can agree on, thus linking these two seemingly contradictory features of patient care. This insight provides an opening to think about "self-neglect" so that our moral intuitions about avoiding harm can be reconciled with our commitment not to act paternalistically (see Holstein et al., 2011).

Relationships between families and their older adult members have received valued attention in the past 10 to 15 years. Despite their deep reliance on autonomy, many ethicists acknowledge that important decisions happen in dialogue with others. Hardwig (1990) has pushed this position the furthest by arguing that family members have equal rights with the older adult. Others (Blustein, 1993) have adopted more modest stances, for example, recognizing that decision making, especially health care, involves moral dialogue, which relies on one's moral community and especially one's family (High, 1991); families are much more than the purveyors of the patient's wishes and preferences (Arras, 1995). High (1991) has convincingly argued that families' interests matter; hence, they ought *not* be dismissed on conflict-of-interest grounds.

This recognition of the family extends to an older adult's end of life. An older adult's decision to die at home rather than in a long-term care setting rarely affects him or her alone. How can the interests of all who may be involved intimately in the older person's life be taken into account? (Ellingson & Fuller, 2001; Kuhn, 2001). What would an ethics of accommodation rather than an ethics of autonomy (Levine & Zuckerman, 1999) look like if it were to account for older adults, families, formal caregivers, and communities? What would it mean to see the relevant stakeholders—the older person, family members, health and social service providers—in a single vision, all included in deciding what to do both preventively and reactively (McCullough & Wilson, 1995).

Using a "**preventive ethics**" approach (i.e., anticipating what might come next, not "preventing" ethics), key stakeholders, including the older person, meet regularly to decide on courses of action that are open to regular adjustments in the fluid situation that so reflects long-term care. **Negotiated consent**, characterized by the "clash and balancing of competing interests" (Moody, 1992), may be the most suitable approach when no one interest stands out and when love and compassion become more significant than autonomy. This view contrasts with the more dominant individualistic, procedural approaches to questions about death, dying, and medical care decision making (Moody, 1992). This dominant view did not offer many challenges to the medical context and the policy apparatus that supports hospitals and medical care. Changes did occur, but they were generally narrow ones that addressed relationships between physician and patient and between social service professionals and clients. One result is that **informed consent** became the central way in which autonomy was enacted in the medical setting, often with the emphasis on consent rather than on adequate information to make the choice informed. Later, as language transformed the patient into the consumer and then the customer, without any analysis of the moral significance of these changes, medicine morphed into a contractual relationship between putative equals. This assumption meant that unrecognized and unacknowledged power relationships were left intact and thus their effects went unaddressed. It also permitted busy nursing home staff to adopt a "minimalist ethic" (Fox & Swazey, 1984), one that only adopted, at best, a mere nod to the provision of care that incorporated any resident or family preferences and that suited their training, time constraints, and professional codes.

MORE QUESTIONS ARISE

Kane and Caplan (1990), in their studies of autonomy in nursing homes, found that residents worried less about major decisions, such as termination of treatment, but did worry about the opportunity to make private phone calls or preserve private space for visitors or for themselves. It should be no surprise that privacy, a feature of our status as adults, is what is often missed the most in nursing home life (Ray, 2008). Agich (1990) redefined autonomy so that it reflected the desire to live in habitual ways and to maintain or remake a sense of self in spite of loss. Accepting that the loss of functional capacities created unavoidable dependencies on others, Agich affirmed that these dependencies did not necessitate the loss of the chance to continue to live in familiar ways. By focusing on interstitial autonomy, he acknowledged "the essential social nature of human development and recognize[d] dependence as a non-accidental feature of the human condition" (p. 12), a point that has been further developed by feminist philosophers (Kittay, 1999; Parks, 2003; Tronto, 1993). This understanding of autonomy regards individuals as concrete and not generalized others (Behabib, 1987) for whom choice is not an abstractly given right but rather a meaningful instantiation of identity. Given this understanding of actual autonomy, to respect individuals means that "we attend to their concrete individuality, to their affective and personal experiences" while also learning "how to acknowledge their habits and identifications" (Agich, 1990, p. 14). In the context of long-term care, it means, to start with, that we offer not merely choice to people, but meaningful choice. These enlarged ethical obligations and the practical demands on caregivers affirm the notion that the good precedes the right. The right to choose is meaningless in the absence of an idea of the good and the possibility to realize that good. Yet, for people in long-term care settings, rights are granted without assurance that they will be able to live their version of the good life. One might take a simple example—when a lifelong vegetarian is offered a choice between a hamburger and a pork chop, it is not a meaningful choice; in fact, it is not a choice at all.

That we live our lives coherently and purposefully matters at any age. For many older people, the effects of chronic illness and the social devaluation that accompanies frailty and inactivity threaten what Taylor (1984) described as "horizons of meaning" (i.e., that which tells us that certain ways of life are deeply preferred to other ways of life). The search for a viable self in conditions of frailty and dependency demands an openness to respond to ethnic, racial, and religious values.

LONG-TERM CARE AS A SPECIFIC CONTEXT

The paradigmatic approach to addressing ethical problems developed in acute care settings. In the 1980s, this approach carried over to the very different long-term care environment, where its suitability is questionable. From micro issues of individual decision making, particularly with regard to autonomy and safety, to issues related to public policy and social justice, justice within families, and the moral implications of vulnerability and dependency, the realities of long-term care created unique moral demands.

VULNERABILITY AND DEPENDENCY

In a Western society devoted almost single-mindedly to freedom, independence, and control, vulnerability, a situation that implies some, if not all, loss of control and power over many circumstances of our daily lives, is an outlier. To be vulnerable is being far removed from the conditions in which familiar views of autonomy operate. In long-term care, a more ancient moral concern, once raised by Socrates, about how to lead a good life may be more relevant in long-term care settings. Hence, a difficult question for our society is how to make that question relevant in conditions that are opposite from those most valued. How can we provide a context in which an individual can find meaning when he or she is unable to live up to the social ideal of independence? To develop a rich account of ethics and aging requires us to think "deeply and candidly" about what equality and dignity mean in the "light of the *full* range of *common* conditions of ability and incapacity, immaturity and decline, symmetry and reciprocity that are part and parcel of human lives" (Walker, 2003, p. 16).

If we do not address these questions in long-term care, we risk isolating residents who are dependent and vulnerable, setting them apart from the strong who will give care without necessarily caring. The feminist ethic of care mentioned earlier embraces a basic value—that "proper care for others is a good, that humans in society should strive to enhance the quality of life in the world so that people can live as well as possible" (Tronto, 1995, p. 142).

In the United States, public support for long-term care has been historically located in the welfare sector. Even though, today, Medicaid pays 42% of the costs of long-term care (primarily financing institutional care, although that emphasis is gradually shifting), programs that serve clients and families are generally starved for resources. Long-term care is generally privatized and basic, delivered primarily by family members and low-wage workers (Player & Pollock, 2001). Attention to tasks and to hours of care makes it difficult to attend to the meaning-making activities that clients may care about above all. Hence, choice is often limited to selecting one home care agency over another or, in some circumstances, using a cash voucher to hire a care worker. Most often, such a choice is limited because the potential user of the service has little information about the agency or individual who will be caring for him or her in the most intimate of ways. This observation illustrates the focus on the choice and not on the information needed to make that choice informed.

This narrow view of autonomy elevates the distinctions that arise from class position. Individuals able to pay privately can, if they have sufficient resources, ignore the incessant attention to the "clock" and hours of care provision and seek the execution or delegation of meaningful choices. As Agich (1990) reminds us "being able to identify with one's choices is a prerequisite for true autonomy" (p. 15). Though an older adult may have lost control over bathing or dressing, if one has the resources, he or she can have some control over how much help she gets and from whom. For these individuals, within the limits of their physical and cognitive functioning, the opportunity to continue developing and expressing their individuality can continue. It is far less possible if one relies on public programs.

For those reliant on publicly funded assistance, overburdened family members and poorly paid caregivers are unable to care in ways that go beyond the instrumental. Ethical values, such as attentiveness, responsibility, responsiveness (Tronto, 2001) or competence, compassion, and care, are difficult to enact. When the provision of instrumental care is deemed acceptable, it becomes particularly difficult to find a listener for stories that facilitate the construction and the reconstruction of identities threatened by loss and change. A relational view of autonomy reminds us that identities can be remade and recreated through the relationships that have given meaning to our lives. Hence, if we accept a richer view of autonomy than the conventional one, we also accept the social nature of the self and the obligation to create opportunities for people who have long-term care needs to find a way to live that supports and sustains their identities. It deepens our moral obligations to include support for maintaining these essential parts of the self. The classic view of autonomy demands much less of health and social service providers because it doesn't require attention to the contextual supports that a relational view of autonomy would demand.

Long-Term Care as Woman's Work

People needing long-term care share another feature of their lives: they are most often cared for by women family members who provide three quarters of the care in the community. Some older people also receive care from paid home care workers, about 99% of whom are women. Wages are low and benefits few. Such care provision is essentialized and billed as "natural"; their work is simultaneously praised and demeaned (Abel, 1991; Twigg, 2004). The primary care receivers are most often also women. For most families, choice is a myth. There is no free choice. Choice seems nonexistent if men are not called on to make comparable choices. Having fewer acceptable reasons for not giving care than do men, women are judged for not providing care (Holstein, 2007). The fact that women do the bulk of caregiving in Western societies disadvantages them in the moment and in the future, as caregivers are unequal to those who do not provide care (Kittay, 1999) and have fewer opportunities to make autonomous choices for themselves. Their careers are often interrupted, wages and future pension benefits are sacrificed, and the risks of poverty in old age are substantially increased. Caregiving places them at serious disadvantage to men, a disadvantage that accumulates over time (see Holstein, 2015).

Yet, women (and many men) are devoted caregivers, insisting that "no one can do it as well as I can." They provide care even if prior relationships were stormy or even abusive. This says something about the power of filial obligation (Brakeman, 1995). It also says something about the inadequate provision of care by the state. In the United States, the care provided by family members, if translated into dollars, amounts to over $300 billion a year (Arno, Levine, & Memmot, 1999). The burden has increased as the state has sought to save public dollars. "Cost containment ... is largely the shifting of the costs of care to patients and families" (Levine & Zuckerman, 1999, p. 148).

DECISION MAKING AND AUTONOMY

McCullough and Wilson (1995) suggest that "concepts such as autonomy, safety, and independence are drawn too starkly and too abstractly in the bioethics literature to be adequate to the complex and shifting realities of long-term care decision-making" (p. 6). Life situations often change dramatically and in ways that prior experiences may have left the older person ill-prepared to address. Trial and error may in fact be the most effective strategy for coming to understand what one's values are in new and difficult circumstances (Kuczewski, 1999). Learning to ask for and receive help may be, for many, among the most difficult of value shifts. Autonomy may best be enhanced by working with the person to adapt to what is no longer possible and by creating an environment that facilitates such adaptation. Although often constrained by the instrumental nature of their work or by the clock, caregivers like to support an individual's value commitments and identifications if only they had the time and if only they felt respected for the work that they do.

Unlike most situations in acute care settings, day-to-day decision making is a central feature of long-term care. The situations are often very complex. Older people and those around them play multiple roles, the possibility for "recovery" is slim, and the long-term future is more likely a deepening rather than an ending of the need for care. This situation differs dramatically from the patient–physician relationship that dominates acute care settings where roles are defined, recovery or at least improvement is the expectation, and the time trajectory is reasonably short. In long-term care, an 83-year-old woman is a client; minutes later she is a mother, grandmother, neighbor, friend. These relationships each have "their own principles that reflect role-specific duties as well as more general concepts that are conducive to mutual self-discovery among the community members" (Kuczewski, 1999, p. 18). Decision making is also complicated and "involves a series of medical, social, and personal decisions, made incrementally over time by multiple decision-makers, rather than a single, well-defined, time-bound decision made, as in acute care, by the dyad of physician and patient" (McCullough & Wilson, 1995, p. 307).

Other features of long-term care further frustrate efforts to apply commonly cited moral rules and principles like autonomy, beneficence, or nonmaleficence. Family relationships are usually decades old, as are the problems. There may be few families that behave in the rational, consensual way that the standard paradigm calls for. The presence of cognitive impairments coexisting with medical conditions further complicate decision making while "safe" accommodations are often experienced as overly regimented and unable to respond to habitual ways of being.

Moreover, although there is a tendency to focus on moments of choice—moving to a nursing home, terminating treatment, violating confidentiality because of perceived danger to the resident, telling the truth to a patient or honoring a daughter's wish not to take away her mother's hope—in fact, the actual process of providing long-term care involves a continuum of constantly arising ethical concerns. How we give a person a bath, the respect we show (or don't show) for the old body, the dignity enhancing (or eroding) ways in which we talk and listen to the older person are all ethical questions that inevitably arise. Long-term care involves relationships, gratitude, reciprocity, love, and fairness, and so it is, above all, about morality.

Despite all these complications, decisions need to be made and actions taken. It is critical to facilitate the process of self-discovery and to identify the range of morally permissible actions and practices (Jagger, 1989). Rather than a resolution, such as terminating treatment for a dying patient, situations that arise in long-term care require "sensitivity, flexibility, discretion, and improvisation to find precisely what responds to the very particular" (Walker, 1992, pp. 28–29). McCullough and Wilson (1995), as noted earlier, recommend a process they call *preventive ethics*. By anticipating what might come next, all stakeholders are better prepared to respond appropriately. In this model, one:

- Identifies stakeholders
- Seeks factual agreement of the older adult's condition
- Elicits the values of the older adult and the family and on this basis seeks their evaluations of the older adult's conditions and realistic alternatives for managing them, including the issue of caregiver burden and costs
- Weighs benefits and harms
- Considers limited obligations in order to promote and protect the interests of others
- Invites reflection on how alternatives affect self-identity of the older adult and family member and the relationships they wish to protect
- Makes recommendations recognizing that they are provisional
- Reviews plans and decisions regularly

Similar to McCullough and Wilson (1995), Kuczewski (1999) embeds his casuistic approach in the ongoing situation suggesting that "routine daily life and social institutions embody moral principles" (p. 19). He argues that a basic ethical framework for older adult care must include candor, as a sign of respect, and responsibility for narrative integrity so that the meaning of an older adult's life is preserved. This latter concept resembles Agich's (1990) sense that one of the most important ways to honor autonomy is to facilitate the older person's ability to live in familiar and meaningful ways in spite of the many changes that may be occurring.

ETHICS AS A CRITICAL PRACTICE: NEXT STEPS

This chapter makes the case for a new view of ethics, one rooted in the daily lives of caregivers and residents in long-term care settings. With this view, ethics is part of the "everyday experiences of thoughtful people" who are an "essential resource for, and check on, the reflections of [others] joined in inquiry, including philosophers" (Pritchard, 2006, p. 8). It is less about theory than it is about how to live well in spite of loss and change. It adopts a social view of the self that grounds autonomy in relationships from which we work toward autonomy competency (Dastani, Dignum, & Meyer, 2004) and which need support to permit continued autonomy. It criticizes the current insistence on discussing public life from a vision of autonomous, equal, rational actors each pursuing separate ends. This is a faulty vision of the self and serves older people in long-term care settings poorly. Instead, based on a feminist ethic of care, it acknowledges interdependent actors who need and provide care in a variety of ways and who have interests and pursuits that exist outside the realm of care (Tronto, 1993).

A feminist ethic of care recognizes that context, understood in social and political terms, is directly related to expansive possibilities for autonomous action. It holds that ignoring context, power relationships, and the variables of class and gender damages an ability to enlist ethics as a force for social change. This understanding of ethics is descriptive, analytical, value laden, and action oriented. As with critical gerontology, critical ethics analyze universal policies and practices for their differential impact on individuals and groups and build a bridge between analyses and action. The world and the possibilities for meaningful choices are very different when viewed from the penthouse apartment or the basement room. Also like critical gerontology, critical ethics ground moral ideals in the lifeworlds of older people. Although at the most abstract level, universal ideals make good sense, in the practical world of long-term care, they miss too much that is important. It is thus essential to pay attention to the particular features of individual lives if we are to justify our ethical approaches.

Because critical ethics are so contextual and particularistic, our ethical responsibilities include establishing—and justifying—claims on society that allow us to meet our responsibilities to ourselves and to others. Moving beyond the older adults with whom we work, it insists that one cannot be a responsible social or health professional in the absence of resources to meet obligations well (Lloyd, 2006; Tronto, 1993). Critical ethics can help assess cultural, social, and political aspects of aging by identifying the normative features of seemingly non-normative areas, such as images of aging. Ethical thinking can expose these areas to an analysis that challenges universalistic assumptions and proposes alternative policies or norms that take differences as well as commonalities seriously. Although public policy cannot take individuals as its focus, it can recognize groups (i.e., women or ethnic and racial minorities; Clement, 1996) that are excluded by "generalizations and idealizations" that "mirror conditions and positions" unlike theirs (Walker, 2003, p. 14).

SUMMARY

Perhaps the most difficult tasks for more critically grounded ethics are to recognize that dependency is part of human life and thus to respect this fact is to facilitate the ability to live well despite dependencies. Positive rights, that is, rights to something rather than the negative right to life without interference, matter little if resources are not available to support their enactment. Further, rights alone do not transform social attitudes about aging and old age or give people the wherewithal to live decently when old. An individualistic ethic has meant that decision making in the clinical realm has taken priority over the social and cultural contexts in which decisions are embedded and that significantly affect the range of choices we actually have and influence how we are seen and treated. This approach positions ethics as an ally in helping more people achieve a good old age, particularly in the challenging arena of long-term care. At the end of life, as at the beginning, love and support are needed as much or more than the chance to decide. And in those areas where decision making is important, context—the system between moments of choice—is critical.

DISCUSSION QUESTIONS

1. What is the role of family making decisions for an older adult in long-term care? Have you been involved in such a situation? If yes, how was it addressed, and (how) did an ethic of care inform the decision-making process?
2. What is the principle of autonomy and how is it an uneasy principle to apply in long-term care settings?
3. How are feminist ethics different from principalism?
4. What is an ethical dilemma in long-term care and how is it usually resolved?
5. When should family preferences supersede the wishes of a family member?
6. How might privacy be upheld in a long-term care environment?
7. Why is a resident's personal narrative so important in supporting his or her autonomy? How might it be used to assist with health care decisions?

ADDITIONAL RESOURCES

PUBLICATIONS

Collopy, B., Boyle, P., & Jennings, B. (1991). New directions in nursing home ethics. *Hastings Center Report, 21*(2), 1–16.

Franklin, L. L., Ternestedt, B. M., & Nordenfelt, L. (2006). Views on dignity of elderly nursing home residents. *Nursing Ethics, 13*(2), 130–146.

Holstein, M., Parks, J., & Waymack, M. H. (2011). *Ethics, aging and society: The critical turn.* New York, NY: Springer Publishing Company.

Kane, R. A., & Caplan, A. L. (Eds.). (1990). *Everyday ethics: Resolving dilemmas in nursing home life.* New York, NY: Springer Publishing Company.

KEY WEBSITES

American Bar Association Commission on Law and Aging www.americanbar.org/groups/law_aging.html

Center for Practical Bioethics www.practicalbioethics.org

Long-Term Care Ombudsman www.aoa.acl.gov/AoA_Programs/Elder_Rights/Ombudsman/index.aspx

World Health Organization (WHO) www.who.int/ethics/topics/longtermcare/en

REFERENCES

Abel, E. (1991). *Who cares for the elderly? Public policy and the experiences of adult daughters.* Philadelphia, PA: Temple University Press.

Agich, G. (1990). Reassessing autonomy in long-term care. *Hastings Center Report, 20*(6), 12–17. doi:10.2307/3563417

Ambrogi, D., & Leonard, F. (1988). The impact of nursing home admission agreements on resident autonomy. *The Gerontologist, 28*(Suppl), 82–89. doi:10.1093/geront/28.Suppl.82

Arno, P., Levine, C., & Memmot, M., (1999). The economic value of informal caregiving. *Health Affairs, 18*(2), 182–188.

Arras, J. (1995). Conflicting interests in long-term care decision-making: Acknowledging, dissolving, and resolving conflicts. In L. McCullough & N. Wilson (Eds.), *Long-term care decisions: Ethical and conceptual dimensions* (pp. 197–217). Baltimore, MD: The Johns Hopkins University Press.

Baier, A. (1994). *Moral prejudices: Essays on ethics*. Cambridge, MA: Harvard University Press.

Beauchamp, T., & Childress, J. (2001). *Principles of biomedical ethics* (5th ed.). New York, NY: Oxford University Press.

Behabib, S. (1987). The generalized and the concrete other: The Kohlberg–Gilligan controversy and moral theory. In E. F. Kittay & D. Meyers (Eds.), *Women and moral theory* (pp. 154–177). Lanham, MD: Rowman & Littlefield.

Blustein, J. (1993). The family in medical decision making. *Hastings Center Report*, *23*(3), 6–13.

Brakeman, S. V. (1995). Filial responsibility and long-term care decision making. In L. McCullough & N. Wilson (Eds.), *Long-term care decisions* (pp. 181–196). Baltimore, MD: The Johns Hopkins University Press.

Capitman, J., & Sciegaj, M. (1995). A contextual approach for understanding individual autonomy in managed community long-term care. *The Gerontologist*, (4), 533–540. doi:10.1093/geront/35.4.533

Clement, G. (1996). *Care, autonomy, and justice: Feminism and the ethic of care*. Boulder, CO: Westview Press.

Cole, T., & Holstein, M. (1996). Ethics and aging. In R. Binstock & L. George (Eds.), *Handbook of aging and the social sciences* (4th ed., pp. 481–497). San Diego, CA: Academic Press.

Collopy, B. (1988). Autonomy in long-term care: Some crucial distinctions. *The Gerontologist*, *28*(Suppl.), 10–17. doi:10.1093/geront/28.Suppl.10

Collopy, B., Dubler, N., & Zuckerman, C. (1990). The ethics of home care: Autonomy and accommodation. *Hastings Center Report*, *20*(2), 1–16. doi:10.2307/3562626

Cooper, D. (2004). *Ethics for professionals in a multicultural world*. Upper Saddle River, NJ: Pearson/Prentice Hall.

Dastani, M., Dignum, F., & Meyer, J. J. (2004). Autonomy and agent deliberation. In *Agents and Computational Autonomy* (pp. 114–127). Berlin/Heidelberg, Germany: Springer Science + Business Media.

Ellingson, S., & Fuller, J. (2001). A good death? Finding a balance between the interests of patients and caregivers. In M. Holstein & P. Mitzen (Eds.), *Ethics and community-based elder care* (pp. 200–207). New York, NY: Springer Publishing Company.

Fireman, D., Dornberg-Lee, S., & Moss, L. (2001). Mapping the jungle: A proposed method for decision-making in geriatric social work. In M. Holstein & P. Mitzen (Eds.), *Ethics and community-based elder care* (pp. 145–165). New York, NY: Springer Publishing Company.

Fox, R., & Swazey, J. (1984). Medical morality is not bioethics: Medical ethics in China and the United States. In R. Fox (Ed.), *Essays on medical sociology* (pp. 645–671). New Brunswick, NJ: Transaction Books.

Goodstein, J. (2000). Moral compromise and personal integrity: Exploring the ethical issues of deciding together in organizations. *Business Ethics Quarterly*, *10*(4), 805–819. doi:10.2307/3857834

Hardwig, J. (1990). What about the family? *Hastings Center Report*, *20*, 5–10. doi:10.2307/3562603

Held, V. (2006). *The ethics of care: Personal, political, and global*. New York, NY: Oxford University Press.

High, D. M. (1988). All in the family: Extended autonomy and expectations in surrogate health care decision-making. *The Gerontologist*, *28*(Suppl.), 46–51. doi:10.1093/geront/28.Suppl.46

High, D. M. (1991). A new myth about families of older people. *The Gerontologist*, *31*, 611–618. doi:10.1093/geront/31.5.611

Holstein, M. (2007). Long-term care, feminism, and an ethics of solidarity. In R. Pruchno & M. A. Smyer (Eds.), *Challenges of an aging society: Ethical dilemmas and political issues* (pp. 156–174). Baltimore, MD: The Johns Hopkins University Press.

Holstein, M. (2015). *Women in late life: Critical perspectives on gender and age*. Lanham, MD: Rowman & Littlefield.

Holstein, M., Parks, J., & Waymack, J. H. (2011). *Ethics, aging and society: The critical turn.* New York, NY: Springer Publishing Company.

Hugman, R. (2005). *New approaches in ethics for the caring professions.* New York, NY: Palgrave/Macmillan.

Jagger, A. (1989). Love and knowledge: Emotion and feminist epistemology. In A. Garry & M. Pearsall (Eds.), *Women, knowledge and reality.* Boston, MA: Unwin Hyman.

Johnson, T. F. (1999). *Handbook of ethical issues in aging.* Westport, CT: Greenwood Press.

Kane, R. A., & Caplan, A. L. (1990). *Everyday ethics: Resolving dilemmas in nursing home life.* New York, NY: Springer Publishing Company.

Kane, R. A., & Levin, C. A. (2001). Who's safe? Who's sorry? The duty to protect the safety of HCBS consumers. In M. Holstein & P. Mitzen (Eds.), *Ethics and community-based elder care* (pp. 217–233). New York, NY: Springer Publishing Company.

Kittay, E. F. (1999). *Love's labor: Essays on women, equality, and dependency.* New York, NY: Routledge.

Kuczewski, M. (1999). Ethics in long-term care? Are the principles different? *Theoretical Medicine, 20,* 15–29. doi:10.1023/A:1009967723214

Kuhn, D. (2001). Is home care always the best care? In M. Holstein & P. Mitzen (Eds.), *Ethics and community-based elder care* (pp. 187–199). New York, NY: Springer Publishing Company.

Levine, C., & Zuckerman, C. (1999). The trouble with families: Toward an ethic of accommodation. *Annals of Internal Medicine, 130,* 148–152. doi:10.7326/0003-4819-130-2-199901190-00010

Lidz, C., Fischer, L., & Arnold, R. (1992). *The erosion of autonomy in long-term care.* New York, NY: Oxford University Press.

Lloyd, L. (2006). A caring profession? The ethics of care and social work with older people. *British Journal of Social Work, 36,* 1171–1185. doi:10.1093/bjsw/bch400

Mackenzie, C., & Stoljar, N. (Eds.) (2000). *Relational autonomy: Feminist perspectives on autonomy, agency and the social self.* New York, NY: Oxford University Press.

McCullough, L., & Wilson, N. (1995). *Long-term care decisions: Ethical and conceptual dimensions.* Baltimore, MD: The Johns Hopkins University Press.

Moody, H. R. (1992). *Ethics in an aging society.* Baltimore, MD: The Johns Hopkins University Press.

Nussbaum, M. (1997). *Cultivating humanity: A classical defense of reform in liberal education.* Cambridge, MA: Harvard University Press.

Parks, J. (2003). *No place like home? Feminist ethics and home health care.* Bloomington, IN: University of Indiana Press.

Player, S., & Pollock, A. M. (2001). Long-term care: From public responsibility to private good. *Critical Social Policy, 21*(2), 231–255. doi:10.1177/026101830102100204

Pritchard, M. S. (2006). *Professional integrity: Thinking ethically.* Lawrence, KS: University of Kansas Press.

Ray, R. E. (2008). *Endnotes: An intimate look at the end of life.* New York, NY: Columbia University Press.

Taylor, C. (1984). *Sources of the self: The making of modern identity.* Cambridge, MA: Harvard University Press.

Tronto, J. C. (1993). *Moral boundaries: A political argument for an ethic of care.* New York, NY: Routledge.

Tronto, J. C. (1995). Care as a basis for radical political judgments. *Hypatia, 405*(2), 141–149. doi:10.2307/3810286

Tronto, J. C. (2001). An ethic of care. In M. Holstein & P. Mitzen (Eds.), *Ethics and community-based elder care* (pp. 60–68). New York, NY: Springer Publishing Company.

Twigg, J. (2004). The body, gender, and age: Feminist insights in social gerontology. *Journal of Aging Studies, 18,* 59–73. doi:10.1016/j.jaging.2003.09.001

Walker, M. U. (1992). Feminism, ethics, and the question of theory. *Hypatia, 7*(3), 23–39. doi:10.1111/hypa.12052

Walker, M. U. (2003). *Moral contexts.* Lanham, MD: Rowman & Littlefield.

Long-Term Care and the Law

MARSHALL B. KAPP

CHAPTER OVERVIEW

The law exerts a significant influence on the quality, accessibility, and affordability of long-term care (LTC) services that are, or that at some future time may be, needed by older Americans. The interaction between the legal system and the various participants involved in the provision and receipt of LTC—consumers, family members, providers, payers, regulators, and advocates—is complex and multifaceted. This chapter attempts to outline some of the most salient aspects of this interaction so as to equip the reader both to more fully and accurately appreciate the roles of the law and lawyers in shaping the LTC environment and to evaluate the actual impact of the legal system on those whom it seeks to benefit, empower, oversee, or punish.

LEARNING OBJECTIVES

After completing this chapter, you should have an understanding of:

- The roles of the law and lawyers in shaping the LTC environment
- How to evaluate the practical impact of the legal system on the professional and personal lives of the various participants in the American LTC system
- Ways to work within applicable legal parameters to improve the quality of care and quality of life for LTC consumers
- How to reconcile effective legal risk management with ethically and clinically good LTC

KEY TERMS

Administrative law
Certificate of need (CON)
Civil tort remedies
Common law
Compensatory damages
Constitutional law
Entitlement rights
Negative rights, positive rights
Parens patriae
Police power
Quality-improvement organizations
Statutory or legislative law

INTRODUCTION

Long-term care (LTC) services are provided in a variety of settings, and consumers often move between settings within the LTC continuum as their needs change from time to time. A difficult set of clinical (transfer trauma) and accompanying legal issues may arise as a result of discharging, transferring, or relocating frail, debilitated older persons unnecessarily and/or without adequate preparation and precautions. This chapter concentrates largely on institutional settings, particularly nursing homes, and on consumer-driven home- and community-based long-term care (HCBLTC) options. However, other aspects of noninstitutional LTC also implicate a variety of important legal issues, most of which are not discussed in depth in this chapter.

DEFINITIONS

The law is composed of a number of distinct but interrelated components, each of which may be relevant to LTC. To begin, **constitutional law** emerges from the written documents that establish the foundational building blocks for the national government and the separate state and local governments. A constitution (including the ways in which the courts interpret and apply the meaning of its language) delineates the powers and constraints of a government vis-à-vis its own citizens. For instance, the Fifth and Fourteenth Amendments to the federal Constitution prohibit a state from depriving persons of life, liberty, or property without due process of law; thus, a state could not take over ownership and control of a nursing home or assisted living facility from private owners just because the state felt it could provide services to older consumers more efficiently than the private providers.

Statutory or **legislative law** is comprised of acts passed by federal, state, and local legislatures functioning under authority conferred by the jurisdiction's constitution. Of course, politics and pragmatic considerations strongly influence how elected legislators utilize their constitutional powers to legislate public policy. Pertinent state statutes would include, among others, those that require licenses to operate LTC facilities or agencies and that set standards for obtaining a required license. Local ordinances, such as those pertaining to fire safety in business establishments and dwellings, also are important in the LTC context.

Legislatures frequently use legislation to delegate to administrative (regulatory) agencies that are part of the executive branch of government and have the power to fill in the vital, particular details necessary for the implementation and enforcement of a broad statutory objective. The laws spelling out those programmatic details (and their judicial interpretations) make up the category of **administrative law**—*rules and regulations*—and must be created (promulgated) according to the jurisdiction's formal Administrative Procedure Act.

Finally, **common law** consists of principles or doctrines enunciated by the courts, on a gradual case-by-case basis, to resolve specific controversies and guide future behavior in circumstances for which existing constitutional, statutory, or administrative law does not provide sufficiently clear direction. Current state doctrines pertaining to the professional liability (i.e., malpractice) of LTC providers, for example, derive chiefly from the common law. The common law may be either abrogated (overturned), reinforced, or modified by subsequent legislation or regulations.

LAW, POLICY, AND ETHICS

It is important to distinguish law from the related concepts of policy and ethics. In a public policy assessment, we are concerned with whether a possible government action is a good or bad idea and whether it is something in which society ought to engage. Is the proposed action the most efficient, effective, and fair way to achieve a legitimate social objective? Ethics presents normative questions about what should or should not be done from the standpoint of moral rightness and wrongness (see Chapter 14). By contrast, law is the civic instrument through which meaningful discussions about public policy and ethics can take place, and the results of that discussion can be carried out in a principled fashion.

Looking in terms of setting boundaries or guideposts for the consideration of policy initiatives and ethical dilemmas, there are three basic issues the law is supposed to answer. First, what am I *required* to do; what are my positive or affirmative obligations? Second, even when there is no legal *duty* to act, what *powers* or *authority* do I have to act in a particular manner if I so choose; what am I *allowed* or *permitted* to do? Third, what *limits* or *restraints* does the law impose on my conduct; what things am I *forbidden* or *prohibited* from doing?

Some matters of good public policy and ethical consensus are not embodied in the law. Conversely, legal provisions are not always consistent with wise social policy or the emerging or dominant ethical consensus of the moment.

SOURCES AND FUNCTIONS OF LEGAL AUTHORITY

On the federal level, Congress's authority to enact statutes (and therefore derivatively the power of federal administrative agencies to make rules) in areas related to LTC stems mainly from two sections in Article I of the United States

Constitution. One provision empowers Congress to collect revenues through imposing taxes and to appropriate those revenues to promote the general welfare. The Medicare, Medicaid, and Social Security programs illustrate the federal government's legislative authority in this regard. Under these programs, the federal government exercises the *power of the purse* to incentivize (in most cases, amounting practically to requiring) LTC providers who want public dollars to behave in a particular manner. Another section of Article I authorizes Congress to regulate interstate and foreign commerce. Statutes such as the Food, Drug, and Cosmetic Act (FDCA) and the Controlled Substances Act (CSA) rely on this authority to regulate which drugs a physician or other prescriber may prescribe for patients.

On the state level, state legislatures and administrative agencies enact statutes and publish regulations primarily under their inherent police powers. The **police power** is a state's innate authority to protect and promote the general health, safety, welfare, and morals of the population. The state police power is underscored by the Tenth Amendment of the U.S. Constitution, which provides: "The powers not delegated to the United States by the Constitution, nor prohibited by it to the States, are reserved to the States, respectively, or to the people." The exercise of state police power may take the form of either direct orders or prohibitions regarding specific provider conduct or financial incentives to encourage particular provider behaviors. Statutes and regulations pertaining to provider licensing, which are enacted to protect consumers from potential harm, are an example of the state police power in action.

By contrast, the common law doctrine of ***parens patriae*** (literally, "father of the country") is the state's inherent authority to benevolently protect people who are so incapacitated that they cannot protect themselves sufficiently. Guardianship laws or civil commitment statutes based on mental illness and dangerousness to oneself would be examples of state action predicated on exercise of the parens patriae power.

SOCIAL FUNCTIONS OF THE LAW

In terms of social function, the law serves several important purposes in the LTC realm. First, the law might try to prevent or mitigate certain potentially dangerous behavior. For instance, federal regulations pertaining to institutional review boards (IRBs) limit the power of families of persons with dementia to enroll these relatives in experimental biomedical or behavioral interventions if the anticipated risk-to-benefit ratio is ethically unacceptable.

Moreover, law can be a tool for establishing and funding health and social programs. Medicare, Medicaid, and the Community Living Assistance Services and Supports (CLASS) program originally contained in the Patient Protection and Affordable Care Act of 2010 (as modified by the Health Care and Education Reconciliation Act) before it subsequently was repealed by Congress, and various state programs paying for particular forms of LTC for eligible individuals are examples of law in this category.

Third, law is a tool for controlling the production and distribution of specific kinds of resources. Licensing statutes for professionals and businesses, as well as legislation creating and financing particular professional education programs (such as government-assisted scholarships for training certified nursing assistants [CNAs]), exemplify this role. Many states still have **certificate of need (CON)** statutes in effect, which require applicants to demonstrate an adequate public need for a particular health service, such as a nursing home, before that service could be created or expanded in the proposed place.

Fourth, laws attempt to make certain that the services received by consumers satisfy minimum quality standards. Quality control is the major justification for statutes and regulations governing the licensure and certification of LTC providers. In developing quality-control requirements, legislators and regulators frequently interact with consumer advocacy organizations, the plaintiffs' personal injury bar (who justify the malpractice litigation system, in part, as one more form of quality-control regulation), and representatives of the different LTC industry sectors. Federal and state enforcement agencies also frequently work with these groups to try to maximize the effectiveness of the legal requirements adopted.

Finally, law can be a tool for creating and enforcing individual rights. Legal rights fall into two basic categories. *Liberties*, or **negative rights**, act as a person's armor against unwanted intrusions initiated by others. For example, an LTC consumer has the right (under the legal doctrine of informed consent, which protects one's autonomy and physical integrity) to refuse unwanted medical interventions. On the other hand, *entitlement* or **positive rights** empower a person to claim some affirmative good from someone else. Medicare, Medicaid, and Social Security create positive benefits for older persons that often come into play in the LTC context. Another pertinent example of law creating a positive right is the requirement in the Americans with Disabilities Act (ADA) that employers and businesses make "reasonable accommodations" in order to employ or serve disabled individuals.

Regarding all of the foregoing social roles, the law serves to reflect, promote, and help shape public norms or values. The law *reflects* and embodies prevailing social attitudes by codifying or enshrining them with formal, official status; we regulate the quality of LTC because society believes, as a moral matter, that consumers should receive LTC of high quality. The law *promotes* social values by enforcing its requirements and prohibitions, including through the use of governmental force if necessary; an LTC provider that violates the law may have its license revoked or suspended. The law helps to *shape* social values by acting as a forceful educator; the use of physical and chemical restraints in nursing homes has been greatly reduced over the past two decades largely because implementation of the law demanding a reduction in restraint use educated society that such reduction could be accomplished safely (see Case Study 15.1).

Case Study 15.1: Mr. Feldman—to Restrain or Not to Restrain?

Mr. Feldman, an 80-year-old wheelchair-bound man, is a resident in a nursing home. He has fallen several times in the past and is currently deemed to be at high risk of falling and suffering significant injury. The facility, with the family's reluctant agreement, has implemented different types of physical restraints, including lap belts and a tray attached to Mr. Feldman's wheelchair, and has positioned Mr. Feldman in the common area where he is more visible to staff. Mr. Feldman is extremely resistant to these interventions and gets very agitated. He just wants to be left alone in his room to look at magazines or watch television. He is moderately to severely demented. If permitted to do so, he is likely to get out of the wheelchair and fall again. The medical director and nursing staff perceive Mr. Feldman will probably suffer physical injury if not restrained or serious emotional injury if he is restrained.

Case Study Discussion Questions:

1. How should the facility and its staff handle this situation?
2. With each of the potential courses of action, what are the possible risks regarding civil liability, regulatory sanctions for violating the resident's rights, and sanctions for violating regulatory provisions regarding accident prevention?
3. Is it realistically feasible for the facility to successfully balance protecting Mr. Feldman's right to make choices and the facility's responsibility regarding resident safety?
4. In a case like this, is the best risk-management strategy also the best ethical solution? The best clinical solution?

SPECIFIC FORMS OF LEGAL REGULATION

LTC in the United States is pervasively regulated legally in a myriad of different respects. The actual (as well as the perceived) regulatory climate powerfully influences the quality, affordability, and availability of services for prospective and current LTC consumers.

Nursing homes and noninstitutional LTC providers must be licensed (i.e., they need permission from the state to operate), and the same requirement is present for individual professionals who work for or with LTC providers. Licensees are subject to sanctions that may be imposed as part of the mandatory state licensing renewal process. Standards pertaining to nursing homes are found not only in state licensing statutes, but also in the federal Nursing Home Reform Act, which was embedded in the Omnibus Budget Reconciliation Act of 1987 (OBRA '87), and the Department of Health and Human Services's (DHHS's) implementing administrative regulations ("Conditions of Participation") and interpretive guidelines for state survey agencies that conduct the annual Medicare/Medicaid survey and certification process under contract to the federal government. Potential punishments for the violation of required standards vary in severity and may include: suspension or revocation of a nursing home's operating license; termination of the Medicare and/or Medicaid provider agreement, which is necessary for the facility's economic vitality; temporary receivership (i.e., a third party is appointed to run the day-to-day functions of the facility); suspension of payment, either for all residents or for new admissions; civil money fines; enhanced state monitoring; mandatory transfer of residents to another nursing home; a directed plan of correction; and/or directed in-service training.

LTC providers receiving reimbursement for patient/client care from the federal government through the Medicare program must cooperate with **quality-improvement organizations (QIOs)**. QIOs are private agencies in each state that contract with the federal Centers for Medicare & Medicaid Services (CMS) to assess provider compliance with professionally recognized standards of care and to work consultatively with those providers toward achieving a better service quality.

Besides being obligated to obey standards established by the federal and state governments, many LTC institutional and agency providers also voluntarily agree to comply with standards published by private accrediting agencies, most prominently The Joint Commission (previously the Joint Commission on Accreditation of Healthcare Organizations, or JCAHO). The Joint Commission is a not-for-profit consortium formed by the American Hospital Association (AHA), American Medical Association (AMA), American College of Surgeons (ACS), and American College of Physicians (ACP). Neither the Joint Commission nor any other private (voluntary) accrediting body, such as the Commission on Accreditation of Rehabilitation Facilities (CARF), provides for nursing homes, home health agencies, hospices, adult day care facilities, case management organizations, or other LTC providers the equivalent of the "deemed status" (making a separate government inspection unneeded) that the Joint Commission holds in the acute care hospital context; however, as noted, a significant number of LTC providers pursue private accreditation nonetheless, largely for its competitive marketing advantages.

Further, criminal prosecutions may be brought by the local district attorney (terminology may vary for this position among different jurisdictions) or state attorney general charging LTC providers and/or their individual employees with mistreatment of consumers and, in the case of deceased consumers, even homicide. Moreover, federal prosecutors acting in conjunction with the DHHS Office of Inspector General (OIG) have initiated a few criminal indictments against LTC providers predicated on the theory that a provider billing the government under the Medicare and Medicaid programs for services when the care delivered was substandard in quality is guilty of attempting to defraud the government in violation of the False Claims Act (18 U.S.C. Sec. 287). The government, in addition, may bring charges pursuant to the Mail and Wire Fraud Act (18 U.S.C. Sec. 1341 and 1343) when the allegedly fraudulent claims have been submitted through the mail or electronically (virtually always the situation today). Violations of the Mail and Wire Fraud Acts are considered predicate offenses (i.e., offenses sufficient to create criminal liability) under the federal Racketeer Influenced and Corrupt Organizations Act (RICO, 18 U.S.C. Sec. 1961). Most states have enacted their own counterparts to the federal False Claims Act (18 U.S.C. Sec. 287), making it illegal to fraudulently bill the respective state Medicaid programs.

Criminal prosecutions brought against LTC providers or their personnel are rather uncommon, but they tend to receive wide publicity when they take place, and they expose the accused party to the possibility of substantial sanctions upon conviction or the entry of a guilty (or no contest, also known as *nolo contendere*) plea. Over and above the criminal penalties, a court's finding of liability under the civil version of the False Claims Act exposes LTC providers to potentially large monetary fines. Additionally, LTC providers may be sued by private individuals acting as "private attorneys general" or "relators" who have the right to bring their own civil False Claims Act or *qui tam* (whistleblower) actions against providers. If the government decides to bring a criminal prosecution based on the relator's evidence, then the relator is entitled to receive between 15% and 25% of the ultimate recovery.

From a statistical perspective, LTC consumers have been underrepresented as plaintiffs in civil lawsuits claiming professional liability or malpractice filed by, or on behalf of, specific consumers against LTC providers and/or their personnel. Older, frail, retired LTC consumers—especially those with short life expectancies—do not generally make attractive clients for plaintiffs' personal injury attorneys who get paid under a contingency fee arrangement; this is because those LTC consumers are not likely to command large **compensatory damages** under the present American tort system. Compensatory damages are a sum of money awarded in a civil action by a court to indemnify a person for a particular loss, detriment, or injury suffered as a result of the unlawful conduct of another. LTC consumers whose care charges are covered under the Medicaid program have not had a financial reason to bring suit because most of any monetary recovery usually would go either to pay the state back for its providing care or for use by the consumer in spending his or her assets down until a new period of Medicaid eligibility became effective.

Furthermore, being able to prove that it was the LTC provider's negligence that proximately or directly caused a consumer's injury could be very difficult in the common situation of a plaintiff who already had multiple, serious underlying medical problems. The availability or nonavailability of proof notwithstanding, a majority of older LTC consumers have neither the physical nor mental wherewithal nor adequate support by family and friends to initiate, prosecute, and survive the personal demands of complex civil litigation.

GROWTH OF LONG-TERM CARE LIABILITY EXPOSURE

At least in the case of nursing homes, this historical paucity of consumers as malpractice plaintiffs is changing. There are a variety of explanations for the changing malpractice environment of nursing homes. Explanations include the enactment of statutes in certain jurisdictions that facilitate or encourage personal injury claims against nursing homes, the enlarged availability of a core of plaintiff expert witnesses for hire, and an increasing willingness of trial courts to award big judgments (frequently including punitive or exemplary damages) in nursing home malpractice cases. The plaintiffs' personal injury bar now vigorously pursues this lucrative practice area representing purportedly injured residents and their families, often in collaboration with residents' advocacy organizations such as the National Consumer Voice (formerly, National Citizens Coalition for Nursing Home Reform [NCCNHR]) or the National Senior Citizens Law Center (NSCLC), LTC ombudsmen programs created under authority of the Older Americans Act (OAA, Public Law No. 89-73) to monitor and investigate possible problems of the nursing home population, consumer groups like AARP, and governmental and private regulators. Legal claims brought against nursing homes or their personnel arise factually from alleged medical care errors and omissions (e.g., allowing the development or worsening of pressure ulcers or medication mistakes), falls and fractures, resident-to-resident assaults, resident abuse, wandering and elopements, and transgressions of residents' rights.

All LTC providers are vulnerable to lawsuits for discriminating against actual or would-be consumers in the provision of services. LTC providers are both physical locations and sellers of public accommodation, as well as recipients of government payments, and therefore must abide by requirements of the Fair Housing Act (FHA, Public Law No. 90-284), the ADA, and Section 504 of the Rehabilitation Act of 1973 (Public Law No. 93-112), as well as their state counterparts, regarding both antidiscrimination prohibitions and the imposition of affirmative obligations to reasonably accommodate disabled persons.

LTC providers encounter the possibility of needing to defend against litigation stemming from allegations that, by providing substandard services, they breached promises made to the consumer in the admission or enrollment contract. The violated promises might have been expressed (put into specific words) or implied by the conduct of the parties.

The business practices of LTC providers may be regulated under federal and state antitrust statutes, which are intended to prevent the sort of anticompetitive conduct exemplified by a hospital steering all of its LTC-needing discharged patients to the home health agency owned by that hospital, even when other licensed home health agencies operate in the vicinity. Business aspects (for instance, the employer role) of LTC providers also may be subject to certain provisions of the Fair Labor Standards Act (FLSA, Public Law No. 75-718) regarding work hours and wages, the ADA, the Age Discrimination in Employment Act (ADEA, Public Law No. 90-202), and the Civil Rights Act (Public Law No. 88-352).

LEGAL IMPLICATIONS OF CONSUMER-DRIVEN HOME- AND COMMUNITY-BASED LONG-TERM CARE

Most consumers who require extensive assistance with their activities of daily living (ADLs) receive assistance in home- and community-based LTC (HCBLTC) settings. In the traditional American model of HCBLTC, most of the important operational facets (the who, what, where, when, and how details) of service financing and delivery have been determined largely by who was paying for the services. When the individual service recipient personally purchases the desired services, that person is treated and bargained with as a consumer (see Exhibit 15.1). However, when third-party payers (usually units of government) get involved, the HCBLTC available to the person with ADL impairments is driven by the policies and procedures of the agencies delivering or coordinating services, within programmatic constraints defined by service funders. Consumers in that situation have limited choice and control about their own LTC once enrollment in the public financing program has occurred.

As noted, the power of the purse is the power to negotiate, and the concept of consumer-driven LTC (in which the consumer is economically empowered to select, hire, supervise, evaluate, and fire his or her own LTC providers according to consumer-determined terms of employment) is not new as applied to older individuals who possess the financial capacity (through personal pensions, invested savings, or private LTC insurance policies) to pay for services themselves. In the same vein, a strong consumer-driven LTC movement had already been developed as far back as the early 1980s in the context of publicly funded LTC for younger seriously disabled persons (such as those afflicted with early-onset diseases or the victims of traumatic injury) who wanted to delineate and control the boundaries of their service plans.

In the recent past, we have witnessed a broad conceptual and practical shift, even for the substantial number of older Americans who rely on public dollars to finance their HCBLTC. This shift has been toward consumer-driven HCBLTC delivery models within which the older person is more empowered to direct both the structural and operational components of the service plan. This shift in policy and practice has been influenced by a variety of social, economic, political, and legal forces.

Publicly financed consumer-driven HCBLTC models vary in detail across the states. These programs are funded through a combination of federally approved state Medicaid waivers authorized by 42 United States Code § 1396n(c), dedicated state appropriations, and private foundation demonstration grants. The exact methods of getting compensation to LTC providers

EXHIBIT 15.1 Examples of Supportive Services With a Legal Component

Suggestions—California's In-Home Supportive Services Program http://www.cdss.ca.gov/agedblinddisabled/pg1296.htm

Cash & Counseling Program http://www.bc.edu/schools/gssw/nrcpds/cash_and_counseling.html or a comparable example of a legal-based LTC-related program.

(e.g., by vendor payments made directly by the government or private insurer, on one hand, versus entrusting consumers with cash or vouchers to spend for themselves, with or without professional counseling, on the other hand) may be different depending on the particular funding and service delivery model.

REGULATION GENERALLY

Under the consumer-driven LTC approach, quality control and direct protection of consumers against provider misconduct still remain legitimate, albeit now secondary, functions of the law. The primary function of the law under consumer-driven LTC is to enable, empower, and facilitate the informed, capable, and voluntary exercise of consumer self-determination within a competitive, affordable marketplace of high-quality goods and services. These legal functions entail both autonomy-enhancing initiatives and the imposition of regulatory limits that are necessary as a matter of consumer protection.

Private arrangements between consumers and independent contractors (independent providers, or IPs) for HCBLTC services set into play an array of risks for the consumer as well as for the in-home LTC worker, such as a private duty nurse (see Case Study 15.2). Sometimes, attempted consumer direction will fail. But even, and perhaps especially, under a vigorous consumer-driven LTC model, a certain core of legal regulation remains unavoidable.

For one thing, access to the courts must remain available to consumers to enforce the promises embodied within private contracts entered into by those consumers with private LTC insurers and sellers of LTC services and goods. Consumers will continue to negotiate and execute such contracts only to the extent they feel confident that the negotiated terms will be enforced legally if the parties fail to voluntarily comply with those terms. Additionally, **civil tort remedies**, namely, money damages, must remain available to particular consumers who are seriously injured because of private provider negligence or intentional misconduct such as physical abuse or financial exploitation.

REGULATING THE INFORMATIONAL ENVIRONMENT

The consumer-driven LTC model depends on consumers who enjoy ready access to adequate, appropriate, understandable information about the risks, benefits, and costs of various alternative services and service providers and who can use that information to meaningfully direct the details of their own HCBLTC. Each consumer should be educated, trained, and supported by objective professional sources to make choices that help to best accomplish the particular consumer's goals and preferences. Legal interventions may productively contribute to this sort of informational environment in several ways.

Case Study 15.2: A Dilemma for Ms. Fernando

Ms. Maria Fernando is an 85-year-old woman who lives alone in her own trailer with six cats. Her medical problems are mild dementia and severe emphysema. She no longer drives a car and cannot walk more than half a block. She has several cousins in her locale who visit Ms. Fernando periodically but who respect her right to live as she wishes. Because she has no savings or possessions other than the old trailer, and a modest monthly Social Security check is her only income source, Ms. Fernando qualifies for her state's Cash & Counseling consumer-directed HCBLTC program. Using the monthly voucher provided by this program, she has hired a young woman to come into her home on a regular basis to bring her groceries and help her with cooking, cleaning, and bathing. The problem is that this woman is very unreliable and often is abrupt and sloppy in performing her assigned tasks and interacting with Ms. Fernando. Ms. Fernando knows how difficult it is in her area to find good help and is afraid to fire this employee for fear of not being able to find a suitable replacement. Being admitted to a nursing home is her biggest fear.

Case Study Discussion Questions:

1. To what extent does consumer-driven HCBLTC, with its reduced external regulation, multiply the risk that many consumers will suffer abuse or neglect?
2. How can these risks be minimized while still affording the consumer substantial control over who provides services and how, when, and where those services will be provided?

First, government requires the collection and public availability of a range of comparative data regarding the quality of services sold by particular LTC providers. More research is necessary to clarify how we can assure reliability and relevance so that consumers really can use this information to choose providers and oversee their performance. The Federal Trade Commission (relying on the statutory authority given to it by Congress, under the Constitution's commerce clause) and its individual state counterparts (based on the state's police power) should establish regulations making false and misleading advertising or other misrepresentations by service and product vendors criminal conduct. False, misleading commercial speech, designed to sell a service or product rather than to take a stand on political issues, is not protected against government restriction under the federal Constitution's First Amendment free-speech clause.

Moreover, any consumers who are defrauded by deceptive practices must be able to demand money damages for their injuries through bringing individual state civil tort claims suits. Also, government needs to be active in setting standards controlling the sales practices of private LTC insurance companies, including regulation concerning product advertising.

REGULATION TO ENHANCE AUTONOMY

Consumer preferences are the essential core—the sine qua non or "but for"—of the consumer-driven LTC idea. Under the traditional LTC model dominated by service agencies and private funders, consumers were compelled to make a trade-off. They gave up choice concerning most of the significant details of their own LTC in exchange for the protection against the risk of harm supposedly provided by an extensive climate of command-and-control ("Thou shalts" and "Thou shalt nots") regulation and tort and criminal liability threats enveloping LTC providers. By comparison, the consumer-driven LTC model somewhat deemphasizes the safety and security function of the law and substitutes in its place a stronger emphasis on the potential of the law to enhance individual autonomy. There is an implied factual assumption that this trade-off of assumed safety for tangible control over LTC details is acceptable—indeed, positively desirable—to the majority of potential LTC consumers and/or their families or other surrogates.

One corollary to this assumption about a preference for increased autonomy (which is fully intertwined with quality of life), even if there may be some cost in terms of the increased potential for the risk of harm materializing (i.e., a threat to the quality of care), is the presumption that most consumers and/or their surrogates have the capacity to make intelligent quality-of-care trade-offs in order to obtain and maintain preferred forms of LTC from preferred providers according to preferred conditions. Consumer autonomy might be exercised either independently, together with family or friends, or by informally delegating decision-making power to another person or persons chosen and trusted by the consumer. Even when a person has been determined to lack sufficient current decisional capacity, consumer-driven LTC is still feasible when the individual has executed, in a timely fashion, legal advance planning instruments, such as a proxy directive or durable power of attorney (DPOA), supplemented by instruction directives or living wills that are applicable to HCBLTC options.

REGULATION TO ASSURE THE AVAILABILITY OF ALTERNATIVES

Consumer choice is meaningful only when consumers enjoy the opportunity to select from, and freely negotiate specific arrangements with, an array of potential providers of LTC goods and services. To foster a vibrant marketplace, government needs to regulate in a manner that assures that LTC providers will remain willing to voluntarily sell their services and goods directly to consumers. These human resource issues include applying to IPs the minimum-wage and maximum-hour provisions of the FLSA, workers' compensation and unemployment insurance regulations, eligibility for Social Security retirement benefits, and federal and state disability insurance programs. To the extent that the legal climate (as well as other pertinent factors) can effectively promote the job satisfaction, safety, and overall well-being of independently hired home care workers, the consumer-driven LTC model is likely to prosper.

BEHAVIORAL MANIFESTATIONS OF THE REGULATORY ENVIRONMENT

The pervasive adversarial legal environment within which LTC is provided in the United States generates a lot of anxiety and apprehension among individual and organizational LTC providers. For the most part, regulators (including plaintiffs' attorneys and the courts) are perceived by providers as police officers with "iron fists," looking for ways to find, catch, and punish bad providers' noncompliance with legal requirements, rather than as collaborators assigned the role of helping providers to improve care and deal with potential problems proactively. To exacerbate this "culture of blame" paradigm, LTC providers often believe that regulators act, at best, inconsistently between and within geographic areas in interpreting and applying the law over time, and at worst, arbitrarily and capriciously, without bothering to make a fair and accurate factual assessment of the situation.

Legal perceptions held by LTC providers matter because those perceptions tend to influence provider behavior in important ways. Some behaviors are positive, such as providers paying more attention to consumer rights, creating more timely and complete documentation of care, and engaging in more vigorous efforts to foster a culture of quality assurance and consumer safety. One noteworthy example of positive provider behavior clearly traceable to legal intervention is the substantial reduction in the prevalence of physical restraints that prevent or inhibit residents from exercising freedom of movement and chemical restraints that unduly sedate residents to the point of immobility in nursing homes following enactment of the 1987 Nursing Home Reform Act (Public Law 100-203, Title IV, Subtitle C).

Some types of behaviors encouraged by providers' anxieties about excessive, irrational legal oversight and providers' own risk of suffering negative legal (and hence economic) consequences may actually impair the quality, accessibility, and affordability of LTC offered and/or provided to consumers. For example, the culture of blame may inhibit efforts to encourage the honest reporting, disclosure, and analysis of errors in the provision of LTC. It also may cause providers to feel compelled to medically over treat particular consumers to their detriment, based on awareness, for example, that state Medicare/Medicaid surveyors may cite providers for deficiencies for failure to achieve a patient's "highest practicable functioning," even when an outcome other than the patient's physical decline and death is unrealistic. Additionally, apprehension about the culture of blame may compel providers to under treat particular consumers to their detriment by, for example, dissuading providers from prescribing adequate levels of narcotics to address patients' pain. An exacerbating factor impinging on good ethical care is that adverse media attention often accompanies legal action brought against any LTC provider.

Even though providers threatened with adverse administrative or judicial consequences often are exonerated at the conclusion of the legal process, for most of them the experience of involuntary involvement in the legal process is generally traumatic. Thus, just the apprehension of having one's conduct questioned in a legal forum, regardless of the likelihood of an eventual positive outcome, is enough to influence provider behavior in a direction sometimes inconsistent with good ethical and clinical LTC of the consumer.

SUMMARY

Government, acting through the instrument of the law, has a strong interest in directing, monitoring, and enforcing the quality and safety of LTC services provided to vulnerable and dependent persons. Within the LTC sphere as elsewhere, the state is expected to exercise its inherent police power to protect and promote the general health, safety, welfare, and morals of the community and its inherent parens patriae (father of the country) authority to protect people from harm who are unable to protect themselves. Moreover, both the federal and state governments have a responsibility to assure that public funds devoted to subsidizing LTC are spent wisely.

This chapter has reviewed some of the ways that government uses the law to try to fulfill its responsibilities in the LTC sphere and the effects of these legal activities on affected actors. Also identified are some of the tensions and challenges that specific legal regulations and processes can pose when the regulator's objective indicators of quality of care and the consumer's subjective perceptions of quality of life diverge, as occurs not infrequently in the LTC context.

DISCUSSION QUESTIONS

1. The fundamental goal of the law in LTC ought to be to make meaningful contributions to improvements in the quality, affordability, and accessibility of LTC to actual or potential consumers and their families. To what extent do you agree with this statement?
2. Particular statutes, regulations, judicial decisions, and legal processes may or may not contribute to improvements in the quality, affordability, and accessibility of LTC to actual or potential consumers and their families. In what ways do specific laws and particular aspects of the legal system positively exert a therapeutic effect on the lives and well-being of their purported beneficiaries? Do laws and legal processes that have been created specifically to confer certain positive benefits on particular beneficiaries actually realize these intended benefits for those intended beneficiaries? Realistically, do the laws in question really "work"? Conversely, in what respects do specific laws and the particular aspects of the legal system act

counterproductively or antitherapeutically to inhibit or detract from the quality, affordability, and accessibility of LTC?

3. We must continually evaluate the positive and negative impacts of the law on its intended beneficiaries, so that those laws may be modified or strengthened as appropriate. What standards and processes should we employ to measure and quantify the therapeutic and antitherapeutic effects of the law in LTC?
4. There may be serious shortcomings in the existing LTC system. To the extent this is true, are those problems best dealt with by a greater volume and/or severity of legal interventions (as compared to, for example, alternative strategies such as educational or financial interventions)? If so, what specific forms of legal intervention are likely to exert the most positive, therapeutic impact on the law's intended beneficiaries? How can lawmakers improve and maximize the use of available data to regulate "smarter" and more consistently and predictably? What is the most constructive balance of the policing role of regulation versus regulators acting as information-sharing consultants engaged in an iterative give-and-take process with the regulated parties? How can these complementary public agency roles be best integrated in pursuit of consumer safety and quality (or both care and life) improvement?

ADDITIONAL RESOURCES

AARP www.aarp.org
American Association for Justice www.justice.org
American Bar Association Commission on Law and Aging www.abanet.org/aging
American Health Lawyers Association www.ahla.org
American Society for Healthcare Risk Management www.ashrm.org
Joint Commission www.jcaho.org/standards
Long-Term Care Ombudsman Program www.aoa.gov
National Academy of Elder Law Attorneys www.naela.org
National Citizens Coalition for Nursing Home Reform (NCCNHR) www.nccnhr.org
National Senior Citizens Law Center (NSCLC) www.nsclc.org
Primary Legal Materials www.findlaw.com
U.S. Department of Health and Human Services, Centers for Medicare and Medicaid Services www.cms.gov/home/regsguidance.asp
U.S. Department of Health and Human Services, Office of Inspector General www.oig.hhs.gov

REFERENCES

Davidson, M. J. (2004). Governmental responses to elder abuse and neglect in nursing homes: The criminal justice system and the Civil False Claims Act. *Elder Law Journal, 12*, 327–354.

Dreher, K. B. (2002). Enforcement of standards of care in the long-term care industry: How far have we come and where do we go from here? *Elder Law Journal, 10*(51), 119–151.

Kapp, M. B. (2003). *The law and older persons: Is geriatric jurisprudence therapeutic?* Durham, NC: Carolina Academic Press.

Miller, E. A., & Mor, V. (2008). Balancing regulatory controls and incentives: Toward smarter and more transparent oversight in long-term care. *Journal of Health Politics, Policy and Law, 33*, 249–279.

Studdert, D. M., & Stevenson, D. G. (2004). Nursing home litigation and tort reform: A case for exceptionalism, *Gerontologist, 44*, 588–595.

United States Government Accountability Office. (2007). *Nursing homes: Federal action needed to improve targeting and evaluation of assistance by quality improvement organizations* (GAO-07-373), Washington, DC: United States Government Accountability Office.

United States Government Accountability Office. (2007). *Nursing home reform: Continued attention is needed to improve quality of care in small but significant share of homes* (GAO-07-794T) Washington, DC: United States Government Accountability Office.

United States Government Accountability Office. (2005). *Nursing homes: Despite increased oversight, challenges remain in ensuring high-quality care and resident safety* (GAO-06-117) Washington, DC: United States Government Accountability Office.

Financing Long-Term Services and Supports in an Aging Society

ROBERT A. APPLEBAUM
EMILY J. ROBBINS

CHAPTER OVERVIEW

Beginning with the rising number of older adults and detailing the increasing costs of long-term care (LTC), this chapter highlights the complex array of mechanisms in place to finance long-term services and supports and the challenges associated with paying for these services. Public funding mechanisms (e.g., Medicare, Medicaid), although covering a significant proportion of costs, are currently ill equipped to handle the influx of older adults requiring care in the coming years. On the other hand, privately funded long-term services (e.g., LTC insurance, out-of-pocket payments) provides consumers with the widest range of care choices; however, this may be unfeasible for the majority of the population. In combination, the large and increasing funds required to support those needing LTC services and supports, the substantial increase in projected need for such services in the future, and current state and federal budgetary challenges create the "perfect storm" for a long-term financing crisis. Improvements in the long-term services system, training and education for caregivers and families, the use of technology in care, and addressing the gap between acute and long-term services are potential solutions to the issue of LTC financing.

LEARNING OBJECTIVES

After completing this chapter, you should have an understanding of:

- The main public mechanisms for financing long-term services and supports
- The primary private mechanisms for financing LTC services and supports
- The challenges facing the United States as they relate to paying for long-term services
- The impact of an aging population on public policy and individuals when needing to provide care for older adults

KEY TERMS

Accelerated death benefit
Capitation
Case mix
Home and community-based services (HCBS)
Home- and community-based waiver program
Local levy programs
LTC insurance
Medicaid
Medicare
Programs of All-Inclusive Care for the Elderly (PACE)
Viatical settlements

INTRODUCTION

Providing long-term services and supports to individuals who experience disability has become a big part of the U.S. economy. With large and growing expenditures in long-term care (LTC), it is important to understand what services are provided and the costs of these services. One important factor in discussing long-term financing is the recognition that, despite very high expenditures on LTC, many consumers know very little about how such care is funded. For instance, in a recent survey by the MetLife Mature Market Institute (2009), more than two thirds of respondents reported that they had **LTC insurance** coverage. One in five indicated that disability insurance would cover the cost of their LTC. One third of the respondents felt that **Medicare** (the national health insurance program for individuals age 65 or older, individuals under age 65 with certain disabilities, and individuals of any age with end-stage renal disease) and **Medicaid** (the joint federal–state program designed to provide health care for individuals with limited income and resources) would cover the total cost of care, and 14% indicated that their current health insurance policy would finance future LTC needs. As will be discussed in this chapter, this is not the case, and in fact, more than nine of every 10 consumers *do not* have coverage for ongoing long-term services and supports.

COST OF LONG-TERM CARE SERVICES

Long-term services and supports are provided in a range of settings broadly categorized as in-home services, residential services, and institutional care. Recent definitions have classified in-home services, community services, and those residential services that maximize consumer independence, such as assisted living, into a category termed **home- and community-based services (HCBS)**. The in-home services of this grouping includes a variety of personal and support services, such as assistance with bathing, dressing, and using the toilet. Community-based services include assistance designed to help an individual and his or her family continue to reside in the community, through such mechanisms as attending an adult day care program (National

Clearinghouse for Long-Term Care Information, 2010). Defining residential services is a bit more complicated. Some residential settings, such as assisted living, are designed to maximize consumer autonomy; in fact, these service settings can receive funding from home- and community-based programs, and thus are treated as community-based care rather than institutional care. Other residential settings, such as board-and-care or domiciliary homes, where individuals do not have private rooms and other environmental choices, such as locking doors, food preparation areas, and a private bathroom, are categorized as institutional settings. Nursing homes and intermediate care settings specifically designed for individuals with intellectual or developmental disabilities are also classified as institutional settings.

The cost of LTC is determined by at least three factors: the amount and type of assistance needed, the setting where services and supports are provided, and geographical location. Some individuals with disabilities receive long-term services and supports from friends and family only and incur no formal provider costs. On the other hand, individuals requiring 24-hour skilled nursing home care can expect to pay on average between $75,000 and $84,000 annually (Genworth Financial, 2013). Those residing in the community receiving an array of formal in-home services, such as personal care, transportation services, meal programs, or adult day care, typically pay anywhere from $250 to $2,500 a month for these services.

Costs vary by the type and amount of services needed. For example, on average, personal care provided by a home health aide is about $19 per hour, and adult day services are approximately $65 per day (Genworth Financial, 2013). Assisted living facility costs are approximately $3,450 per month, and again vary by region, type of facility, and the consumer's needs (Genworth Financial, 2013). The range of LTC costs cannot be understated. Some individuals with private resources choose to remain at home despite substantial need and can incur annual costs of more than $100,000. On the other hand, many individuals, with the help of family members, may be able to remain in the community with in-home service packages of only a few hundred dollars per month. Nursing home care also varies dramatically by state, with the median annual cost of a nursing home in Alaska reported at $222,000, compared to $46,000 in Texas (Hauser, Fox-Grage, & Ujvari, 2012; for a complete overview of how costs vary across the United States, see Genworth Financial [2013]). Thus, the level of disability, the availability of family support, and the geographic area are all important factors in determining the overall cost of the home-care package.

PAYING FOR LONG-TERM CARE

There are both informal and formal mechanisms for delivering and paying for long-term services and supports. Despite a large increase in formal LTC, the majority of LTC delivered in the United States is unpaid care provided by family and friends, with an estimated value of these services being more than $450 billion (Hauser et al., 2012; see Chapters 3 and 4, this volume). The substantial growth in the population in need of long-term assistance, particularly the increase in older people over age 80, has resulted in a rapidly expanding formal LTC industry, which was estimated to be valued at more than $225 billion in 2009 (Eiken, Burwell, Gold, & Sredl, 2012; Georgetown, 2007; MedPAC, 2010).

LTC is financed through a range of public and private mechanisms. In the public sector, Medicaid (almost 50% of total LTC costs) and Medicare (20% of total costs) are the two largest payors. The Veterans Administration (VA) is also an important public funder of long-term services and support for military veterans, providing more than $3.5 billion for both in-home and institutional services (Tritz, 2006; U.S. Department of Veterans Affairs, 2009). These Veteran Administration expenditures, along with other state and federal public programs, account for about 2.5% of total LTC expenditures. In the private sector, individual out-of-pocket payments and private LTC insurance account for approximately 18% and 7% of all LTC financing, respectively (Georgetown, 2007). Other private expenditures, such as United Way, and other philanthropic foundations represent the final 2.5% of LTC funding. A description of the major funders of LTC is provided in the following sections.

MEDICAID

Enacted in 1965, **Medicaid** is a joint federal–state program designed to pay health costs of individuals with limited income and resources. Medicaid is one of the largest domestic programs in the U.S. federal budget, spending more than $413 billion in 2011. Interestingly, although Medicaid spent more than $114 billion on LTC in 2012 (Kaiser Family Foundation, 2013a), accounting for 28% of total Medicaid expenditures, the LTC benefit was not even included in the initial Medicaid legislation (Truffer, Klemm, Wolfe, Rennie, & Shuff, 2012). The intermediate care benefit for nursing home care was added in 1968, and the **home and community-based services waiver program**, known as HCBS Waivers, which—for those meeting Medicaid requirements—provides services that allow individuals to remain in their own home or live in a community setting, was enacted in 1981. Medicaid is financed by both the federal government and individual states through a formula based on the per capita income of the state, such that a high-income state, such as New York, would pay a full 50% of the program whereas a low-income state, for example, Mississippi, could have a state share as low as 17%. The program is administered by each state, but the federal government requires states to provide certain health and LTC services, including hospital and nursing home coverage, whereas other services are state options, such as dental and vision care.

In 2011, Medicaid spent 52.5% of its LTC budget on institutional care, either nursing homes or intermediate care facilities for individuals with intellectual or developmental disabilities. About 30% of Medicaid LTC funds were allocated to home- and community-based waiver programs, with another 11% of LTC funds used for the personal care option (Eiken et al., 2012). Four percent of the Medicaid LTC budget was allocated to home health care.

Medicaid is a social welfare program and as such has strict eligibility requirements. To be eligible to receive Medicaid LTC services, an individual must meet both low-income and disability thresholds. Although income and asset eligibility criteria vary by state, in general an individual must have income below the poverty level and assets between $1,500 and $5,000. In recognition of the need to have higher income in order to pay for day-to-day living expenses, states have the option of allowing those individuals residing in the community who are in need of LTC to have a higher income threshold (up to 300% of the monthly Supplemental Security Income amount, which was $674 per month in 2010). Asset limitations cannot be modified. Individuals requiring Medicaid assistance and residing in a nursing home essentially pay their entire incomes to the Medicaid program and receive a monthly allowance, typically $40 to $50 per month, for personal expenses.

In addition to meeting income guidelines, to be eligible for Medicaid support for nursing home care or HCBS under the Medicaid waiver, individuals must have a severe functional limitation. For instance, can an individual dress or bathe him- or herself independently? Again, the criteria vary by state, but in general, an individual must have impairments in at least two activities of daily living, such as bathing, dressing, transferring from bed to chair, getting to the toilet, or eating independently. Severe cognitive impairment can also qualify as a disability. The personal care option and home health coverage also have requirements to receive services, but they are not as restrictive as nursing home or waiver eligibility standards. Because of the high cost of nursing home care and the lack of private insurance, Medicaid has become the major payor of nursing home care, with about six in 10 nursing home residents paid for from this source.

Although institutional care is still the largest LTC Medicaid category, there has been a significant shift in Medicaid financing in recent years. In 1997, 76% of all Medicaid LTC expenditures were allocated to institutions, whereas in 2009 the proportion was 55% (Eiken et al., 2012). Again, state variation is dramatic (see Figure 16.1), with Oregon spending 25% of its 2011 Medicaid budget on institutional LTC, compared to Alabama's institutional expenditures of 62% of its 2011 Medicaid budget (Kaiser Family Foundation, 2013b).

Nursing homes receive a *per diem* payment per resident; the daily rate is specific to each facility. The rate is set by each state and is typically determined by a range of factors, such as condition of the resident, to assess the likely amount of assistance that person would need (termed **case mix**), facility staffing levels, capital costs, geographical area, type of services covered, and funds available to the state. In some states, such as Ohio, a quality-of-care component is also included in the payment. The average daily Medicaid payment rate in 2011 was $178, ranging from $233 per day in Hawaii to $120 per day in Illinois (Hauser et al., 2012).

Medicaid has become a major part of state budgets, accounting nationally for more than one fifth of entire state expenditures. With LTC expenditures making up about one third of total Medicaid spending, in combination with a growing older population with disability, states recognize the intense challenges faced by

FIGURE 16.1 The proportions of Medicaid funds allocated to individual services.

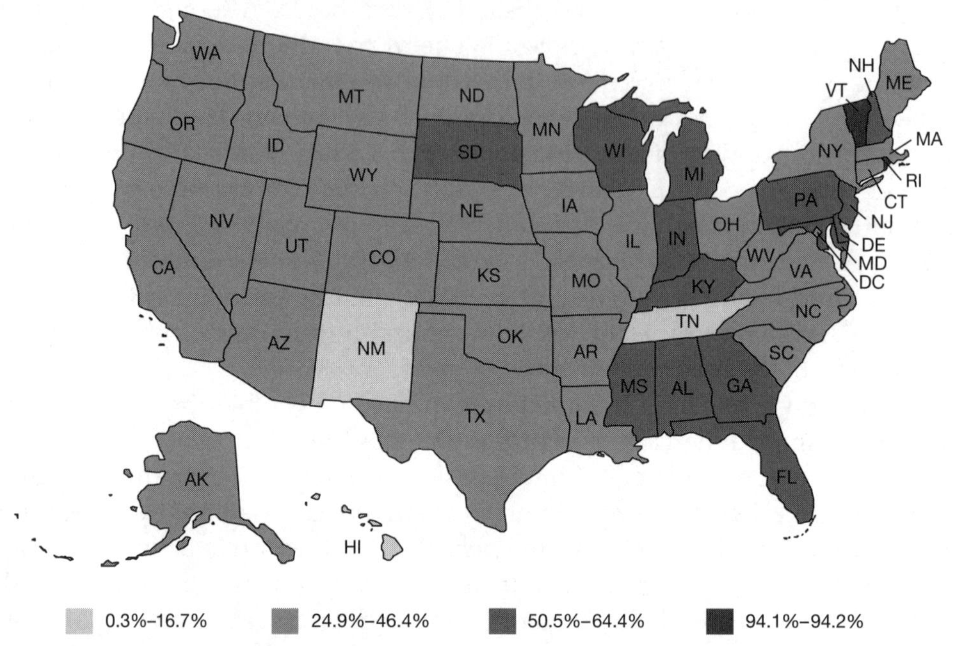

Source: Kaiser Family Foundation (2013a).

Medicaid as our nation ages. Exacerbating this challenge are recent trends that show a growth in the number of individuals under age 60 who are experiencing a long-term disability and are using formal long-term services and supports (Mehdizadeh, Applebaum, Nelson, Straker, & Deacon, 2013).

MEDICARE

Also enacted in 1965 under Title 18 of the Social Security Act, Medicare is a federal program designed to provide insurance coverage for older adults with a demonstrated work history qualifying them for Social Security. With $502 billion in expenditures, the insurance program is funded through a variety of sources, including a payroll tax on employees and employers (1.45%), beneficiary premiums and cost sharing, and general tax revenues. The program was primarily developed to provide coverage for acute medical care—it was not designed to pay for LTC. The program includes four coverage areas: Hospital Insurance (Part A), Supplementary Medical Insurance (Part B), Medicare Option (Part C), and Prescription Drug Coverage (Part D). Although Medicare is not designed to cover LTC, several components of the program do include traditional LTC elements.

The Medicare Skilled Nursing Home Benefit is the largest component of Medicare allocated to LTC, with expenditures of $27.4 billion in 2010 accounting for about 11% of total LTC expenditures (Talaga, 2013). As a result of changes in hospital reimbursement, through the implementation of a prospective payment system (method of reimbursement in which Medicare payments are made based on a predetermined, fixed amount), the average length of stay for Medicare hospital recipients has dropped by about 5 days. This change has resulted in a dramatic expansion of nursing home expenditures under Medicare, increasing from $10.4 billion in 1999.

Despite directing these funds to nursing home care, the Medicare benefit is designed as acute care rehabilitation coverage. In fact, an individual is not eligible for the Medicare nursing home benefit unless he or she has spent 3 days in the hospital with an acute care ailment and the nursing home stay is directly related to that hospitalization. For consumers meeting these criteria, Medicare will cover the first 20 days in the nursing home at no charge to the beneficiary. Between day 21 and day 100, Medicare requires a cost share of $157.50 (2015 amount), and after day 100, Medicare coverage ceases. Because individuals covered by Medicare are receiving rehabilitation services, the average Medicare reimbursement rate is considerably higher than either private pay or Medicaid rates of reimbursement. For example, a recent study in Ohio found that the average Medicaid reimbursement rate in 2007 was $174 per day, whereas the Medicare daily rate was $351 (Mehdizadeh, Applebaum, Deacon, & Straker, 2009).

Reimbursement changes have resulted in a shift in how nursing homes are being used. Many individuals enter nursing homes for rehabilitative care under Medicare. For example, a study by Mehdizadeh et al. (2009) found that after 3 months, only 43% of all those entering Ohio nursing homes were still residents, and after 6 months, fewer than one third remained as residents. A large portion of these short-term residents enter the nursing home via the hospital and receive Medicare short-term care prior to returning to the community (Mehdizadeh, Nelson, & Applebaum, 2006). The shift to reimburse hospitals prospectively has increased short-term nursing home use, and as will be noted in the next section, has had a similar effect on home health utilization.

The Medicare Home Health Benefit provided $18.4 billion in coverage in 2011, up from $8 billion in 2001 (Talaga, 2013). In 2009, there were more than 10,400 Medicare-certified home health agencies, growing from just over 7,000 in 2001 (MedPAC, 2010). Medicare home health benefits fall under both Part A and B of the Medicare coverage plan. Services include nursing, home health aides, and a range of therapies, such as physical and speech therapy. To receive home health care, a physician must order the specified services, and limits are placed on the type, frequency, and duration of home health services depending on the condition and circumstances of the beneficiary. Medicare home health is designed primarily as complementary to the acute care condition experienced by the consumer. In some instances an individual can receive Medicare home health benefits for an extended period of time lasting 6 months or longer. There is no cost share requirement for the home health benefit.

As is the case for the nursing home benefit, home health expenditures have dramatically expanded as a result of the prospective payment system, and this has further blurred the lines between acute care and LTC services.

In many instances, older people with chronic disability may receive services from both HCBS providers for assistance, such as personal care, and certified home health agencies for nursing, therapies, and in some instances, overlapping home health aide care. Although many questions arise about the home health services delivery system, it appears evident that there will be continued pressures to reduce hospital stays and even to expand outpatient medical procedures, suggesting that there will be expanded use of Medicare home health in the future.

The Medicare Hospice Benefit spent more than $15 billion in 2012, up from $2 billion in 1999. Currently, there are 3,400 Medicare hospice providers in the United States. The hospice benefit is targeted to individuals in the last 6 months of life, although about 20% of hospice users require services for more than 180 days. Hospice care does not require a deductible under Medicare. Although the majority of hospice care is short in duration, there is a growing trend for such services to be provided over an extended period of time, once again blurring the lines between short- and long-term services and supports.

OTHER PUBLIC FUNDING MECHANISMS

In addition to the two major public funding sources for LTC, Medicaid and Medicare, there are several smaller public contributors (accounting for less than 5% of the total LTC bill).

The Veterans Administration

The Veterans Administration (VA) provides an array of LTC services to veterans, from homemaker/home health aide services to fully skilled nursing home care. LTC services for veterans whose disability is determined to be a result of their military service are provided at no cost to them. Veterans whose disability is determined to be nonservice related must make copayments for LTC services. There are three levels of copays for veterans. *Inpatient care,* which includes nursing home care, respite care, and geriatric evaluations, has a copayment ranging from $0 to $97 per day depending on the veterans' individual financial status. *Outpatient care services,* which include adult day care, respite care, and geriatric evaluations, range in cost from $0 to $15 per day. Finally, *domiciliary care,* designed for veterans who require care falling between acute care and fully skilled nursing home care, consists of respite services, geriatric evaluation and management by an interdisciplinary team of professionals, community residential care, home health care, adult day care, and homemaker/home health aide services, and ranges in cost from $0 to $5 per diem. For all types of care, days 0 to 21 are free of financial obligations and are fully covered by the VA. Days 22 to 180 require copay based on the veteran's income. Financial responsibility for care required over 181 days is determined by the individual's income and assets, less $89,280 in liquid assets for spousal resource protection (U.S. Department of Veterans Affairs,

2009). LTC through the VA can be provided in a number of locations: a VA nursing home, a community nursing home, a State Veterans Home, or domiciliary. Care provided outside of the VA network is not covered by VA funds. The VA also provides a monetary benefit termed "Aid and Attendance and Housebound Benefit" as a supplement to those receiving a VA monthly pension. The benefit is available to those who require assistance from another person to perform personal functions, such as bathing or dressing, or to those who are housebound.

The Older Americans Act

The Older Americans Act (OAA), passed in 1965, allocates a substantial portion of its $1.7 billion allocation to HCBS. Major HCBS funded by the OAA include Aging and Disability Resource Centers that provide information and referral assistance and long-term options, including counseling; home-delivered meals; care coordination and case management; homemaker, personal care and transportation services; and a series of services in support of caregivers. Although about two thirds of OAA funds are allocated to HCBS, the entire legislative allocation of $1.7 billion, when factoring in inflation, has remained flat funded for the past three decades, with the 1980 allocation at $1.1 billion (Administration for Community Living, 2010). Yet, over this time period, the older population has doubled in size. Nevertheless, the OAA provides infrastructure support for the aging network, and although underfunded, it remains a core foundation for the service delivery system for older people.

Programs of All Inclusive Care for the Elderly

The **Programs of All-Inclusive Care for the Elderly (PACE)** is designed to assist individuals age 55 and over to stay at home in the community and live as independently as possible. This program uses a combination of Medicare and Medicaid funds to cover all medically necessary care and services, both acute and long term (Centers for Medicare and Medicaid, 2008). To be eligible to receive assistance from PACE, an individual must be at least 55 years old, live in a PACE organization service area, meet the state certification for nursing home level of care, and be able to live safely in the community with the services provided by PACE. Services provided under PACE include, but are not limited to, primary care; acute care needs, including emergency services; prescription drugs; nursing home; home health care; physical and occupational therapy; adult day care; meals; dentistry; social services; transportation; and any additional services deemed necessary by the PACE health care team. Individuals can also receive Medicare, Medicaid, both, or neither, and still remain eligible for PACE funding. If an individual is not covered by Medicaid, he or she is charged a monthly premium for LTC services and Medicare Part D (the prescription drug benefit) equal to the Medicaid **capitation** amount; that is, the predetermined amount that Medicaid has agreed to pay providers for each individual under its care. The goal of the PACE program is to assist individuals to remain in the community for as long as possible. Consequently, only approximately 7% of PACE participants reside in a nursing home (National PACE Association, 2010).

State-Funded Home- and Community-Based Care Services Programs

State-funded home- and community-based care services programs are designed to provide support services to older adults to help maintain independent community living. As each state is generally responsibly for the funding and eligibility of its HCBS program, there is considerable variability among the programs. Programs are financed in a variety of ways. The majority of programs are funded through general state revenues (taxes). Other programs (such as the HCBS program in Pennsylvania) use alternative methods, such as state lottery revenues, to fund programs. For these programs, basic eligibility requirements are that individuals be age 60 or over, in need of respite services, have limited finances, and have impairments in some activities of daily living (ADLs) and some instrumental activities of daily living (IADLs). Individual financial contributions for services also vary by state. In Massachusetts, for instance, individuals with incomes above $1,806 per month are required to pay the total cost of care, but those with limited income or intermediate health care needs must pay a 15% copay for services rendered. State-funded home- and community-based care programs generally conduct a needs assessment of the individual applying for the program and develop an individualized service plan for care. Services provided by state-funded HCBS programs include homemaker, personal care, day care, home-delivered meals, transportation, and other community support services as required by the care plan. The top five states in order of HCBS program financing in millions of dollars are Pennsylvania ($182.2), Massachusetts ($171.5), Illinois ($155.2), New York ($95.3), and Florida ($67.2; Houser, Fox-Grage, & Gibson, 2009). Some states, such as Alabama, Mississippi, Montana, New Hampshire, and Ohio, have limited or no HCBS programs and are ranked at the bottom of the state-funded HCBS programs list (Houser et al., 2009).

Levy Programs

Local levy programs are an alternative funding mechanism used in some states (see Case Study 16.1). In part because of the limited funds available from the OAA for in-home services, and in part because some states have no or limited state home care programs, local tax levies have been used as an approach in select states. In our review of this approach, we found 12 states that have used this approach, with one state, Ohio, generating $165 million in 2011 (Payne, Applebaum, & Straker, 2012). In Ohio, local funding brings in more than double the amount the state receives from its OAA allocation. Typically, these programs require voters to return to the ballot box every 3 to 5 years to reauthorize senior levy programs. States use the funds collected via levies to fund an array of services, such as nutrition, home-delivered meals, transportation, in-home services, information and referral, case management, senior center administration, home modification,

Case Study 16.1: Ohio Levy Programs

The history of the levy programs used to fund aging services in Ohio provides an interesting example of the power of individual advocacy. In the early 1970s a woman named Lois Dale Brown, who had been an active social services volunteer in Clermont County, Ohio, approached county commissioners about a concern that she had about the growing older population. She wanted to build a senior center that would provide an array of services to this growing older population. The commissioners liked the idea, but responded that they did not have the funds available for such an effort. She then asked whether the project could be funded through a property tax levy. The commissioners responded that although they liked the idea under the current state law they could not use property tax levy funding for such a purpose. Hearing this, Ms. Dale Brown spent the next 2 years convincing state legislators that this was an appropriate use of property tax revenues. After a successful change to the state law she returned to Clermont County and was able to get a levy passed to create Clermont Senior Services, an organization that continues to effectively serve elders today. Building on the Clermont success, other counties also used such levies to support senior services. Today, in Ohio 73 of the state's 88 counties have property tax levies, which raised more than $165 million last year to support services for seniors. Although it does not happen every day, the lesson is don't underestimate the power of one person to make a difference.

Case Study Discussion Question:

1. Do you think that using property tax levies is a good approach to funding in-home services? What are the advantages and disadvantages of such an approach?

adult day care, prescription assistance, volunteer coordination, and provide low-income seniors with dental, hearing, and vision services. The challenge with levy programs is twofold. First, local municipalities must work to educate voters and political officials on the need and benefit of the levy. Second, because levies are property-tax based, lower income residents who own their dwellings may be negatively affected.

PRIVATE EXPENDITURES

Out-of-pocket payments are the third largest payer of LTC services and supports and account for roughly $37 billion of LTC financing (Georgetown, 2007). The majority of individuals with LTC needs live in the community and are cared for by unpaid family members and friends (Kaye, Harrington, & LaPlante, 2010);

the economic value of unpaid family caregivers is $450 billion annually (Hauser et al., 2012). For individuals who wish to pay for LTC services independently, there are a number of private options to consider. For those in good health, private LTC insurance or relocating to a continuing-care retirement community, which provides a community living arrangement with housing, health care, and social services for older people in a stepped-care environment, may serve as the best option. For those in poor health or with a terminal illness, accelerated death benefits or **viatical settlements** (whereby a terminally ill person sells his or her life insurance policy to a third party for less than its mature value, in order to benefit from the proceeds while still alive) may provide the best way to pay for LTC services. There are also payment options that can be accessed when health is not a primary consideration, such as annuities, home equity conversions, trusts, and life settlements.

PRIVATE FINANCING OPTIONS

Long-Term Care Insurance

Long-Term Care Insurance (LTC insurance) emerged in the 1970s as a way to decease the burden on public funding mechanisms, to reduce financing risk for consumers, and to fill the gap in LTC coverage left by Medicare. To utilize LTC insurance payments, individuals purchase policy coverage up front specifying dollar-per-day coverage amounts. To access benefits, a claim must be submitted and approved by the insurance carrier before services are provided. Originally, policies were limited to nursing home-only coverage and were quite expensive. Current policies have improved coverage considerably, with the majority of policies now offering coverage for home health, assisted living, and nursing home care. LTC insurance premiums are based on age and health status; older, less healthy individuals pay more for coverage than do younger, healthier individuals. Over the years, policy premiums have become more affordable. Now, the typical policy offers $100 per day nursing home coverage, $50 per day home-care coverage, and numerous amenities, such as inflation protection or unlimited lifetime benefits for an increased premium. Approximately 9% of individuals age 40 to 70 have an LTC insurance policy.

In 1993, to further enhance the appeal of private LTC insurance, the Partnership for Long-Term Care was initiated. This is a joint public–private program that allows individuals to purchase private LTC insurance policies and then, once the benefits of the policy are exhausted, to qualify for Medicaid and retain a predetermined level of assets (determined by the type of policy purchased), bypassing Medicaid spend-down requirements. Originally, the Partnership for Long-Term Care program was initiated in four states, California, Connecticut, Indiana, and New York. The goals of the program are to decrease reliance on Medicaid and to encourage individuals to purchase private LTC insurance policies. Under the program, individuals purchase a state-backed LTC insurance policy that allows them to retain some of their assets and still qualify for Medicaid once their LTC insurance benefits are exhausted. In 2005, due to the success of the program, the

Partnership for Long-Term Care was expanded and currently all 50 states are in the planning, development, or early-implementation stages.

Accelerated Death Benefits

Individuals who are in poor health or who are terminally ill have limited choices when applying for programs that assist in paying for LTC needs; thus, accelerated death benefits are a good option to consider. An **accelerated death benefit** is a life insurance death benefit paid in cash in advance of death and is provided tax free. This option is included with some life insurance policies, although individuals may have to pay an additional or extra premium to utilize this product. There are different types of accelerated death benefits depending on the purpose; for instance, individuals who are terminally ill may have different benefits than those who have LTC needs or those who are confined to a nursing home. Generally, benefits are capped at 50% of the death benefit.

Reverse Mortgage: Home Equity Conversion

Health status is not a consideration when applying for a home equity conversion; therefore, this is an attractive LTC payment option for many people. A reverse mortgage is a special type of home equity loan that many individuals use to pay for home- and community-based care or to purchase LTC insurance. With a reverse mortgage, individuals receive cash in a lump sum, monthly payment, or credit line, against the value of their home without having to sell it. The reverse mortgage becomes due when an individual dies, moves out, or sells his or her home. There are no restrictions on the use of the funds received from a reverse mortgage.

Trusts

Another private option for paying for LTC is a **trust.** A trust is an agreement under which money or other assets are managed and controlled by one person (or company) for the benefit of another person. Depending on the specific goal, a variety of trusts can be created. For the purpose of paying for LTC, there are two particular types of trusts, *a charitable remainder trust* and *a Medicaid disability trust.* A charitable remainder trust is generally used by wealthy individuals with specific types of assets that they want to donate to a public charity or charities at fair market value. Individuals making the donation receive tax deductions on the gifted amount, and the donor receives payments from the trust that can be used for LTC. When the donor dies, all remaining money goes to the charity or charities. A Medicaid disability trust is created to enhance the quality of life of an individual with a disability who qualifies for public benefits. This type of trust is limited to disabled persons *under* 65 years old. Under a Medicaid disability trust, assets are managed by a nonprofit organization and the individual is exempt from standard Medicaid eligibility rules. For a summary of the main financing mechanisms of LTC, see Table 16.1.

TABLE 16.1 Main Sources of LTC Financing

PROGRAM TITLE	FUNDED BY	LTC CONTRIBUTION (%)	ELIGIBILITY REQUIREMENTS	BENEFITS/COVERAGE
Public Programs				
Medicaid	Federal and state governments	50%	Income* below poverty level and assets between $1,500 and $5,000; two ADL* or cognitive impairments	Nursing home residents: cost of care paid in full
Medicare	Federal government via payroll tax, beneficiary premiums and cost sharing, and general tax revenues	20%	10 years of eligible employment; age 65+; end-stage renal disease	Part A: Hospital insurance; nursing home coverage requires 3-day postacute hospital stay; first 20 days covered in full; days 21–100 cost-share; day 100+ Medicare coverage ceases
VA	Federal government		Military service connection	Service-related disability: full LTC coverage; non-service-related disability: copayment required
OAA	Federal grants		Age 60+	Home- and community-based services
PACE	Medicare and Medicaid	2.5%	Age 55+; live in PACE area; meet state certification for care; ability to live safely in community with PACE services	All Medicare and Medicaid covered services

(*continued*)

TABLE 16.1 Main Sources of LTC Financing (*continued*)

PROGRAM TITLE	FUNDED BY	LTC CONTRIBUTION (%)	ELIGIBILITY REQUIREMENTS	BENEFITS/COVERAGE
HCBS	State funded (e.g., taxes, lottery)		Age 60+; in need of respite services; limited finances; some ADL impairments; some IADL impairments	Copayment required**; homemaker; personal care; day care; other necessary community support services
Private Programs				
Out-of-pocket	Individual	18%	Not applicable	Determined by the individual
LTC insurance	Individual	7%	Plans based on age and health of individual	Nursing home; assisted living facility; home health care; coverage varies by plan but typically pay $100/day for nursing home care and $50/day for home health care
Philanthropic foundations	Individuals/ organizations	2.5%	Varies by organization	Varies by organization

ADL, activities of daily living; HCBS, home- and community-based services; IADL, instrumental activities of daily living; LTC, long-term care; OAA, Older Americans Act; PACE, Programs of All-Inclusive Care for the Elderly; VA, Veterans Administration.

* income amounts vary by state

** cost-sharing requirements vary by state and program

FINANCING ISSUES AND CHALLENGES FOR AN AGING SOCIETY

This chapter has highlighted the complex array of mechanisms in place to finance LTC services and supports and the challenges associated with paying for these services. In combination, the increasing funds required to support those needing LTC services and supports, the substantial increase in projected need for such services in the future, and current state and federal budgetary challenges create the "perfect storm" for a long-term financing crisis.

A review of LTC expenditures in the context of current inflationary patterns and projected demographic changes brings experts in LTC policy to a consensus conclusion that the current approach to financing LTC is simply unsustainable. We cannot double or triple the size of the older population that will need long-term services and supports and simply continue the current approach to delivering and financing LTC. Estimates from a recent study in Ohio indicate that if the state made no changes in its current approach, the Medicaid program, which is now one quarter of the entire state budget, could approach 50% of the state budget over the next 10 to 15 years (Mehdizadeh, 2010). Such a scenario is not feasible, because states have many competing elements vying for a share of the budget, including schools, roads, prisons, and other human services. This problem is common in literally every state in the nation. What then, can states and the nation do to prepare for this financing crisis? There are a number of options.

IMPROVE THE EFFICIENCY AND EFFECTIVENESS OF THE LONG-TERM CARE SYSTEM

LTC has been expensive, but questions have been consistently raised over the past three decades as to the efficiency and effectiveness of approaches used. First and foremost has been long-standing criticism that the U.S. system has relied too heavily on institutional care. For example, although the intermediate care option became a mandatory Medicaid service in 1968, it was not until 1981 that Congress even allowed HCBS, and to this day most of these services require a special waiver from the Center for Medicare & Medicaid Services (CMS) for funding. Nursing home care continues to be an entitlement, whereas HCBS are dependent on state allocations and federal waiver approvals. This means that the present LTC financing system makes it easier for states to place individuals in the most expensive care setting (nursing home) and harder to support them in less expensive care settings (HCBS).

Although many states and the CMS have responded to this challenge by shifting how Medicaid LTC funds are spent, the overall system is still highly inefficient. For example, 92% of older adults are not eligible for Medicaid when living in the community (Mehdizadeh et al., 2013); however, almost two thirds of all nursing home residents are paid for by Medicaid. There are very few public LTC resources available for moderate income or middle-class Americans prior to entry into an LTC facility. One of the challenges for states and the federal government is to develop supports for those individuals prior to relying on the Medicaid program.

ENHANCE INDIVIDUAL, FAMILY PLANNING, AND TRAINING EFFORTS IN LONG-TERM CARE

Historically, the U.S. health and welfare system developed as a hybrid, attempting to balance individual, employer, and governmental responsibility. In the area of LTC, our policies have essentially emphasized individual responsibility or reliance on Medicaid, a welfare program designed for the medically indigent. Such a system has resulted in considerable inequity across the population, because some individuals have used legal, and in some instances, illegal means to tap into Medicaid funds by shielding private assets, whereas others have used individual resources to pay for their care. In addition to the lack of fairness, such a system results in incentives for individuals and families to rely on public resources sooner than necessary. What is needed is a system that provides encouragement and support to individuals and families to remain as independent as possible in the community. A moderate amount of support for an individual could substantially delay the need for institutional assistance. Data from across the United States show that there is considerable variation in both bed supply and the use of nursing homes (Houser et al., 2009, 2012). Reducing nursing home use has the potential to save states and the federal government billions of dollars each year.

IMPROVE THE USE OF TECHNOLOGY IN PROVIDING LONG-TERM CARE SERVICES AND SUPPORTS

Another important way to improve the efficiency and effectiveness of the LTC system is through technology (see Chapter 8). Although still at the early stages of innovation, some promising areas have already been developed, and many are under development. For example, Toyota and Honda have been developing personal care robots to assist with household, personal care, and even health care tasks. The television show *The Jetsons* advanced the idea of Rosie the personal robot, and it appears quite likely that this will be a reality in the future.

Other advances already under way include the use of in-home security devices, such as heat and water sensors, door alarms, and even cameras, to enhance home safety for caregivers and older consumers (Kinney, Cart, Murdoch, & Conley, 2004). Retirement communities have already begun to build into new construction innovations such as mechanisms to detect whether a resident has not left her bedroom or bathroom in a specific period of time.

Our society has experienced tremendous technological changes over the past three decades. The computer, cell phone, automobile, Internet, and many other aspects of our lives have changed appreciably. How can these changes and the developments to come be used to help individuals maintain independence in their own homes and communities? Although many questions exist, it is clear that technology can serve as one of the answers to the complex LTC challenges facing an aging population.

IMPROVE THE LINK BETWEEN ACUTE AND LONG-TERM CARE

One of the biggest challenges facing the health and long-term well-being of the older population is the limited coordination, communication, and integration between acute care and LTC systems. Because the funding mechanisms for acute care and LTC have been separate, the delivery systems for each type of care have also developed separately. A result of this lack of coordination is that many physicians are unaware of the LTC system, and communication between sectors is often limited. Although there have been some initiatives to address this problem, such as the PACE program discussed earlier or some state-integrated care models, such as Minnesota's Senior Health Options (MSHO), Arizona's Long-Term Care System (ALTCS), and Wisconsin's Partnership Program (WPP) (McGeehan & Applebaum, 2007), overall the problem remains. The problems faced in the arena have been well documented by noted gerontologist Robert Kane who, reflecting on a career in geriatrics and LTC, described the frustration in attempting to get the two systems to work together to assist his mother (Kane & West, 2005). One of the hopes of health care reform is that under the new funding stream the linkages between the acute care and LTC systems will be improved.

DEVELOPING PREVENTATIVE PROGRAMS TO ADDRESS THE GROWING CHALLENGES OF AN AGING SOCIETY

Approaches to providing LTC services and supports have generally been reactive rather than proactive. There has been little effort to develop preventative interventions, despite considerable expenses for nursing home care. Recent efforts by the Administration on Aging through the Area Agency on Aging network to provide programs focused on evidence-based practices for falls prevention and disease management are the first real steps taken to address this issue. The evidence on the effects of falls, both personal and monetary, has been clearly identified, yet our investment in falls prevention has been microscopic in comparison to other service expenditures. As the size of the older population increases, it will be imperative to address mechanisms to prevent, limit, or delay the need for long-term services and supports. Shifting some funds into preventative activities is not only better for individuals, it is one of the only ways that we will be able to provide the needed assistance to an aging America.

SUMMARY

As the baby boomers move into old age, it is clear that today's long-term challenges are a small prelude to the potential problems of tomorrow. These demographic changes, along with increases in disability rates for those under 60, mean that whatever problems we have today will be small in comparison. With most states already spending one quarter of their entire state budgets on Medicaid, the doubling of those likely to need long-term services and supports presents an ominous forecast for the future. In recent work for legislators in

Ohio, our own research estimated that if no changes were made in the state's approach, Medicaid would grow to more than 50% of the entire state budget by 2040 (Mehdizadeh et al., 2013). Adding to these challenges is our inability as a nation to come to consensus on financing long-term services and supports. The repeal of the CLASS Act, which was the LTC coverage part of the Affordable Care Act, provided an example of how difficult it is to develop national policy in this area. Finally, in case we needed another example to demonstrate our inability to agree on how to finance LTC, the recent report of the Bi-Partisan Commission on Long-Term Care could not even address financing issues because the members were divided on the potential approaches (U.S. Senate, 2013). Although the solutions to delivering and financing long-term services and supports are not yet determined, what is clear is that the United States will experience a large increase in the number of individuals likely to need long-term services and supports.

DISCUSSION QUESTIONS

1. Describe the differences in eligibility and types of services offered through Medicaid and Medicare.
2. This chapter provides brief descriptions of several funding mechanisms for LTC. In your opinion, which two or three resources best fit the needs of the growing older adult population? Why?
3. What are some of the benefits and challenges for older adults (with LTC needs) who choose to remain in the community? How might this impact their aging experience?
4. Policies and practices are often reformed in order to meet the needs of older adults. If you were chosen by a committee to help reform LTC funding, what changes would you suggest to help prepare states and the nation for the growing number of LTC users?
5. Describe ways in which improvements in technology will lead to changes in how older adults receive care in both the community and LTC settings.
6. Family members play an essential role in providing financial, physical, and emotional support for older adults. Additionally, families help older adults navigate through and select needed services to either move into an institution or remain within the community. What could be done, on the local, state, or national level, to help older adults and family members prepare for such a transition?

ADDITIONAL RESOURCES

For a complete overview of how LTC costs vary by state (and financing mechanism), see Genworth Financial. (2013). *Cost of care survey: Home care providers, adult day health care facilities, assisted living facilities, and nursing homes* (10th ed.). Retrieved from www.genworth.com/dam/Americas/US/PDFs/Consumer/corporate/130568_032213_Cost%20of%20Care_Final_nonsecure.pdf

REFERENCES

Administration for Community Living. (2010). *Administration on Aging (AoA)*. Retrieved from http://www.aoa.acl.gov/AoA_Programs/OAA/Introduction.aspx

Centers for Medicare & Medicaid Services. (2008). *Quick facts about Programs of All-inclusive Care for the Elderly* (CMS Publication No. 11341).

Eiken, S., Burwell, B., Gold, L., & Sredl, K. (2012). *Medicaid HCBS waiver expenditures: FY 2004 through FY 2009*. Cambridge, MA: Thomson Reuters.

Genworth Financial. (2013). *Cost of care survey: Home care providers, adult day health care facilities, assisted living facilities, and nursing homes* (10th ed.). Genworth Financial. Retrieved from www.genworth.com/dam/Americas/US/PDFs/Consumer/corporate/130568_032213_Cost%20of%20Care_Final_nonsecure.pdf

Georgetown University Long-Term Care Financing Project. (2007, January). *Medicaid and long-term care*. Washington, DC: Georgetown Health Policy Institute.

Houser, A., Fox-Grage, W. & Ujvari, K. (2012). *AARP across the states: Profiles of long-term services and supports* (9th ed.). AARP. Retrieved from www.aarp.org/content/dam/aarp/research/public_policy_institute/ltc/2012/across-the-states-2012-full-report-AARP-ppi-ltc.pdf

Houser, A., Fox-Grage, W. & Gibson, M. (2009). *Across the states, profiles of long-term care and independent living*. Washington, DC: AARP.

Kaiser Family Foundation. (2013a). *Total Medicaid spending (FY 2012)*. Kaiser Family Foundation. Retrieved from http://kff.org/state-category/medicaid-chip/medicaid-spending

Kaiser Family Foundation. (2013b). *Distribution of medicaid spending on long term care (FY 2011)*. Kaiser Family Foundation, State Health Facts. Retrieved from http://kff.org/medicaid/state-indicator/spending-on-long-term-care/#table

Kane, R. L., & West, J. C. (2005). *It shouldn't be this way: The failure of long-term care*. Nashville, TN: Vanderbilt University Press.

Kaye, S., Harrington, C., & LaPlante, P. (2010). Long-term care: Who gets it, who provides it, who pays, and how much? *Health Affairs*, *29*(1), 11–21.

Kinney, J., Cart, C., Murdoch, L., & Conley, C. (2004). Striving to provide safety assistance for families of elders. *Dementia*, *3*(3), 351–370.

McGeehan, S., & Applebaum, R., (2007). The evolving role of care management in integrated care models. *Case Management Journals*, *8*(2), 2.

MedPAC. (2010). *Healthcare spending in the Medicare program*. Report of the Medicare Payment Advisory Commission. Retrieved from www.Medpac.gov

Mehdizadeh, S. (2010). *Disability in Ohio: Managing the projected need for long-term services and supports*. Oxford, OH: Scripps Gerontology Center.

Mehdizadeh, S., Applebaum, R., Deacon, M., & Straker, J. (2009). *Providing long-term services and supports to an aging Ohio: Progresses and challenges*. Oxford, OH: Scripps Gerontology Center.

Mehdizadeh, S., Applebaum, R., Nelson, M., Straker, J., & Deacon, M. (2013). *Maybe elephants can dance, two decades of progress in delivering long-term services and supports in Ohio*. Oxford, OH: Scripps Gerontology Center.

Mehdizadeh, S., Nelson, M., & Applebaum, R. (2006). *Nursing home use in Ohio: Who stays, who pays? Brief Report*. Oxford, OH: Scripps Gerontology Center.

MetLife Mature Market Institute. (2009). *Long-term care IQ: Removing myths, reinforcing realities*. MetLife Mature Market Institute. Retrieved from https://www.metlife.com/assets/cao/mmi/publications/consumer/long-term-care-essentials/mmi-long-term-care-iq-removing-myths-survey.pdf

National Clearinghouse for Long-Term Care Information. (2010). *Where is long-term care provided?* Retrieved from www.longtermcare.gov/LTC/Main_Site/Understanding_Long_Term_Care/Services/Services.aspx

National PACE Association. (2010). *National PACE Association.* Retrieved from www.npaonline.org/website/article.asp?id=4.

Payne, M., Applebaum, R., & Straker, J. (2012). *Locally funded services for the older population: A description of senior-service property-tax levies in Ohio.* Oxford, OH: Scripps Gerontology Center.

Talaga, S. (2013). Medicare home health benefit primer: Benefit basics and issues. *Congressional Research Service* (7-5700). Retrieved from www.crs.gov

Tritz, K. (2006). *Long-term care: Trends in public and private spending.* CRS Report for Congress, The Library of Congress. Washington, DC: Congressional Research Services.

Truffer, C. J., Klemm, J. D., Wolfe, C. J., Rennie, K. E., & Shuff, J. (2012). *Actuarial report on the financial outlook for Medicaid.* Office of the Actuary, Centers for Medicare and Medicaid Services, Department of Health and Human Services. Retrieved from http://medicaid.gov/Medicaid-CHIP-Program-Information/By-Topics/Financing-and-Reimbursement/Downloads/medicaid-actuarial-report-2012.pdf

U.S. Department of Veterans Affairs. (2009). *VA health care eligibility and enrollment.* Retrieved from http://www.va.gov/opa/publications/benefits_book.asp

U.S. Senate. (2013). *Commission on long-term care: Report to Congress.* Washington, DC: U.S. Government Publishing Office.

Understanding Long-Term Care Policy

RICHARD H. FORTINSKY
NOREEN A. SHUGRUE

CHAPTER OVERVIEW

Currently, there is no unifying long-term care policy in the United States. Public policies at the federal, state, and local levels have developed in an incremental and fragmented fashion, influenced in large part by the interests and persuasive powers of the many constituents of the long-term care system. This fragmentation in long-term care policy, especially in the public sphere, was cogently summarized nearly 30 years ago as a "complex cube" of funding streams, populations needing long-term care, and settings in which long-term care is delivered (Oriol, 1985). This chapter describes a framework for understanding long-term care policy development in the early 21st century by describing the highly political process by which long-term care policy decisions are made and the inter-relationships among the major types of long-term care policies, the types and levels of decision makers in the long-term care arena, and the interest groups that influence its formation. The chapter summarizes many of the historical milestones in long-term care policy making and major current policy issues. It concludes with a description of major trends in long-term care policy making on which some consensus appears to be forming.

LEARNING OBJECTIVES

After completing this chapter, you should have an understanding of:

- The impact of public policy decisions on persons needing long-term care
- The types of public policies affecting long-term care
- The different levels of governmental and nongovernmental policy makers
- The variety of interest group politics that influence long-term care policy decisions

KEY TERMS

Executive branch
Financing policy
Health resources policy
Interest group
Judicial branch
Legislative branch
Public policy
Regulatory policy
Service organization and delivery

INTRODUCTION

"Politics is the art of the possible," according to the remark most often attributed to Otto von Bismarck (Shapiro & Epstein, 2006). His observation is an apt description of the political process by which long-term care policy is made. By this point in the book, it should be quite apparent that there is no unifying long-term care policy in the United States. Instead, public policies at the federal, state, and local levels have developed in an incremental and fragmented fashion, influenced in large part by the interests and persuasive powers of the many constituents of the long-term care system. There are many theories of policy process, but most recognize that policy development is accomplished through the gradual accumulation of knowledge by groups variously known as "issue networks" or "policy subsystems" (Miller, Mor, & Clark, 2010). In the case of long-term care, these constituent groups include long-term care recipients and their families, caregivers and advocates, providers of all types, taxpayers, academic researchers, and public officials in both **executive** and **legislative branches** of government responsible for providing, financing, and regulating long-term care services. The **judicial branch**, too, has influenced policy through court decisions in cases brought by other actors in the long-term care arena.

At times, long-term care policy has focused on financing specific services in the continuum of care discussed in Chapter 1, at other times the focus has been specifically on one population group needing long-term care, and at still other times on regulatory oversight of services financed by public funds. The purpose of this chapter is to examine the politics and dynamics underlying **public policy** formulation and implementation in relation to individuals with long-term care needs. In an effort to complement rather than duplicate contributions of other authors in this book, this chapter presents and elaborates on a framework for understanding where public policy originates, what and who influences its development in the long-term care arena, and how major public policies concerning long-term care have been shaped to date. This framework is intended to illuminate the complex interplay among policy makers, **interest groups**, and the political climates and sensibilities that have influenced long-term care policy development to date. Figure 17.1 illustrates this framework as a three-dimensional "cube" of long-term care policy development for the early 21st century,

FIGURE 17.1 Framework illustrating three domains comprising the cube of long-term care policy development.

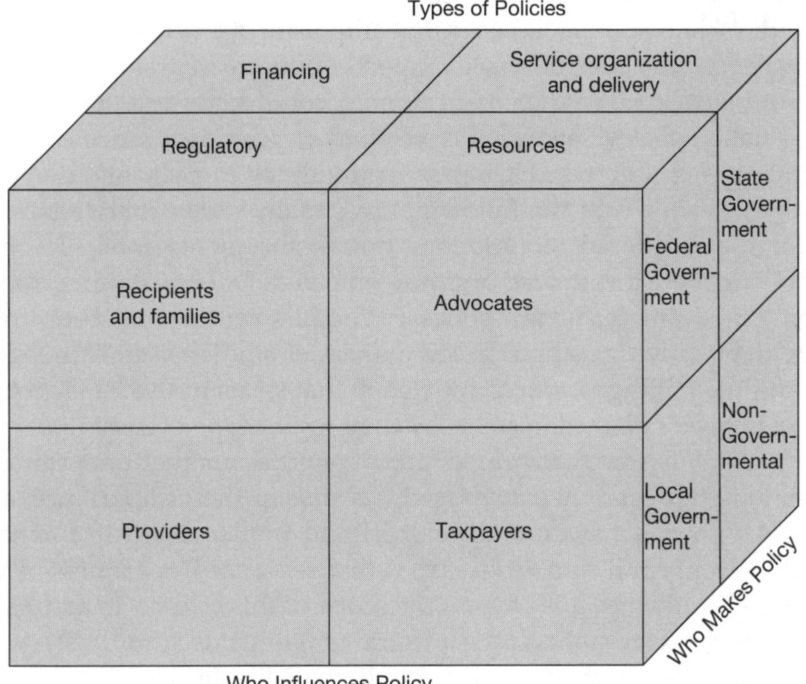

Source: Adapted from Fortinsky (2005).

adapting the original complex cube of long-term care introduced by Oriol (1985). As Figure 17.1 shows, the three domains of long-term care policy development include the types of policies developed, levels of policy development, and the various constituencies who influence policy development. Dynamics underlying long-term care policy development can be characterized as the interplay among one or more components of each of these three domains or dimensions of the cube. Most of the remainder of this chapter elaborates on these three dimensions of long-term care policy development. Populations needing long-term care are discussed in greater detail throughout this book; therefore, the following section briefly summarizes these populations in order to retain the focus of long-term care policy development on those who require services.

POPULATIONS NEEDING LONG-TERM CARE

The population with long-term care needs has much in common. Nevertheless, in policy discussions, this population has often been categorized according to age and type of disability, in part to target services more precisely, but also because advocates historically were concerned with advancing the interests of one population while failing to recognize parallels with other groups. Examples of populations for which separate policies have been developed include persons with developmental disabilities, persons with chronic mental illness (see Chapter 13), older adults with physical disabilities, younger persons with physical disabilities, and adults with cognitive impairments. Other groups with long-term care needs who have been segregated in policy discussions include people with brain injuries, HIV/AIDS, neurological conditions, and end-stage kidney disease. Public policies have been developed to provide a range of home- and community-based services (HCBS) for individuals in each of these classified groups and, as shown in the following text, many states operate parallel programs for these different populations due to the incremental way in which public policies were formulated and implemented. One heartening trend in the development of long-term care policy in the 21st century has been the recognition by many advocates and policy makers of similar needs among various groups and the willingness to shape policy that treats individuals according to their level of need rather than solely by their age or type of disability.

Veterans of the American armed forces comprise another important population with long-term care needs. Indeed, because of their importance, an entire set of public policies has been developed and implemented to finance, organize, and deliver health care services to veterans via the Department of Veterans Affairs (DVA). Although it is beyond the scope of this chapter to address details of DVA long-term care policy, DVA programs will be used to illustrate broader points about types of public policies affecting long-term care.

TYPES OF LONG-TERM CARE POLICIES

Public policies in the health arena can be grouped into four major types, depending on the aspect of health care with which they are primarily concerned—financing, service organization and delivery, regulation to ensure service quality, and health resources availability. Some legislation includes more than one type of policy.

FINANCING POLICY

Financing long-term care services has given rise to some of the most heated debates as well as some of the most progressive thinking and creative solutions in the long-term care arena. Medicare, Medicaid, and the Veterans Administration are examples of public financing policies in that they specify funding mechanisms to pay for health-related services, the types of services that are eligible to receive funding, and the target populations eligible for funded services. But **financing policy** goes well beyond public payment systems to include private financing of needed services (both paid and unpaid). Private financing of long-term care needs may come from long-term care insurance, personal assets, reverse mortgages, and unpaid care from family members or others. Chapter 16 provides an in-depth look at the costs of long-term care and the many public and private mechanisms used to finance it. In this chapter, we discuss how financing policy involves the interplay between various schemes of public and private financing in the health sphere, and how they have contributed to the development of a continuum of care for persons with long-term care needs. Questions that arise in the financing policy debate include: Is long-term care a public or private responsibility? How can public and private resources complement each other to achieve equitable outcomes (Stevenson, Cohen, Tell, & Burwell, 2010; see Exhibit 17.1)?

EXHIBIT 17.1 Policy illustration—the CLASS Act

The CLASS Act: What is the role for government in financing long-term care?

One policy issue that illustrates many of the themes in this chapter is the continuing debate over the proper role of government in financing long-term care. This debate culminated in the passage of the Community Living Assistance Services and Supports ("CLASS") Act as part of the 2010 Affordable Care Act, the intense controversy over its sustainability, and its subsequent repeal in 2012.

Should long-term care be a public or private responsibility, or some combination of the two? To what extent should government funds be expended to provide long-term care, or to provide a mechanism for the public to fund its own needs? For the poor, and for those who spend enough assets on long-term care to become poor, these questions have mostly been answered through Medicaid's provision of long-term care benefits, though issues remain concerning its institutional bias. Persons with substantial wealth can usually finance their own care. For those in between who wish to provide for current or anticipated future needs, however, there is considerable debate about government policy. At one end, some argue that long-term care is a private responsibility that families should plan for and shoulder with some combination of informal family care, expenditures of personal assets, and purchase of private long-term care insurance to avoid impoverishment. At the other extreme, some argue for a mandatory social insurance program analogous to Social Security in which all would be covered and all would pay.

The CLASS Act seemingly split the difference by creating an innovative yet controversial voluntary, government-run long-term care insurance program. Supporters, including many unions and consumer advocates, praised the advantages of a program that focused on home care over institutional care, and in which people could not be denied coverage or charged higher premiums based on health or disability, claiming that it would ultimately save Medicaid dollars. Opponents decried it as a "Ponzi scheme," and actuaries warned of an "insurance death spiral" in which adverse selection would result in an insurance pool with mostly high risk

(continued)

EXHIBIT 17.1 Policy illustration—the CLASS Act (*continued*)

people. A 2011 paper by the President of the Society of Actuaries concluded in part that:

> The CLASS Act attempts to solve problems in America's long-term care financing system without first accounting for why that system has failed. CLASS addresses the symptoms (problems of access, quality, reimbursement, and institutional bias) without fixing the problem (easy access to Medicaid-funded LTC).
>
> (Moses, 2011, p. 22)

After more than 2 years of policy debate, unable to meet the statutory requirement that the program remain fiscally solvent for at least 75 years, the CLASS Act was repealed in December 2012. The repeal does not, fortunately, return the policy debate to square one, as the process has generated a great deal of data and discussion. The country is still far from consensus on policy issues, however, and the same legislation that repealed CLASS created a new 15-person Long-Term Care Commission to define the long-term care problem; examine financing, delivery, and workforce issues around long-term care; and present its findings to Congress.

The 15-member Commission released its final report to Congress in September of 2013. In addition to findings and recommendations on service delivery and workforce issues, the Commission addressed financing by offering two highly opposing approaches: private insurance options and social insurance (Commission on Long-Term Care, 2013). Private options would include allowing families and individuals to set up savings funds analogous to the existing section 529 education savings accounts. Social insurance options would include modifications to both Medicare and Medicaid. It is significant to note that the report was endorsed by only nine of the 15 commissioners, leaving a strong minority in opposition to the report and doing nothing to resolve the issue of the government's role in long-term care financing.

The Commission recognized that extensive work remains to be done and recommended creation of a longer tenured national advisory committee to continue its work and to "ensure provision of a sustainable and integrated range of public and private financing mechanisms to meet the needs of people with functional and cognitive impairments" (Commission on Long-Term Care, 2013). It also recommended that the 2015 White House Conference on Aging be convened in coordination with the National Disability Council to consider long-term care.

Any such commission or conference faces the daunting task of determining the proper role of government in national long-term care policy in light of the policy debate between individual and collective responsibility. Major options include expanding Medicaid, providing additional incentives for the purchase of private long-term care insurance, and revisiting a public long-term care insurance program, either a voluntary program like CLASS or a mandatory program such as that required for acute care under ACA (Weiner, 2013). As a policy matter, the issue is likely to endure for many more years.

SERVICE ORGANIZATION AND DELIVERY POLICY

Public policies may also authorize the development of direct health care services and mandate how these services will be organized and delivered. At the federal level, for example, the Veterans Administration Medical Centers, nursing homes, and associated inpatient and outpatient health services were established pursuant to these types of public policies. At the state level, these types of policies created hospitals and group homes for persons with chronic mental illnesses (see Chapter 13 for more details about chronic mental illness).

Most of these public policies have limited their service organization and delivery authority to specific settings of care, such as acute care and outpatient care, and do not focus on how care might be coordinated between these settings and settings outside their authority. For example, the question of how services within and outside the DVA should be coordinated for veterans who use services in both systems has attracted intermittent attention in the health policy arena over the past several decades, but to date there are no public policy resolutions or program directives to enhance such service coordination for our nation's veterans, including those with long-term care needs.

For the broader long-term care population in the United States, service organization and delivery has been most hampered by the lack of effective public policy directives regarding how Medicare-funded and Medicaid-funded services might be organized and delivered to achieve greater coordination from the viewpoint of a continuum of care. This so-called "dually eligible" population of over 9 million individuals utilizes a disproportionate share of both Medicare and Medicaid resources, in part because they are more likely to be in fair or poor health and have multiple chronic conditions (Neuman, Lyons, Rentas, & Rowland, 2012). Policy changes intended to better coordinate care are difficult to enact because the same dually eligible individuals often receive similar Medicare-reimbursed and Medicaid-reimbursed services over the same time period (Fortinsky, Fenster, & Judge, 2004), and the two programs operate independently, with separate administrative and service limitations that do not address complex needs in an integrated fashion (Gold, Jacobson, & Garfield, 2012).

Efforts to improve service coordination for the dually eligible population began in earnest with passage of the Balanced Budget Act of 1997 (BBA 97; Pub. L. 105-33, 111 Stat. 251). BBA 97 legislation facilitated the development of integrated delivery models incorporating acute and long-term care services for persons aged 55 and older eligible for long-stay nursing facility care. These were based on the original On Lok model founded in San Francisco in the early 1970s to provide comprehensive services in the community to keep frail seniors in their homes and on subsequent demonstration sites for the Program of All-Inclusive Care for the Elderly (PACE). The BBA 97 also enabled Medicare and Medicaid funds to be pooled in order to improve service organization and delivery at PACE provider sites. Health and long-term care providers and insurers who partner to form PACE sites must be willing to accept the negotiated financing terms set by federal Medicare and state Medicaid programs in order to participate as a PACE site. These terms are usually expressed as per enrollee per month capitated rates. According to the National PACE Association's website (www.npaonline.org; accessed June 1, 2015), in 2015 there were a total of 114 operational PACE sites in 32 states, including demonstration sites established before the 1997 BBA authorized the PACE model as a permanently recognized provider type under both the Medicare and Medicaid programs. The 1997 BBA legislation related to PACE site replication represented the most progressive move to date toward health service organization and delivery for the dually eligible population on a national level and helped set the stage for future advances in public policy that would improve further the continuum of care for persons with long-term care needs. Nevertheless, PACE replication sites are limited in number and in geographic scope compared to the size and needs of the growing dually eligible national population.

More than a decade would pass until additional federal legislation was enacted to help stimulate state-level creativity in organizing and delivering care to the dually eligible population. As a direct result of the 2010 Patient Protection and Affordable Care Act (ACA; Pub. L. 111-148, 124 Stat. 119), in early 2011 the Center for Medicare and Medicaid Innovation (also created by ACA) at the Centers for Medicare & Medicaid Services (CMS) issued a call for proposals from state Medicaid programs and their designated partners to begin integrating health and long-term care services for this costly population. As of August of 2013, as the 3-year "State Demonstration Proposals to Integrate Care and Align Financing for Dual Eligible Beneficiaries" were beginning, seven state proposals had been approved, 14 were pending with CMS, and several others were considering seeking federal approval. This shift marks an important step forward in the policy-making process because the evidence generated by these state-level social experiments or demonstration programs will be able to further inform policy development for all states as the dually eligible population continues to grow in size.

For Medicare beneficiaries more broadly, there is a modest history of using Medicare financing options to influence changes in the organization and delivery of health care services. Under the Tax Equity and Fiscal Responsibility Act of 1982 (TEFRA; Pub. L. 97-248, 96 Stat. 324), health maintenance organizations (HMOs) and other health care providers were encouraged to assume risk for Medicare beneficiaries by providing mandatory and, optionally, additional services for a capitated rate. TEFRA initiated a voluntary movement of HMOs and other health care providers into the Medicare managed care market. This 1982 TEFRA initiative stamped the imprint of the private sector on Medicare; depending on one's political viewpoint, federal Medicare policy formulation since then has been viewed as either the "privatization" of Medicare or as offering consumers more choices for Medicare coverage.

The movement toward private sector involvement in Medicare accelerated with passage of the 1997 BBA, which codified these private sector Medicare plans as Medicare + Choice, or Medicare Part C plans. Between 1997 and 2001, many Medicare managed care providers left the market primarily due to insufficient Medicare reimbursement rates (Brown & Sparer, 2003). In an effort to stimulate private sector interest in Medicare participation, in 2003 Congress passed into law the Medicare Prescription Drug, Improvement, and Modernization Act

(Pub. L. 108-173, 117 Stat. 2066) which re-branded Medicare + Choice as "Medicare Advantage" (MA). More important, this new law offered health care providers and insurers financial incentives to sponsor an MA plan by providing surplus reimbursement rates as high as 14% above traditional Medicare reimbursement rates. In response, the MA marketplace expanded rapidly, and plan providers offered expanded benefits to traditional Medicare enrollees, including participation at reduced rates in the Medicare prescription drug program that began in 2006 under the same 2003 legislation. These new policy-driven incentives led to a rapid rise in the enrollment of Medicare beneficiaries into MA plans; the number of MA enrollees almost tripled between 2005 and 2013, growing from 5.3 million to 14.8 million, the latter figure representing 29% of the entire Medicare population (Mathematica Policy Research, 2013).

In yet another policy decision made by Congress in response to concerns about surplus MA plan payments in times of fiscal austerity, under the 2010 PPAC Act, surplus payments to MA plans will be gradually reduced over a 10-year period. It remains to be seen whether this policy decision will result in MA plans pulling out of the market and a reduction in the number or proportion of Medicare beneficiaries enrolled in MA plans.

From the viewpoint of Medicare beneficiaries with long-term care needs, MA plans were also expected to offer or improve service coordination for their enrollees, which could theoretically help link acute and postacute care with long-term care services. However, recent evidence has shown that MA enrollees with disabilities, some of whom might require long-term care services, were disenrolling disproportionately from MA plans due to lack of satisfaction with MA services given their needs (Riley, 2012). Therefore, it remains unclear whether the trajectory of MA plan growth will be matched by noticeable and helpful changes in the organization and delivery of services to those individuals in the Medicare population with long-term care needs.

REGULATORY POLICY

An important example of public policy in the area of regulation is the Omnibus Budget Reconciliation Act of 1987 (OBRA '87; Pub. L. 100-203, 101 Stat. 1330), which significantly strengthened the capacity of federal and state agencies to monitor the quality of care provided in long-stay nursing facilities. OBRA '87 was implemented following a highly influential report from the Institute of Medicine (IOM) that demonstrated the delivery of relatively poor quality of care in America's long-stay nursing facilities and proposed a comprehensive set of recommendations designed to improve nursing facility quality (Institute of Medicine, 1986). As a result of OBRA '87, a uniform resident assessment and care planning system, called the Minimum Data Set (MDS), was implemented nationwide in 1991. Though designed to create individual care plans and improve quality, the MDS data was also envisioned to be used for regulatory functions (Institute of Medicine, 1986).

Riding on the momentum created by OBRA '87, CMS has continued to engage in efforts to initiate **regulatory policy** to improve quality throughout all sectors of health care. In 2002, CMS implemented the Nursing Home Quality Initiative as a matter of public policy. This initiative involves the publication and wide dissemination of quality-of-care "report cards" for all nursing facilities, using data from the MDS form developed as a result of OBRA '87. A similar effort in home health care followed in 2003 when CMS introduced the Home Health Quality Initiative (HHQI) policy initiative, with quality "report cards" based on data from the federally mandated Outcome and Assessment Information Set (OASIS). Though these initiatives are not necessarily aimed at coordinating services, they mark important advances in quality monitoring because they focus on health-related outcomes (e.g., whether or not the service recipient improved in level of functioning or experienced a decrease in the severity of symptoms).

Despite many improvements in quality of care that accompanied implementation of the MDS, there have been persistent criticisms that introduction of this measure did not deal with quality-of-life issues, did not require residents to be interviewed directly, and that state and federal regulatory systems remained too limited (Rahman & Applebaum, 2009). A new version of the MDS, version 3.0, was implemented in 2010 and featured additional quality-of-life measures, resident interviews, and more standardized assessment procedures. It remains to be seen how effectively the revised MDS will address regulatory concerns.

HEALTH RESOURCES POLICY

The Public Health Service Act of 1944 (Pub. L. 78-410, 58 Stat. 682) was amended in 1973 to authorize the establishment of the Health Resources and Services Administration (HRSA), located within the U.S. Department of Health and Human Services. Just as CMS is responsible for implementing policies formulated by Congress in the realm of health financing policies, HRSA is responsible for implementing policies formulated by Congress in the realm of health resources policies. HRSA includes a Bureau of Health Professions, which is responsible for helping to assure access to quality health care professionals in all geographic areas and to all segments of society through appropriate preparation, composition, and distribution of the health professions workforce. This bureau also has the responsibility to improve access to a diverse and culturally competent and sensitive health professions workforce.

Over the past decade, pressing health resource policy issues affecting the population with long-term care needs have included a shortage of nurses, a shortage of paraprofessionals such as home health aides and personal care providers, and a shortage of health care providers with expertise in geriatrics (Kovner, Mezey, & Harrington, 2002; Sochalski, 2002; Ward & Berkowitz, 2002). In addition to initiatives implemented by the health professions themselves, HRSA has responsibility for implementing training programs to attract individuals to work in these professions. This personnel shortage may also be viewed as a crisis in the recruitment and retention of a qualified long-term care workforce (Lehning & Austin, 2010). A highly publicized and potentially influential 2008 report from the IOM warned that the nation faces an impending workforce crisis as the number of older patients with complex medical needs outstrips the ability of health care providers to care for them (Institute of Medicine, 2008). Although not limited to long-term care needs, this report made numerous recommendations about expanding both the number of workers and training opportunities of the health care workforce.

The workforce shortage is particularly acute in long-term home care. The Bureau of Labor Statistics projects that personal care aides and home health aides will be the first- and second-fastest growing professions between 2010 and 2020. Their ranks are projected to grow by about 70% during those years, a rate much faster than the anticipated growth for most occupations (U.S. Department of Labor, 2013). Total direct care workers in long-term care, both in-home and nursing home workers, are projected to reach nearly 5 million by the year 2020, more than all teachers from kindergarten through 12th grade (3.9 million) or law enforcement and public safety workers (3.7 million) (Paraprofessional Healthcare Institute, 2013).

Projected openings do not necessarily mean that there will be enough workers to fill the jobs. Policy makers and health care employers at all levels are struggling to fill openings, particularly in the lower paid long-term care occupations, typically staffed by people who are less likely to have health insurance and benefits and more likely to live below the poverty line than the typical worker (Institute for the Future of Aging Services, 2007).

Finally, it is important to note that **health resources policy** also pertains to building construction to support the delivery of health care services. For example, the Hill–Burton Act passed shortly after World War II funded the construction of acute care hospitals and nursing homes. The National Housing Act and its amendments in the 1950s created apartment-style living quarters for persons with disabilities and older adults, with design features intended to support their independent living (see Chapters 9 and 10). These policies were concerned with the "bricks and mortar," or "hardware" aspects of health resources, and offered little guidance about the types and organization of services to be provided within the walls of the facilities (i.e., the "software").

LEVELS OF LONG-TERM CARE POLICY DEVELOPMENT

Long-term care policy formation occurs primarily in four places: federal, state, and local (including county and municipal) governments and nongovernmental entities, such as foundations and insurance companies that sell long-term care insurance. Within each of the three levels of government, policy may be made in any of the three branches: the executive branch (including the governor and agency heads), the legislative body, and the judicial system. Interactions among levels and branches of government can be both complex and overlapping, with lines between policy formation and implementation often blurred. In particular, the federal/state interplay on the most consequential policy issues deserves further exploration.

At the federal level, although Congress formulates much public policy, responsibility for policy implementation and oversight is in the hands of federal and state agencies. Jurisdictional responsibility for implementing and monitoring legislation varies considerably, with federal responsibility for Medicare; joint federal/state responsibility for Medicaid; and federal, state, and local responsibility for the Older Americans Act.

In addition to federal legislation, players at the federal level influence policy through funding (e.g., the Older Americans Act) and regulation (e.g., quality standards for nursing homes and approval of state Medicaid Waivers for HCBS). However, states are generally recognized to be the primary drivers of long-term care policy, providing not only 50 "laboratories" for testing public policy that may result in creative approaches, but also substantial variation from state to state (Kane, 2008).

At the state level, legislatures formulate policies regarding how certain federal monies, such as Medicaid, will be expended and how state revenues might be used to fund new initiatives. Over the past 25 years, a large number of state legislatures have enacted policies to expand HCBS for persons with long-term care needs. In some cases, financial and medical eligibility criteria for state-funded programs created by these policies are less stringent than eligibility criteria for Medicaid-funded HCBS, although the range of services available under these programs may be identical. State legislatures also formulate policies specifying sources of revenue that could be used to pay for new programs. For example, in Pennsylvania, state lottery revenues are earmarked for social and health-related services available to the older population.

Public policies at the state level are also formulated by executive branch agency administrators to modify the ways that Medicaid funds are used to make services available to the state's population. For example, all Medicaid Waiver programs originate at the state level by agency administrators who must formulate evidence that expanded HCBS will be cost-effective in relation to long-stay nursing facility or other institutional services for the projected population served. State applications are submitted to federal administrators at CMS for approval, but state-level policy makers are responsible for introducing these initiatives.

State executive branch organizations vary considerably, and policy making for different target populations often occurs in different agencies, such as those for aging, developmental disabilities, mental health disabilities, and visual disabilities, with inconsistent results. Since the year 2000, many states, such as Texas, Vermont, and Washington, have undergone consolidation and reorganization of executive branch agencies to establish better budget and policy controls over long-term care policy making and implementation. States with greater consolidation of policy, financing, quality, and service delivery functions have reaped the benefits of more flexibility, including the ability to manage institutional services and HCBS within the same agency, and better cross-fertilization of ideas and practices across disability groups (Kane, 2008).

To illustrate the extent to which state agency administrators have formulated public policy for persons with long-term care needs, Table 17.1 shows the number of states that had operational Medicaid HCBS Waiver programs in federal fiscal year (FFY) 2010 for different populations with long-term care needs, total Medicaid expenditures for all states combined for each HCBS Waiver program in FFY 2010, and the compound annual growth rate in Medicaid expenditures from FFY 2005 through FFY 2010 for each of these HCBS Waiver programs for all states combined. In FFY 2010, nearly every state had a Medicaid Waiver program for people with intellectual or developmental disabilities (ID/DD). Most states ($n = 42$) had a combined Medicaid Waiver program for older people and younger adults with disabilities (A/D); 27 states had a separate Medicaid Waiver program for younger adults with disabilities. Fewer states had separate Medicaid Waiver programs solely for older people ($n = 12$), people with HIV/AIDS ($n = 14$), medically fragile children ($n = 13$), and people with brain injuries ($n = 19$). In states with multiple Medicaid Waiver programs, each program has its own administrative structure within state government (Eiken, Burwell, Gold, & Sredl, 2011). A few states, including Vermont, Rhode Island, and Arizona, have moved from separate population-based waivers to "comprehensive" waivers providing similar services for all populations regardless of type of disability.

Table 17.1 also shows that in FFY 2010 the largest amount of HCBS Medicaid Waiver program expenditures by a wide margin were for programs for the population with ID/DD (more than $25 billion), followed by A/D waiver programs (more than $6 billion). Nearly every type of Medicaid Waiver program experienced significant growth in expenditures between FFY 2005 and FFY 2010, especially programs for older people, people with brain injuries, and medically fragile children. In contrast, during this period the Medicaid Waiver program for people with HIV/AIDS experienced a substantial decline in expenditures. Taken together, trends in these Medicaid HCBS Waiver programs stand as the most visible and pervasive examples of how persons with long-term care needs have benefited from public policy formulation and implementation at the state level designed to maintain individuals in their own homes or other community settings outside of nursing facilities.

A related area of state public policy formulation is the appropriate balance between long-stay nursing facility and home- and community-based care, because Medicaid spending on nursing facility care nationwide accounts for more than 60% of all Medicaid long-term care spending for older adults and people with physical disabilities. That percentage varies dramatically by state, with states as low as 35% (Minnesota) and others as high as 86% (North Dakota) in 2011 (Eiken, Sredl, Gold, Kasten, Burwell, & Saucier, 2013). Most states have attempted to redress this imbalance by crafting public policies to limit the supply of nursing facility beds and to expand home- and community-based care programs for different long-term care populations, as shown in Table 17.1. A few states have taken more dramatic measures to reduce nursing facility service, especially Oregon, which for many years has aggressively moved to discharge nursing facility residents and serve them in a variety of community-based settings, including adult foster care and assisted living (Hernandez, 2007).

There are numerous examples of joint federal/state policy initiatives in the long-term care arena. In many cases, the federal government sets strategic policy and offers opportunities through grant funding for pilot or demonstration projects in the states. One early example is the Cash and Counseling demonstration of the 1990s, which tested the efficacy of offering cash allowances or personally

TABLE 17.1 Number of States With Medicaid Home and Community-Based Services (HCBS) Waiver Programs for Different Targeted Long-Term Care Populations, Total Expenditures for Each Program, Federal Fiscal Year (FY) 2010, and Compound Annual Growth Rate for Each Program from FY 2005 to FY 2010

TARGETED LONG-TERM CARE POPULATION	NUMBER OF STATES WITH MEDICAID HCBS WAIVER PROGRAM* FY 2010	TOTAL EXPENDITURES, FY 2010 (IN MILLIONS)	COMPOUND ANNUAL GROWTH RATE, FY 2005–FY 2010 (%)
People with intellectual disabilities only	9	$5,902	9.4
People with developmental disabilities (including intellectual disabilities)	38**	$19,474	8.1
Older people and people with physical disabilities	42**	$6,078	9.9
People with physical disabilities only	27	$1,796	12.2
Older people only	12	$1,022	16.4
People with brain injuries	19	$505	17.7
People with HIV/AIDS	14	$54	-2.8
Medically fragile children	13	$189	20.7
People with mental illness	4	$26	19.1

Source: Eiken et al. (2011).

*In some categories, Vermont, Rhode Island, and Arizona are not included in these numbers, but provide similar services as part of a comprehensive Section 1115 waiver.

**Includes the District of Columbia (Washington, DC).

controlled budgets to long-term care consumers in place of agency-provided services. With initial funds from the Robert Wood Johnson Foundation, Medicaid consumers were allowed to choose the type and amount of services that best met their needs, emphasizing consumer choice and control over a more bureaucratic model (Doty, Mahoney, & Simon-Rusinowitz, 2007). The successful results of the demonstration in four states (Arkansas, Florida, New Jersey, and New York) have led to replication of the cash and counseling practice in many other states over the past decade.

Another prominent example of a federal/state program designed to increase the use of HCBS and reduce the use of institutional services is the Money Follows the Person (MFP) demonstration, initiated in 2005 with funding through CMS. MFP increases state Medicaid-matching funds to support nursing home residents who wish to return to the community and to strengthen states' capacity for serving community long-term care needs (Mathematica Policy Research, 2012). As of 2011, forty-four states and the District of Columbia had implemented MFP demonstration programs, with three new states awarded planning grants in 2012.

A third example of joint federal/state long-term care policy making is the collaborative effort between CMS and the federal Administration for Community Living (ACL), formerly the Administration on Aging, to streamline access to long-term care services through state-level Aging and Disability Resource Centers (ADRCs). CMS and ACL set the national vision of streamlined access to information and support for community-based living in 2003 by providing start-up funds to 12 states to implement the vision, adding additional states in succeeding years. With continued federal support, including $50 million in funding through the 2010 Affordable Care Act, there are now ADRCs in every state. States, in turn, have implemented the consumer-driven system of long-term supports in a variety of ways through cooperation among state and local organizations and are expected to sustain the initiatives with state funding (O'Shaughnessy, 2011).

Public policy at all levels of government can also be formulated in the judicial branch through litigation and court decisions. In 1999, the U.S. Supreme Court decided the landmark case *Olmstead v. L.C.*, 527 U.S. 581 (1999), which held that the retention of persons with disabilities in institutional settings in Georgia was discriminatory and a violation of the Americans with Disabilities Act of 1990 (Pub. L. 101-336, 104 Stat. 327). The *Olmstead* decision exemplifies a federal-level public policy that has had far-reaching effects for the population with long-term care needs. Mentioned in earlier chapters, *Olmstead* directed states to discharge from institutional settings individuals with developmental and mental health disabilities who were determined to be candidates for residence in community-based settings, provided that the placement could be reasonably accommodated and taking into account resources available to the state and the needs of others with similar disabilities.

The *Olmstead* ruling has had implications far beyond the population with mental health disabilities that was the subject of the original litigation. It stimulated more than 60 "*Olmstead* lawsuits" in at least 28 states raising similar issues on behalf of people who are institutionalized or at risk of institutionalization because of a lack of community-based services (Ng, Wong, & Harrington, 2009). It has also set in motion formal state-level initiatives across the country, frequently known as state "*Olmstead* plans" to transition eligible individuals with a wide range of disabilities from long-stay nursing facilities and other institutional facilities into community settings, as well as to make communities more accessible to persons with disabilities. And it has set the stage for meaningful change in the organization and delivery of services to persons with long-term care needs, particularly in states where movement in this direction has been incremental at best.

At the local level, elected officials with legislative authority include county commissioners and city and town officials. Examples of policy initiatives that can help address persons with long-term care needs are integration of Older Americans Act funds with county-level funds to help coordinate long-term care services and local referenda that propose to fund long-term care services from new local tax revenues (see Chapter 16 for more information about local tax levy financing programs for long-term care services). Agencies that typically make policy on a local level include Area Agencies on Aging and Centers for Independent Living, each of which serves constituents with long-term care needs. Local housing policy also has a significant effect on the ability of persons with long-term care needs to live in the community (see Chapter 9). In the judicial arena, local probate or surrogate courts make policy about conservatorships and other means of meeting the long-term care needs of people deemed unable to make those decisions for themselves. It is beyond the scope of this chapter to elaborate fully on county and local levels of policy making, but these efforts are increasing with the aging of the baby boom cohort, as their health-related needs and those of their parents are replacing concerns related to educating their children in local schools.

Although most long-term care policy is made in the governmental arena, private interests also play a role, by themselves or in partnership with government policy. For example, insurance companies that sell long-term care insurance make policies about underwriting, coverage, benefit levels, and cost that in turn affect the propensity of customers to provide for their own future needs through insurance. The question is often asked to what extent long-term care financing should be a private responsibility versus a public one (Stevenson et al., 2010)? Government policy makers may encourage certain marketplace arrangements through regulation or through public–private partnerships, such as the Partnership for Long-Term Care, a joint effort by many state governments and private insurers that encourages citizens to protect their assets through long-term care insurance while saving the state Medicaid long-term care costs. To date, over 40 states have set up Partnership programs in the hopes of relieving pressure on overburdened Medicaid programs (Andrews, 2009). Some private foundations, such as the Robert Wood Johnson Foundation, aim to improve health policy and practice, including long-term care policy, through philanthropy and grant-making activities.

WHO INFLUENCES PUBLIC POLICY DEVELOPMENT?

Public policy unfolds in a highly interactive political process, regardless of the level of policy formulation. In fact, by its very nature, the entire legislative process often begins with ideas or proposals submitted to policy makers by citizens or by leaders of interest groups representing specific constituencies. As legislative policy makers and their staff members disseminate drafts of bills, interest groups with opposing views insert themselves into the political policy-making process. The same is true for policy making in the executive branch, as constituents and advocates press their cases in the regulation and rule-making process, and at the judicial level, where legal briefs are filed and arguments made by opposing sides. Thus, public policy development is influenced first and foremost by interest group politics, with many groups operating from a position of enlightened self-interest.

Although the players in the long-term care political process are many, four of the most prominent categories include (a) long-term care recipients and their families; (b) advocacy groups for older adults or people with various disabilities; (c) long-term care providers of all types, including institutions or facilities such as nursing homes as well as the long-term care workforce, which may or may not be unionized; and (d) taxpayers who pay the cost of publicly financed long-term care.

The number of interest groups influencing the long-term care public policy development process has grown dramatically over the past two decades. In addition to numerous national and local organizations focused on issues pertaining to older adults, there are also scores of interest groups representing other populations needing long-term care (e.g., persons with developmental disabilities or mental illness), and they have focused their lobbying efforts primarily on maximizing independent living, assuring equal access to employment and educational opportunities, and optimizing community inclusion of persons with disabilities. The efforts of these interest groups were rewarded with the passage of the Americans with Disabilities Act of 1990, a landmark piece of federal legislation for persons with disabilities (although not exclusively addressing long-term care needs of this population).

From the viewpoint of elected or appointed officials charged with formulating public policy, it is welcome when many or most such interest groups support a similar position on a policy topic. In the past, this rarely occurred in practice; however, during the 1960s sufficient consensus was reached, so that major federal legislation was passed affecting the vast majority of individuals with long-term care needs. Three of the most influential public policies that directly affect most individuals with long-term care needs to this day—Medicare, Medicaid, and the Older Americans Act—were born at the same time in 1965. At that time, the national political climate was highly oriented toward addressing the needs of the population, in areas of life as wide ranging as civil rights and health-related needs. In the health arena, federal policy makers responded to calls from a broad spectrum of interest groups, ranging from consumer advocacy organizations to physician and hospital professional associations, to craft public policy that would offer health insurance coverage (Medicare) and a wide range of community-based supportive services (Older Americans Act) to older Americans, as well as health insurance coverage for poor Americans and people with disabilities of all ages (Medicaid). At that time, costs associated with implementing these new public policies were not viewed as insurmountable barriers, blunting potential opposition from taxpayer interest groups.

Since that time, however, taxpayer interests have become much more prominent in long-term care policy debate at all levels, as the affordability of public benefits has decreased. Cost containment has become a major feature of the political climate surrounding public policy development, while the population requiring long-term care has grown dramatically and the range and expertise of interest groups have grown in size and political effectiveness. Medicare and Medicaid grew rapidly, straining federal and state budgets, and the Older Americans Act has not fully achieved its initial goals due to insufficient financing. Consequently, there has been a much less unified view in recent years, compared to the situation in 1965, that the needs of vulnerable populations should be an overriding priority in fashioning public policy.

At the state level, interest groups representing different populations requiring long-term care influence elected officials and state agency administrators responsible for formulating public policy. Advocacy groups representing persons with developmental disabilities and younger adults with physical disabilities are particularly influential in promoting policy options that lead to independent living. Medicaid HCBS Waiver programs have served as important instruments of public policy in this regard, and Table 17.1 provides evidence in terms of expenditures about the relative success different interest groups have had in helping grow these programs for their constituents requiring long-term care.

Providers of long-term care are not only a crucial link between those who receive long-term care services and those who pay for them, but also constitute interest groups in their own right, with a significant impact on long-term care policy decision making. Within the provider community there are a wide range of diverse interests. Providers include both institutions (such as nursing homes, assisted living facilities, group homes, and home health agencies) and individual paid providers. Individual members of the long-term care workforce include professionals, such as nurses, social workers, occupational and physical therapists, and direct care workers, who provide most of the "hands-on" care, including certified nursing aides, home health aides, and personal care workers (Stone & Harahan, 2010).

There is no one "provider" voice in the long-term care policy debate. Institutions, such as nursing homes, have a strong interest in preserving the viability of their business model and receiving adequate compensation for their services. Home health agencies have a stronger interest in supporting rebalancing efforts that support more long-term care users in community living settings. Unionized workforce members have a difficult time preserving wage and benefit progress when Medicare and Medicaid are slashing reimbursements to their employers. And the direct care workforce, who form the centerpiece of the long-term care workforce, often experience the most low-wage, low-benefit, high turnover, physically and emotionally demanding work (Stone & Harahan, 2010; U.S. Department of Labor, 2013). They struggle to affect policy in ways that allow them to achieve parity with hospital or other institutional workers.

From the viewpoint of the continuum of care framework, a critical lesson from this brief review of interest groups is that as long as different constituency groups act only in their own interests and influence policy development accordingly, the promise of more unified long-term care policies and a true continuum of care for the entire population with long-term care needs may continue to be elusive. As such groups work together and find a common voice in the policy debates, the prospect of more comprehensive and effective policy making grows brighter.

EMERGING TRENDS IN LONG-TERM CARE POLICY

This chapter began with the admonition that there is no unifying long-term care policy in the United States. The encouraging news is that consensus is steadily building at every level of policy making, and among numerous public policy stakeholders, regarding a core set of guiding principles and practices for long-term care organization, delivery, and financing. These principles and practices hold promise for the establishment of more consistent long-term care policies across the states and ultimately for the achievement of better outcomes for individuals and families needing and receiving long-term care services."

"REBALANCING" OR "BALANCING" THE SYSTEM

Much of the policy debate over long-term care is now framed in terms of its effect on the institutional/HCBS balance, with policy aimed at serving more people in and providing more funds for community-based settings. Federal and state governments and advocacy groups are setting goals for "rebalancing," that is, shifting long-term care utilization and expenditures toward community settings where most people prefer to receive services, and creating a more equitable system that is largely oriented away from institutions while assuring quality in all components of the system (Robison, Shugrue, Porter, Fortinsky, & Curry, 2012; see Case Study 17.1).

Case Study 17.1: Can This Widow Remain in Her Home?

Mary Masterson is 77 years old, widowed, lives alone at home, and relies on Social Security checks as well as a small annuity payment for her monthly income. She has been hospitalized twice in the past year for flare-ups of congestive heart failure, and once for a fall in her bathroom. She has been weakened considerably by numerous other medical conditions, including diabetes, arthritis, and osteoporosis, and has started to have trouble remembering to take all 10 of her prescription medications. She also takes several nonprescription over-the-counter medications and vitamins that are not documented in her medical record. Her daughter, who lives nearby, works fulltime and does her best to help her mother with daily activities and to provide transportation for Mary, but is increasingly concerned about her mother's ability to live independently. Mary desperately wants to remain in her home but is aware of her declining health. Mary is also aware that her daughter's health is becoming jeopardized by helping her while holding down a full-time job.

Because of her recent hospitalizations and increasing weakness and forgetfulness, at her last office visit Mary's primary care physician told her and her daughter that they should consider looking into getting help in the home if Mary is to continue living there. Mary's physician did not know about where she or her daughter should begin to find out about possible help.

Case Study Discussion Question:

1. What long-term care policies and programs discussed in this chapter might be useful for Mary and her daughter?

The primary policy mechanisms for enhancing noninstitutional supports are Medicaid's three main HCBS programs: waivers, personal care services, and the home health benefit. As noted earlier in this chapter, states have had widely varying success in rebalancing by reducing the percentage of Medicaid spending that pays for institutional care. A recent study of 15 years' worth of Medicaid data (1995–2009) explains some of this variance in terms of state policy decisions (Kaye, 2012). The study concluded that gradual rebalancing can greatly reduce overall spending compared to what would have been spent in the absence of rebalancing, while increasing the number of people receiving services. More rapid rebalancing may also serve more people, but risks spending more than would have been needed without rebalancing due to the infrastructure costs of the new programs. States that cut HCBS spending due to budget crises, the worst approach, are likely to increase overall long-term care spending as people who lose home services are institutionalized (Kaye, 2012).

INDEPENDENT LIVING/CARE IN THE LEAST RESTRICTIVE SETTING

The *Olmstead* decision was a major catalyst in the effort to allow all people with long-term care needs to live and receive supports in a setting that allows them the most autonomy. Independent living has for many years been a major thrust of interest groups representing children and younger adults with physical, mental, and developmental disabilities requiring long-term care. Needs of older adults have more often been cast by interest groups as favoring home- and community-based care over long-stay nursing facility care. Independent living across the life span has become a more effective principle in the political process surrounding policy development because it speaks directly to a public policy goal from the perspective of those whose needs are the true targets of public policy.

CONSUMER CHOICE AND SELF-DIRECTION

Because the Cash and Counseling demonstration proved so effective in allowing consumers to direct their own care, many more long-term care services and supports now allow consumers to choose options that best meet their own needs. Over the past 15 years, a number of states, including Connecticut, Georgia, Maine, and Minnesota, have introduced consumer direction into Medicaid-funded home-based services for persons with disabilities. Younger persons with disabilities have spurred these initiatives to a much greater degree than have older persons. These initiatives enable care recipients themselves to arrange and supervise personal care assistants and other in-home service workers without the requirement of an independent care supervisor or case manager. Although numerous challenges remain in assuring that consumer direction yields high-quality care and controlled expenditures, this principle is becoming more popular with older adults over time as the baby boom cohort advances in age (Ruggiano, 2012).

MORE INTERACTION/LESS COMPETITION BETWEEN OLDER ADULTS AND PEOPLE WITH DISABILITIES

Finally, more people with long-term care needs across the age and disability spectrum, along with their families and advocates, have come to appreciate similarities in need and outcome and have worked together to effect desired policy change. Similarly, government agencies supporting persons with long-term care needs are moving away from silos toward more integrated policy development, by merging or working together more cooperatively. In particular, there is growing support for limiting age-specific and disability-specific Medicaid waivers and moving toward more universal criteria based on need rather than age or disability. As of 2012, for example, Arizona, Rhode Island, and Vermont operated their HCBS Waiver programs through comprehensive global Section 1115 waivers that cover all populations and services (Kaiser Commission on Medicaid and the Uninsured, 2012).

SUMMARY

Although long-term care policy development remains fragmented in the early part of the 21st century in the United States, several trends toward coordination of efforts among policy stakeholders appear evident in terms of the dimensions of the long-term care policy development cube discussed in this chapter. State governments remain clearly in the lead among levels of innovative long-term care policy development, but federal government–initiated financial incentives to states to create novel ways of organizing and delivering home- and community-based long-term care to Medicaid-eligible populations have grown considerably under the 2010 Affordable Care Act. Additionally, the MFP program that began in 2005 is driven by federal financial support to states to discharge Medicaid-eligible nursing home residents and create new housing and supportive service infrastructures to accommodate these individuals in the community. States are responding by developing more coordinated service systems involving governmental and nongovernmental health and social service providers. Although state variation in long-term care policy development will remain the rule, within states there are numerous signs that long-term care is less fragmented than in past decades and that state comparisons will be possible in broad terms across programs, such as MFP, that were initially stimulated by infusions of federal financial support stemming from federal long-term care policy directives.

Along the dimension of who influences policy, the rise of the person-centered care movement has resulted in the active and growing involvement of service recipients and families, advocates, and providers in shaping their states' long-term care policies and programs oriented toward increasingly coordinated home- and community-based care and away from long-term nursing home care. Providers of nursing facility services are being challenged through state policy to diversify their service lines into the community setting at the risk of losing occupancy and failing financially due to decreased demand for their type of long-term care service delivery.

In terms of long-term care resource policy, workforce development policies to stimulate the supply of long-term care professionals and paraprofessionals will likely grow in frequency and creativity across the states. Federal and state resource policies that in previous decades supported construction of facilities to provide centralized long-term care are being replaced by education and training programs for new and experienced health and social providers needed to serve growing numbers of long-term care recipients living at home with substantial levels of disability.

Finally, regulatory policy development in long-term care appears to be increasingly outcome oriented, with coordinated care systems held accountable for well-defined performance markers established at the inception of programs and tracked routinely by state and federal governmental agencies, primarily those representing Medicaid insurance coverage for long-term care. Increased movement toward integration of Medicare and Medicaid financing, organization, and delivery for dually eligible populations within states is being accompanied by required performance measures chosen and regulated by states but monitored as well by the federal CMS. These regulatory trends are intended to maximize community involvement, functional capacity, and independent living among long-term care populations. More traditional regulations, such as survey and certification of nursing facilities and home health agencies to ensure minimum levels of care quality, will likely continue in their present forms, but "report cards" available to the public will facilitate competition to improve care quality. In growing areas of long-term care, such as assisted living and companion and homemaker services, regulation policies are less well-developed but are likely to grow quickly in the near future and include mandatory quality-of care-related requirements combined with outcome-oriented performance measures that are likely to be developed by a variety of policy stakeholders with vested interests in these types of services.

In conclusion, states will continue to serve as policy development laboratories and enforcers of long-term care regulations, but other levels of governmental and nongovernmental stakeholders will retain vested interests in how long-term care is financed, organized, and delivered. Trends toward greater involvement of service recipients and families, advocates, and the general public in long-term care policy development, and the slow rise of market forces as competition among providers is encouraged with outcome-based performance measures, are likely to dominate the long-term care policy development landscape well into the 21st century.

DISCUSSION QUESTIONS

1. Name the four primary types of public policy affecting long-term care, and describe the primary function of each.
2. What is the role of interest groups in creating long-term care policy?
3. How and why is long-term care policy in the United States so fragmented?
4. Describe three principles you would favor to guide long-term care policy making, and discuss the effect that each would have on legislation. Cite examples if possible.

ADDITIONAL RESOURCES

PUBLICATION

AARP Public Policy Institute. (2008). *A balancing act: State long-term care reform* (Report #2008-10). Washington, DC: AARP.

KEY WEBSITES

Administration for Community Living www.acl.gov
Centers for Medicare & Medicaid Services www.cms.gov
Kaiser Family Foundation Health Policy http://kff.org

REFERENCES

Andrews, M. (2009). "Partnership" policies for long-term care hold promise—and pitfalls. *Kaiser Health News*. Retrieved from www.kaiserhealthnews.org/Stories/2009/July/10/LTC.aspx

Brown, L. D., & Sparer, M. S. (2003). Poor program's progress: The unanticipated politics of Medicaid policy. *Health Affairs, 22*, 31–44.

Commission on Long-Term Care. (2013, September 30). *Report to the Congress*. Retrieved from http://www.gpo.gov/fdsys/pkg/GPO-LTCCOMMISSION/pdf/GPO-LTCCOMMISSION.pdf

Doty, P., Mahoney, K. J., & Simon-Rusinowitz, L. (2007). Designing the cash and counseling demonstration and evaluation. *Health Sciences Research, 42*(1), 378–396.

Eiken, S., Burwell, B., Gold, L., & Sredl, K. (2011). *Medicaid 1915(c) waiver expenditures: 2011 update*. Cambridge, MA: Thomson Reuters.

Eiken, S., Sredl, K., Gold, L., Kasten, J., Burwell, B., & Saucier, P. (2013). *Medicaid expenditures for long-term services and supports in 2011*. Cambridge, MA: Truven Health Analytics.

Fortinsky, R. H. (2005). Public policy. In C. J. Evashwick (Ed.), *The continuum of long-term care* (3rd ed., pp. 265–277). Stamford CT: Delmar Thomson Learning.

Fortinsky, R. H., Fenster, J. R., & Judge, J. O. (2004). Medicare and Medicaid home health and Medicaid waiver services for dually eligible older adults: Risk factors for use and correlates of expenditures. *The Gerontologist, 44*, 739–749.

Gold, M. R., Jacobson, G. A., & Garfield, R. C. (2012). There is little experience and limited data to support policy making on integrated care for dual eligible. *Health Affairs, 31*(6), 1176–1185.

Hernandez, M. (2007). Assisted living and residential care in Oregon: Two decades of state policy, supply, and Medicaid participation trends. *The Gerontologist, 47*, 118–124.

Institute for the Future of Aging Services. (2007). *The long-term care workforce: Can the crisis be fixed?* Washington, DC: Institute for the Future of Aging Services.

Institute of Medicine (1986). *Improving the quality of care in nursing homes*. Washington, DC: National Academies Press.

Institute of Medicine (2008). *Retooling for an aging America: Building the healthcare workforce*. Washington, DC: National Academies Press.

Kaiser Commission on Medicaid and the Uninsured. (2012). *Medicaid home and community based service programs: 2009 data update*. Kaiser Family Foundation. Retrieved from http://kaiserfamilyfoundation.files.wordpress.com/2013/01/7720-06.pdf

Kane, R. (2008). States as architects and drivers of long-term-care reform for older people. *Generations, 32*(3), 47–52.

Kaye, H. S. (2012). Gradual rebalancing of Medicaid long-term services and supports saves money and serves more people, statistical model shows. *Health Affairs, 31*(6), 1195–1203.

Kovner, C. T., Mezey, M., & Harrington, C. (2002). Who cares for older adults? Workforce implications of an aging society. *Health Affairs, 21*, 78–89.

Lehning, A. J., & Austin, M. J. (2010). Long-term care in the United States: Policy themes and promising practices. *Journal of Gerontological Social Work, 53*, 43–63.

Mathematica Policy Research. (2012). *Money Follows the Person: 2011 annual evaluation report*. Cambridge, MA: Mathematica Policy Research.

Mathematica Policy Research. (2013). *Tracking Medicare health and prescription drug plans monthly report for June 2013*. Princeton, NJ: Mathematica Policy Research.

Miller, E. A., Mor, V., & Clark, M. (2010). Reforming long-term care in the United States: Findings from a national survey of specialists. *The Gerontologist, 50*, 238–252.

Moses, S. A. (2011, January). *The CLASS Act and the future of long-term care financing*. Presented at the Society of Actuaries Living to 100 Symposium, Orlando, FL.

Neuman, P., Lyons, B., Rentas, J., & Rowland, D. (2012). Dx for a careful approach to moving dual-eligible beneficiaries into managed care plans. *Health Affairs, 31*(6), 1186–1194.

Ng, T., Wong, A., & Harrington, C. (2009). *Home and community-based services: Introduction to Olmstead lawsuits and Olmstead plans*. University of California at San Francisco Center for Personal Assistance Services. Retrieved from www.pascenter.org/olmstead/

O'Shaughnessy, C. (2011). Aging and disability resource centers can help consumers navigate the maze of long-term services and supports. *Generations, 35*(1), 64–68.

Oriol, W. E. (1985). *The complex cube of long-term care*. Washington, DC: American Health Planning Association.

Paraprofessional Healthcare Institute (PHI). (2013). *Occupational projections for direct-care workers 2010–2020*. New York, NY: PHI.

Rahman, A. N., & Applebaum, R. A. (2009). The nursing home minimum data set assessment instrument: Manifest functions and unintended consequences—Past, present, and future. *The Gerontologist, 49*, 727–735.

Riley, G. F. (2012). Impact of continued biased disenrollment from the Medicare Advantage program to fee-for-service. *Medicare and Medicaid Research Review, 2*(4). doi:http://dx.doi.org/10.5600/mmrr.002.04.a08

Robison, J., Shugrue, N., Porter, M., Fortinsky, R., & Curry, L. (2012). Transition from home care to nursing home: Unmet needs in a home- and community-based program for older adults. *Journal of Aging and Social Policy, 24*(3), 251–270.

Ruggiano, N. (2012). Consumer direction in long-term care policy: Overcoming barriers to promoting older adults' opportunity for self-direction. *Journal of Gerontological Social Work, 55*(2), 146–159.

Shapiro, F. R., & Epstein, J. (2006). *The Yale book of quotations*. New Haven, CT: Yale University Press.

Sochalski, J. (2002). Nursing shortage redux: Turning the corner on an enduring problem. *Health Affairs, 21*, 157–164.

Stevenson, D. G., Cohen, M. A., Tell, E. J., & Burwell, B. (2010). The complementarity of public and private long-term care coverage. *Health Affairs, 29*, 96–101.

Stone, R., & Harahan, M. F. (2010). Improving the long-term care workforce serving older adults. *Health Affairs, 29*(1), 109–115.

U.S. Department of Labor, Bureau of Labor Statistics. (2013). *Occupational outlook handbook: 2012–13 edition*. Washington, DC: Department of Labor. Retrieved from www.bls.gov/oco/

Ward, D., & Berkowitz, B. (2002). Arching the flood: How to bridge the gap between nursing schools and hospitals. *Health Affairs*, 21, 42–52.

Weiner, J. M. (2013). After CLASS: The long-term care commission's search for a solution. *Health Affairs*, 32(5), 831–834.

Epilogue

PAMELA B. TEASTER
GRAHAM D. ROWLES

> *We are such stuff as dreams are made on; and our little life is rounded with a sleep.*
>
> —William Shakespeare, *The Tempest,* Act 4, Scene 1

In Chapter 1, you were introduced to three family stories, those of Grandma Brewster, Anders Swenson, and Mark A. Lincoln. We return to them now. These stories, using pseudonyms, were based on real-life situations and represent care recipients, caregivers, and the promise and peril of caregiving. In the first scenario, Grandma Brewster experienced fairly conventional circumstances when encountering the continuum of care. Recall that she was a widow but had loving family surrounding her. Her family rallied to help provide her care needs until it became unrealistic for them to do so and unsafe for her. She was fortunate, in that she retained her cognitive capacity, but her physical health declined over time. Dying peacefully and painlessly in one's sleep at a good old age and surrounded by loving family, as Grandma Brewster did, is the dream of philosophers (Callahan, 1995), poets (Bryant & Stilson, 1817), and, we suspect, most of you who have read this book.

The second story, of Anders Swenson, born with Down syndrome, portrays a person who was fortunate enough to be embraced by smart, caring, and dedicated parents. Anders's parents embodied current concepts of supported decision making and person-centered care discussed within this text, demonstrating how ideas have crystallized into action precisely because of the population of persons with intellectual disabilities whom Anders represents. Though his father's life was shortened by leukemia, Anders remains supported by his mother while living with an enviable degree of independence. His care trajectory, up to the point at which the vignette concludes, is a model of what it means to care. What is left unknown, but alluded to, is what happens to Anders should his mother predecease him. According to a statewide survey of 3,256 households in Kentucky conducted by Rowles, Sands, and Horne (2007), parents' concern about what happens to their child with a disability should the parents die prior to the child is viewed by the citizens of the Commonwealth as the number one issue with respect to the needs of older adults, outstripping transportation, housing, and employment needs.

The final vignette about Mark Lincoln not only involves more travails than the others but also necessitates informed and caring family members directing his care, albeit at a distance. Mark's path of physical and mental decline is not unusual for adults who survive to be among the oldest-old, although women typically live longer than their male spouses and more than one child is usually helping with care provision for an older parent (often, one lives near the parent and others are more distant). Evident in this scenario are the multiple responsibilities that daughter Kaylee had to assume—those of caring for her father, her spouse, her children, and completing her work. Attending to these responsibilities required delicate balancing and rebalancing. Mark was fortunate, in that Kaylee worked hard to preserve his autonomy, especially by supporting his great desire to remain in the town in which he had resided his entire adult life, even though it meant that they were not immediately present in each other's lives. Though Mark might have lived longer had he not experienced a precipitous fall, his trajectory of decline would most likely have eventually necessitated his move from an assisted living facility to a nursing home. At that juncture, he may have had to leave his beloved town so that Kaylee and her family could better direct his care.

Modeled in the three introductory vignettes and at the heart of this volume is the complex interplay of ideas and action involved in the ethical imperative to care for others (see, especially, Chapter 14). We return to the ethical and moral imperative to care for others here in our epilogue, as we believe it undergirds how we have approached our presentation of the continuum of long-term care. We embrace the types of care delineated by Tronto (2001), as we find them especially applicable to all those involved in addressing the long-term care of adults, from the hands-on friend to the policy maker in Washington. Fisher and Tronto (1990, p. 40) define care as a "species activity," one that is "a distinct and human activity that includes everything that we do to maintain, continue, and repair our 'world' so that we can live in it as well as possible." Care is de facto complex and incorporates individual as well as societal concerns. Care as an activity demands a level of quality commensurate with the values of those engaged in it. Care occurs in community and facility settings and is not relegated to one gender, one socioeconomic level, one government, or one society. Care, yes, long-term care, embraces and involves all.

Important and instructive to readers of this text on the continuum of long-term care are the phases of care that Tronto identifies, phases that explicate how to go about care work as well as its relational dimensions: caring about caring for, caregiving, and care receiving. "Caring about" is paying attention to the need for care. Members of Grandma Brewster's family cared about her. The phase involving "caring for" occurs when someone or something assumes the responsibility for meeting an identified need, for example, when Anders Swenson's parents arranged for Anders to be well educated so that he could be as autonomous as possible. "Caregiving" is the phase in which individuals, organizations, or both meet a person's material needs, such as when a nursing assistant at Mark Lincoln's assisted living facility measured and brought him medications, an activity that Tronto notes involves a level of competence (Tronto, 2001).

Finally, and an aspect too often unaddressed but critical for a full understanding of the care collective (Teaster, 2003), is "care receiving," which involves the response to and responsiveness of the recipient of care. Instructive for the continuum of care discussed by the authors of this book, "In a way, since any single act of care may alter the situation and produce new needs for care, the caring process in this way comes full circle, with responsiveness requiring more attentiveness" (Tronto, 2001, p. 63).

Thus, our ethical imperative—to do what we ought to do—in the provision of long-term care is to continue to develop new ways of care that are responsive to the needs of those who are involved in providing it and receiving it. In this way, we again realize that caring for others is not new at all, but rather the needs of care recipients have changed. Never before in history have persons lived so long with disabilities and with chronic disease. Families and family structures are more diverse than in previous generations, and, so, with their changing nature create the concomitant changes in the way that they can and do care for others. The very same can be said for financial structures and for governments.

Changes in the way we treat care recipients and alterations in the structures and pathways for doing so are notable and instructive. Haber (Chapter 2) reminds us that early structures for care seem harsh to 21st-century readers, but she is careful to emphasize that the nature of this phase of care, long-term care, is an iterative one. Consequently, from a model of care in which those in need were regarded as vagrants and driven from one town to another, we have enlarged our thinking far beyond the conception of warehousing, far beyond treating an illness or condition, and toward the idea that long-term care should have at its center the care recipient who directs care and is supported in doing so. We are embracing a model in which residential long-term care is regarded, not as purely medicalized, but rather, a model that holds central the concept of "home," as well as the honor and respect afforded it (Holstein & Mitzen, 2001; Thomas, 1994). Moreover, in an attempt to involve both care providers and care recipients, new technologies and conceptions (e.g., smart homes, assistive devices, robots) are no longer aspirational care but instead part of the evolving reality of long-term care. And who knows what might exist on the horizon? For example, will Droids deliver our medicines to us, within an hour of contacting a virtual pharmacy?

We conclude our epilogue as we began it, stressing that in the next iteration of long-term care in an aging society, the individuals, the systems, and the approaches about which we have written will morph significantly from those presented here. We maintain that the core values of respect for elders, optimizing health and well-being, preserving autonomy, and promoting responsibility to and responsivity to costs, both pecuniary and human, make imperative that at the center of long-term care in an aging society is the person for whom we care about, we care for, and give care. In doing so, and bound together in the care collective, care receiving directs it all.

REFERENCES

Bryant, W. C., & Stilson, W. (1817). *Thanatopsis*. New York, NY: G.P. Putnam's Sons.

Callahan, D. (1995). *Setting limits: Medical goals in an aging society with a response to my critics*. Washington, DC: Georgetown University Press.

Fisher, B., & Tronto, J. (1990). Toward a feminist theory of caring. In E. K. Abel & M. K. Nelson (Eds.), *Circles of care: Work and identity in women's lives* (pp. 35–62). Albany, NY: State University of New York Press.

Holstein, M., & Mitzen, P. (Eds.). (2001). *Ethics in community-based elder care*. New York, NY: Springer Publishing Company.

Rowles, G. D., Sands, H. R., & Horne, A. S. (2007). *Kentucky Elder Readiness Initiative: A survey of Commonwealth residents, preliminary statewide report*. Lexington, KY: Graduate Center for Gerontology, University of Kentucky.

Teaster, P. B. (2003). When the state takes over a life: The public guardian as public administrator. *Public Administration Review*, *63*(4), 396–404.

Thomas, W. (1994). *The Eden Alternative: Nature, hope and nursing homes*. Sherburne, NY: Eden Alternative Foundation.

Tronto, J. C. (2001). An ethic of care. In M. B. Holstein & P. B. Mitzen (Eds.), *Ethics in community- based elder care* (pp. 60–68), New York, NY: Springer Publishing Company.

Glossary

Accelerated Death Benefit *(16)* A life insurance death benefit paid in cash in advance of death and provided tax-free. This option is included with some life insurance policies, although individuals may have to pay an additional or extra premium to utilize this product.

Accessory Dwelling Units *(9)* These arrangements are rooms or a set of rooms in a single-family home in a single-family area designed or arranged for use as a separate dwelling unit and have been established by law.

Activities of Daily Living (ADLs; *1, 6***)** A widely used set of measures of an individual's ability to function independently. This measure is customarily broken down into two components. Personal activities of daily living (PADLs) involve assistance with getting out of bed, bathing, dressing, toileting, feeding, and grooming. Instrumental activities of daily living (IADLs) involve grocery shopping, managing medication, meal preparation, transportation, managing finances, legal assistance, mobility, and arranging appointments.

Administrative Law *(15)* Law created by legislatures to delegate to administrative (regulatory) agencies, which are part of the executive branch of government, that allow the power to fill in vital, particular details necessary for the implementation and enforcement of a broad statutory objective.

Adult Day Services (ADS; *7***)** Often referred to as adult day care, these are programs that support the health, nutritional, social, and daily living needs of adults with functional limitations in a group setting during daytime hours.

Adult Day Services Plus *(7)* Case management services offered to adult day services (ADS) participants and their families, including counseling, education, support, and referral. These services are provided by trained staff members in ADS, such as social workers and nurses. The goal of ADS Plus is to improve family caregiver well-being, increase service utilization, and reduce costly nursing home placement.

Affordable Care Act *(5)* The Patient Protection and Affordable Care Act (ACA) addresses preventable hospital readmissions through various programs. These include the Community Care Transitions Program, which targets improved discharge planning and follow-up care in the community for persons at high risk of readmission and the Medicare Independence at Home Demonstration Program, which will test the use of interdisciplinary teams in the home for persons with chronic conditions and disabilities.

Age-Friendly Neighborhoods or Communities *(1)* A neighborhood set up to help older adults live safely, enjoy good health, and stay involved in their lives. Examples include well-lit sidewalks, buildings with automatic door openers and elevators, and older adult-friendly neighborhood activities (e.g., volunteerism, walking).

Aging in Place *(1, 7, 8, 9, 13)* Sustaining residence in a specific location at home or within the community while experiencing changes associated with aging.

Almshouse *(2)* First founded in Boston in 1664, the almshouse became a well-known and easily recognized institution in scores of cities throughout the 18th century. Within its walls could be found the most problematic of the needy: the orphan without a family, the insane whose care had become too difficult for his or her kin, the widow who had outlived her relatives, and the diseased whose sickness was incapacitating.

Ambient Assisted Living *(8)* Ambient assisted living (AAL) environments move beyond the components of smart homes because they create a residence in which the environment is embedded with a single integrated system of networked sensors that are programmed specifically to the needs and preferences of the user(s).

Americans with Disabilities Act (ADA; 2**)** A law enacted in 1990 and amended in 2009 that prohibits discrimination based on disability. Under this legislation, discrimination against a disabled person is illegal with regard to employment, transportation, public accommodations, communications, and government activities.

Area Agencies on Aging *(7)* Established under the Older Americans Act (OAA) in 1973, Area Agencies on Aging (AAA) are located across the United States and provide a wide range of services to older adults and their families, such as helping to arrange for home- and community-based services, empowering informed decision making, and linking needs with services to foster independence.

Assisted Living *(4, 13)* A residential option that provides help with activities of daily living (i.e., bathing, dressing, transferring, toileting, eating) and instrumental activities of daily living (i.e., housework, preparing meals, taking medication, shopping for groceries, using the telephone, paying bills, and caring for pets) for those who do not yet require full-time medical service or skilled nursing care.

Assisted living settings are privately occupied apartments with features, such as a full bathroom, kitchenette, and locking doors, in which the residents control their space, furnishings, time of activities, and care plans. Assisted living settings are recognized as residential options that bridge home care and more intensive skilled care provided in a nursing facility. Definitions have continued to evolve because uniform standards across states do not exist.

Assistive Technology *(8)* Any device or piece of equipment, whether acquired commercially off the shelf, modified, or customized, that is used to increase, maintain, or improve functional capabilities of individuals with disabilities (Technology-Related Assistance for Individuals with Disabilities Act of 1988—P.L. 100–407).

Attachment to Place *(9)* Attachment to place is indicated by the large percentage of older persons who have stayed in their homes for long periods of time. It is at the core of people's housing preferences and a significant influence on their views about long-term care.

Autonomy *(14)* Freedom from external control or influence; maintaining independence in order to pursue and act on life choices. In the health care arena, this term is often associated with the writing of John Stuart Mill.

Board and Care or Adult Foster Care *(10)* Type of old-model assisted living property found in smaller buildings. The accommodations are more likely to consist of bedroom-like units. Multiple residents may have to share toilet facilities and/or bathing areas found in another part of the building.

Capitation *(5, 16)* A system in which a provider is reimbursed a specific amount annually by the insurer for each patient enrolled in the plan.

Care and Caring *(1)* *Care* (n.) is the provision of what is necessary for the health, welfare, maintenance, and protection of someone or something. One could conceivably take care to care. *Care* (v.) is to look after or attend to the needs of others or to be concerned about their needs. *Caring* is displaying kindness and concern for others, particularly persons who are in need of care.

Caregiving Career *(4)* A perspective on caregiving that views the family caregiving process as a dynamic and complex trajectory in which the caregiver experiences a number of "transitions," or turning points, as the chronic disability of the care recipient progresses and generally worsens. Such transitions include preparation for and acquisition of the caregiver role, enactment of associated tasks and responsibilities, and eventual disengagement from the role.

Case Mix *(16)* Type or mix of patients residing in nursing homes. The nursing home rate is set by each state and is typically determined by a range of factors used to assess the likely amount of assistance that a person would need (termed "case mix"), facility staffing levels, capital costs, geographical area, type of services covered, and funds available to the state.

Case-Mix Groups *(5)* Categories of patients with certain characteristics and utilization patterns that are used to justify the health insurance prospective payment system rate codes.

Centers for Medicare & Medicaid Services (CMS; *6***)** The U.S. federal agency previously known as the Health Care Financing Administration (HCFA) that administers Medicare, Medicaid, and the Children's Hospital Insurance Program. It is located within the U.S. Department of Health and Human Services and provides coverage for 100 million people annually.

Certificate of Need *(15)* Many states require applicants to demonstrate an adequate public need for a particular health service, such as a nursing home, before that service is created or expanded in the proposed place.

Certification *(11)* Credential required for reimbursement by Medicare or Medicaid. Certification for one or both programs is recommended by the State Survey Agency, which conducts an inspection of the facility in question and provides its findings to a Centers for Medicare & Medicaid Services (CMS) Regional Office. The vast majority of nursing homes are dually certified, accepting both Medicare and Medicaid. Because Medicare is regulated by the federal government, the CMS Regional Office makes the final determination regarding certification.

Chronic Illness *(1)* A chronic illness is one that lasts three months or more, as defined by the U.S. National Center for Health Statistics. Typically, it is not possible to prevent or cure chronic diseases; they do not "go away."

Civil Tort Remedies *(15)* Civil tort remedies, namely, money damages, remain available to particular consumers who are seriously injured because of private provider negligence or intentional misconduct, such as physical abuse or financial exploitation.

Collaborative Care *(12)* Collaborative care is a key to success for members of the provision of hospice care and includes the hospice team, the long-term care team, family and friends of the patient, and the patient.

Combined Models of Care *(7)* Programs that combine the social and medical models of care in long-term care settings, such as ADS. Although many ADS centers may describe themselves as either "social" or "medical" models, most centers have at least some elements in their programming that indicate an amalgamation of both approaches to care.

Common Law *(15)* Principles or doctrines enunciated by the courts, on a gradual case-by-case basis, to resolve specific controversies and guide future behavior in circumstances where existing constitutional, statutory, or administrative law does not provide sufficiently clear direction.

Community Living *(13)* To live in one's own home or in a community-based homelike setting.

Comorbidity *(6, 13)* The existence of two disorders or illnesses occurring in the same person, simultaneously or sequentially.

Compensatory Damages *(15)* Sum of money awarded in a civil action by a court to indemnify a person for a particular loss, detriment, or injury suffered as a result of the unlawful conduct of another.

Compression of Morbidity *(1)* Concept that derives from Fries' hypothesis that the burden of lifetime illness may be compressed into a shorter period before the time of death if the age of onset of the first chronic infirmity can be postponed.

Conditions of Coverage and Conditions of Participation *(5)* Health care organizations are required to meet certain eligibility criteria established by the Centers for Medicare & Medicaid Services which allows them to begin or continue involvement in Medicare and Medicaid programs. These conditions include staffing, reporting requirements, quality-assurance obligations, and structural characteristics, among other conditions. Compliance is expensive and requires strict adherence by all staff to Medicare policies and processes.

Constitutional Law *(15)* Written documents that establish the foundational building blocks for the national government and the separate state and local governments. A constitution (including the ways in which the courts interpret and apply the meaning of its language) delineates the powers and constraints of a government vis-à-vis its own citizens.

Consumer-Directed Home Care *(5)* A model of care (also known as *cash and counseling*) that enables home care consumers to recruit and manage their personal care helpers, who may be paid family members. Such care promotes individual choice about type and provision of home care services.

Continuing-Care Retirement Communities *(10)* Originally known as life care communities, these age-restricted properties accommodate older persons with all levels of assistance and care needs in independent living, assisted living, and skilled nursing facilities found on a campus-like setting.

Critical Gerontology *(14)* Critical gerontology is a framework for scientific understanding that cannot be divorced from either values or subjective aspects of the lived experience of the older person.

Culture Change Movement *(1, 4)* A philosophy resulting from a recent shift in focus of long-term care from uniformity and medical issues toward client-centered care and quality of life.

Dementia *(13)* A mental health disorder indicating significant cognitive impairment in memory, reasoning, and thinking abilities.

Demographic Transition *(1)* This refers to the transition from high birth and death rates to low birth and death rates as a country develops from a pre-industrial to an industrialized economic system.

Depression *(13)* A mental health disorder that includes a prolonged state of feelings of hopelessness and unhappiness that involves symptoms of depressed mood, loss of interest or pleasure in previously enjoyed activities, decreased motivation, feelings of guilt or low self-worth, disturbed sleep or appetite, low energy, and poor concentration.

Design Interventions *(1)* Innovative designs for living spaces that allow a person with a disability to be able to live and navigate in a space. Examples are grab bars in showers, lowered sinks, and extra-wide door frames.

Disability *(1, 6)* A physical or mental impairment that substantially limits one or more major life activities.

Dual Eligibility *(11)* Term used to describe persons who qualify for both Medicare and Medicaid. According to the Centers for Medicare & Medicaid Services, the term "dual eligible" refers to those utilizing "Medicare Part A and/or Part B who are eligible for some form of Medicaid benefit." For example, Medicare pays days 1 to 20 in a skilled nursing facility, and Medicaid may cover the daily copay for days 21 to 100, depending on an individual's beneficiary group.

Dual Specialization *(4)* This phenomena occurs when direct care staff provide personal, hands-on care, and when family members remain responsible for a care-recipient's psychosocial support.

Durable Medical Equipment *(6)* Certain medical equipment such as a walker, wheelchair, or hospital bed that is ordered by a doctor for use in the home.

Eden Alternative *(4)* An institutional long-term care alternative designed to improve quality of life for residents by creating a more homelike environment. Instead, the Eden Alternative aims to create a vibrant surrounding where residents can interact with their surroundings. To this end, animals are a regular part of the lives of the residents, and gardens are planted for both dietary benefits as well as social and spiritual reasons. Additionally, children play a large role in the Eden Alternative, and planned programs such as onsite childcare centers and summer day camps are included.

Elder Abuse *(3)* The infliction of physical, emotional, or psychological harm, financial exploitation, sexual abuse, or intentional or unintentional neglect.

Elder-Friendly Communities *(9)* Aging-friendly cities that combine the design features inherent in Universal Design along with the neighborhood-based service models of NORCs or the Village Model. A crucial component of Elder-Friendly Communities that links well-designed home and streets with surrounding accessible services is pedestrian-friendliness.

End-of-Life Care *(12)* Hospice care for those who have chronic disease(s) or symptoms or functional impairments that are irreversible and progressive that may lead to death.

English Poor Law *(2)* Passed in 1601, colonial governments decreed that families were required to provide for the needs of their relatives; kin were to take in the orphaned or infirm; and the old were to be sheltered alongside their offspring.

Environmental Design *(8)* Physical configuration of built environments.

Epidemiologic Transition *(1)* Resulting from demographic transitions (e.g., an increasingly older population), this involves phases of changes in patterns of illness and death.

Ethical Analysis *(14)* Employing systematic methods of ethical examination to examine moral problems.

Ethical Dilemma *(14)* An ethical dilemma concerns the need to choose from among two or more morally acceptable options or between equally unacceptable courses of action, when one choice precludes selection of another.

Evidence-Based Intervention *(3)* An intervention with proven feasibility, efficacy, and effectiveness with many groups of persons based on extensive research and evaluation.

Executive Branch *(17)* The branch of government, whether federal, state, or local, that is responsible for implementing and enforcing laws passed by the legislative branch and interpreted by the judicial branch.

Fall *(13)* An inadvertent and sudden postural change toward the ground. Often the sign of other health problems or environmental hazards.

Family Caregivers *(3)* Generally unpaid individuals who care for family members or friends requiring assistance due to illness or disability.

Family Involvement *(4)* Family involvement is multidimensional and can include a range of components such as visiting, provision of personal or instrumental care, socioemotional support, monitoring, decision making, and advocacy.

Federal Nursing Home Reform Act (OBRA '87; *2***)** The Omnibus Budget Reconciliation Act of 1987 (OBRA '87) was passed by the U.S. Congress to address insufficient care provided by nursing homes. The act requires that nursing homes receiving federal aid provide for each resident: individualized personal care plans, access to high quality of life and care, freedom from unnecessary restraints—physical or chemical, and maintenance of daily activities (e.g., walking and bathing).

Feminist Ethics *(14)* An approach to ethics building upon the notion that traditional ethical theorizing undervalues the unique moral experience of women and so seeks to use a feminist approach to transform it.

Financing Policy *(17)* A policy that specifies funding mechanisms to pay for health-related services, the types of services that are eligible to receive funding, and the target populations eligible for funded services.

Formal Care *(1, 3)* Care provided in home and facility settings that includes but is not limited to visiting nurse services, homemaker services, respite care, and home health aide services. Care outside the home setting includes, but is not limited to, adult day care, senior centers, assisted living, nursing home care, and hospital care.

Functional Independent Measure (FIM®; *6***)** A systematic tool for measuring disability and determining how much assistance an individual requires with activities of daily living (ADLs).

Functional Status *(1)* Measures of ability using tools that assess dimensions of an individual's physical, cognitive, emotional, and social status.

Geographical Dispersion *(1)* This concept has to do with the diffusion of where family members are located in proximity to where an older person is living. Greater dispersion creates more caregiving at a distance.

Gerontechnology *(8)* The study of older adult use and interaction with technology.

Health Resources Policy *(17)* Public policy relating to resources available for the provision of health care, including access to quality care and health care professionals.

Hierarchical Compensatory Model *(3)* A model that describes a preferred order as to who provides care. This order is typically based on the closeness of family relationships. Family care is expected to be performed by the closest available and capable family member with spouses as first choice, followed by children, other kin, and friends or neighbors, with formal helpers last. For older adults who are more severely impaired and/or need more assistance, or when the availability of informal helpers is limited, there is more fluidity and overlap between family and paid helpers.

Hill–Burton Act *(2)* An Act passed by the U.S. Congress in 1946 that supported the construction of hospitals.

Home- and Community-Based Services (HCBS; *16***)** A grouping of in-home services, community services, and residential services that maximize consumer independence, such as assisted living.

Home and Community-Based Services Waiver Program *(16)* One of many options available to states to allow the provision of long-term care services in home and community based settings under the Medicaid Program. States may offer a variety of services under this waiver program.

Home Care *(5)* Nonmedical services that are provided in the home such as light housekeeping, meal preparation, and medication reminders.

Home Health Care *(5)* Services that are usually medical or clinical and are provided in the home, including various therapies and skilled nursing care.

Home Modifications *(9)* Physical adaptations to home environments in areas such as entryways, kitchens, bathrooms, and stairwells, that can make it safer and easier to perform tasks and carry out activities of daily living.

Homer Folks *(2)* A welfare advocate of the 1930s who argued against the notion that the old should end their days in the almshouse simply because they were poor.

Hospice *(12)* A model for quality compassionate care for people facing a life-limiting illness. Hospice provides expert medical care, pain management, and emotional and spiritual support expressly tailored to the patient's needs and wishes.

Hospice-Supported Consult Model *(12)* A model of hospice care for residents of long-term care that allows palliative care consultant providers from a contracted hospice to consult upon the request of the resident's attending physician. This model often draws on the existing hospice–community relationship.

Household Issues *(14)* Problems that arise in the everyday worlds of older people, family members, the community, and long-term care settings.

Housing and Services Model *(10)* A model whereby states license or certify both the appearance of new-model apartment-like properties and their long-term care assistance. Few states regulate assisted living as a service model.

Impairment *(1)* A general or specific weakening, damage, or deterioration, usually the result of injury or disease.

Independent Living Communities *(10)* Once labeled as "congregate housing," these residence-like settings provide hotel-like hospitality services such as meals, housekeeping, laundry, transportation, and recreational activities. Independent living communities are less likely than assisted living residences to accommodate physically or cognitively impaired residents.

Informal Care *(1, 3)* Assistance provided by a broadly defined and inclusive network of family and friends. This network is typically unpaid and includes care by spouses and unmarried partners; biological and nonbiological children, grandchildren, nieces, nephews, and other family kin, neighbors, church members, and close friends.

Informed Consent *(14)* Freely and clearly given consent by a legally competent individual to participate in a medical procedure or other activity.

Inpatient Rehabilitation Facility (IRF; *1, 6***)** An inpatient rehabilitation hospital or a rehabilitation unit in an acute care hospital that is licensed under state laws to provide intensive rehabilitative services.

Instrumental Activities of Daily Living (IADLs; *6***)** Activities that are required for one to live independently (e.g., preparing meals, doing housework, shopping, managing money, using the telephone, and taking medication).

Intellectual and Developmental Disabilities (IDD; *7***)** Disabilities that impact intellectual and/or physical functioning and adaptive behavior, often resulting in substantial limitations in learning, self-care, independence, and self-sufficiency.

Intentional Community *(9)* A community that offers an alternative to aging in place in a lifelong home. In an intentional community, residents commit to living together with a shared common purpose or goal. Although older adults may have to relocate from their homes in this model, they can remain in their own communities, accessing familiar services, maintaining meaningful relationships, and maximizing their financial resources. Intentional communities that provide for supportive aging include cohousing and shared housing.

Interest Group *(17)* A group with common interests that uses advocacy to influence opinion among policy makers or outcomes of public policy. Also known as an advocacy group or a lobbying group.

Intergenerational Programming *(7)* As defined by the National Council on Aging, intergenerational programs are activities or programs that increase cooperation, interaction, or exchange between generations, particularly the younger and the older generations.

International Classification of Functioning, Disability, and Health (ICF; ***6*****)** The World Health Organization's (WHO) framework for measuring health and disability at both individual and population levels.

Judicial Branch *(17)* The court systems, whether federal, state, or local, that are responsible for interpreting laws passed by the legislative branch and enforced by the executive branch.

Kerr–Mills Act *(2)* Legislation passed in 1960 that allocated funds for older adults who, although not poor enough to receive old-age assistance, still could not cover the cost of their medical care; the Act also provided support for those in skilled nursing homes. The Act dictated that states, rather than the federal government, determined the level of eligibility.

Kin Dependency *(4)* The situation that occurs when informal caregivers continue to provide the bulk of assistance even with the introduction of formal support.

Legislative Branch *(17)* The branch of government, whether federal, state, or local, that is responsible for making the laws that are enforced by the executive branch and interpreted by the judicial branch.

"Less Eligibility" *(2)* A principle that dictated that the environment of the almshouse could not meet or exceed conditions found beyond the institution's walls so that "unworthy individuals" would not seek shelter when they could theoretically provide for themselves. The upshot was that conditions within institutions were purposefully intended to be inhospitable.

Lifestyle *(1)* The way in which a person lives, such as living a healthy lifestyle to optimize aging.

Local Levy Programs *(16)* These programs offer an alternative funding mechanism for long-term care that is used in some states. In part because of the limited funds available from the Older Americans Act for in-home services, and in part because some states have no or limited state home-care programs, local tax levies have been used as an approach to fill the financial gap.

Long-Term Care *(1)* Environmental, medical, and personal care plus social support provided on a recurring or continuing basis to persons who have lost or never acquired some degree of functional capacity. A variety of medical and nonmedical services that help meet health or personal needs for people who have an illness or disability.

Long-Term Care Community-Based Model *(12)* A model used by nursing homes to integrate palliative care best practices through education and/or a designated team that operates within the community setting.

Long-Term Care Continuum *(1)* An integrated model of long-term care providing a comprehensive and linked set of environmental conditions, informal assistance, and formal supports and services focused on meeting the health, personal care, and social needs of individuals as their capabilities and circumstances change.

Long-Term Care Insurance *(16)* Insurance that emerged in the 1970s as a way to decrease the burden on public funding mechanisms to reduce financing risk for consumers, and to fill the gap in long-term care coverage left by Medicare.

Long-Term Care System *(1)* A linked set of supports, services, and integrating mechanisms that guide and track the provision of both informal and formal physical and mental health and social services to persons in need of long-term care.

Managed Care Plans *(5)* Insurance plans that provide health insurance by contracting with providers and facilities to develop a network that offers less expensive care to enrollees than conventional insurance plans offer. There are three main kinds of managed care plans, which include health maintenance organizations (HMO), preferred provider organizations (PPO), and point of service plans (POS).

Medicaid *(2, 10, 16)* A joint federal–state program enacted in 1965 and designed to pay health costs of individuals with limited income and resources.

Medicaid Home and Community-Based Waiver Programs *(5, 7)* State-administered programs that allow for federal Medicaid reimbursement for services to individuals in need (e.g., older adults, individuals with disabilities) that are not traditionally covered through Medicaid. These services are designed to facilitate community living and often include adult day and home health services.

Medical Model *(7)* Often viewed as the traditional model in long-term care settings, such as nursing homes and adult day centers, medical models of care focus primarily on the physical and medical needs of individuals. Medical models of care often combine elements of social models of care, and combined models are increasingly becoming more the norm.

Medicare *(2, 16)* Enacted in 1965 under Title 18 of the Social Security Act, Medicare is a federal program designed to provide insurance coverage for those older adults with a demonstrated work history that qualifies them for Social Security benefits.

Medicare Managed Care Plans or Medicare Advantage Plans *(5, 6)* Public and private organizations contract with the Centers for Medicare & Medicaid

Services (CMS) to provide four different health insurance options as part of Medicare Part C, including coordinated care or traditional managed care, which consists of health maintenance organizations (HMO), preferred provider organizations (PPO), and point of service plans (POS); Medicare medical savings account plans; private fee-for-service plans; and religious fraternal benefit plans.

Mental Illness *(13)* Decline in mental health status, traits, and ability that leads to impairment in everyday functioning.

National Family Caregiver Support Program (NFCSP; *3***)** Under the aegis of this program, local Area Agencies on Aging receive federal funding through State Units on Aging to provide supportive services to grandparent caregivers aged 60 and older. Services support the needs of grandparent caregivers and include health screenings, respite, socialization, permanency planning (i.e., developing a plan for the grandchild's permanent living situation), family counseling, financial and legal support.

Naturally Occurring Retirement Communities (NORC; *9***)** Neighborhoods where high concentrations of older people have moved or have aged in place that were not planned as retirement communities. An NORC could be in an urban high-rise condominium complex, a low-income apartment building, a suburban village of townhomes, or an exurban single-family neighborhood—anywhere that people have aged in place and/or other older people have decided to move due to proximity to services they desire.

Negative Rights, Positive Rights *(15)* Operating under the concept of informed consent, negative rights allow the refusal of an act or action to prevent it from occurring. Positive rights entitle a person to claim an affirmative good from an entity (i.e., Americans with Disabilities Act, Medicare, Medicaid, and Social Security).

Negotiated Consent *(14)* Negotiated consent is an approach to upholding decisional autonomy when no one interest trumps all others.

Negotiated Risk Agreements *(10)* This refers to a legal instrument incorporated into assisted living regulations that addresses tenants' liability exposure for risky behaviors.

New-Model Assisted Living Properties *(10)* New-model assisted living properties are typically corporate-owned facilities that are occupied by a relatively large number of residents, found in modern buildings that offered greater resident privacy. They accomodate persons with a wide range of impairments, but because of costs, are less likely to accept residents dependent on Medicaid. This group contrasts with other facility clusters that tend to be smaller, older, often "mom and pop" establishments that serve lower income elders who are more likely to share their units.

New Technologies *(1)* Related to design interventions, new technologies are tools and machines that allow persons with compromised functioning to be able to live and move safely in an environment. An example is surveillance technology.

Nursing Facility *(11)* A type of health care facility licensed by the state that offers room, board, nursing care, and some therapies. Also encompassed in this term are skilled nursing facilities, which provide around-the-clock nursing care and other specialized services such as speech pathology and physical therapy.

Nursing Home *(1, 4, 11)* As defined by Medicare, a nursing home is a "permanent residence for people who are too frail or sick to live at home or as a temporary facility during a recovering period."

Old-Age Homes *(2)* Begun in the early 1800s, these specialized homes were established to provide long-term care for those regarded as upstanding citizens and, especially, for native-born elderly people.

Older Americans Act (OAA; *7***)** Enacted in 1965, the OAA established the Administration on Aging (AoA) and state agencies on aging to address the social and health needs of older adults and their families with the overarching goal of promoting independence and independent living.

Old-Model Assisted Living Properties *(10)* Usually subsumed under the general "assisted living" label, but often referred to as board and care/adult foster care, these facilities are more likely to be housed in smaller buildings. Their accommodations are more likely to consist of bedroom-like units. Multiple residents may have to share toilet facilities and/or bathing areas found in another part of the building.

***Olmstead* Decision** *(2, 13)* *Olmstead v. L. C.* (98-536) 527 U.S. 581 (1999) resulted in a Supreme Court ruling that made it discriminatory to institutionalize a person with a disability, including mental illness, as long as that person wishes to live in the community and is capable of benefitting from the setting.

Omnibus Budget Reconciliation Act of 1987 (OBRA '87; *2***)** Legislation that required institutions receiving Medicare or Medicaid funds to guarantee that residents could maintain the "highest practicable, mental, and psychosocial well-being." Not only were the supervisors of homes to be concerned about the nature of care, they had to expand their focus to assure that individuals had a high quality of life. Staff had to be trained, restraints had to be limited, and family members were to have a voice in the care of their relatives.

Original Medicare (Part A; *6***)** Original Medicare pays health care providers directly for Part A (hospital insurance) and/or Part B (medical insurance) benefits. Once the deductible is met, Medicare covers 80% of approved charges with the patient responsible for the remaining 20%. In addition, Part B has a monthly premium. In Original Medicare it is possible to add optional prescription drug coverage by purchasing Medicare Part D. Medicare Supplement insurance, known as a Medigap policy, can be purchased to fill "gaps" in coverage and reduce out-of-pocket costs. The majority of seniors (72%) are enrolled in Original Medicare.

Outdoor Relief *(2)* Historically, a type of assistance provided to poor older adults in the form of money, food, clothing, or goods that was given in lieu of entering an institution.

Overseers of the Poor *(2)* Individuals who were either appointed or elected to take care of poor older adults in the community. These overseers were empowered by local statute to provide for indigents with public funds.

Palliative Care *(12)* An approach to health care that improves the quality of life of patients and their families facing the problems associated with a life-threatening illness through the prevention and relief of suffering by means of early identification and impeccable assessment and treatment of pain and other problems—physical, psychosocial, and spiritual.

Palliative Care Consult Model *(12)* In this model, nonhospice-affiliated palliative care workers consult with providers to create complete assessments on request of the resident's attending physician.

Parens Patriae *(15)* A common-law doctrine recognizing the state's inherent authority to benevolently protect people who are so incapacitated that they cannot protect themselves sufficiently (literally, "father of the country").

Person-Centered Care *(1, 11)* Treatment and care provided by individuals or entities that place the individual at the center of his or her own care. Person-centered care also takes into account needs of the individual's caregivers.

Person-Centered Principles *(10)* Principles of living and decision making that put the wishes and interests of the resident in long-term care at the center of activities and decisions. Facilities that follow these principles foster environments that are enjoyable, comfortable, and pleasurable (not unlike their original homes) and residents can feel like competent individuals who are in control of their lives and environment.

Physiatrist *(6)* A physician who specializes in physical medicine and rehabilitation (also called PM&R) and focuses on the prevention, diagnosis, and treatment of disease or injury.

Plan of Care *(12)* An individualized plan developed to meet the needs of the patient and/or family. Each member on the care team brings discipline-specific expertise as well as superior communication skills to help develop and implement the plan.

Police Power *(15)* Power of the state to protect and promote the general health, safety, welfare, and morals of the community, and in this case, persons in the long-term care community.

Poorhouse *(2)* Facility run by the government to provide housing and for those in need.

Postacute Care *(6)* Specialized follow-up services provided outside medical offices and hospitals (e.g., inpatient rehabilitation facilities, skilled nursing facilities, and at home through home health care) to support a patient's ongoing medical management, rehabilitation, or skilled nursing care.

Preservative Care *(4)* A type of care provision in residential facilities in which the role of family members is to help maintain the identity of the relative via engagement with facility staff or other activities. This role may include monitoring, advocacy, and decision making on behalf of the resident.

Preventive Ethics *(14)* A "preventive ethics" approach (i.e., anticipating possible ethical issues, not "preventing" ethics) enjoins key stakeholders, including the older person, to meet regularly to decide on courses of action that are open to regular adjustments in long-term care situations.

Primary Caregiver(s) *(3, 4)* The person or persons responsible for the majority of hands-on care for the older or disabled family member. There is often an unspoken understanding that primary caregivers are the main persons in charge of the care (completing everyday tasks and errands) and service coordination for an impaired family member.

Principalism *(14)* A practice in which ethical decisions are made using four main ethical principles – autonomy, beneficence, nonmaleficence, and justice.

Programs of All-Inclusive Care for the Elderly (PACE; *7, 16***)** Optional under Medicare and Medicaid, PACE provides frail older adults who meet requirements for nursing home placement with comprehensive service options designed to enable them to receive care while continuing to live in the community (e.g., home, assisted living).

Progressive Surrogacy *(4)* A system in which family members remain involved in numerous and escalating decisions regarding a care recipient's daily living, his or her physical and social environments, treatment and health care decision making, and crisis and end-of-life care.

Prospective Payment System *(5, 6)* A reimbursement system based on service categories with set payment amounts; fees are set for hospitals in advance for costs associated with care for a specific diagnosis as opposed to the prior practice of reimbursing for days of care irrespective of patient diagnosis.

Public Policy *(17)* A course of action that is taken by an organization with governmental authority with regard to a specific issue. It may include laws, regulations, judicial decisions, and funding priorities.

Quality-Improvement Organizations (QIOs; *15***)** Private state agencies that contract with the federal Centers for Medicare & Medicaid Services to assess provider compliance with professionally recognized standards of care and to work consultatively with those providers toward achieving a better service quality.

Regulatory Policy *(17)* Public policy that compels or limits certain prescribed behavior and imposes penalties for noncompliance.

Rehabilitation *(6)* Physical treatments designed to facilitate the process of recovery from injury, illness, or disease to as normal a condition as possible.

Residential Normalcy *(10)* Places where persons enjoy comfortable and pleasurable surroundings (not unlike their original homes) and, despite their physical or cognitive limitations, still feel like they are competent individuals who are in control of their lives and environment.

Respite or Respite Services *(3, 7)* Any service or assistance that provides a family caregiver with the opportunity to take a break from his or her care responsibilities.

Reverse Mortgage *(9)* A loan that allows homeowners age 62 and over with high equity (i.e., a relatively small or fully paid mortgage) to convert part of that investment into cash. No repayment is required until the homeowner dies or no longer uses the home as a principal residence. There are few restrictions on the use of the funds generated from a reverse mortgage; they are often used to purchase in-home care, to upgrade the home to accommodate a caregiver, and/or to finance costly supportive features such as a fully accessible bathroom or an elevator.

Secondary Caregivers *(4)* Persons who often give support and assistance to primary caregivers by providing psychoemotional, instrumental, and financial support. Secondary caregivers may become involved in various types of assistance for the care recipient but not to the same extent as the primary caregiver.

Self-Care Interventions *(1)* Self-care interventions are intentional activities that promote individual physical, mental, and emotional health.

Serious Mental Illness *(13)* A diagnosable mental, behavioral, or emotional disorder that meets criteria in the *Diagnostic and Statistical Manual of Mental Disorders*, Fifth Edition (*DSM-5*). It results in functional impairment that substantially interferes with or limits one or more major life activities.

Service Organization and Delivery Policy *(17)* A policy that specifies how direct health care services will be organized and delivered.

Skilled Nursing Facilities (SNFs; *6, 13***)** Facilities, often characterized as "nursing homes," that provide long-term care services to assist with limitations that significantly impair self-care and ability to engage in activities of independent living. SNFs may be part of nursing homes or hospitals, but they are not traditional nursing homes. They provide skilled health care rather than custodial care.

Smart Growth *(9)* A town-centered approach focused on transit and pedestrian convenience. Housing and commercial uses are mixed together in the same neighborhoods, on the same block, or in the same buildings, providing usability to people of all ages and abilities.

Smart Home *(8)* A residence that is augmented with technology to observe the environment, monitor the ongoing status of residents, support activities of daily living, promote physical independence, and reduce caregiver burden.

Social Model *(7, 10)* Often viewed as alternative or complementary to the medical model of care, social models of care focus on the interpersonal and psychosocial needs of individuals and families.

Social Security *(2)* Enacted in 1935 under the Roosevelt administration as a federally administered social insurance and benefit program. Its benefits now include retirement income, disability income, Medicare and Medicaid, and death and survivorship benefits. The Social Security Act has been liberalized on numerous occasions since its passage but remains a cornerstone of retirement or disability income for scores of Americans.

Special Care Units (Memory Support Neighborhoods; *10***)** A physically separated area dedicated to serving persons with dementia in a special care unit (SCU). The residential units tend to be smaller in these specialized dementia wings and may consist of only studio or bedroom units as opposed to an apartment. Shared occupancy is more common. Entry and exit doors of these living areas are often secured by locks, alarms, or passcode systems to prevent residents from wandering. Some SCUs also have "safe and interesting walkways, and appropriate levels of auditory and visual stimulation, to yield improved outcomes, such as reduced agitation and enhanced quality of life."

Special Care Units *(10)* A physically separated area in a long-term care facility dedicated to serving persons with dementia.

Spend Down *(11)* The process of reducing assets in order to qualify for programs or services. For example, prior to qualifying for Medicaid support, it is often necessary for an individual to deplete savings and dispose of fixed assets.

Statutory or Legislative Law *(15)* Acts passed by federal, state, and local legislatures functioning under authority conferred by the jurisdiction's constitution.

Substitution Model *(3, 4)* A model of long-term care based on an assumption that, given the option, families choose or substitute formal care in place of providing care within the family.

Supplementation Model *(3, 4)* A model of long-term care that views formal care as complementing the informal care provided by family, thereby lessening the time-consuming and potentially exhausting demands on family caregivers without replacing informal care provision.

Survivorship Curves *(1)* Graphs showing the number or proportion of individuals surviving to each age for the population of interest; the curves can be constructed for a given cohort based on a life table.

Task-Specific Model *(3)* A model of care that suggests that the appropriate provider of long-term care support is dictated by the type of task with which help is needed. For example, family is seen as best suited for assisting with nontechnical, nonmedical tasks and tasks that cannot be easily scheduled, such as toileting and transferring from chair to bed. Paid providers can best manage tasks requiring specialized knowledge and training that can be scheduled, such as wound care. The allocation of tasks reflects a clear division of labor with task segregation occurring between family and paid helpers.

Telehealth *(5)* The process of monitoring of a patient's condition through remote computer access and updating a central nursing station through a wireless network.

Third Age *(1)* The Third Age is a designation for the time that active retirement begins. There are even reference to a fourth age, which is reserved for the oldest old.

Universal Design *(8, 9)* Universal design is an all-encompassing concept promoting design in homes and public spaces that is accessible, adaptable, and usable by persons of all ages and abilities.

Viatical Settlements *(16)* For those in poor health or with a terminal illness, accelerated death benefits or viatical settlements (whereby a terminally ill person sells his or her life insurance policy to a third party for less than its mature value in order to benefit from the proceeds while still alive) may provide the best way to pay for long-term care services.

Village Model *(9)* The Village Model offers an approach to aging in place that allows for communal experience, resource sharing, and care provision without physical relocation.

Visitability *(9)* Concept consisting of three main components needed to make a home accessible to residents, friends, and relatives who have limited functioning: zero-step entrances to the home, wide interior doors, and at least a half bathroom on the ground floor (toilet and sink). Visitability is aimed toward single-family homes, duplexes, and triplexes, and is not expected to provide a totally accessible living space.

Index